KEEP • SHARE • RETURN

The Magicians of Main Street:
America and its Chambers of Commerce
1768-1945

Chris Mead

John Cruger Press

Oakton, Virginia

Library of Congress Cataloging-in-Publications Data
Mead, Christopher, 2014.
Magicians of Main Street / Chris Mead.
p.   cm.
ISBN: 978-0-9903033-0-5
Printed in the United States of America.
Book design by Roxanne Rash
For updated news and comments on the book visit *www.magiciansofmainstreet.com.*
Published by
John Cruger Press
Oakton, Virginia

To Laura

Early Responses to *The Magicians of Main Street*

"Long before the enfranchisement of municipal governments, chambers of commerce or their equivalents ran the show. In many ways, they still do. In this never-a-dull-moment contribution to the re-emergent field of American business history, Chris Mead presents an action-packed narrative of high-mindedness, enlightened self-interest, and, now and then, chicanery."

Kevin Starr, University of Southern California

"Is war good for business? Many people seem to believe this, with a glaring exception: businesspeople. The consistent opposition of chambers of commerce to military adventures is just one of the fascinating findings of this history of a vital but little-appreciated American institution."

Steven Pinker, Johnstone Professor of Psychology, Harvard University, and author of *The Better Angels of Our Nature: Why Violence Has Declined*

"Alexis de Tocqueville in his classic *Democracy in America* expressed wonderment at the proliferation of voluntary associations in the United States. Among them were chambers of commerce, the first of which was founded in New York in 1768, before the American Revolution. In *The Magicians of Main Street*, Chris Mead tells how chambers of commerce across the nation shaped America from colonial times to the end of World War II. This is a story, previously untold, essential to understanding how America became what it is."

Michael Barone, Resident Fellow, American Enterprise Institute; Senior Political Analyst, *Washington Examiner*; co-author, *The Almanac of American Politics*

"This book is a major contribution for understanding local chambers of commerce on both sides of the Atlantic. Not only the first in-depth treatment of U.S. chambers from 1768 to the modern era, it is also a thorough coverage of many engaging events and initiatives ranging from the Miss America Pageant to influences on the outcome of Presidential elections. Academics, practitioners and members of chambers, not to mention the public, owe Chris Mead an immense debt for this original work."

Robert J. Bennett, Professor of Geography, Cambridge University

"This history of the United States as seen through the lens of the chambers of commerce across time and across the country is an impressive accomplishment, admirably written and referenced. It makes clear that while the chambers often engaged in local boosting, they played a much more significant role in American economic development, from defending local interests to fighting for civic improvements."

Donald A. Ritchie, author of *The U.S. Congress: A Very Short Introduction*

Early Responses to *The Magicians of Main Street*

"Chris Mead's engaging narrative reveals the pivotal role chambers have played in shaping some of our most pivotal historical events. Through a series of fascinating untold stories that are sure to surprise you, Chris shines a light on the chambers' diverse role in shaping America's business development - from supporting the laying of the first transatlantic cable, to providing funding for Charles Lindbergh's Atlantic flight, to inventing modern commodities trading. He connects this fascinating history to the chambers' critical role in shaping our nation's business success today. Their advocacy on behalf of the millions of small business owners that power our economy is the lasting legacy of America's chambers of commerce."

Gail Goodman, CEO of Constant Contact and author of
Engagement Marketing: How Small Business Wins in a Socially Connected World

"Chris Mead's *Magicians of Main Street* reads like a secret history of American commerce. It takes an institution rarely studied and chronicles its critical role in the many of the boldest innovations of the past couple of centuries. Leavened by stories of failure and foolishness as well, Mead gives the chambers the kind of historical treatment they rarely get from pundits, but is much deserved."

Joel Kotkin, Fellow in Urban Studies, Chapman University;
Author, *The Next Hundred Million: America in 2050*

"This lively account of the unduly untold story of American chambers of commerce fills a considerable gap--not only in American business history, but in American history itself, which as Chris Mead amply demonstrates was significantly inflected by their activities. Beginning in 1768 with the New York Chamber of Commerce, thousands of like groups nationwide collectively fostered some of the country's signal achievements, even as their activities both inform and reflect the successive concerns of American economic, political, and social history."

Karl Kusserow, John Wilmerding Curator of American Art, Princeton University;
Editor and co-author, *Picturing Power - Portraiture and Its Uses in the
New York Chamber of Commerce*

Early Comments from Chamber Executives

"Chris Mead has captured the heartbeat of America ....the vital and significant role that chambers of commerce have played in our nation's history. He writes with clarity that 'a chamber of volunteers' committed to community and country can lead, transform, and strengthen our Republic."

Rob Wonderling, President and CEO, Greater Philadelphia Chamber of Commerce

"Chris Mead illustrates how chambers have built more than just strong businesses—they have built strong communities. He captures the extensive work of chambers, from their European roots and their American founding in the pre-Revolutionary War colonies, to their impact through two World Wars. *The Magicians of Main Street: America and its Chambers of Commerce* is an important reflection on the role chambers have served developing prosperous nations and the cities and states within them."

Kelly Brough, President and CEO, Denver Metro Chamber of Commerce

"An amazing body of work, Chris Mead's *Magicians of Main Street* offers – for the first time – a compendium of the pivotal roles chambers have played in building American communities and, thereby, the nation itself. For those of us who are chamber of commerce practitioners, this exhaustively researched book serves as a cornerstone in the foundation on which we have built our professional lives and provides a valuable lens through which we can view the history and development of our communities."

David Adkisson, President and CEO, Kentucky Chamber of Commerce

"Chris Mead's *Magicians of Main Street* provides incredible insights and a firsthand look into initiatives chambers of commerce have engaged in throughout history. This walk through the ages provides foundational knowledge of who we are as chambers, the critical roles served, and the importance of this great industry. It further provides a compass for the path that chambers can and must take moving forward continuing the tradition of service with excellence, shaping our communities, and leaving a legacy for generations to come."

Aaron Cox, CEO, Texas Chamber of Commerce Executives

"A fantastic uncovering of the organization that makes things happen in communities across the United States. You have to read it to find the 'magic' that chambers of commerce have unveiled in their cities and towns. This is the first time that this collective wealth of knowledge and influence has been captured. Kudos to author Chris Mead for highlighting the magic many think just appears before their eyes (or just happens)!"

Betty Nokes, President and CEO, Bellevue, Wash., Chamber of Commerce

"You can always trace all devilment to a Chamber of Commerce."
—Will Rogers

Acknowledgments

It takes a village to raise a book. And it takes just about a town or a city to raise a full-length history chronicle out of the hands of a first-time author. Many people helped with this effort.

This group participation is perhaps surprising, as the book began as an almost comically isolated and uninformed effort. But at every turn, people helped, and some helped over a period of years. Among the early believers in the project were Jason Stern and his wife Bonnie. Jason and Bonnie saw something in the story of Main Street chambers that was not being told in books at the time. He mentioned the idea to many people and persuaded Donald Ritchie, the noted expert on the history of the U.S. Senate and author of several well-regarded books on American history, to take a peek at an early draft. Don was kind enough later to read through the entire manuscript. Another person Jason brought into the picture was Frank Hodsoll, former chief of the National Endowment for the Arts. These men's incisive comments, along with Jason's and Bonnie's, helped the infant book project progress.

Colleagues at the Association of Chamber of Commerce Executives (ACCE) were indulgent supporters of their co-worker's obsession. It would take a listing of the staff directory to cite all who aided me, in ways big and small, but one should be singled out here. Tamara Philbin, ACCE's chief operating officer, read a group of my collected chamber stories and said it was jarring to move from one tale to the next with no chronological context. This simple comment forced me to realize that the entire project had to be structured somehow as a single history, with each story set in some logical sequence and more or less placed into its contemporary context.

She essentially called for a book that was four or five times as difficult as the project I thought I had embarked on. Thank you, Tamara. Really! The project began taking on more of the coloration of U.S. history as a whole. It became, accidentally, about much more than chamber membership renewal rates in 1923 or coffeehouse arguments in 1768.

Tens of thousands of Internet-stored documents were consulted for this project. Also of course I worked with libraries holding real-live books, chamber minutes, and other records, and am grateful for the help of their diligent staff. It was exciting to walk into the South Carolina Historical Society in Charleston to look at the early records of the Charleston Chamber of Commerce. Faye Jensen, the director, on hearing that the author was curious about George Alfred Trenholm, whispered, "You know he was Rhett Butler." It wasn't news to me at that point, but somehow it was a thrill to hear those words whispered in that place. She and her staff were exceedingly helpful. So were Matt Strauss at the Heinz History Center in Pittsburgh, David Kessler at the Bancroft Library at the University of California at Berkeley, and Lucas Clawson at the Hagley Museum and Library in Wilmington, Del. The Library of Congress staff was always friendly and instructive. And Kim Dori of my local library, the Chantilly branch of the Fairfax County, Va., Public Library system, along with her colleagues, aided me in more than one pinch.

Current and former chamber of commerce executives, consultants, and companies serving chambers from across the United States were extraordinarily generous. They furnished local chamber histories, minutes, ideas, comments, and, no little thing at all, encouragement. It is impossible to list them all, but some of them include (and I apologize for those passed over as a result of challenged memory circuits):

Dave Adkisson, Jeff Barnett, Jerry Bartels, Lane Beattie, Jan Hart Black, Jim Blasingame, Marilyn Blessie, Lee Blitch, Dick Blouse, Candace Boothby, Simon Brackley, John Brewer, David Brown, Kelly Brough, Austin Burke, Phil Bussey, Jay Byers, Bob Canter, Lenny Caro, Dick Castner, James Chavez, Chip Cherry, Jay Chesshir, Jay Clemens, Jonathan Coe, Dan Colantone, Dave Cooley, Bill Cooper, Tom Cosby, Aaron Cox, Jim Coyle, Tim Daman, Pat Dando, Richard Dayoub, Barb Denny, Bryan Derreberry, Kat Dewrell, Jim Dinegar, Roland Dorson, Larry Dowell, David Eads, Mark Eagan, Mike Edwards, Rob Engstrom, Chuck Ewart, Dick Fleming, Len Flesner, Leslie Foley, Gemma French, John Garman, Mike Gaymon, Dick Gibson, Sami Glascott, Catherine Glover, Randy Gordon, Glen Gould, Susan Graf, Carroll Gray, Oz Griebel, Leron Gubler, Rich Hadley, Philip Hageman, Win Hallett, Chip Hallock, Jim Heeter, Rod Henry, Jack Hornbeck, Brad Hicks, Mac Holladay, Gerald Holman, Ellen van der Horst, Dianne Hrobsky, Bill Hubbard, David Jameson, Patrick Jankowski, Marc Jordan, Kara Kelley, Joe Kelly, Frank Kenny, Dave Kilby, Debbie Klein, Mark Kleinschmidt, Brad Lacy, Cindy Larsen, Steve Leahy, Wally Lee, Marlene Lellock, Pete Levi, John Limbach, Leo Liu, John Long, Doug Loon, Doug Luciani, Rick Lutovsky, Paul Magaril, Matt Mahood, Connie Majure-Rhett, Mike Manning, Doug Marsh, David May, Eddie McBride, Barbara McNees, Matt Meadors, Brandon Mendoza, Chris Messina, Mary Ann Miller, Leslie Milloy, Bill Mock, John Moore, Ken Moore, Jeff Moseley, John and Nancy Myrland, Mike Neal, Matt Nemerson, Gary Newton, Maria Nieves, Laura Oblinger, Tiffany Ott, Phil Parker, Richard Perez, Doug Peters, Teresa Pinto, Joyce Powell-Johnson, Bob Quick, David Rattray, Joe Reagan, Mike Reagen, Tony Rescigno, Pete Robinson, Mike Rollins, Joe Roman, Jerry Roper, Andrew Rudnick, Dick Rush, Rick Russo, Frank Ryll, Charles van Rysselberge, Steward Sandstrom, Susanne Sartelle, Kim Scheeler, Dan Schenkein, Ralph Schulz, Harvey Schmitt, David Sciamanna, Carlo Scissura, Steve Scoppetta, Kyle Sexton, Eldonna Shaw, Pat Sheeran, Tony Sheridan, Mike Simas, Steve Snyder, Neil Spirtas, Dale Steenbergen, Casey Steinbacher, Steve Stevens, Bob Thomas, Bill Thornton, Gary Toebben, Jim Tollefson, Tom Torti, Joe Unterreiner, Jim Vaughn, Ceci Velasco, Joan Verplanck, Allie Williams, Craig Williams, Roy Williams, Sam Williams, Jim Wolfe, and Rob Wonderling.

Three respected chamber leaders who are deceased also helped the author frame some of its issues early in the process of thinking about chamber history: Rusty Hammer, Mike Hauser, and Robert Blankenship.

Canadian chambers provided useful perspective on their brethren to the south: John Dolbec, Todd Letts, Darcy Rezac, and Martin Salloum.

From the chamber world overseas, other people provided help and encouragement and perspective. These included Victor Fedotov, David Frost, Jack Stopforth, Uriel Lynn, Ze'ev Lavie, Anthony Parkes, and Alexey Voytenok. Parkes, managing director of the ICC World Chambers Federation, provided several key contacts. None was more important or valuable to this book than Cambridge University Professor Robert Bennett, the world's leading authority on the history of chambers of commerce. Bennett's most ambitious work on chambers, *Local Business Voice: The History of Chambers of Commerce in Britain, Ireland, and Revolutionary America, 1760-2011*, was of great value in providing perspective and understanding. Moreover, his comments on the manuscript of this U.S. book were extremely helpful.

Outside the chamber of commerce world in the United States, these people were among those blowing on the sails of this struggling schooner: my book club friends and neighbors who kindly read the manuscript and gave useful comments: Richard Gibbons, Darrin McCullough, and Bill Rigger; business-education expert Brett Pawlowski; high school classmate Steve Givens; philanthropic consultant and now Ford Foundation Vice President Hilary Pennington; Lyz Crane from ArtPlace; Kim Phillips-Fein, author of the fascinating *Invisible Hands: The Businessmen's Crusade Against the New Deal*, whose book led me to the remarkable Leonard Read; Woodbury University's Rick Nordin; Dave Elbert, whose *Standing on the Shoulders of Giants* helped me understand the chamber in Des Moines; Partners for Livable Communities founder Bob McNulty; and author Joel Kotkin, who kindly featured a couple of my articles on his Web site, NewGeography.com. Civic strategist Otis White, moreover, helped the author in his attempt to address the book to an audience broader than chamber executives, chamber members, and urban experts.

Another key supporter in this effort was Ryan Petty, an economic developer and former chamber executive who lives in Tacoma, Wash., and who is by night a publishing guru. Both Ryan and I were releasing books at about the same time, and Petty was generous enough to share his insights on the rapid changes in the world of book publishing and distribution. Jim Blasingame, a noted writer and publisher on small business topics, also helped greatly.

Greater Raleigh Chamber of Commerce President Harvey Schmitt once suggested to a *Wall Street Journal* reporter that he talk with the author regarding chamber economic development efforts in the past. That reporter, Conor Dougherty, saw an interesting story in my peculiar passion for chamber of commerce history. The resulting article, "Don't Yawn: Chambers of Commerce are Really Quite a Kick," was featured on the front page of the *Journal* on August 17, 2012. As much as any other single thing during the book writing project, this article with its gentle ribbing helped provide an energy boost needed for completing what would be a seven-year effort.

Roxanne Rash, a colleague from ACCE, agreed to take on the demanding after-work job of graphics, illustration, and design director for the book. She took particular delight in finding photos and drawings no one else knew about – the perfect complement to the kinds of stories the book was attempting to reveal. Another ACCE colleague, Sarah Myers, handled final galley-proof editing and indexing.

My good friend and neighbor Cynthia Bailey came out of the blue to volunteer to be the overall editor of this book. She was just what the chamber doctor ordered: someone with a great feel for and love of the English language, and not too many preconceptions about chambers of commerce. This should be a story not just for insiders. She came on board at a stage when the book's course had been charted, but she nevertheless steered it away from many a rocky channel and shark-infested shoal. Responsibility for any remaining errors of fact or of writing style or diction lies with the author alone.

My extended family, with plenty of obsessive writers sprinkled in it, encouraged and otherwise helped me in many ways. Uncle Billy Mellette, cousin Mike Martinez, brother-in-law Jim Wise, and father-in-law Douglass Lewis were all there for their fellow writer. So were others in their respective families, including Joe and Elizabeth Lewis, who also kindly read the manuscript.

In my immediate family, two more writers gave much encouragement and many helpful comments. One was my father Loren Mead, whose books on churches and congregations were remarkably parallel to this book in that they analyzed groups of people at the local level. Loren and I had many a conversation on what this chamber material meant. The other was my older brother, Walter Russell Mead. Perhaps Walter's best-known book, and my favorite, is *Special Providence: American Foreign Policy and How it Changed the World*. This book describes contending groups of people in the American saga and how their interactions produced an amazingly, but not automatically, successful foreign policy. Among other things, Walter generously mentioned this book project on his popular blog at *The American Interest* magazine.

My mother, Polly Mead, played no minor role. She encouraged me from about age five to be a writer. She made every sacrifice to help me and my siblings receive a good education. She herself became a published poet. Sadly, she died on September 16, 2013, before my book was published, but she was anxious to see it progress. I will never forget either her love of the creative process or her love of me. My sister, Barbara, also supported the effort, and my younger brother Philip, an emergency physician, helped on more than one occasion to make sure that my health would hold up to the inevitable strain.

Mick Fleming, the president of the Association of Chamber of Commerce Executives, was extremely supportive of his writing-obsessed subordinate. Although nearly all the research and writing of the book took place on early mornings and weekends, there were inevitable intrusions on the workday, not to mention challenges to the stamina of the author. Mick was willing to accept the occasional bumps as he ably piloted the association through the recession and other challenges, large and small. He was a believer in the project and more than once alerted chamber executives to the research. Moreover, he provided timely and helpful comments on the manuscript and never once, in seven years, asked the author to pass over the mistakes that past chambers have made. Like the author, Mick wanted to see the real story and not a pretend one. Toward the end of the project, he uncovered a treasure trove of old ACCE materials that added many details to the story, particularly from the mid-1920s to 1945.

My children, Katherine, Grace, and John, put up with their virtual ink-stained father's quest for longer than they should have. And their mother, my wife Laura, was the most patient of all. Once she called this book his "girlfriend" and indeed many times she had to look the other way as he followed this unusual and captivating mistress. But while I cared deeply about his book, the only one I have really loved, all along, was not named "chambers of commerce," but was a beautiful and extraordinary woman named Laura Lewis Mead.

Foreword

So, I stroll into Chris Mead's office next door to mine one quiet morning in 2009 and he tells me he heard another great story about a chamber of commerce that was prominent half a century ago. Increasingly, as he completed road trips or phone calls, he had mentioned these funny or amazing episodes and we chuckled or shook our heads in amazement.

That day's tale was about the Miss America pageant that the Atlantic City Chamber had dreamt up in the 1920s. We were left somewhat speechless gazing at a picture he found showing two dozen curly-headed flappers on the beach, clad in bathing costumes heavy enough to sink Michael Phelps. The project had carried Atlantic City into the headlines in a somewhat naughty context for the times.

Chris was always picking up such stories while visiting with the Association of Chamber of Commerce Executives members. During that conversation, he casually joked, "Somebody should write a book." The rest, as they say, is history . . . literally.

A year or so later, when Chris was in the midst of early drafts of the rapidly expanding publishing venture that was to become *The Magicians of Main Street*, *The Wall Street Journal* requested an interview with me to talk about this very "interesting" person on my team who was engaged in an avocation (writing the history of American chambers) that related to his vocation (raising money for the association serving chambers).

"Why do you think he's doing this?" asked the reporter when he showed up at the office. "Are you paying him for it?" I answered that ACCE was neither investing in the book project, nor paying him for the hours he was spending on it. I think I told him that chambers get under your skin when you spend time with them, and certainly had got under Chris's. I didn't know exactly why Chris was doing it, but I understood his passion for the task. He was right: somebody should tell this story.

Many people think that chambers are somehow responsible for the weather on the day of the big game, or the welcome parade when an American Idol finalist comes home. In reality, the history of chambers of commerce in this country embodies the building of the modern American economy. Town by town. Project by project. Decade by decade.

Marc Jordan, a remarkably resilient and talented chamber leader, who is still active in his forty-second year in the profession, encapsulates the mission and work succinctly: "Chambers do the things in a town that everybody thinks just happen." I would modify Marc's remark by adding: The chambers in the 18th and 19th centuries did the things that could not have been done any other way.

The daunting task Chris has undertaken will make it clear that chambers orchestrated, motivated, suffered, innovated, celebrated, and conspired through almost every halting step and frantic sprint of American economic expansion. This was especially true during the 178 years covered in *The Magicians of Main Street*, during which the role of government in the economy was much more limited than it is today.

This book is much more than a collection of gee-whiz episodes and entertaining stories about guys in suits who hype their towns. The book is more because chambers are more.

Chamber of commerce missions have always been two-pronged: profitability for members today and prosperity for community tomorrow. This bi-polar purpose statement, phrased in various ways but largely consistent across place and time, makes the portfolio of chamber work remarkably diverse. That diversity appears throughout *Magicians*.

There are stories about crises of conscience as communities attempt to deal with the Native Americans who were here before white settlement. Global concerns occupied the boards of the chambers Chris examines, as peace and war hung in the balance during the presidential terms of Washington and almost every White House occupant. It is extremely enlightening to read the accounts of chambers of commerce single-handedly attacking infrastructure demands of the nation's growing population and economy. School buildings, railroads, water systems, and airports move from inspiration to drawing board to reality through the accounts of collective business action described herein. The work portfolios between 1768 and 1945 have been wide and deep.

Much of the magic captured in the book relates to what one might call 'community harmony and happiness.' While this might at first appear to be the soft or light side of chamber work, it is every bit as vital to prosperity as land development or harbor construction. Gatherings, events, and festivals help build the culture and provide the glue that creates communities in the first place and keeps them together over time.

The book captures efforts to create magnet events from world's fairs to locally focused art fests. It is also clear that the gatherings of business leaders, whether to discuss post-war recovery or new labor laws, helped communities deal with and address challenges too big for any one company to handle alone. Forums, conferences, and other meetings are described in the book, all of which reduce friction among merchants and employers, a critical function of every chamber.

Such gatherings also allowed chambers and communities to come to consensus on issues and to stimulate advocacy (few called it "lobbying" in those days) to achieve desired outcomes. Through chamber of commerce gatherings and discussions described in the book, we see how communities found a shared lexicon and a collective voice with which to speak to everyone from the media to the President.

Just as the book highlights an ever-present tension between the needs of companies and those of the community, it also makes clear that immediate priorities and future-focused dreams were often at odds. The author sometimes, such as when covering the beginnings of the Progressive movement, portrays business being dragged to the altar, but then becoming enthusiastic partners in good government, anti-corruption initiatives. In some chapters, it's clear that chambers of commerce were visionary and ahead of their times. This was certainly true in regard to the importance of aviation, urban development and education reform. It was less evident in their reaction to the threat of Nazism in the 1930s, when business groups and individual companies tended to lean toward neutrality.

The few times that Chris had crises of conscience of his own arose when he was forced to deal with episodes of bad behavior by these usually admirable organizations. From the beginning, he asked me, as both his employer and as a sometime leader of American chambers, whether he should or could fully tell these stories of bad judgment, bad action and bad outcomes. Chris was tortured over these delicate and indelicate issues, like the treatment of Native Americans as communities spread across the continent, the xenophobia during the two World Wars, and the cutthroat competition exhibited between two communities vying for a rail line or defense contract.

We both came to the conclusion that he might as well not bother doing the book if he wasn't going to tell the whole story – warts and all. Chambers of commerce are fallible entities, full of fallible individuals, run under consensus governing models. Given these limits, as well as what passed for wisdom in their times and highly volatile context in the youth and adolescence of our nation, they did the best they could. In hindsight, they were sometimes dead wrong. Chris had to tell these unpleasant stories, even if some influential people, including this reader, might prefer that the truth might somehow be retroactively changed. Without including these negative references, who would believe the larger positive story of *The Magicians of Main Street*?

The book is about collective action, both good and bad, but it is also about inspirational, as well as flawed, individuals and unusual characters. And, importantly, it is about personal leadership.

Today, economic development and community building are often deemed the purview of trained professionals. During the first two centuries of our chamber history in America, they were personal.

In every chapter of this book, people – individual leaders – step up. To be fair, some step forward for personal or company gain, but most do so out of a spirit of civic pride and the expectation of civic engagement that seems alien in the twenty-first century. It's not that we don't have selfless leaders today; of course we do. Present-day volunteer leadership, however, tends to be more narrowly focused. Those who step forward likely to do so in regard to a cause or a neighborhood that is dear to their hearts, rather than a larger collective good and community-wide advancement. The causes also seem more immediate – "Stop beach erosion to save tourism." or "Pass the gas tax to enable us to fix the bridges." or "Support/oppose this candidate who will help/hurt everything."

I view this not a criticism of our current civic affairs, which are shaped by factors ranging from global corporate ownership to convoluted political jurisdictions. Rather, it is an acknowledgment of the pace of change and the urgency of the problems we face as a nation and regions in this particular historic moment.

Throughout *The Magicians of Main Street*, the reader can't help but absorb the sense of history many of the characters and organizations seemed to display. They seemed to know that building the tunnel west of Denver would change Colorado development forever – so they supported it. In these pages, individuals speak out about the need to address education reform in order to ensure a prosperous future for city and nation. And, they push for community livability because of their desire to have a place people love forever, not just because they want band music for their own summer nights on the village green. In Chris's research, we see businesses investing in chambers as much for the futures of the places they live as for the companies they own.

If I had any influence on this project, which I'm not at all sure was the case, it was to remind Chris that the book would suffer if the editorial decisions were supply-driven. To some degree, of course, history is always influenced by who bothered to write down and save the stories and data. The richness of the histories available from some chambers is matched by a paucity of information about others. Coverage of cities of like New York,

Philadelphia and Charleston is more robust because their chambers of commerce existed long before the first American trappers even roamed the Rockies.

To avoid the risk of having the book being unrepresentative of the chamber movement as a whole, Chris dug deeply through mountains of sometimes obscure texts and primary source material. He spent weeks at the Library of Congress and other libraries, hundreds of hours on the phone, and immeasurable web time seeking out the legacies we knew to exist in communities that had not been as prescient about the need to preserve archives.

The result of this extensive research and analysis is impressive, but also fun. The leading magician of this book, Chris Mead, weaves hundreds of stories into one compelling, entertaining narrative. That creative and inquisitive style ensures that the powerful messages of hope and cautionary tales found in every chapter can be recognized and appreciated, rather than relegated to the reference shelf. This story has never been told before and now it has been told in a way that will engage anyone who is interested in community development and leadership . . . forever.

Michael Fleming
President and CEO
Association of Chamber of Commerce Executives

Contents

What is a Local Chamber of Commerce?

Chamber of commerce: an association, primarily of people in business, to promote the commercial interests of an area

Random House Webster's Unabridged Dictionary, 2014 (online)

Chambers in the United States stand at the crossroads of business and politics. These institutions came into existence primarily to safeguard and extend opportunities for business. Their specific missions vary according to their community, leadership, and laws. Moreover, especially in the past century, many chambers' roles have been broadened from precisely targeting of business needs (e.g., getting the new overpass built to let in more freight, keeping taxes in check, pushing for downtown retail development) to community-wide initiatives that only have an indirect, although sometimes powerful, impact on business: K-12 education improvement, job training, attracting talented young people to town, or promoting affordable housing. The chamber of commerce has morphed, to some extent, into a chamber of community, although the business watchdog v. community benefactor dichotomy has existed in some form since the very beginning of this institution.

This book refers primarily to local chambers of commerce in the United States, with some reference to similar chambers in Canada and elsewhere. There are local chambers in most countries of the world. Chambers vary even more widely across the globe than they do in North America, but most chambers in the world can be divided into one of two major categories: public-law and private-law chambers.

Public-law chambers require every business to register with the chamber. Hence these are quasi-governmental entities, more a part of than apart from government. Still, they are a voice on behalf of business. On account of their receiving fees from all businesses, they tend to have large budgets. The Paris Chamber of Commerce, for example, has an annual budget of more than $600 million per year – larger even than the annual budget of the United States Chamber of Commerce (about $200 million in 2011, including its affiliates; the number is roughly $50 million or more higher in election years). The countries where public-law chambers exist include many of the places that have legal systems based on the

Napoleonic Code, which tends to emphasize the central authority of the state more than do countries following the British common-law tradition.

Private-law chambers have voluntary membership, which means that they are constantly in the process of trying to obtain and keep members. The United States, Canada, Great Britain, Norway, and many other countries have this type of system. While these private-law chambers are regulated entities – most U.S. chambers, for example, are 501C 6 organizations to permit lobbying – their regulation is less stringent than is that of the public-law chambers. These freewheeling organizations are less an arm of the state than a finger nagging at it (or beckoning to it).

Few things in life are simple, and in the case of chambers, it's become clear that the public-law/private-law dichotomy isn't as precise as it perhaps once appeared to be. Private-law chambers sometimes take on public functions, and many public-law chambers are trying to be, or at least studying the idea of becoming, more private. One study has broken up chambers into a half-dozen categories, with the strictly private-law chambers appearing in 72 countries and the other five groups represented in 122 countries.[1]

Even in just one country, there are many chambers of commerce. The United States has 7,086 chambers of all types, according to the 2013 edition of the *World Chamber of Commerce Directory.*[2] There are another 588 in Canada. But it's difficult to pinpoint every chamber, especially the smallest and newest ones, including many that are ethnic, "green," neighborhood, transnational, women's, gay and lesbian, and other specialized organizations. Chamber staffing may range from zero (as is the case for thousands of chambers, which are entirely run by volunteers) to 80 or more. In the United States, local chambers of commerce (including county, regional, municipal, and neighborhood) with two or more full-time employees probably number no more than about 3,000.

What exactly do local chambers of commerce in the United States do? Most of them divide up their activities in four or five main areas: Government relations/lobbying, membership, communications, events, and other activities such as affinity programs (offering health insurance or other products to members) or economic/tourism development. Of these, the core activity is usually considered dealing with government, a job that's often more easily accomplished via a group of businesses (a chamber) rather than by a single business on its own.

Introduction

The curious thing about the United States, as Alexis de Tocqueville remarked in *Democracy in America*, is that this land of the free is swirling with groups. As molecules bump against each other faster as they are melted, so the people of the melting pot moved faster under freedom, reconstituting themselves with rapidity and ingenuity to solve the problems of the new land. Peoples formerly bound by rules of custom and monarchy or aristocracy found new liberties as immigrants and discovered new ways to interact with others. The land of the individual quietly became, also, the land of the group. And one of those kinds of groups was the chamber of commerce – a relatively new idea that the Americans refashioned according to their needs and interests. These American chambers would have a lasting impact on their country.

Many chamber dues payers were far from wealthy, but it's certainly fair to say that the average chamber member, and even more so the average chamber board member, was better off than the average citizen in the periods examined here. Chambers of commerce hence sometimes operated as an aristocracy lite, a restraining, Senate-like, calming influence on the body politic. They exercised a healthy skepticism of government programs most of the time, unless their members thought those programs were likely to have a material impact on local economic prospects.

Still, to focus only on the wealth of some chamber members, or on their general (and far from monolithic) tendency toward political conservatism, or on their seeming fixation on detailed aspects of civic and commercial life, is to miss the wider picture of what these groups did. Nathaniel Hawthorne grasped the strange contradiction of chambers of commerce – the inherent conservatism of business juxtaposed against the fantastic plans these people occasionally realized. "It is dangerous to listen to such dreamers as these," he wrote.[1] Chambers, it turned out, could unite clusters of enterprises or will cities out of the pine needles and crickets. Once they came to consensus on a project, it had a good chance of happening. These groups of doers, perhaps not surprisingly, could get a lot done.

Chambers of commerce often functioned as the venture capitalists and entrepreneurs of civic life. If a camel is a horse created by a committee, then these business organizations generated more than their share of dromedaries. Their sandy footprints are everywhere, from the Golden Gate Bridge and across the Father of Waters to the sea bottom at Hell Gate in New York's harbor. Your city council, or your city itself, may derive from a group of men who once sat around a table singing or passing a hat to collect pledges.

Why should this essentially be the first full-length history of American chambers of commerce? Appendix A points to 13 different explanations of why we forget these organizations. There are many reasons. We find individuals more interesting than groups, high ideals more uplifting than idealism mixed with other motives, clear and suddenly exercised power more exciting than the drip, drip, drip of influence exercised over years or decades, foreign wars more interesting than peace on the home front, death more interesting than taxes. We have blind spots of historical understanding. We can't see the car approaching us on the right. But that doesn't mean it's not there.

Following chambers through American history is like watching Forrest Gump, only there's a forest of Gumps. Chambers had a hand, sometimes an invisible one, in many great and small enterprises. From humble beginnings just before the American Revolution, they gradually put together a resume of achievements that few individuals – perhaps just four or five great Presidents – could match in total, cumulative impact on U.S. society.

Chamber members took action on things they were excited about, or afraid of, or desperate to acquire. These were all, of course, simply human beings. The man in the gray flannel suit, or in the three-cornered hat, or in the high starched collar, or the woman in pumps, had passions just as abiding as those of the stevedore and the sharecropper. And those passions found expression in the national life with traces easily discernible today.

Two high-profile chambers – the Chamber of Commerce of the State of New York and the U.S. Chamber of Commerce – get plenty of attention in this narrative, as they did in many of the periods covered here. Never, however, did either chamber call all or even most of the shots for the business organizations in the country. The bewildering variety and occasional cussedness of the other chambers makes them interesting to learn about and often instructive. Together, those thousands of other American chambers did more than any single chamber has, probably anywhere.

Following more than a million chamber members over nearly 200 years, in what were eventually about 3,000 chambers of commerce in the years up through World War II, is a demanding task. Choosing a few hundred illustrative examples out of many thousands is more of an art than a science, and deciding which stories to amplify is even more a judgment call. The process is necessarily imperfect, much like watching a river in near darkness. But by glimpsing the glints of moonlight on this quiet and sometimes turbulent chamber water, we can get a sense of its power and direction and force.

The book opens with a very brief look at the beginning of trade and commercial organizations in other parts of the world, and then in the United States. The much longer examination of the American chambers is the heart of the book, starting in some detail just before the Revolutionary War and ending at the year 1945. In the years from George III to Roosevelt II we will learn much that can help us understand not only chambers' and our past, but our present and future as well. A brief epilogue will take us, at Jet Age speed, from 1945 to the present day.

The North American story begins quietly, slowly, as a few windswept chambers of commerce grapple with the Wild East maelstrom of trade and conflict on the Atlantic. Somehow the plucky and cantankerous organizations survive, or at least give birth to descendants, and begin a steady march across a continent that doesn't belong to them. Almost by osmosis, and usually by accident, and perhaps at first unnoticed by the reader, they begin creating many of the institutions and capacities that we now take for granted in modern life.

By the end of World War I, they have changed the nation irrevocably, so much so that their hand often is hidden by their own creations as they continue to quietly remake their communities. They grapple with a Depression for which the cure is, not Prozac, but the response to a talented, charismatic mass murderer who looks strangely like Charlie Chaplin. These "weak" institutions soldier on, some declining, some not, but most of them able to outlive any tyrant, from Al Capone to Adolf Hitler.

These American chambers appear weak because they depend on voluntary engagement. And it is that kind of weakness that is, to a large extent, the strength of their country. Autocrats, beware of nations of shopkeepers – and also of nations full of shopkeepers' and businesses' organizations.

The things these chambers did or helped accomplish were wide-ranging and, when seen together, profound. One chamber started the Farm Bureau; another streamlined how charitable donations were handled, influencing the creation of Community Chests and the United Way; another brought the first movie producer to southern California; still another was the moving force behind the largest concrete structure in the world; while one more first brought up the proposal for a flexible monetary system that became the Federal Reserve Bank. A beach chamber started the Miss America Pageant; a mountain chamber sponsored the first music folklore festival.

Then there was the chamber responsible for 20,000 deaths in the Mississippi Valley, and the "real Rhett Butler," who brought in so many European arms to the Confederacy that many thousands of Yankee soldiers would never make it back home. And there was the "Lion of the Vigilantes," a business leader who imposed order while elected officials made an art of ballot-box stuffing and letting arsonists burn down much of their city to steal from the ashes. And these of course are simply a few samplings of the organizations' actions. These chambers had merchants who knew how to make change.

Indeed, in the period from the nation's birth to World War II, chambers of commerce managed significantly to influence the country's politics, physical infrastructure, culture, and economy. Usually they did this without attracting a great deal of attention. These weren't secret societies, by any means. But they discovered that when you grapple with the details of civic life, people are more than willing to let you alone for a while. And when the publicity does come, it's usually a congressman or mayor or President who's cutting the ribbon or taking the flak. All this isn't that bad from the perspective of the businesses making up the chamber. That is, provided that someone is building the dam or approving the variance so that Acme Manufacturing Company will come to town.

Some believe it's impossible to generalize about chambers of commerce. There is a saying, "When you've seen one chamber, you've seen one chamber." Chambers of commerce do vary greatly from one another. But every snowflake is different, too, and the weather report doesn't say, "Trillions of completely different flakes are descending, so we won't attempt to describe them by crude measures such as inches of precipitation." Let's examine, then, the chamber landscape throughout this period. We have already indicated two things: they have been less prominent in the public eye than, say, politicians, and they have valued getting results of one kind or another.

Volunteers and What They Cared About

U.S. chambers are voluntary organizations. This has led to years of misery in courting, coaxing, begging businesses to do their part and be a part of the chamber. Why go through all this agony of dues collection? It's because those collections represent a kind of vote, and a vote that can matter. One example is the New York and Boston chambers' resolutions in favor of the Jay Treaty in 1795, which, according to critics at the time, had a disproportionate effect on the nation's deliberations over that pact. One can't be the "voice of business" without having heard that voice, without having received some concrete indication of business's support.

As voluntary groups, chambers benefit from what one might call the "democracy of the elbow." That is, influence beyond the power of a single vote can come to those who are willing to devote the elbow grease needed to effect change. You can extend your influence in the community by stepping up to help in some way. Chambers, over many decades, had volunteers who did just that. These chambers supplemented the power of their volunteers with paid staff, especially after the Civil War. Money can substitute for or augment the time of volunteers. Nothing, however, can substitute for the chambers' members caring about whatever issue is at hand. If key members of the chamber don't care, the chances are that the issue will pass unaddressed, or that some other civic organization will take up the cause.

Old soldiers never die, and neither do some chamber obsessions. Chambers with a fixed program or project can come back, for years and years, longer even than a human life, trying to get things done. Look at the New York Chamber's struggle for a stable currency based on gold; picture also the Las Vegas and Los Angeles chambers' fixation on harnessing the power and the water of the Colorado River. Both in the case of the gold and the river, the firing of tiny neurons in the brains of these chambers' members slowly blasted away millions of tons of rock. A watercourse may take hundreds of millions of years to dig out a channel; if it took the Houston Chamber two or three lifetimes to do the same thing, that's quite rapid by Mother Nature's standards.

Public Works and Transportation

One of the dominating concerns of chambers historically, lampooned by the occasional critic, has been on public works and transportation projects. Can any serious observer, after seeing what they managed to do in their first 178 years, not stop and wonder at the power of this obsession? Think of the ports that were dredged, sometimes multiple times, at the urging of the local chamber. Think of the canals that snaked across the nation's skin, soon overtaken by railroads, usually with chambers all along the way cheering them on, often after passing the hat for some improvement or other, and sometimes after making sure that the improvement went their way and not that of a rival town.

These chambers seldom found an obstacle they wouldn't try to cross. When the Isthmus of Panama was too much of a barrier for a canal, the New York and Philadelphia chambers asked for shipping lines to terminate on either side of it. When it was time for a canal there, dozens of chambers pushed the project, and the Cincinnati Commercial Club and the New York Chamber of Commerce had a hand in furthering Philippe Bunau-Varilla's dream of a great machete chop through Panama. Then it was time for big fairs, promoted by the chambers in San Diego and San Francisco, to celebrate the canal's opening in 1914.

Some communities owed their civic lives to the chamber obsession with transportation. Denver's progress would have been held back indefinitely if its board of trade had not passed the hat for a link to the Transcontinental Railroad. Houston might be a small village in Texas if not for the transformation of its snag-infested bayou to a great ship channel. Los Angeles would be, literally, a backwater if its chamber hadn't fought fiercely for a port and then, with its waves lapping 18 inches above the sand, got it deepened.

The Atlantic wasn't too big to cross. The Savannah Chamber's members spearheaded the first steamship across it, in 1819, and the New York Chamber cheered as Cyrus Field and Peter Cooper lay the first cable under it. In 1927, the St. Louis Chamber helped Charles Lindbergh fly the *Spirit of St. Louis* across the chilly waves to Paris, while the Brooklyn Chamber had to settle for Berlin.

Chambers shouted for the Pony Express, only to have another of their obsessions, the telegraph, overtake it. The New York Chamber first grasped the winning concept of how the Transcontinental Railroad would be financed, but it was the Boston Board of Trade that, among the chambers, first took a big group on it, at the cost of one unhappy antelope. Great distances were for chambers simply another cost of doing business. The San Francisco Chamber hailed ships from every land, and the skinny riders that docked their sweating ponies in Sacramento, and those marvelously sweet crystals from Hawaii that would one day seduce the islands into union with the Union.

These groups of business people were not amateurs in the movement of people and things. Chambers played a critical role in the good roads movement, years before Henry Ford first laid a wrench on a car; financed the first regularly scheduled airline flight, from St. Petersburg to Tampa; and set up hundreds of airport committees of chambers, meeting in some cases over decades, and responsible for where millions of passengers land today. The nation's first superhighway struggled toward birth at the end of the Depression, courtesy of Harold Ickes and the Pittsburgh Chamber of Commerce. Other contemporary public works projects bearing the early fingerprints of chambers included the Golden Gate Bridge, Hoover Dam, and Grand Coulee Dam. Even the pioneering government organization that built so many public works and inspired so many similar organizations, including the TVA and Robert Moses's Triborough Bridge Authority, namely the Port Authority of New York and New Jersey, grew out of a chamber (the New York Chamber of Commerce).

Perhaps we should forget these things, as most people have. The main advantage of remembering is that it's useful to see how some things got done. Chambers of commerce didn't do everything in almost any of these cases. But all of these, and hundreds more, projects would not have happened when they did, and how they did, without the intervention of these business organizations. And quite a few of these projects, one suspects, would not have happened at all.

Indeed, it's difficult not to see the work of chambers in a hundred aspects of American life today. Perhaps the same could be said if, instead of chambers, we were looking at other groups of people. There are all kinds of influences on our lives and this country. But the chambers have been one of them, and they have shown their hand over a couple of centuries. It's possible to see many of their interests and their problems, their triumphs and their mistakes, and their likes and dislikes. One of their areas of focus, clearly, has been transportation and public works, but there have been others.

Boosting

Scratch a chamber, and you'll usually find a Frank Wiggins in there somewhere. Wiggins was the chamber executive who conjured up the American fascination with, and migration to, Los Angeles around the turn of the 20th century. Come to our community; start a business here; invest in us; visit our attractions. These kinds of boosting activities happened from an early time, long before Wiggins, at least since the Lexington Society for the Promotion of Emigration in 1797. Grown-up chambers, or chambers in grown-up cities, tended to put more polish on the appeals. But seldom did the appeals end completely as communities matured, any more than a mature company gets rid of its sales department.

The chambers' efforts at community self-promotion were sporadic at first, then built up steadily. The expansion of the railroad network – facilitated by many of these same chambers – was a huge help. Railroads often gave free passes for promotional trips, and there were plenty of those excursions. By the 1880s, such groups as the Salt Lake Chamber and the Los Angeles Chamber were taking not just people, but exhibits on the road. And the Tulsa traveling road show in 1905, complete with a young, soon-to-be-famous entertainer and his rope, helped that chamber will its community out of the prairie dust.

There were fairs, and more fairs, and exhibits in those fairs, and struggles to attract the Egg, Butter and Cheese convention and the reunions of Civil War units. There were macabre tussles over human remains, with the Richmond Chamber proudly successful in grabbing what was left of Jefferson Davis, and Deadwood breathing life into Deadwood Dick by pretending he died. Hawaii boosters hawked pineapple juice on the boardwalk in Atlantic City; St. Petersburg boosters measured bathing suits on women in a battle with imaginary village scolds. These chambers wanted more human beings, dead or alive.

As the early chambers passed the hat to entice railroads to lay track to their towns, so they passed it to get manufacturers. Many a city today owes a major industry to some old board of trade's "bonus" for a factory in that line of business. Fort Worth's mammoth stockyards arrived this way; Southern California's aircraft industry grew partly out of a chamber-organized air show in 1910. The South's industrialization in the first half of the 20th century drew much of its strength from chambers' economic development efforts.

The growing sophistication of chamber efforts in tourism and economic development led to the creation of specialized organizations to further the activity. Chambers set up industrial bureaus and tourism bureaus, some of which were semi-independent or completely separate organizations. A number of these organizations found streams of funds separate from chamber membership dues or funding drives. Soon, thanks to such initiatives as Balance Agriculture with Industry in Mississippi, those seeking new factories could more easily tap government funds. For tourism, the big breakthrough in securing government funding would not occur until after World War II, when the bed tax would emerge and spread faster than bedbugs, while biting just as hard.

But for both tourism and corporate recruitment efforts, it was increasingly clear that thoughtful activities, beyond simply sending out glad-handers' brigade, were needed to help generate the business every community wanted. Chambers were involved in thinking through what would best promote their towns and cities. And their capital or superfund campaigns for economic development, harking back to Forward Atlanta in the Twenties, would begin to change many an American civic landscape after World War II.

Dealing with Government

Chambers of commerce, by and large, were skeptical about government, but not dismissive. They frequently criticized it, whether it was over the British failure to stop Yankee privateers in 1780 or Tammany Hall's failure to operate honestly in – well, pick a year. These business organizations were avid watchdogs; they represented enough community influence, in many cases, to be able to stand up to corrupt or inept public officials.

Chambers members usually preferred smaller government and lower taxes, but not always. When it was time to pay for the bridge or railroad crossing, business people would rather have the whole community pitch in, via taxation or the issuing of bonds, rather than pass the hat solely among themselves. They often supported the building of more public schools – and would pull out all the stops to grab a university if the opportunity came up, and perhaps especially a state-funded university.

And to capture the state capital, as the Oklahoma City Chamber did in 1910: what a succulent plum for the community! This was true even if, as the Sacramento Chamber found, it required eternal vigilance to keep the capital and its jobs safely in town. There was nothing wrong with using other taxpayers' money to build the local economy.

When government was too intrusive or expensive, however, chambers could raise their voices as high as anyone's. The Charleston Chamber's anti-tariff outcry in 1827, the Taxpayers Convention in South Carolina in 1871, the U.S. Chamber's screams of protest at the antics of Franklin Roosevelt's first two or three administrations - these are only a few examples of business-organization rage. Sometimes getting angry worked, and sometimes it didn't.

For all their skepticism of government, chambers, like other interests in their country, had a hand in expanding it. Chambers were involved in establishing institutions already noted above (the Federal Reserve Bank, Farm Bureau, Port Authority of New York and New Jersey), along with such organizations as city manager and commission government, in hundreds of communities each; the National Weather Service; the U.S. Department of Commerce; the Interstate Commerce Commission; and the Food and Drug Administration.

Crime and Civil and Labor Unrest

When government failed to keep the peace, business people and their organizations occasionally would step in. San Francisco's William T. Coleman was nearly as handy with pick handles and ropes as he was with California trade statistics. Marshall Field sweetly presented new dresses to ladies and a shiny Gatling gun to strikers.

Sometimes these efforts at fighting local crime and disorder had national consequences. In 1894, the New York Chamber funded the Lexow Committee investigation of New

York's police that led to the appointment the following year of a new, clean-as-a-whistle superintendent, Theodore Roosevelt, whose effective work as a cop helped get him a vice presidential nomination under William McKinley. The revived Vigilance Committee of the San Francisco Chamber created such a climate of antiunion divisiveness and fear that it may have cost visiting Presidential candidate Charles Evans Hughes the election in 1916. In 1919, the Boston Chamber tried to help impose order during the police strike, and its (and others') failure to stop the rioting – along with a rare burst of eloquence from Silent Cal - helped propel Massachusetts Governor Calvin Coolidge to the Presidency.

Sometimes a criminal was just plain bad for business. Al Capone fit that category, and so Robert Isham Randolph and the Secret Six went after him by means fair and foul. The Florida Chamber didn't like the reputation that Charles Ponzi was giving to the local real estate industry and helped put him back where he belonged, in an exclusive gated community underwritten by Massachusetts taxpayers.

Generally speaking, the labor movement, or at least the closed shop, was anathema to most chambers and their members. There were exceptions to this, and sometimes chambers were successful at negotiating an end to labor stoppages. The U.S. Chamber's Eric Johnston was a poster boy for peaceful relations with unions. But most chambers wished that labor organizing would simply go away. Some chamber leaders, notably Tate Brady of the Tulsa Chamber, played rough with union members when they came to town.

Racial and Ethnic Friction

American racial and ethnic relations were a sad story from 1768 to 1945, and chambers were a part of it, although sometimes they gave a good account of themselves. The New York Chamber attempted to persuade Arthur Tappan to stop proselytizing against slavery and would have preferred almost anything to war over that issue. But the same chamber argued for emancipation in 1862, and at various points in its history championed the rights of immigrants, including the Chinese on the West Coast. Unfortunately, the fabled business organization abandoned its best traditions in 1934, when it endorsed the report of an anti-Semitic and immigrant-phobic "expert," Dr. Harry Laughlin. That report, questioning the genetic value of some of the people coming into the United States, was ammunition for those wishing to keep Jews and others from leaving Europe's troubled shores and landing in the United States.

Southern chambers, by protesting with good reason against hyper-taxation and misrule, helped their region shake off Yankee troops and meddling after the Civil War. But this ultimately led to disenfranchisement of blacks and an environment that tolerated the imposition of Jim Crow laws. A more positive spirit emanated from Sherman-scarred Atlanta, and from chambers in places such as Greenville, Miss., and Memphis, where business people saw it in their enlightened self-interest to try to create a better place for blacks and whites alike.

Chambers seldom bore direct responsibility for riots, but we do hold them accountable for how they reacted to those disturbances. The horrific race riot in Tulsa in 1921 was a blot on the community that remains today. The chamber shared in the shame, not so much for Tate Brady's apparently violent "watchman" activity, as for naming him head of a group to determine the fate of the black neighborhood, and for refusing outside aid to the stricken

African-American community. This chamber, however, later turned on the KKK, as did other chambers in many parts of the nation. Extremism and violence, ultimately, were a disaster for business, and chambers looked hard for alternatives.

An early example of accommodation between the races, one that presaged activities after World War II, was the Harlem employment compact in 1938. This agreement between storeowners and black civic groups, involving Adam Clayton Powell Jr. on one side and Col. Leopold Philipp and the Uptown Chamber of Commerce on the other, promised greater employment to blacks in local stores, but was ultimately unsuccessful, in part because of the poor economic environment. Nevertheless, the idea of chambers negotiating with aggrieved leaders of the black community would come up again, in a big way, during the civil rights era.

Among the strangest and saddest examples of chamber race relations was the involvement of the Los Angeles Chamber of Commerce in pushing for putting Japanese-Americans under confinement during World War II. While most of the nation also was angrily racist after the Pearl Harbor attack, the Los Angeles Chamber's leaders aggressively and cleverly pushed a public affairs strategy that advanced this agenda, and fast. This anti-Japanese-American approach was in contrast to how the chamber had acted in the past, and to how it would act in the future, regarding Asian-Americans.

War and Peace

Chambers of commerce historically have shown a marked ambivalence to seeing their nation go up against major opponents in war. The "merchants of peace" at the chambers in New York and Boston may have made the difference in the razor-thin margin of passage of the Jay Treaty in 1795, ending the chance for a war that could have broken the country permanently apart at that perilous time in the nation's history. In 1895, the New York Chamber intervened again, this time in opposition to the President, and may have averted war over Venezuela (although it is hard to imagine that the normally moderate Grover Cleveland would really have let war happen over such an issue).

Before the Revolutionary War, the Civil War, World War I, and World War II, major chambers essentially said, "Let's think this over." Business organizations, as a rule, did not seek fights with powerful countries. It was too risky. Surely arbitration or compromise would bring about a better result.

Studies indicate that a significant *level of commerce* between two nations generally inhibits the chance of their going to war. And so it may not be surprising that *chambers of commerce* also shrink from war – not always, but often. As such, chambers have played a seldom noticed role in American foreign policy, on balance, it appears, angling their country toward peace.

Peace through trade, however, isn't always the best policy. Tom Watson's befriending Hitler and bolstering IBM's German subsidiary was, in retrospect, a disastrous mistake. A chamber leader can hurt his or her country by burnishing the reputation of autocrats with evil intentions.

Once just about any war was declared, chambers turned out to be not merely patriotic, but avid fighters for their country. It was American material wealth as much as Americans' fighting skills that caused the Yankees to win the world series of wars. And chambers did much to convert industry to a war footing. If, in the process, they got a military base or two that would power the local economy for decades to come, so much the better!

Other Chamber Activities

Naturally, it is difficult to summarize all the activities of 3,000 or more chambers in a short space. In just one area, entertainment, the list of things the chambers started, or ran for an extended period, or helped attract, or financed, quickly lengthens: the Miss America Pageant and the nation's first folk music festival, as previously mentioned; innumerable other beauty contests and baby shows; the Lake Placid and Los Angeles Olympics; boxing matches including such heavyweights as Jack Dempsey, Gene Tunney, and Georges Carpentier; Bonneville salt-flat automobile speed dashes; airplane and balloon races; the Cherry Blossom Festival in Washington, D.C.; the Shenandoah Apple Blossom Festival; spring training baseball in Florida and Georgia; the Winter Carnival in St. Paul; Punxsutawney Phil; the "Daddy of Them All" Frontier Days rodeo in Cheyenne; various world and regional fairs; parades of all kinds; and so on.

Practical Men and Women

Lord Keynes once said, "Practical men, who believe themselves to be quite exempt from any intellectual influences, are usually the slaves of some defunct economist." Many of our cities and their proud and independent inhabitants are the unwitting heirs of some defunct commercial club or board of trade. Our cities, our population, our industry, our airports and seaports and roadways and rail lines, our forms of local government, our education systems, our military base infrastructure, our charities, our downtowns, and in many cases even the ways we look at civic life, have been partly and sometimes significantly shaped by the activities of early chambers of commerce and their descendants.

What is our verdict on the life of chambers over this period? "Ye shall know them by their fruits," said Jesus (Matthew 7:16). Many of these chambers' fruits will be recounted in this book, and readers may differ in their assessments. For the author, looking back, it's hard to separate these chambers from the growth of their country.

Much good came from what they did. They followed more or less the attitudes and outlooks of the society that surrounded them, with occasional, sometimes glaring, exceptions. In the case of some of the exceptions, however, the chambers may have behaved better than perhaps their members would have if acting alone.

Chambers benefited, sometimes, from what we might call the "group effect" of behavior: people tend to act more decorously, more selflessly, when other people are watching. Transparent collection plates get more donations. Chamber-member companies, today, have credit ratings roughly 70 points higher than those of the average company in their state.[2] The New York Chamber's motto, "Not born for ourselves alone," indicates a striving for being better than selfish urges might suggest.

Does this mean that chambers from 1768 to 1945 were packed with saints in training? Hardly. We will see plenty of examples of their shortcomings. And, strengthened by the moral or social image of these chambers, some bad actors got away with bad things. Moreover, some good people, or people who thought they were good, did bad things. No one could or should ever accuse chambers or their members of perfection.

Still, on balance, these business organizations, for all their flaws, helped their equally flawed country and communities develop. Americans have an optimistic side, much of that expressed by, and perhaps some it coming from, chambers of commerce. Who can't admire the Memphis Chamber secretary talking about the cotton trade in 1861, as mighty and unstoppable as the great Mississippi, or the San Francisco Chamber president saying, after the earthquake and fire of 1906, "It could have been worse"? There is a certain charm in that dogged civic courage.

Perhaps it is optimism – not the old brass-band sort, but some scrubbed-up, modern relative of it – that continues to induce stressed business people and employers to come together to think about their organizations' and their communities' futures. Something of the spirit of 1768 and of 1945 persists in many of these little crowds, which meet by the thousands across the nation. Perhaps these chamber members keep talking and planning because they really believe something can be improved, even though others may consider it a waste of time. Whatever it is precisely, there's something in that innate, positive conviction that sooner or later, at this board meeting or the next, or at a retreat, or at the annual dinner, will impel someone to blurt out something.

And what is that "something"? It's a sentence that begins with three very Tocquevillian words. These are the three words of the "helium hand," of the volunteer, of the person who doesn't know what he or she is getting into, or getting others into. These words make a terrible sound that eats at sleep and overturns budgets and, once in a while, changes history. And those words are, of course, as they have been more or less for a couple of centuries:

"Why don't we . . .?"

Beginnings

Commerce

In the beginning, there was commerce. Chambers came later. Indeed, in its simpler forms, such as exchanging berries for meat, commerce has existed since people have. More sophisticated trade began to grow up after some tribes started specializing in farming. And as early as 5,000 or 6,000 B.C., fairly complex long-distance commerce was taking place, according to archaeological evidence.[1] About 3,300 B.C., written records began to be kept in Mesopotamia and provide evidence of a thriving waterborne trade along the Tigris and Euphrates rivers and beyond.[2]

Trade fostered the growth of a class of clerks and civil servants to keep track of the activity. We have evidence that a government-connected board of trade existed as much as 4,000 years ago. Archeologists have found that the palace of Mari, in present-day Syria, featured in 2,000 B.C. a sophisticated section that handled commerce:

> There was a Foreign Office and a Board of Trade in the administrative palace of the kingdom of Mari. More than 100 officials were involved in dealing with the incoming and outgoing mail, which amounted to thousands of tablets alone.[3]

Of course, there were occasional disputes among traders. Here is a complaint registered on a clay tablet in the Sumerian city of Ur, circa 1,800 B.C. by a copper merchant named Nanni:

> You said, "I will give good ingots to Gimil-Sin. That is what you said, but you have not done so; you offered bad ingots to my messenger saying "Take it or leave it." Who am I that you should treat me so? Are we not both gentlemen?"[4]

The arbitration of such disputes, together with other activities performed by the clerks and government officials of this period, would later be handled by the infant chambers of commerce in the Western world.

Trade and conflict were never far apart. Homer's *Odyssey* involves a long sea voyage, with glimpses of many alluring islands and products and creatures, after the Trojan War. The Peloponnesian War between the rival camps of Athens and Sparta was, to a large extent, a struggle over grain trade routes.[5] The Punic Wars between Rome and Carthage also were, almost literally, trade wars.

But it was in times of peace that trade grew most rapidly. Trade historian William Bernstein notes that after the battle of Actium, when the Roman Empire was united peacefully under Octavian (later Augustus Caesar), there was an explosion of trade with places as far afield as China.[6] Roman roads, Roman coins, and Roman soldiers made it safe to conduct business over long distances. Lighthouses, anti-pirate patrols, and Roman colonies made shipping practical as well. Latin, as the *lingua franca* of the western half of the empire, smoothed the difficulty of transactions. There was even divine assistance, from the god of trade, Mercury, from whom is derived our word "commerce" (from *merx* for merchandise; *com* is a prefix meaning "with" or "together").

There were business organizations to go along with this Roman trade. As early as 495 B.C., Rome had a *Collegium Mercatorum*, or commercial exchange. When Spain was a colony of Rome, a group of merchants from Malaga assembled an organization in Rome to advise the government as a kind of trade council or chamber of commerce.[7] And local pride and boosting was not absent from these Rome-centric times: even St. Paul boasted that he was from "no mean city."[8] (His city of Tarsus, today's Mersin, was a major port.)

After the Roman Empire fell, European trade was disrupted by endemic violence and political instability, but trade flourished in other regions where order prevailed. The explosion of Islam, founded by the visions of a trader, Mohammed, created a network of exchange stretching from modern-day Indonesia to North Africa. And in the thirteenth century, behind the steaming horses of the Mongol warriors lay thousands of miles of safe territory for authorized merchants, allowing Marco Polo to journey all the way from Europe to China, India, and Mongolia, meeting communities of merchants and witnessing a vast network of international trade.

Traders congregated, naturally, around markets and in port areas. And in many ways, their contacts were very close, some based on family ties and some on ties of clan or even of caste. Artisans and merchants formed special groups of society in cultures in such places as the Indian subcontinent and the islands of Japan. Such groups sometimes made special appeals or suggestions to their rulers on how to maintain or promote business.

The Emergence of Guilds

As Western Europe emerged from the destruction of the Roman Empire and into the somewhat more settled Middle Ages, its trading activity began to pick up. With it came guilds of tradespeople and merchants. These guilds helped regulate commerce within their area of specialty, kept trade secrets, and interacted with other guilds as needed to promote commerce. From these guilds, some see the ancestors of not only some chambers of commerce but also of trade associations and of unions. Yet while many of these guilds had a focus on local business similar to that of chambers of commerce in later days, they differed in that they were an arm of government: the guilds had official charters protecting their rights to regulate trade, set prices, and so on.

One such guild was in Bruges, Belgium, known as the Brokers Guild, which was made up of people we might call medieval freight forwarders. These individuals were responsible for moving goods through the thickets of tolls, varying coins and currencies, highwaymen, and other obstacles to trade in the late Middle Ages. Records on the Guild date back to the middle of the 13th century. Its members were given a monopoly of the deals on freight movement in the County of Flanders. Originally, guild members were not permitted to own businesses, but this restriction was rescinded in 1293. At this time, the energetic Brokers Guild, which received membership dues from guild members, shared many characteristics with later chambers of commerce, including powers of arbitration. In fact, in 1665, the organization changed its name to "Chamber of Negotiation and Commerce being also the Privileged Brokers Guild."[9] But this guild, as did all or nearly all other guilds, derived its powers directly from government, and hence wasn't quite the same animal as the voluntary-membership chambers of commerce that would one day spring up on both sides of the Atlantic.

There was much other organized commercial activity in northern Europe. The Hanseatic League, from the 12th to the 16th century, was a kind of union of merchants stretching from London to Russia. Each city along the path of its Baltic trade routes had a group of traders who participated in the system maintained by the League.

Venice was another place where commerce began taking on a life and institutions of its own. Much of the Venetian Empire was built on its flourishing trade, and the merchant princes who ran the island city also ran their ships across the waters of the Mediterranean and other seas. These seafarers advanced trade through such Italian innovations as double-entry bookkeeping and sophisticated trade financing. The leading merchants essentially became the local government, as would occur elsewhere in towns where trading was the dominant activity.

The First Chamber of Commerce

It was in France where the modern term "chamber of commerce" would emerge. On August 5, 1599, in Marseilles, the first organization to have that name (*chambre de commerce*) was created. The town council had found it "no longer possible to combine commercial with municipal functions" and set up the new, separate organization.[10] This powerful group received royal recognition in 1650 and was involved in everything from harbor maintenance, to sending trade missions abroad, to chasing down pirates. (Two centuries later it would have a hand in the creation of the Suez Canal.)

A chamber of commerce was founded in Paris soon after that in Marseilles. It was to play a role in the development of the New World. Samuel de Champlain relied on it greatly for support as he looked for backers for the infant settlement in French Canada. At a critical moment in 1618, when his support in Rouen had weakened, the Paris Chamber helped Champlain obtain backing from the king and other influential people in Paris.[11]

These business organizations seem to have filled a need. In 1700 Louis XIV authorized the creation of several more French chambers that would nominate deputies to the new Royal Council of Commerce in Paris.[12] While these chambers and other guilds and associations were suppressed with the French Revolution in 1789, Napoleon revived them and encouraged their spread outside France. The Corsican dictator, however, was no admirer of independent or quasi-independent institutions of any kind, including those of merchants. He once wrote to his minister of police, Joseph Fouché, that "the deliberations of the Chambers [of commerce] are invariably valueless."[13] The man who called Britain "a nation of shopkeepers" saw merchants more as a source of revenue or plunder (and the distinction between the two was never terribly clear to Napoleon) than of advice.

The Evolution of Business Organizations in the British Isles

The British Isles, too, were becoming busier with organizations of traders. Guilds of European merchants may have been introduced to England after the invasion of William the Conqueror in 1066. William's arrival stimulated cross-channel trade and the need to service it. There are early references to merchant guilds in the decades after the invasion.[14] By 1318, according to a later commentator, there was a briefly organized national assembly of merchants under King Edward II.[15]

Local merchant guilds in the British Isles began evolving into complex and occasionally powerful organizations. Sometimes, as in Venice, they became the local government. In other cases, they did not control all of government but exercised extraordinary influence nonetheless. In Bristol, the merchants' guild seems to have turned into a remarkable trading organization known as the Society of Merchant Venturers. This group funded John Cabot's 1497 voyage to Newfoundland and received a formal royal charter in 1552.[16]

Since 1621, Great Britain had a governmental trade council, often called the Board of Trade, which served as an adviser to the king. Indeed, among its other functions, the Board of Trade was the main point of liaison with the American colonies on behalf of the Crown. But the Board of Trade, as a direct part of government, was not a true chamber of commerce. Moreover, the Board of Trade was made up of just five to 10 appointed officials, all from the British aristocracy, and had no voluntary or external membership.[17]

During the 17th and 18th centuries, ideas about chambers and chamber-like organizations gradually began to take deeper root in the British Isles. James Whiston proposed the idea of a "commercial parliament" beginning in 1681. Another writer, Charles Davenant, went further and suggested an independent, elected body of merchants, a "council of commerce," which was proposed to Parliament and almost adopted in 1695. Finally, drawing on these two earlier thinkers, Malachy Postlethwayt, a well-regarded and popular author who was "the Keynes of his day," advanced many commercial concepts. One of his popular books was the *Dictionary of Commerce* (1751), in which he discussed a national council of commerce. In *Great Britain's True System* (1757), he wrote of local French chambers and said they would be of "inestimable advantage" if adopted in Britain.[18]

The British and their transatlantic cousins may have listened to Postlethwayt's advice on French chambers, but they didn't copy the French. Rather than mimic the quasi-governmental style of French chambers, in which companies had to be licensed by their chamber and in which the chamber was the officially acknowledged commercial authority of the community, business organizations in the English-speaking regions on both sides of the Atlantic evolved more or less spontaneously into administratively weak, but politically influential, organizations. The English-speaking chambers had little if any direct authority. But they were allowed to raise their voices against authority. And, in the centuries ahead, they certainly would.

Raising Voices on Both Sides of the Atlantic

Even before Postlethwayt's ideas on chambers were well known, there emerged in the Americas some business organizations with attributes of modern chambers of commerce, such as governance rules and lobbying. One of them was a society formed in 1733 to resist the British Molasses Act. Chamber historian Robert Bennett notes of the Boston group:

This was reconstituted in about 1760 to resist renewal of the Act and to be a general Boston Society for Encouraging Trade and Commerce within the preserve of Massachusetts Bay (BSETC). It had formal governance procedures and broad lobby objectives, in almost every respect acting as a *de facto chamber*, and was a direct forerunner of the first Boston Chamber of 1785.[19]

There were other ad hoc or temporary groups that had some chamber-like features. In 1750, merchants came together as an association in Halifax, Nova Scotia. We have little knowledge of their activity, but the group certainly existed and has been claimed, with perhaps some exaggeration (given that there was the more substantive group in Boston in 1733), to be the first chamber of commerce in the New World.

Here is the main testimony about the Halifax group:

> In the month of August, 1750, three hundred and fifty-three settlers arrived in the ship Alderney; and in September following, three hundred German Protestants, from the Palatinate, in the ship Ann. The Governor and Council were embarrassed in providing for their support, and found it necessary to enter into pecuniary arrangements with the merchants of the town, who at this early period had formed themselves into an association for the benefit of trade.[20]

Things weren't easy for the merchants or the settlers then: the following spring, in the nearby community of Dartmouth, Indians scalped a number of settlers and carried away others as prisoners.[21] The merchants' organization (like many chambers of commerce) seems to have lapsed into inactivity soon after its founding, but apparently the idea was not lost. A more formally constituted group appeared in 1786 and another in 1804.[22]

Into the 1760s, the incipient chamber development remained at least as active on Europe's side of the Atlantic, where the chamber idea had originated and where most of the merchants were. In 1763 there was a Committee of Merchants in Dublin, although it was not until 20 years later that the city could boast a full-fledged chamber.[23] Similar committees appeared elsewhere in Ireland – in Cork, Waterford, Limerick, and Belfast. And in England and Scotland, such groups appeared in Edinburgh, Glasgow, Greenock, Leith, and Exeter. Moreover, there was a potters' chamber set up in north Staffordshire in 1767.[24]

In 1767 the English-speaking world seems to have obtained its first organization officially called, without modifiers except the local place name, a "chamber of commerce." In the English Channel, the Jersey Chamber of Commerce was formed in 1767; its first meeting of which we have a record was on February 24, 1768, at the King's Head Tavern in St. Helier.[25] The organization was devoted to trade, especially with the leading trading partner of the island, Newfoundland. In 1769 there was likely a similar chamber founded on the island of Guernsey.[26]

At the very time when English-speaking business groups were beginning to form and to taste some limited freedom from governmental authority, the Atlantic theater had grown more troubling for everyone involved in trade. Commercial tensions between King George III and his American colonies were heating up. And a couple of colonial chambers would be right in the thick of it. Could the new concept of a free chamber, a chamber that could speak its mind to anyone, survive war, occupation, and schism? The years ahead would test that idea.

The new colonial chamber members would excitedly discuss political and economic ideas in taverns where they often sipped, not just beer or whiskey, but the stylish, invigorating drink of coffee, and, occasionally, its sister beverage, tea. . .

New Chambers in
a New Nation

1768-1815

The American chamber story begins, as so many stories do, with a war. The government of Great Britain had spent heavily to win the Seven Years War, which lasted from 1756 to 1763. This worldwide conflict included some heavy fighting in North America (where the struggle is sometimes called the French and Indian War). British soldiers remained garrisoned in the New World after the fighting and their government, not surprisingly, sought means of paying for their upkeep.

Why not tax the colonists to pay for the forces protecting them? This appeared only fair to many in Parliament, and was logical given the relatively high living standards on the western shores of the North Atlantic. But the colonists objected, pleading poverty and exhaustion from the war.

Unfortunately, the case of the colonists may have been undercut by the wealthier ones among them. American merchants had lavishly entertained British soldiers after the war's successful conclusion. The colonists' protestations of poverty rang hollow. As John Pintard, who was to serve later as secretary of the New York Chamber of Commerce, related:

> The plea [of poverty] was rebutted in Parliament by an appeal to the elegant entertainments given by the citizens of New York to the officers of the British army, and the dazzling display of silver plate at their dinners, equal if not superior to any nobleman's, which hospitality and exhibitions were adduced as proof of the wealth and prosperity of the Colonies.[1]

If Pintard's observation is correct, then surely these were some of history's most expensive meals. It was only two years later that Parliament issued the Stamp Act, which called for taxation of a wide variety of printed materials and documents and aroused the fury of the colonists. Whether or not the New York merchants were in any way to blame for starting this new conflagration, however, they did have to cope with the act's aftermath. And in so doing, they not only started a chamber of commerce, but also, indirectly, had a hand in starting a war.

On October 31, 1765, the day before the act was to be enforced, a group of New York merchants convened at the Burns' Coffee House and resolved not to trade with Britain until the Stamp Act was repealed. More than 200 of them signed the document.[2] This meeting of merchants, with a specific resolution and outcome, has plenty of resemblance to a chamber of commerce meeting, and indeed could be considered a precursor to the founding of the local chamber, by many of the same merchants, three years later. The 1765 non-importation threat worked; merchants in other colonial cities followed suit, alarming traders in Britain, who induced their government to back down and repeal the Stamp Act the following year.

Some of these New York traders would later remain loyal to the British government and some would become revolutionaries. But on Halloween in 1765, they had united in a single act of measured defiance. Their action would quickly inspire others in New York and throughout the colonies, including many who were far more radical than they.

One of the leaders of these merchants was John Cruger, who was also a member of the General Assembly of New York and mayor of the city. As a member of the Assembly's Committee of Correspondence, he had penned eloquent protests against missteps by the British authorities, including the "Declaration of the Rights and Grievances of the Colonists in America" after the Stamp Act was promulgated.

John Cruger

Cruger, while devoted to the rights of his fellow colonists, also wished to preserve order. When, after November 1, 1765, it was clear that local activists would attack the office of Lieutenant Governor Cadwallader Colden to seize the hated stamps, he intervened and persuaded Colden to surrender the stamps. Colden's acquiescence, and the moderation of British General Thomas Gage, defused the tension. Mayor Cruger even wrote a letter of thanks to General Gage for avoiding bloodshed.[3] It was this kind of moderation that would distinguish the activism of chambers in succeeding years. Most merchants had something to lose in armed conflict and usually would avoid serious trouble if they could.

But the troubles continued. The New York Assembly quarreled with Parliament and was dissolved by Governor Sir Henry Moore on February 11, 1768. On April 5 of the same year, Cruger and his fellow merchants met together again. This time it was to form a new organization, one that was born in the uncertainty of the period, but that would last long after it, through peace and war. The association was called the New York Chamber of Commerce.

Chambers of commerce, as we have seen, had existed for more than a century in Europe, but there was something different about the new ones emerging in the English-speaking areas on both sides of the Atlantic. They were relatively independent of government authority and able to voice the opinions of their members. They represented commercial interests in an occasionally hostile and never easy mercantile environment.

The New York Chamber was an energetic exponent of the concerns of its merchants. Even its motto was oddly appealing, calling for feelings beyond self-interest from its members: *Non nobis nati solum* ("Not born for ourselves alone"). Created at a time when the currents of freedom were running strong, the chamber had no specific obligation to, nor financing from, government.

The chamber did, however, apply for and receive in 1770 a charter of incorporation from King George III, via the offices of Lieutenant Governor Colden.[4] This document, full of the flowery prose of the era, informed the king that the chamber, which already had been meeting to good effect, could "answer and promote the Commercial and consequently the Landed Interest of our said growing Colony." The document asked for powers from the king, but these powers were simply to allow the group to organize itself: to elect officers, to have a corporate seal, and to erect buildings out of common funds. This was an advisory group, something of a merchants' think tank, not a royal bureau.

Not Born for Ourselves Alone:
Seal of the New York Chamber of Commerce

The lack of specific powers was, on examination, a remarkably creative thing. It was analogous to the discovery of the number "zero." When nothing was possible, anything was possible. Possessing almost no explicit power, a merchants' group could dream up practically anything to help, harass, encourage, stymie, or otherwise interact with the people with the "real" power over commerce and the community. This new organization was really something new and different.

The growing sense of independence among the colonials, then, was manifested in a chamber that was itself independent – independent but with a sense of responsibility toward the local economy. This idea of a free, detached chamber, able to comment on the economy and try to improve it, but without specific powers to do so, proved so influential that even after a Revolutionary War that was also a civil war, the infant organization somehow survived.

Cruger was named president of the new chamber in 1768 and was reelected unanimously the following year, when he was also elected speaker of the reconstituted Assembly of the Colony of New York. He would remain speaker of the Assembly until it was dissolved in 1775. Through Cruger and his colleagues, the chamber would be tied intimately to the coming war. Moreover, Cruger's nephew, Nicholas, had brought in an ambitious young business associate from the West Indies who would also be closely connected to the war and who would become a great friend of the chamber, a young man named Alexander Hamilton.

The New York Chamber essentially was born into conflict, with its merchants aiming to distance themselves from the growing radical sentiment against the mother country. A new non-importation embargo, opposed by most merchants, was the immediate threat that brought the chamber into being in 1768. As would be the case for this chamber and many others in future years, the merchants' aim was reform, not revolution.[5] Indeed, the New York Chamber handled many prosaic items of business in its first years, such as creating prizes for fish catches and improving standards for local currency.

As an institution, the chamber was not directly involved in many matters connected with the growing tensions with Great Britain, although certainly some of its members, such as Cruger, were deeply enmeshed in political events. No doubt one reason for the chamber's relative lack of political activity was that its membership (like the population of New York) was split on the question of independence from Great Britain. Indeed, more of its members were loyalists than revolutionaries. After the battle of Lexington, the chamber held one more meeting, on May 2, 1775, and then went into dormancy.

Southern Exposure

Several hundred miles to the south, another group of merchants was also feeling the tensions of the revolution. On December 2, 1773, in the port of Charleston, a British ship, the *London*, arrived in the harbor with 257 chests of tea. Similar ships had gone to Boston, New York, and Philadelphia. New York and Philadelphia protesters had sent the ships back home; in Boston, of course, a group of merchants and artisans dressed as American Indians had dumped the tea into the sea. In Charleston, those opposed to the right of Parliament to tax the colonists were anxious to see that not a penny of tax was collected on this tea and that the exotic drink be boycotted.

The merchants of Charleston, like those in other cities, were split in their loyalties. But the weight of the traders' opinion was in favor of moderation. This contrasted with the other two major classes in town, the planters and the artisans, both of which were more revolutionary in their sentiments. Some of the merchants owned a portion of the tea in the harbor and had an interest in it being sold, and some were recently from Britain or the West Indies and had no particular attraction to the idea of independence of the American colonies. Moreover, many merchants feared that if the tea was sent back to Britain or dumped into the sea, then the ever-ready class of smugglers would take over this business and undermine the position of legitimate traders.[6]

On December 9, 1773, several of the more loyalist-leaning merchants held a meeting to further their cause. They continued to confer during the month, and "formed themselves into a Society, by the Name of the Charles-Town Chamber of Commerce," according to the local newspaper.[7]

These were among the wealthiest merchants of this booming port city. John Savage, an attorney, came originally from Bermuda, and was a partner with Gabriel Manigault in a successful venture that traded tea and other items. Miles Brewton, its vice president, was the leading slave trader in Charleston.[8]

These men and their colleagues found some success with their chamber's first initiative: they managed to reach a draw with the South Carolina radicals on the tea issue. Some of the tea could be unloaded, although it was to be only warehoused for the time being. Thus, Charleston became the only port in which British tea reached American soil. (Nevertheless, the tea was not sold until three years later, when the revolutionaries managed to market it).[9]

In its early years, the Charles-Town Chamber of Commerce accomplished a few things beyond this act. The economy of the entire colony – indeed, of the 13 colonies – was in disarray because of the disruption of trade with Britain. In 1774, the chamber supported an effort to create certificates of indebtedness – promises to pay creditors once tax money was collected by the troubled South Carolina colonial government.[10] In 1775 it took some action on bills of exchange.[11]

With the start of the Revolutionary War in 1775, there isn't a great deal more known of the activities of this chamber, except that John Savage remained president until he left the city. British forces occupied the city from 1780 to 1782 and, when they left, took thousands of loyalist citizens with them. A total of 300 ships departed, leaving Charleston with a huge hole in its economy and in its civic leadership.[12]

The loyalist coloring of the original chamber could have led Charleston to abandon the idea of having another chamber. But in 1784, the Charleston Chamber was reconstituted with a group of merchants who were patriots. The first leader of the new chamber, in fact, had been a patriot naval commander in the Revolutionary War: Dutch-born Alexander Gillon. He had captained a ship he named *South Carolina*, helping with the capture of New Providence in the Bahamas. The *South Carolina* was a privateer, namely a wartime pirate-like vessel cruising the high seas in search of enemy prizes, making Gillon one of the first, but not the last, of the Charleston chamber leaders to be involved in this aggressive form of naval "trade."

The Rump Chamber

Privateers were a big part of the wartime action in Charleston – as they were in New York. In fact, during the Revolutionary War, so many captured ships were brought into the British-occupied New York harbor that they were a key reason for the revival of the New York Chamber of Commerce after its war-related closure in the middle of 1775. There needed to be some organization to help deal with all the loot. This contraband was composed of ships and cargo captured not by patriot, but by loyalist privateers.

The loyalist members of the old chamber came together on June 21, 1779, and addressed a letter to the British commandant in New York, Daniel Jones, asking for permission to revive their organization. Not only had the good policies of the British increased commerce, they said, but the "success of Private Ships of War" had also led to a need for a group so that "the many mercantile differences which so frequently happen may be adjusted."[13]

Just how much loot was there? Three months earlier, on March 8, Governor Tryon had announced the extraordinary volume of activity:

> I have already issued one hundred and twenty-one Commissions to as many private Vessels of War, - that in the short space of Time elapsed since the eighteenth of September last the Prize Vessels arrived here amount to above six hundred thousand Pounds Lawful money of New York, at the ancient currency of eight Shillings a milled Dollar.[14]

No doubt a great deal of this massive booty was seized from the ships of the patriot members of the New York Chamber of Commerce. Loyalist privateers were cruising for patriot prizes, while patriots were doing the reverse. The members of the New York Chamber of Commerce thus played an active role in the naval conflicts the Revolutionary War – apparently on both sides. The chamber that would one day fulminate against the very idea of privateers during the Civil War was a hotbed of them in the war of the nation's birth.

The New York Chamber of Commerce had lost about a third of its members to the patriot cause and others to flight from the troubled New York area, but the loyalist members who remained knew how to defend their interests. The group's president, Isaac Low, was a respected merchant who had sided with Cruger and others in the early protests against Parliament's excesses. But his heart was with the mother country. John Adams had taken his measure accurately after meeting him just before the Revolution, in August 1774, when he wrote in his diary:

> Mr. Low, the chairman of the Committee of Fifty-one, they say, will profess attachment to the cause of liberty, but his sincerity is doubted.[15]

Isaac Low indeed was a loyalist at heart, and declared his loyalty to Britain after the patriots declared the opposite. Low was briefly arrested early in the Revolutionary War. He had retired to Raritan, New Jersey but was caught up in a roundup of people suspected of corresponding with the enemy. Low managed to convince General George Washington, who had initiated the crackdown, that he was innocent. After his release, and the capture and occupation of New York by the British in September 1776, Low moved back to New York, where he was considered the key figure behind the revival of the chamber in 1779.[16]

Privateers would remain the critical issue for the "rump" chamber. The patriots turned out to be just as good at stealing enemy ships as the loyalists were. Years later, the Boston Board of Trade cited figures showing that rebel privateers during the American Revolution captured 200,000 tons of British goods, raising insurance premiums from 5 to 40 percent.[17] On behalf of the New York Chamber, Low wrote in 1781 to British Admiral Marriott Arbuthnot asking for better protection against patriot privateers. Low argued eloquently that the New York vicinity was the prime target of the enemy raiders: "the best Cruizing Ground for the Enemy, perhaps in the World, is within a small distance of Sandy Hook."[18]

Admiral Arbuthnot considered this a Low blow. Like many authorities after him in the Americas, the admiral took issue with the meddling of the local chamber of commerce. "It gives me no small concern that you should suppose I have been in the smallest respect inattentive to this service in the Arrangement of the King's Ships," he remonstrated.[19] Low sent a conciliatory reply which, however, also emphasized that New York had more trade to protect than did the more northerly port of Halifax.[20] In this and many a war to come, local chambers of commerce would be unable to put aside completely their city pride and economic self-interest as they took part in international conflicts.

This wasn't by any means the limit of the work of the loyalist New York Chamber during the war. It offered a reward to men who agreed to sign up for duty on the King's ships, while it protested when threatened by the British Navy's impressment of sailors from its successful privateers. It helped the British locate patriot privateers and gave a reward to an intrepid mail captain who had escaped the clutches of the rebels.

The chamber even offered to help with the menacing problem of how the British stored gunpowder. The British Navy had kept a "Powder-Ship" in the New York harbor that had blown up after lightning struck it, causing considerable damage to property on the shore. The helpful chamber suggested the use of a patriot's invention – Ben Franklin's lightning rod – to prevent a recurrence on the next Powder-Ship.[21]

But the patriots, aided by their French allies, turned all the efforts of the King's soldiers and sailors to naught. The loyalist chamber's energetic and resourceful efforts on behalf of the mother country had been in vain. On November 25, 1783, General Washington and his troops entered the port city.

Isaac Low and most of the other loyalist merchants in the chamber had left town. This could have been the end of the chamber. But just as in Charleston, where the concept of the chamber had been tainted by its loyalists, in New York the patriot merchants decided they needed this institution despite its loyalist interlude. In the spring of 1784, 40 merchants sent a petition to the New York Legislature asking for a renewal of its charter under the new government, with a new name, the Chamber of Commerce of the State of New York. Their petition was granted.[22]

A Parting Glance

It is worth a parting glance at the two American chambers of commerce and their role in the Revolutionary War. The members of the New York and Charleston chambers, despite having key leaders who were patriots, were chiefly on the side of the mother country. The New York Chamber's members had pushed for reform, but when push came to shove, Isaac Low and many of his chamber colleagues had come down on the side of Great Britain. The Charleston merchants had aimed not to dump British tea into the water, but to bring it ashore.

Was there a reason that these two chambers, the first in what would become the United States, leaned more toward the enemy than toward revolution? In retrospect, and after viewing North American chambers of commerce in action over more than 200 years, we can see some logical reasons for their actions. Over the years, most chambers would shrink from revolution and open war. Their basic inclination would be toward peace. After all, trade worked best under peaceful conditions. Sometimes, when Americans look back, they may wish that these institutions were more forthright in prosecuting what they now consider to be the "right" wars. But at the time, especially for people with a conservative bent who preferred reform to revolution, and who abhorred the massive, destructive results of full-scale conflict, some quiet alternative to war was usually these merchants' choice.

In later years, in a stable United States, chambers would tend to be all-out in their attempts to aid their country in war – once war was declared. (In the prelude to war, by contrast, chambers tended to weigh in for peace and/or arbitration.) At the time of the Revolutionary War, however, it was not quite so clear what "their country" was. To any conservative person, Great Britain must have appeared to be more logical choice for a stable guarantor of business and prosperity for North Americans. The prudent choice for merchants surely was to aim for a peaceful solution before war was declared, and then, perhaps, to choose the side of the greatest power on the globe, the British. That so many of the merchants of occupied Charleston and New York chose this approach is not a surprise. Indeed, the merchants' point of view against revolution was not far from that of the average American colonist of the times; there were plenty of fighters on both sides who entered the lists reluctantly and who would have preferred peaceful reform to bloodshed.

Perhaps what is a surprise is how quickly – almost instantly – the patriot merchants, once the war was over, reestablished chambers of commerce in their communities. There was something useful and reassuring about these institutions. They seemed to provide an element of stability and reform to a fractious society that often made things difficult for business. Chambers of commerce might be among the last in war - but they could be first in peace.

Chambers in the Early United States

Transportation, security, and infrastructure, all critical to commerce, had appeared on the agendas of North American chamber meetings since at least 1768. These concerns continued after the Revolutionary War. Indeed, they continue more than two centuries later.

The chamber in New York, still usually referred to by its familiar, old name (the New York Chamber of Commerce), had plenty to do as the infant United States of America emerged. The organization came out against smuggling, in part because customs revenues were one of the few sources of income for the government.[23] It also requested that the state government petition Congress for relief against the pirates of the Barbary Coast.[24]

When John Hancock and other Boston merchants asked in 1785 that the New York Chamber urge the federal government to effect a trade treaty with Great Britain, the chamber decided to recommend holding a public meeting on the topic at City Hall. It was felt that the chamber alone was not of sufficient authority to advise the U.S. government such a significant matter of foreign policy.[25]

Surely one of the more interesting activities of the new chamber was its hosting of a speaker on January 3, 1786. The man was Christopher Collis, who envisioned a canal to connect New York with the Great Lakes. Others had had similar ideas, but Collis's plan was fairly specific and had received some encouragement from members of the legislature. His statement to the chamber noted:

> Your memorialist has formed a design of opening an intercourse with the interior parts of the United States, by an artificial inland navigation, along the Mohawk River and Wood Creek to the great lakes – a design which must evidently extend the commerce of this city with exceeding rapidity beyond what it can possibly arrive at by any other means; a design which Providence has manifestly pointed out, and which, in the hands of a commercial people, must evidently tend to make them great and powerful; and which, though indefinite in its advantages, may be effected for a sum perfectly trifling when compared with the advantages.[26]

The chamber approved of his idea but indicated it had no funds to help him. Three decades later, it would take an ambitious New York governor, DeWitt Clinton, to champion successfully the building of the Erie Canal, beginning in 1817 and ending in 1825. That scheme, considered harebrained by many, also would win the approval of the hard-headed merchants of the New York Chamber of Commerce.

The Return of the Charleston Chamber

In Charleston, the reconstituted chamber was a strong proponent of plans for the Santee Canal, the first canal in North America to connect two separate river valleys. This canal joined the Santee and Cooper rivers, permitting cotton shipments from upcountry to reach the port. The project attracted a who's who of South Carolina supporters, including the "Swamp Fox" himself, the Revolutionary War hero Francis Marion. The endeavor was approved by the legislature and opened in 1801. The Santee Canal saw significant barge traffic, although design flaws led to its running dry at times.[27]

The Charleston Chamber's members faced several trading problems in the early years of the new nation. For example, the British in 1783 barred U.S. ships from trading with the British West Indies, which otherwise would have been a natural and nearby market for the Charleston traders. The Charleston organization communicated both with the New York Chamber of Commerce on these problems and with merchants in Philadelphia and a Committee of Merchants in Boston, a chamber-like group that included Declaration of Independence signer John Hancock.[28]

Feelings ran high against the British, who seemed to be continuing the war with exclusionary, mercantilist trade policies that victimized the former colonists along the Atlantic. The Charleston Chamber's members decried British policies as "repugnant with Evils." It even seemed that the British were out to get the Americans: the British showed "a disposition to ruin if possible the Merchants, & real citizens of the Union & by every means in their power both abroad and by their Agents here to check the rising Consequence Credit & Interest of a large and extended Empire in its infancy, form'd by Nature for Agriculture & Commerce."[29]

In August of 1785, the chamber convened a public meeting on the trade problem. As a result, a "Committee of Citizens" created a resolution requesting that South Carolina offer the U.S. Congress the powers to negotiate trade treaties with foreign powers.[30] Thus at this early stage, South Carolinians and the Charleston Chamber wanted a stronger, not weaker, national government, in order to protect them from a predatory Great Britain. Indeed, merchants' urgent need, not just in Charleston but elsewhere in the new republic, for some sort of national (not only state) defense against the depredations of the great foreign powers, was one of the primary motives for the scrapping of the weak Articles of Confederation in favor of the stronger Constitution in 1789.

The new leadership of the Charleston Chamber attempted to diversify the city's trade from Britain and its possessions, but the job was difficult. The chamber worked through Alexander Gillon to find opportunities in Holland and through Thomas Jefferson for markets in France. As early as 1784, the chamber formed a special committee to gather the economic information requested by Jefferson; work was complicated by the lack of trade records, "all the Books of the Custom House being Carried away by the British."[31] The most memorable result of these efforts was the importation of many species of flowers, some with origins in the Far East. Such efforts made Charleston's plantations more beautiful, but didn't do a great deal for building the local economy.[32]

In the middle of 1790, the Charleston Chamber was in need of a boost, too. Several members resigned and in July, there was a motion made to dissolve the chamber. Fortunately, this motion was postponed, and in September the motion was withdrawn and the chamber brought on a number of new members.

This revival was timely. On March 30, 1791, the following resolution was approved:

Resolved, that the Chamber of Commerce is of Opinion that the Merchants of Charleston should address the President of the United States on his Arrival, and entertain him with a public Dinner, and that a Committee be appointed to draw up an address to him and to take Subscriptions from the Merchants in the City, for the Purpose of defraying the Expences and conducting the Business of the Dinner; and that they be empowered to invite such public officers and others, as they may judge proper.[33]

Indeed, on May 7 the chamber hosted President Washington to a gala dinner in Charleston. It was complete with a baroque address from the merchants (signed on their behalf by Edward Darrell, the chamber's president) and an equally polite, if shorter, response from Washington. Thus right after almost succumbing to apathy, the chamber members hosted the father of their country.

An interesting wrinkle to the world of chambers in the United States emerged in these early years of the Republic. Up to this point, the country's chambers and similar groups had concentrated mostly on overseas trade and the currency, transportation, and other systems supporting it. There was no major organization that focused on domestic industry. But in 1787, a Philadelphia merchant and politician named Tench Coxe – an active individual who had established a short-lived chamber in Philadelphia in 1784[34] - founded an organization called the Pennsylvania Society for the Encouragement of Manufacture and the Useful Arts.[35] This organization promptly awarded an inventor named John Hague 100 pounds for improvements in spinning cotton fibers.[36]

A clever mill worker in England, Samuel Slater, read a news article about this award and decided his skills would be better remunerated in the United States. As the British government was fiercely protective of that nation's textile know-how, Slater disguised himself as a farm laborer to emigrate to the former colonies in 1789. There, before long, he had entered into business with Moses Brown of Providence and began setting up dozens of cotton mills in Rhode Island and Massachusetts.[37] The American textile industry was born almost overnight, thanks in part to a helping hand from a cash award made by a kind of business organization that was new to the United States.

The Pennsylvania Society for the Encouragement of Manufacture and the Useful Arts wasn't exactly a chamber of commerce, but it was as close an approximation as Philadelphia had at the time. (In fact, in later years that city would have two separate organizations, one focused mostly on domestic business and the other on trade, until they finally came together in 1845.) Moreover, the Society communicated with other commercial groups: e.g., Tench Coxe in1792 asked for trade data from the Charleston Chamber.[38]

Coxe's local-industry focus made particular sense in inland locations where the opportunities for international trade were limited and domestic production was critical. This may explain why a group with the name of the Meadville Society for the Encouragement of Domestic Manufacture and the Useful Arts was founded in 1807 in that small town in western Pennsylvania. This organization is considered to be the forerunner of today's chamber of commerce in Meadville. Eventually, most U.S. chambers of commerce would focus both on the selling of things (commerce) and on the making of them (industry).[39]

The Jay Treaty

The French Revolutionary Wars beginning in 1793 brought hostilities between France and Great Britain, leading to problems for neutral merchants from the United States. British warships would seize American sailors and commandeer U.S. merchant ships that they believed were abetting the enemy; the French took American ships also. Just like their federal government, chambers of commerce in the United States would grapple with these problems for another two decades.

President George Washington favored the maintenance of neutrality, despite the humiliations and disruptions at the hands of the British and French. He feared that an aggressive reaction by the United States could lead to war with the principal source of the trouble, the British. Such a conflict could tear apart the unstable republic, which had enough problems of its own without a war. Memories of Daniel Shays' anti-tax rebellion in 1786-87 in central and western Massachusetts, suppressed by the state militia, were still fresh. The Constitution had only been ratified in 1788, and the former colonies were barely united under its unproven structure.

Washington's peaceful approach had support in some trading communities. On July 22, 1793, a group of Boston merchants met in Faneuil Hall to express support for the President's neutrality policy.[40] But this didn't mean they believed they should simply ignore the offenses of the British and French. They met again on September 12 and formed a committee to collect, and send to the President, "authenticated evidence of injuries done to our commerce by the armed vessels of any belligerent power."[41]

The merchants' leader was Thomas Russell (1740-1796), a remarkably civic-minded man who seemed to have followed a lucky star. As a young man in 1762, he had travelled to the West Indies on a trading mission and been captured by the French. Transported to Martinique, he was imprisoned, but happened to be carrying with him a letter of introduction to a prominent local individual – a letter he had not expected to use on the journey, but brought just in case. The letter brought about his release and gained him powerful friends. Russell went on to have a successful mercantile career, being the first Boston businessman to trade with Russia, and was a member of the State Council.[42]

On March 17, 1794, Russell and his colleagues founded the Boston Chamber of Commerce. He was its first president. Working through an institution, as opposed to simply holding meetings and making declarations, was probably viewed as the best way to influence public policy. Indeed, there was something semi-official and vaguely important about the new institution that would both strengthen its allies and infuriate its opponents.

The Boston Chamber was founded 21 years after the emergence of the Charleston Chamber of Commerce. It would take only 23 days for the next chamber to be established. This was the New Haven Chamber of Commerce, set up by 26 local merchants on April 9, 1794. The group's president was Elias Shipman, a merchant.[43] This chamber would engage many of the leading citizens of New Haven in the coming years, including dictionary pioneer Noah Webster.

The New Haven merchants were deeply concerned about the war between France and Great Britain. The British, in particular, were seizing neutral ships and impounding them. In early 1794, no fewer than 19 ships of New Haven merchants were being held by the British.[44]

There was fear on the high seas but also opportunity. Elijah Austin was one of the animating spirits of the new Connecticut institution. He had mesmerized the port city the previous year when one of his ships came into the harbor, laden with exotic porcelains and silks from China. This was the first shipment from China to arrive in New Haven. So excited was the community that it was easy for Austin to find the money to start building a bigger ship that, when complete, would return to China. It was already being built in the first half of 1794.[45]

Hence the New Haven merchants set up the chamber not only out of fear of the British and French navies, but out of excitement at the possibilities of trade elsewhere.[46] Yankee merchants lost little time in their attempts to open new markets. But clearly the north Atlantic remained the bread and butter of these merchants and it was under serious threat.

Tensions with the British were white-hot. In a last-minute attempt to prevent war, President Washington dispatched John Jay in May 1794 to try to negotiate a treaty with Great Britain. Alexander Hamilton had drafted the basic terms, hoping to maintain peace and commerce with Britain, even if at the cost to some rights of neutrality. On May 9, just three days after Jay had been given his instructions for the negotiations, the New York Chamber of Commerce, headed by its president, the merchant Comfort Sands, passed resolutions supporting the mission.[47]

The nation nervously awaited the results of Jay's trip. But life went on. In New Haven, Elijah Austin was fully engaged in his trading business, and on June 19, 1794, he opened up a chest of clothes from the West Indies. A younger employee, Henry Hubbard, was helping him. Two days later, Hubbard died of yellow fever. Austin succumbed to the same affliction just two more days later in New York.[48] While at the time no one knew the cause of this dread disease, it was assumed that something about the West Indies cargo, or in the chest itself, had caused their demise.

Austin's friends in New York somehow got his body back quickly to New Haven for burial. It was discovered that his estate was insolvent. Perhaps had he lived to see the bigger ship return from China, he might have resolved his debts. In any event, the case involving his property embroiled not only New York Chamber President Comfort Sands (who happened to be Austin's agent in New York) but also, eventually, Alexander Hamilton himself, who would soon resign from Washington's government to practice law in New York.[49] Hamilton and Sands were to have other, critical connections during this period as well.

John Jay and the British signed the treaty on November 19, 1794. While it did not resolve all the issues involving impressment of sailors and ship seizures, it provided for the better recovery of more than $10 million in ships and property seized by the British. The treaty also provided for the withdrawal of British troops from the Northwest Territory (western Pennsylvania and the area north of the Ohio River) and called for arbitration to resolve disputes such as the border between Canada and the United States and wartime debts.[50] More important for President Washington, the treaty ended, for the time being at least, the risk of war with Great Britain.

At the same time, because it failed to prevent the capture of other American ships or future impressment of U.S. sailors, many people saw Jay's handiwork as a stain on the new nation's honor. The primary group to take offense at the terms of the treaty was the emerging party that was loosely called Republicans or Republican-Democrats – Jefferson, Madison, Monroe, and others who distrusted the wealth of the Yankee traders and the power of the U.S. government. The Republicans (not to be confused with the party of the same name that emerged in Lincoln's day) had more faith in revolutionary France than in aristocratic Britain, and they were correct in viewing that the Jay Treaty would, at the very least, complicate relations with France. Was this the way to treat the nation that had helped the Americans win independence just 11 years earlier?

Popular unhappiness with the treaty's terms erupted in 1795. Citizens held angry meetings throughout the young republic, and caustic commentary filled the newspapers. Without doubt, the prevailing opinion was against the document.

One organization, however, bucked the tide. The New York Chamber of Commerce, still headed by Comfort Sands, celebrated Jay's arrival back in New York, where he had been elected governor. On January 2, 1795, the chamber authorized the purchase of gunpowder for Jay's welcome.[51] The following month, it hosted a gala dinner for the treaty's chief proponent, Alexander Hamilton, who by this time had resigned from Washington's government. Hamilton received nine cheers, whereas Washington and Adams received just three apiece.[52] Hamilton, who even in private life continued to work for the ratification of the treaty, would find this chamber a critical ally for the greatest foreign policy success of Washington's Presidency.

Alexander Hamilton

The Senate began discussing the Jay Treaty in early June; it appeared it might not be ratified, which likely would lead to war with Great Britain. From Mount Vernon, Washington complained to Hamilton on July 29 that "the cry against the treaty is like that against a mad dog; and every one, in a manner, seems engaged in running it down."[53] Hamilton hardly needed telling; that same month, in trying to take the floor at an anti-treaty rally, he was reportedly hit in the head with a rock and he challenged Democratic Society leader James Nicholson to a duel, although they did not fight it.[54]

On the same day that Washington wrote Hamilton, the President sent a letter to Secretary of State Edmund Randolph with similar concerns about the fate of the treaty, noting that "I have never, since I have been in the administration of the government, seen a crisis, which in my judgment has been so pregnant with interesting events." But he acknowledged that there was hope for the treaty's proponents: "From New York there is, and I am told will further be, a counter current."[55]

That "counter current" was the New York Chamber of Commerce. On July 21, 1795, it held a special meeting on the treaty. Its minutes noted: "This meeting was the most respectable ever held in the Chamber of Commerce (upwards of seventy members being present). After the treaty was read, resolutions approving thereof were adopted with only ten dissenting voices."[56]

The New York Chamber's resolution appeared to cause a shift in momentum in the debate. On August 11, 1795, the Boston Chamber of Commerce, led by President Thomas Russell, held its own meeting on the treaty and passed unanimous resolutions supporting it. The chamber's members agreed to publish these resolutions in newspapers and to send them to President Washington.[57]

Other groups followed suit, including merchants in other cities who gathered for the purpose of expressing their approval of the treaty, and the momentum quickly shifted. The leading role of the chambers and the merchants was not lost on the opponents of the treaty. Indeed, their dismay is an indicator of the influence that the New York and Boston chambers had on the debate. The radical pamphleteer Tom Paine, for example, railed against the "snivelling" [sic] address of the New York Chamber of Commerce.[58]

Thomas Jefferson wrote to James Monroe that despite the overwhelming opposition to the treaty's terms, a few merchants were in favor of it. He went on: "The Chamber of Commerce in New York, against the body of the town, the merchants in Philadelphia, against the body of their town, also, and our town of Alexandria have come forward in it's [*sic*] support."[59]

Several months later, James Madison, writing to James Monroe, looked back and concurred that initially the treaty was extremely unpopular and that its proponents were "struck dumb by the voice of the nation." But then something had happened:

> At length, however, doubts began to be thrown out in New York, whether the Treaty was as bad as represented. The Chamber of commerce proceeded to an address to the P., in which they hinted at war as the tendency of rejecting the Treaty, but rested the decision with constituted authorities. The Boston Chamber of Commerce followed the example, as did a few inland villages.[60]

Jefferson's partisans were scratching their heads at how a few merchants could defeat so many popular demonstrators against the treaty. An author writing under the name Mentor totaled up the numbers of those publicly demonstrating against the treaty (about 25,000) compared with those in favor of it (about 1,000). The extreme examples of the outsized influence were in New York and Boston, where, Mentor claimed, only 33 and 32 merchants, respectively, came out for the treaty.[61] In these cities, of course, it was the chambers of commerce that led the efforts to support the treaty. There was something very new and perhaps special about the political influence of these organized bands of merchants, which had few specific powers and not even great numbers of members, but which did have an uncanny ability to catch the ear of legislators and other politicians.

At the same time, it would be a mistake to give full credit to chambers of commerce for the Senate's ratification of the Jay Treaty, by exactly the required two-thirds majority (20-10), in mid-August of 1795. First, President Washington had put his office on the line in support of the treaty, and the father of his country continued to have great prestige even in the midst of a ferocious partisan battle. Second, of the four chambers of commerce in the nation at the time, only those in Boston and New York had officially and publicly backed the treaty. (Granted, a future member of the New Haven Chamber of Commerce, Noah Webster, was a fierce partisan for the treaty through the Hamilton-backed Federalist publication, *American Minerva*.) Third, a number of non-chamber groups, of merchants and of ordinary citizens alike, also supported the treaty.

Finally, the fiercest proponent of the treaty was not the chambers nor independent merchants, but a man who was their hero. This was the greatest partisan politician of the Federalists, the only man whose combative skills matched those of the Republican-Democrats – Alexander Hamilton. It is even possible that it was Hamilton who prompted the New York Chamber of Commerce to come up with those history-making, perhaps history-changing, resolutions. There is no doubt that the New York Chamber's resolutions were a perfect complement, perfectly timed, to Hamilton's efforts to get the treaty ratified.

Already we have seen that Hamilton was immensely popular with the chamber's members. Moreover, he knew New York Chamber President Comfort Sands well, even renting a house from him.[62] The two had known each other during the Revolutionary War, when Hamilton was a key aide to Washington and Sands's firm had supplied the Continental

Army, once earning a rebuke from Washington for allegedly overcharging for goods. Sands had been a director of the Bank of New York, which Hamilton had founded. The two of them were involved in Elijah Austin's troubled estate. And Sands was a part owner of a ship named *Hamilton* (which, unfortunately, had been seized by the French in 1794).[63]

At a later date, on a different matter, Hamilton bragged to his friend Gouverneur Morris that he had prompted the New York Chamber to write the U.S. Congress: "I *induced* [Hamilton's emphasis] the Chamber of Commerce to send a memorial."[64] (A "memorial," a commonly used term at this time, was the rough equivalent of an "open letter" or "report" by a modern association or business organization.) If Hamilton had influenced the chamber on this lesser matter in 1802, it is certainly reasonable to conclude that he also did so in 1795, when the fortunes of the Presidency and indeed the peace of the nation were at stake.

Regardless of Hamilton's role, the New York Chamber's resolutions still turned the tide in favor of the Jay Treaty. As in so many other cases throughout history, a chamber played a significant role in a drama that included other actors. And while history has mostly forgotten what the New York and Boston chambers did, President Washington did send each of them a note of thanks. His notes to Comfort Sands and Thomas Russell, respectively, included one paragraph in each letter that was almost identical:

> While I regret the diversity of opinion which has been manifested on this subject, it is a satisfaction to learn, that the commercial part of my fellow citizens, whose interests are thought to be most directly affected, so generally consider the treaty as calculated, on the whole, to promote important advantages to our country.[65]

Washington had it right: the associations of merchants were supremely suited to comment on a treaty that involved their members. Had these merchants pontificated about slavery or whiskey or Indians, few would have listened. But on a matter involving their ships, they deserved to be heard. And apparently they were.

The Jay Treaty, as we know from hindsight, did not solve the nagging problems of British impressments and searches of neutral ships. But it did allow the young nation to grow stronger by keeping it out of war. Interestingly, there was a curious parallelism to the Jay Treaty's course: on the British side of the Atlantic, its chambers of commerce were actively involved in the issue, too, and those chambers made sure that the ultimate solution was similarly pragmatic and not inflammatory.[66]

The young North American country did, indeed, put on muscles after the treaty was signed. Trade greatly increased: U.S. shipping skyrocketed from 54,000 tons annually in 1790-92 to 236,000 tons in 1800, as Henry Adams approvingly noted in his *History of the United States*.[67]

Although relations with Great Britain had been stabilized, those with France grew worse. After John Adams assumed the Presidency in 1797, anti-French sentiment grew close to hysteria with the passage of the Alien and Sedition Acts. The New York Chamber of Commerce was swept up in the Federalist-fueled passions and worked with Governor Jay to bolster the fortifications of the New York harbor, but the dreaded U.S. war with Napoleon never came.

Into the Interior

The chambers in New York, Charleston, New Haven, and Boston all faced the Atlantic Ocean and, during the early years of the Republic, most of their attention, naturally, was focused on maritime trade. But settlers and traders were penetrating the interior of the country and opening it up to commerce. The chamber concept would follow them. And it turned out that chambers were well suited to the life of the inland communities, where frequently the concern was less about how to repel British boarders than how to attract German farmers.

Deep within the North American continent, a chamber-like organization was set up in St. Louis in 1793. Here, a group of merchants was dealing with a diverse group of trading partners – namely the Osages, Arikaras, Mandans, and other tribes of Native Americans. The European and American traders needed to organize in order to safeguard their business.

In the Louisiana Territory in 1793, the Spanish authorities had temporarily halted trading for fur and other goods, as it had become chaotic and dangerous, with different tribes and Europeans in a violent struggle for markets. St. Louis merchants then formed a trading association which, in the following year, successfully petitioned the authorities to form "The Company of the Explorers of the Upper Missouri."[68] This company effectively set prices for furs and other merchandise and created a virtual monopoly for St. Louis-based traders.

The articles of incorporation of the company make constant reference to the board of trade (*comercio*).[69] Such a board of trade, complete with elections and a government relations initiative, had some of the attributes of more established chambers of commerce. While this board seems to have disappeared, perhaps coincident with the U.S. purchase of the Louisiana Territory in 1803, for a while at least, it functioned as a trade-promoting organization, if not a true local chamber in that 1) it had significant powers derived from government, and 2) its influence spanned a geographic area larger than a single community.

Another organization arose in 1797 in Lexington, Kentucky, and left a still slight but more lasting imprint. The group did not call itself a chamber of commerce, but its activities are a dead ringer for what American chambers of commerce continued to do in succeeding years: to promote the community as a good location for business. The Lexington group organized itself at the house of John Postlethwaite on September 8, 1797, just five years after the state was founded. The official name was The Lexington Society for the Promotion of Emigration.[70] Not surprisingly, today's chamber, known as Commerce Lexington Inc., considers itself the progeny of its ambitious 1797 ancestor.

Why the focus on promotion? For cities in the interior of the country, the growth of commerce was dependent less on the regulations and practices of international trade than on attracting business from people already on the continent. Chambers in the interior of North America became, to a large extent, business promoters or, in later terminology, economic developers.

The Lexington group was energetic. Although the population of the town was only 1,475 in 1798, the Emigration Society was determined to raise that number substantially. It collected and published information that would show others the economic opportunities of the area. Here is one example of its work:

AVERAGE PRODUCE OF ONE ACRE OF LAND.

Of wheat sown in corn-ground, 25 bushels; in fallow-ground, 35; corn, 60; rye, 25; barley, 40; oats, 40; potatoes, Irish, 250 – sweet, - ; hemp, 8 cwt.; tobacco, 1 ton; hay, 3 tons.

LEXINGTON MARKET PRICES.

Wheat, per bushel, $1; corn, 20 cents; rye, 66 cents; barley, 50 cents; oats, 17 cents; potatoes, Irish, 33—sweet, $1; hemp, per ton, $86.66; tobacco, per cwt., $4; hay, per ton, $6.[71]

It wasn't enough simply to collect the material and have it printed and advertised; the group even translated material into German and handed it out to immigrants on the East Coast.[72] The organization also did its best to quash talk that hurt its image, such as that area residents were moving out. The Society noted of a report saying Kentuckians were flocking to the Louisiana Territory:

> The report is notoriously ill grounded, and we can boldly assert that of the great number who have, by the artful representations of the interested, been induced to visit that country, *very few* indeed have settled on any part of the Mississippi, whilst the far greater proportion have returned, disgusted with the Spanish government, and with an increased affection for Kentucky.[73]

Interestingly, just two years before the Lexington society was founded, a young "emigrant" named Henry Clay moved to town. On April 11, 1797, four months before the society was founded, he married Lucretia Hart. Her father, Colonel Thomas Hart, a rope merchant and landowner, would be the founding president of the new organization.[74] Throughout his long political career, Clay would become a key promoter of the West, much as his merchant father-in-law was. And Clay would be a champion of the sort of "internal improvements" – canals, roads, bridges, railroads – that would capture so much of the energy of American chambers of commerce.

Apparently Lexington's emigration society was onto something. It wasn't enough for happy residents to send word back to friends and relatives that Lexington was a good place to settle. Organized effort, providing facts and figures and commentary, made it more likely that the word would spread – and not just to acquaintances but to complete strangers. The society quickly found imitators.[75]

One of them was the Washington Emigration Society in Mason County, Kentucky, also begun in 1797. This organization held monthly meetings and it, too, published material in the *Mirror*. Like later chambers of commerce, it looked askance at excessive litigation, and deplored the wrangles over land titles in the area: "A stranger who comes to purchase must be alarmed at the infinity of disputes, and is on that account deterred from purchasing and perhaps leaves the country in disgust."[76]

While the Kentucky emigration societies would fade away, and appear to have aimed more at a single issue (attracting residents) than at general business or community promotion, they captured the spirit that many subsequent chambers would champion. Organized groups of business people were capable of attracting more residents and business to their communities. The growth of towns and cities, it turned out, was not solely a function of whatever natural features were in the area, such as good soil or a navigable river. A good chamber of commerce, in some cases, could entice potential residents and business people just as effectively as could Mother Nature.

Troubles on the Atlantic and the Mississippi

The coastal chambers of commerce faced many difficulties as the nation's third President, Thomas Jefferson, took office in 1801. The Jay Treaty had averted war and kept trade flowing, but there were continued British violations of neutral shipping. These problems would fester, culminating in the War of 1812. In the meantime, the sharp trade disputes, somewhat paradoxically, both inspired the birth of new chambers and destabilized the merchant community along with some of the early chambers.

The Boston and New York chambers, so prominent in the movement to pass the Jay Treaty in 1795, were less visible as the new century dawned. The Boston Chamber's founding president, Thomas Russell, died in 1796, and some of the spirit of his chamber seemed to die with him. The New York Chamber's president from 1794 to 1798, Comfort Sands, had come under increasing financial pressure, thanks mainly to the British and French seizures of ships in which he had a share, and he was declared bankrupt in 1801. Attendance at New York Chamber meetings declined, in part because of yellow fever epidemics and in part because of the disruptions of trade, until the chamber finally closed its doors in 1806, not to reopen for 11 years.[77] In some of the most tumultuous years in the history of American trade, perhaps the greatest chamber of them all was almost completely out of the action.

But the spirit that John Cruger and his colleagues had felt in 1768 had been passed on to others. The New Haven and Charleston chambers continued to function effectively. A chamber in Hartford, Conn., influenced by the example of the New York Chamber, functioned briefly from 1799 to 1804.[78] And on February 9, 1801, the Philadelphia Chamber of Commerce was founded. It would prove to be one of the most active commercial organizations in the United States, if not the most active, for several years.

The founding president of this chamber was Thomas FitzSimons, an Irish-born Catholic who was one of the framers and signers of the Constitution and was a prominent merchant. He was a very generous man, having loaned money to many of his friends, including Robert Morris, the man who more than any other financed the American Revolution, and who, like Sands, was declared bankrupt in 1801. FitzSimons was appalled at the violations of neutral shipping and he used the new chamber as the vehicle for expressing his concerns, which were shared by his fellow chamber members.

Only eight days after founding the chamber, he wrote an official chamber letter to the Secretary of the Navy, Benjamin Stoddert, complaining of British seizures of shipping in the West Indies. Insurance premiums on shipping to Havana, he noted, had jumped from 10 percent to 30 percent in just a few days, and in New Providence alone there were 40 British privateers preying on shipping.[79] On October 10, FitzSimons wrote to President Jefferson that Spanish cruisers were seizing American ships entering the Mediterranean.[80] Spain at the time was controlled by Napoleon and the Spanish ships' captains claimed that the Americans were trying to supply the British garrison at Gibraltar. Once again, American merchants were being victimized by both sides in the great European war. FitzSimons and his chamber would continue to draw attention to the attacks on American shipping over the next few years.

The Philadelphia Chamber also engaged in other activities. In early 1802, it petitioned Congress to repair the piers in the Delaware River and otherwise protect ships in the harbor during the winter.[81] The appeal was successful, and in 1805, the Pennsylvania Legislature empowered its Board of Wardens to levy a fee of four cents per ton on ships leaving the Philadelphia harbor to cover the cost of these improvements.[82] Even after FitzSimons himself was declared bankrupt in 1805 – he had lent money to too many friends – the chamber continued to be a strong advocate for trade in one of the leading port cities of the nation.

The Philadelphia Chamber of Commerce wasn't alone in its appeal for better trade practices and its attacks on foreign powers' lack of respect for neutral shipping. The other chambers concurred. While the New York Chamber of Commerce's voice was gradually becoming weaker as it faded into dormancy, the New Haven Chamber of Commerce made up for it, vigorously protesting everything from discriminatory British duties in the West Indies to President Jefferson's appointment of an apparently incompetent customs inspector.

Feelings were running high. Henry Dagget, president of the New Haven Chamber of Commerce, fairly shouted in this 1806 memorial against ship seizures and impressments:

WE HOLD IT TO BE EXTREMELY IMPORTANT THAT ALL NATIONS SHOULD COMBINE AGAINST SUCH INNOVATIONS UPON THEIR RIGHTS; and *in particular that the United States, whose geographical position gives them the best chance of maintaining neutrality, during wars in Europe,* SHOULD FIRMLY RESIST EVERY ENCROACHMENT UPON THE RIGHTS OF NEUTRAL COMMERCE.[83]

Dagget's voice was joined by that of Noah Webster, who authored some of the protests and memorials of the New Haven Chamber of Commerce.

Not all the news was bad. There was one foe on the other side of the ocean whom we could beat: the Barbary Pirates. The rulers of Morocco and Tripoli had been demanding bounty for passing through their waters and took American ships that didn't pay them. Under Captain Edward Preble, the Americans successfully brought these regimes to heel in 1803 and 1804. Chambers of commerce naturally cheered this result. In 1805, the New York Chamber, in one of its last actions before suspending its meetings in 1806, honored Captain Preble with a dinner after his triumphant return to the United States.[84]

Captain Preble got a dinner from a chamber; another Barbary hero, his subordinate Stephen Decatur, got a wife. On May 2, 1801, a new chamber of commerce had been founded at Norfolk, Virginia.[85] Its president was a self-made man, a local civic leader and iron maker named Luke Wheeler. Wheeler had a beautiful daughter, Susan, whom he had sent off to boarding school in Baltimore, and who had been courted by none other than the brother of Napoleon Bonaparte, Jerome. Aaron Burr had made unsuccessful passes at her. Susan hadn't fallen for the Frenchman or for the mercurial Burr, but she immediately became interested in Decatur after visiting his ship in his absence and seeing a miniature portrait of him. A few days later, meeting the real thing, she fell in love. She and Stephen were married in 1806.

Both Luke Wheeler and his hero son-in-law would be dragged into a major event off Hampton Roads, Virginia, in 1807. In an incident that was a deeply humiliating to all Americans, a British ship, the *Leopard*, attacked a U.S. Navy ship, the *Chesapeake*, killing three men and wounding 16. The British commander plucked a few men off the ship that he claimed were British citizens and forced them into service on the *Leopard*.

The incident elicited particular anger in the Norfolk area. The *Chesapeake* had been built by Norfolk area shipwrights and the wounded from the ship were brought to a local hospital, where one of them died. Preparing to defend themselves and to show their defiance to the British outrage, local citizens formed a Committee of Safety. Luke Wheeler was on the committee.[86]

Meanwhile, Stephen Decatur sat in court martial over the captain of the *Chesapeake*, James Barron, with unfortunate results for both men. Barron was ruled deficient in his duties. Decatur would go on to become an even greater hero in the War of 1812. Barron, however, felt humiliated by the ruling of the court martial, and in 1820 challenged Decatur to a duel and killed him.

Two Embargoes

For the maritime trade of the United States, the *Leopard* incident was last straw. President Jefferson had to do something about the flagrant violations of American sovereignty on the high seas. He ordered a closure of U.S. ports – the famous embargo that crippled the U.S. economy and was frequently called the "Dambargo."

The embattled chambers along the coast did what they could to mitigate the consequences. The Philadelphia Chamber of Commerce requested an exemption from the embargo to permit shipments of provisions to the West Indies, but was refused.[87] This chamber also attempted to aid unemployed local seamen, with limited success.[88]

A southern chamber also committed to help unemployed seamen find jobs, although it couldn't handle all the demand for assistance. It aimed to assist southerners and asked the northern seamen to go home.[89] This was a new organization: the Savannah Chamber of Commerce, founded on December 13, 1806.

Eighty-five "merchants, traders, factors and insurance brokers" had come together to promote trade in this Georgia port. Among the members was the wealthy entrepreneur William Scarbrough, who was interested in new technology and may have had something to do with a system of weights and measures introduced by the chamber in its initial year to track shipments at the port of Savannah.[90] (Savannah had witnessed another technological marvel a few years earlier, in 1793, when Yale graduate Eli Whitney had visited the nearby plantation of the widow of Revolutionary War General Nathaniel Greene, Catherine, and come up with an invention called the cotton gin.) This chamber's timing wasn't perfect – the 1808 embargo snuffed out maritime trade except for smuggling – but the chamber had an extraordinary survival instinct and managed to stay in operation not only through the embargo but also through the Civil War and other tumultuous events of the next two centuries.

Far away, another southern chamber was born in 1806. Just three years after the Louisiana Purchase, New Orleans merchants had come together to promote trade at the mouth of the Mississippi. But before the year was out, they were clamped by a strict embargo of trade, more than a year before Jefferson's embargo.

The reason for this halting of commerce was not the British, nor the French, but a domestic threat: Aaron Burr. Reports that Burr was coming down the Mississippi in flatboats with soldiers terrorized the people of the city. It was said that Burr, having failed to ascend to the Presidency of the United States, intended to create his own empire in the West.

The U.S. general in charge of the region, James Wilkinson, was a cure perhaps worse than the disease. Indeed, he had been named to his post by Jefferson at Burr's recommendation and was accused of plotting with Burr. Few if any U.S. military men have left behind a reputation of greater duplicity or high-handedness. Apparently trying to prove his loyalty to the United States by his harsh methods against Burr, Wilkinson demanded extraordinary powers, including suspension of the right of *habeas corpus*, the imposition of martial law, and even the impressment of local sailors, to thwart the dreaded Burr.

The members of the New Orleans Chamber of Commerce were willing to help, up to a point. They met, upon request by the authorities, on December 9, 1806, where Wilkinson and Territorial Governor William Claiborne apprised them of the situation. The merchants agreed to an immediate embargo on ships leaving the harbor. They even raised money to feed and clothe their sailors who would enter the service of the U.S. government under Wilkinson's command.[91]

Wilkinson's harsh policies, however, proved to be much too strict for the governor and the local citizens. The general demanded the use of the merchants' sailors for a full six months – a ridiculous request, given that Burr's attack appeared to be only a temporary emergency. In these and other extreme demands, Wilkinson quickly aroused increasing opposition from all quarters in New Orleans.

Burr never came down the river. His conspiracy, if that's what it was, fizzled. On December 31, Claiborne called off the embargo.[92] Wilkinson went on to undistinguished service in the War of 1812. And the New Orleans Chamber of Commerce remained in business, at least for a few years, as settlers poured into the Louisiana Territory and enriched the economy of the new West.

In March 1809, just before leaving office, President Jefferson signed the act repealing his embargo. The cessation of trade had devastated the economies of the port cities and discouraged their chambers of commerce. One of them, however, didn't give up on trade.

A Testy Disposition

The Philadelphia Chamber of Commerce enlisted the help of entrepreneur Jonathan Grout, Jr. to set up a set of signals from Reedy Island, at the head of the Delaware Bay, to Philadelphia. This contraption, known as a semaphore system, was based on technology known in Europe for more than a century. Grout's project involved a series of towers with men on each who monitored, with telescopes, the positions of the arms of the towers facing them. The men would move the arms of their tower to align with those of the preceding tower, thus transmitting signals faster than any other way then available. The project began operating on November 9, 1809. The purpose was to report the approach of ships as quickly as possible to the docks in Philadelphia.[93]

There were two problems with the innovation, however. One, no doubt, was the expense of maintaining such a complicated, labor- and capital-intensive system. The other problem was Jonathan Grout's personality. He had a "testy" disposition and seems to have had a difficult time keeping clients.[94] The Philadelphia system soon fell into disuse.

Similarly in disuse, the chambers of commerce in the United States and its territories kept an extremely low profile during the War of 1812. The Charleston Chamber of Commerce had ceased operating in about 1803.[95] The New York Chamber of Commerce was not meeting either, and, once the protests against British and French practices were forgotten and the fighting had begun, the other chambers appear to have been nearly silent. Only after the war, when the commerce of the nation was once again secure and there was almost half a continent to explore and develop, did American chambers of commerce begin to flex their muscles again and see what they could do.

The Challenges
of Peacetime

1816-1836

After the War of 1812, few chambers were still noticeably active, perhaps just those in Philadelphia, New Haven, and Savannah. Apathy, yellow fever, and wartime confusion had claimed most of the others, including the chambers in New York and Charleston. But within just a decade, the latter two chambers would revive with a bang, and at least two others (in Albany, N.Y. and Baltimore) would be operating. These unusual institutions filled a need. They never really died, but rather went dormant. Indeed, by the 1820s, both the New York and Charleston chambers had "died" twice (once during the Revolutionary War and once in the first decade of the 19th century), and yet both somehow had come back to life after each experience.

Part of the reason for the continued life in the U.S. chamber movement was the gradual spread of the chamber concept overseas. It was hard to forget completely about chambers of commerce when one's trading partners were members of their own local groups. Napoleon's advance through Europe had planted chambers far and wide, and even though these differed from New York's independent-chamber model, they successfully coordinated local enterprise and performed services for trading partners. Public-law chambers[1] moved beyond France to such cities as Cologne (1803), Rotterdam (1803), Frankfurt-on-Main (1808), Warsaw (1809), and Metz (1815).

In the British Isles, the voluntary, private-law chamber concept caught on, appearing in such communities as London (1782 to 1800), Liverpool (1774 to 1796), Dublin (1783, to fade and be reestablished in 1820), Glasgow (1783), Belfast (1783, re-founded in 1802), Manchester (1774, 1793, and 1820), Limerick (1807), Newcastle (1813), and Waterford (1787 and 1804).[2] The British chambers clearly recognized the importance of trade with the Americas. Indeed, the Glasgow Chamber was founded at the conclusion of the U.S. Revolutionary War in large part out of concern for the disruption of Glasgow's dominance of the American tobacco trade. British merchants and U.S. Consul James Maury formed the American Chamber of Commerce in Liverpool in 1801 because of the high volume of trade between that city and the United States.[3]

To the north, Canadian chambers also slowly took root. Halifax got a revived chamber in 1804, while Quebec had a chamber briefly in 1776 and a Committee of Trade in 1809. St. John, New Brunswick, got a chamber in 1817, and Montreal in 1822. Formal organizations of business people were becoming a worldwide phenomenon, impossible to ignore by anyone well versed in international commerce.

Still, the spread of the concept in other countries didn't make the job of U.S. chambers much easier. American business organizations in the years after the War of 1812 faced double pressures – integrating with the burgeoning global economy and grappling with a raucous domestic political and economic environment. In the period bookended by Andrew Jackson (i.e., from the year after his victory at the Battle of New Orleans in 1815 to his last full year as President, in 1836), these chambers lost many a political battle, especially on tariff rates and on the nation's banking system. But they emerged from the turbulent period more or less intact. They had a solid chance to grow along with their rambunctious, optimistic country, whose opportunities usually seemed to outnumber its mistakes.

On March 4, 1817, Cornelius Ray, who had been the president of the New York Chamber of Commerce when it stopped operating in 1806, called the organization together for its first meeting in 11 years.[4] No doubt there was much to discuss: Governor DeWitt Clinton was proceeding with his dream, and that of many others, to build the great Erie Canal. This was the moon landing of its era, an epochal project that, when completed in 1825, almost instantly would transform New York City into the unquestioned commercial capital of the Western Hemisphere.

Some had a feeling of what this canal meant. New York Chamber secretary John Pintard made a prediction, considered extravagant in 1823, that 14 years after the completion of the canal, New York City's population would double. In fact, it surpassed that prediction, rising from 123,706 in the 1820 census to 312,852 in 1840.[5] Sipping the wealth and energies of the heart of the nation through the straw of this muddy canal, New York would swell to amazing size, leaving Boston, Philadelphia, and Charleston far behind.

While the Erie Canal was a marvel, it wasn't the only technological dream of its time. In Savannah, the energetic and flamboyant William Scarbrough, one of a committee of seven that had drafted the rules for that city's chamber of commerce, commissioned another modernistic project: the building of a steamship that would be the first such vessel to cross the Atlantic Ocean. He insisted on naming it the *Savannah*, wanting his city to have credit for such a notable achievement.[6]

While he furnished much of the money, many chamber friends helped finance the venture. Of the four other directors of the Savannah Steam Ship Company, two were with Scarbrough as fellow members at the start of the chamber in 1806, Robert Isaac and Joseph Habersham. So were a number of investors in the project, including Benjamin Burroughs, Robert Mackay, and Robert Mitchell.[7]

Scarbrough's ship left Savannah on May 22, 1819. The passengers had more dangers than those of the sea to worry about. One Savannah resident wrote his wife in London, asking that Scarbrough's irrepressible wife not be allowed to sing "or she will frighten the good people of England."[8]

The ship took only 29 days to reach Liverpool, where it was mobbed by excited crowds. Off Ireland, the ship was chased by another ship, the *Kite*, out of concern that the Georgia vessel was on fire.[9] Most of the time the ship used steam power, but part of the time it used its sails in order to conserve fuel. The vessel went on to Copenhagen, Stockholm, and St. Petersburg before returning more or less intact to the United States.

SS Savannah

Unfortunately, the pioneering ship's career was short-lived: the *Savannah* was dismantled after that initial voyage. Scarbrough was said to have been financially ruined as a result, although other causes no doubt contributed: the Panic of 1819, for one, and his legendary household extravagance, for another. Still, Scarbrough was ahead of his time. It would be another couple of decades before steamships regularly crossed the Atlantic.

The Panic of 1819, one of a series of financial setbacks in the United States during the 19th century, was sharply painful. Chambers of commerce and their members did what they could to survive in the absence of the kinds of government aid we take for granted today. Merchant groups pushed for a national bankruptcy bill to standardize practices across states and prevent individuals from hiding their assets from creditors. Among those involved were the chambers in New York, Philadelphia, and New Haven.[10] But Congress didn't pass the proposed legislation; at this time most legislators weren't prepared to view the bankruptcy clause in the Constitution as giving the federal government sweeping powers over the states. Tariffs, however, were another matter entirely.

The Struggle over Tariffs

The idea of free trade was relatively new as America grappled with tariff policy in the wake of the War of 1812. Adam Smith's *Wealth of Nations* was published in 1776, while David Ricardo's *Principles of Political Economy and Taxation*, introducing the theory of comparative advantage, appeared only in 1817.[11] But these ideas were powerful and spread quickly. Among their strongest adherents were merchants, who were happy for new weapons in traders' age-old struggle against tariffs. It was the merchants who had to pay tariffs and who lost customers because of the resulting higher prices.

Moreover, it wasn't simply the educated elite who were capable of seeing a bad tariff bargain. Tariff rates, and the affected products, were public information. It didn't take an economist to point out whose unseen hand was fingering your wallet.

Tariffs were the primary source of revenue for the government, which was the main reason they had been increased during the War of 1812. After the war, in 1816, higher rates were institutionalized, including a 25 percent tariff on cotton and woolen goods. Part of this was to combat British dumping, at cut-rate prices, of the many goods that had piled up in warehouses during the great war with Napoleon (and the little war with the United States).

Yet there were pressures not just to maintain the higher rates from 1816, but to increase them in 1820. The prime mover behind this was Henry Clay, whose "American System" envisaged the interior of the United States flourishing under a tariff wall that fostered domestic industry. Others supported the idea, too, especially the growing community of manufacturers who benefited from a shield against British imports.

The Philadelphia Chamber of Commerce took a leading role in fighting the idea of an increase in tariffs in 1820. It called to merchants up and down the coast to come together and discuss a response to a Congressional move for a 5 percent tariff hike. In Boston, the Philadelphia Chamber's call to action brought a large group of merchants together. They found a champion for their free-trade cause, Daniel Webster.[12]

In Baltimore, merchants supported the Philadelphia Chamber's move also. They met on September 13, 1820, and decided to send a group to a proposed meeting in Philadelphia. They also decided, on the same day, to form the Baltimore Chamber of Commerce, under the leadership of Robert Gilmor.[13] Baltimore merchants had come together before on an ad hoc basis, including in 1806 to produce a lengthy memorial (signed by "Robert Gilmor, and twenty five others") to the President and Congress to protest British violations of American neutrality.[14] But there were advantages to being organized into an institution. After all, this wasn't going to be the only tariff bill they might be called upon to address.

The chambers in Baltimore and Philadelphia, and the merchants in Boston, were joined in their opposition to a tariff hike by the newly reestablished New York Chamber of Commerce and other groups. Nevertheless, the tariff bill passed the House. It wasn't, however, enacted. This was as close to success as these chambers would come on tariff issues in the next dozen years.

Henry Clay once again became Speaker of the House in 1823 and oversaw a proposal to raise duties in 1824 to 35 percent on imported iron, wool, cotton, and hemp.[15] By this time, Daniel Webster had switched camps and favored tariff hikes, supporting the growing manufacturing industry in his region against the merchants. The weight of opinion in the North and West of the United States backed the measure.

But northern merchants (as opposed to manufacturers) knew what was bad for them. The New York Chamber of Commerce, for example, provided an eloquent memorial to Congress, noting that the new tariff raised money that wasn't needed; favored some industries over others, thereby violating the Constitution's aim "to promote the general welfare"; protected manufacturers that already had a significant tariff wall; could invite retaliatory duty increases by Great Britain; and unfairly treated the South.[16]

The Nullification Crisis: Dress Rehearsal for the Civil War

The new, high tariff schedule was indeed unfair to the mostly non-manufacturing South, but few southerners realized at first just how bad it was. One southerner, however, did understand the discrimination caused by tariff walls. Jacob Newton Cardozo was an interesting man. For starters, he had changed his middle name from Nunez to Newton (which occasionally led to some confusion, as his brother was named Isaac). He came from a distinguished, although not wealthy, family of Sephardic Jewish background. His father had fought as a patriot in the Revolutionary War and settled in Charleston.[17]

Although Jacob Cardozo had only a basic Charleston public education, he was an expert in economics and trade. He was familiar with the writings of Adam Smith, David Ricardo, and other economists, and was a prolific writer and publisher. He believed strongly that legislation should not favor one class over another.

In fact, Cardozo was intimately involved in a conflict over fairness in South Carolina created by planters and others who were jealous of the success of local merchants. In 1822, the Legislature had "imposed onerous taxation on the mercantile body," as he later put it.[18] When shippers and traders gathered the following year to protest the measure, this revived the Charleston Chamber of Commerce. Cardozo was a part of the revival movement and joined a committee that wrote a memorial to the Legislature causing a reversal of the tax policy.[19] His focus on fairness, the chamber, and memorials to legislators would be seen again, with far greater ramifications, during and after the debates on the Tariff of 1828.

Clay and his legislative team managed to get the 1824 tariff bill passed. It was a clear defeat, despite the efforts of most of the nation's chambers of commerce, and the forces of protection grew stronger.

By 1827, the pressure for higher tariffs had reached a boiling point. A complex set of negotiations had yielded plans for duties of 50 percent on woolen and other goods. The resulting Tariff of 1828 would be called by southerners – and others - the "Tariff of Abominations." Jacob Cardozo and the Charleston Chamber of Commerce strongly contested the idea. Cardozo has been credited with carrying the anti-tariff protest plan to the chamber[20] and was on the committee to draft a memorial to Congress on the issue. Indeed, he may have written the memorial himself.[21]

On June 12, 1827, before the legislation had been passed by Congress, Charleston Chamber President David Alexander introduced the chamber's memorial on the tariff proposal. This was the first free-trade memorial to Congress from the South.[22] Alexander's cover letter acknowledged that while the chamber was first with the issue, only the public's outcry would make a difference.[23]

The Charleston memorial itself made many of the points of earlier anti-tariff-hike documents from other chambers of commerce and merchant groups. But it added great emphasis on the unfairness of the new tariff regime to the South. The increased duty on coarse wool products, for example, would fall only on southern planters, who clothed their slaves in these products. The tariff plan would play havoc with the economy of the South.

It would also disrupt the politics of the South and thereby of the Union. The chamber's memorial ended by questioning just how much loyalty citizens should have to a political power that acted unfairly toward them. It noted that "there are limits to legal obedience" and that the "affection" people usually feel toward their form of government should not be presumed upon or abused. The memorial's final sentence is ominous, quietly warning of the danger that South Carolina (if not the entire South) might reevaluate ties to the Union if the federal government continued to treat it unfairly:

> But your memorialists would be wanting in one of the highest of their obligations which their present office imposes on them if they did not forewarn the legislature of the union against a too confident dependence on the unimpaired strength of that affection, whilst there continues to be neither pause nor rest to the spirit which has dictated our prohibitory and exclusionist policy.[24]

This idea that states would have a right to secede, to "nullify" their involvement in the Union, was not new. In the South, the concept had arisen mostly because of fears that the

North was trying to end the institution of slavery. Those fears were eased with Henry Clay's Missouri Compromise of 1820, which more or less patched over differences between the North and South on the expansion of slavery to new states.

The tariff issue, however, was different. It was clear that the "Tariff of Abominations" was unfair. On this issue, South Carolina, and indeed the entire South, was entitled to righteous resentment at high-handed treatment of the North and West. The tariff went against all the new ideas of free trade and, in effect, taxed the South to help the North.

The call from the Charleston Chamber of Commerce had plenty of support. South Carolina Senator Robert Hayne, who had aided Cardozo when he had had financial difficulties,[25] had opposed the Tariff of 1824 and also that of 1828. He addressed the Charleston Chamber in 1827, apparently shortly before the chamber issued its memorial to Congress, saying the proposed tariff would devastate the southern economy with "a commercial calamity compared with which war itself would almost lose its terrors!"[26]

Hayne continued to promote the anti-tariff cause, and the right of the state to secede. In 1830 he entered into what has been called the greatest debate in the history of the U.S. Senate, over the issue of the states' rights to overturn federal policies. His opponent, and the person whom history would declare the winner, was Daniel Webster, who closed his lengthy oration with the famous words, "Liberty and Union, Now and Forever, One and Inseparable!"

But it was John C. Calhoun, the South Carolinian who served as vice president under both John Quincy Adams (1824 to 1828) and under Andrew Jackson in his first term (1828 to 1832), who proved the stronger champion of the South on the tariff question. Calhoun had become a free trader in 1828, and grew increasingly disaffected with the federal government in which he served, eventually resigning from the vice presidency under Jackson.

Calhoun propounded the doctrine of nullification so eloquently, and his fellow South Carolinians agreed with him so eagerly, that in 1832 the state legislature passed an act invalidating federal tariff laws. Only after President Jackson sent U.S. Navy warships to Charleston harbor (aided, to be sure, by a more conciliatory tariff outlook back in Washington) did the state back down.[27] Henry Clay crafted a compromise tariff in 1833 that defused tensions on the issue, and from then on, tariffs might be contentious, but would not be an incitement to civil war.

Tariffs were taken off the table as an explosive sectional issue, but the damage had been done. Southerners, especially South Carolinians, had seen that they had been victimized by the North, and that when they stood up for their rights, they were ultimately accommodated. The threat of secession had caused the North to step back.

For Jacob Newton Cardozo, all this was not good news. He had alerted the chamber, and the city of Charleston, to the unfairness of the Tariff of 1828. But he had opposed the idea of nullification. Others, inside and outside his chamber, had used Cardozo's arguments not just to attack an unfair tariff, but to attack and undermine the legitimacy of the young republic.

Movement on Land and Water

Although Jackson's warships had temporarily intimidated commerce at the angry Port of Charleston, other ports were booming. American transportation, in general, was on a roll. The Erie Canal was a case in point. Before it was built, it cost $120 to ship a ton of flour from Buffalo to New York City. After its completion, it cost just $6.[28]

And then came the railroads. In the late 1820s and 30s, the iron horse was just a splay-footed foal, but growing fast and clearly one day headed for the races. Meanwhile, steam power propelled more and more ships up rivers and along coastlines, even as sailing ships still commanded the great oceans. It was the beginning of a golden age of transportation.

Chambers of commerce would chase after the opportunities, not always as fast as the newest ships and trains, but sometimes fast enough to beat their neighboring communities. Moreover, they combated natural perils and plucked out physical obstacles in their way. There was a strange symbiosis of these stationary chambers of commerce with the accelerating movement of people and goods.

With the Great Lakes now having a clear path to the Atlantic via the Erie Canal, two chambers of commerce anticipated the next bottleneck to be attacked: the land barrier in Central America that separated the Atlantic and Pacific oceans. In 1827, the New York and Philadelphia chambers sent a memorial to President John Quincy Adams suggesting a regular ship service through the Gulf of Mexico to the mouth of the Chagres River, in what is now Panama.[29] Similar service was envisioned on the Pacific. These shipping lines would indeed be inaugurated, although not until just over two decades later, under pressure from hordes of 49ers.

New York was now in an almost impregnable position. By 1825, it had not only one of the finest natural harbors in the world, but also its world-renowned canal to Lake Erie. Philadelphia had neither. And the problem of Philadelphia's Delaware Bay harbor was acute. The chamber of commerce determined to fix it.

This was the same chamber that had been pushing, almost since its establishment in 1801, for better piers and other improvements along the Delaware River. But the greatest problem of all was the hazard at the mouth of the river. Ships anchored there were vulnerable to fierce Atlantic storms. The Philadelphia Chamber of Commerce drew up reports and memorials detailing the wrecks of ships there. It asked for Congressional support for funding for a protective breakwater. The chamber even created a special committee on the structure.

In a two-year period ending in December 1825, no fewer than 51 ships had been wrecked within ten miles of the proposed breakwater, with the loss of everything aboard.[30] Even so, it took some doing, and much pushing by the Philadelphia Chamber and its political allies (including the New York Chamber of Commerce), to secure federal funding of $250,000 for the initial year and comparable amounts through most of the years up to 1840. Work commenced in 1828 under the direction of the noted architect William Strickland.

The first structure of its kind in this hemisphere, and the second largest in the world, the protective breakwater was more or less complete from a practical standpoint in 1840, according to Strickland, although additional work was done later. Despite some criticism, it seems to have served its basic purpose well. More than 835,000 tons of stone had been put into the Delaware Bay by 1840. The number of aggregate days that ships spent in shelter behind the structure rose from 866 in 1833 to 5,661 in 1839.[31] There was, finally, safe harbor in Delaware Bay. The basic structure still exists today.

Ships were the lifeblood of international trade, but railroads were clearly going to be a force in domestic transportation and commerce. The first rudimentary train powered by a locomotive and carrying freight had appeared on the other side of the Atlantic, in Wales, in

1804. It was not until 1830, however, that the first commercially successful railroad existed, also in the British Isles, running from Liverpool to Manchester. In that same year, there were only 23 miles of railroad tracks in the United States, a number that would jump to 2,818 in 1840 and 30,626 by 1860.[32]

The members of the Charleston Chamber of Commerce were among the first to see the railroads as their opportunity to open up markets in the interior of the state and beyond. On February 4, 1828, a special committee of 10 at the chamber was created to investigate the feasibility of setting up a railroad between Charleston and Augusta, Georgia, in order to "intercept the cotton that was going by water from Augusta to Savannah."[33] This wouldn't be the first time that railroads would be used as a competitive weapon in commercial battles between cities.

The chamber committee concluded that the railroad was a good idea, and in May of 1828, the railroad company elected its board of directors, half of whom were chamber members.[34] On December 25, 1830, service began on a part of the route, involving the first steam locomotive ever used for business in the United States. In 1833 the 136-mile route was completed, the longest railroad line in the world under management by a single company (the South Carolina Canal and Rail Road Company).

Unfortunately, not unlike the Savannah steamship, this was a high-tech project that was ahead of its time. The railroad was not as successful as the promoters hoped, in part, no doubt, because Charlestonians had decided that the tracks shouldn't go all the way down to the wharf.[35] The city's attraction for vacationers and tourists was assured, perhaps at the cost of its future as an industrial center. At the other end, the railroad stopped just short of its destination of Augusta; Georgians correctly deduced the nefarious plot to steal their waterborne trade and prevented the extension of the tracks into their city. The railroad had one other unfortunate distinction: it was the site of the first railroad fatality in the United States, when, in June of 1831, the train exploded, killing a worker.[36]

The New York Chamber of Commerce also became active on railroads. The chamber in 1834 strongly endorsed the plan, already chartered in 1832, for a railroad from Lake Erie to the Hudson River, and authorized and approved funding for a pamphlet promoting the project. This eventually led to the creation of the Erie Railroad, which helped develop the southern part of New York State, including the cities of Binghamton and Elmira, and eventually merged into other lines.[37]

These were only the opening rounds in chambers' struggles against, and fascination with, the railroads. The new iron connections could, in theory, turn any town into a city, or, if they bypassed a city, turn it back into a town. Railroads were one of the leading obsessions of chambers until just after World War I, when other forms of transportation took over. Surely no other industrial development in the 19th century had a greater impact on which communities forged ahead at rib-rattling speed and which ones gazed longingly at the disappearing caboose of their opportunity.

Breaking the Bank

Banks – as critical for the national expansion as railroads – received plenty of attention in this period. One of them attracted more than its share of interest. The Second Bank of the United States, a Philadelphia institution headed by the resourceful and headstrong

Nicholas Biddle, became a consuming controversy for much of Andrew Jackson's presidency. It received deposits of U.S. government funds and was one of the leading financial institutions of the nation, although by no means as powerful as today's Federal Reserve System. The bank's 20-year charter expired in 1836 and Jackson was adamant that it should not be renewed. He ultimately won a protracted struggle against Biddle, aided by a popular feeling that finance should be democratized and not concentrated in the hands of a few East Coast bluebloods.

Andrew Jackson

The Philadelphia Chamber of Commerce supported Biddle completely. Indeed, the chamber in January 1834 issued a memorial to Congress that strongly protested the Jackson administration's policy of removing funds from the bank, pointing out the financial chaos that was resulting. Foreigners were losing faith in U.S. credit, workers were being laid off, and canals, railroads, and other projects being delayed or abandoned.[38]

At the top of the signatures of the memorial was Robert Ralston, the president of the chamber. A well-respected merchant, Ralston had been head of the chamber from 1820 to 1825 and again became the head in about 1830.[39] He was one of the first citizens of Philadelphia. In 1834 he was also the chair of the Second Bank of the United States.[40] (Biddle was the president.) In short, Ralston and Biddle, and bank and chamber, were joined at the hip. Given Jackson's extreme animus toward Biddle, it is hardly surprising that the President paid little attention to the remonstrances of the Philadelphia Chamber.

Of course, it wasn't just the Philadelphia Chamber of Commerce that advocated commercial peace and stability and the renewal of the bank's charter. The New York Chamber of Commerce, the new Philadelphia Board of Trade, and many others supported Biddle's bank. Indeed, 200 different groups came forward to plead for the bank, but these were just gusts of wind to Old Hickory. When the storm of public opinion, and merchants' complaints, was near its peak, Jackson was visited by a delegation of New York business people who complained they were practically insolvent. Jackson angrily harangued them for 15 minutes and told them to go ask Biddle for money; he had plenty of it. The browbeaten group left Jackson's office, after which he summoned one of them back. "Didn't I manage them well?" he exclaimed. Jackson simply wanted someone to share his chuckle over his performance with the group.[41]

Jackson was not a man who would bend to the reasoned words of the Philadelphia Chamber of Commerce, any more than he would stand for South Carolina to secede over tariffs. His mind was made up. The chambers of commerce of the time, which consisted mostly of the kind of well-to-do business people that Jackson was happy to take on, were no political match for the victor of the Battle of New Orleans. Jackson's destruction of the nearest thing the country had to a national bank, it's believed by many economists, contributed to the disastrous Panic of 1837 and, some say, to the periodic return of sharp, nationwide financial setbacks, until the Federal Reserve Act (strongly advocated by chambers at the time) was passed in 1913.[42]

A Nation of Organizations

In 1831, a young Frenchman arrived in the United States with a commission to study American prisons. He would become the most notable French visitor since another young aristocrat, the Marquis de Lafayette, had crossed the Atlantic to serve in the Revolutionary War. The new arrival, Alexis de Tocqueville, came only six years after Lafayette's triumphant return tour of the United States in 1824 and 1825, when the aging general received tremendous acclaim wherever he went, including welcomes from the New York and Philadelphia chambers of commerce.

Tocqueville journeyed with his lifelong friend, Gustave de Beaumont, in a more quiet fashion. His observations of the new country, captured in his book *Democracy in America* (1835), were so acute that they remain the closest thing to a mirror that the United States has ever had. He saw an energetic country with more citizen participation in ordinary affairs than there was in Europe:

Alexis de Tocqueville

> Americans of all ages, in all stations of life, and all types of disposition are forever forming associations. There are not only commercial and industrial associations in which all take part, but others of a thousand different types . . . In every case, at the head of any new undertaking, where in France you would find the government or in England some territorial magnate, in the United States you are sure to find an association.[43]

Tocqueville did not use the term "chambers of commerce," but he sensed the overall organizational ferment in the United States at that time. And indeed, the 1830s were to be a productive period for the formation and rejuvenation of business organizations. A host of factors, from financial uncertainties to the growth of traffic on rivers and rails and the rapid movement into the interior of the continent, led to a need for business people to come together and plan.

It was in 1833, coincidentally the year of Tocqueville's return to France, that Philadelphia blew the starter's whistle on a new phase of business organization in the United States. A group within the Philadelphia Chamber of Commerce had been unable to get the traders, headed by the venerable Robert Ralston, to open their association up not just to merchant shippers, but to business people of all kinds. The splinter group met on October 15 and decided to form a new organization, the Philadelphia Board of Trade. At its meeting a week later, Thomas P. Cope, a Quaker merchant who was as respected as Ralston in the business community, was unanimously elected the president of the group, with 242 votes.[44]

Philadelphia's commercial community had been split prior to this. In the tariff debates of 1824 and 1828, the free-trade memorials of the Philadelphia Chamber of Commerce had been contradicted by the opposing opinions of ironmongers and other business people in the community.[45] Many men of affairs whose interests focused on the interior of the country favored Henry Clay's "American System" of high tariffs coupled with domestic improvements such as canals and railroads. Such a point of view could hardly be more opposed to that of the Atlantic trade-focused, low-tariff advocating Philadelphia Chamber of Commerce.

The tariffs protected domestic manufacturers. In Philadelphia (as well as in other cities, notably Boston), the business community had reacted to the commercial supremacy of New York, thanks in large part to the Erie Canal's completion, by turning its attention from trade to manufacturing. The new industrial efforts were successful for the most part, leading to a large constituency in favor of tariff walls. And the Philadelphia Board of Trade seems to have embraced that protectionist point of view. "It has always been in favor of protective tariffs, and has expressed itself clearly on the subject a number of times," a subsequent history noted approvingly.[46]

Less than a month after its opening meeting, the Philadelphia Board of Trade had sent a delegation to the Internal Improvements Convention in Warren, Ohio. The organization in 1836 would help push for rail links that became the Philadelphia and Erie Railroad, and in 1848, successfully urged the incorporation of the Pennsylvania Railroad. Not forgetting its international trade roots, the group also pushed for a new customs building and various improvements along the Delaware River.[47]

It wasn't long before the Philadelphia Chamber threw in the towel. It became submerged in the larger and more active Philadelphia Board of Trade in 1845. The combined organization, although situated in a coastal city, would carry on the interior-focused, open-the-country, clear-out-the-obstacles outlook that had been evident years ago in Kentucky's Lexington Society for the Promotion of Emigration. The two groups, separated by 36 years in their founding, were united in the person of Henry Clay, who married into the first group, and whose ideas inspired the second.

What's in a name? The "board of trade" appellation was not new, but this appears to have been the first time that business people in a major North American city had used it. The British Board of Trade was a venerable governmental council. Not surprisingly, local British chambers greatly favored the "chamber of commerce" term, both to avoid confusion with their government and so as not to be seen as aping it or pretending to be it.

In the New World, however, it was different. No government department with roots in Canada or the United States was called the Board of Trade, even though the British Board of Trade was responsible for the island nation's colonies. "Board of trade" had an authoritative ring to Americans and Canadians, no doubt in part from its governmental origins, which was surely appealing to the arrivistes in the New World. (To be sure, "chamber," too, had a vaguely authoritative feel, as in "Chamber of Deputies" or the "Senate Chamber.") And given that North America's chambers of commerce and boards of trade had little if any true authority, it wasn't a bad idea to adopt a name that implied a bit of clout. In any case, the name "board of trade" was adopted in 1833 by the new Philadelphia group.

In his extensive diary, Thomas Cope several times expressed satisfaction with the organization he headed. But Cope had his hand in many civic activities in his association-friendly city. Indeed, as a young man he had known the father of Philadelphia (and American) associations himself, Ben Franklin. Franklin had organized groups of tradesmen called "juntos" that acted much like modern networking groups or chambers of commerce.[48]

The "board of trade" name spread rapidly, till one observer wrote that in 1858, between Portland, Maine and San Francisco, he could ascertain there were 20 boards of trade, compared with just 10 chambers of commerce.[49] There wasn't much, if any, difference at this time between a "chamber of commerce" and a "board of trade," although the newer boards of trade often found themselves ensconced in the marketing of agricultural products. This was in part because these newer organizations frequently were situated in inland areas where farming was by far the dominant sector.[50]

Tensions Over Slavery

Tariffs inflamed North-South relations for a time in the 1830s, but the festering problem of slavery also increased tensions between North and South, and chambers within these regions were not immune to the growing hostilities. The brothers Lewis and Arthur Tappan, wealthy silk merchants, were not especially active in commercial organizations, although in 1825 Arthur had been a member of a Pearl Street merchants' group that gave Governor DeWitt Clinton silver vases in thanks for his work to create the Erie Canal.[51]

But the brothers were unusually public-spirited and were strong abolitionists. The two helped establish the American Anti-Slavery Society (AASS) in 1831; Arthur Tappan was its founding president. In the mid-1830s, the brothers bankrolled a massive AASS propaganda campaign: in 1835 alone, they had 1 million anti-slavery tracts printed and distributed, North and South.[52]

Southerners were furious. People made impassioned speeches against New York and hunted for AASS materials in slave quarters. In Charleston, vigilantes raided the post office and took out mail bags from New York, using them for a great bonfire in which they burned an effigy of Arthur Tappan.[53]

Southerners began a boycott of the Tappan brothers' company. The fracas threatened to involve other New York businesses too, however. For one thing, a successful boycott would bankrupt the company, harming its creditors. For another, some southerners broadened the boycott to include all New York businesses.

Delegations from the New York Chamber of Commerce and city authorities visited Arthur Tappan, pleading with him to change course. On one occasion, when they mentioned the harm his actions were causing to his creditors, he seemed be conscience-stricken and was silent for a moment. Then he said, "You demand that I shall cease my anti-slavery labors, give up my connection with the Anti-Slavery Society, or make some apology or recantation – I WILL BE HUNG FIRST!"[54]

No one hung Tappan, and tensions were reduced when the New York postmaster stopped permitting AASS materials to be shipped to the South. But the boycott had come close to bankrupting the Tappans. Spurred in part by this frightening experience, in which the interests of creditors were so important, in 1841 Lewis Tappan would found the Mercantile Agency. This firm set out on the novel activity of collecting and selling business credit information.[55] Many years later, it would be known as Dun & Bradstreet.

It is Dangerous to Listen to Such Dreamers as These

1837-1860

Andrew Jackson's war on the Second Bank of the United States destabilized, at least for the short term, the country's financial system. Nicholas Biddle's bank was irreparably weakened, and local banks in other parts of the country took up some of the slack with looser lending standards. Chambers of commerce expressed concern about the lack of a national bank and feared this deficiency also meant a lack of financial discipline.

On May 10, 1837, two months after Martin Van Buren had taken office as President, a financial panic erupted. Bankers in New York, worried about inflation, had demanded payment only in gold and silver coins. Loans were called in and hard currency disappeared from circulation. The nation faced economic disaster.

There surely was a sense of "I told you so" among many chambers of commerce, which had largely supported the Second Bank of the United States. After the crisis hit, the chambers in St. Louis and New Orleans called for the reestablishment of a national bank.[1] Those in Boston, New Orleans, and New York complained that given the shortage of hard currency, it was virtually impossible for importers to pay the tariffs required to bring goods into the country.[2] These memorials and resolutions may have felt good, but accomplished little: Van Buren was committed to pursuing the policies of the President under whom he had served, and this meant not having a national bank. And importers would have to continue to pay tariffs with hard currency.

Feelings ran high on the issue of the ailing financial system. In June, the New Orleans Chamber of Commerce held a meeting on the topic, which was said to be the largest group ever assembled in that city. An executive of a local bank asked for a vote on who supported the idea of a national bank and who didn't. Apparently that individual was the only person in the entire gathering who opposed the idea of a national bank.[3]

In the absence of a national bank, it fell to private citizens to try to fix the alarming run on gold. And as would occur 80 years later, it would be a member of the New York Chamber of Commerce who did much to contain the damage. James King was a financier and trader who had been a major figure in the construction of the Erie Canal and who had spent time working in England as well. Active in the chamber and very civic minded, King visited London in October 1837 and persuaded the directors of the Bank of England to advance one million pounds to his firm. The advance permitted New York banks to resume making payments in gold, easing the financial strain considerably, both in New York and elsewhere in the nation.[4]

Despite King's rescue effort, economic activity remained subdued for five years after the Panic. But life went on and chambers of commerce did their best to beat a path to the world's door. People imagined new, great cities where villages stood before. There was something bold about chamber members' dreams for their cities.

Nathaniel Hawthorne captured this contrast between business conservatism and audacity. A few years after the Panic, in *Mosses from an Old Manse*, he imagined a fantasy museum of portraits, and entered into a gallery of the images of businessmen:

> Judging them as they stood, they might be honored and trusted members of the Chamber of Commerce, who had found the genuine secret of wealth, and whose sagacity gave them the command of fortune. There was a character of detail and matter-of-fact in their talk, which concealed the extravagance of its purport, insomuch that the wildest schemes had the aspect of everyday realities. Thus the listener was not startled at the idea of cities to be built, as if by magic, in the heart of pathless forests; and of streets to be laid out, where now the sea was tossing; and of mighty rivers stayed in their courses, in order to turn the machinery of a cotton-mill. . .
>
> "Upon my word," said I, "it is dangerous to listen to such dreamers as these! Their madness is contagious."[5]

Many fortunes were lost, in 1837 and afterward, as chambers of commerce and their members chased after dreams of urban growth. But great cities and enterprises grew, too. And often people found themselves struggling, not against human competitors, but against nature.

Mississippi River System Chambers

The New Orleans Chamber of Commerce members knew a lot about the whims of nature. They knew of sand, snags, silt, and mud. How did one control a river that carried the dust and twigs of half the nation? And how did a chamber of commerce, with little direct authority of any kind, command something as mighty as the Father of Waters?

While it may not have been easy, something needed to be done. The exploding steamboat traffic along the river and the ships coming in from the Gulf of Mexico required reliable channels at reliable depths. The New Orleans Chamber of Commerce, which and been reestablished in 1834 after a hiatus, had requested help from the federal government to keep the riverbed as clear as possible. And the government responded, as it had in other port cities, in part because of the financial incentive: more traffic meant more tariff revenue, and tariffs remained the leading source of income for Washington. A total of $285,000 was appropriated for the task, to be carried out by the War Department.

But the government's response was inadequate: first, a recommendation for an unaffordable ship canal, and then, the assignment of two small boats to dredge the river. As the New

Orleans Chamber and its engineer consultant, Albert Stein, pointed out, dredging doesn't work well on rivers, which are constantly depositing silt. It's better to direct the current (by means of piles, jetties, and piers) against the riverbed and away from the banks, than to try to scoop up an unending flow of mud.

Nevertheless, at least for a time, two federal dredging boats, Canute-like, were helplessly trying to fight the mud-carrying capacity of the mighty Mississippi. Two boats, of course, weren't enough for this task. One contemporary author noted that it would take about 10,000 large ships to dredge and remove all the mud that the Mississippi quietly carried each day as it made its way past New Orleans to the sea.[6]

A few hundred miles upstream, the St. Louis Chamber of Commerce was as interested in the river as was its sister chamber to the south. With the advent of steamboats, people could travel down the Ohio River, then upstream along the Mississippi to St. Louis, and then either take off overland toward the West or travel further by water via the Missouri or the Mississippi River. St. Louis was indeed the Gateway to the West, and the chamber of commerce's leaders were acutely aware and proud of this fact.

Edward Tracy, the president of the St. Louis Chamber in 1838, was asked by Congress how many people travelled by boat from Louisville to St. Louis. "It is impossible to form a correct estimate," he responded. "The number is immense. I have known upwards of two thousand to arrive in twenty-four hours."[7]

Some no doubt returned to Louisville; many others continued west. A stream of commerce and people, almost as powerful as the rivers that bore it, was pouring into the sparsely settled lands on the far side of the Mississippi. And along the Ohio and Mississippi Rivers, a string of new chambers quickly emerged to help serve the traffic.

In 1838, two chambers were founded along the Mississippi, one far to the north of St. Louis, the other about equally far to the south. In the north, the Galena Chamber of Commerce was created at a meeting of merchants on February 2. The chief industry of the Illinois town was lead mining ("galena" is the name for lead ore), and a hard-living crew of thousands of miners were active in the town until the California Gold Rush drew many of them away. The chamber was active for several years, including in the founding of the city government in 1841 and in petitioning for improvements on the Upper Mississippi.[8]

In the South, Nathaniel Anderson and Louis Trezevant, two local merchants, led in the founding of the Memphis Chamber of Commerce in 1838.[9] This organization would soon fade, but would be revived in 1860. While their community, next to the Mississippi, didn't also sit beside a major tributary to the great river, Memphis did command a bluff that helped make it a strategic location in peace and war.

The Ohio River saw more chambers rise up. In 1839, a chamber was created in Louisville, Kentucky, although the city had had a similar organization earlier.[10] The 1839 chamber lasted only till 1843, however. Among the primary concerns of the chamber was the Louisville and Portland Canal, which took boats around the nearby Ohio River rapids.

Cincinnati previously had some business organizations, but the first significant chamber in the community was sparked by an advertisement in the *Cincinnati Daily Gazette* on October 15, 1839. The ad, signed by 76 individuals and companies, requested a meeting at the local Young Men's Mercantile Library Association.[11] The chamber emerged from that meeting and would quickly become one of the leading business groups in the country.

In Wheeling, Virginia, a board of trade existed in the early 1840s and perhaps before then. It energetically and successfully pushed for the building of a bridge across the Ohio River. The resulting railroad bridge was built in 1849, using a technology that was revolutionary at the time: suspension engineering. At 1,010 feet in length, it was a wonder of the times, despite drawing opposition from Pittsburgh interests that didn't want any obstructions in the Ohio River.[12]

Back in St. Louis, the chamber focused with great concentration on the obstructions to its vital river traffic. Its consultant, A.B. Chambers, provided a report in giving powerful arguments for the removal of snags in the river. Citing Captain Henry Shreve, Chambers noted that a snag boat could remove 20 snags per day and would cost only $2,000 per month. At only about $4 per snag, this must have appeared a good investment to just about anyone. Chambers decried the injustice of federal improvements all around the United States without the allocation of a penny to the heartland's river system, serving 6 million people. Of all the areas receiving federal improvement funds, only those at Buffalo and the Delaware River (Philadelphia's outlet to the sea) had anything like the trade of St. Louis. Without the removal of the snags, the Mississippi River's shipping costs increased by 1 percent, a tariff upon both importers and exporters to the benefit of no one.[13]

A.B. Chambers, and chambers of commerce, saw the need to pluck out the trade barriers in the nation's waterways. It is difficult to say which chamber of the many candidates – Philadelphia, Charleston, St. Louis, or New Orleans, to name a few – worked hardest to keep its waterways open. But in 1840, a chamber would be born that would rival any of them, if not surpass them, in its obsession with the free flow of goods and people over water.

A Path to the Sea

Houston's beginnings were inauspicious. The city was founded on a yellow fever-infested piece of land by a snag-infested creek in August of 1836, just four months after Texas won its independence from Mexico. Although it was designated the capital of Texas through 1840, the town then lost that distinction. The Texas legislature moved the capital to Austin. Meanwhile the Texas currency had sunk to 50 cents to the U.S. dollar and New Orleans merchants cut off credit to the town. To top it off, there was an infestation of rats.

In 1838, citizens petitioned the legislature to approve a charter for a local chamber of commerce. Unfortunately, they had put their request in the hands of "Honest Bob" Wilson, a boisterous senator who once declared he hoped that God would strike dead anyone who voted against his proposal for open meetings. He was expelled from the Texas Senate but was triumphantly reelected, at which point he led a drunken parade through Houston's downtown, with other legislators threatening to pursue him down the street with guns and bowie knives. The fracas subsided, but it wasn't until a new, more sober senator, Dr. Francis Moore Jr., presented the proposed charter in 1840 that Houston had its chance for a Republic of Texas-approved chamber of commerce.[14]

Texas President Mirabeau Lamar signed the charter on January 28, 1840, along with a similar one for Matagorda, Texas. The Houston group, in a town beset by problems, soon set to work. "The Houston Chamber of Commerce became the coordinator of community development for a frontier village that was dying," said a chamber summary many years later. After the town was designated the "Port of Houston" by the legislature in

January of 1842, giving Houstonians the right to clear obstructions from Buffalo Bayou, the chamber raised $2,000 to do just that.[15] Not long afterward, in 1849, the chamber organized a major reception for the first steamer, the *Ogden*, to reach the port direct from New Orleans.[16]

This was the beginning of a process, lasting until the present day, of cultivating Houston's 50-mile pathway to the Gulf of Mexico. For more than 170 years, the chamber often led the action, and rarely was absent from it. This community focus on an avenue to the sea, and on other civic improvements, did not go unnoticed, even at the time. As early as 1857, a newspaper in Columbia, Texas, commented:

> The history of San Felipe, Velasco, San Luis and Columbia (all on the Brazos River) shows that situation is no guarantee of future greatness. They were all well situated – their owners lacked enterprise. Compare Columbia to Houston! The one situated at the head of tide water on the largest river in the state, the center of the richest planting section of the world – Houston on a shallow bayou, naturally incapable of navigation to any extent, surrounded by post oak, pine barrens, and boggy prairies – one has all the advantages of situation, the other of an energetic people.[17]

The Great Lakes Chambers

Far from Buffalo Bayou, Buffalo, New York was one of the boom towns of the 19th century. Its future was transformed when a group of townspeople, led by a charismatic businessman and judge named Samuel Wilkeson, performed herculean labor in Lake Erie and turned an inhospitable inlet into a protected harbor for ships. They erected piers and moved sand, mud, and rocks, beating out the town of Black Rock as the site for the western end of the Erie Canal.

The task had begun when local business people formed the Buffalo Harbor Company in 1819. It was an association of business people, but aimed purely at the end of improving the port and capturing the Erie Canal. It wasn't called a chamber of commerce or board of trade and had no aims beyond canal- and port-related activity.

In fact, the Great Lakes had no chambers of commerce as late as 1841. Perhaps not surprisingly, the first two notable chambers of commerce in the Great Lakes were founded where water connections to the Atlantic were closest. In the case of Canada, this was Kingston, Ontario, where the St. Lawrence River meets Lake Ontario. (While at this time the river was not completely navigable, it was the best water route to the sea available.) There the Kingston and District Chamber of Commerce was established in 1841.

On the U.S. side of the border, Buffalo was the Great Lakes community with the best access to the Atlantic, thanks to the Erie Canal. Hence it was not a coincidence that a chamber of commerce was founded there in 1844. Buffalo had more than enough business to warrant a formal association of business people.

The founder of Buffalo's chamber knew the harbor very well. As a poor boy, Russell Heywood had started work by selling molasses candy on the docks. His business grew until he owned his own store. In 1844, as a prominent merchant in one of the great new cities of the 19th century, he saw the need for a chamber of commerce. He expressed his thoughts clearly in a speech in June 1845 when the Buffalo Board of Trade dedicated its new building. His talk, which is preserved, shows that knowledge of chambers of commerce and their role in world trade had somehow penetrated to the interior of the United States and to a former candy hawker on the docks of a frontier village. "All cities throughout the world of any note have their chamber of commerce or board of trade," he said. He went on:

> Buffalo is now one of the largest grain markets in the world and is destined to be the largest, when half of the western prairies are brought under the plow, with three hundred ships, fifty steamboats, and hundreds of merchants trading with her; surely what has been indispensable in other cities since the Middle Ages, must be essential to Buffalo.

His next rationale for starting the organization would bring a glint of recognition from Adam Smith and a frown from today's antitrust regulators:

> Meeting on 'Change' gives you an opportunity of comparing views and establishing uniform prices for the day.

But there were other advantages beyond fixing prices (which at the time was legal):

> You mingle together and become better acquainted with each other, and rub off many sharp corners of jealousy and selfishness. By promptness at the hour all persons that have business with you will expect to meet you here instead of spending hours, as is frequently the case, in pursuit of you about the city.

Other advantages included the reading room, the registry of arriving ships and boats, and the chance to advertise the sailing times of one's own ships.[18]

In the same year (1845), two chambers were founded – by the same person, Sir Isaac Buchanan - on Lake Ontario's Canadian side, in Toronto and Hamilton. On the U.S. side of the lakes, three chambers were formed in a single year, 1848: the Oswego (N.Y.) Board of Trade on Lake Ontario, the Cleveland Board of Trade on Lake Erie, and the Chicago Board of Trade on Lake Michigan. Like zebra mussels, chambers had found a hospitable environment and they spread rapidly.

Chicago's Revolution

The Chicago Board of Trade (BoT) proved to be an interesting specimen. It was 1848 when this organization was formed in an ambitious but remote community by the backwaters of Lake Michigan. There was something special about this fast-growing town, and something special about its chamber of commerce.

The Chicago Board of Trade was set up in March of 1848, made up of 82 members from all types of business.[19] It was shucked from the same cob as the chambers and boards of trade that were popping up all over the Midwest. Members "passed resolutions concerning canal tolls, telegraph services, harbor improvements, and other matters affecting the city's economy."[20] Like most chambers, as a voluntary organization, it had little actual power. The Chicago Board of Trade did, however, have the ability to tackle a problem. Just as the New

York Chamber of Commerce spent a great deal of its early energies on trying to assure the quality of fish and other commodities, so did the BoT try to improve the quality and image of its grain that, thanks to the railroads, Great Lakes, and Erie Canal, could reach the East Coast and even Europe.

The BoT's first efforts were directed towards shifting from a volume-based bushel measurement to a weight-based bushel. Measuring by weight was the more reliable method of calibration, and the newfangled grain elevators that were clustering in the city needed a uniform way to measure their contents.[21] The voluntary BoT was unable to enforce a weight-based measure, however.

Things came to a head with the huge European demand for grain brought on by the Crimean War. Traders flooded the BoT's daily meetings (which previously had had a hard time getting attendance) and in 1856 it finally began issuing regulations to smooth the process of trading.[22] Grain was also classified not just by weight and type but by quality.

Relatively quickly the organization refined its classifications and measurements to such an extent that grain became a fungible commodity, as oil is today. It didn't matter if the wheat came from Farmer Jones' land or Farmer Fred's, so long as it could be identified as a specific grade and type. All of a sudden, grain could be mixed, making it easier to collect, store, sell, and ship.

By 1859 the BoT had applied to the state and received a charter for the legal right to set standards for members, arbitrate their disputes, and impose decisions.[23] It had become a "quasi-judicial entity" and therefore at least a part of the organization ceased to be a traditional, voluntary chamber of commerce. Yet it continued to exercise some civic functions, as would be clear for example when it raised money for troops during the Civil War.

Without a doubt, this group of business people was, originally, a standard, garden-variety American chamber of commerce. But when it changed, it changed the world. As the scholar William Cronon has noted:

> By 1859, then, Chicago had acquired the three key institutions that defined the future of its grain trade: the elevator warehouse, the grading system, and, linking them, the privately regulated central market governed by the Board of Trade. Together, they constituted a revolution.[24]

This board of trade, born in the year of revolutions (1848), did more than its share to remake the economy. The chamber had set up the world's first (and still by far the largest) modern commodities exchange. The innovations continued over the years, with the creation of futures trading and countless other improvements. Indirectly, through setting up this thoroughly modern institution, Chicago's original chamber changed agriculture, shipping, trading, and indeed capitalism itself.

Some of the changes reverberated just 90 miles up Lake Michigan in Milwaukee. No doubt impressed with the success of the Chicago traders, businessmen created their own exchange, the Milwaukee Chamber of Commerce, in 1858. This group tackled rail and harbor improvements, as well as other tasks. Most notably, the Milwaukee Chamber introduced the "the pit," an octagonal floor space with steps on the inside and on the outside. The pit soon migrated to other commodity trading establishments and symbolized for the public the manic excitement and commotion of these places.[25]

Chambers of commerce, as Buffalo's Russell Heywood had seen, were becoming *de rigueur* for towns and cities on the move. They were popping up from Wilmington, Del. to Wilmington, N.C., from Watertown, N.Y. to Columbus, Ga., and in Nashville, Tenn., Richmond, Va., and Portland, Me. The institutions were creeping into the social fabric of the nation, adapting themselves to environments as diverse as this awakening country could offer.

Indeed, as in Houston, a chamber could be born in a remote place that wasn't in the United States, but one day would be. Far away from American soil, in the Kingdom of Hawai'i, another organization was born: the Hawaii Chamber of Commerce. On October 15, 1850, just a few months after King Kamehameha III had declared Honolulu to be a city and the capital of the Hawaiian Islands, a group of merchants gathered at the store of Starkey, Janion & Co. to create their institution.[26] It dealt with various trade and harbor safety issues and was consulted on the repeal of the unusually high $5 per gallon tax on imported liquor, which apparently led to more smuggling and didn't succeed in its alleged purpose of cutting down native consumption of alcohol.[27] (The King reduced the duty to $2.50.) Someday, a tariff on a much different item would mean everything to this kingdom and to this chamber.

The Lion of the Vigilantes

Far from Honolulu, across many lapping leagues of rolling waves, lay the land of the Golden Gate. Few communities were as distinctive as San Francisco in 1849 during the Gold Rush. The population of the town soared perhaps 50 percent in the first two months of the year, to about 3,000 people, as immigrants poured in on the way to the goldfields near Sacramento. The place was in chaos. As a chamber document from December 1850 noted:

> Society was in a state of utter disorganization, which became worse and more terrible as the autumn and winter months brought more thousands to the place. There was neither a proper government for the State, nor recognized municipal authorities who could have protected the citizens and established order and made provisions for the systematic extension of the town and the reception of the coming crowds.[28]

For anyone involved in business, imposing some order was essential. Not coincidentally, the city and the chamber were established on the same day: May 9, 1850.[29]

One of the key roles of the chamber was to arbitrate the commercial disputes of its members at a time when the territory's legal system was just being formed. As in some other communities, the chamber imposed a modicum of law in a legally challenged environment.

But the chamber's formal trade promotion activities weren't enough, in the eyes of many merchants and others who sought order for the port city. Lawlessness was so prevalent, and public officials so corrupt (ballot box stuffing being a high art in this boom town), that people began to search for alternative answers to establishing public order. Such a group needed a leader.

The man who would become the standard-bearer of this extralegal movement was William Tell Coleman. Coleman would belong to the San Francisco Chamber at some early date (although probably not as a charter member) but also, beginning in 1858, to the New York Chamber, where he was active in supplying the Eastern merchants with statistics and

William Tell Coleman

other information on industry in California. Later, in 1873, this master dispatcher of fast-flying clipper ships would become president of the San Francisco Chamber.[30]

Coleman was the perfect extralegal enforcer for merchants. He had a long history of knowing what he wanted and going after it. At age seven, he had demanded that he be allowed to take a neighboring girl home to be his wife. (The dumbstruck father demurred.)[31] Nor was he afraid to use force for what he considered right. In his early twenties in the Wisconsin territory, he organized a group of men to fight a lumberjack bully and his cronies who were trying to prevent logs from reaching the merchant who had contracted for them. Coleman took on the bully himself in hand-to-hand combat and won, inspiring the ne'er-do-wells to run for the woods.[32]

He had a personal magnetism that was almost palpable – a George Washington-like *gravitas* that drew men toward him, especially in times of crisis. Robert Louis Stevenson encountered Coleman while the Scottish author was in San Francisco working on his book *The Wrecker*. Stevenson described Coleman as a man who could tame a wild town full of people happy to burn down buildings to loot them or to hang merchants from the gallows. Wrote Stevenson, giving the merchant a name that would stick: "That lion of the Vigilantes had but to rouse himself and shake his ears, and the whole brawling mob was silenced."[33]

Coleman also was a gentleman. When he travelled through the Utah territory on his way to the California goldfields, he put on a dinner in honor of Brigham Young in gratitude for the Mormon leader's generosity in offering supplies and food to the bedraggled party. Possibly no other wagon train group ever did this for Young. And Coleman compensated his kind hosts with commodities they didn't have in abundance: flour, bacon, coffee, tea, and sugar.[34]

In February of 1851, still fairly new in town and only 27 years old, Coleman, along with others who were fed up with crime, gathered where San Francisco Mayor John Geary was trying to speak. Coleman defied the pussyfooting mayor and led his group of vigilantes to put on a brief trial for two suspected criminals. One of them escaped their custody while the other – against Coleman's wishes – was given a temporary reprieve because some believed he only looked like the true murderer they were after. The man everyone wanted to string up was named "English Jim" Stuart; the person still in jail claimed he was named Berdue.[35]

Perhaps Mayor Geary and his elected and appointed cronies could have established some order at this point. But they didn't, and things got worse. A group of Australian criminals known as the Sydney Ducks had been terrorizing the town with such tactics as burning down buildings and looting whatever was left inside. On May 4, 1851, a huge fire erupted, burning down three quarters of the town. Much loot from the burned structures was found afterward in "Sydney-Town," the part of San Francisco where the criminals lived. This was the last straw.[36]

On June 10, 1851, a group of businessmen and their associates formed a new association, the Committee of Vigilance of San Francisco, to begin more systematically taking on crooks. Although not a chamber of commerce in the strictest sense, the vigilantes were merchants just like Coleman. Indeed, many of them were members of the chamber that had been formed just 13 months earlier. Of the signatories suggesting a chamber of commerce in a newspaper posting in 1849, more than one third were to be members of the Vigilance Committee.[37] The property owners who made up the chamber, not surprisingly, wanted an end to the destruction of their property.

At the sound of a bell, they would assemble to take action. It didn't take long before they heard its sound. As Coleman later recounted:

> They had scarcely adjourned half-an-hour before the bell was tapped. On reaching our head-quarters I found a number of gentlemen had returned, and soon after there was brought in a very large, rough, strong and vicious-looking man called Jenkins, an ex-Sydney convict who had been detected in the theft of a safe &c. from a store on one of the wharves. He was well known as a desperate character, who had evaded justice on many occasions here, and whose record, easily proven, would entitle him to the severest punishment.[38]

Soon, John Jenkins was hanging outside a second-story window of the Merchants Exchange building, the same building where the San Francisco Chamber met.[39] The Vigilance Committee had claimed its first victim.

In 1851 vigilantes finally got their private enemy No. 1, English Jim, while also sending a fast horse to keep his lookalike Berdue from being strung up by the law in nearby Marysville. After a trial that English Jim himself called "damn tiresome," 400 men walked with him to the wharf on Market Street. There they hung him from a derrick.[40]

Two Sydney Ducks exposed by English Jim's confessions, Sam Whittaker and Robert McKenzie, soon were sprung from jail and strung up. Then things calmed down. The lawless lawmen of San Francisco began meeting ships at the docks to turn away any Australians up to no good. Coleman and his associates went back to their normal business lives. They even founded an institution to enhance their camaraderie and their peaceful pursuits: the Mercantile Library.[41]

This could have been the end of the story, but San Francisco had plenty of anarchy still to serve up. In November 1855, a gambler and killer named Charles Cora brought a stunningly beautiful prostitute to the theater, placing her prominently in a box, instead of the stalls where such women usually sat. This disturbed the wife of a U.S. Marshal, William Richardson. Outside, Marshal Richardson exchanged harsh words with Cora, but Cora, as was his wont, accentuated his arguments with a bullet. Richardson died and Cora was shuffled off to jail.[42]

Most expected Cora to get away with it. An ally of Cora's was James Casey, a businessman who had managed to become elected to the Board of Supervisors via an unusual facility with ballot boxes.[43] But Casey's corruption was exposed by an editor, curiously named James King of William. The editor, among other remarks, noted that Casey was a former inmate of Sing Sing Prison in New York. Casey didn't appreciate this publicity. So Casey shot and mortally wounded James King of William, and was himself escorted to jail.[44]

Now there were two miscreants in jail, along with renewed fears that they would escape justice. But William Tell Coleman, after a two-year absence, was back in town. He was quickly named head of the revived Vigilance Committee. Coleman and his vigilantes defied the governor and the local militia commander, a banker named William Tecumseh Sherman. Although the jail holding Cora and Casey was guarded by 150 men, Coleman's force comprised 2,500 men who marched with strict discipline toward their assigned places. When there appeared to be a standoff, the vigilantes wheeled up a cannon, aimed it at the jail, and quietly loaded it with shot and powder. Casey and Cora were released, after protest, into the hands of the vigilantes. After brief extralegal trials, each man was hanged.[45]

William Tecumseh Sherman, soon to be the scourge of the South, disapproved of the proceedings. But his militia had not shown up for work. Meanwhile, Coleman's forces were "orderly in the extreme," as Sherman would later write. The vigilante "pork-merchants" (Sherman's term) soon got tired of midnight committee meetings and, after a couple of additional hangings, went back to their day jobs. Sherman, who had resigned his militia commission in disgust with the local goings on, went back to St. Louis.[46]

Just as chambers of commerce had traditionally filled in the cracks of government, doing on a private basis what the public couldn't or wouldn't do, so the San Francisco vigilantes had created a system of rough justice to replace a system riddled with corruption. These vigilantes had many ties to the local chamber. Indeed, the San Francisco Chamber of Commerce would look on this "vigilance" tradition with pride and would call on it two more times in the future. And Coleman's men inspired many other communities in the rough-and-tumble West, leading to some of the activities that, in turn, were to spark a host of Hollywood Westerns in the next century.

Cleaning Things Up

It wasn't just the San Francisco Chamber of Commerce that attempted to clean up its town and remove criminal elements or shady dealers. Many business organizations, in this era of loose regulation and weak central authority, looked for law and order, or at least fair dealing and some measure of public safety.

Steamboat boilers were one concern. These engines sometimes exploded, leading to deaths and horrific injuries. (Mark Twain once persuaded his brother Henry to ride on a steamer, only to lose him in a huge explosion.) Chambers in New Orleans and elsewhere called for safer boilers.

The Cincinnati Chamber of Commerce came out against another disruption of river commerce: steamboat runners.[47] These were people who, for a fee, would badger people on the docks to travel on a steamboat different than the one they had intended to board. Sometimes these unscrupulous men would separate baggage from passengers, or husbands from their wives. They were even known to tell the gullible that a particular steamboat was safe because it had no boilers.[48]

A different kind of runner plagued New Orleans: "the sailor boarding house runners." These were groups of "land pirates" who would raid incoming ships and strip sailors of their possessions. The New Orleans Chamber of Commerce appointed a committee to look into the matter:

> The Committee are credibly informed that in almost every instance on the arrival of a vessel from sea she is, before being made fast, immediately boarded by gangs of desperate men, numbering from half a dozen to twenty or thirty, who rush on board in defiance of the officers

of the ship, enter the forecastle or sailor's house, forcibly take possession of the effects of the crew, viz: their clothes, bedding, chests, etc.[49]

The chamber, not surprisingly, recommended measures to stop the abuses.

Human nature wasn't much better on the East Coast. Aided by the Savannah Chamber of Commerce, which provided moral support as well as $430 for legal fees, the mayor of the Georgia port city began waging war "upon the land-sharks who keep sailor boarding houses, and abduct seamen from vessels about to sail, in order to hire them again to some other vessel."[50] Meanwhile, the Cleveland Board of Trade inveighed against a group of Canadian ruffians who boarded the brig *Concord* when it was docked in Sarnia, Ontario, and shot its captain.[51]

The Railroad Giant Awakens

Chambers of commerce, whether on oceans, rivers, or lakes, had shown themselves adept at opening pathways for boats and ships. Improvements in railroads, however, made this exciting alternative to waterborne transportation increasingly practical. And while not everyone could have an Erie Canal, almost any community could aspire to be a stop on a railroad line. Moreover, with the settlement of the Oregon Territory's border with Britain in 1846 and the new territories acquired after the Mexican War (1846-48), people could envision rail lines stretching thousands of miles, and imagining their town or city at a critical junction.

John Roebling, the great engineer and bridge builder of the time, pointed out in a talk to the Pittsburgh Board of Trade in 1847 that rail transportation was beginning to overtake water. Coal was being shipped by rail from Pottsville to Philadelphia for less than $1 per ton per 100 miles, which compared favorably with steamboats' rates of 40 cents to $1 per ton per 100 miles. And rail had other advantages that ultimately would win out: "But whether steamboats charge a few cents more or less, will little influence the transport of the great west, while the saving of transshipment and commission, and the certainty, rapidity and safety of conveyance, are of much greater moment to the merchant and the traveler."[52]

What would quickly become the largest rail system in the country, the Pennsylvania Railroad, was incorporated in 1846 with significant help from Thomas Cope and the Philadelphia Board of Trade.[53] The BoT continued to push hard for the completion of the railroad to Pittsburgh, as well as for other improvements to the rail system of the region. The word "railroad" appears no fewer than 52 times in the BoT's annual report for the year ending in February 1859.[54]

The merchants of Boston, without a chamber since 1843, created the Boston Board of Trade in 1854. It was managed by Isaac Chapman Bates, a full-time chamber secretary, something the mighty New York Chamber could not boast at the time.[55] It's likely that hiring a full-time secretary was part of Boston's attempt to outgun New York on transportation. Bates was, or soon became, an expert on railroads. Both Boston and Philadelphia would continually seek railroad improvements to compete with New York, which had the huge transportation advantage of the Erie Canal.

Bates was energetic. His annual report for 1857 ran no fewer than 670 pages. When a critical link to Chicago, a new suspension bridge across the Niagara River, was open for rail traffic in the spring of 1855, he visited the site personally to help untangle the vast snarl of rail cars waiting to cross – stretching 10 to 20 miles in either direction. A similar traffic jam in the spring of 1856, caused by a snowstorm, had tied up 60 percent of the rail cars of the New York Central and threatened to suck up the others. Bates went back to the site and did his best to ease the bottleneck, keeping his Boston members informed of the situation.[56] For business people of this era, and for their chambers of commerce and boards of trade, proper railroad connections were critical.

The Greatest Project of Them All

In 1786, as we have seen, the New York Chamber of Commerce had given its bully pulpit to Christopher Collis, who had conceived of a plan for a canal to the Great Lakes. When the actual canal was completed in 1825, New York was more than ever connected with the trade of the interior of the nation. It's not surprising that it would be this chamber that would support the idea of a railroad that would tie the continent together even more than the canal did, stretching from the Great Lakes to the Pacific Coast.

As with Collis, the New York Chamber of Commerce took up the call of an individual with an idea. Two generations later, it was Asa Whitney, a successful merchant from New Rochelle, New York. After 1844, Whitney single-mindedly and forcefully advocated the idea of a transcontinental railroad. Originally he envisioned the tracks starting at Lake Superior but the plan evolved into a railroad emanating from Lake Michigan, where railroads were in the process of reaching from the East. Two aspects of his plan set it apart from most others of the time: self-financing (the railroad would be paid for by the sale of public lands on either side of the tracks) and economy of the route (a survey would determine the shortest distance from Lake Michigan to the Pacific Coast with the fewest obstacles).

The New York Chamber appointed a committee to examine plans for transcontinental railroads and concluded that of all the ideas out there, only Whitney's was practical. The committee suggested, however, that Whitney's financial benefit from the project should be curtailed and that the railroad should be the property of the United States. In this it was overruled by the chamber as a whole; its members believed that no one would dedicate his life to such a project without some financial benefit.[57]

The New York Chamber's August 7, 1849 resolutions on behalf of Whitney's idea were brief but forceful and were presented to the U.S. Senate on Christmas Eve.[58] But the time wasn't right. Congress was tied up in negotiations over slavery, ending in what became known as the Compromise of 1850. Ultimately Whitney's plan would not be acted upon, even though his idea for land-grant-financed railroads would be widely copied, with the first such project occurring in 1858.[59] Whitney was only slightly ahead of his time, and of all the dreamers who imagined rails spanning the nation, he was the most prescient.

The South wanted a transnational railroad, too. And the members of the Charleston Chamber of Commerce retained a strong interest in railroads, despite their extensive attention to their city's harbor and despite the limited success of the railroad to Hamburg, S.C. that their chamber started in 1828. Part of the focus on rails was because Charleston had a limited hinterland; the Appalachian chain cut off South Carolina from waterborne trade with the interior of the country. To get beyond the mountains and reach to the West,

Charlestonians had to rely on railroads. Moreover, rails also offered the prospect of uniting the slaveholding states, as other sets of rails were tying the North and the West together.

One of the chamber's members in this period was James Gadsden, who was president of the South Carolina Railroad Company during the 1840s. Gadsden joined the chamber in 1842 and remained a member until his death in 1858. He envisioned a transcontinental railroad for the South, stretching from Charleston to San Diego. When it became clear that the United States needed additional land from Mexico to build such a railroad, he was able to complete the transaction. Gadsden was appointed U.S. Ambassador to Mexico in 1853 and arranged for the purchase of 30,000 square miles of territory in what is now southern Arizona and New Mexico and includes such cities as Tucson, Yuma, and Lordsburg. While the railroad was never built, the Gadsden Purchase added a significant and valuable piece of land to the United States.

St. Louis v. the Future

The members of the St. Louis Chamber of Commerce knew that St. Louis was a choice piece of real estate. At the confluence of the Mississippi and Missouri Rivers, the city commanded the water routes that were opening up the West. It's no wonder the chamber for so many years, like its counterpart in New Orleans, had been working so hard to pluck out the obstacles in the river. The Gateway to the West had to be wide open in order to attract maximum traffic and business.

In the mid-1850s, a challenge emerged to the importance of the rivers: a railroad bridge across the Mississippi, the Rock Island Bridge, which reached from Illinois to Davenport, Iowa. It was completed in 1856, despite intense opposition from the St. Louis Chamber of Commerce. The bridge united the Chicago and Rock Island Railroad with the Mississippi and Missouri Railroad in Iowa, which was to stretch from Davenport across the state to Council Bluffs – opening a lightning path for commerce all the way from Omaha to New York City. All of a sudden, where was St. Louis's choke point on trade in the interior of the country?

Engineers sited the bridge based on an 1837 topographical survey by a young Army lieutenant, Robert E. Lee, and other studies. The six-span bridge was 1,581 feet long – far shorter than anything that could have been erected downstream at St. Louis, where the Eads Bridge, completed in 1874, would be 6,442 feet long.

Franklin Pierce's Secretary of War, Jefferson Davis, had tried to stop the Rock Island Bridge, not wanting rail traffic to take a northern route before a southern route was completed. But his effort to keep the railroads from using the former military site of Rock Island failed. The bridge was in place – but although there was a celebration in 1856 to commemorate the crossing, the event was perhaps premature.

On May 6, 1856, just 15 days after the celebration, the steamer *Effie Afton* crashed into the bridge, catching fire and burning up. The bridge was put out of commission, at least temporarily, because it caught fire, too. While the crash was an apparent disaster for the northern-rail advocates, it was a victory for river traffic. As a lawyer for the bridge company later noted, "Why, there was a shouting and ringing of bells

A sketch of the crash and burning of the *Effie Afton*

and whistling of all the boats as it fell. It was a jubilee, a greater celebration than follows an excited election."[60]

Yet only four months later, the bridge was back in operation. The *Effie Afton*'s owner sued for damages in a case that all saw as a contest between rail and river, *Hurd v. Rock Island Bridge Company*. The St. Louis Chamber of Commerce energetically supported the plaintiff, and some said, may have prompted him to sue in the first place.[61]

This was a celebrated case, one of the most famous in the career of the experienced lawyer who took the lead role on the side of the bridge company. Against the combined might of the steamboat interests along the river, led by the St. Louis Chamber of Commerce, this lawyer somehow managed to convince a few members of the jury that railroad bridges were not an obstruction to commerce, but an extension of it. He suggested the surge of migration to the West had rights equal to north-south traffic. And the need for the railroad was clear: "It is in evidence that from September 8, 1856 to August 8, 1857, 12,586 freight cars and 74,179 passengers passed over this bridge," the lawyer said. And for the four months of the year when the river iced up, the railroad was still there to serve the public.[62]

Abraham Lincoln
Attorney, 1857

It was a magnificent performance by the attorney. The jury was hung, which essentially meant that the railroads had won this battle. It was a major step forward for the railroads and their great junction city, Chicago.

The extraordinary case, watched with interest not just along the Mississippi River, but across much of the nation, added to the reputation of the eloquent lawyer, Abraham Lincoln. His client, the bridge company, was vilified for planting an obstruction in the river. And yet later the same lawyer would be famous for sending forces to clear the river of an even more imposing obstacle – the Confederate army in Vicksburg – after he had become President of the United States. With the Union victory in July 1863, Abraham Lincoln famously wrote, "The Father of Waters again goes unvexed to the sea." It turned out that the President and the chamber had something in common: neither really wanted snags in their river.

The St. Louis Chamber had been thwarted by Abraham Lincoln in the *Rock Island Bridge* case, but it wasn't finished. It raised $37,000 for a legal challenge to the bridge,[63] which was ultimately unsuccessful. And an agent for the St. Louis Chamber of Commerce, J.W. Bissell, was actually jailed in 1860 for conspiring to burn the bridge. Although Bissell was later acquitted, there had indeed been an attempt to burn down the bridge.

The bridge survived and the northern rail route proceeded to develop rapidly and later became part of the route of the original Pacific (Transcontinental) Railroad. St. Louis, by opposing progress, became caught in a losing race with the up-and-coming city of Chicago, which not only had the northern rail route but also, through its position on Lake Michigan, a waterborne trade route through the Erie Canal all the way to the Atlantic.

In retrospect, what could St. Louis have done? Surely someone was going to build a bridge across the river eventually. It would have been a gargantuan task to build a trans-Mississippi bridge in St. Louis in the mid-1850s, however. When Eads completed his bridge there in 1874, the structure was considered an engineering marvel, as it still is today. The northern route was almost predestined to win because it had a much narrower part of the river to cross.

In addition, St. Louis had the misfortune to be in the volatile border area between the North and South. Tensions in Missouri and neighboring Kansas were hot in the mid-1850s and only got worse in the years immediately before the Civil War. The northern route bypassed these problems and was a secure base for rail traffic for the North throughout the Civil War. A southern route would have been difficult to complete before the war and impossible to operate consistently during it.

In hindsight, there may not have been much St. Louis could have done to stay even with the upstart city to its northeast. Still, the St. Louis Chamber of Commerce might have mitigated the damage by being less stubborn. The city became too well known for fighting progress rather than embracing it. Its rival, Chicago, seldom made that mistake.

Kansas City Here I Come

Missouri soon had another community with a penchant for railroads: Kansas City. This community saw a new chamber formed on October 21, 1856: the Kansas City Association for Public Improvement. Its name soon changed to the Chamber of Commerce of the City of Kansas. A chamber member named Col. R.J. Van Horn wrote a memorial to Congress in the late 1850s arguing that Kansas City was the natural site for railroads, including an intercontinental railroad.[64] Two decades later he reflected on the achievements of the early chamber in Kansas City:

> Various railroads centering here were mentioned as having been secured through the efforts of the organization; the opening of the Indian Territory, as far as it has gone, was also attributable to the same earnest effort; as well as the fact that many schemes inaugurated by rival towns for the injury of Kansas City had been successfully defeated.[65]

Indeed, this infant chamber, so apparently concerned about its rivals in other towns, packed a punch of its own. The Kansas City Chamber and the local business community succeeded in getting the Pacific Railroad to "aim its tracks" at Kansas City as early as 1858; this precocious victory may have predetermined those that followed. After the Civil War, Kansas City's business leaders managed to win the first rail bridge over the Missouri, outdistancing their rivals in St. Joseph and Leavenworth, each of which had had probably more than three times Kansas City's population. Leavenworth, the more logical candidate, was hurt by a divided business community.[66] The early organization paid off, and the Kansas City chamber men won rail primacy for their city, a hammerlock on regional transportation infrastructure that has lasted nearly a century and a half.

Chambers of commerce, then, in the years before the Civil War and the years after it, were of course not involved in military hostilities with one another. But the competition for business was at times almost as fierce. Where the rails went determined where the business went. A bridge wasn't just an engineering project; it was a path to the future, if not also a blow aimed at metropolitan competitors. A new railroad line for a community was, or sometimes appeared to be, a virtual yellow-brick road.

From One Struggle to Another

There was one contemporary fight even fiercer than the river v. railroad battle. It was over slavery in Kansas. In the mid-1850s anti-slavery settlers formed the majority in the territory but were attacked by pro-slavery advocates from Missouri. After a brief respite in the fighting, it was rumored that a pro-slavery group, the Kickapoo Rangers, were about to enter Kansas from Missouri and create mayhem once again.

A group of merchants from Lawrence, grasping at straws, appealed to the St. Louis Chamber of Commerce for help. Their letter, reprinted in the *New York Times* on February 28, 1856, tried to cater to the profit motive of the St. Louis businessmen. Hold back the marauders, said the Lawrence correspondents, and Lawrence and St. Louis could prosper together. Let the evildoers attack, and there would be consequences. Trying to sound threatening, the Lawrence businessmen fortified their argument with italics:

> For, *if by an unnatural and coercive policy on the part of any of your people, we are induced to open new thoroughfares for trade with other cities, and invest our wealth in opening railroads and telegraphic communications with the same, the weight of your imprudence will recoil only upon your own heads, and in due time we shall escape the fiery ordeal unscathed.*[67]

At this time, the Rock Island Bridge was almost complete, and the Lawrence merchants no doubt sensed the weakness of St. Louis. The Missouri city's near-monopoly as a river trading depot was under threat from the rails. The Lawrence merchants, if attacked by Missourians, could lay tracks north to Iowa or otherwise circumvent their southern tormentors. Railroads could be a weapon in this war over slavery. (And in a different way, railroads most definitely would be used in war in just a few years.)

In fact, business people in neither Lawrence nor St. Louis could do much about the incursions into Kansas. The situation had moved beyond the reach of chambers of commerce. And as would become clear later, the St. Louis Chamber itself was split over the issue of slavery.

Global Breakthroughs in a Tense Time

Chamber of commerce members felt the growing tensions over slavery as much as their countrymen and women did. But progress didn't stop; new markets were opening and new technologies developing. In the years just before the Civil War, there were things to celebrate and anticipate.

One of them was the opening of the Japanese market. In 1853 Commodore Matthew Perry had taken a powerful fleet to Japan and, the following year, forced the Tokugawa Shogunate to agree to trade with the West. For the New York Chamber of Commerce, this was great news. The chamber presented the victorious commodore in 1855 with a collection of china, together with silver utensils, goblets, etc., valued at between $6,000 and $7,000 at the time (about $160,000 in today's prices).[68]

Even more exciting was the laying of the first transatlantic telegraph cable. The two people most responsible for the endeavor, Cyrus Field and Peter Cooper, were both connected with the New York Chamber of Commerce.[69] The accomplishment was lauded by the chambers in Liverpool, St. John's (Newfoundland), and, of course, New York. The New

York Chamber of Commerce gave medals to the captain and crew of the U.S. cable-laying ship, the *Niagara*, and, in an August 1858 resolution, pronounced the cable to be "the greatest event of the age."[70] Unfortunately, the cable shorted out the following month. Nevertheless, with some help from the chamber, Field got it operating again just after the end of the Civil War.[71]

The laying of the Atlantic Cable

For San Francisco, the lack of a telegraph across the Great Plains was a serious problem. News travelled very slowly and impeded commerce with the East. The inauguration of the Pony Express in April of 1860 changed everything. Fast-riding, wiry horsemen, such as the man later known as "Buffalo Bill" Cody, carried mail and telegraph dispatches across the Great Plains, reducing the time for coast-to-coast communications to just 10 days. This was so exciting to the San Francisco Chamber of Commerce that it requested daily deliveries "by Pony time."

A committee of the chamber had figured out that two riders, daily carrying 40-pound sacks of half-ounce letters, could handle 934,400 letters in a year.[72] This would mean that the main means of getting mail to San Francisco, the excruciatingly slow steamer route via Panama, wouldn't be needed any more. Moreover, the two riders would be safer than one among the dangers of the West.[73]

In December of 1860, the chamber's proposal was presented to Congress,[74] although it had little effect. The government closed down the expensive and often dangerous Pony Express operations on October 26, 1861, just 18 months after the service had begun. Telegraph lines had reached across the Great Plains on October 24. Posses of electrons were outrunning the fastest horses in the West.

Trying to Avert War

The Republican Party opened its second convention on May 16, 1860, in the booming city of Chicago. There was something fitting in this choice of venue. The country was bursting with commercial activity, even as it was convulsed over the issue of commerce in human beings. The mood was ebullient. The Chicago Board of Trade provided, and the delegates accepted, an invitation to take them on an excursion on Lake Michigan at 5:00 pm. A delegate proposed three cheers for the ladies of Chicago, and his fellow conventioneers "compromised" with one cheer.[75]

But of course, the convention had other business. It nominated Abraham Lincoln as its candidate for President, a man whose opposition to slavery, combined with his folk wisdom and kindly disposition, had made him popular in many parts of the North and West. Lincoln's election in November would convince most of the leaders in the South that it was time to secede from the Union.

There were last-minute attempts to stitch the country back together after Lincoln's election. Among them were resolutions by many different groups of citizens and business people seeking to concede virtually every issue to the South. More than 800 members of the Milwaukee Chamber of Commerce approved one such measure.[76]

On January 17, 1861, businessmen meeting at the New York Chamber of Commerce created such a petition. Afterward they quickly sought signatures for it, gaining more than 40,000.[77]

In late January a high-level delegation brought it to Washington, where it went nowhere. Why, opponents asked, should there be a "compromise" over the election of a President? Lincoln had not even taken office and had done nothing yet against southern interests.

There was something fishy about this petition. Newspapers identified it with the New York Chamber, since the meeting had been held there, and most if not all of the prominent people in the room were members. But this was not an official chamber meeting and was not authorized as such. In fact, Matthew Maury brought this up at the February 7, 1861, meeting of the chamber, seeking clarification as to whether it was an official meeting or not.

It wasn't an official meeting, admitted Peletiah Perit, the president of the chamber. But he said that the merchants who had been at the meeting were chamber members. (In fact, on the invitation to the meeting, the list of nine prominent business people involved included each of the top three officers of the New York Chamber: Peletiah Perit, Royal Phelps, and Abiel Low.[78]) The southern-leaning Richard Lathers proposed a resolution that the chamber could host the petition committee for "any more meetings they may choose to hold in forwarding the laudable and patriotic object in which they were engaged." The resolution was approved. Hence the chamber winked at this pro-peace group it had admitted, and did nothing in public to disassociate itself from the petition committee.[79]

The failure of the petition in Washington wasn't the end of the New York merchants' push for peace. William E. Dodge, a prominent businessman and chamber member and a determined advocate for peace, attended the "Peace Convention" at the Willard Hotel in Washington beginning on February 4. This was a meeting convened by former President John Tyler with many representatives from the border states, along with some sympathetic northerners.

The proceedings didn't get far, in part because President Abraham Lincoln dropped by from time to time and made clear his disagreement with those who would placate the southern secessionists. William E. Dodge spoke up at one point while Lincoln was in the audience. Dodge said he was a "plain merchant" sent to the convention by the New York Chamber of Commerce (an interesting assertion, given the chamber's admission that it had not officially sponsored the peace petition committee).

He told Lincoln: "It is for you, sir, to say whether the whole nation shall be plunged into bankruptcy; whether the grass shall grow in our commercial cities."

"Then I say it shall not," Lincoln responded. "If it depends upon me, the grass will not grow anywhere except in the fields and in the meadows."[80]

The Peace Convention sputtered to an end in late February, 1861.

The semiofficial, but extremely energetic, efforts by New York Chamber members to stop the Civil War are a part of history – although not of any official New York Chamber history. Now that most people in the United States, North and South, see the Civil War as a just one, we cannot help but look down on what appears to be the appeasement of slavery and secession just before the war started. This wasn't, in our modern view, the most courageous moment of the New York Chamber of Commerce. But at the same time, this was and remains a clear and powerful demonstration of business groups' desire to maintain peace, to cling to "business as usual." There had been before, and would still be afterward, a strong chamber tendency to try to avert large-scale wars. It's interesting that even William E. Dodge's fear-mongering warning of "bankruptcy" would be repeated, just before World War II, by the president of the U.S. Chamber of Commerce.

Meanwhile, further into 1861, the push for peace still wasn't quite over yet. One of the hot-shot younger members of the New York Chamber had another card up his sleeve. He had embarked on a mission to convince the nascent Confederacy that union was still possible.

Coming Together
and Coming Apart

1861-1865

It was worth a try. Colonel Richard Lathers, that prominent southern member of the New York Chamber, addressed the Mobile Chamber of Commerce, and endeavored to let these southerners know that they had friends in the North and that together they should try to patch up their quarrel. The fate of the Union was too important to leave to a few abolitionist firebrands in Massachusetts or Kansas. Lathers was one more chamber man trying to keep the peace.

Lathers, originally from Georgetown, S.C., was the founding president of the Great Western Insurance Company. Originally he was to be part of a delegation of three ad hoc peacemakers from the North, but the other two were unable to come. (One of them, former President Millard Fillmore, had taken ill.) So it was Lathers alone who went through the South, addressing skeptical but usually friendly groups in key southern cities and meeting Jefferson Davis and other Confederate leaders in Montgomery.

He had just finished the written part of his speech in Mobile and was shifting to personal remarks when there was a murmur in the crowd. Someone had brought in some news. The Confederates had fired on Fort Sumter, S.C.

Lathers had the bad luck to be offering a message of peace on the opening day of the Civil War, April 12, 1861. There wasn't much point in continuing. The meeting was closed with a vote of thanks to him.

Nevertheless, he was slow to give up. He tried to keep a similar engagement a couple of days later at the New Orleans Chamber of Commerce. But the morning of the meeting, the mayor paid him a call and said he was an 'alien enemy' and had better take the 2:00 p.m. train out of town. He obeyed.[1]

Lathers arrived safely in New York, but his chamber there already had been busy. Most of the members of this chamber no longer shared Lathers' ambivalence about the conflict. The New York Chamber of Commerce was at war.

On April 19, the New York Chamber of Commerce held a special meeting on the war. Resolutions already had been drafted, but it was decided to postpone their reading until there was a larger, public meeting on Saturday, April 20, in the appropriately named Union Square.[2]

The patriotic rally on April 20 in New York was important for many reasons. It was said later to be "probably the largest public meeting ever to be held in America" up to that point.[3] Stirring up patriotic sentiment in New York was critical, both because of the military manpower of the city and state, and because of the city's political importance. New York was known to be a hotbed of Democratic and Copperhead (peaceful) sentiment. For the New York Chamber of Commerce to spearhead a pro-Union rally at this point, and later, was no doubt appreciated by President Lincoln, who so recently had opposed the chamber's not-so-subtle push to appease the South.

The resolutions promised the full support of the chamber in the war effort. In addition, the resolutions condemned, at some length, Jefferson Davis's decision to permit privateers on the high seas to attack northern shipping. Indeed, it was Davis's act that made the war somewhat personal for members of the New York Chamber of Commerce, many of whom had direct or indirect interests in the Yankee ships and their cargo. The resolutions didn't even consider the Confederate maritime predators worthy of the name of "privateer":

> *Resolved*, That the proposition of Mr. Jefferson Davis to issue letters of marque to whosoever may apply for them, emanating from no recognized Government, is not only without the sanction of public law, but piratical in its tendencies, and therefore deserving the stern condemnation of the civilized world. It cannot result in the fitting out of regular privateers, but may, in infesting the ocean with piratical cruisers, armed with traitorous commissions, to despoil our commerce and that of all maritime nations.[4]

To help stamp out the depredations of the southern pirate ships, the chamber called for the federal government to "blockade every Southern port, so as to prevent the ingress and egress of such vessels."[5] This resolution received more than the usual acclaim from listeners. "Immense applause" followed its reading.

Throughout the war, the New York Chamber would pay special attention to the privateer issue. Nothing seems to have upset its members more. The concern showed up in all sorts of ways. For example, in the fall of 1860 Captain John Wilson, while at the helm of the *Minnie Schiffer,* had effected the daring rescue of 500 passengers from a burning ship, the *Connaught.*[6] But once he had "turned pirate" for the Confederacy, the chamber removed his portrait from its walls.[7]

Despite its obsession with privateers, the organization would also lend the weight of its opinions and support to the entire war effort of the Union. This was important not only from a financial and war supplies standpoint, but also from a political one. Not everyone in New York City was as ardently behind the war effort as the chamber was.

During its initial meeting on the war, the chamber took concrete steps to back the war effort. Learning of the need to equip troops for the front, the group raised $21,000 in 10 minutes. It also promised to quickly subscribe the remaining $9 million of government borrowing to fund the conflict.[8]

The New York Chamber announced it would send copies of its resolutions to other chambers of commerce. But merchants already had met in the Boston Board of Trade offices on April 18 in order to "consider upon the best means of preserving the Union, and upon addressing the Massachusetts delegation in Congress." They formed committees and planned a petition to Congress.[9] The war would quickly involve every business organization in the country, one way or another.

The Confederates believed as much in their cause as the Yankees in theirs. The Charleston Chamber of Commerce, for one, was deeply embedded in the conflict. The shelling of Fort Sumter was occurring in the

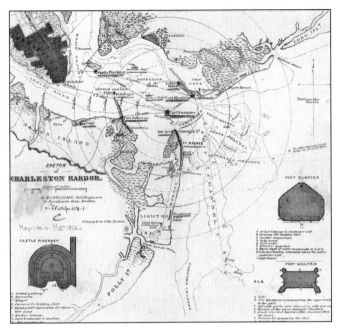

Charleston Harbor

very harbor that the chamber had lovingly worked to create and expand. One of the pioneers of the chamber in this regard was George Alfred Trenholm. In 1851, as president of the chamber, he requested to the superintendent of the U.S. Coast Survey that the harbor's chart be traced for local use.[10] The expert who was asked to do much of this work was John Newland Maffitt. He must have done a good job because Trenholm and the chamber had honored him and his colleagues with a public appreciation dinner in 1852. This Trenholm-Maffitt team, effective in peacetime, would prove to be equally adept in war.

Interestingly, the Charleston Chamber of Commerce has a claim to having been the organization that created the first Confederate flag that was publicly flown in South Carolina, and likely the first such flag seen by Yankee troops. On March 4, 1861, the first "Stars and Bars" flag had been approved and flown in the Confederate capital of Montgomery, Alabama. Instructions on how to make it were then telegraphed to Charleston. Lee Howard, a deputy naval officer, was quoted in the *Charleston News* later as saying he asked the chamber's porter, Christopher Nelson, to make the flag. The next morning, on March 6, 1861, Howard was pleased to see it flying over the Custom House.[11] The chamber's Nelson claimed he had raised it. There it flapped defiantly at the Yankee troops stationed at Fort Sumter. Shortly afterward, it was taken aboard a steamer, *Carolina*, becoming the first ship out of the Charleston harbor (and possibly the first seagoing ship anywhere) bearing the Confederate flag.

As the North and South geared up for war, their chambers did what they could, even though their commercial activities necessarily took a back seat to the war effort. The New York Chamber of Commerce and the Philadelphia Board of Trade both requested that the federal government protect their harbors, and action was taken at least in the case of New York.[12] The Cincinnati Chamber of Commerce called for repairs to the damaged Baltimore & Ohio Railroad so as to improve Union access to the sea from the interior.[13]

During the first year of the war, one chamber in the South showed that it had not completely lost its chamber stripes despite the onset of hostilities. Surely one of the great classics of chamber optimism is the Memphis Chamber's review of the year ending in August 1861. Secretary J.N. Toof noted that "Memphis has suffered to an incomparably limited extent, and . . . the aggregate of her trade has been larger than in any previous year." He went on:

> The rapid and unparalleled growth of Memphis during the past five years has, to many, appeared to be unsubstantial and precocious – the result of fortuitous and fortunate circumstances, which the first revulsion in the affairs of the country would dissipate or seriously disturb – but the commercial statement we present, considered with the important events of the year, proves that the currents of our trade are as sure and unfailing as that of the mighty Mississippi, on which much of it is borne – fluctuating with the seasons, but nothing interrupting their flow.[14]

That mighty, uninterrupted flow of trade was quickly bottled up on October 22, 1861, by an order from Confederate Major General Leonidas K. Polk. He put an area near Memphis under military rule and forbade grain shipments from it, so as to keep the supply for the army. On October 30, 1861, Toof and his president, Thomas Hunt, complained in a letter to Jefferson Davis that Polk's action was both illegal and counterproductive. Instead of lowering food prices for the army, as intended, Polk's obstruction of trade had raised grain prices in Memphis by 33 percent.[15]

Optimism, however, still survived in chambers in the South. The Macon, Georgia, chamber was founded in February of 1861, and in July its president called for a commercial convention to be held there on October 24.[16] (Not much seems to have come from that idea for a meeting, however.) In December 1861, the legislature approved the petition for a Selma, Alabama chamber. And the Atlanta Chamber of Commerce sent a missive addressed to the "Chamber of Commerce of London, England" (although a modern London chamber was not founded until 20 years later) touting the southern cause, the South's adherence to free trade principles, and, also – this was a chamber, after all - the advantages of the promising Georgia city. A *New York Times* writer had great fun with Atlanta's pretensions but clearly was incensed that the letter was taken seriously on the other side of the Atlantic:

> It would hardly have occurred to us to make such a document the subject of note, were it not that the London journals have taken this piece of Southern bombast *au pied de la lettre*. If Bohemia were to issue a circular to the European Powers, arrogating to herself to dictate concerning maritime law, blockades, and the Rights of neutrals, it would probably strike those journals as slightly grotesque. And yet the ridiculous cockeral [*sic*] circular of a Chamber of Commerce of a little wooden village in Georgia, is made the subject of long and solemn discussions! Their sense of humor and their knowledge of the relations of American commerce have certainly room to develop.[17]

Chambers could not completely lose their promotional stripes in the North, either. The Boston Board of Trade could match anyone in its fervor for fighting the secessionists. But it also took care to protect home base. On November 23, 1861, a special committee of the Board of Trade wrote to U.S. Quartermaster General M.C. Meigs asking him to set up a Bureau of Clothing and Equipment for New England. Of course, a little boosting was *de rigueur*: "The water power of the Merrimac and Saco alone is sufficient to supply the clothing for one hundred millions of people," the committee wrote.[18]

New England could make military items more cheaply than could anyone else, the Boston men stated, but it appeared that Philadelphia and New York were getting more contracts than Boston was. The businessmen complained: "Boston is the second commercial city of the United States, and may of right – we are constrained to aver – may of right – claim to be placed on an equality, in this behalf, with New York, Philadelphia, and Cincinnati."[19] Just because there was a War Between the States didn't mean there was an end to the War Between the Cities; the Boston Board of Trade and other chambers would continue to jockey for urban position during the Civil War.

In a painful echo of the unfolding war, and of the thousands of families whose loyalties fell on opposite sides of the conflict, the St. Louis Chamber of Commerce split apart on January 9, 1862. Chamber Secretary W.B. Baker had brought in a new group of prospective members, apparently with the plan of giving the chamber a pro-Union majority. But the secessionists literally "blackballed" all the applicants. (According to the rules, five black balls would disqualify any applicant.) At this, the Union-leaning members walked out, intending to start their own chamber.[20]

The strong hand of the Union was beginning to make itself felt in the West. By early February, General Henry Halleck stamped out the St. Louis problem by forcing chamber members to swear allegiance to the Union. Apparently the brave wielders of black balls became suddenly timid: "the great rebels of the Chamber of Commerce came right up to the rack," *The New York Times* gleefully reported.[21] Conditions in another border state, Kentucky, were improving to the extent that Louisville merchants were creating a new chamber of commerce there.[22]

In the troubled waters of the East, southern ships continued to wreak occasional havoc. One of the most fearsome was the world's first ironclad ship, the *Merrimac*.[23] This menacing vessel was impervious to the attack of just about every wooden ship. Fortunately for the North, an inventor named John Ericsson had fashioned an opposing craft, the *Monitor*, which soon sailed after the *Merrimac*. The two ships clashed at Hampton Roads, Virginia, on March 8-9, 1862. The battle was a draw, and neither ship saw serious combat afterward. Nevertheless, other Yankee ironclads soon were afloat. Fears that the South's brief advantage in technology could jeopardize the entire fleet of the North gradually dissipated.

The New York Chamber's members were jubilant. At a special meeting on March 12, just three days after the historic battle, the chamber voted resolutions praising the captain and crew of the *Monitor* and its Swedish-born inventor. John Ericsson, who was present at this meeting, explained that his funny-looking craft, which some called a "cheesebox on a raft," was eminently seaworthy, despite having a hull that rose only a foot above the waterline. The revolving turret (nine feet above the waterline) kept the vessel afloat. "There can be no danger of her swamping. It is like a bottle with a cork in it," he told the New York merchants.

(Unfortunately, events proved him wrong; the *Monitor* later capsized in a storm while it was being towed.) And he added that if Captain Dahlgren had allowed the *Monitor* to use wrought-iron shot, or if the gunners had aimed lower, the Yankee ship would have sunk the *Merrimac* at that first engagement.[24]

On April 6-7, 1862, a terrific struggle took place at Shiloh (also known as Pittsburg Landing), Tennessee. Despite an initial rout of the Yankees, General William Tecumseh Sherman had stood fast and turned defeat into victory. But the cost was terrible: this was the bloodiest battle ever fought to that point on American soil.

On hearing of the battle and the enormous casualties, the Pittsburgh, Pa., Board of Trade organized the "Pittsburgh Sanitary Committee," which sent two steamers to Pittsburg Landing, carrying 30 nurses and surgeons. The cost of the operation was $6,000, and it was said to have saved hundreds of lives,[25] earning the thanks of Secretary of War Edwin Stanton.[26]

The victories in the West reopened trade routes that had been disrupted by the conflict. On June 9, 1862, Cincinnati Chamber President Joseph C. Butler telegraphed Secretary of Treasury Salmon P. Chase that Butler wished to announce trade could flow as far as Memphis, and all the way to New Orleans once Vicksburg was taken. Chase responded on the same day in the affirmative regarding Memphis, noting, "Tender to the Chamber of Commerce, and to my fellow citizens of Cincinnati, my heartiest congratulations on the partial reopening of our rivers, soon, I trust, to be completed. *May they never again be closed to American commerce.*"[27]

The war was proving to be much bloodier and longer lasting than either side had expected. On July 1, 1862, President Lincoln drew his trump card, the vastly greater population of the North, and requested an additional 300,000 Union soldiers. This prompted echoes of patriotic support in many parts of the North, including from commercial organizations. At a meeting at the Board of Trade offices in Philadelphia, $45,000 was pledged toward raising 10 regiments. "No person subscribed less than a thousand dollars, and some subscribed as high as three thousand," reported the *New York Times.*[28] The Chicago Board of Trade raised $15,000 and an artillery battery and began recruiting a regiment.[29]

Buffalo heard the call as well. There, the pain of the war was fresh. On May 31, 1862, a regiment from Buffalo, the 100th, had led its division in the Battle of Seven Pines, Virginia.[30] The men of the 100th were in the vanguard of 6,000 Union troops under General Casey, attempting to hold off 30,000 rebel troops. The troops had charged into the rebels, who were protected by barricades of slashed tree limbs. The Yankees were ordered to retreat, and the real killing began as the rebels followed after them.[31]

Of the 960 men of the regiment who charged into combat, 210 returned to camp that night.[32] The regiment had almost been exterminated. The news hit Buffalo hard. There the Buffalo Board of Trade stepped into the battle. On July 25, responding to the President's call for new enlistments, the Board of Trade met and decided to support the regiment both with money and with recruiting help. It raised $22,000 and soon had a recruiting ad out that boasted, "$20,000 for EXTRA BOUNTY and PREMIUMS!" The "gallant 100th" would hereafter be known as the Board of Trade Regiment.[33]

These original Buffalo soldiers, thanks to a diligent and honest chronicler named George Stowits, would become among the better known of the chamber-backed fighting units in the war. By August 1862 the regiment had grown to a strength of 451 because of the return of missing and wounded men. The Board of Trade's drive added 345 more, getting the regiment to a respectable size again.[34] And the Board's continuing help would prove valuable as the tired young men followed a bloody trail through the rest of the war.

Among the many patriotic rallies in the North during July of 1862, the one spearheaded by the New York Chamber of Commerce on July 15 was the largest and most prominent. Various commentators compared it to the previous, chamber-sparked rally, also at Union Square, on April 20, 1861. Estimates of that 1861 crowd had ranged up to 250,000. Whether or not the July 1862 meeting was larger than the first meeting (opinions differed), the mood was more somber and determined the second time around. It appeared that all classes in New York were united against the foe: millionaires and laborers stood together and listened to speech after speech. The spirit of the rally, as intended, no doubt induced many new enlistments into the Union armies.

While the New York Chamber of Commerce was in full battle dress, its feisty opponent in the South, the Charleston Chamber of Commerce, had fallen on hard times. Like many chambers during the war, including the one in Atlanta, the Charleston Chamber ceased operating. The chamber's ledger book for February 9, 1863 showed $730 in dues received during the past year and $3,042.50 in arrears. Its annual meeting, held the same day, apparently resulted in a decision to close the chamber for a while.[35] This decision to suspend operations, however, did not in the least signal that chamber members themselves were giving up the war effort.

"Heard With Amazement"

The Confederacy's "piratical cruisers" began to take a toll on American shipping during 1862, aggrieving Union merchants no end. Things came to a head in October, when the *Alabama* burned the U.S. merchant ship *Brilliant*

A.A. Low

CSS Alabama

after taking its cargo and three British seamen who volunteered to cruise with the privateer. Abiel Low, the second vice president of the New York Chamber and a leading merchant, introduced an angry series of resolutions at a special meeting on October 21. The thundering resolutions against the *Alabama*'s attacks concluded with a charge that Britain was complicit in the attacks:

> Resolved. That this Chamber has heard, with amazement, that other vessels are fitting out in the ports of Great Britain, to continue the work of destruction begun by the "Alabama;" an enormity that cannot be committed on the high seas without jeoparding [*sic*] the commerce and peace of nations.[36]

To be sure, the British government wasn't building these ships, but it was tolerating their construction. Abiel Low and his cohorts wanted to embarrass British leaders into better behavior, into closer supervision of the work going on at the docks in Liverpool and elsewhere. They also wished to deter the French from similar privateer-aiding activities, and may have had some success in this.[37]

But the key target of the New York Chamber was Great Britain. If this was amateur Anglo-American diplomacy, it fit a pattern. The merchants of New York had dealt closely with the British government since even before their Stamp Act protests of 1765, and they had pushed for the passage of the Jay Treaty in 1795. James Gore King's bringing back one million pounds from the British banks in 1837 was a kind of financial diplomacy. The close commercial ties of New York and London would soon be cemented by a young binational banker who joined the New York Chamber in late 1862, J. Pierrepont (later Anglicized to Pierpont) Morgan. These New York merchants depended for their commercial lives on a healthy relationship with Great Britain.

And they left few stones unturned in their British political meddling. For example, chamber members contributed to a fund for English workers who were unemployed because of the cessation of the cotton trade thanks to the U.S. blockade of southern ports.[38] In March of 1862 they had publicly honored John Bright, the Birmingham Member of Parliament who championed free trade, manufacturers and merchants, and good Anglo-American relations.[39] And they worked their sources in Great Britain effectively, having ties not only to merchants in the Liverpool Chamber (where southerners also had contacts) but to public and private figures in the island kingdom.

In July of 1862, the New York Chamber passed resolutions honoring Samuel Goddard, an American based in Birmingham who was writing pro-Yankee commentary for the newspapers and who was in contact with John Bright. Goddard wrote back in response:

> I wish to say that my exertions have been directed mainly to prevent any intervention in favor of the rebels; and my attention has been given to the highest quarters in France, and to the government ministry of England, as well as to influential men, and the people generally, and I believe these exertions have not all been in vain.

Goddard also requested in his note that the New York Chamber "not to give any publicity to the resolution in my favor, for, although so highly honorable, it might detract from my efficiency as a voluntary agent, and there is yet great work to be done."[40]

With its resolutions condemning the building of privateers, the New York Chamber was taking a very public, and somewhat inflammatory, stance. It did not fail to elicit reactions from across the water. The *London Times* responded indignantly, "What has England to do with this?" It went on:

> Are we to shut-up our shipyards as well as our factories as a homage to the Federal lust of conquest? The New-York Chamber of Commerce, and especially Mr. Low, who seems to be their mouth-piece, would appear to be of this opinion. They have "heard with amazement" that other ships are being built in England and Scotland which may possibly become at a future time Confederate vessels of war.[41]

This sparked a furious response from *The New York Times*, for it was common knowledge that Confederate maritime predators had come off British docks and with British knowledge.[42] Postwar investigations would show precisely how much British authorities knew about the activity. It appeared that there was little that the Yankees could do.

After the rebel steamer *Nashville* sank the valuable New York packet ship *Harvey Birch* on November 16, 1862, the New York Chamber of Commerce once again fulminated against the Confederates' predation. Its leaders wrote a letter to President Lincoln urging that he send steamers to European waters to protect American shipping there. And it dispatched a delegation to Washington to discuss the matter with the President.

One of the chief spokesmen of the small delegation was none other than Colonel Richard Lathers, the man who was addressing the Mobile Chamber of Commerce on the opening day of the Civil War. He and his colleagues, along with New York's Congressional delegation, were ushered into the White House to make their case. Lathers read out the letter and elaborated on it. He thought he was succeeding in his petition.

Then President Lincoln, clad informally in slippers, responded, "Very well put, young man, but the blanket's too short." Lathers was taken aback. Lincoln continued:

> If you should ever sojourn in a tavern at my old home in Springfield, of a cold winter night, you might be put in a room without furnace or stove, and if you were tall like myself and desired to cover your chest with the blanket you would uncover your feet, and if you desired to protect your feet you would then have to uncover your chest. That is the present condition of our small navy. If we fully protect the Confederate harbors from blockade running, we cannot cover the China Seas and other distant grounds where the rebel cruisers are to be found.[43]

Lincoln graciously postponed his Cabinet meeting by two hours so that the group could have further discussions with those officials, in case they should discover that the New York group's idea was workable after all. But it became clear to all that Lincoln's intuitive perception was right on the money. The U.S. Navy just wasn't big enough. The blanket was too short.

The Cabinet discussions had included talks with Treasury Secretary Salmon P. Chase and with a fellow New Yorker, Secretary of State William Seward. Curiously, in view of the nature of the petition, Lathers' memoirs do not mention here the Secretary of the Navy, Gideon Welles. Perhaps there wasn't a meeting, or perhaps it didn't go well.

Gideon Welles was not a fan of the New York Chamber of Commerce. Like many public officials before and after him, he resented the meddling of these chamber amateurs. Granted, the bad blood arose because some of them considered *him* an amateur. He wasn't a shipowner. However, he was a gifted and honest administrator, and most historians consider him to have acquitted himself well in the job.

His diary of January 5, 1863, simmered:

> There is a set of factious fools who think it is wise to be censorious, and it is almost as amusing as it is vexatious to hear and read the remarks of these Solomons. One or two of these officious blockheads make themselves conspicuous in the New York Chamber of Commerce . . .[44]

Spurred by fury at the attacks of rebel privateers, and by anger at blockade running, in early 1863 the New York Chamber of Commerce urged the President to issue letters of marque to ships that would essentially become Yankee privateers. These ships would hover off the coast of Bermuda and Nassau to intercept the blockade runners. The President turned down the suggestion after senators informed him that this could incite war with Great Britain.[45]

The hysteria over the rebel predator ships may have been exaggerated. In July of 1863, New York Chamber officials admitted that over two years the destruction of Yankee shipping amounted to only 61,000 tons out of a total of 3,000,000, or only about one percent per year.[46] But the chamber had continued to hound Gideon Welles with advice and memorials on how to deal with the foe.

George Alfred Trenholm
aka "Rhett Butler"

And just who was this foe? There were many people on the other side, of course. But the mastermind of the South's naval arsenal was George Alfred Trenholm, former president of the Charleston Chamber of Commerce and one of its most active and committed members.[47] Trenholm headed a shipping and trading firm called John Fraser & Co. The company had international connections, including a subsidiary in Liverpool, Fraser, Trenholm & Co. The Liverpool subsidiary's chief, a South Carolinian named Charles Prioleau, was a prominent member of the Liverpool Chamber of Commerce – and of the Charleston Chamber.

The Charleston firm's large oceangoing ships were bottled up by the Union blockade. Trenholm therefore offered other services to the Confederacy. The most important service of all was financial: having specie deposited in Charleston that could be converted into letters of credit to obtain foreign currency in England. The Confederacy's purchasing agents in England then were able to obtain much-needed military supplies and other goods for shipment to the South.

Goods from Britain would have to run the federal blockade, and by 1862 most of the ships from British ports that were engaged in the business would dock in Nassau or Bermuda, where their cargoes would be offloaded onto faster, sleeker ships. Trenholm was the leading operator of those smaller ships. He began the Nassau business when a large British steamer, the *Gladiator*, was stranded there with a cargo that included 20,240 Enfield rifles and other supplies. He offered to take the cargo into the Confederacy by using two of his small steamers, the *Cecile* and the *Kate*.[48] The lucrative business blossomed from there and ultimately he had as many as 60 ships slipping through the Union dragnet.

Trenholm had a useful associate: his old friend from the U.S. Coast Survey, John Newland Maffitt. Maffitt had joined the Confederacy and proved to be of great service to Trenholm and others fighting the Union on the water. Maffitt, on Trenholm's recommendation, captained the *Cecile*, and later would skipper the rampaging *Florida*, the ironclad *Albemarle*, and other Confederate ships.

The blockade-running business, supplied from England with the help of Trenholm's financial services and much of it carried on his ships, was never enough for the needs of the Confederacy. Still, it provided sufficient munitions and other goods to prolong the war and kill tens of thousands of Yankee troops. It greatly enriched Trenholm, who later was the inspiration for Rhett Butler, the wealthy blockade runner in *Gone with the Wind*.

Trenholm also arranged for the building of Confederate ships, including the *Alabama*, which left the Liverpool port several days early to avoid seizure by British authorities. This ship went to sea on July 29, 1862, and dispatched at least 55 Yankee ships. The *Alabama*, indeed, as we have seen, angered Abiel Low and his colleagues at the New York Chamber of Commerce more than any other ship on the ocean.

The captain of this destructive vessel, Raphael Semmes, had his own opinions on the New York Chamber, as he noted in his memoirs:

> From papers captured on board this vessel [the *Crenshaw*], we learned that the New York Chamber of Commerce – whose leading spirit seemed to be a Mr. Low, one or two of whose ships, if I mistake not, I had burned – was in a glow of indignation. Its resolutions were exceedingly eloquent. This Chamber of Commerce was a sort of debating society, which by no means confined itself to mere commerce, as its name would seem to imply, but undertook to regulate the affairs of the Yankee nation, generally, and its members had consequently become orators. The words "privateer," "pirate," "robbery," and "plunder," and other blood-and-thunder expressions, ran through their resolutions in beautiful profusion.[49]

The New York Chamber seems to have amused Semmes as much as it annoyed U.S. Navy Secretary Welles. But perhaps it was the chamber that had the last laugh on Semmes. In August of 1864, the Yankee *Kearsarge* sank the *Alabama* off the coast of France. The New York Chamber of Commerce subsequently spent $25,000 on medals and cash rewards for that captain and crew of the *Kearsarge*. The Boston Board of Trade chipped in another $21,000.[50]

The Road to Union Victory on Land

In early 1863, the Buffalo Board of Trade regiment was stirring back to life. After the Seven Pines battle, its remaining soldiers had spent a brief respite out of combat, in camp in Virginia. There, the arrival of mail was usually welcome, except when "now and then a father and husband whose heartless wife was ever thrusting the thorns of complaint into the already overburdened heart, demanding, without reason, money, when the thing was a stranger in camp for months."[51] Sometime after January of 1863, these troops turned into rebels themselves, refusing to work without whisky rations, and then stealing a barrel of it.[52] But most of the time they were peaceful, and the "faithful knights of water and soap" proved to be adept and determined at cleaning their clothes when the opportunity arose.[53] They would soon face more fighting.

Antiwar rioting in New York City, 1863

The almost simultaneous, and decisive, Union victories of Gettysburg (July 3, 1863) and Vicksburg (July 4) made it appear that the tide of the war had finally turned. But not everyone wanted to continue the fight. On July 13 through 16, massive working-class riots erupted in New York City in reaction to the draft. While the New York Chamber of Commerce remained 100 percent behind President Lincoln (if not so much behind Secretary Welles), its patrician members clearly did not represent everyone's views in the city. The New York Chamber underlined its support for the war, and for order in the city, by donating $10,000 to the relief of police and firefighters who had been injured in the riots.[54] William T. Coleman, that energetic vigilante and bicoastal chamber member, gave a critical personal assist to the authorities in putting down the riot.[55]

With the victory at Vicksburg, the Union's control of the western region was tightened, and chambers of commerce were acutely aware of which side was winning the struggle. The Cincinnati Chamber of Commerce expelled 33 members who refused to take the oath of allegiance to the United States government.[56] Memphis was thoroughly tamed, although its chamber argued gamely that the federal government could not fairly both term the region to be in a state of insurrection and also collect taxes from it.[57] But in general, things were so much better for the Union cause in Memphis that on August 25, General Grant was feted in the chamber of commerce offices with a public dinner filled with almost embarrassingly lavish praise. He wrote a grateful letter to the local citizens' committee afterward, pleased at the "first public exhibition in Memphis of loyalty to the government which I represent in the Department of the Tennessee."[58]

Outside the immediate theater of the war, business went on. On August 13, 1863, the Portland, Maine, Board of Trade cheerfully hosted chambers and boards of trade from as far afield as Milwaukee, Chicago, Detroit, Quebec, and Montreal. About 250 guests came and were feted with a brass band, an excursion among the nearby islands, and of course a display of local products and a "hand-shaking" with local citizens. The festivities included a clam bake involving "sixty bushels clams, ten bushels potatoes, sixty dozen ears corn, two hundred and fifty lobsters, ten bushels oysters, twenty codfish, eighty dozen eggs, eighty quarts baked beans, one hundred gallons coffee, sixty gallons ice cream and a good supply of other 'fixings' necessary to enhance the 'feast of wit and flow of soul.'"[59] This bounty, of course, would have been inconceivable in most of the war-weakened South.

But there was a rival to Portland that wasn't south of the Mason-Dixon line. Before the guests had arrived in Portland, word got back to the Boston Board of Trade that this shindig was in the works. Needless to say, the Boston group took action. It quickly got hold of the visitors, obtained free passes from the railroads, and was able to entice many of the travelers to go back via Boston on the return trip. Portland may have made a stealth attack, but Boston could parry it.[60]

In Milwaukee things appeared as bright as they were at the Portland bash. The Chamber of Commerce of Milwaukee reported cheerfully in 1862 that "last year mercantile failures in this city have been fewer and for a less amount than in any other city of the Union, in proportion to population and business."[61] Two years later, the same chamber petitioned the Senate for a wagon road from Idaho to haul gold from the West.[62]

But these prosperous business people may have been too comfortable. When a woman named Mrs. Bickerdyke visited the Milwaukee Chamber to ask for donations for sick and wounded soldiers, she was turned down on the grounds that the chamber already had equipped a regiment. She became livid:

> And you, merchants and rich men of Milwaukie, living at your ease, dressed in your broadcloth, knowing little and caring less for the sufferings of these soldiers from hunger and thirst, from cold and nakedness, from sickness and wounds, from pain and death, all incurred that

you may roll in wealth, and your homes and little ones be safe; you will refuse to give aid to these poor soldiers, because, forsooth, you gave a few dollars some time ago to fit out a regiment! Shame on you – you are not men – you are cowards – go over to Canada – this country has no place for such creatures![63]

The shamed merchants decided to support her efforts after all.

While life in parts of the North was good, the Buffalo Board of Trade regiment was headed into more trouble. It had been shipped to South Carolina, where its soldiers witnessed fighting in the siege of Charleston and, from July to September of 1863, participated in the bloody and unsuccessful struggle to capture Fort Wagner. (This was the same battle portrayed in the 1989 movie *Glory*.) Sergeant Flanders of Company A planted the Buffalo Board of Trade colors on the fort but was killed, after which Corporal Spooner retrieved the torn emblem.[64] The Board of Trade sent a new one to replace it.[65]

Early in 1864, the Buffalo Board of Trade regiment began a series of hard-fought battles in Virginia. By about this time the Board of Trade had recruited a total of 511 men for the regiment, but it wasn't enough to cover the losses. Moreover, as the New York City draft riots had shown, there was increasing reluctance to serve in this protracted conflict. It would take 354 draftees to plug the holes that the Board of Trade couldn't fill with volunteers. Eventually 1,825 men would serve in this regiment, with many of them victims of Minié balls, bayonets, artillery fire, or disease.[66]

The Board of Trade kept up its assistance, providing fresh regimental colors that were an agony for tired troops to carry through swamps and thick forests. The colors attracted their share of complaints. In times of battle, though, for some reason these burdens became worth dying for.

And then there were the wounds. The Buffalo Board of Trade did much to make sure its regiment had the proper medical supplies. Sometimes, however, the care of a human being at the front was the most important of all. In October 1864, as the regiment grappled with rebel forces in what was to become the siege of Petersburg, Major Stowits was wounded. His book records:

> The field hospital, in charge of Surgeon Kittenger, whose skill as a surgeon has been acknowledged, was crowded with sufferers, lying on boards on the ground; while Clara Barton, that noble, self-denying woman, passed along with her attendants, supplied with what refreshments the wounded soldier craved, weak with loss of blood and stiff with exposure. In the morning the lumbering ambulances began to transport us to steamer at Deep Bottom for Fortress Monroe, where some of us lived and others died.

> The name of Clara Barton is written in the memory of every suffering soldier that ever felt the weight of her finger's touch on his anguished brow, or took from her hands the life-giving draught. Her presence, power and will has calmed many a terror-stricken soul, and quieted the heart's flutterings.[67]

Grant's armies were slowly closing in for the kill in Virginia. Further south, progress was more rapid. General William Tecumseh Sherman, never especially successful in business, was proving to be something of a reverse chamber of commerce. His strategy of striking at the economic heart of the South, carving a streak of chaos and destruction through the middle of Georgia on his march to the sea, culminated in a celebrated telegraph from Savannah to President Lincoln on December 22, 1864. It read:

> I beg to present you as a Christmas-gift the city of Savannah, with one hundred and fifty heavy guns and plenty of ammunition, also about twenty-five thousand bales of cotton.

Sherman composed that telegraph at the home of the president of the Savannah Chamber of Commerce, cotton merchant Charles Green.[68] The Union general had accepted the offer of this house for his temporary office and quarters both because of its comfortable size and opulence and because Green, as a British citizen, would not be reviled as a traitor by his neighbors for giving up his home to a Yankee.

Green had another motive for hosting Sherman: keeping his cotton. Many of the bales of the precious fibers sat in local warehouses belonging to Green. The chamber president was something of an expert on warehousing. As early as 1842, when he was secretary of the chamber, Green had submitted a lengthy committee report to the federal government that dealt with how much the government need be involved in the setup and ownership of warehouses.[69] But in 1865, despite Green's hosting the scourge of Georgia, the chamber's opinions counted for little. On January 19, as president of the chamber, Green wrote a letter to Britain's ambassador to the United States, Lord Lyons, protesting that the cotton owned by British subjects in Savannah was being taken away by soldiers without vouchers.[70] Green's loss was President Lincoln's gain, and the British merchant didn't recover his cotton. (He did, however, remain in business and was still dealing with other federal issues as president of the chamber as late as 1876.[71])

The war, of course, had resulted in staggering losses for many people, especially in the South. There was pressure in Congress to create a national bankruptcy bill to help business people recover from the dislocations of the war. However, in early 1865, commercial organizations raised objections. The Philadelphia Board of Trade and the Boston Board of Trade, fearing the loss of up to $200 million in money owed to northern creditors by southern debtors, asked that such legislation be postponed.[72] And indeed a national Bankruptcy Act was not passed until later, in 1867, although it seems to have pleased no one and it was repealed in 1878.[73]

Whether or not the South could ever repay northern merchants, the North needed to put an end to the war. The final assault on Petersburg occurred on April 2, 1865, when Yankee troops overran Fort Gregg. The 100th was in the forefront of this final major battle with the Army of Northern Virginia. The troops of the Buffalo Board of Trade rushed the fort, led by their color bearers, who were killed. Major James Dandy, in command of the regiment, picked up the fallen emblem and erected it on the fort. He fell, mortally wounded. But the colors of the Buffalo Board of Trade remained, the first Union insignia to fly over the fort.[74]

Lee was forced out of Petersburg with his bedraggled army, but the cause was hopeless. On April 9, 1865, he surrendered to Grant at Appomattox. The war was nearing its close.

There wasn't much wealth to recover from the exhausted and smoking South. But across the North and West, the economic energies unleashed by the war were undiminished. Indeed, in July of 1865, just two months after the final surrender of the Confederacy, dozens of U.S. and Canadian chambers of commerce came together in Detroit to discuss trade and transportation issues. This meeting would lead to the creation, only three years later, of the first federation of chambers in the United States, the National Board of Trade. The Civil War was over and the work of building the greatest economic colossus in history was getting under way.

Reconstruction and Renewal

1866-1876

Cyrus Field appreciated international projects. He was in Egypt, looking at the works for the greatest engineering feat of the time, the Suez Canal. He was the official delegate of the New York Chamber of Commerce to a meeting convened by the moving force behind this project, Ferdinand de Lesseps.

De Lesseps had called for a "Conference of Representatives of Chambers of Commerce" to begin meeting in Alexandria, Egypt, on April 6, 1865. A total of 85 people attended, including delegates from 62 chambers of commerce from 14 countries. The group toured the Suez diggings and was impressed. At other delegates' request, Field wrote a report for their signature. It noted optimistically: "In our opinion the construction of a ship canal across the Isthmus is only a question of time and money." Field went on to send various documents, charts, and other papers from the project to the New York Chamber of Commerce; while de Lesseps effusively thanked the chamber for its participation and encouraged it to tell its members about the great project.[1]

Thus, in the same month that Lee surrendered to Grant at Appomattox, the New York Chamber was looking past the Civil War to the world beyond and the massive economic opportunities that were unfolding. De Lesseps was shrinking the world with his water bridge from Europe to Asia. And similarly, Field (with the help and the encouragement of the New York Chamber) would soon make additional attempts, and ultimately a successful one, to lay a working telegraph cable on the Atlantic floor, bringing North America and Europe much closer together.

And yet for the New York Chamber and other business organizations in the United States, it was the North American market where the opportunities were greatest. In this atmosphere of optimism and excitement, if also of war weariness, a group of chambers of commerce and similar commercial groups convened in Detroit on July 11, 1865. The organizers proudly claimed that the 43 groups represented there (28 from the United States, 15 from Canada) comprised "every known organized commercial board in the United States and the British American Provinces," excluding those in the South and border states, where these institutions were still in disarray.[2]

According to one of the participants, Hamilton Hill of the Boston Board of Trade, this meeting was different from the various commercially oriented conventions of the past. This one had hardly any politicians; it was "the first occasion when the business men of the United States have come together to consult upon those practical questions underlying the national prosperity".[3] The meeting, Hill noted, was of particular interest to the people of the West, who were anxious to have more outlets to the sea.

The problem was another canal – not the Suez, but the Erie. The vast grain output of the Great Lakes states was being compressed and sipped through a narrow straw that linked the West to the Atlantic. The Erie route was the cheapest way to transport Western grain to the East Coast and to Europe, but it wasn't cheap enough. Speakers envisioned more railroads and other improvements, including a Niagara Ship Canal that would connect Lake Ontario and Lake Erie on the U.S. side. (This project, a dream of many chambers for many subsequent years, never came to pass because it aroused hot opposition from supporters of the Erie Canal, who saw it as potential competition.)

Feelings ran strong on the Erie Canal's chokehold on commerce. Joseph Aspinall, the president of the Detroit Board of Trade, apparently offended a number of his guests from the East when he said:

The West has long felt the exorbitant transfer charges and tax levied by the State of New York upon its products passing through the Erie Canal, which is assessed regardless of the demand or value of the property at the place of destination, which, together, oftentimes exceed the Canal and Hudson River freight to New York, or lake transportation of one thousand miles, sometimes equaling the latter and the Ocean freight from New York to Europe together, or even what the Western farmer realizes upon coarse grains at the place of production.[4]

Lewis Allen of the Buffalo Board of Trade received applause later in the meeting when he said Aspinall's charge was "false in its expression and unjust in its conclusions."[5] The following month, N.S. Benton, the auditor of the Erie Canal, thundered in an open letter to Aspinall that the Detroit Board of Trade president was either ignorant of the facts or on purpose uttering "palpable untruths." Benton complained:

If New-York holds a local position advantageous to exterior trade and interior traffic, is this a crime for which she must or should be denounced and punished?[6]

Thus, the recent, catastrophic war clearly had not erased sectional or economic tensions in the United States. Westerners resented the skinny strip of water in New York State that had made their grain shipments possible but also wrapped them in a relationship of dependence. Those in the West found natural allies in the Eastern cities competing with New York.

Boston and Philadelphia, for example, as they did before the Civil War, had a strong economic interest in finding rail or water pathways to circumvent the dominance of the Erie Canal and New York City. It's therefore not surprising that the boards of trade in Boston and Philadelphia were the leading advocates of the creation of a national organization made up of chambers of commerce. Such an association, in theory, would examine all kinds of channels for commerce, and not just the one that New York monopolized. After the Detroit meeting in 1865, the boards in Boston, Philadelphia, and other cities - but with only tepid support from the New York Chamber - pushed for what was to become the National Board of Trade.

The North and the West may have had problems in the immediate aftermath of the Civil War, but these, of course, paled in comparison to the confusion in the border states and the anguish in the South. In May of 1865, the leaders of the Nashville Chamber of Commerce complained to President Andrew Johnson that the merchants of Louisville were trying to recruit the Fourth U.S. Army Corps to their city, even though its troops and commissary owed a lot of money to Nashville merchants.[7] Meanwhile, the Cincinnati Chamber reported that while the military authorities had ordered hogs to be slaughtered and sold in Lexington and Louisville, the stubborn creatures instead had gone to Cincinnati, where the markets and meat packing facilities were better.[8] The war was over, and even pigs were choosing the free market over military authority.

Southern Living

In the South itself, conditions were miserable. Atlanta, that ambitious "wooden village" whose chamber had touted its virtues to London during the war, had shown that its wood would burn brightly. Indeed, it was from a hill near Atlanta that Sherman had looked down on the flaming city and proclaimed, "War is hell."

In 1865 about one quarter of Atlanta's women were widows.[9] The chamber, moreover, had disappeared during the war. But its feisty, booster spirit was very much alive. In later years, the chamber would even tout Sherman's targeting and burning of the city as evidence of the city's critically important location.[10] And as early as 1866, a group of merchants had formed a board of trade whose members met daily. Moreover, the Atlanta Chamber of Commerce would emerge in 1871.[11] Like Scarlett O'Hara scooping the earth of Tara and vowing to rebuild, so the citizens and merchants of Atlanta were intent on fighting their way back to prosperity.

While Scarlett was busy in Atlanta, "Rhett Butler" had his hands full in Charleston. George Alfred Trenholm, his son William, and 20 colleagues managed to revive their chamber on February, 1866. The chamber needed work: while its books listed assets of $2,511.51, most of the money ($2,500) was invested in Confederate bonds, and the cash ($11.51) was in Confederate currency.[12]

George Trenholm offered the very first resolution for this revived chamber. The short document, which the chamber approved, encouraged the people of Cincinnati to continue their efforts to construct a railroad toward Charleston.[13] It was time to start building again.

There was nonetheless a cloud hanging over the members of the Charleston Chamber: many of them feared prosecution by federal authorities for their activities during the Civil War. On March 12, 1866, they addressed a letter to President Andrew Johnson and asked for clemency for the offenders, who had a reason for their waterborne wartime escapades:

> In their distress and perplexity, and having no other avenue open to them for employment in the only profession of which they had any knowledge, or that offered the means of preserving their families from want and suffering, many of them engaged in the trade of running the blockade.[14]

With the war over, these and other business people couldn't move on because "the want of confidence among individuals, arising out of the insecurity of person and property against arrest and seizure, paralyzes all the operations of industry."[15]

Fortunately for Trenholm and his colleagues, the threat of arrest gradually receded under the Johnson administration. Trenholm himself had been jailed after the war, and had appealed to President Johnson on June 6, 1865, for a pardon. He was paroled by special order in October 1865 and finally pardoned on October 25, 1866.[16] While his incarceration was brief, the federal government was implacable in its pursuit of his company, Fraser Trenholm & Co., which declared bankruptcy in 1867.[17] Trenholm, however, remained one of the first citizens of Charleston, and was reestablished in banking by 1870. He and his son William would have more to say about the future of this venerable but creative chamber.

The Golden Age of the Iron Horse

On November 29, 1864, more than 700 soldiers of the First and Third Colorado Cavalry approached a settlement of friendly Cheyenne and Arapaho Indians. These Native Americans had acquiesced in treaties drastically shrinking their lands to make way for a massive migration of gold prospectors and others to the Colorado Territory. But the soldiers nevertheless attacked the Indians at Sand Creek, killing more than 100 of them, mostly women and children. The troops' brutality and the grisly relics they brought back to Denver shocked many Americans and led to the resignation of the territorial governor, John Evans.

Why the attack? There had been much fighting with other Indian groups, and atrocities on both sides. Evans, worried about the transfer of Union troops to Missouri, was concerned that Indian hostilities would grow worse. Moreover, he wanted the Transcontinental Railroad (then known as the Pacific Railroad) to pass through Denver on its way to San Francisco. Continuing strife with Native Americans, or even the perception of it, was hardly going to help in attracting the railroad.[18] He and his men appear to have wanted to sweep away the entire issue, with all potential human obstructions brushed out of the way. Thus, at least part of the reason for one of the most shameful massacres of peaceful Native Americans in the history of the United States was simply economic development – or more pointedly, greed.

Evans was the kind of man who got what he wanted. A wealthy physician, he had founded the Illinois Republican Party and befriended Abraham Lincoln; the city of Evanston, Illinois, is named for him. He had a hand in founding not only Northwestern University, but also the University of Denver. His partner in setting up the University of Denver, then called Colorado Seminary, was his good friend, the Rev. John Chivington, known as the "Fighting Parson." It was Chivington who led the massacre at Sand Creek, in the same year (1864) that he and Evans had set up the seminary.

The violence on the Colorado frontier gradually faded, although the story of the massacre remained, longer lived than any of its perpetrators. Meanwhile, Denver's railroad problem persisted. Indeed, in 1866, despite negotiations with Evans, Union Pacific executives chose Cheyenne over Denver as the transit point for the great project. Their decision was perfectly rational, as the path of the Pacific Railroad would be straighter if it went through Cheyenne, and Wyoming's Bridger Pass was much lower than the mountains around Denver. And while Evans and his colleagues might have been able to remove a few peaceful Native Americans, they couldn't budge Pike's Peak.

Although this routing decision was a logical one for Union Pacific, it was a disaster for Denver. Not being connected to the only efficient means of shipping goods was as close to a death sentence as a city could get. Local citizens saw a possibility of organizing a Colorado railroad that would reach up to the Union Pacific. But this group didn't have the necessary money: $600,000. Business people began to move out of the city. The Kansas Pacific made overtures to the city, but its price was higher: $2 million.

By the fall of 1867, the situation was desperate. As a later chamber chronicler wrote:

> Denver had to have a railroad if it was to survive as a city. So on November 13, 1867, John Evans and John Smith and General John Pierce and others marched up the stairs of Cole's Hall on Larimer Street, and before they had marched down again the Denver Board of Trade had been born, with the ambitious job of securing for Denver a railroad.[19]

The group made a plan for a $500,000 capital project, organized the Denver Pacific Railroad Company on November 19, 1867, and collected the first $300,000 over the next three days. The fledgling Denver Board of Trade had ensured that its city would survive. Less than three years later, the first locomotive arrived in town, and other railroads quickly followed, aided by the Board.[20] Denver thus immediately became one more illustration of the curious symbiosis between chambers of commerce and transportation, and specifically between chambers and railroads.

Far-off Scranton, Pennsylvania, had railroad problems of its own. Just after the Civil War, this city had more iron and steel furnaces (28) than any other community in the nation except Johnstown, Pa. But it had only one railroad, the Delaware, Lackawanna and Western (DLW), which was no friend of local merchants. The DLW made them pay the same price for any shipment up to 100 pounds, whether it weighed nine ounces or 99 pounds.

In December 1867, 13 local men wearing beaver hats met together over a Scranton grocery store to form a Merchants Association. The following year, they changed its name to the Scranton Board of Trade (BoT) and faced their most pressing problem head on: they appealed to the DLW to lower its rates. The answer was a firm "no."

The DLW's intransigence prompted the Scranton BoT to action. Three of the Scranton group's leaders met with the freight manager of the Erie Railroad, the line that the New York Chamber of Commerce had helped start, running from New York City to Buffalo, and asked whether the Erie Railroad would be willing to build a spur down to Scranton to tap into this industrial boom town. The answer was "yes." Although the route was indirect, the merchants indeed got a lower freight rate. Faced with this competition, the DLW agreed to lower rates as well.[21]

Chambers of commerce and boards of trade began to grow up quickly as railroads spread across the nation. Although a single businessperson was usually powerless when confronting a railway official, a group of businessmen could occasionally make a difference. Sometimes they enticed railroads to town, sometimes they fought rate discrimination, and sometimes, as in the case of Scranton, they did both. Chambers of commerce suddenly became more essential than ever. In many towns and cities, there were few if any entities other than the chamber that could stand up to the railway board.

The Golden Spike

The great rail event of the age, of course, occurred at Promontory Summit, Utah, on May 10, 1869, when Leland Stanford hammered a golden spike into the completed Pacific Railroad. The chambers in New York and San Francisco immediately exchanged congratulatory telegrams.[22] Travel across the continental United States, which had taken a vexatious and dangerous six months before this event, now took just one week. The nation suddenly had become a true continental power, and every city and its chamber of commerce longed to be connected to the grid.

The first chamber of commerce to take an official tour across the new train path was the Boston Board of Trade. The Pullman brothers (George M. and A.B.) were so excited about this cross-country rail trip of prominent business people that they volunteered to build a group of special train cars to accommodate the group in comfortable style.[23] On May 23, 1870, a group of 130 people - Board of Trade members, their spouses, half a dozen children, and a few others - set off from Boston, cheered by 5,000 well-wishers. They rode with the president of the Detroit Board of Trade for part of the way, met with the leaders of the Chicago Board of Trade, and drank in the scenery of their route.

Crossing the Great Plains from Omaha, they saw federal troops and heard of what they thought might be trouble: "A party of one hundred Indians, we were told, crossed the track at Potter station the night before we were there, with war-paint on their faces and mischief in their hearts."[24] But they experienced no problems with Native Americans. In Salt Lake City, they were addressed by Brigham Young himself, who "explained and defended some of the peculiar views of his people."[25] They continued to San Francisco, where the chamber of commerce feted them and from which they fanned out to other nearby towns.

Board of Trade Secretary Hamilton Hill carefully noted interesting economic and business facts along the way, including the sudden growth of Iowa's population and the booming lumber industry in the Rockies. One of his more interesting observations was the relatively depressed condition of San Francisco. The Pacific Railroad had very suddenly ended San Francisco's monopoly on many products needed by the people of the West. Now the East could compete with cheaper products, and it did. But overall, most believed that in the long run, the railroad would add to the prosperity of San Francisco and California.

On June 26 the Boston group reluctantly turned homeward. They saw groups of hundreds of Indians on horseback on their return trip, as well as wildlife. One of the excursionists bought an antelope to take back home, but it died 20 miles from Boston. Still, overall the experience was a fascinating one – a "complete success" in Hill's words.[26]

The complete success referred to a single trip, not to Boston's railroad strategy. Hill believed that Boston was far behind where it should be in the development of railroad links to the rest of the country. Hence the Boston trip was not just a chance to view the reunited nation, but to see the possibilities of railroads.

Secretary Hill believed that Boston, while it might not catch up with its "rival" (New York City), could gain plenty of business thanks to the growing importance of rails. These metallic veins of commerce diminished the relative significance of New York's Erie Canal. Despite its disastrously slow start in railroad building, Hill thought Boston had an opportunity to improve its competitive position. He argued that "when the railroad lines converging in this city have been made altogether what they ought to be, these railroads will make Boston."[27]

For San Francisco, even more than for Boston, railroads were of vital importance. Hence it was a matter of great concern when the Central Pacific Railroad tried to persuade Congress to give it Goat Island (today known as Yerba Buena Island) as a terminal. This island, about halfway between San Francisco and Oakland, would have essentially cut off San Francisco's access to transcontinental freight and made Oakland the western terminus of the national rail system.

Not surprisingly, the San Francisco Chamber of Commerce fought fiercely against the Central Pacific ploy. In 1872, the chamber unanimously approved a resolution asserting that Central Pacific's proposal "may be treated with the hostility which selfish scheming against private and public rights deserves at the hands of the Congressional guardians of the people's interests."[28] The San Francisco Chamber and its allies beat off the railroad's challenge, showing once again that chambers of commerce could occasionally win battles against the powerful railroad companies.

The New York Chamber of Commerce entered the lists as well. Members were concerned that the railroad companies were gouging them with unfair freight rates, giving other cities a comparative advantage in the struggle for more shipping business. Pulling together a number of other local commercial groups, such as the Cotton Exchange and the Produce Exchange, the chamber created the Cheap Transportation Association on November 20, 1874.[29] The name was changed the following year to the more respectable-sounding American Board of Transportation and Commerce, but the aim remained the same, namely to check the railroads, to blow the whistle on the whistle-blowers.

A Flurry of Organizing

"Nearly every town of 20,000 inhabitants maintains its Chamber of Commerce," noted H.T. Johns, secretary of the St. Paul Chamber of Commerce, in his chamber's annual report for 1873.[30] In the 1870 Census, there were 71 communities with 20,000 or more inhabitants, and indeed the smallest of them was . . . St. Paul.[31] This community was enamored of its energetic chamber, but it wasn't alone. Having a chamber of commerce or board of trade was becoming a matter of civic pride. More broadly, as the United States emerged from the chaos of the Civil War, people felt a need for coming together again, for institutions that would foster unity and peaceful progress.

Apart from those already mentioned above, these communities (to name only a few) featured new or refurbished chambers or boards of trade by 1870: Little Rock, Richmond (Va.), Jacksonville (Fla.), Newark (N.J.), Trenton, Dubuque, Lincoln (Neb.), Providence, Madison, Portland (Ore.), San Diego, Nashville, two Wilmingtons (N.C. and Del.), Chattanooga, and Charlotte. The concept of business organizations not only survived the war, but it flourished.

The formation of the National Board of Trade (NBoT) in 1868 helped people focus on just what these organizations were and what they did. This group, born out of the July 1865 meeting in Detroit and subsequent conclaves, had its first official gathering in Philadelphia in June of 1868. A good portion of the meeting had to do simply with who got to be included and who didn't, and how much representation they should have.

The Maine Shipbuilders Association was allowed to sit, but not to vote; this did not sit well with the shipbuilders at all. But as Hamilton Hill from Boston pointed out, the shipbuilders came to the meeting "only as a single and a special interest," and not as a general business group. Moreover, they came from Maine and not from a specific community in Maine. And so they were barred from membership.[32]

What about a produce or merchants' exchange? Here, Hill was inclined to be inclusive, noting that "the Corn Exchange, or Produce Exchange, as it exists in our seaboard cities, is the corresponding body to the Board of Trade as it is found in the West." And as these organizations handled the broad array of local agricultural production, they could be classified as general business organizations.[33]

A group's level of activity also mattered. One delegate, for example, challenged the Richmond Board of Trade's right to come. "Some of these institutions are mere reading-rooms," he said. Satisfied that Richmond's group was real, the audience acquiesced to its coming.[34]

The attempts to define just what chambers of commerce or boards of trade were surely had some value. But the continuing arguments on who shouldn't be included, and who should be officers and who should have voting rights, presaged some of the difficulties this organization would face in the future. "I am very much afraid if we look after our own dignity too much, we shall kill the Association," said Philadelphia's George Buzby wisely.[35] The NBoT would not die for many years, but it never truly lived as the preeminent business organization in the nation. It chose a path of exclusivity that ultimately led to a dead end.

Still, the meeting had a number of positive aspects. Members talked about the perennial desire to get the federal government to help with local canals and river and port dredging. They dealt with the Civil War debt and the need to strengthen the currency. In addition, they promoted the proposed shift from the bushel to the 100-pound "cental" – an idea that eventually caught on to some degree – more, at least, than the more radical notion of adopting the newfangled metric system.

A contemporary writer summarized the following year's meeting, in Richmond in 1869, as a reach toward uniformity. Delegates asked for nationwide standards (or at least a move toward more similar state standards) on measurements, licensing, corporation laws, coinage, tariff and revenue laws, and other areas. Ultimately, these attempts to smooth out the wrinkles of interstate commerce were a drive toward completing what the blue-clad troops had enforced a few years earlier: "a Union, strong and great, an indivisible nation."[36]

Chamber of Commerce Weather

In 1844, Samuel F.B. Morse sparked a technological and information revolution when he sent the words "What hath God wrought" skittering along a wire from the U.S. Capitol to Baltimore. His modern telegraph system quickly spread around the globe, often at the urgings of local chambers of commerce that wanted their cities connected to this electronic web. There were all kinds of uses for the new technology, from carrying financial news to helping railroad companies manage the movement and freight of their trains. One of the most interesting uses was weather prediction.

The telegraph made it possible to collect weather data from many places within a short time. From that data, it was possible to make forecasts. This sort of data collection and prediction began in Germany in 1835 with the rudimentary telegraph networks of the time but was greatly accelerated when Morse's superior system spread around the world, creating hundreds of potential weather tracking stations.

By 1860, the Smithsonian Institution had a large number of U.S. locations providing weather information and was transmitting a weather bulletin. Merchants were even creating their own weather reports based on data they collected.[37] The advent of the Civil War, coupled with a disastrous fire at the Smithsonian, prevented further progress.

Cleveland Abbe, a weather expert, took charge of the Cincinnati Observatory in 1868 and immediately called for a renewed focus on weather data collection via telegraph. The Cincinnati Chamber of Commerce enthusiastically endorsed the idea and agreed to pay for a three-month pilot program. On September 1, 1869, making use of data from first 10 and later 30 stations in the region, the chamber underwrote the publishing of a daily newsletter, *The Weather Bulletin of the Cincinnati Observatory.*[38]

"This was, I believe, the first systematic attempt in the United States to make the weather reports practically useful to our commercial communities," Abbe later wrote.[39] As such it attracted a lot of attention. But it needed greater support. After the three-month period was up, Abbe had continued to publish the information using his own resources and the donated services of telegraph employees.[40]

Joseph Gano, the president of the Cincinnati Chamber, and other chamber leaders promoted the idea at the Richmond meeting of the National Board of Trade in November 1869. These businessmen and their chambers helped support a proposal to Congress to produce a complete national weather reporting system under the control of the War Department. The measure was approved and then signed by the President in February, 1870; the institution eventually became the National Weather Service.[41] Hence the Cincinnati Chamber of Commerce, in helping so much to get the project started, did its best to disprove the later adage that "Everybody talks about the weather, but nobody does anything about it."[42]

A Boom Town Burns Down

On Sunday, October 8, 1871, a fire began burning out of control in Chicago. The conflagration continued for two days, destroying about 17,500 structures (including the entire business district), killing 200 to 300 people, and leaving about 90,000 homeless. The Great Chicago Fire was an amazingly rapid and powerful strike against the fastest growing American city of the age, almost as if to punish its famously brash spirit.

And yet that spirit led the way out of the debacle. The Chicago Board of Trade's beautiful home, known as the Chamber of Commerce Building, "the finest hall used for commercial purposes in the country," had been obliterated.[43] Nevertheless, the Board's directors quickly determined to create a new facility as good as the one they lost, and construction began immediately. "The Chamber of Commerce have struck the first blow," reported *The New York Times* on the city's reconstruction efforts.[44] Board of Trade Vice President Charles Culver said later, "In my opinion, no one thing did more to remove doubt as to the reconstruction of Chicago than the announcement made on the very week of the fire, that men were at work on the new Chamber of Commerce building."[45]

In just a few months, the Board of Trade sounded a note of such chamber optimism, good spirits, and willingness to look past grim realities (and the tenth month of 1871), that it could rank with the Memphis Chamber's bullishness on cotton shipments in 1861:

The year, although darkened by an almost unparalleled catastrophe, must, in a general business view, be regarded as a most satisfactory one, perhaps exceeding in substantial advancement any of its predecessors. In all branches of the city's trade the first nine months of 1871 witnessed great prosperity.[46]

Within a year, the Chamber of Commerce building was complete. It was magnificent. And the attitude of the Board of Trade was more ebullient than ever. Wrote Secretary Charles Randolph in 1872:

The membership of the Board is largely in excess of a year since; and at the near approach of the close of one year after the "great fire" there is a general feeling of satisfaction that so great a calamity should have left so few unhealed wounds, and all share in high hopes for the constantly brightening future, and feel that no period in the past has been more full of promise for future great prosperity and advancement.[47]

Chicago indeed rebuilt, and over the years became famous for not just the amount of construction but for the quality and care put into erecting its great buildings. The Board of Trade could claim to have had a hand in setting the stage for the architectural wonders to come. It had shown that creating an attractive, expensive building right out of the ashes could make a statement not just about the importance of commerce, but about the fireproof spirit of the community.[48]

There was another silver lining to the clouds of smoke: the great support received from other communities, including their chambers of commerce. The New York Chamber of Commerce held a special meeting while the fire was still burning, on October 9, 1871, and determined to raise funds for relief of Chicago. The total amount contributed by the chamber and its donors was a considerable sum: $1,030,000.[49] Among the other chambers that assisted were those of Milwaukee, Galveston, Honolulu, and even Cardiff and Newport in Wales, Staffordshire in England, and Le Havre in France.[50]

Reform

It took organization to put Chicago back together. A powerful organizing impulse, moreover, led people to start, strengthen, or simply join chambers after the Civil War. That same impulse led many of them to try to rationalize divergent social and especially government activities into something they considered more ethical and/or efficient. No doubt it is human nature to assume that problems lie in the behavior of others rather than ourselves. In the North, South, and West, it was usually other people – not chamber members or others of similar established rank in society - whose behavior needed to be fixed. In the West, it was the Native Americans and their agents in the Bureau of Indian Affairs; in the North, notably in New York City, it was the unruly immigrant population and its often corrupt political leaders; and in the South, it was the various state administrations of Yankee "carpetbaggers," cooperating southern "scalawags," and emancipated blacks.[51]

The West and Native Americans

The Sand Creek Massacre illustrated how one future chamber leader, then-Governor John Evans, was as ruthless and cruel an enemy as any Native American could have. But not all business people felt similarly toward the original inhabitants of the continent. Far from the scenes of battle and massacre, chambers and their members sometimes expressed sympathy toward Native Americans in the West.

Leading business people from the East found a receptive ear in President Grant when they called for reform of the notoriously corrupt agents of the Bureau of Indian Affairs (BIA). In March of 1869, a group of philanthropists led by William Welsh, a member of the Philadelphia Commercial Exchange (and the brother of John Welsh, who was president of the Philadelphia Board of Trade), visited the President. They indicated that only 25 percent of federal money allocated to Native Americans on reservations actually reached them. Grant then appointed a nine-member board of oversight of the BIA, with members that included such leading executives as Welsh himself and William E. Dodge, president of Phelps, Dodge & Company and the president of the New York Chamber of Commerce.[52]

Other chambers' members, however, expressed views on reform that were opposed to those of Welsh and Dodge. At the January 1874 meeting of the National Board of Trade, delegates discussed a resolution calling essentially for the immediate breakup of the tribal lands in the Indian Territory and the opening up of most of this vast country for settlement. The region comprised most of what today is Oklahoma, along with some surrounding lands, and was larger than the state of Missouri. The NBoT resolution proposed that most local Indians would be given homesteads so that they could become regular U.S. citizens, although a few tiny reservations might dot the region.

NBoT Vice President B.R. Bonner, from the St. Louis Board of Trade, expressed what he considered a win-win proposition, namely that the Native Americans would get civilization, and the whites would get most of their land:

> In giving to the Indians civilization, we also develop one of the most beautiful and fertile sections of our country, which will be inhabited and populated by the white people of the country, and all the blessings of commerce, of education, of social culture, and material advancement and development, will ensue.[53]

J.E. Marsh from the Kansas City Board of Trade added that the Indian Territory stood as a giant barrier to commerce. For example, it was prohibitively expensive to run railroads through it, since the railroads couldn't profit by selling the land beside the tracks. This blocked Kansas City's access to the Gulf of Mexico through the port of Galveston. And cattle drovers could not take their herds through the area without risking taxes, stampedes, and theft.[54]

The National Board of Trade group agreed to support the resolution.[55] And while their recommendation wasn't accepted during Grant's presidency, most of it was eventually adopted. The seizing of the Indians' land, as had happened so many times before, no doubt would have occurred in this case with or without the support of these chambers and boards of trade. The "reform" was most famously carried about by whooping "Sooners" when the crack of rifles on April 22, 1889, opened up some of the choicest parts of the Territory for white settlement. Economic justifications – frequently provided by nearby chambers of commerce – would be used for the breakup of these and other formerly tribal lands, and the continued destruction of a way of life that predated Adam Smith, railroads, and chamber dues.

Removing Boss Tweed

The East had a famous institution connected with a Native American: Tammany Hall, a corrupt New York City political organization curiously named after a long-dead chief named Tamanend. Reformers saw Tammany Hall under William M. ("Boss") Tweed as a den of thieves. The machine was kept in power largely by the votes of Irish, German, and other immigrants who appreciated its service to their communities while largely ignoring its considerable appetite for graft.

Thomas Nast cartoon skewering Boss Tweed's corruption, October 22, 1871

In 1871 *The New York Times* uncovered massive fraud emanating from the office of Controller Richard B. Connolly. Connolly had clear connections to the Tweed organization including to Mayor Oakey Hall, a Tweed associate. At one point in the controversy, when the PR battle was going against the mayor, he suggested that the New York Chamber of Commerce form an independent committee to look into the allegations. The chamber prudently refused. Unless Mayor Hall handed over the appropriate documents, any committee would be kept in the dark and would shield the mayor and the controller from scrutiny.[56]

The chamber called together a Committee of Seventy, composed largely of its members, to assure that reform efforts would go ahead and Tweed's graft would be exposed.[57] While *The New York Times*, cartoonist Thomas Nast, and Samuel Tilden played the lead roles in taking down Boss Tweed, the chamber was a key ally. And it was a chamber member, William Havemeyer, who won election as a reform candidate for mayor in 1872.

The New York Chamber also pushed successfully for reform in an area that hit its members right in the pocketbook – customs house collections. The chamber found that fees on services there were much too high and managed in 1872 to obtain a 35 to 40 percent reduction in its warehousing fees. Investigations into the activities of the customs house did not shed a favorable light on its chief, Chester Arthur. But Arthur cooperated with the study.[58]

Arthur was later dismissed from his job by President Benjamin Hayes in an attempt to remove a plum post from the patronage system in New York politics. Arthur's reputation remained clouded when he became President of the United States in 1881. But he had shown he could tackle reform while working with the New York Chamber, and indeed as President he sponsored one of the leading reform bills in American history, the Pendleton Civil Service Reform Act.

Outside New York, other chambers were also involved in reforms, or at least in calling attention to abuses. The Newark Board of Trade complained that after the city had spent $1 million on a system for drinking water, the water wasn't fit to drink.[59] In St. Paul, the chamber led in a reform of the city charter so as to make the City Council more responsible and transparent in its allocations of taxpayer funds.[60] In the District of Columbia, the Board of Trade hosted a meeting of people who were angry at government abuses and aimed for a better apportionment of spending between the federal and local government (a debate that has continued, off and on, for more than a century).[61]

The Taxpayers' Revolt

Discontent with government had reached the boiling point in the South. Military occupation led to inevitable abuses of authority, while the new Republican-controlled state governments frequently were accused of corruption. And the accusations weren't simply based on animosity from those who lost the war.

Not surprisingly, a certain coastal city in South Carolina led the charge against the depredations of Yankee-imposed government. It was from Charleston that leading southern citizens first openly and in an organized fashion called into question the legitimacy and fairness of the regime they believed had been imposed on them.[62] And it was two business groups, the Charleston Chamber of Commerce and the Charleston Board of Trade, that were in the vanguard of the protests.

On March 30, 1871, the Charleston Chamber of Commerce held a meeting on the tax-and-spend Republicans in the state legislature. "The extraordinary and needless expenditure of the public money amounts almost to rapine and plunder," declared acting president S.Y. Tupper. "Education, character and experience are ignored and excluded from office by an intolerant negro majority, banded together and controlled by the arts of those who are strangers to us in name, feeling, sympathy and interest."[63]

The group proposed the holding of a Taxpayers Convention in Columbia to protest the fiscal disaster. On March 31, 1871, the Charleston Board of Trade held a similar meeting, the largest in its history. Richard Lathers, now residing in his native state of South Carolina, attended and recalled it in his memoirs. BoT Vice President George Walter complained that from 1860 to 1870, the state's spending had increased from $400,000 to $4 million per year, and the state's debt from $5 million to $15 million, while property valuations had shrunk from $500 million to $190 million. The state's propertied individuals were being taxed out of everything they had.[64]

The Taxpayers Convention in Columbia, called together by the two Charleston business groups, took place on May 9-12, 1871.[65] Both the Charleston Chamber of Commerce and the Board of Trade sent delegates. George Trenholm presented information on the dire fiscal situation of the state.[66] The meeting became, in essence, a protest against the misrule of the Reconstruction Era.

The southern white propertied classes were publicly complaining that they were being frozen out of government and that this was unfair. They pointed to the fiscal mess as the consequence of cutting them adrift. And by focusing on the waste and inefficiency of the administration in Columbia, they pursued a theme with which people in the North, or indeed anywhere, could sympathize: opposing bad government.

While little changed in the short term, the long-term effects of the meeting were significant. A measure of the political effectiveness of the Taxpayers Convention was that it was imitated. In September of 1871, a similar meeting was held in Austin, Texas, while South Carolina had another meeting in 1874 and Mississippi in 1875. The New Orleans Chamber of Commerce, moreover, vocally criticized the spending practices and corruption of the federally backed state government in Louisiana. A part of the impetus for President Hayes's removal of federal troops from the South in 1877, formally ending Reconstruction, was a sense that the governments that the Yankees had imposed were not only unwelcome, but fiscally incompetent.

Hence it was better to leave it to the southerners to run the South. Unfortunately, it was almost exclusively the white southerners who would be empowered in the Jim Crow era that would soon follow. As former Confederates regained public office, they began, in state after state, to restrict the ability of blacks to vote, and ultimately ushered in an oppressive, segregated system that some said was not a great deal better than the slavery that preceded it. This southern apartheid system did not even have the benefit of promoting rapid economic growth. The South's economic and population expansion would lag behind that of the North for decades, until one day the fresh air of integration would mix with the cool breeze from air conditioners, the South's political culture would be more aligned with that of the North, and capital and people from around the world would seek out the sun-soaked land of the fed-up taxpayers.

Fixing on Gold

The nation's finances and currency were a constant concern after the Civil War. The reunited states had a colossal federal debt and there was frequent debate over the role of gold, silver, and paper in the monetary system. The New York Chamber of Commerce and most of its sister organizations around the country favored a hard-money stance, pushing for the paper "greenback" currency to be redeemable in gold, if not immediately, then as soon as feasible.

In 1873, the currency concerns grew more extreme as a financial panic spread around the world and hit the United States hard. On September 18, the great Philadelphia house of Jay Cooke and Company, which was financing the Northern Pacific Railroad, declared bankruptcy. The New York Stock Exchange closed for 10 days as the financial shock waves reverberated across the nation.

Most chambers stuck to their hard-money stance. Two of the best-known business organizations in the country were firmly in the saddle. While the Chicago Board of Trade briefly suspended options trading, it soon got back to business and later reported that not a single one of its members went under because of the crash.[67] The New York Chamber of Commerce was steered by the firm hands on its finance and currency committee, headed by Samuel Ruggles and including such members as Cyrus Field, William Seligman, and its rising young banker, J.P. Morgan.[68]

With President Grant's support, Congress passed the Resumption Act in 1875, which called for a return to gold-backed currency in 1879. Although most chamber leaders supported the move, there was plenty of opposition among debtors, who stood to gain from inflation, from silver mining interests, and from the capital-starved regions in the South and West. Even in New York there was opposition to the hard-money move. In fact, the man next in line to the presidency of the New York Chamber of Commerce, ex-mayor George Opdyke, was a soft-money man.

This was one chamber for which, with rare exceptions, there was only one monetary standard: gold. And Opdyke paid the price for not being a "gold" member. Normally he would have quietly glided, uncontested, into the presidency of the chamber. But an opposition ticket of hard-money candidates, headed by Samuel Babcock, arose and defeated him. The election was all about whether the currency should be backed by gold or not.[69]

Eventually Opdyke resigned from the chamber. He was recruited to head the much less prestigious New York Board of Trade, organized in September of 1874,[70] where he was seen presiding over a dinner in 1875. This dinner had an embarrassingly small turnout for an organization boasting 1,400 members. "Covers were laid for 200 guests, and only 50 were present," reported the *New York Times* snarkily.[71] The fall from the New York Chamber's gold standard was sudden and steep.

Chambers Come of Age

The New York Chamber of Commerce celebrated its 100th anniversary in 1868. And it was apparent that chambers had become established in the public imagination. As always, politicians viewed the kibitzing of business groups with mixed feelings. But they listened. The pro-free-trade Parliamentarian John Bright noted at an annual dinner of the Associated Chambers of Commerce in Great Britain:

> I believe it is objected by some persons that great questions are for the Legislature, and not for Chambers of Commerce. I should like to ask what Parliament would be, if it were not for that public opinion which not only instructs it, but impels it forward?[72]

That chambers were intimately connected to their government was underlined by President Grant himself, who during his Presidency visited the chamber or board of trade in Cincinnati, Toledo, Chicago, and Wilmington, Del. And certainly local chambers were mostly aligned with his largely pro-business policies. Business organizations had developed a reputation for working with government when it suited them, especially on their eternal quest for transportation improvements. Noted one contemporary critic:

> When merchants gather together in a board of trade, they first "demand" rigid economy of the Government, and then press an appropriation for dredging some local sand-bank.[73]

What was increasingly clear was that chambers were beginning to see their mandate as going far beyond sand banks. It wasn't just the promotion of the weather telegraph or the interminable wrestling matches with railroad companies or even the reform of local government. Chambers began getting involved in all kinds of activities. The Boston Board of Trade, for example, inspected local pork processing plants;[74] the Charlotte Chamber of Commerce pushed for grades in schools and different classrooms instead of one-room schoolhouses;[75] and the San Francisco Chamber of Commerce held talks with Alaskan natives on seal killing.[76]

The St. Paul Chamber of Commerce, albeit a young organization in a young city, exemplified the trend of expanded activities for these business organizations. In 1874, a new secretary summarized the matters that the chamber had considered in the prior year, and it ranged from locating new factories and a university in the city to erecting fireproof buildings for public records.[77] Quietly, with almost no one noticing, these institutions were becoming embedded in many aspects of American life.

The Nation's 100th Birthday Party

The creation and attraction of fairs, festivals, and expositions to promote cities was already becoming an activity of chambers of commerce. In the 1870s, leading members of the Philadelphia Board of Trade paved the way for a massive undertaking for the time: the Centennial Exposition. Congress had approved a plan for Philadelphia to host the 100-year birthday celebration of the United States of America in 1876. But while there would be some moral support from the federal government, as well as a loan, private fundraising was absolutely essential to make the project succeed.

The group in charge of raising funds, the Centennial Board of Finance (CBF), was made up largely of leading members of the Philadelphia Board of Trade (PBoT). John Welsh, the president of the BoT for 15 years, led the charge as chair of the Board of Finance; Frederick Fraley, at this time the vice president of the National Board of Trade, was the secretary-treasurer of the CBF.[78] Welsh and his team worked locally to secure support but also looked to other markets. On one occasion five Centennial Board of Finance members (all PBoT members), including Welsh, visited the New York Chamber of Commerce and garnered pledges of its support for the giant birthday celebration.[79] Welsh later received a $50,000 award, which he gave to charity, for his services for the 1876 centennial event.[80]

While there were problems with the fundraising – the U.S. government successfully sued to get its $1.5 million loan back – there was enough money on the table to create a massive and popular fair in Philadelphia from May through November, 1876. More than 10 million visitors attended, including President Grant and his wife. A massive Corliss steam engine powered much of the machinery at the fair. Among the products and inventions exhibited publicly for the first time were the telephone, the Remington typewriter, Heinz ketchup, Hires Root Beer, and a plant that showed great promise in controlling erosion – kudzu.[81]

Bringing Hawaii Closer to the Mainland

Although kudzu was a Japanese import, it was another Pacific area product that captured the attention of the Honolulu and San Francisco chambers of commerce: sugar. The Hawaiian Islands produced sugar in abundance, and much of it entered the U.S. market through the Golden Gate. There was only one problem: sugar producers in the United States, notably in Louisiana, had (with the help of the New Orleans Chamber of Commerce) made sure there was a strong protective tariff on sugar imports. Somehow the tariff would have to be circumvented if the Hawaiian crystals were to find their logical home in the stomachs of American children.

In 1867, the Honolulu Chamber of Commerce suggested the idea of trade reciprocity between Hawaii and the United States.[82] Its leaders doggedly pursued the effort, despite being turned down in 1867 and 1873. The San Francisco Chamber also supported the idea.[83]

Reciprocity (which would eliminate the sugar tariff) really was just a halfway house, however. Such treaties could later be revoked or altered. The permanent answer to the problem would be Hawaii's becoming a territory of the United States. In pushing for reciprocity, both chambers were setting a course toward eventual union between Hawaii and the mainland, even if not every chamber member or citizen understood this. Once Hawaii became addicted to the vast sugar market in the United States, it would be almost impossible to break the habit.

Although reciprocity was well short of union, it was a major step. And President Grant and King Kalakaua agreed upon the Reciprocity Treaty of 1875. In return for opening its markets to Hawaiian products, the United States asked for something, and got it: land covering the area of what today is known as Pearl Harbor.

Progress on Yellow Fever

Fostering the flow of trade was as important on the Gulf of Mexico as in the Pacific Ocean. Members of the New Orleans Chamber of Commerce were dismayed – like other merchants in coastal areas – at the costs of lengthy quarantine restrictions in their port. When ships came in from the Caribbean or Central or South America, sometimes there was yellow fever aboard. If that fever spread to New Orleans, at least before 1870, it spelled disaster for the local population. But starting in the early 1870s, the New Orleans Board of Health experimented with a new form of containment of yellow fever, namely, disinfection of ships and houses with carbolic acid. When the homes of infected people were quickly treated with carbolic acid, the fever's spread was drastically diminished. For the first time ever, New Orleans had a way to stop the horrific epidemics that periodically swept through it.

The New Orleans Chamber of Commerce eagerly embraced this reform. Not only would the new practice make unnecessary long detentions of ships in quarantine, but the city itself would be freed from fear of the disease that had haunted it since the first epidemic in 1796.[84] Here was an economic development bonanza.

A member of the Louisiana Board of Health, G.W.R. Bayley, who was an expert on the new carbolic acid disinfection, knew how much his techniques would be valued by local business people. In an address to the New Orleans Chamber of Commerce, he stated:

> It is believed to be possible and practicable to prevent epidemics of yellow fever in New Orleans, and if so it needs no argument to show what would be the beneficial effect upon the commerce of the city as a result.[85]

Indeed, he was convinced his department had recently rescued the city:

> The evidence is abundant – indeed, overwhelming – that New Orleans was saved from a terrible yellow fever epidemic in 1873 by the efforts of the Board of Health, its sanitary corps, and its use of disinfectants.[86]

Bayley's analysis of the problem was sure to appeal to a *local* chamber of commerce:

> The disease is local, and must be destroyed, and its spread prevented by local remedies.[87]

The chamber issued resolutions calling on the General Assembly of Louisiana to approve of this new approach to yellow fever, including the removal of the "time-detention called for in the existing quarantine law."[88] In other words, ships treated by this method didn't have to wait for expensive weeks in the harbor. In fact, detention was only so long as required to complete the disinfection.[89] They could land their goods or steam upriver much sooner, now that the city had a means of stopping epidemics in their tracks. The chamber got its wish and the legislation passed.

The New Orleans Chamber of Commerce and the Louisiana Board of Health were pushing forward a reform that appeared to be scientifically proven and efficient. New Orleans finally had control of its persistent yellow fever problem. Or did it?

Jeff Davis, Economic Developer

The New Orleans Chamber wasn't alone in its interest in economic development. At least since the Kentucky emigration societies in 1797, U.S. business organizations had been doing their best to attract business to their communities. After the Civil War, this work continued, and indeed sped up in some places. Through distribution of pamphlets to other chambers' reading rooms, taking excursions to other cities and encouraging others to come to one's own city for a conference of some kind, chambers attempted to keep the spotlight on their communities.

The railroad magnate Leland Stanford started a major California marketing program in 1868. His chief allies were members of the San Francisco Chamber of Commerce, including William T. Coleman. The idea was to set up an International Emigrant Union in Baltimore, where the North German Lloyd line of steamers had just set up a landing point. Here California boosters could meet with people fresh from Europe and encourage them to take the excellent rail connections soon to reach all the way across the continent to San Francisco.[90]

In 1869 the San Francisco Chamber set up a similar promotional office, the California Emigrant Union, to receive the new residents and to beat the drums for more of them. The California office had a budget of $36,000 per year and ran till the end of its charter in 1899, when it was succeeded by an even larger organization called the International Colonizing Company. Many people in California, although they may not realize it, have ancestors who came to the state thanks to the railroad/chamber boosters' alliance of the late 19th century. Among the "colonies" of the CEU were Pasadena, Fresno, and Lompoc.[91]

Chambers and boards of trade worked hard to grow and attract new industry. The St. Paul Chamber of Commerce was involved in a buckskin glove project and other pursuits – not to mention the relocation of Hamline University from Red Wing, Minn.[92] (Chambers, especially in Texas but also across the nation, would become expert at capturing colleges.) The board of trade in Springfield, Illinois, had a hand in obtaining the Springfield Watch Company and the Alexander corn planter factory.[93] Then as now, business people saw the arrival of a new manufacturing facility as a vital boost to the community.

Economic development fever was muted during the difficult years after the Panic of 1873, but it had not by any means disappeared. In fact, even in the Mississippi Valley, the cradle of the Ku Klux Klan, there was a spirit of encouraging growth. In early 1876, the New Orleans Chamber of Commerce helped support a convention on immigration to the southern states. One of the key organizations involved in the conclave was a New Orleans-based group called the International Chamber of Commerce and Mississippi Valley Society. This ambitious economic development group wanted to bring the world to the lower Mississippi region. Its president was none other than Jefferson Davis himself.[94]

Unfortunately, the International Chamber didn't get far with its plans. The bitter realities of racial conflict in Louisiana no doubt got in the way. As a writer for the *New-Orleans Republican* noted:

> Immigration invites itself to the best places. In the case of our own State, when lawlessness in the country parishes has been subdued, when men wishing to make homes are met with words of welcome, instead of shot-guns and the masked riders of midnight, immigrants will find a way here without jetty passes or the particular society presided over by Jefferson Davis.[95]

As the writer implied, racial oppression wasn't normally a magnet for investors. And when violence was added to the mix (although certainly not by Davis himself), economic development would be another lost cause.

Taming Disorder

1877-1886

Dinner of Champions

The annual dinner of the New York Chamber of Commerce was always a major event, but the gathering at Delmonico's on May 15, 1877 was particularly significant. U.S. President Rutherford B. Hayes had accepted an invitation to come. This was just over two months since his inauguration as President following a contentious election race with New York Governor Samuel Tilden, a Democrat. Hayes had lost the popular vote but won election thanks to some contested Electoral College ballots. Following his win, in a gesture seen as a compromise with the Democrats (although he had intended to do this anyway), Hayes agreed to withdraw the last federal troops out of the South. This was the formal end to the turbulent Reconstruction era.

Hayes was not the only national figure at the dinner, by any means. Others in his administration who were there included Secretary of State William Evarts, Secretary of the Interior Carl Schurz, Attorney General Charles Devens, Controller of the Currency John Jay Knox, General William Tecumseh Sherman, and Major General Winfield Scott Hancock. This wasn't a small affair for either the federal government or for the New York Chamber of Commerce.

For the members of the chamber, as for President Hayes himself, this dinner was a chance to salve the wounds of the North and South and to move the nation forward into a new period of peace, economic growth, and international trade. North and South, and Republican and Democrat, could unite in a common spirit of enterprise. It was only appropriate that the hosting organization had fought hard to avoid the Civil War, and then fought even harder to win it.

Things got off to a bad start when, before the event, it was rumored that the chamber had waited before finally inviting the losing candidate Tilden to the dinner. (Chamber Secretary George Wilson denied this rumor and expected Tilden to come to dinner, although the ex-governor actually didn't attend.)[1] Then, as people were arriving, the old entrepreneur and silver advocate, Peter Cooper, who had built *Tom Thumb* (the first locomotive for the first American railroad), helped finance Cyrus Field's trans-Atlantic cable, and founded the Cooper Union, discovered his place was taken and wandered aimlessly until the chair thief was unseated.

At dinner came a bigger gaffe. Chamber President Samuel Babcock called bluntly for sounder national financial policies:

> Twelve years have passed since the termination of our civil war, and while it resulted in releasing from bonds four millions of human beings, it inflicted upon us a system of financial measures which has since put under bonds forty millions of people.[2]

This play on the word "bonds," equating the suffering of four million slaves with that of the nation's attempt to pay off war debts, offended not a few in the audience. Even *The New York Times*, normally a staunch chamber supporter, caught the reaction:

> This sentiment [Babcock's remark], it is only proper to say, was greeted with loud cries of "No, no." So loud and determined was this demonstration that Mr. Babcock made no further political allusion . . .[3]

Yet Babcock's ham-handed wordplay indicated the depth of his passion, and that of his chamber, for policies of sound money and adherence to the gold standard. The "inflationists" Peter Cooper and George Opdyke, both present that evening, were the exceptions. Long after Babcock retired from his position, the New York Chamber of Commerce would be one of the most persistent advocates for sound money based on a single precious metal.

Indeed, as any perceptive guest at dinner could have surmised, if ever there were a wizard in this Emerald City, manipulating public opinion and private enterprise to preserve hard money and full repayment of debts, surely he was a member of the New York Chamber of Commerce. And he would be tireless in the coming decades, despite having many other issues to address. Ultimately this "wizard," or this collection of individuals who were transfixed by the importance of the gold standard and "honest money," would in succeeding decades help shape the American financial system for the indefinite future.

The Great Railroad Strike

While the diners at Delmonico's looked forward to better times, those times were still not very good. A lingering recession, if not depression, had followed Panic of 1873. This downturn had hit the overbuilt railroads especially hard, causing them to clamp down on wages. On July 14, 1877, workers in Martinsburg, West Virginia, declared they had had enough. Learning their pay would be cut a second time, they went on strike against their employer – the same railroad for which Peter Cooper had built *Tom Thumb* many years before, the Baltimore and Ohio.

The disturbances quickly spread to Cumberland and Baltimore, then to Pittsburgh and other parts of Pennsylvania, and on to St. Louis and Chicago. Protests quickly turned violent and resulted in dozens of deaths and the shuttling of federal troops – along the same railways that had sparked the strikes – to the scenes of trouble. It took 45 days to end the upheaval.

Businessmen were appalled and angry at the damage. The Pennsylvania Railroad's Thomas Scott famously said of the strikers, "Give them a rifle diet and see how they like that bread."[4] Resolutions urging President Hayes to use federal troops to put down the insurrections and prevent their recurrence were passed by the Philadelphia Chamber of Commerce, Philadelphia Board of Trade, the Maritime Exchange, and the Baltimore Corn and Flour Exchange.[5]

The Wild Midwest

Chicago, the railroad hub of the nation, not surprisingly was the scene of some of the worst trouble. Albert Parsons, the leading labor advocate in the Windy City, addressed a crowd of 30,000 strikers and their sympathizers on July 21, 1877. He favored state control of railroads and much of the rest of the economy and urged members of the crowd to join the socialist Workingman's Party of the United States. (This party was an affiliate of the International Workingmen's Association, founded in 1864 by Karl Marx and Friedrich Engels.[6]) While he had not proposed violence and the crowd was peaceful, Parsons found his opponents were incensed.

He was immediately fired from his job as a printer at the *Chicago Times*, and would discover that he would be blacklisted from other employment for another two years. Moreover, two men, saying the mayor wanted to see him, escorted him to a building where he soon faced, not Mayor Monroe Heath, but Police Superintendent Michael Hickey and a group of about 30 men in civilian clothes. Many of these men were from the Chicago Board of Trade. Superintendent Hickey harangued Parsons, as did many in the crowd, for two hours. Some advocated lynching or jailing him, but others advised that this would just incite the workers all the more.

Finally Hickey escorted Parsons out of the room. As they left, the chief said, according to Parsons' autobiography:

> "Parsons your life is in danger. I advise you to leave the city at once. Beware. Everything you do or say is known to me. I have men on your track, who shadow you. Do you know you are liable to be assassinated any moment in the streets?" I ventured to ask him who by & what for? He replied "Why those Board of Trade men would as leave hang you to a lamp post as not."[7]

Indeed, although Parsons would survive this encounter, the Chicago Board of Trade was not finished. When disorder reigned in the streets, the Board persuaded the reluctant Mayor Heath to allow citizens' patrols to keep the peace. But these groups, even when reinforced by General Philip Sheridan and his U.S. cavalry troops who had recently fought the Sioux, could not stop further bloodshed.

The Chicago police did the actual fighting, and were liberal with bullets. While no police died, 18 were injured. Thirty strikers and sympathizers died and 200 more were wounded.[8] Chicago suffered more casualties than any city except possibly Pittsburgh.

A few months later, Secretary Charles Randolph acknowledged in the Board of Trade's annual report that the original protests involved "the true representatives of labor in efforts to redress real or supposed wrongs" by the railway bosses. But the demonstrations had been hijacked "by the baser elements of society for the purpose of inaugurating a reign of terrorism and plunder."[9] He wrote nothing about the rage of his own members.

In fact, Randolph's somewhat detached and reasoned tone betrayed some common ground with the protesters. The Chicago Board of Trade's leadership had no affection for the management of the nation's railroads. Indeed, the chambers and boards of trade in most of the United States were beginning to weave together their perennial complaints about price discrimination and other abuses into a hard-hitting strategy to tame the Iron Horse. And, to a significant extent, they would succeed.

Nevertheless, whatever sentiments that chamber or board of trade members might share with workers regarding the management of the railroads, the shock of the civil disturbances lingered. Now there was a new reason to support, or indeed to form, a chamber of commerce: to build a bulwark against labor agitation and social unrest. Employers might jointly set up citizen patrols, as the Chicago Board of Trade did, or share information on labor agitators, or even in some cases blacklist striking workers or their leaders from future employment. Inside the velvet glove that might welcome new companies to town or publicize the successes of local industry, there was now, in many chambers and boards of trade, an iron fist poised to strike strikers.

The businessmen of Chicago, however, had not had an ideal organization to help them handle the crisis. The Chicago Board of Trade included many of the leading entrepreneurs in town as members, such as Marshall Field, Philip Armour, Cyrus McCormick II, and George Pullman. But none of the individuals just named was on the Board's board.[10]

Moreover, the Board of Trade was not primarily an organization to look after the civic affairs of Chicago; it had pioneered modern commodities trading and this was now its primary *raison d'etre*.[11] Its annual reports were full of hogs and oats and wheat; by contrast, for example, those of the New York Chamber of Commerce began with a nearly book-length section on its activities that touched on civic, state, national, and even international affairs. The Chicago Board of Trade's scope of activity was purposefully narrow.

The Commercial Club of Chicago

Therefore it is perhaps not surprising that this booming city, famed for its enterprising civic spirit, and smarting from labor and social upheaval, would spawn, on December 27, 1877, a new institution that would look more broadly at the affairs of the city. Seventeen individuals met that day to form the Commercial Club of Chicago. Their ranks were quickly boosted to 60, where the membership was capped.

The group contained many of the prominent members of the local business community. Other such elite clubs existed in town; this one differed from them in that it performed civic work with business interests in mind. It was patterned after the Commercial Club of Boston, which had grown out of the Boston Board of Trade in 1868.[12]

Marshall Field

According to its constitution, the Club was created "for the purpose of advancing by social intercourse and by a friendly interchange of views the prosperity and growth of the city of Chicago."[13] Its founding president was Levi Z. Leiter. But the true power behind it was Leiter's business partner – who would buy him out in 1881 – the retailing legend named Marshall Field.

Field was one of the geniuses of American merchandising. He is said to have originated two of the most famous sayings in the industry: "Give the lady what she wants" and "The customer is always right." But when it came to labor activism, he was not so generous in spirit.

For Field, the striker was always wrong. He would provide a hard edge to many of the policies proposed by the Commercial Club and to the reactions of the business community to labor disputes. Field, in fact, also headed the Citizens' Association that had aided the police in patrolling the city. After the troubles, that association gave money to the police for weapons including "four twelve-pound Napoleon cannons, some lighter artillery pieces, and a Gatling gun."[14]

Still, Field's creativity also would permeate the new club, helping it perform civic miracles that would have an influence far behind the shores of Lake Michigan. The same business people who would help smash labor unrest would sow things of beauty along the avenues of this metropolis of grain and growth. As in another unruly city, Florence during the Renaissance, the merchant princes had both a soft side and a hard side.

Trouble at Haymarket Square

While the Commercial Club of Chicago was just beginning to dedicate itself to truth, beauty, and firearms, the community's original chamber – now more of a commodities exchange than a chamber, but still the city's leading symbol of business leadership and power – was in full flower. In 1880 the Chicago Board of Trade's leaders unanimously determined that they needed a new building. Surprisingly, they had already outgrown the edifice they had boldly constructed in the ashes of the Great Fire of 1871. One stone symbol of hope and the promise of capitalism would yield quickly to another. This was a city where growth was just on this side of catastrophic. The new building would be sited very close to where, only 46 years previously, "a large black bear and forty wolves were killed in a strip of timber."[15]

The new building of the Chicago Board of Trade (BoT) was a marvel: an edifice costing upwards of $1.5 million and featuring a 300-foot-tall tower, frescoes, statues, and colored granite staircases. Its cornerstone was laid on December 13, 1882.[16] So proud were the members of the BoT at its erection that they planned a three-day celebration of its opening in April, 1885. Celebrations, certainly, weren't unknown at this dynamic exchange; for example, the messenger boys and clerks had a custom of dumping flour on the black-suited traders on New Year's Eve.[17]

Festivities began on the evening of April 28 with a concert, attended by 12,000 people, in the building's Exchange Hall. The following morning, 3,500 leaders of the city and of other communities and chambers of commerce sat to hear speeches about the past and the future of the great Board of Trade.[18] A sumptuous dinner was to cap this impressive day.

But Chicago's radical leftists and anarchists had another plan. Such people were seething at the idea of a celebration at the "Board of Thieves." They sent out this circular asking for a meeting on Market Street:

> After the ceremonies and sermons, the participants will move in a body to the Grand Temple of Usury, Gambling and Cut-Throatism, where they will serenade the priests and officers of King Mammon and pay honor and respect to the benevolent institute. All friends of the bourse [exchange] are invited.[19]

The circular's writer had a wry sense of humor, but some in the group meant business. One of them was Albert Parsons, the same man who was told in 1877 that the Board of Trade members were just about ready to string him up. Parsons allegedly said to a group of about 2,000 protesters just before the march began:

> Have we got the right to live? Do we want our natural rights? Then, if you do, let every man lay up a part of his wages, buy a Colt's navy revolver, a Winchester rifle, and learn how to make and use dynamite. Then raise the red flag of rebellion, and strike down to the earth every tyrant that lives upon this globe."[20]

The group, singing the *Marseillaise*, moved toward the brand-new monument to capitalism, the BoT Building. They denounced the capitalists within and their "twenty dollar supper."[21] Just as the building was a symbol of the greatness of the business of Chicago to the BoT members, it was a symbol of theft of the rightful property of the working classes, according to the anarchist and socialist demonstrators.

Clearly the protesters wanted to spoil the celebration. One reporter wrote that one of the demonstrators, August Spies, showed him "a large piece of dynamite and a long piece of fuse which [Spies] said he had intended to place under the Board of Trade Building if he had been permitted to get near it."[22]

Police were quickly summoned and steered the demonstrators away from the building. But there were scattered incidents of violence and there was a heightened sense among police and business people alike that the city was under threat. The crisis passed, but the tension remained.

On May 4, 1886, a group of demonstrators congregated in Chicago's Haymarket Square. The peaceful gathering to promote the eight-hour day was close to ending when someone threw a bomb at the police, killing Officer Mathias Degan. The police opened fire, sparking a wild melee. After it was over, eight policemen were dead and 60 injured (most, it's now believed, from the panicked firing of the police into the crowd). As for civilians, the toll isn't as clear, but the numbers may have been even greater.

It was the biggest piece of news in the country since Lincoln's assassination.[23] The event shocked people everywhere and caused an outpouring of rage (never far from the surface) against the anarchists and socialists who seemed to have caused the trouble. Authorities in Chicago quickly captured eight radicals, including Parsons and Spies, and put them on trial for the bombing.

The Chicago Board of Trade's position on the trial was never in question. Its annual report covering the year fairly shouted, "All honor to the heroic police force, which, in that dark hour on the 4th of May, 1886, stood undismayed in Haymarket square like a wall of adamant for public safety!"[24] The grateful BoT gave $13,000 to the families of the police who were killed or wounded. Referring to the dead police and what he perceived as the successful quelling of the radical violence, BoT Secretary Stone wrote: "Seven hearts were stilled. The red tide was stayed. Justice waits."[25]

Justice, it turned out, was on extended holiday. A jury was picked that almost guaranteed conviction. The foreman was an employee of Marshall Field, the apostle of giving the lady what she wants and giving anarchists what they didn't.[26] The judge made rulings that were patently unfair to the accused, although in the fevered spirit of the times, not many people outside the labor movement noticed or cared.[27]

No one could pin the bomb on any of the accused. Yet, primarily because of their incendiary words – many of them captured by reporters and witnesses during the high-profile Board of Trade Building demonstration the previous year - they were all convicted. Seven were sentenced to death and the eighth, Oscar Neebe, to 15 years in prison.

After the appeals process ended fruitlessly for the defendants, Illinois Governor Richard Oglesby commuted the sentences of two of the defendants, Samuel Fielden and Michael Schwab, to life in prison. There was a movement among some leading businessmen to push for clemency for the remaining defendants, for clearly none of them had thrown the bomb. But Marshall Field, the most powerful mogul in the metropolis, intervened at a critical movement and turned the tide of opinion back towards execution.[28]

One of those on death row, Louis Lingg, killed himself in prison with a smuggled bomb. The other four – Albert Parsons, August Spies, Adolph Fischer, and George Engel – were publicly hung on November 11, 1887. Police Superintendent Hinckley was prophetic a decade earlier: the Board of Trade men had wanted to see Parsons strung up, and ultimately they and their allies in the police and the courts got the job done.

As time passed, the injustice of the process became clear to more and more people. A movement aided by a young lawyer named Clarence Darrow succeeded finally in persuading Governor John Peter Altgeld to pardon the remaining defendants (Fielden, Schwab, and Neebe) in 1893. This pardon, controversial even at this stage, had a PR advantage: it occurred during the Columbian Exposition, helping smooth the rough edges of a city wanting to show the world its refinement.

The Haymarket incident clearly set back the labor movement in the United States, perhaps by decades. Throughout the period leading up to it, and in the reaction to it, groups of business people played much more than a cameo role. The Board of Trade, the Commercial Club, and the Citizens Association were both targets of the wrath of anarchists and socialists and instruments of their control and punishment. The unofficial field marshal of the forces of reaction was, without a doubt, Marshall Field, but he had plenty of troops.

In part, these actions of groups of business people were inevitable. Laborers gathered in groups to oppose increasingly large concentrations of capital, and business people came together in part to oppose labor. Chambers of commerce naturally took the side of business, and no doubt acquired many new members and additional influence as a result.

Six-Guns, Sulfur, and the Board of Trade Saloon

Violence, unfortunately, wasn't a monopoly of Chicago or any other community in this period, and in the West, it was still plentiful. The nation's frontier was shrinking fast in the 1880s, aided by the railroads, migration, and the itchy trigger-fingers of the law. Chambers, often called by the still stylish name of "board of trade," popped up in communities that were clinging to civilization by the fingernails. These organizations sought many things, but one of the most precious was simply to be able to get through the day without being shot.

Tough towns started to clean up, one by one, and a board of trade was an emblem of new-found respectability. Dodge City started a board of trade in 1886, and there was a move to start one in Tombstone in 1892.[29] The concept of such commercial groups had even reached the point of wry humor in names: in Leadville, Colorado, Doc Holliday was a regular at the Board of Trade Saloon (and once shot one of its bartenders).[30] Another local drinking haunt was called the Chamber of Commerce.[31]

Deadwood, S.D., a ramshackle, wild mining camp, got its (real) board of trade comparatively early, in 1881. The Deadwood BoT was the brainchild of Seth Bullock, who came to town in 1876. Bullock and his partner planned to peddle goods to the miners that had flocked to the town on hearing tales of the existence gold from none other than General George Custer.

Bullock got something of a crash course in frontier life:

> Less than a day after Bullock and Star arrived in the goldcamp, McCall shot Wild Bill Hickok to death in the No. 10 Saloon. The next morning, an impromptu court of prospectors acquitted McCall, an apparent move to ensure that Deadwood remained lawless. At the same time, Indians were massing in the Black Hills in preparation for an attack on the settlement. The escalating violence did not sit well with Bullock's decorous sensibility, and the sight of a Mexican bandit riding through the streets brandishing a severed Indian head just hours after Hickok's murder was enough to convince Bullock to address the town's crucial need for law and order.[32]

Soon Bullock was sheriff. He had a knack for keeping the peace. Often he patrolled without a gun. This was an enforcer with charisma, much like San Francisco's William T. Coleman.

For his adopted town to take off, Bullock wanted it to have a business organization. Indeed, his voice was the "loudest and most persistent" of those calling for a board of trade. In January of 1881, 50 business men met at the local Phoenix Building and agreed to create the Deadwood Board of Trade. *The Black Hills Daily Times* wrote, "a board of trade for Deadwood has been Seth Bullock's pet hobby, and now that we have one, we suppose he is happy."[33]

Seth Bullock

The group took on many tasks, most of them, at least at first, not successful. But one did get off the ground: a flour mill. Several members put up $5,000 so the town wouldn't have to import expensive flour from outside. Board of Trade flour soon was a local brand.[34]

Bullock didn't put aside his enforcement work. Once in 1884 while he was patrolling the range, he came across one man leading a captive. The bound man was a horse thief by the name of Crazy Steve. The captor was an easterner by the name of Teddy Roosevelt. Roosevelt had come west to try (unsuccessfully) to raise cattle. Bullock and Roosevelt became lifelong friends. Indeed, Roosevelt would appoint Bullock to lead a group of his Rough Riders.[35]

Bullock helped tame his town, becoming a local fixture and eventually a national figure, portrayed in such epics as HBO's *Deadwood*. He stopped fistfights, organized militias to keep the Indians at bay, and once dumped sulfurous canisters into a mine to break a strike. The miners sheepishly came out. But he also built up the business of the town, including erecting a popular 64-room hotel that is still in use today.[36] Like other board of trade men in his time, he was a generalist: he could enforce order and grow the economy at the same time.

The Committee of Safety

San Francisco, too, was a community where the merchants didn't shrink from a fight if it meant keeping the peace in town. As in Chicago and other cities, San Franciscans encountered a wave of unrest during the disturbances of 1877. Here the labor agitation primarily took the form of anti-Chinese activity. A Chinese laundry was burned on July 23, several others were sacked, and many property owners were concerned that if many of the 300 Chinese laundries in town were put to the torch, the whole city (mostly made of wooden buildings) would go up in flames.[37]

General John McComb, who headed a state militia contingent of 1,200 recruits, requested a meeting of leading citizens at the San Francisco Chamber of Commerce offices at 2:00 pm on July 24. The merchants and McComb believed that the city's police force of 150, even when combined with the militia, was insufficient to prevent a large-scale riot and/or fire. William T. Coleman, the veteran organizer of vigilantes, and president of the chamber in 1873-74, was in the room, although he had little to say.[38] Nevertheless, given his standing in the community and his experience with extralegal solutions, he was unanimously voted the president of the organization created on the spot, the Committee of Safety.[39]

Coleman took charge, issuing proclamations and securing arms from the War Department. Believing that armed troops walking the streets might raise rather than reduce the level of tension, however, he kept them drilling but not in front of the public. Instead, he adopted a more home-made solution, as he indicated in a later report:

> I appreciated the difficulties often arising by having military forces in the presence of mobs, excepting only as a dernier resort, when they are needed for actual and effective service. This was in harmony, too, with the nature of our call and organization, to be and act in support of the police, and not of the military. I accordingly gave orders for the purchase of 6,000 hickory pick-handles, to be shortened and converted at once into large, first-class police-clubs, and to arm every man as a special policeman with clubs and side-arms.[40]

This instant police force with its Coleman staves was ready by nightfall of July 25, 1877, and went on patrols in the days afterward. Coleman noted that he had 5,438 volunteers available, of whom about 1,500 were on duty at any given time. Many of the troublemakers left town, seeing that Coleman's forces had the upper hand. But plenty of troublemakers were left.

By the next day, tensions were high. Angry workers were creating disturbances here and there with seeming impunity. When Coleman's recruits met during the evening, they were ready for action:

> It was evident that the army of volunteers were impatient for something to do. This impatience was manifested at first by pounding the floor with their pick-handles.[41]

Coleman channeled this anger and energy toward the struggle at hand. The following day there were several fights between the rioters and the amateur lawmen, and some fatalities. Tensions simmered until the 30th, when the Committee adjourned – but, pointedly, did not disband.[42] These merchant-policemen would be available if needed in the future.

Coleman was not a cardboard vigilante out of the Western gunslinger mold that, in large part, he inspired. (Moreover, his 1877 activities were not vigilantism but support of the overwhelmed law enforcement establishment.) He was more thoughtful and urban – a civic entrepreneur. This was the thinking man's tough guy. Coleman later would recall of his experiences:

> Among the phenomena notable in California annals, from pastoral days to the present indus-
> trial epoch, none possesses greater sociological interest than the vigilance committees of 1856,
> and the committee of safety in 1877.[43]

"Chinese Houses Here Burning"

Although Chinese immigrant workers had done much of the heavy lifting on the Pacific Railroad, they were victims of a great deal of discrimination and ill treatment, not only in San Francisco but along the entire West Coast. In 1882, moreover, the Chinese Exclusion Act, which greatly restricted their ability to stay in the United States or be joined by their friends or relatives from China, came into effect. The New York Chamber of Commerce – including A.A. Low, who had led the chamber during the later years of the Civil War and who was a veteran trader with China - had strenuously opposed the legislation. The New Yorkers stood against the restrictions even though sentiment in California was overwhelmingly in favor of Chinese exclusion: a later document of the New York Chamber cited an 1879 California vote of 883 for Chinese immigration and 154,638 against, with similar patterns in Nevada.[44] The ballot involved, however, was of dubious clarity, probably causing an exaggeration of the admittedly racist spirit abroad in the Far West.

In 1885, a branch of the Knights of Labor began agitating for forcible removal of the Chinese remaining in Washington Territory. Chinese workers were coming into the territory from British Columbia, and more were expected when the work on the Canadian Pacific Railway was complete. General J.W. Sprague, president of the Tacoma, Wash., Chamber of Commerce, complained to President Grover Cleveland about the lack of enforcement of the Chinese Exclusion Act. He asked for help from the U.S. Navy and other assistance to stem the Chinese immigration and preserve order.[45]

Things quickly got worse. A couple of days later, on November 5, 1885, Assistant U.S. Attorney C.H. Hanford put it more succinctly in a note to territorial Governor Watson Squires: "Chinese houses here burning. You ought to do something for Seattle quick."[46] Federal troops soon arrived, but in February 1886, anti-Chinese riots in Seattle were so serious that Governor Squires declared martial law. This was fortunate: the move prevented a gang from carrying out its plans to hang Thomas

THE CHINESE NEW-FOUND FRIENDS WILL KNOCK IN VAIN.

Cartoon depicting New York Chamber's support for Chinese immigrant workers.

Burke, the new Seattle Chamber's young secretary who was trying to protect the Chinese.[47] This chamber, formed just in 1882, of course backed Squires's measure.[48] Order was finally restored, in part because so many Chinese had been put onto ships heading out of the area.

Although anti-Chinese agitation reached a fever pitch, Chinese business people maintained a toehold in the nation. Chinese merchants in both New York and San Francisco later thanked the New York Chamber of Commerce for its support of their cause. And there was a full-fledged Chinese Merchants' Exchange on Sacramento Street in San Francisco in 1884, two years after the Exclusion Act.[49]

Mayhem on Main Street

Throughout this turbulent period, chambers of commerce and boards of trade included some of the most prominent people in town – but they remained subject to human passions. The Cincinnati Chamber of Commerce witnessed a public horsewhipping of one of its members, right on its trading floor, on New Year's Eve in 1878. Merchants quickly subdued the cowhide-wielding terrorist and he was put in jail. The victim, Charles Maguire, at first said he was being attacked because of some business venture gone awry. But it turned out that Maguire had been much too friendly with his assailant's wife. Maguire was lucky; his rival was carrying a gun, and clearly might have solved the dispute "in Kentucky fashion."[50]

On October 13, 1882, St. Louis Chamber President Charles E. Slayback ran to the *Post-Dispatch*, where the editor, Colonel John A. Cockrell, had just shot Slayback's brother through the eye. In that room, "a very affecting sight occurred, Charles lifting the body from the ground and weeping bitterly."[51]

The dead brother, Colonel A.W. Slayback, had intended to kill Cockrell over a dispute about something that had run in the newspaper. Cockrell drew first and killed Colonel Slayback, but was almost dispatched himself by an angry friend of the dead man, W.H. Clopton. Fortunately for Cockrell, someone put a gun to Clopton's head and told him, "Lower your weapon or I shall kill you!" Clopton slunk out of the room, but he otherwise likely would have fired his pistol. After all, he was "the same man who horsewhipped the aged Senator Jewett in this town in this city a few days ago."[52] This community, although named for a saint, was no easy place in which to run a chamber of commerce.

A Gift for a President's Widow

Violence in this period touched even the occupants of the White House. One of the most traumatic experiences for the nation after the Civil War was the shooting and subsequent death of President James A. Garfield in 1881. The New York Chamber of Commerce set up a fund to provide for the widow and her children, one of whom, Harry, would contribute something to the chamber movement himself one day. The chamber managed to raise an extraordinary $360,000 (about $8.03 million in today's dollars), for which Lucretia Garfield was extremely grateful.

She used some of the money to build an addition to the family's Ohio farmhouse. On the second floor, she set up a library to house her husband's Presidential papers. This became the first Presidential library.[53]

Garfield's insane assassin, Charles Guiteau, heard of the munificence of the New York Chamber. "The rich men of New York gave Mrs. Garfield $200,000 or $300,000," he said. "It was a splendid thing – a noble thing. Now I want them to give me some money."[54]

Winged Defeat

The *Emily B. Souder*, a steamship also equipped with canvas sails, pulled into the New Orleans harbor after a voyage from Havana via Key West. Thanks to the hard work of the Louisiana Board of Health on the containment of yellow fever, with its recommendations championed by the New Orleans Chamber of Commerce, the laws now permitted ships to move into the port and upriver without "time detention" unless a quarantine officer specifically requested it. The modern miracle of carbolic acid treatment would mop up any problems of the pesky, but now controllable, disease.

It was the end of May, 1878. The medical inspector held the *Souder* up for just a few hours and then let it steam up to a berth in downtown New Orleans. An ailing crew member, John Clark, who later bragged that he "had beaten the quarantine officer," staggered into a boarding house and died soon afterward, his skin a shade of yellow. Another crew member died shortly thereafter. Dr. Samuel Choppin, president of the Louisiana Board of Health, recognized these as yellow fever cases, but didn't report the news to the Tennessee Board of Health, as he had promised he would in the case of an epidemic.[55] No doubt he believed he had the problem contained.

In June and July, New Orleans authorities permitted 18 ships coming from Havana to enter their harbor, plus 15 from South America. Several continued upriver toward the great city on the Tennessee bluffs, Memphis. And a number of these vessels had passengers who felt ill. By the end of July, there were people stricken with yellow fever in Memphis, although authorities did not report the existence of the disease there until August 14.[56]

The disease exploded. It turned out to be the worst outbreak of yellow fever in American history. Memphis was ravaged by the fever and people fled the city *en masse*, spreading the disease even further. The city's population of 47,000 in July became just 19,000 in September, and 17,000 of these had yellow fever.[57] Ultimately, about 5,000 people died in Memphis alone, and total deaths in the Mississippi Valley reached 20,000.[58]

Memorial to those killed by yellow fever in Memphis, 1878

Calls for help went out across the nation and many chambers of commerce responded. General Cyrus Bussey, the president of the New Orleans Chamber of Commerce, wasted no time in coming to New York to appeal to the most powerful chamber in the land. He attended a special meeting of the New York Chamber on August 23. There he explained the devastation caused by the disease and the chance that it might not abate "until the setting in of frost."[59]

General Bussey said the spread of the epidemic "was due in great part to the overconfidence of the people in general, and of the Board of Health in particular." He seems to have laid no blame on the shoulders of his chamber, which had been the Board of Health's champion for the liberalized quarantine regulations. He suggested that it would be a good idea to send money to New Orleans physicians, who were the best in the South at treating yellow fever.[60]

The response of the New York Chamber was gratifying. It created a relief committee of 25 whose treasurer, J. Pierpont Morgan, dispatched checks totaling $171,919.13.[61] Other chambers also gave money to help.

But the damage had been done, especially to Memphis, many of whose refugees never returned. Indeed, one historian credits the yellow-fever mosquito with possibly making Atlanta the "New York of the South" instead of Memphis.[62] Only a couple of decades after the epidemic, Tennessee's competing Nashville Chamber of Commerce touted the virtues of its city, which, although far enough south to be warm, was "far enough north to be safe from Yellow Fever."[63]

Stopping the Railroad Robber Barons

Today we have a tendency to view business in the Gilded Age as rapacious and without a thought to the public interest. In terms of the railroads, this idea isn't far off the mark. This was an unusual industry, which sought and received subsidies from communities and governments, and attracted every kind of get-rich-quick investor and speculator. Other businesses did not have such perks or, arguably, bring aboard so many shady operators. Indeed, entrepreneurs and executives in just about every other line of work were furious at such evils as freight discrimination, overcharging, cash bribes and free trips for politicians, rate pooling, and financial shenanigans including stock watering (adding more shares of company stock to take over the firm or to extract more dividends from the business) and misleading reports of profits and losses.

Chambers of commerce were very clear in their disdain of such activities. In 1879 the National Board of Trade's delegates voted 42 to 3 in favor of some form of national regulation of the industry.[64] The Railroad Transportation Committee of the New York Board of Trade and Transportation[65] reported that "the public wealth is being concentrated in a few hands by a system of taxation, under the guise of taxes and tolls for transportation, compared with which the tolls exacted by the robber-Barons of the feudal ages were petty."[66] Although railroads essentially had created the great metropolis of Chicago, the Chicago Board of Trade had many harsh words for their management, such as these of Secretary Charles Randolph in January 1881:

> Reflecting men stand aghast as they observe link after link forged and firmly welded in the great chains which a few individuals hold, and so effectually control as to be a standing menace to the commercial prosperity of the country, and to its best and highest interests.[67]

The railroads might ignore what some business organizations might say about them – but when the powerful New York Chamber of Commerce spoke, it was a good idea to listen. The chamber created a Committee on Railroad Transportation in January of 1878 to monitor railroad price discrimination against New York City. Even at the meeting where this committee was announced, the president of the New York Central, William Henry Vanderbilt (son of the great transportation mogul Cornelius Vanderbilt), showed up and defended his company. "I grant that we have been actuated by selfish motives, but what adds to our business helps New York's commerce," he said.[68]

Chamber President Samuel Babcock and his colleagues continued to antagonize Vanderbilt and went on to oppose the railroads on several fronts: spearheading an anti-monopoly conference in Utica, pushing with the New York Board of Trade and Transportation for a state regulatory authority, crusading against bribery of politicians, and ultimately calling for, with others, a national body to regulate the railroads. The chamber's activism elicited bursts of anger from the railroad chieftains – a good sign that this organization (whose voice was "far mightier than any that has been raised in Congress," according to Maine Senator James G. Blaine[69]) was drawing blood.

William Vanderbilt, who had endured a good deal of verbal abuse from his domineering father, seems not to have been schooled well in the language of diplomacy. He once was quoted, famously, as saying, "The public be damned."[70] In a joint letter he wrote with another railroad chieftain, he went straight after the New York Chamber of Commerce:

> The growth of a disregard of the rights of property in this country is very marked, and railroad corporations offer favorable forms of attack. The encouragement, by such a body as the Chamber of Commerce, to such ideas will not stop at rail-road corporations, but will reach all kinds of associated capital, and will not be stopped before it reaches all property. This growing tendency to socialistic principles is one of the most dangerous signs of the times, and if not checked, will produce scenes of disaster that would now appall the country.[71]

While the chamber's special committee bridled at the accusation (which Vanderbilt's counsel Chauncey DePew later inflated to "Communistic"), it must have amused not a few people to hear the New York Chamber of Commerce's magnates referred to as socialistic. Vanderbilt's bullets were missing the mark, while the chamber's were hitting theirs.[72] As the railroads' opponents won victory after victory in the state legislature in New York and elsewhere, it was quietly becoming clear in the early 1880s that the railroads would have to live under increased supervision.

State railroad commissions were forming in many states, including in New York in 1882 (with one of the commissioners required to be appointed by the New York Board of Trade). And a consensus was growing that national regulation was necessary. Indeed, in 1887, Congress passed the Interstate Commerce Act, one of the landmark steps in federal regulation of private industry. This act created the Interstate Commerce Commission (ICC), an organization to which chambers would appeal again and again in future years, sometimes successfully, asking for relief from alleged railroad freight discrimination.

The ICC legislation had the overwhelming support of the nation's chambers of commerce, from New York to San Francisco. In popular histories of the United States, the victory for railroad regulation is attributed to populism – especially angry farmers, who indeed were in the vanguard of the movement. But business and chamber support for the ICC was also deep and abiding, and clearly contributed to the legislation's success. At this pivotal moment in American business history, chambers of commerce were asking for a significant ramp-up of the federal regulation that in later years many of them would decry. In a sense, W.H. Vanderbilt was right: what the New York Chamber of Commerce and others were advocating would not stop at the railroads. The genie of increased federal and state regulation would prove most unwilling to squeeze back into the lamp.

Supervision of Business in a Freewheeling Era
Railroads were not the only aspect of business requiring some oversight, at least in the view of chambers of commerce. At the request of its chamber and board of trade members, the

National Board of Trade took a stand in 1879 against the adulteration of food and drugs. It also offered a $1,000 prize for the best program "to prevent injurious adulteration and regulate the sale of food without imposing unnecessary burdens upon commerce."[73] Spurred in part by the yellow fever epidemic of 1878, people were worried about the spread of disease through food and drugs. Business organizations' concerns for regulating food harkened back to the New York Chamber of Commerce's war on bad fish and flour in colonial days, and to the boards of trade and produce exchanges that now sold enormous quantities of food and grain, clearly specifying weights and measures of quality. It would not be until 1906, however, that there would be Congressional legislation (the Pure Food and Drug Act) to set national food safety standards.

Another regulatory push had to do with wilderness land. The idea of setting aside land for state or national parks – and keeping most business out of them – was relatively new in the Gilded Age. Only the area around Hot Springs, Arkansas (under Jackson's Presidency), Yosemite Valley, California (under Lincoln's), and Yellowstone (under Grant's) had been carved out for national preservation. In New York, a movement was under way to preserve Niagara Falls. Then, in 1883, the New York Chamber of Commerce began pushing publicly for state preservation of the Adirondack Forest.

This vast area of 6.1 million acres, today the largest park in the continental United States,[74] is an enormous watershed for the Hudson Valley. Chamber members and scientists feared that if unrestricted logging took place, the soil would lose its ability to hold water and the flow of the Erie Canal and the Hudson River would be disrupted. For some, if not most, chamber members, there may have been little concern for keeping parkland – but a threat to the Erie Canal was mortal danger to the economy of New York City, which owed its rise to preeminence in commerce more to the canal than to any other single factor.

New York newspaper editorialists were calling for preservation of the Adirondack Forest in the fall of 1883. The plans of the Adirondack Railroad Company to traverse the region spurred concerns for the future of the forest. On December 6, at a meeting of the New York Chamber of Commerce, Morris Jesup, sounding more like an environmentalist than a prominent businessman, raised the alarm and appointed a special committee. On December 20, the chamber released a booklet, *Save the Adirondack Forests and the Waterways of the State of New-York.*[75]

Very soon afterward, Jesup and his committee members were meeting with state legislators.[76] The chamber continued to pursue the topic energetically, fighting such encroachments as horse-drawn wagons that could carry out logs.[77] The New York Board of Trade and Transportation joined the fray in 1884 and pushed equally hard – perhaps even harder – and seems to have been largely responsible for the creation of constitutional, permanent protection for the park in 1894.[78]

We Are Fit for Habitation

Chambers outside New York cared about the great outdoors, too. And many were very proud of their local environments. The St. Paul Chamber of Commerce's annual reports had made several touchy comments over the years about its weather not being really as cold as people thought. No wonder members were incensed when, in 1885, a New York reporter wrote that St. Paul was "another Siberia, unfit for human habitation in winter."[79]

The chamber turned lemons into lemonade, or perhaps ice into ice cream. Defiantly, the business people set up a winter fair in 1886 to prove that people did live in Minnesota in the wintertime. The St. Paul Winter Carnival was an instant hit, featuring an ice palace and other attractions. It continues today, drawing about 350,000 visitors per year.[80]

Southern Voices

The end of Reconstruction had freed the North to pursue its manic economic development and had permitted the South's dominant whites to chart a course of their own. In the mid-1880s, two different speeches reflected two contrasting views of the South and its potential. One was pessimistic and backward-looking, while the other was optimistic and forward-looking. Together, these talks shed much light on both the Old South and the New.

The year 1884 marked the 100th anniversary of the reconstituted Charleston Chamber of Commerce, after its patriots under Commodore Alexander Gillon had reassembled the institution within their new nation, the United States. To commemorate this significant moment, the chamber's leaders chose a distinguished member, William Trenholm, to discuss the past century and its implications.

William Trenholm was the son of George Alfred Trenholm, the great chamber leader and terror of the Yankee blockade of the South. It was William who joined his father to recreate the devastated chamber in 1866. He had lived through the ups and downs of the chamber, Charleston, and the South, and he had come up with some basic insights on the nature of commerce and his community.

Trenholm knew that the key problem of business in South Carolina and Charleston was evident from the earliest days after the American Revolution: "Unfortunately for Charleston's commercial career, the people of the State neither valued nor respected trade."[81] The state enacted measure after measure that depreciated the currency or otherwise weakened the position of creditors. Merchants had no stable financial environment in which to operate. On top of this, the traders bore more than their fair share of the taxes of the state. In myriad ways, agriculture was coddled and commerce distrusted. It was (although Trenholm didn't bring up the nation's third President) a state that followed the economically eccentric farmer- and planter-embracing visions of Thomas Jefferson.

Trenholm bemoaned the consequences of squandered opportunities. A state that didn't appreciate business was unable to foster it. "With a wonderfully indented coast and full two thousand miles of safe and easy inland and deep river navigation, she [South Carolina] has produced no sailors and established no fisheries," he noted.[82] The same lack of enterprise was found in forestry and local manufacturing. And in a state that glorified the production of the land, land prices were stagnant, far below those in other regions of the country.[83]

Trenholm observed that with merchants lacking social and political standing, the successful ones either bought land and slaves and became leisurely planters, or they departed the state altogether. This exodus removed valuable expertise from Charleston's merchant community, leaving those who remained without the wisdom that might have prevented some of the speculative failures of past years. A brief "sunburst" of success in the 1850s was wiped out by ill-conceived business failures, and a revival that began around 1860 was cut short by war and then by a rapacious Reconstruction.[84]

William Trenholm concluded his sobering speech with an attempt to be constructive. He advocated better transportation infrastructure, a focus on Charleston's key geographic position linking the United States with South America, and a revival of the great traditions of the chamber. In the end, however, his pessimism was more convincing than his optimism.

Indeed, Charleston and the South faced continuing problems. While the North was producing iron, the South was still manufacturing irony. Trenholm ended up doing exactly what he criticized. He moved out of the state, eventually becoming an active member of another chamber (the New York Chamber of Commerce), as well as the U.S. Controller of the Currency.[85]

Careless with Fire

A more convincing optimism emerged from that home of widows and ashes, Atlanta, and one of its energetic and likeable prophets, Henry Grady. This bright spirit did not live long, but he spoke well. His vision, a good deal more gripping than Trenholm's, inspired his adopted city and especially its business people. If chambers of commerce had patron saints, and New York's was Alexander Hamilton, then Atlanta's was Henry Grady.

Henry Grady

Grady was the editor of the *Atlanta Constitution* when he visited New York to speak at a dinner of the New England Society shortly before Christmas in 1886. He was known as a booster of the South and of Atlanta and was an apostle of moderation in race relations (although by no means advocating full equality between whites and blacks). While on that December night at Delmonico's he didn't speak before a chamber, as Trenholm had in Charleston, Grady could have noted in the audience many well-known members of the New York Chamber of Commerce, including Samuel Babcock, Morris Jesup, J. Pierpont Morgan, F.B. Thurber, and Charles Tiffany.[86]

At a critical moment in the talk, Grady suddenly saw in the audience a man who was a frequent guest, and great friend, of the members of the New York Chamber of Commerce: General William T. Sherman. This of course was the man whose treatment of Atlanta was legend. Not missing a beat, Grady remarked:

> I want to say to General Sherman – who is considered an able man in our parts, although some people think he is a kind of careless man with fire – that from the ashes left us in 1864 we have raised a brave and beautiful city; that somehow or other we have caught the sunshine in the bricks and mortar of our homes, and have builded therein not one single ignoble prejudice or memory.[87]

Grady's amazing facility for reconciliation went further, and invoked the memory of his father, a Confederate soldier slain in the conflict:

> In my native town of Athens is a monument that crowns its central hills – a plain, white shaft. Deep cut into its shining side is a name dear to me above the names of men, that of a brave and simple man who died in brave and simple faith. Not for all the glories of New England – from

Plymouth Rock all the way – would I exchange the heritage he left me in his soldier's death. To the foot of that shaft I shall send my children's children to reverence him who ennobled their name with his heroic blood. But, sir, speaking from the shadow of that memory, which I honor as I do nothing else on earth, I say that the cause in which he suffered and for which he gave his life was adjudged by higher and fuller wisdom than his or mine, and I am glad that the omniscient God held in the balance of battle in His Almighty hand, and that human slavery was swept forever from American soil – the American Union saved from the wreck of war.[88]

Grady's talk, today known as the "New South Speech," argued that the liberation of the slaves had been a welcome democratizing force and was good for the South: "a hundred farms for every plantation, fifty homes for every palace, and a diversified industry that meets the complex needs of this complex age." He said of the South that "The shackles that had held her in narrow limitations fell forever when the shackles of the Negro slave were broken."[89]

As an editor and speaker, Grady propounded these positive, forward-looking views throughout the South and, as on this occasion, in the North. But in Atlanta, especially, his ideas seem to have taken root. The Atlanta Chamber of Commerce, after Grady's untimely death in 1889 at the age of 39, self-consciously attempted to keep the Grady spirit. Racial moderation, overtures to the North for investment and workers, and a focus on building up industry would be themes to which it would constantly return, often invoking the name of the inspiring editor.

Gathering Strength

Power in Numbers

In their 120-year history up to 1887-88, American chambers of commerce had encountered periods of retrenchment, usually because of war or financial depression, and periods of expansion and exuberance. Starting around 1887, the year after the Haymarket incident in Chicago, another wave of growth began, one that washed over the entire country, although with particular force in the West. There were many reasons for the upsurge: concern about labor unrest, the desire to join together to solve civic and social problems, increasing prosperity, and the competitive struggle for markets and population.

From 1887 to 1893, the number of major cities that began or revitalized their chambers of commerce is remarkable. These included, to name only a few: Salt Lake City, Los Angeles, Detroit, Indianapolis, Richmond, Atlanta, Cleveland, Boston, Phoenix, Kansas City, Oklahoma City, Syracuse, Birmingham (Ala.), Omaha, Raleigh, and Jackson (Miss.). But it wasn't just big cities and big chambers. Other new business organizations included the Catlettsburg (Ky.) Chamber of Commerce, the Coatesville (Pa.) Board of Trade, and even the Sing Sing (present-day Ossining, N.Y.) Board of Trade.

The sheer number of chambers of commerce was noteworthy. Colonel J.A. Price of the Scranton Board of Trade informed the National Board of Trade in 1889 that he had uncovered 526 commercial organizations in the United States with a total of 95,000 individual members.[1] (These included trade associations as well as chambers.) The following year, he came back with a more complete list, one that must have stunned his listeners: a total of 1,171 such groups in 45 states and territories, and including 234,200 individuals.[2]

"It is found that local organizations have been forming with astonishing rapidity everywhere, through every State of the Union, with intent upon some local, municipal, district or State improvement," Price said.[3] Then he made the point that others would see and capitalize on in the coming decades: there was potential political power in this mass of influential citizens:

Should a proper and well arranged system of cooperation among these organizations ever be affected [*sic*], it will constitute the most influential commercial organization on the surface of the globe.[4]

The National Board of Trade (NBoT), with only 33 organizational members at this time, clearly had a great deal work to do if it were to fulfill its potential as the uniting body of commercial groups in the country. This did not mean that it, and others, could not begin to start tapping the power of this network of nearly a quarter of a million civic leaders, not to mention their companies. But a truly powerful national commercial organization was still some years away.

Nevertheless, the NBoT members had dreams of glory. This did not always endear them to the most powerful chamber in the country, the New York Chamber of Commerce. In 1888, the NBoT went so far as to insist that the New York Chamber's delegates should attend the entire three-day NBoT conferences and not duck out for other purposes. As a result of this perceived effrontery, the New York Chamber sent no delegates that year.[5]

Things got worse. In November 1891 the New York State Board of Trade (BoT) was formed in Rochester. The New York Chamber was invited to join it, but the chamber's counsel found in the fine print of the state BoT's rules that its members must belong to no other bodies. Becoming completely subordinate to any group, let alone a brand-new one with its scope limited to a single state, was unimaginable for New York Chamber members. They not only declined the offer to join the state Board of Trade, but withdrew from the National Board of Trade.[6]

Still, such struggles among organizations were signs of increased activity. The energy of the times found its way into the New York Chamber as well. While it retained its limit of 1,000 members, those it did accept were of unusually high stature. In December of 1887, both Andrew Carnegie and telephone mogul Theodore Vail joined the chamber; over the next five years, others who came aboard included John D. Rockefeller, railroad magnate C.P. Huntingdon, financiers Jacob Schiff and August Belmont (the latter a horse racing fan for whom the Belmont Stakes is named), former Comptroller of the Currency and Charleston Chamber member William Trenholm, wholesaler and future Secretary of the Interior Cornelius Bliss, railroad sleeping car maker George Pullman, retailer George Macy, and even the occasional friend and sometime soft-on-silver nemesis of the chamber, former U.S. Senator John T. Sherman.[7]

Senator Sherman's brother, General William Tecumseh Sherman, entered the New York Chamber through another door. A longtime friend of the organization and guest at its dinners, he was invited to join as an honorary member in November 1889, along with a compulsive tinkerer by the name of Thomas Alva Edison. Both accepted.[8] In between presidencies, Grover Cleveland joined as an honorary member; later, as President-elect for the second time, he called the organization "our Chamber of Commerce."[9] Another entrant to the club was former Ambassador to France Whitelaw Reid. While giving Reid the honor, New York Chamber President Charles Smith called the honorary membership distinction "an American merchant's patent of nobility, the 'Iron Cross of American commerce.'"[10]

These were heady times for business organizations. The American nation was turning into a world power, in large part because of its growing industrial might. Modern life seemed to require more organization, more scientific thinking, more business – and more and better chambers of commerce.

The Boston Chamber of Commerce was one of many such groups attempting to organize itself better in order to extend its reach and influence. To point the way, Boston Chamber President Alden Speare shared with his members a letter from the chamber that really seemed to be doing things right: the venerable Cincinnati Chamber of Commerce, with 2,299 members, many of whom met *daily*.[11] While these chambers differed from modern chambers (and many of their contemporary chambers) in carrying on significant trading activities, the insights provided by the letter of Cincinnati Chamber Superintendent Sidney Maxwell have some applicability to any attempt to organize groups of businesses.

Maxwell noted the need to appeal to the commercial interests of members in order to keep them coming back:

> Extraordinary and spasmodic means may be used for the purpose of bringing together frequently the membership of a commercial body, but they will not be permanently effectual without personal interest being actually secured.[12]

A person's business must first be addressed before he can be depended on to look at more general concerns. Hence a community's specialized trades and industries needed to have opportunities to do business among themselves, separately. Without this concession to self-interest, the larger group cannot last.

But the larger group – the chamber – is important, too. It has the power to defend even the weakest of the trades that it represents. So the different trades must unite in the chamber to be most effective and influential. Maxwell suggested:

> In my estimation, the ideal Chamber of Commerce . . . is one in which the largest encouragement is given to the organization of individual trades, so that just as early as possible each department of business may feel that it is permitted to address itself to the consideration of its own interests, feeling at the same time that it has all the sanctions of the general body for its preservation, defense and development.[13]

Many a modern chamber executive and board member will recognize similar problems of reconciling different industries and lines of business with the overall requirements of the chamber. Similarly, modern commercial organizations must weigh the desires of members to "get some business" with the need to preserve the chamber's broader, general mission. As with any organization, chambers must balance the needs of the individual with the imperatives of the group.

Maxwell's thoughts, and the Boston Chamber's interest in them, show how chamber executives and board members were conscious that intelligence and planning could be applied to their organizations. A contemporary with similar ideas lived in Indianapolis. Colonel Eli Lilly was the founding president of the Commercial Club of Indianapolis in 1890, a group that eschewed the old "brass band" approach to trumpeting a city's merits in order to attract business. Instead, Lilly and his colleagues aimed at promoting growth through "scientific" means involving statistics, maps, and careful study of which industries would do best in the local economy.[14]

Brass band or not, however, capturing business was never far from the top of chambers' list of objectives. Colonel Lilly in 1892 wrote a gushing letter of congratulations to the secretary of the Commercial Club, William Fortune, when it appeared that Fortune had snagged a big convention of Civil War veterans and their families: "Well, I suppose the die is cast and that you have captured the Grand Army of the Republic – a job by the way that was too great for the whole Southern Confederacy."[15] The 1893 event broke all records, with 300,000 visitors, and Fortune's expert management reportedly left a surplus that became the kernel of the first permanent convention and visitors bureau activity of any American city, a later writer claimed.[16]

The Beginnings of State Chambers of Commerce

For years there had been one "state" chamber in the United States: the Chamber of Commerce of the State of New York. However, its name was misleading. This chamber, which (under its original name, the New York Chamber of Commerce) predated the United States and indeed the existence of "states" in North America, was focused mostly on the needs of the major businesses in New York City. Its state concerns had to do primarily with items that affected the city, such as the Croton Reservoir, the Erie Canal, or the railroad network. It even took on the preservation of the Adirondack wilderness not simply for aesthetic reasons but so as to protect the waterways feeding New York's harbor. Moreover, the chamber spent much energy on issues going far beyond Albany: sugar tariffs, Chinese immigration, Civil War financing, and British ship seizures, for example.

Toward the end of the 19th century, business people began to form organizations claiming, with varying degrees of accuracy, to represent their state. A Utah Board of Trade existed in 1879 and published a guide, "The Resources and Attractions of the Territory of Utah."[17] Ten years later, in October 1889, the New Orleans-based Chamber of Commerce and Industry of the State of Louisiana sent four delegates to the National Board of Trade meeting in Louisville, where they were admitted as members.[18] The following year the state group also attended the National Board of Trade meeting, this time in New Orleans, where its delegates asked for federal action to improve the Mississippi River.[19]

The trend continued. The Maine State Board of Trade had its first meeting on September 10, 1889.[20] On October 30, 1890, 33 business groups, with a total of 99 delegates, formed the Massachusetts Board of Trade.[21] The Connecticut State Board of Trade held meetings in 1890 and in subsequent years.[22] The New York State Board of Trade, as we have seen, was formed in November of 1891. The Virginia State Board of Trade held an initial meeting in June 1892 and the Richmond Chamber of Commerce determined to join it.[23] The Cleveland Chamber of Commerce, itself in a mode of reorganization and revitalization, led in the creation of a state board of trade in Ohio in 1893.[24] Although most of these initial efforts would falter, Ohio's chamber has remained in business to this day.

People were beginning to understand that statewide business organizations could be valuable as critics or advisors of the governments in their states. In the West in particular, state boards of trade were created in large part to attract more residents and industry. Utah, California, and Nevada each had had a state board of trade by 1890. The Nevada State Board of Trade published a booklet that recalled the work of the Kentucky immigration societies nearly a century earlier. Not only did the Nevada boosters want to promote their territory, but they wished to correct misconceptions about it:

Nevada has been outrageously slandered by ignorant writers and speakers, and the broadest jokes and sarcasms of our own wits have been accepted as reliable information by millions of people who know less about one of the States of the Union than they do about the Congo country.[25]

Ultimately, state chambers were less effective at boosterism than were city chambers. It took money and energy to attract new people and businesses. Those most willing to work on this usually had some local self-interest. Promoters in Los Angeles, for example, would be more likely to make money if they enticed people to their own city rather than to somewhere else in the state of California. City promotion began in earnest in the late 1880s, as we will see, and local chambers were in the vanguard. State chambers would play a role in business attraction, but their primary activity would come in other spheres and in future years.

A Rail Car Named Salt Lake City

In Utah, the Mormon leadership had instituted a boycott of non-Mormon businesses – one that was in effect even when Brigham Young addressed the Boston Board of Trade delegation in 1870. But the Utah Territory was opening up to outside influences and sought statehood. The boycott ended in 1882 and plural marriage was forbidden in the new state constitution of 1887. In the same year, no doubt reflecting the spirit of openness to change, three major new chambers were founded: in Salt Lake, Provo, and Ogden.[26]

These chambers worked to promote their communities but had other tasks as well. Reflecting the mining interests in the region, the Salt Lake Chamber came out in favor of "free silver." And the Provo Chamber teamed up with the Salt Lake Chamber to oppose a threatened reduction in the tariff on lead and wool. One of the 30 founding members of the Provo Chamber, a young man named Reed Smoot, complained that decreasing the wool tariff would be equivalent to "a law compelling the slaughter of all the sheep."[27] Smoot was a fan of tariffs. Four decades later, while a Republican senator from Utah, he coauthored the now infamous Smoot-Hawley Tariff Bill. That 1929 bill raised tariff levels on 20,000 products so high that American exports and imports were reduced by more than half.

The Salt Lake Chamber had a well-known visitor on May 9, 1891: President Benjamin Harrison, who was on a campaign swing. He had some nice words of encouragement for the chamber:

> I wish you all success in this enterprise, and I hope you may grow until its membership shall embrace all of your commercial classes, and that its influence may do for your business here what the water of your mountain streams has done for the plains – make them grow longer and more productive, and at the same time expel from them those mean jealousies which sometimes divide men.[28]

Harrison's appeal to unity was especially appropriate for this chamber, which may account for the "prolonged applause" after his remark. Throughout the state, reconciling the fractious Mormon and "gentile" (non-Mormon) commercial communities was a high order of business. For the Salt Lake Chamber of Commerce, this was an explicit goal, mentioned in its very first meeting and underlined in its motto, "No politics or religion in the Chamber."[29]

But the "mean jealousies" were fragmenting this chamber even before President Harrison's speech. Chamber President and former Governor Caleb West had visited Washington, D.C. in April 1890 and indicated he supported the Cullom Bill, which would take away the vote from Mormons. Word got back to Utah and the chamber and local newspapers were up in arms.[30] The religious tensions continued, combining with bad economic times to cause the Salt Lake Chamber to drop from 500 members in its first three years to only about 200 in 1893.[31]

Still, a seed had been planted. The local business people had clearly shown that the chamber of commerce was a logical place for Mormons and gentiles to work together and bring the community together. And the chamber had done something else with far-reaching implications.

On June 6, 1888, a rail car left town with this sign on either side: "Utah Exposition Palace Car; The Resources of Salt Lake City, the Gem City of the Rocky Mountains; Free exhibit sent under the auspices of the Salt Lake Chamber of Commerce." The car travelled the country for three months, distributing 14 tons' worth of publications on Utah and its leading city. It is credited with bringing thousands of new residents to Salt Lake City. More importantly, it inspired other chambers to even larger promotion efforts.[32] Of these chambers, none outdid a little booster organization, set up in the fall of 1888, called the Los Angeles Chamber of Commerce.

California Dreaming

In the middle 1880s, Los Angeles had experienced a sharp economic downturn, thanks primarily to the collapse of real estate prices. Nonetheless, this relatively undiscovered part of the United States, freshly opened by the railroads to increased settlement, was ripe for promotion. What it needed was skilled farmers to make the land productive and the economy strong, and a strong business-minded organization to make that happen.

A group of local business people gathered together to talk about what a chamber of commerce might do to improve the prospects of the region. For these California burghers, publicity was the most important single task of the chamber. Once people knew about the wonders of their region, they would come. One businessman, Clarence Warner, who had been connected with the Santa Fe Railroad, suggested a sort of rolling exhibit of the produce of the land. The rail car would travel into the Midwest to tempt the experienced farmers there to try their hand in sunnier southern California. Other, stationary exhibits would reinforce the message.[33] Warner's vision would be startlingly realized by the new chamber, as would many of the ideas of the other founders. This was to be a chamber of practical dreamers.

The person who made the motion to create the Los Angeles Chamber of Commerce, on October 15, 1888, was a newspaperman: Colonel H. G. Otis, the editor of the *Los Angeles Times*.[34] Before long, Otis's writers would be penning the leaflets and brochures that would blanket the nation. Many of the publications were handed out at the rolling California on Wheels exhibit, which visited most significant cities in the Midwest and drew about 1 million visitors over two years ending in 1890.[35]

Just six years after the business organization's founding, San Francisco veteran journalist Charles Irish noted that Los Angeles trailed only Chicago in its self-promotion.[36] That was high praise for the small southern California community and its chamber. To be even compared with Chicago, with its phenomenal growth and its world-famous Columbian Exposition of 1893, was a great compliment.

To tap into the excitement of Chicago and its coming exposition, the Los Angeles Chamber of Commerce sponsored an "Orange Carnival" there in 1890, featuring oranges and other southern California produce. The chamber printed 20,000 tickets and was overwhelmed by the results of its own promotion. Massive crowds arrived on opening day, until "squad after squad of police were ordered to the scene to prevent a riot." Ultimately this orange event drew in 100,000 visitors.[37]

The following year's carnival, however, was clouded in tragedy and mystery. Chamber Secretary H. Jay Hanchette, a former newspaper man, managed the 1891 Orange Carnival. When his work in Chicago was over, he departed on foot for the train station, and was never seen again. Hanchette was happily married and left behind two sons. Although his disappearance was never resolved, his path to the train station went through a rough Chicago neighborhood, and most concluded that he was murdered and his body disposed of.[38]

Hanchette was ultimately replaced by his understudy at the Orange Carnival, Frank Wiggins. A strait-laced Quaker, Wiggins became the chamber's superintendent of exhibits. His mild-mannered demeanor disguised Barnum-like skills of promotion.

At the Columbian Exposition in 1893 in Chicago, the chamber executive conjured up a larger than life-sized elephant sculpture lined with of 850 pounds of walnuts, and he created a gigantic tower of oranges. Despite hundreds of competing exhibits from all over the world, Wiggins's displays were viewed by millions. After the exposition, the chamber continued its Los Angeles promotion program through advertisements and brochures. The chamber distributed 2 million written promotional pieces by the turn of the century, reaching perhaps one in five Americans through these methods.[39] Its efforts put the dusty desert town on the map.

The chamber also began to push hard for a port at San Pedro, opposing C.P. Huntingdon's plan for a port at Santa Monica, near land he intended to buy for Southern Pacific. The business organization, moreover, urged the U.S. annexation of Baja California (until the resulting uproar embarrassed it), and pushed for new and better industry. In 1893, after gyrations in the market for oranges, it organized local growers into a cooperative called the Southern California Fruit Exchange, today known as Sunkist.[40]

The Los Angeles Chamber of Commerce, from its founding in 1888, had set a new standard of community promotion and activism that inspired other chambers. But it had no monopoly on energy or creativity, even in southern California. In 1888, chambers were founded in Long Beach and Pasadena. And one project of the San Diego Chamber of Commerce captured attention.

The Ladies Annex of the San Diego Chamber of Commerce

In 1889, George Nolan, the secretary of the San Diego Chamber of Commerce, came up with the idea of enlisting a group of women to aid the chamber.[41] Little did he know what he had started. A month or two after its inauguration, as a writer tartly noted, "The Annex is now larger than the Chamber to which it is annexed." She added that the chamber had better watch out or "folks will speak of the Chamber of Commerce of the Ladies Annex."[42]

That writer was probably Flora Kimball, an amateur horticulturalist and a feminist who was the founding president of the Annex. Kimball claimed this organization was the first such women's group connected with a chamber in the entire country.[43] She was used to being a pioneer. She had been the first female master of a local farmers' group (known as a grange) in the nation.[44] She founded a number of other local organizations, and chaired the program the day in June 1895 when Susan B. Anthony came to town and spoke to the San Diego Woman's Club.[45] When she died in 1898, Kimball was probably the most famous woman in California.

The Ladies Annex shared the boosterism of the chamber itself. As Mrs. Carrie Williams wrote:

> We are annexed to the Chamber of Commerce with the avowed purpose of aiding them in developing the wonderful and very numerous resources of this most wonderful of all the regions of God's green earth. Yes, this is a wonderful land, and all the green-eyed glances cast upon it by her Northern sisters cannot lessen her charms or make her less enchanting. San Diego stands unrivaled, a *diamond-tipped feather* in the Western wing of the American eagle.[46]

The members of the Ladies Annex spent a good deal of time on horticultural activities, including collecting the items for the California on Wheels and stationary exhibits of agricultural goods. (Although the Los Angeles Chamber of Commerce was the leading force behind the rolling exhibit, other groups in the state also participated.) Soon, however, they came upon an even bigger project: cleaning up and beautifying a large tract of land that the chamber had helped persuade the city to purchase: a 1,400 acre site, much of which is the area today known as Balboa Park:

> The tract is so large that San Diego city men have not felt themselves able to tackle it yet. Not so the women. The ladies of the Annex have resolved to commence work, not on all of it at once, but on ten acres to start with.[47]

It wasn't long before a new secretary of the San Diego Chamber of Commerce was criticizing their efforts, saying they had pruned trees and shrubs too closely. They gently explained why their methods were correct.[48] The Annex gradually faded away, moving out of the chamber offices and into history. No doubt the loss of Flora Kimball, who had moved on to other activities and organizations, was part of the reason.

The Passing of Public Men

On December 6, 1889, former Confederate States President Jefferson Davis died. Many southern chambers of commerce mourned his passing. One of them did something about it.

The Richmond Chamber of Commerce held a meeting on June 18, 1891 that approved resolutions to build a monument to the dead President. The resolutions included a plan to let Mrs. Davis know about the work and that "should Mrs. Davis deem it proper to consign the remains to this people," Jeff Davis's bones would be interred in the city where he had been best known to the world.[49]

The chamber formed a committee to seek the remains, which were resting in New Orleans. This was important, in part because the absence of Davis's body was an obstacle to fundraising. Eighteen months previously, Richmonders had begun raising money for the

Jefferson Davis Memorial, Richmond, Va.

monument but had suspended their efforts when Mrs. Davis had said it was "inexpedient" for her to make a decision within a year regarding the moving of her husband's remains.[50]

Fortunately, this time, after the committee met her, she gave her consent. As a result, reported the chamber, "his honored remains have recently been removed here from New Orleans and re-interred in our beautiful Hollywood," an achievement that "was one of the most impressive and gratifying events which ever occurred in the history of our city."[51] Jefferson Davis, who had discovered economic development in the Mississippi Valley, now would become in death, thanks to the chamber, an underground supporter of tourist attraction in his wartime home of Richmond.

In early 1891, U.S. Secretary of the Treasury William Windom died at Delmonico's Restaurant. He had just finished his address at the annual meeting of the New York Board of Trade and Transportation. He sat down, "swooned," and collapsed, probably from a heart attack.[52]

On Valentine's Day of 1891, General William Tecumseh Sherman, an honorary member of the New York Chamber of Commerce, passed away in New York at the age of 71.

General William T. Sherman statue on Fifth Avenue, New York

True to his warlike form, he took a Confederate general with him: General Joseph E. Johnston died a month later from a fever contracted as a result of serving as a pallbearer in Sherman's funeral. Johnston had been hatless out of respect, believing that Sherman would have done the same for him.[53]

The New York Chamber of Commerce held a special meeting in commemoration of the Union general, a distinguished honorary member and friend. The grief of the members ultimately had a very public expression: the chamber commissioned a bronze statue of the General Sherman that today sits at the Fifth Avenue entrance to Central Park. The sculptor, Augustus Saint-Gaudens, created the larger than life likeness at his studio in Paris. The statue is considered a masterpiece.

Tightly Closed Pockets

Many thousands of miles away in Russia, a severe famine struck the Volga region in late 1891. The future Nicholas II, son of the reactionary Czar Alexander III, was in charge of raising money to ameliorate the disaster. He and his father bungled the effort to fight the famine, causing immense suffering and pushing many people, among them a young man later known as Lenin, toward extremism in politics.

Americans, including the venerable and dedicated Clara Barton, pulled together for the relief effort. Naturally, the New York Chamber of Commerce's members took an interest in helping with this disaster, as they had with so many others. They raised funds – but with a wrinkle.

At the chamber's monthly meeting on February 4, 1892, after many testimonials in favor of aiding the Russians, the president of Kuhn, Loeb & Co., Jacob Schiff, spoke:

> Mr. Chairman, I hesitated and was in doubt whether or not I should come to this meeting, for, as you are aware, I belong to that race which has suffered so terribly at the hands of the Czar's Government.[54]

Schiff went on to say that although the Jewish people had endured much at the hands of the Czar, he would be willing to contribute to the fund, provided that the corrupt Russian officials did not get their hands on it. He noted that "the Jews will tightly close their pockets" if the money went directly to their oppressors in the Russian government.

Jacob Schiff

Money was raised and sent to Russia via private channels. But the chief royal fundraiser, Nicholas, learned nothing from Jacob Schiff's attitude. When the Prince Nicholas became Czar Nicholas II, he carried on the anti-Semitic policies of his father. Jacob Schiff, a determined man, as he had shown at the New York Chamber on more than one occasion, was incensed at the Czar's continuation of the pogroms that terrorized the Jews of Russia. He decided, as he put it in the chamber meeting back in 1892, to "tightly close" his pocket.

When Russia went to war with Japan in 1904, Schiff did his best to ensure that the Czar could not borrow money for the conflict.[55] As he noted at the time: "I pride myself that all the efforts, which at various times during the last four or five years have been made by Russia to gain the favor of American markets for its loans, I have been able to bring to naught."[56] And he arranged financing for a $200 million bond issue on behalf of the Japanese government. The money alone was a boost to the morale of the Japanese, but it also permitted the Asian island nation to bolster its forces on land and to acquire and equip the ships that decisively defeated a motley Russian fleet at the battle of Tsushima. For the first time in modern history, an Asian nation had overcome a European power in war.

The humiliation of the defeat destabilized Russia, encouraging unrest that simmered on past the opening of World War I. Under the pressure of German arms, the wobbly Russian regime finally collapsed. Not long afterward, the Czar and his family were shot.

Regime Change in Hawaii

Another Pacific Ocean-related event would unfold sooner. The McKinley Tariff of 1890 removed the duties on sugar imports, replacing them with a "bounty" or subsidy to be paid to U.S. sugar producers. All of a sudden, the Hawaiian growers saw their tariff advantage eliminated. Under the preferential system that had been pushed by both the Honolulu and San Francisco chambers (and opposed by most other chambers), the sugar producers on the islands had managed a massive trade. It totaled about 120,000 tons in each of the final years before the tariff change became effective. More than 90 percent went to the Port of San Francisco.[57]

The loss of much of this trade was a blow to the entire economy of the islands. More than a few people knew that there was one way to rectify the situation: arrange for the islands to be annexed by the United States. If Hawaii were a territory of the North American country, the growers could benefit from the same bounty paid to U.S. sugar beet and cane planters (two cents per pound), available to no one else in the world. In other words, as far as the American sugar bounty was concerned, if you can't beet 'em, join 'em.

The popular King Kalakaua died in 1891 and was succeeded by Queen Liliuokalani. She quickly aroused nearly universal criticism, including from the Honolulu Chamber of Commerce, for a lottery scheme connected with interests in Louisiana. She also signed an equally unpopular opium licensing bill. She initiated the drafting of a new constitution, one that strengthened the monarchy and disenfranchised some of the foreign business people on the islands. Her effort was motivated, at least in part, by the desire to block annexation by the United States. Many planters and merchants were alarmed.

On the morning of Saturday, January 14, 1893, the Chamber of Commerce of Honolulu was abuzz with rumors that the queen would promulgate the new constitution in the afternoon.[58] The palace had been warned of strong opposition to the move. That afternoon, the queen's ministers (who were allied to the foreign cause) quickly left the palace when they realized the queen did not intend to back down. On January 17, the foreigners mobilized a group of militants, the Honolulu Rifles, and also called in the U.S. Marines from the harbor, saying that life and property needed to be protected.

The call for help was unnecessary; the streets of Honolulu were peaceful. But the presence of the Marines was a signal to the queen that her cause was lost, and she surrendered. A provisional government of the foreign rebels took over.

The provisional government sought U.S. annexation of the islands, and the San Francisco Chamber of Commerce strongly backed it up. But opponents saw the seductive dream of annexation was mostly based on the sugar subsidy. As Congressman Harter of Ohio said of the pressure to annex Hawaii:

> The whole scheme is a job intended to benefit a few sugar planters who are anxious to secure a 2 cents a pound bounty paid by the United States on the native product. We will knock out that bounty shortly, and then you'll hear no more about annexation.[59]

Harter may have been correct about the main motive behind annexation, but he was wrong about knocking out the sugar subsidy. It's still going strong after more than a century.

President Grover Cleveland was furious at the revolt and at the actions of the Marines and opposed any territorial grab. It was not until the Spanish-American War, in 1898, that President McKinley reluctantly acceded to overwhelming pressure for annexation. Hawaii became a territory of the United States.

The chambers in San Francisco and Honolulu did not appear to have any direct role in the coup. But by successfully advocating trade reciprocity in previous decades, they had helped inaugurate the special sugar arrangement - one of the sweetest trade deals of the century - that inexorably bound the two economies closer together. Hawaiian sugar exports to the United States grew from less than 1,300 tons in 1861 to 120,000 in 1890.[60] That nearly 100-fold growth in trade was a major asset that the business community felt it needed to protect - at almost any cost.

The Great Fair

The Columbian Exposition of 1893 in Chicago was one of the most remarkable fairs of all time, making a lasting imprint on American culture and society. It was to mark the 400th anniversary of Columbus's discovery of the Americas. (As with many such celebrations, it was delayed. It missed the original target date of 1892 by one year.) About 21 million people visited the event. It featured the first Ferris wheel, the first commercial movie theater, and, of course, the Los Angeles Chamber of Commerce's pyramid of oranges and its giant walnut-coated elephant. Many other chambers of commerce exhibited the wares of their communities or lobbied their cities and states to pay for displays.

The business community of Chicago was involved from the beginning. The Commercial Club of Chicago's "early advocacy and support for the World's Columbian Exposition," according to a club historian, was one of its greatest achievements.[61] Club members also played significant roles in the fair. Lyman J. Gage was the original director of the fair and was succeeded by W.T. Baker, who concurrently served as the president of the Chicago Board of Trade. Other club members who were active in supporting the fair included Marshall Field, George Pullman, and John Doane.

The chief architect and planner of the fairgrounds, Daniel Burnham, was not a member of the Commercial Club at this time. (He was elected into the 60-member association in 1901.[62]) But his visionary creation on the shores of Lake Michigan impressed the leaders of the business community. Burnham's success in 1893 would lead to a project with the Commercial Club after the turn of the century that would set the standard for modern city planning.

Among the many aftereffects of the great fair in Chicago was a stimulus for more fairs. A string of similar projects began to take shape. All but one (the World's Fair in St. Louis) were less ambitious than the Columbian Exposition. Most, however, made a significant impact on their local economies and bore the fingerprints of the local chamber in their conception, execution, or both.

Fighting Back Against the Panic of 1893

The nation's booming economy came to a crashing halt in 1893 (in time to hurt the gate receipts of the Columbian Exposition but not to derail it entirely), when speculation and overbuilding contributed to the collapse of several railroads and other companies. A side effect of the upheaval was a run on the nation's gold supply. Investors feared that silver, which had been more in demand since the Sherman Silver Purchase Act of 1890, wasn't worth 1/16th of its weight in gold. The Act had required the U.S. government to step up its silver purchases.

In June the financial situation was critical, with money almost impossible to find and interest rates at a staggering 80 percent. Five bank presidents, all members of the New York Chamber of Commerce, formed a Clearing House Loan Committee that provided $41 million of loan certificates in order to provide liquidity (and confidence) to the market.[63]

Nonetheless, the situation was still unstable. The New York Chamber of Commerce advocated the repeal of the Sherman Silver Purchase Act of 1890, which, it was felt, inflated the value of silver and thereby cheapened gold.

The chamber lobbied hard for repeal of the Act. Chamber President Charles Smith proudly attributed the rapid passage of the repeal bill in the House to an almost unprecedented campaign. Copies of the chamber's resolutions in favor of the bill, and urging action to support it, were sent to 420 commercial associations and 4,430 bank and trust companies. Moreover, chamber members sent 30,000 letters to individuals and companies with the same message.[64] It took a bit longer to get the bill through the Senate, but ultimately the effort was successful.

These lobbying letters were sent to the South and West.[65] Politicians in the East backed the gold standard; it was the West (or at least Midwest) and South where the swing votes lay. The New York Chamber of Commerce was acting much as a national chamber would, reaching far beyond its city and state to promote a change affecting the entire United States.[66]

On banking and financial questions, New York needed the votes of the rest of the country. For a while the New York Chamber still might be able to lead the gold-standard battle virtually alone, but ultimately it would be better served to have representation from the places where it sought support. For national lobbying campaigns, a national chamber made the most sense. The gold-standard and related financial battles would continue for another couple of decades, until finally, and not by coincidence, a national banking system and a true national chamber would emerge at almost the same time.

Gold over Silver

Averting complete financial collapse in 1893 didn't end the nation's financial problems. The depression following the panic was severe and caused widespread unemployment and the failure of many businesses. Another run on the nation's gold supplies, more worrisome than the one in 1893, led to the intervention of J.P. Morgan (now a vice president of the New York Chamber of Commerce) in February 1895. Morgan personally met with President Grover Cleveland and promised to stanch the flow of precious metal out of the United States. He and his consortium succeeded.[67] Later, Cleveland praised the members of the New York Chamber for their efforts to "save the country from the havoc of financial madness."[68] Clearly, however, a financial system that required the personal intervention of a few private bankers to save the currency of their nation was far from stable.

The continuing crises and economic hard times had the effect of polarizing opinions on currency reform. Most of the chambers of commerce in the country stood with the New York Chamber on maintaining the gold standard. These groups, predominately Republican-leaning, viewed the silver heresy as undermining confidence in gold and perpetuating an environment of economic uncertainty and financial crisis. Lined up against them were those individuals, especially farmers and small business people in the South and West, who thought that the hard-money bankers of the East monopolized capital and starved the nation of its economic potential. This group, primarily Democratic-inclined, included many debtors who would benefit from the inflation that would likely result from the infusion of more silver into the nation's financial system.

The two points of view were personified in the candidates for the Presidential election of 1896: William McKinley, the hard-money Republican, and William Jennings Bryan, the free-silver Democrat. For the New York Chamber of Commerce's members especially, this was an election that they could ill afford to lose. In March 1895, the month after J.P. Morgan's intervention in the markets, the chamber set up a committee to begin a campaign for "sound money." This campaign preceded Bryan's nomination for President but coincided precisely with the popular demand for free silver and became an implicit attack on Bryan's candidacy.

The chamber's push for sound money was its most powerful lobbying move since its inception in 1768. The Committee for Sound Financial Legislation printed and distributed "more than sixty million pages of the best sound money literature," according to its chair, Henry Hentz. Even as the Los Angeles Chamber was overheating the printing presses promoting golden sunshine, the New York Chamber was pushing for golden currency. The New York leaflets were sent "singly to individual addresses," at great expense but guaranteed to reach individual voters. Moreover, 2.5 million people were reached each week through articles and commentary that the committee offered to newspapers. This phenomenal effort was "almost exclusively directed to the South and West."[69]

Here, as earlier in the decade, the New York Chamber of Commerce was acting much as a national chamber would. It reached far beyond Manhattan and Brooklyn – even far across Lake Erie and on the other side of the Mississippi. Without doubt, its members hoped to influence the Presidential election of 1896.

McKinley did win the election – the first Republican president to gain a majority of the popular vote in 24 years. But his margin was not especially dramatic – 600,000 votes (7.1 million to 6.5 million). Although the New York Chamber's effort didn't hurt McKinley's campaign, Mark Hanna, McKinley's campaign manager, is primarily credited with the win over Bryan. Hanna raised $3.5 million, five times the amount spent by the Democrats.[70] Of course, Hanna knew where his allies were. Indeed, he met with the chamber's "Sound Money Committee" on August 19, 1896, no doubt to coordinate final tactics of the two complementary campaigns.[71]

The win over the "Boy Orator of the Platte" was gratifying. Bryan could have been addressing the New York Chamber of Commerce when his Democratic nomination speech, the most famous in American political history, concluded:

> You shall not press down upon the brow of labor this crown of thorns, you shall not crucify mankind upon a cross of gold.

When he lost, the chamber members felt as if they had successfully dodged a silver bullet. Still, the victory might only be temporary. Bryan and his policies could be easily revived, and thus this was the moment to lock in sound money policies.

The New York Chamber of Commerce found an unexpected ally in the middle of the country: Hugh Hanna (no relation to Mark Hanna), an Indiana manufacturer. On November 18, 1896, just after McKinley's election, Hugh Hanna addressed the Indianapolis Board of Trade and suggested a group of chambers from the Midwest meet in order to chart out a course for sound monetary strategy in the future. Why from the Midwest? The *New York Tribune* summarized Hanna's reasoning as follows:

He said that since the Far West will not move in the direction desired, and such a movement instituted by the East would be met with the prejudices that pervade the West, it was left to the business men of the Central West to inaugurate a movement by which, he predicted, some desirable ends may be obtained.[72]

The bankers from the East would be thrilled at this valentine from the heartland. And the Midwesterners were barely getting started. The Indianapolis Board of Trade, heeding Hanna's call, asked for a meeting of Midwestern boards of trade, which occurred in Indianapolis on December 1. This group, in turn, recommended a national meeting in Indianapolis, representing boards of trade and chambers of commerce from every community in the nation with 8,000 or more people.[73]

That larger meeting took place, beginning on January 12, 1897. It involved 294 delegates from 28 states.[74] This was the biggest gathering of U.S. chamber leaders up to this time. (One of its indirect effects was to cast a troubling light on small size of the meetings of the National Board of Trade.) It is considered one of the seminal developments in the history of the U.S. monetary system.

The group came up with recommendations to stick to the gold standard, to gradually retire U.S. debt, and to begin to create a banking system that would reliably allocate capital through the United States at uniform rates of interest.[75] The last item essentially was a call for a national banking institution, one that eventually emerged in 1913 as the Federal Reserve Bank. A leader in the lobbying effort for the Federal Reserve also was active in these Indiana deliberations, J. Laurence Laughlin of the University of Chicago. Both monetary reform efforts, in 1897-88 and in 1912-13, would be spearheaded by Midwestern chambers and opinion leaders, not – at least on the face of it – by the bankers and the leading chamber of New York.

A subsequent Indianapolis monetary convention in January of 1898 successfully got Congress to take up these subjects. The ultimate result was legislation which, while falling short of establishing a national banking system, did uphold the supremacy of the gold standard. The nation by this time was less inclined to put its faith in silver; the depression following the Panic of 1893 had abated and soon Klondike gold was pouring into the coffers of the nation's banks and its government.

The leaders of the New York Chamber of Commerce, always anxious to show that their desired monetary reforms came from somewhere other than New York, were so appreciative of Hugh Hanna's efforts that they made him an honorary member in April of 1900. They also struck a medal in his honor. During the discussions of Hanna's contributions to the nation, he was compared not once, but twice to Alexander Hamilton himself.[76]

Hanna may have been no Hamilton, but he and the nation's chambers of commerce had helped set the nation's monetary system on a course that would continue far into the future. Moreover, their surprisingly effective joint action via the Indianapolis conventions indicated that these business organizations could do more together. Local chambers, when they cooperated effectively, could indeed have a national impact.

The Home Front

While addressing national issues from time to time, local chambers continued to do what they did best: looking after things much closer to home. Much like cleaning house, reforming corrupt municipal governments was a never-ending task. In this area, the New York Chamber had a bigger job than most.

Tammany Hall's corruption had reached embarrassingly high levels in the early 1890s. Finally, the New York Chamber of Commerce took action. It helped fund a study of police corruption and organized a Committee of Seventy to promote reform. This group launched a mayoral candidate, William L. Strong, who defeated the Tammany nominee, Hugh Grant, in November of 1894. Indeed, the Committee of Seventy's reform team, soon to include an energetic police commissioner named Theodore Roosevelt, virtually swept the election.[77] The cleanup of municipal government helped pave the way for other reforms, including the beginning of the New York subway system (spearheaded by the chamber) and the consolidation of the governments of New York City and Brooklyn (an idea that had been explored in the chamber and that was "decisively shaped" by New York's business elite[78]).

Encouraged by the New York example, no doubt, Philadelphia citizens created a reformist Committee of Ninety-Five at the beginning of 1895; one of its members was Frederick Fraley, the president of the National Board of Trade.[79] As far away as La Crosse, Wisconsin, the board of trade investigated the city's finances, although it was careful to state:

> From the first it should be plainly stated that no suspicion of personal venality has been suggested against any of the common council or the several departments; there is, however, a strong conviction of blunders and mismanagement by the operating departments, and if such conviction is warranted, should be located and remedied.[80]

Often the cleanup was literal. In Sacramento, the chamber, set up in 1895, almost immediately set out to find cleaner water for the city. In Spokane, the Chamber Secretary Storey Buck noted that there were claims that "meat has been sold in Spokane markets from cows that have died natural deaths" and indicated the chamber would look into recommending solutions to the problem of unsafe meat.[81]

Getting Around

While the nation's rail system was largely built, there was always more to do in order to move people and freight. In New York, there was an urgent need for better transportation to reach crowded downtown Manhattan. A growing consensus indicated that the only way to move people efficiently was to go underground. For this, trains needed to be electric; otherwise, the smoke of burning coal would asphyxiate passengers. London had such an underground train in 1890. New York's efforts, however, had stalled.

The attempt to create the subway was led by the New York Chamber's former president and the former mayor of New York, Abram Hewitt. His efforts were stymied until in 1894 the chamber took up the task and created a committee to tackle the work. The committee hatched a plan whereby the project would be financed with 3 percent interest rates provided to the city, versus the 6 percent available to private capital. As such, the project could be built inexpensively enough to pay for itself from fares.[82] Carefully keeping the effort out of the grasp of Tammany, the chamber had a commission created with eight members, six of whom were chamber members, including the chamber president.[83]

The plaque of the founding of the New York City subway, "Suggested by the New York Chamber of Commerce"

The project moved forward and became the basis of one of the world's largest subway systems. Although Tammany Hall tried to wrest control of the project from the chamber, in the early, formative years of the subway, it failed. The New York Chamber of Commerce was able to lay claim to one of its greatest achievements and to one of the leading urban transportation advances in the United States.

Other cities had their own transportation issues to tackle. For example, the Washington Board of Trade in the nation's capital had a Committee on Bridges with an aggressive agenda. In 1895, it was pushing for a "Memorial Bridge across the Potomac."[84]

The Los Angeles Chamber of Commerce showed at an early date what would become an obsession of the chamber and of southern California in general. Indeed, the chamber's records at the turn of the century reveal that the organization had been pushing for roads for 10 years, if not since its inception in 1888:

It [the chamber] has assisted the good roads movement by advocating every practicable form of legislation that has been proposed, by holding public meetings and by circulating literature on that topic. It is pleasing to note that in the past ten years a vast improvement has taken place in the condition of the highways in Los Angeles County.[85]

The Los Angeles Chamber's leaders knew nothing of Henry Ford – or of the "little old lady from Pasadena," or the flashy cars driven by rappers in the 21st century. Nonetheless in the 1890s they were busy preparing the way for what would become the world's best-known automobile-powered urban culture.

As we have seen, the chamber in Los Angeles also had pushed hard for a port, fighting with Southern Pacific and the U.S. Congress to get an outlet to the ocean. Much of the water at the target site, San Pedro, 20 miles south of Los Angeles, was only 18 inches deep. Groused Maine's Senator William Frye to the people of Los Angeles: "You have made a great mistake in the location of your city. You should have put it at some point where a harbor really exists, instead of calling on the U.S. Government to give you something which Nature has refused!"[86] Such words deflected off the LA Chamber like water off a dredge's back. One day the world's largest supertankers would float comfortably on what was once a foot and a half of water. For the Los Angeles Chamber, what existed was less important than what might exist someday with a little effort, and preferably with a sprinkling of federal funds.

Houston business and civic leaders, as we have seen, had a harbor fixation of much longer standing. They had been obsessed with a path to the sea since 1840. The Houston Chamber of Commerce in the 1840s and 50s, the Houston Board of Trade and Cotton Exchange in the 1870s, and Houston Business League in the 1890s and beyond, all took a hand in deepening or widening the Buffalo Bayou.

In 1895 an Army Corps of Engineers expert told Houston officials that the federal government wouldn't help dredge the Buffalo Bayou until the sewage there was cleaned up. The

Houston Business League thereupon lent its support to a successful effort for a $300,000 bond issue to take care of this problem.[87] But that was only one step.

In 1898 the Houston Business League's leaders, together with other Houstonians, appealed to Congress to lobby for a 25 foot deep ship channel. Congress appropriated only enough money to get to 17.5 feet.[88] Still, it was something and it moved Houston closer to the ideal watercourse.

Galvestonians mocked Houston's effort to have a world-class port. When Galveston merchant Sampson Heidenheimer lost six bargeloads of salt in the rain en route to Houston, the *Galveston News* cackled:

> Houston at last has a salt water port. God Almighty furnished the water; Heidenheimer furnished the salt![89]

As if on cue, a huge hurricane hit Galveston on September 8-9, 1900. The wind and waves flattened the city, which would never regain its primacy in Texas seaborne commerce. As many as 8,000 were killed. Houston clearly was a safer port, and it would be the main focus of future investment in port facilities in east Texas. The years of work, much of it chamber-led, on deepening the channel were going to pay off spectacularly.

Galveston after the hurricane

Exposition Fever

After the Columbian Exposition of 1893, many other communities attempted to hold impressive fairs, even if not quite on the scale of the great Midwestern city; most could not aspire to the status of a world's fair. Nevertheless some of these events drew hundreds of thousands or even millions of visitors. Often, chambers of commerce were involved. After all, what better way could there be to put one's city on the map?

The first great exposition after Chicago's was the Cotton States and International Exposition of 1895 in Atlanta. Even in a weak economy, the Atlanta Chamber of Commerce and Fulton County were able to raise $550,000 for this fair, which ultimately brought $2.5 million worth of spending to the area (versus an investment of $11 million and total spending of $27 million in Chicago).[90] In a community of only 100,000 people, the Atlanta achievement had a major impact on the city and state, and reinforced the "New South" visions of both Henry Grady (who had helped spearhead a smaller cotton exposition in 1881, in which the chamber had played a supporting role) and of the Atlanta Chamber of Commerce.

This kind of attention was hard to attract any other way. One source excitedly mentioned that clippings of 25,000 different newspaper articles about the exposition had been collected, and estimated that these were probably no more than a fifth of the total.[91] Although other cities in the region were larger (New Orleans, Louisville, and Memphis, not to mention the District of Columbia and Baltimore), Atlanta had proclaimed itself as a leader in the emerging economy of the awakening South.

Another great city championing the New South, Nashville, took up the torch next. Tennesseans had thought of having a celebration to commemorate the centennial of the founding of their state in 1796. The Nashville Chamber of Commerce, which resulted from the combination of the Commercial Club and the Board of Trade in 1894, took charge. On July 8, 1895, "after a stirring speech by chairman Tulley Brown," the chamber's members declared that Nashville should be the site of the celebration.[92] The event, which took place for six months in 1897, was considered a great success. President McKinley attended, and thanks to one attraction at the fair, to this day Nashville boasts its own Parthenon – a monument modeled after the original structure in Athens, Greece.

The Parthenon replica built for the Tennessee Centennial and International Exposition

Old meets new: electric lighting on the Parthenon and Pyramid, Tennessee Centennial and International Exposition, 1897

In 1895, Nebraska's silver-tongued favorite son, William Jennings Bryan, called for a Trans-Mississippi Exposition in his state in 1898. Soon afterward, a meeting at the Commercial Club of Omaha confirmed the interest of local citizens, and the club campaigned to bring meetings to the city during the fair. Many other civic groups and business people also were involved. A total of 2.6 million people attended, including – again - President McKinley. McKinley, indeed, to his ultimate peril, was a big fan of "civic patriotism" and of such fairs.

At a time when commemorative expositions were clearly popular, it's not surprising that people found the 100th anniversary of the Louisiana Purchase in 1803 to be a great opportunity for a show. St. Louis took the reins at an early date. David R. Francis, a former mayor of St. Louis, governor of Missouri, and secretary of the U.S. Department of the Interior, addressed the Business Men's League of St. Louis in 1896 with this suggestion: "St. Louis is the gateway of that great territory [Louisiana Purchase], and she should celebrate its centennial in 1901 by a great international exposition, second to none ever held in the world."[93]

Francis was wrong about the year, but right about the concept. And it was not a coincidence that the leading public man of Missouri brought the proposal to its leading civic group. The Business Men's League was the most active business organization in town, and ready for a challenge. It handled the early fundraising tasks quickly and well, paving the way for Francis to lead a successful effort to get Congress to appropriate funds for a large fair after the turn of the century – shortly after the smaller but still ambitious Pan-American Exposition scheduled for Buffalo in 1901.

Civic events didn't have to be giant fairs. They could be small parades or other events that showcased the particular culture of their areas. The Los Angeles Chamber of Commerce, among its many activities to promote Southern California, had contemplated the idea of some sort of festival:

Another project which was advanced in 1889, and debated at some length, was for an annual festival, somewhat resembling the Mardi Gras in New Orleans, but characteristic of the City of Los Angeles, and in keeping with the institutions and past history of Southern California. No definite plan was formulated and no effort made to carry out this project; but it is interesting to note that five years later it was put into execution in the Fiesta de Los Angeles, and the Rose Tournament of Pasadena, which continued for several seasons to give pleasure to our people and to attract thousands of visitors.[94]

While it's probably too generous to credit the Los Angeles Chamber of Commerce with having sparked two extremely popular festivals, there is no doubt that mercantile interests and associations, in general, had a hand in the development of both events. The Merchants' Association of Los Angeles, founded in 1893, created the Fiesta de Los Angeles on April 12, 1894, and it turned out to be a major success. The *Los Angeles Times* crowed:

> In place of looking to San Francisco for inspiration and example, it is time for the merchants to cut loose and start a new era of prosperity upon a broader plane. In the future the rotteness [*sic*] of San Francisco must shoulder her own responsibilities. Los Angeles is a new world formed with higher motives, broader principles, and greater ambitions. The Chicago of the West – the ambitious, prosperous city of the western Hemisphere.[95]

Los Angeles may or may not have had broader principles than San Francisco, but its weather made possible a great abundance of flowers. And it was ultimately a flower festival that would surpass even the popular Fiesta de Los Angeles and become perhaps the premier annual gathering in Southern California for a century to come. The Tournament of Roses was begun by the Valley Hunt Club, a high-toned social and sporting group, but it soon found the project too big to handle. The Pasadena Board of Trade (later the Chamber of Commerce) managed the event for a few years. Festival organizers then and in the future would discover that chambers of commerce had the staying power and often the where-withal to guide an event through its early (or later) struggles. Soon the event was passed over to a local citizens' group, the Pasadena Tournament of Roses Association.[96]

Even the recently Wild West was a good place for a festival. Cheyenne's economy was not doing well in 1897. Mayor William Schnitger determined something needed to be done and so he appointed key business people to the Cheyenne Board of Trade. A Union Pacific passenger suggested a fair. The Board of Trade and the community came up with Frontier Day, an event on September 23 that included a mock stagecoach holdup, steer roping, a wild horse race, and bronco riding. Attendance was about 4,000, including 1,500 coming in on the train.[97] It was a remarkable success and became an annual event. The chamber continued to support it, directly and indirectly, over the years. Today, the festival attracts about 500,000 people per year and is known as the "Daddy of 'em All," the original rodeo and Western festival that inspired so many others.

Gold Strike in the Klondike

It was in August, 1896, that either Kate Carmack or Skookum Jim found some yellow particles in a creek off the Yukon River in Canada, near Alaska. The timing was ironic; only a month before, William Jennings Bryan had given his "Cross of Gold" speech at the Democratic National Convention. People were soon heading into banks in Seattle, Portland, and San Francisco and coming out with gold-backed currency. The rush was on.

People were hurrying to a very cold place. Indeed, by early November of 1897, the Yukon River had frozen, restricting the food shipments to the prospectors. President W.S. Mason of the Portland Chamber of Commerce sent a telegram to Secretary of War Russell Alger offering to donate provisions and supplies to the miners – if the War Department would only get the items to the miners before the "ice fetters" of the Yukon loosened in the spring.[98] The following month, Mason telegraphed Senator McBride that Portland citizens had donated at least 100 tons of food.[99]

On December 16, Congress appropriated $175,000 for a relief expedition. The city, and indeed the country, was abuzz with questions on how best to help the miners. The Spokane Chamber of Commerce stepped in, dispatching to Washington, D.C. an "energetic newspaper man," Frederic Marvin. This gentleman urged the War Department to consider sending the relief column through an old telegraph route that passed through Spokane. This was the best way to reach the miners, Marvin urged.[100] But it turned out that the Washington, D.C., bureaucracy moved at glacier speed. The War Department determined that reindeer would be needed to reach the goldfields, so Secretary Alger ordered them from Norway. This, of course, took time.

By March 1, these creatures were set for a high-speed train trip across the country to Seattle. It was quite an assemblage of Scandinavian life: not only 529 reindeer (20 to 25 per railcar), but also 113 Norwegian, Finn, and Lapp attendants and their families. "The trip is intended to be made with no more than the ordinary stoppages of a first-class train, but more stops may have to be made if the reindeer prove to be poor travelers," noted a reporter.[101]

In early March, however, the Secretary of War called off the relief shipment, saying the miners had enough food. Moreover, by the time the reindeer would have reached the goldfields, it would be nearly springtime anyway. Certainly the hardships of the miners had been real, and some had starved.

Those who supplied the Klondike miners did well. It's not surprising, then, that in 1898, Juneau, Alaska, was a flourishing town, with 3,000 inhabitants and a chamber of commerce. Indeed, L.G. Kaufman, the secretary of the Chamber of Commerce of Juneau, Alaska, also apparently known as the Alaska Chamber of Commerce, wrote a detailed report about his community for the U.S. Department of Labor. His glowing but painstakingly fact-filled report even numbered the various businesses in town. By far the leading establishment was "saloons" (30), followed by "attorneys at law" (18), and then, not surprisingly, "general merchandise and Yukon outfitters" (12).

Kaufman finished his report with both a bright look at his city's opportunities and a delicately veiled criticism of the famous hardships and distribution challenges just faced by the Yukon district. Juneau had no need of reindeer relief, as his final sentence implied:

> The chief virtue of prospecting on the coast of southeastern Alaska is the ability to keep in constant communication with a distributing point for supplies and the general evenness of the climate, which is not nearly as severe as the great majority of mining settlements throughout the world.[102]

There's No Place Like Nome

One place in Alaska was well known for its low temperatures: Nome, on the west coast, not far south of the Arctic Circle, was frigid and remote. This town got its first log cabin in 1898; two years later, it had as many as 20,000 people, thanks to the gold rush. A chamber of commerce emerged in the forest of stakes and shovels and, on June 24, 1900, requested that Brigadier General George Randall provide law and order until the United States District Court could establish itself. The general obliged the following day, although it took only a month until Judge Arthur H. Noyes arrived, and the town was officially incorporated in November.[103]

The Nome Chamber's work was far from done. In late January of 1901, a crisis hit:

A story that rivals the horrors of the Black Hole of Calcutta was told at the Chamber of Commerce meeting Monday night – sixteen men and a woman huddled together in a maimed and mutilated condition from frost-bite, in Slishkovich's cabin on Pilgrim River, unable to lie down because of the crush, and with the added horror of starvation facing them.[104]

The chamber dispatched help, although it turned out that the situation, while severe, wasn't as dire as originally reported. But the community was so remote and so cold that it courted trouble every winter. It was Nome that, in 1925, faced a diphtheria epidemic that spurred a race of dogsleds to bring serum to town. (That rescue effort, in turn, inspired the famous Iditarod race that still involves chambers today.) When Charlie Chaplin sat down with a knife and fork in the silent comedy *The Gold Rush* (1925), preparing to devour a boot, he was not departing far into fiction.

Far to the south of Nome, Juneau, and other Alaskan communities, a chamber of commerce determined on a plan. The Los Angeles Chamber of Commerce sent 10,000 copies of a promotional brochure to the mining districts of the Yukon. The Los Angeles Chamber knew exactly what it was doing: "emphasizing the advantages of the Southern California climate in a place where they would be most keenly felt."[105] No doubt there were some weary prospectors who decided to trade their gold nuggets for golden sunshine, their dreams of untold wealth for visions of oranges, walnuts, and roses.

An American Idea

The New York Chamber of Commerce had played a critical role in 1795 in keeping the United States out of war with Great Britain. The chamber had supported the Jay Treaty at a time when it appeared on the way to defeat. A century later, in 1895, the chamber took out its cudgels once again and fought for peace.

Great Britain had opposed Venezuela in the South American country's territorial dispute with British Guiana. President Grover Cleveland took a hard line, considering British meddling in this dispute as a violation of the Monroe Doctrine of 1823. That doctrine called for European powers not to colonize the New World and to stay out of land disputes.

In a speech delivered to Congress on December 17, 1895, President Cleveland decried Britain's seeming rejection of the authority of the Monroe Doctrine and declared the United States must "resist, by every means in its power" British encroachments on Venezuelan territory. He was prepared for war:

In making these recommendations, I am fully alive to the responsibility incurred, and keenly realize all the consequences that may follow.

In concluding, the President thundered with indignation:

> There is no calamity which a great nation can invite which equals that which follows a supine submission to wrong and injustice and the consequent loss of national self-respect and honor, beneath which are shielded and defended a people's safety and greatness.[106]

The markets fell on the news, and Americans, including members of the New York Chamber of Commerce, were surprised at the bellicose remarks.

People on both sides of the Atlantic feared that the two great powers would fight over territory that neither of them particularly cared about. In this period of jingoism, many saw national honor to be at stake. It was almost as if the United States were looking for a country to fight.

The New York Chamber of Commerce almost immediately called a meeting to consider the options. Even to summon a meeting on this topic appeared to be an attempt to second-guess the President. Some considered this semi-treasonous, given that we were dealing with a foreign power.

An editorialist at *The New York Times*, a paper that ordinarily supported the chamber, took strong exception to the clearly independent outlook of the merchants' organization:

> If the Chamber of Commerce may review the action of the President and of Congress, already taken in the House and assured in the Senate, in respect to a declaration of national policy, where shall we fix the limit of its powers of review and dissent? Must the General of the army in the field – if we ever do have a war, which may God forbid – issue his orders subject to the approval of the Chamber of Commerce of the city of New-York? Will the Chamber attend our fleets and countermand the orders of our Admirals?[107]

Watch out for such "patriots of the ticker," the editorialist warned.[108]

Irish World, an Irish-American newspaper, later looked back on the New York Chamber's call for arbitration and thundered that the action gave "such aid and comfort to England as was possible to give under the circumstances" and showed the organization's "traitorous spirit."[109]

The chamber was not dissuaded. On January 2, 1896, it approved resolutions calling for the nation to consider the advantages of arbitration to solve international problems such as this one. It again faced opposition – but time was now on its side. With a chance to reflect, fewer people saw the need to rush into hostilities. Moreover, there were other lands – Hawaii and Cuba, for example – competing for the nation's attention.

Some U.S. chambers, and many British ones, registered their assent to the pacific stance of the New York Chamber of Commerce. But the significant break came when Congress proposed arbitration as a good idea. Parliament then jumped in wholeheartedly, with the ex-Prime Minister William Gladstone lauding the U.S. initiative. New York Chamber member Charles E. Smith was in Britain at the time. A member of Parliament turned to him and said, "The American idea has conquered."[110]

The appeal to arbitration, however, was an idea of unclear origin. The London Chamber of Commerce also had a role in this high-stakes drama. The London Chamber was fully established in 1881 and was a robust and vigorous organization. Its initiatives in commercial education would influence many chambers across the Atlantic and around the world. Moreover, its members took the unusual step in May 1899 of inviting their New York counterparts to dinner in recognition of the excellent relations between their two chambers and governments.[111]

The London visit, originally intended for 1900, took place in June of 1901. The delegation of 38 New York Chamber members, including their president, Morris K. Jesup, even met with the King and Queen, despite the fact that the court was still in mourning for Queen Victoria, who had died on January 22.[112] The VIP treatment continued with a magnificent dinner, with 300 guests including U.S. Ambassador Joseph Choate, on June 5.

At that dinner, Lord Brassey, president of the London Chamber, offered a toast to the New York Chamber. His remarks included this revealing comment:

> When difficulties had arisen in relation to Venezuela, the London Chamber of Commerce appealed to the New York Chamber to use their good offices in the cause of a peaceful solution. They responded to the call. We desired to mark our deep sense of the service rendered. It has brought us together this evening.[113]

The elaborate dinner for the New York Chamber's members was, apparently, a gracious thank-you for the Americans' work on averting war over Venezuela.[114] Now that the tensions had passed, and the Anglo-American friendship was at a high point, it was safe to mention in a passing toast that the New York Chamber's bold peacemaking move had not been an American idea after all.[115]

Two Men, One Idea

In the growing prosperity and ebullient optimism of the period leading up to the turn of the century, one group stood out with fewer opportunities and more restrictions than it had experienced a quarter century before: Black Americans. Southern governments had severely limited black voting rights and set out to reduce the contact between the races. Lynchings were a continuing outrage that ripped the legal and social fabric of the region. The violence also dissuaded northern investors from moving to the South. Race relations, however, were not a great deal better in the North, where, although African Americans had more legal rights, they also faced prejudice.

W.E.B. Du Bois

W.E.B. Du Bois, born in Massachusetts, was the first African American to obtain a Ph.D. degree from Harvard University. He was impatient with the low status of blacks in the United States, North and South. In 1899, while teaching at the all-black Atlanta University, he organized a conference called "The Negro in Business." This two-day event, on May 30 and 31, featured the results of a study he had led on the nature of black enterprise in the South, complete with statistics and classifications of the kinds of work performed by these businesses.[116]

Du Bois, like many of his contemporaries, envisioned blacks coming together for mutual betterment. If white society wasn't being fully cooperative, blacks could create prosperity on their own. The conference's resolutions urged "Negro Business Men's Leagues . . . in every town and hamlet."[117]

Here was an extraordinary endorsement of the idea of chambers of commerce. If the concept worked for white men, why shouldn't it work for black men? Du Bois seized on the hot chamber name of the time, the Business Men's League, as the moniker for his group.

Du Bois pursued the idea somewhat. Later in 1899 he was made the director of a bureau on business by the Afro American Council.[118] But Du Bois was more interested in ideas, and in finding a way to empower his people, than in the specifics of business organizations.

Another African American leader, Booker T. Washington, quickly took hold of the concept. Washington was something of an apologist for segregation, and believed in blacks

concentrating on achievement in business and education before tackling the thorny issues of interracial politics. Washington had built up a small empire around his Tuskegee Institute and associated enterprises. As the best-known black leader of the time, he had the contacts and the name recognition to make a success of Du Bois's suggestion. Without crediting Du Bois – and attracting plenty of criticism for appropriating the younger man's idea – Washington pursued the concept on his own.[119]

Booker T. Washington became the founding president of the National Negro Business League, which held its first meeting in Boston on August 23-24, 1900. About 300 delegates were there. He saw this organization as showcasing the kinds of people who would serve as inspirations to all African Americans:

Booker T. Washington

> This meeting will prove a great encouragement to our people in all parts of the country, bringing together, as it does, the men and women of our race who have been most successful in life. The most humble black boy will be made to feel what you have done he can do also.[120]

The organization, including many local chambers that functioned more or less as chapters of the national group, would grow significantly in the years before the First World War.

Taking Stock: Chambers at the End of the Century

In June of 1900, the New York Chamber of Commerce expanded its membership rolls to 1,500, after earlier in the decade raising the number from 1,000 to 1,250. It had just finished raising $1 million for its own building and had received an invitation to visit the London Chamber of Commerce. Since just 1893, the chamber and its members had accomplished several major tasks, any one of which would have been among the top achievements of any other business organization in the country: leading the fight against free silver; stopping the outflow of gold to Europe; toppling Tammany Hall's leaders and replacing them with reform candidates; initiating the New York subway system; promoting the consolidation of Manhattan, Brooklyn, and other areas into a greater New York City; and successfully calling for arbitration in the dispute with Great Britain over Venezuela.

Yet even in New York, this chamber was not alone. The city (including Brooklyn, with which New York City amalgamated in 1898) had many trade associations and several boards of trade by the century's end. There were local groups, such as the East Chester Board of Trade, the North Side Board of Trade, the Harlem Chamber of Commerce, the Staten Island Chamber of Commerce, and the Grand Street Board of Trade. There were transnational groups: the Italian Chamber of Commerce (founded in 1887 with help from the Italian government, but catering extensively to Italian-born merchants in New York; a similar group was set up the same year in San Francisco[121]) and the Spanish Chamber of Commerce.[122] Booker T. Washington would soon have a Negro Business League there.

And there were broad-based groups that had some aspirations to the kind of status that the New York Chamber enjoyed. One was the New York Board of Trade and Transportation, which remained active. A new organization emerged in 1897, moreover: the Merchants' Association of New York, which actually was broader based than its name implied, and one day would far surpass the New York Chamber in membership and range of activities.

Thus the Tocquevillian urge to associate and organize was alive and well among business people in New York City in 1900. It was also alive and well in the rest of the country. One state alone, Montana, which had a population of just 243,000 in 1900, boasted 17 commercial organizations.[123]

Chambers were finding their way into just about every American community of note. As Chauncey Depew told the Detroit Chamber regarding chambers of commerce and boards of trade:

> It is but a few years since they existed only in the large cities. Now they have been created in every village of more than a thousand inhabitants.[124]

Depew, the New York Chamber member and former U.S. senator for New York, was speaking in 1895. This was a time in which a new vigor seemed to animate business organizations, with business men's leagues and similar groups coming to such communities as St. Louis, Sacramento, Birmingham, Atlanta, and Houston. The country's wealth and population were swelling and business people wanted their towns and cities to keep pace.

After Colonel Price's untimely death in 1892 at age 48, it was Edward A. Moseley of the Interstate Commerce Commission who let his contemporaries know just how many commercial groups there were in the country. Not including granges (agricultural groups) or railway associations, his compilations in the mid- and late 1890s showed around 2,000 business organizations in the country, most of them local chambers of commerce, boards of trade, or commercial clubs.

This was, to many Americans at the time, an amazing statistic. As New York Chamber of Commerce President Alexander Orr noted, the number of U.S. business organizations had grown from just four in 1800 to 2,000 in 1900, a 500-fold increase. "What they have accomplished for the people of this country is simply incalculable," he wrote. He gave them credit for the phenomenal rise of the American economy over the 19th century.[125]

Yet in this era of proliferating and growing business organizations, some things had not kept pace. The National Board of Trade only had about 40 members and was a pale reflection of the civic energy all around it. In 1900 it was still headed by Frederick Fraley of

Philadelphia, who had been born in 1804, during Thomas Jefferson's first term as President.

With the NBoT as weak as ever, the country still had no truly national chamber of commerce. And although many, if not most, of the greatest deeds of the New York Chamber were behind it, countless local chambers were barely getting started. These new chambers' greatest achievements – and mistakes – would occur in the years to come.

A New Energy

President William McKinley was shot on September 6, 1901, at an international-al exposition of the kind he enjoyed and that were so often popularized and patronized by chambers of commerce. During the Pan-American Exposition in Buffalo, anarchist Leon Czolgosz approached the President, covering his pistol under a handkerchief, and fired two shots. Eight days later, the President died.

Chambers of commerce, of course, condemned the murder of the President. He was a kindred spirit to many local leaders. McKinley had been a proponent of the civic patriotism popular among business organizations of the time. And he was seen by most as a friend of business.

His successor Theodore Roosevelt, by contrast, was quick to criticize business trusts and to regulate corporate activities he deemed a threat to society and to fairness. Yet Roosevelt had something in common with chambers. He appreciated their role in bringing out the best in business people and in restraining the impulse for single-minded pursuit of wealth at any cost to the community.[1]

Indeed, Roosevelt, whose father had been a member of the New York Chamber of Commerce, thought well of that organization. This was despite the fact that its members includ-ed such trust builders as J.P. Morgan, John D. Rockefeller, and Andrew Carnegie. At the chamber's banquet on November 11, 1902, the President said:

> There are very different kinds of success. There is the kind of success that brings with it the seared soul – the success which is achieved by wolfish greed and vulpine cunning – the success which makes honest men uneasy or indignant in its presence. Then there is the other kind of success – the success which comes as the reward of keen insight, of sagacity, of resolution, of address, combined with unflinching rectitude of behavior, public and private. The first kind of success may, in a sense – and a poor sense at that – benefit the individual, but it is always and necessarily a curse to the community; whereas the man who wins the second kind, as an incident of its winning, becomes a beneficiary to the whole commonwealth. Throughout its history the Chamber of Commerce has stood for this second and higher kind of success.[2]

The Department of Commerce and Labor

One important way to strengthen chambers, and businesses in general, would be to have their interests represented better in the federal bureaucracy. Having a special federal department devoted to business was not a new idea. Chambers of commerce longed to have a place in the government where their concerns could be aired and where trade statistics and other useful commercial information could be gathered. Indeed, the concept for such a department had been brought up consistently by the National Board of Trade ever since its founding in 1868, and even at the initial Detroit meeting where the NBoT was conceived in 1865.

But the NBoT advocated many things, most of which never came to pass. Starting a new federal department was a major undertaking that required widespread support. Senator William Frye of Maine began introducing bills to start such a department as early as 1891, but he, too, did not make much headway in the early years.

Something changed after the turn of the century. The New York Chamber of Commerce, which had a solid batting average on the issues it chose to address, took up the cause of the new department. Shortly thereafter, perhaps unsurprisingly, the department came to be – with the chamber's friend and admirer, Teddy Roosevelt, endorsing the concept.

The New York Chamber first entertained the idea in a meeting on January 3, 1901. John A. Kasson, the special commissioner plenipotentiary of the United States, addressed the group with his support for such a bureau. Kasson had been negotiating various reciprocity and other trade agreements and acutely felt the need for more input from business people. He said everyone was hurt by the lack of a place for merchants to share their insights with federal officials:

> This divorce, this want of relationship, of mutual influence, of cooperation between the men who have the knowledge and the Government which has the responsibility of legislative action, is a positive public misfortune, a source of error and incompleteness in framing both laws and treaties, so far as these affect business interests.[3]

Kasson noted that the Senate Commerce Committee's chair, William Frye, was in charge of a bill to create such a department. But the new federal organization, if it were created, would be only half the solution to the problem of a lack of communication. The other half involved creating an organization of chambers that could communicate effectively with the government. Kasson had found that the dozen chambers he had attempted to work with had been unable to provide the kinds of basic information he needed. He recommended that there should be some sort of national grouping of the chambers, with a paid secretary in Washington, to collect the information and opinions required by the federal government.[4]

Kasson thus sketched an outline of two mirror organizations, one of business, the other of government, aimed at furthering the national economy. His vision was not too far from what ultimately occurred: the creation of a Department of Commerce and of the U.S. Chamber. But there was work to be done to make the vision real.

The New York Chamber had a clear interest in furthering Kasson's hopes for a new federal department. (The U.S. Chamber idea, for an organization that might someday overshadow the New York Chamber, was less appealing, at least for now.) The New York Chamber supported increased trade and its members felt, like Kasson, that a Washington-based bureau would facilitate the kinds of reciprocity agreements and other pacts that Kasson was attempting to negotiate. In November of 1901, the chamber issued a unanimous resolution in favor of the concept and announced it would send the document to President Roosevelt, members of Congress, and chambers of commerce and boards of trade all across the nation, requesting their cooperation in securing passage of the legislation.[5]

When the New York Chamber spoke, other chambers listened. By December, the San Francisco Chamber had received its copy. The northern California chamber's board determined, on January 9, 1902, that the New York Chamber's resolution should be "reiterated." The San Franciscans distributed copies to the California delegation in Washington, urging those members of Congress to support such legislation.[6]

The National Board of Trade had continued to lobby for similar legislation, with a major push beginning in March 1901, although its efforts were probably less significant than those of the New York Chamber. At the same annual meeting (in January of 1902) at which the NBoT discussed its efforts to create the department, it held forth on the St. Louis Merchants Exchange's suggestion that the NBoT be dissolved after the meeting because it was weak and ineffective.[7] The organization's members decided to keep the NBoT alive, although it continued to dodder along with a good deal less influence than that of the great chamber in lower Manhattan.

What gave the strongest impetus to the creation of the new department was a word from President Roosevelt. He told Congress that such a department was needed, saying that wage earners needed a system of support just as farmers did. The new Secretary of Commerce and Industries should "deal with commerce in the broadest sense; including among many other things whatever concerns labor and all matters affecting the great business corporations and our merchant marine."[8]

Roosevelt's address had a strong, positive effect on the push for the department. Indeed, it may have been the most timely and effective plea by a President "in the whole history of the growth of Executive Departments," according to a contemporary expert.[9] Interestingly, and probably not coincidentally, this plea occurred on December 3, 1901, less than a month after the New York Chamber's resolution and its transmission to the President. Congress approved the new federal bureau, called the Department of Commerce and Labor, and in February of 1903 it began operating.

A Variety of Chambers

Chambers were continuing to proliferate, although many of them lacked the sophistication of the New York Chamber, the Philadelphia Board of Trade, or the Los Angeles Chamber. For example, in August of 1902 a group from the South Baltimore Business Men's Association, while on an outing in Ocean City, got into a brawl in a bar. One of the delegation jumped on another man's back and the fighting commenced. John Kelly from Baltimore, attempting to make peace, was bitten on the ear.[10]

The more decorous East Baltimore Business Men's Association had a sumptuous annual dinner earlier in 1902. Its menu featured an interesting concoction of misspelled French with English trimmings: "Filet de Bouff aux Mushrooms." But no one went home unsatisfied. The menu concluded with: "Fruit. Ice Cream. Assorted Cake. Wine. Cigars. Beer." And the 150 guests were treated to a full recital of the organization's achievements during the year.[11]

The venerable Cincinnati Chamber of Commerce handled matters large and small. It criticized the enforcement of a new state law "containing certain restrictions in the trade in Skunk Skins, considered prejudicial to the fur trade of the State, and specially injurious to our local trade in such skins."[12] On January 15, 1901, the chamber entertained, on the floor of "'Change" (the Merchants' Exchange), the dashing young war correspondent, Member of Parliament, and Boer War veteran, Winston Churchill.[13] On May 5 of the following year, 'Change was visited by a Boer, H.D. Viljoen, who was touring the country to promote the cause of the losing side in the troubling South African war.[14]

Rails, Roads, and Lakes

Transportation remained a focus of chambers of commerce in the early 20th century, as it had been since their earliest days. With the nation's railroad network more or less mature, chambers focused more on freight discrimination issues, siting and improvement of train stations, and urban rail issues. But interesting new problems did come up. In October of 1903, the Connecticut State Board of Trade, supplementing its other program topics such as "The Tramp Problem," included a meeting session on "The Control of Horseless Carriages in Our Highways and Streets."[15]

Deepening rivers and harbors was a continuing chamber concern as well. Here, too, there was a unique issue that captured many chambers' attention. Chicago had a 28-mile Sanitary Canal, a bold reversal of the course of the Illinois River, that diverted city's sewage from the static Lake Michigan into the moving waters of the Mississippi River system. What if that Sanitary Canal were deepened and widened into a great ship canal, one that would allow ships on the Great Lakes to sail all the way down to the Gulf of Mexico?

This was a grand idea, one that added sparkle to a whole constellation of cities in the nation's midsection. The project would break the aggravating monopoly of the Erie Canal (and hence New York City) on the commerce of the lakes. Places such as St. Louis, Chicago, and New Orleans would instantly be granted new wealth and prestige. At a time when the whole world looked forward with interest to the building of a canal across Central America to link the Atlantic and the Pacific, why not also think big and bring the Great Lakes to the great southern gulf?

This idea kept coming up. It caused a fracas at the January 1904 meeting of the National Board of Trade, when George Anderson of the Pittsburgh Chamber of Commerce erupted at the delegates' desire to end discussion of the project. He said this might lead to the end of the NBoT. "We came here for work and not child's play," he said. "Do it [end the discussion] if you dare."[16] The group attempted to compromise but would not endorse the deepened canal. One of the key points was uncertainty about its costs. As James Carter of the Boston Merchants' Association said, "I do not see how we can vote intelligently upon this without knowing whether this is a $10,000,000 proposition or a $200,000,000 proposition."[17]

While the idea persisted for several years, and resulted in the founding of the Lakes-to-the-Gulf Deep Waterways Association in St. Louis in 1906, it faced a basic problem other than simply cost. It was that the deepening of the Sanitary Canal could drain the Great Lakes like a giant bathtub. The Milwaukee Chamber of Commerce later quoted a report indicating that water flow of 20,000 cubic feet per second would lower the level of Lake Erie by 11 inches and Lake Huron and Lake Michigan by 13 inches.[18] This reduced water level, among other things, would require additional dredging of harbors all through the Great Lakes just to reach their former depth. Ultimately a compromise solution was found, but not for several more decades.

The Intracoastal Waterway

There was, however, another canal project that began its sinuous course toward reality. In 1905, the long dreamed of Intracoastal Waterway from Texas to Florida became the focus of the Victoria Business Men's Association and other chambers in Texas and Louisiana. A waterway system, just inside the coast, would shield cargo from Gulf storms and permit barges and other low-draft vessels to move bulk goods cheaply.

Roy Miller was an important ingredient to the success of the early intracoastal canal efforts. An agent for the St. Louis, Brownsville & Mexico Railroad, he knew of farmers' frustration at seeing their crops spoil while waiting for transportation to Houston or Galveston. The city where he was based, Corpus Christi, needed a deep-water port, he believed. To agitate for the port and for better transportation, he revived the Corpus Christi Commercial Club. While nearby cities coveted the same deep-water amenity, Corpus Christi eventually won out, in large part due to Miller's obsession with the issue.[19]

Miller also saw the need for an intracoastal canal to move freight in and out of Corpus Christi. He may have been alerted to the idea by its early champion, C.S.E. Holland, the president of the Victoria Business Men's Association. The meeting they called in Victoria in the summer of 1905 set in motion many like-minded people on the path to the "ocean lite" method of transportation. The group formed the Interstate Inland Waterway League, which ultimately became the Gulf Intracoastal Canal Association. Holland was elected president of the new league.[20]

"Without the association, there might never have been a canal," a historian of the canal has written. "From camping on the doorstep of the nation's Capitol to prodding sluggish county governments, encouraging the donation of necessary rights-of-way and the rebuilding of bridges, this organization served as the leading proponent of the GIWW [Gulf Intracoastal Waterway]."[21] The project, made up of a thousand sub-projects, has been called the "1,000 mile miracle."[22] It took decades to complete, but – aided by World War II, which created a demand for torpedo-free transportation – it was finally finished in 1949 from Brownsville, Texas to Apalachee Bay, Florida.[23] No doubt the miracle was aided by Miller's magic; he would become one of the most powerful lobbyists in Texas, working with a myriad of politicians, including an ambitious young man from the Texas Hill Country, Lyndon Baines Johnson.[24]

The Panama Canal

The Panama Canal was the greatest engineering feat of its time. Ferdinand de Lesseps had tried to make a go of such a canal in the 1880s but failed because of disease that killed more than 20,000 workers and engineering challenges that were beyond the technological capabilities of the period. But anyone who looked at a map could see what the New York and Philadelphia chambers had argued in 1827 – that some form of expedited passage across the narrow Isthmus of Panama would save shippers a great deal of money and time.

After the French paused in their struggle, the Americans, strengthened by a sense of imperial and hemispheric destiny, picked it up. Chambers of commerce, as was inevitable in an infrastructure undertaking of this magnitude, were involved in too many ways to count. A project such as this would bring untold riches to the cities that could host the ships going to and from the canal area.

In 1892 there had two been major conventions on an Isthmian Canal, one in St. Louis and the other in New Orleans, which build up excitement for a renewed attempt at a canal. The New Orleans Board of Trade had organized the meeting in its city at the suggestion of Colonel T.T. Wright, a Henry Grady-like New South enthusiast from Nashville. More than 600 people attended the event on November 30, 1892, including a "liberal delegation" from the New York Chamber and 31 from the San Francisco Chamber.[25] The New Orleans BoT would later claim that this was the seminal event in the revival of American interest in a Panama Canal.[26] While the Panic of 1893, along with the exposure of French attempts to bribe members of Congress, had doused these fires of interest, they continued to smoulder.

Technological and political developments made the great canal project more feasible by the turn of the century. One of the key figures to champion the canal, and the man who would tip off the Americans to the possibility of fomenting a revolt in the Colombian province of Panama, was a Frenchman named Philippe Bunau-Varilla. Bunau-Varilla had been involved in de Lesseps's original canal-building effort and in a failed revival attempt. Now he would throw his lot in firmly with the United States.

During the summer of 1900, while Bunau-Varilla was dining alone in a nearly empty restaurant in Paris, someone from the only other occupied table asked him to join the men there. There were three businessmen from Cincinnati, including Harley Thomas Procter of Procter & Gamble.[27] When Bunau-Varilla told them of his thoughts on a canal through Panama rather than through Nicaragua, they were surprised to hear the information. In December he received an invitation to speak at the Commercial Club of Cincinnati.[28]

The next month Bunau-Varilla arrived in New York, where Procter met him and together they travelled to Cincinnati. The Frenchman gave his first speech in English on the Panama question at the Commercial Club on January 16, 1901. It was a smash hit – he converted the crowd from skepticism to enthusiasm. Other speaking invitations soon followed.[29]

One meeting seemed particularly effective. He wrote of this April speaking engagement:

> The event that had the widest echo during this rapid and decisive struggle [Panama vs. Nicaraguan route] had certainly been my lecture before the New York Chamber of Commerce. The unrivalled authority of that assembly, which counts among its members the most powerful men in the United States, had enhanced the authority of my thesis and multiplied its echo a hundred-fold.[30]

Soon, urged on by the big-project and big-stick enthusiast President Roosevelt himself, the United States government proceeded to grapple with the Panama project (as opposed to the Nicaragua route), beginning the major work in 1907 and concluding in 1914. There would continue to be many connections of chambers to this project. The Army engineer who made a success of it, General George Goethals, would become involved with the New York Chamber in many capacities afterward, while his right-hand man and canal publicist, Joseph Bucklin Bishop, would write a glowing but interesting history of that chamber in 1918. And two California chambers would promote major fairs to celebrate the great mid-hemispheric lock and rock project. While the Erie Canal's completion in 1825 occurred in a relative vacuum of chamber leadership, the Panama Canal was built when chambers were energetic and nearly omnipresent. This time around, business organizations were dying to be a part of the big dig of their era.

Building the Local Economy

Chambers everywhere were looking for new businesses to come to town. The Fort Worth Board of Trade had settled on its niche in the 1890s – meat-packing and the cattle industry – having brought a meat packer to Fort Worth and sponsoring, beginning in 1896, the Southwestern Exposition and Fat Stock Show.[31] The BoT engineered a major coup in the summer of 1901, helping raise $100,000 in cash incentives to bring two huge meat packers to the community: Armour & Co. and Swift & Co.[32] The new arrivals helped generate a massive construction boom – a 230 percent increase from 1904 to 1909, according to the city, far outpacing Dallas's 47 percent and San Antonio's 45 percent construction increases.[33] Ironically, it was in Fort Worth in 1909 that a group of chamber secretaries condemned the practice of paying cash bonuses to industrial promoters and wishing that "means could be found to run them out of the state."[34] Yet at least in the Swift-Armour case, the money wasn't a bad deal for the community.

In fact, paying cash bonuses to attract firms was endemic. It was a natural outgrowth of chambers' and boards of trades' earlier attempts to lure railroads with financial incentives. Even in small communities, the cash register opened. For example, in a town of 3,000 people in the Great Lakes region (called "Blankton" by the author of a Ph.D. thesis on it), a group of business people formed a board of trade in 1906 and set about trolling for companies. They quickly secured four out of 10 they had considered. The board's key weapon was a $20,000 war chest for improvements and cash bonuses, which the group had persuaded the town's citizens to raise from taxes, by a vote of 387 to 57.[35]

Everywhere, chambers wanted more factories. The Business Men's League in Clarksville, Tennessee, reorganized as the Clarksville Chamber of Commerce in 1905, complete with a new motto: "More Smokestacks & Whistles." It soon began its attempt to recruit new industry to town.[36]

Recruiting was handled not only by chambers of commerce but by relatively new organizations specializing in business attraction. The Gettysburg Development Company was formed in October 1899, even before the Business Men's League was created the following June.[37] In Cincinnati, the venerable chamber supported the creation of the Cincinnati Industrial Bureau in late 1900.[38]

In tourism, also, new organizations emerged that were partly separate from the local chamber. We have already seen how the Commercial Club of Indianapolis pioneered the idea of a permanent convention and visitor attraction activity after its Grand Army of the Republic success in 1893. In Honolulu, the chamber set up and administered the Joint Tourist Committee, aided by government funds, in 1903.[39] The Denver Chamber set up a new organization in 1904, the Denver Convention League, to attract meetings. It succeeded, signing up 42 conventions in its first year.[40]

Not only factories and conventioneers, but schools, colleges, and universities were fair game for the boosters of the era. In 1903, a group of Kalamazoo merchants founded The Press Club to lobby for Western State Normal School to come to their community. They succeeded.[41] The name of The Press Club became the Kalamazoo Chamber of Commerce, and the school evolved into Western Michigan University, which today has about 30,000 students.

Similarly, in Davisville, California, business people got together in 1905 to create a chamber in order to attract University Farm School. The Davisville (now Davis) Chamber of Commerce succeeded, beating out dozens of other communities, and celebrated with fireworks.[42] The school today is called the University of California at Davis and has about 30,000 students.

These weren't the first examples of communities competing to attract schools. That was an age-old American activity, dating back at least to 1717, when the institution today known as Yale University shopped itself to the cities of Connecticut, with New Haven winning the prize while Hartford got the new statehouse and the unfortunate New London received the dubious consolation prize of a courthouse.[43] What was relatively new in the early 1900s was that many chambers were becoming seriously involved. And their activity would only grow in the coming years.

Finally, there was that old standby of U.S. economic development, obtaining land from Native Americans. There was still choice land yet to acquire, and much of it was in the remaining Indian Territory of Oklahoma. The Muskogee Commercial Club took on this job head-on in 1904, recommending that Indian lands be available for sale, with some restrictions. It quickly found allies from others in Muskogee, as well as from neighboring commercial clubs and chambers of commerce.[44]

The strategy worked. Soon the Muskogee Commercial Club had issued a promotional booklet on the new territories with the subtitle, "The land of the red man calls for the white man's plow."[45] In 1912, the organization announced in *Nation's Business* that its unique achievement was "reducing from an ownership in common to individual ownership almost 20,000,000 acres of land in Eastern Oklahoma, through legislation at Washington."[46]

The chamber members in another Oklahoma town, smaller than Muskogee, realized their community was so insignificant and remote that no one was going to visit them; they would have to go out calling. And so they did, as a participant later described their journey:

> Years ago I remember an incident of a never-heard-of hustling little town that was hardly known as far as the county line. It was located about 30 miles from where I was born and raised. They wanted to do something that would attract attention to their little town. This stunt I'm going to tell you about may not be new now, but I believe it was then. They hired a special train for 10 days and made a trip to what to us was back East, St. Louis, Indianapolis, Chicago and Kansas City. It took just about all the town could raise, but every businessman dug up all he could. They loaded the luggage car with things their country could raise.
>
> The reason I remember this case so well was because I had the good fortune to be invited to go along, and it was one of the first cases of me and my little rope making a public appearance.

Well, it was a joke – a hundred men getting off a train, marching with a band, boosting a place nobody had ever heard of. But business men in the places we paraded commenced to realize that there must be something in our town or we couldn't do all this.

Now if you are anxious to know whatever became of this tank town it's Tulsa, Oklahoma, which would have been a real town even if its people weren't greasy with oil, for it is founded on the spirit of its people.[47]

So wrote Will Rogers of the train trip of 1905, followed by more ambitious trips in 1908, 1926, and 1929, that did, indeed, put Tulsa on the map. Tulsa's civic drive and its ambitious commercial club, according to local lore and to the opinions of many outsiders, enabled it to rise above the sea of small towns around it. All those towns were near the oil wells that popped up like spring grass all over the area after the Glenn Pool was discovered in 1905. But only Tulsa, said its proponents, had the civic commitment to clean up and add cultural and transportation amenities to make its community a place where the oil company executives and foremen would choose to make their homes.

"It Could Have Been Worse"

At 5:12 am on Wednesday, April 18, 1906, the earth shook in San Francisco Bay. The quake, about 7.9 on the Richter scale, toppled dozens of buildings in San Francisco. The quake cracked open gas mains, causing fires to erupt all over the city, while also breaking water pipes, so that it was almost impossible to fight the conflagrations. This was truly a catastrophe, with deaths today estimated at more than 3,000 and damage in the hundreds of millions of dollars.

The Chamber of Commerce of San Francisco felt the effects as much as anyone. Its offices were destroyed and much connected with its history was lost.[48] And of course, its members found their businesses, if they still existed, in complete disarray. The fires continued for four days.

The chamber, however, showed the same kind of optimism that had been exhibited by the Chicago Board of Trade in 1871 after the Great Fire. One week after the quake, the San Francisco Chamber had new offices in the undamaged Ferry Building. "When we look about us we can say that while in April, 1906, we met with a great disaster, it could have been worse," wrote President William Marston in the chamber's annual report. "We shall rebuild this city and increase our commerce, which this Chamber will promote by all means available."[49]

Remarkably, the chamber actually gained 100 members during 1906. And the city's business increased from 1905 to 1906. Moreover, the chamber's Washington representative was busy uncovering many opportunities for federal appropriations for the beleaguered community.[50]

Aid poured in from chambers across the nation. Across the bay, the Oakland Chamber of Commerce, founded only five months before the quake, immediately went to work. President Edson Adams formed a relief committee that provided food and shelter to 100,000 refugees, more than 65,000 of whom ended up as permanent residents of the East Bay city.[51] The New York Chamber, so often generous in times such as these, had raised $782,000 within three weeks.[52] The Los Angeles Chamber collected another $300,000.[53] Many other chambers followed suit in smaller amounts.

Santa Rosa's downtown was completely destroyed in the same quake. Almost immediately, a group of business people, including a prominent local banker, Frank Doyle Jr., founded a chamber of commerce. The chamber issued a press release that sugared over the disaster and didn't even mention the word "earthquake." The Southern Pacific Railroad, which was responsible for bringing many newcomers to California, had urged chambers to emphasize the fires, which were preventable, over the earthquake, which, of course, was not.[54]

But while the Santa Rosa Chamber of Commerce may not have been forthright about the extent of the disaster, it was to exhibit vision of another kind. As merchants began to rebuild, Doyle suggested that they widen the main street of the city, 4th Street, to accommodate the new vehicles known as automobiles.[55] This was the first, but not the only, significant transportation innovation that Doyle and his chamber would champion.

In San Francisco, the community and the chamber followed the same approach as Santa Rosa, minimizing the effects of the earthquake and concentrating their reports on the fire and on their quick recovery. But in one respect, the chamber was exceedingly tough. Prompted by public complaints that insurers were not paying out effectively on the claims of their policyholders, the chamber commissioned an exhaustive report detailing as precisely as possible the performance of each insurer.

The author of the report, Professor Albert Whitney of the University of California, pulled few punches. "The earthquake damage in San Francisco stands as a monument almost entirely to cheap, dishonest and sincerely ostentatious construction," he wrote.[56] And he pointed out which companies that had absconded from town, running away from their financial obligations.

But on the whole, given the problems, the insurance industry had performed fairly well. The combined earthquake and fire created a situation that was "the most difficult in the whole history of fire insurance."[57] It was the largest fire on record, for one thing. On top of that, there was of course an earthquake, and there was massive destruction of records, including those of the insurance companies.

Whitney singled out one local company, ironically called the Fireman's Fund, for special praise. With many of its clients facing damage from the disaster, the fund didn't have enough money to satisfy in full all the claims of its policyholders. It paid all it could and then distributed new stock certificates that, if and when their value appreciated, would eventually repay the remainder of its obligations.[58] This firm's honest and creative approach won it many new friends and clients.

Three Secretaries, One Profession

The occasional disaster couldn't obscure the increasing order and knowledge being brought to bear on modern life from many quarters. The dawning 20th century brought with it an explosion of knowledge and an increasing specialization in many fields. One of those fields was that of the paid administrators of chambers, known then chiefly as "secretaries." Some chamber secretaries, as we have noted, had been paid employees even before the Civil War. But now they became more conscious that their job was distinctive and important. Three of them attracted particular notice during this period, and their examples illustrated not only where chambers of commerce had been as organizations, but where they had arrived, and even where they were headed.

George Wilson: Preserving the Spirit of the Chamber

The man who had guided the New York Chamber of Commerce for so many years, George Wilson, died on October 8, 1908 at the age of 69. He had served the chamber for 51 years, missing only four meetings in that entire period[59]. Wilson had joined the chamber as assistant secretary in 1858, working on its first annual report. He became secretary in 1868.

George Wilson, secretary, New York Chamber of Commerce

The Wilson years had encompassed remarkable changes in the great city. As Wilson himself wrote in the chamber's 50th annual report, his metropolis had seen "a half century of such commercial development as has not been witnessed in the history of the world."[60] The chamber had been in the thick of it. Yet Wilson, through the change, had seemed to embody the virtues and style of the old days. Indeed, only after he died did the annual reports' title pages refer to their state as "New York" rather than "New-York."

What kind of man was this, who stood for so long with the greatest chamber of its time? He was clearly modest and self-effacing, and seemed to be viewed more as a skilled butler than the master of the house. Although Wilson produced excellent transcriptions and summaries of chamber meetings, his name rarely appeared in the annual reports save in reference to something the members said about him or did for him.

Yet this man had character and it was reflected in the chamber. He was modest and dignified, but when he spoke, it was with the authority of one who is fully prepared with the facts. Accommodating to a fault, he "drew the line where he thought the interests of this Chamber, in the preservation of its precedents and principles were involved."[61] Some of the fierce independence of the chamber no doubt was due to this man, who "distrusted all entangling alliances."[62]

He could be emotional – and nearly broke down when, in 1902, the chamber's members passed the hat and surprised him with a gift of $10,800.[63] But mostly he conducted himself with quiet dignity, letting others do the talking while he gathered information, compiled reports, and conducted the basic operations of the chamber.

His eulogists saw him as charming, much-loved, and unfailingly diligent. "He was omnipresent," said one.[64] Never, however, was he the center of attention. At the special meeting called at the time of his death, only 110 attended. (The next regular meeting had 255 people, and the subsequent annual dinner 426.)[65] One of his eulogists, Charles Schieren, generously suggested that his portrait be added to the glittering gallery of captains of industry in the chamber's halls – a gallery that Wilson had done much to maintain and augment. Meeting chairman George Seward responded, "The picture of Mr. Wilson is already here, Mr. Schieren."[66]

Jacob Schiff asked, and the chamber's membership agreed, that Wilson's chair in the hall of the chamber building be draped in black for 30 days. The organization continued along with its new secretary, Sereno Pratt, who soon added a few changes to the chamber, making it a bit more like other chambers, with a monthly bulletin and a small helping of the boosterish enthusiasm that was animating so many other business organizations. The New York Chamber would move on. It had lost perhaps not a great man but a good one, and yet one who, as much as any single individual, had made this chamber the leading local business organization of its day.

Frank Wiggins: The Greatest Booster of Them All

If George Wilson represented some of the best qualities of the chamber executives of the past, Los Angeles's Frank Wiggins exemplified many of the ideal attributes of the chamber executives of the present. Wiggins did many things, but above all he was a booster. With backers such as General Harrison Otis, a founder of the chamber and owner of the *Los Angeles Times*, Wiggins shook a sleepy Los Angeles and woke it into a dream. Long before Walt Disney created his fantasy kingdom in Anaheim, Wiggins had cast a spell on millions of Americans, luring them across a sea of sand to his magical mirage.

Almost anyone could create brochures, commandeer a press, and send the items to the four corners of the earth. And what group of chamber leaders didn't regularly praise their city and region? The difference, in Frank Wiggins's case, was keen, and yet practically grounded, inspiration, and a depth of excitement about his adopted city that few could match.

Wiggins, indeed, may have owed his life to Los Angeles. Desperately ill with lung disease, he had left his father's saddlery business in Earlham, Indiana, in 1886 to die – or at least convalesce – in southern California. He immediately married his cousin, who doubled as his nurse.

The magic sun and air of the West began to cure him, slowly. It took him three years, until 1889, before he was healthy enough to hold a job. He soon became employed at the brand-new Los Angeles Chamber of Commerce as its superintendent of exhibits.

Wiggins fell in love with the sun, fruit, and flowers of his new home. He promoted the Southland as if his fragile life depended on it. Like Dorothy walking from her black-and-white Midwestern world into the colorful land of the Munchkins, the dour Quaker of Earlham was amazed at what he saw. Wiggins became a cheerleader, indeed the chief cheerleader, for this university of abundance.

His was an intensely visual imagination. For others, oranges and grapefruits were locally grown produce. For Wiggins, they were life-giving passion fruits. Just to look at them conjured up beautiful, sunny days and a land of almost unlimited plenty. For Midwestern farmers, accustomed to a hard life working wheat or corn and struggling through cold winters, Wiggins offered a riot of color and crops. The opportunities in southern California had to be seen to be believed.

Frank Wiggins (center) stirring the pot

In fact, it was the visual and tactile senses that led to a practical people's hearts. Newspapers might be distrusted, but the look, feel, and taste of a real orange could not be made up. As Wiggins explained to a group of California growers on the eve of the St. Louis World's Fair:

The picture or the thing itself is more effective than the printed word with the great mass of people. . . So must an attractive exhibit of products be more effective than the most forceful description of the same. People may doubt the accuracy of written statements regarding our resources and attractions – our enormous pumpkins and our blooming orange groves, with snow-capped mountains in the background. They may even doubt the authenticity of the picture of these things; but when they can see and handle and even taste our products, then even a doubting Thomas must be convinced.[67]

Oranges could be grown, of course, in hundreds of communities; Wiggins had no monopoly on them. But he was perhaps unique among the promoters of his time in the extent to which he prized them. His three orange arrangements at the Chicago World's Fair alone required 375,000 oranges over the extent of the exposition.[68] As we have seen earlier, Wiggins's chamber had organized Sunkist, the growers' cooperative that brought relative stability to the industry, and which began to produce alluring, artistic, scenic covers for the crates of the fruit shipped all over the nation, putting the California dream in millions of homes.

Wiggins believed in oranges - as well as in walnuts, roses, grapefruits, and pumpkins. And his deities often were larger than life. It was Wiggins who had invented the giant elephant made of walnuts that came to the World's Fair in 1893 and returned to the permanent exhibit in Los Angeles. In that same permanent exhibit, visited by 185,000 people annually by 1907[69], was a giant tower of ears of corn, shaped into a giant ear, and a statue of a huge bottle of wine, made up of many smaller bottles.

The chamber secretary's vision of produce was similar to that of his conception of Los Angeles – the bigger the better. And in a young nation flexing its industrial and agricultural muscles, it was a vision that others could share. At the St. Louis World's Fair in 1904, the Birmingham Commercial Club had exhibited the world's largest cast-iron statue, a giant image of Vulcan to symbolize that city's metal-mongering prowess. And of course, in everyone's imagination lingered the great figure looming over the New York harbor since 1886, the Statue of Liberty.

But Los Angeles was the biggest dreamer of them all. It was a town that, with much imagination, was fashioning itself into a giant city. And Wiggins, as much as anyone else in this southern Californian patch of desert, wielded the wand.

Perhaps it was only a matter of time before Wiggins and the chamber would run across the *industry* of images. In 1907, Colonel William Selig, an entrepreneur in the popular new field of movies, received a brochure from the Los Angeles Chamber of Commerce. The flyer touted the southern Californian community's 350 days of sunshine.[70] Selig, impatient with bad weather in Chicago, dispatched a crew to Los Angeles to take advantage of its sun. Others quickly followed him, with the chamber doing all it could to attract them. By 1915, Wiggins's organization was bragging that 80 percent of the nation's movies were being made in the city.[71]

Wiggins sought other business as well. He cooperated in the push for a project, strongly advocated by his board members, to bring water from the Owens Valley, 230 miles away, to Los Angeles – and then clamored for even more water, from the Colorado River. His chamber also targeted the new field of aircraft, and the automobile, too, pushing for more and better roads. And always, he angled for more residents and tourists to come to his earthly paradise.

On October 18, 1924, a vacationing Wiggins died on a boat returning from Havana. He had worked for the chamber for 35 years and headed it for 28 of them. The institution had about 1,000 members when he began working there, and 7,500 by the early Twenties.[72] The city's population skyrocketed from 50,000 in 1890 to 576,000 in 1920, and would reach a staggering 1.2 million by 1930.

Frank Wiggins

William Mulholland, who built the Owens Valley aqueduct and other projects, once joked that the only way to stop growth in southern California was to kill Frank Wiggins.[73] But even Wiggins's death couldn't stop the great city he had helped build. Los Angeles was still on its growth spurt in 1924, and went on to become the second largest city in the nation. During World War II, when the city was bursting at the seams with wartime development, a writer for *Life* magazine would describe Wiggins as "the greatest city booster who ever lived."[74]

Ryerson Ritchie: Spreading the Civic Word

Ryerson Ritchie was a master at capturing community spirit. He was able to take chambers and turn them into engines of community growth and development. At the peak of his career, during the two decades from 1893 to about 1912, he transformed, one by one, the chambers in Cleveland, Detroit, Boston, and San Francisco. Ritchie was a true Progressive Era expert whose knowledge took root and remained even after he left town – a good thing, as Ritchie left town frequently.

Born in 1858, he began his career in Montreal, then was involved with the chamber in Cincinnati for three years, spent seven years with the commercial club in Kansas City (1886 to 1892), then six in Cleveland (1893 to 1899), a few years in private business in Cleveland, then five years with the chamber in Detroit (1903 to 1907), two in Boston (1908 to 1909), and no more than two or three in San Francisco (where he resigned in 1912).

Frank Wiggins and Ryerson Ritchie were, in at least two ways, polar opposites. Wiggins championed one town; Ritchie worked on behalf of many. Wiggins was a booster; Ritchie emphatically wasn't.

To illustrate his disdain of boosterism, Ritchie observed that to Japanese chamber officials who recently had travelled to many cities around the United States, Americans appeared to be "a nation of braggarts." Chambers at every stop emphasized why their community was the best. Ritchie complained, "In the East as in the West, we have the Boosters' Club, the Boosters' League, the Chamber of Hustlers and a variety of associations with equally appropriate nick names; and they are all supposed to be conducted by staid intelligent business men."[75]

Instead of talking about being the best, Ritchie argued, American chamber executives and members should quietly *become* the best. They should organize and make their communities so advanced, so well run, that people and businesses would naturally flock to them. And here, the man who was against boosterism became something of a self-booster. He indicated that the cities adopting his principles grew faster than others did.

In a talk before the San Francisco Chamber of Commerce and published in 1912, Ritchie pointed out the population rankings of five cities in 1890, 1900, and 1910:

1890	1900	1910
Cincinnati	Cleveland	Cleveland
Cleveland	Buffalo	Pittsburgh
Buffalo	Cincinnati	Detroit
Pittsburgh	Pittsburgh	Buffalo
Detroit	Detroit	Cincinnati

Note how the "proud old city of Cincinnati" fell in the rankings, Ritchie said. Its commercial organizations were in disarray and at odds, and so the city couldn't grow like its competitors. Buffalo, too, had not been able to get its civic act together.

The star pupils were Cleveland, Pittsburgh, and Detroit. All three had followed Ritchie's precepts and had risen in the rankings. Of course, he had served as secretary at both Cleveland and Detroit. Pittsburgh had copied Cleveland's example, he noted. Clearly, Ritchie said, those cities that followed his advice would outgrow their competitors. He even took some credit for Detroit's success in snaring the automobile industry and Cleveland's in capturing iron ore instead of Buffalo.[76]

This was a man who knew he was right. It may have been his ego and assertiveness, so different from George Wilson's charming character, which propelled him from city to city. In Detroit, two newly merged organizations split off from the Board of Commerce in 1907 "owing to personal differences with the secretary."[77] And by the time Ritchie's San Francisco speech was published in the National Municipal Review, he had already resigned from the San Francisco Chamber, with only the shortest of departing-secretary notices in the chamber's bulletin.[78] Perhaps the San Francisco Chamber's members heard his population musings mixed with anti-boosterism and thought of Frank Wiggins to their south, who was eating their population lunch with about as much boosterism as one city could conjure up.

Although Ritchie was not as great a man as he thought he was, he was, nevertheless, a civic genius. With Wiggins, and possibly Wilson, he was one of the leading chamber executives of his time. His Midas touch made many business organizations become much better than they had ever been before. He was imitated and studied in cities from Honolulu to Dayton to Rochester, N.Y. Indeed, most business organizations today owe much to the modern chamber model that Ritchie pioneered.

One of the first tasks for Ritchie and his fellow reformers was to unite the main business organizations in town under the banner of the chamber. In each of his "big four" reform efforts, the process began with a consolidation. In Cleveland in 1893, it was the Committee on the Promotion of Industry coming together with the Board of Trade[79]; in Detroit in 1903, five different groups coalesced into the Detroit Board of Commerce[80]; in Boston in 1909, the Merchants' Association and the Chamber of Commerce joined[81]; and in San Francisco in 1911, the Merchants Association, the Merchants Exchange, the Downtown Association, and the Chamber of Commerce combined.[82]

In each of these cases, the whole was greater than the sum of the parts. In Boston, for example, while the Merchants' Association had had 1,810 members and the Chamber of Commerce 1,000 (with some duplicates between the two organizations), the combined group had 4,500 members by 1911 and was touting itself as the largest business organization in the country.[83] Its inaugural annual dinner in 1909 was addressed by President Taft himself.

The civic energy released by this fusion process was explosive. For example, the Cleveland Chamber, with 82 committees and 450 volunteers on them, by 1905 had already pioneered city planning, consular reform, smoke abatement, and workplace safety, among other issues. Its work on charities, already imitated in places as far afield as Detroit and Honolulu, would ultimately affect civic philanthropy throughout the nation, influencing War Chests, Community Chests, and the United Way. The chamber even held viewings of the bodies of two of its distinguished (and deceased) members, John Hay and Senator Mark Hanna. This description of some of the "less significant" of its 1905 activities gives a sense of the breadth of its work:

> The working out of a comprehensive plan for the renaming and renumbering of the streets of the city, which is now under trial; the promotion of a department of the city for the planting of shade trees on the streets and their care and preservation by the City Forestry Department; the passage of an ordinance regulating vehicles; the bringing about of the use of granite instead of sandstone in the new Federal Building in the course of construction; the protection of fish in Lake Erie during spawning season; the study of taxation in the State; the improvement of local transportation facilities; the development of an adequate system of dockage along the lake front for the protection of the city's commerce; the study of the public schools and the extension of their usefulness; the promotion of a new Union Station in connection with the group plan; the prevention of fraudulent solicitation of unauthorized persons for improper charitable enterprises through a Bureau of Information maintained by the Chamber.[84]

By this time Ritchie had already left Cleveland for Detroit, but the Ohio city's chamber continued to carry on his work with undiminished commitment.

The chamber expert barely touched down in Boston in 1908-09, but his impact was extraordinary. The Hub's best and brightest were soon remarkably active in the chamber that Ritchie had wrought. The organization's 62 committees had such luminaries as Louis Brandeis contributing his time on railroad freight discrimination, Frederick Law Olmstead Jr. chairing the committee on city planning, Edward Filene (the retailer with an "Automatic Bargain Basement") chairing the industrial relations committee and active on other committees, and Arthur D. Little heading the Committee on Quality Stamp. The

Cleveland Chamber of Commerce, ca. 1900

president of the chamber was James Storrow, a prominent local investment banker and a founder of General Motors, for whom Storrow Drive is named.

No topic intimidated this chamber. It worked to deepen the Boston harbor, reduce air pollution, and even fight the common cold.[85] Yet despite all its activity, members had a certain consciousness that the energy behind it was more significant than anything in particular that it might achieve. The chamber reported that "its most far-reaching and proudest accomplishment is itself."[86]

Ritchie could take pride in having sparked such a civic revolution. And he did. He told his San Francisco audience, "The Boston chamber has some excuse for believing that the Hub will be a modern Utopia by 1915."[87]

Perhaps Ritchie could have added that his proudest accomplishment was himself. His basic concept was for powerful, united chambers to tackle a multitude of urban problems in a rational, businesslike, but spirited manner, thereby sparking economic growth of a lasting kind.

What was new about Ryerson Ritchie? The great New York Chamber had pioneered the idea of a few committees, each with a few good men, working on a few civic projects. Ritchie democratized that vision and made everyone in business a potential reformer. Thousands of eager business people could pool their energy and turn their cities, if not into Utopia, at least into something remarkable and inspiring.

Three Secretaries: A Postscript

Wilson, Wiggins, and Ritchie each were much admired for very different styles and achievements. Wilson's character, deferential but with a base of integrity and dependability, was precisely what his strong-minded members wanted. He left few visible fingerprints on the record of his chamber, and he may have preferred it that way.

Wiggins took the boosterism of his members and raised it to levels that no board of directors had any right to demand. He was so pro-Los Angeles, so focused on attracting more people and business, that his volunteer leaders joked about it. His achievements spoke for themselves and he was known for being an exceptional professional. He was comfortable with his success and didn't thirst after greater recognition. Outgoing President Robert Bulla said proudly in 1916 that Wiggins had turned down salary offers from other cities, some for more than three times what he was being paid by the Los Angeles Chamber.[88]

If Wilson's ego was too subservient for modern managerial tastes, and Wiggins's about right, Ritchie's was a little too big for his or any era. He was neither the student of, nor the peer of, his board members and members. He was their teacher. He might not be able to grow a city the way that Wiggins could grow Los Angeles. But Ritchie's chambers were Los Angeles's equals in nearly everything else. As Wiggins built up his city to a remarkable extent, so Ritchie, despite his faults, built up chambers of commerce.

Civic Energy to Spare

Even as Ryerson Ritchie and others were merging business organizations together, in different cities new chambers grew up where there seemed to be a need. The Chicago Association of Commerce (CAC) was founded in 1904 and expanded with the speed of handshakes. Business people in this great city, after all, would give birth to the Rotary Club in 1905, a civic networking idea that shot around the world in a short time. For banker Harry Wheeler and other founders of the CAC, Chicago had pressing urban requirements that weren't being addressed by the small and exclusive Commercial Club (with just 60 members), the local Merchants Club, or the commodity-centric Chicago Board of Trade. The CAC, as we will see, became a hotbed not only of local but of national change.

New York, as in so many things, was a special case. It had what was, in the view of President Roosevelt and many others, the greatest business organization in the nation. Why should the city attempt to improve on the Chamber of Commerce of the State of New York?

The problem with this chamber, for all its glittering history and achievements, was that it was too exclusive. It had room for a mere 1,500 local business people, but Greater New York had hundreds of thousands of people who conducted business and wanted to see their city improve. John D. Rockefeller might be happily ensconced in his chamber of commerce, but what organization could the average businessman join so as to make contacts and to make New York a better place?

The Merchants' Association of New York, set up in 1897, was founded nearly simultaneously with the 1898 creation of greater New York City out of Manhattan and nearby urban areas. The association's simple motto was "To foster the trade and welfare of New York." The group grew steadily and rapidly, aided by a civic spirit many didn't think existed in the metropolis. "**Are you doing your share?**" asked its bulletin boldly on the eve of a membership drive in late 1912. The same issue reprinted this poem on page one:

Boost New York
Get a move on, get together;
All you people who reside
In the boroughs of this city,
Get awake to civic pride.
For a city of five millions
Should beat others in a walk.
Get together, then ye people:
Give a boost to old New York.

Get together, get a move on;
Help New York to get her own.
'Tis a work for all her people,
Not a few who stand alone.
Boom the city with your efforts;
Work cuts far more ice than talk.
Get together, all ye people;
Give a boost to old New York.[89]

The *New York Globe* gushed, "The most useful organization in New York in all that pertains to New York's material welfare is the Merchants' Association." Not to be outdone, the *New York Herald* editorialized, "Not in a generation has there been such an awakening to the business needs of this great municipality." The association's bulletin listed its membership-drive recruits with the headline, "Hundreds of Recruits to Fight for New York."[90] Let

Chicago and Los Angeles and Kansas City – even Boston – brag about their rah-rah spirit. New York, too, had civic pride and a spirit of pitching in for the public good.

The group's secretary, an attorney named S. Cristy Mead, shared much of the reformist outlook of Ryerson Ritchie. Mead was a bit stuffy (once insisting that a chamber secretaries' group sing the national anthem a second time with more fervor) and not a particularly original thinker, but was much more personable than Ritchie. He seemed to have, like Ritchie, the ability to draw enthusiasm out of his volunteers. But that enthusiasm seemed less to lead to conflict (as so often happened in Ritchie's case) than to steady movement toward solid civic improvements.

S. Cristy Mead

The nation's newly muscular chambers of commerce tackled problem after problem, in more fields than business organizations had ever confronted before. But one of them, if bemused at the spirit of the Merchants' Association, didn't take its eye off a ball it had been watching for more than a century. The New York Chamber of Commerce couldn't shake its obsession with the nation's currency.

Inelasticity

It was Jacob Schiff, the man who had just withheld currency from wartime Russia, who worried most about currency shortages in the United States. On January 4, 1906 he told fellow members of the New York Chamber that monetary conditions over the past 60 days were "nothing less than a disgrace to any civilized country." Interest rates had varied from 10 to 125 percent.[91]

Schiff emphasized that this instability was not only a disgrace but a serious threat. "I do not like to play the role of Cassandra, but mark what I say. If this condition of affairs is not changed, and changed soon, we will get a panic in this country compared with which those which have preceded it will look like child's play," he said.[92]

What was the cause of this wild fluctuation? It wasn't speculation, which other countries had in greater degree without the same interest-rate instability. And it wasn't a shortage of currency. The basic problem was "inelasticity" – banks' inability easily to move money from one institution to another. Schiff, concerned that the Treasury Department was merely going to add money into circulation without unclogging the nation's financial arteries, asked that the chamber's Committee on Finance and Currency look into a better approach. The chamber's members unanimously agreed.[93]

The committee came back the following month with a viewpoint very similar to Schiff's. But while he praised the group's "able" report, he thought it wasn't enough merely to file the document. "We, as the leading Chamber of Commerce in the United States, owe a greater duty to our country. We must do something," he said.[94] He recommended, to applause, that Chamber President Morris Jesup appoint a special committee of five to work with other organizations and make recommendations to be given, via Treasury Secretary L.M. Shaw, to the President, Theodore Roosevelt.[95]

Schiff could not join the new committee, as he was called to Japan for earthquake relief efforts of the American Red Cross. But the special committee was formed and reported to the chamber. The group's study included an interesting reminder that the U.S. economy was still heavily based in agriculture. Every fall, banks' cash reserves fell short as financing was required to pay farmers and move their goods to market. To cover the reduction in their deposits, the banks called in loans at precisely the time when the economy needed the money the most. Conversely, in the spring the eastern banks experienced a cash surplus. All of these seasonal fluctuations could be smoothed if the country had some way to use the U.S. Treasury's funds to flow to and from banks as needed.[96]

Prompted by Schiff, the New York Chamber of Commerce was moving toward the idea of the creation of a national bank, or national banking system. This idea was anathema to many Americans, who, like President Andrew Jackson many years before, feared vesting this much power in the federal government. And the New Yorkers themselves had no desire to instigate another great national currency battle of the kind they had in helping defeat William Jennings Bryan and "free silver." But the weakness of the nation's monetary system was apparent to all who were willing to look closely.

And then suddenly, at harvest time in 1907, the nation was seized by a great financial panic. Schiff's Cassandra-like warning had been timely. It took superhuman efforts of another member of the New York Chamber, J.P. Morgan, to pledge his own money to counter the panic, and to lead his and other New York banks to stanch the losses and restore order. The massive disruption showed the entire nation that something was wrong and needed to be fixed. People might disagree on the solution, but now at least everyone knew there was a problem.

It would take a determined effort to educate the American public about the need for some national solution to the inelasticity that Schiff and the New York Chamber had so clearly identified. But a monetary plan emanating from the banks of New York, or even from the New York Chamber, was going to be a political non-starter. Just as in the fight against free silver, the bankers needed a champion from the heartland. Instead of the Indianapolis Board of Trade, this time the movement would come from further west. Indeed, the youthful Chicago Association of Commerce led an effort almost immediately after the panic, urging commercial bodies such as the Cleveland Chamber to petition Congress and the President to take action on the "currency question."[97]

As efforts proceeded to stir up interest in banking reform, the Midwest remained the center of attention. President Taft, who took office in March of 1909, agreed with the need to educate the public, especially west of New York. In September 1909, on the eve of his own tour of the West, he told the Boston Chamber of Commerce that he approved of Rhode Island Senator Aldrich's plans for a central bank that "shall be kept free from Wall Street influences."[98]

The West, or at least the Midwest, needed to have a strong voice in the proposed banking reform, but the East was critical, too, both for ideas and money. The American Bankers Association, with most of its membership in the East, was a key player in lobbying and education efforts. The New York Chamber, the New York Merchants' Association, and the East-leaning National Board of Trade all were involved in efforts to promote a better monetary system.

Paul Warburg was the leading representative of the New York Chamber in the banking reform movement. He was a partner at Kuhn Loeb, where Jacob Schiff was the senior partner, and Schiff was his wife's brother-in-law. Warburg helped carry the torch of reform from the East to the politically vital Midwest. He, along with other New York bankers promoting Senator Aldrich's banking reform plan, settled on Chicago as the base for a national education and lobbying effort.[99]

The handoff to Chicago was handled with an act worthy of Kabuki theater. On May 29, 1911, the board of the Chicago Association of Commerce passed this resolution:

> *Resolved*, That the Chicago Association of Commerce, recognizing the distressing effects of panics on trade, capital and labor, the consequent need of a sound banking system in the interest of all the people in the country, and the suggestion made for a National Reserve Association, hereby requests [certain named members] to form a National Citizens' League, the object of which shall be to give organized expression to the growing public sentiment in favor of, and to aid in securing the legislation necessary to insure an improved banking system for the United States of America.[100]

Couldn't such a reform league simply form itself? Why the chamber involvement? It was a disarmingly simple strategy: the Chicago Association of Commerce provided one more layer of insulation from the New York origins of the push for monetary system change. The CAC helped lend the appearance of heartland support for the effort. In fact, the new organization, whose full name was the tongue-twisting National Citizens' League for the Promotion of a Sound Banking System, received its largest share of contributions from New York.[101]

Harry A. Wheeler, vice president of the Union Trust Company in Chicago and a past president of the CAC, admitted that the CAC's role wasn't exactly its own idea:

> The Chicago Association of Commerce only accepted a responsibility imposed on it by the other commercial bodies of the nation to take the initiative in the conduct of a campaign to which their support had been pledged. The only part taken by the Association, as such, was to launch the new League. This done, it surrendered all control to the Board of Directors of the League.[102]

The leader of the National Citizens' League (NCL) was none other than J. Laurence Laughlin, the University of Chicago professor who had been the propagandist-in-chief for the anti-free silver struggle. The NCL became an extraordinarily active organization. In the first six months of 1912 alone, it distributed nearly a million pamphlets and hundreds of newspaper articles.[103] Its lobbying impact for what became the Federal Reserve Act was enormous; one observer considered it second only to the American Bankers Association (ABA) in its ability to promote the legislation.[104] But of course, the ABA on its own – just like the New York Chamber of Commerce – couldn't truly claim to represent a popular movement. It took a chamber-blessed organization from the Midwest to provide the needed aura of legitimacy.

Still, this Tinkers-to-Evers-to-Chance play – from the New York Chamber to a Midwestern chamber to Laughlin and his printing presses – was an awkward way to promote monetary reform, either for free silver or for a national banking system. Essentially, Schiff,

Warburg, and the New York Chamber of Commerce had been attempting, in a somewhat convoluted way, to act as a national chamber of commerce would. Not surprisingly, once the U.S. Chamber was organized in 1912, the League was dissolved into it. The U.S. Chamber could finish the work of promoting nationwide support for what would be a nationwide banking system.

Waterways and Roadways

For chambers of commerce, one immutable rule held true in both the 19th and 20th centuries: every community's waterway must be dredged, and then dredged some more, preferably at someone else's expense. In 1910 even the tiny Mount Vernon (N.Y.) Chamber of Commerce wanted its aqueous access accentuated. The chamber anxiously awaited a visit from Col. W.M. Black, an Army engineer, to see about "relief from the troublesome rocks" in East Chester Creek.[105]

Massachusetts Senator Henry Cabot Lodge knew the drill. Once these requests reached Congress, legislators combined them, Bismarck-like, into a veritable pork sausage. "A river and harbor bill is a bill that is sure to pass because it is made to pass," he told the New York Chamber of Commerce.[106] But despite all the competing claims for federal largesse, there were ways of jumping ahead in line.

A key method, which Houston may have originated (according to a later chamber history), was to raise local funding to pay for some of the desired improvements. This chamber and its antecedent organizations had focused for decades on finding a path to the sea. After Galveston was devastated by hurricane in 1900, and the Spindletop well gushed in 1901, causing Houston's port activity to explode, more people realized that Houston's scheme was not harebrained after all. Still, the appropriations weren't sufficient to the need.

The Houston Business League (which became the Houston Chamber of Commerce in 1910) organized a delegation to visit Washington with the local-funding supplement idea. On June 25, 1910, Congress agreed to spend half of the $2.5 million cost of the creation of a 25-foot ship channel, with "local interest to pay half thereof." The idea worked, and the impressive Houston Ship Channel was launched, paid for by Uncle Sam and his nephews and nieces in Houston.[107]

The Houston idea didn't take long to spread. President Taft, at an October 1909 banquet of the port-obsessed Los Angeles Chamber of Commerce, spoke at great length about the harbor and praised the city for its having voted bonds to supplement hoped-for federal appropriations. Congress, he said, appreciated that local resolve and willingness to pay for improvements: "The Lord helps those who help themselves," he said.[108] In the century to come, hundreds of chambers of commerce would follow the Houston and Los Angeles examples to attract federal funding for all manner of projects.

Meanwhile, the Los Angeles Chamber had been deeply involved in a local project of remarkable audacity, the creation of a 230-mile aqueduct from the Owens Valley. In 1905 the chamber had given a strong endorsement to the proposal for such a project, which was championed by board member and former mayor Fred Eaton.

In December 1908, the chamber called Chief Engineer William Mulholland to account for progress on the water project:

Mr. Mulholland met the committee of this body with some trepidation. It is human nature, whether in Maine or California, for taxpayers to demand results, and these immediately. "Well," he answered, "we have spent about $3,000,000 all told, I guess, and there is perhaps 900 feet of aqueduct built. Figuring all our expenditures, it has cost us about $3,300 per foot" – this defiantly. He waited for the words to sink in; then added, "But by this time next year I'll have 50 miles completed, and at a cost of under $30 per foot, if you'll let me alone." "All right, Bill," said the chairman. . . "Go ahead. We're not mad about it."[109]

Owens Aqueduct under construction, 1912

The project, completed in 1913, allowed the city to grow. But it had its critics, including those who complained about the profits that Eaton and others had made on Owens Valley real estate. (The movie *Chinatown* provides a dark and fictionalized view of the entire effort.) And the near drying up of the Owens Valley was a sad result. As Will Rogers put it later:

Ten years ago this was a wonderful valley with one-quarter of a million acres of fruit and alfalfa. But Los Angeles had to have more water for its Chamber of Commerce to drink more toasts to its growth, more water to dilute its orange juice and more water for its geraniums to delight the tourists, while the giant cottonwoods here died. So, now this is a valley of desolation.[110]

The cottonwoods didn't vote; Los Angeles citizens had approved the bond issue for the $23 million project by a 10 to 1 margin. This water-challenged city would soon be thirsting for even more water, and the chamber would champion that cause as well. Other chambers in the region, too, would see the need for a means to tap the seemingly abundant waters of the Colorado River.

Land transportation was as important as ever, and despite the novelty of automobiles, railroads retained vital importance to most communities. Chambers continued their perennial struggles against freight discrimination, albeit now channeling most of their disputes through the Interstate Commerce Commission that they had helped create. And even after the turn of the century, chambers were involved in raising money to attract railroads. This effort wasn't always successful. A survey of Texas chamber executives in 1909 revealed that 80 percent of their organizations were raising bonuses or stock subscriptions for new railroads, but only 4 percent could report that they actually had new railroad mileage as a result.[111]

Automobiles were becoming increasingly important to most communities. The chamber in Abilene, Texas, which in 1912 pushed for more hitch racks for horses in town, the following year was pushing for an auto route to Fort Worth.[112] Chambers in Colorado, Texas, and elsewhere successfully advocated the creation of state highway commissions to rationalize the checkerboard pattern of road building that resulted when counties built their own roads willy-nilly.

For modern readers, it's difficult to comprehend the impact of the automobile in the early 20th century. Once people realized that the horseless carriage was here to stay, they knew that their community's future depended on being able to host the traffic. Hence cities and towns pushed for the rapid expansion of their road network.

As a U.S. Chamber expert, Grosvenor Dawe, told the Good Roads Association in 1912, the preceding 15 years had seen an explosion in the number of chambers of commerce and in the "agitation" for good roads. The two phenomena, he believed, were intimately connected. Communities, especially small towns, did not want to be bypassed by the automobile. Chambers of commerce could maintain the pressure to obtain the good roads their towns needed.[113]

One way to participate in the burgeoning automobile industry was to sponsor auto shows or to hold races. Proud of its booming car and auto parts businesses, the Indianapolis Commercial Club began to hold shows in 1910.[114] Its efforts, however, were quickly overshadowed by the race put on a few miles from town, soon to be called the Indianapolis 500. After 1912, when the Commercial Club combined with several other civic groups to form the Indianapolis Chamber of Commerce, the new organization from time to time would become involved in the popular race, including, in 1917, working to keep it from leaving the state.

Many miles away, a promoter named Bill Rishel had persuaded the Commercial Club in Salt Lake City to sell tickets to watch a barnstorming race driver speed across the Bonneville Salt Flats for the first time. The driver, Teddy Tetzlaff, set a world record of 141 miles per hour in his 1907 debut on a salt surface. In later years the Salt Lake Chamber would become even more involved with the saline speedway.[115]

Chambers also began exploring air travel, not always with promising results. In 1909, the Sacramento Chamber of Commerce paid host to a visiting blimp. Locals were so excited that they drove across a farmer's field to watch. The farmer angrily demanded $100 in damages, but was talked down to $5, which the chamber paid.[116] In 1911, the Washington Chamber of Commerce invited a flier named Harry Atwood to come to the capital city; he flew all over town but the chamber refused to pay his expenses, so private citizens tried to raise the $1,000 themselves. Meanwhile, chambers in other cities promised Atwood they would pay his expenses if he would visit their cities.[117]

The Los Angeles Chamber of Commerce turned out to be the most successful promoter of air travel. It helped put together the first air show in the United States, which attracted a quarter of a million visitors over 11 days. The event brought airplane makers and flyers from all over the world. Historian

The meet that hijacked an industry

Kevin Starr would write almost a century later: "In January 1910, organizing an international air show at Dominguez Hills, the Los Angeles County Chamber of Commerce virtually hijacked the newly developing aviation industry in its entirety to Southern California."[118]

Modern City Planning

The 1893 Columbian Exposition in Chicago had popularized the idea of planned cities. Many chambers of commerce, imbued with the organizing spirit of the age, embraced city planning. Chambers and boards of trade in Cleveland, Boston, Dallas, and Washington, D.C. advocated this fashionable kind of development. Daniel Burnham, who supervised the 1893 Chicago project, was connected with many efforts, as was the famous landscape planner, Frederick Law Olmsted, and his son, Frederick Law Olmsted, Jr.

In Washington, D.C., the Washington Board of Trade was a prime mover in the creation of the Mall area near the Capitol, aided by both Burnham and the elder and younger Olmsteds. The planners successfully pushed, for example, for the removal of the railroad tracks that cluttered the Mall. In Cleveland, the chamber got Burnham involved in the creation of Public Square. Boston's newly energized chamber after 1909 had the junior Olmsted head its city planning committee, and although the result was some downtown improvement, it was not the broad metropolitan planning structure that the chamber and Mayor Fitzgerald advocated.

No little plan: Plan of Chicago, 1909

The greatest city plan of the era was Burnham's effort for Chicago. He first mentioned the idea to the Commercial Club in 1896, which clearly was interested. The Merchants Club, too, was intrigued with the concept. In 1907, the two organizations merged into a single group, still named the Commercial Club of Chicago, in large part to get Burnham's work off the ground. Burnham did not take a salary, but the Club provided $100,000 for staff and expenses. He then hired Edward Bennett to turn many of his ideas into drawings.[119]

Burnham made no little plan. The result, published by the Commercial Club in 1909, transformed much of downtown Chicago and the lakefront. His plan is still consulted today, as "one of the most fascinating and significant documents in the history of city planning."[120] Burnham captured much of the optimism of the Commercial Club and his contemporaries in Chicago, who saw a vast, unruly sprawl of 2 million people and many thousands of structures and believed it could be tamed and improved for the common good.

More Industry, More Tourists

Every chamber of commerce, even the most enthusiastic about following the do-gooder civic precepts of Ryerson Ritchie, had a secret Frank Wiggins lurking inside it. The eternal desire to entice more people and industry was difficult to repress, even if chambers wanted to. Business people in the young 20th century desired more business and would go to great lengths to get it. As countries around the world jockeyed for advantage over one other, so did cities and their chambers in the United States. "It was a deadly serious business, this booster spirit, this fight of each city for a place in the sun," noted a Buffalo Chamber history covering this period.[121]

Financial commitment often was part of the struggle for industry. The hands that passed the hat to bring in the railroad could – and did – reach out for contributions to induce factories to come to town, or, at the very least, to print up brochures touting the benefits of the community. Soon after the Panic of 1907, chambers stepped up their promotion efforts.

In 1910, the Tulsa Commercial Club began assembling a war chest of $200,000 to "locate new industries."[122] Perhaps the club was motivated partly by all the activity in Oklahoma City, including the successful effort to land two meat packing factories (more or less the equivalent of attracting a semiconductor fabrication facility today). The Oklahoma City Chamber of Commerce managed to find a $300,000 "bonus" for each of the two firms, Morris and Co. and Sulzberger and Sons, and got an estimated 2,500 to 3,000 jobs plus $7 million in investment as a result.[123]

And thus the business attraction sweepstakes proceeded. The Buffalo Chamber of Commerce came up with a war chest of $100,000.[124] Toledo, however, seems to have been too slow on the draw:

> Charles F. U. Kelly has "passed up" Toledo, O., as the location for his proposed tire and rubber company. He has notified the president of the Toledo Chamber of Commerce to call all deals off, as the delay of Toledo citizens in raising the $100,000 asked of them indicated too much indifference. Kelly says a city further west subscribed $200,000 for his project within ten minutes after it was presented.[125]

The Boston Chamber of Commerce, coming up with $500,000, had a unique twist to its fund: the money was to be used not for loans to companies, but to serve as a credit guarantee enabling those firms more easily to borrow money from banks.[126]

The funds-for-factories fever reached the Pacific Northwest. The Seattle Chamber of Commerce proudly noted the "Roll of Honor" of donors for its "Special Finance Campaign," aimed not only at snaring new employers and conventions but also at paying for regular chamber operations. The total amount: $74,250.50.[127] A subsequent chamber announcement thanked "Japanese Business Men" for their additional contributions to the fund, ranging from $120 from C.T. Takahashi and M. Furuya to $12 from each of 22 different business men.[128]

Little Rock carried a big stick. It may have beaten all contenders. In 1911 its chamber raised $1 million to attract business.[129]

College Capture, Continued

Chambers continued to prowl for the prey known as normal schools and colleges. In Greenville, N.C., working in tandem with local state senator James L. Fleming, locals set up a chamber of commerce for the express purpose of capturing East Carolina Teachers Training School. The chamber put together a Committee of Eighty to lend weight to the campaign and garnered the support of chambers in nearby communities.[130] The state indeed awarded the school to Greenville in 1907; today it's called East Carolina University and has 28,000 students.

In Texas, competition for colleges literally heated up in 1910 when a religious academy burned down in Waco, and sought to rebuild elsewhere in the state. Fort Worth beat out Waco and Dallas for the institution, now known as Texas Christian University. The winning package came from the Fort Worth Board of Trade, the Fairmount Land Company, and local churches. The bid included 50 acres of land, $200,000, and a guarantee of a street car line and utility service.[131] TCU, with a student body of 9,000, still calls Fort Worth home.

Although Dallas may have lost the chance to capture TCU, it wasn't idle. As a Dallas Chamber of Commerce history notes:

> It was brought to the [Chamber] Board's attention that Texas Methodists had begun weighing the advantages of relocating Southwestern University from Georgetown to North Texas. Chamber board members actively lobbied for the school, and – although the Church voted 21-13 to leave the University in place – the five Texas Methodist conferences were impressed enough by Chamber efforts and community support to establish a new school in Dallas called Southern Methodist University, which opened its doors in 1911. In appreciation, the new school administrators invited the [chamber's] Board to make up the receiving line at the school's first graduation ceremony.[132]

Concomitant with the creation of SMU in Dallas, the Methodists were seeking to set up a college in the Southeast. The Atlanta Chamber of Commerce stepped in. It pledged $500,000 and an attractive site if Emory University were located in Atlanta. Coca-Cola magnate Asa Candler contributed an astonishing $1 million to the cause. He also had useful affiliations: he was the former president of the Atlanta Chamber of Commerce and his brother was not only a Methodist bishop, but head of the Methodists' Educational Commission.[133]

Technical and professional schools were also targets for the chambers of this era. In Memphis, the Business Men's Club assisted with the relocation of the University of Tennessee's School of Pharmacy to Memphis in 1909, and U.T.'s College of Medicine and Dentistry to Memphis in 1911.[134] In Omaha, the Commercial Club worked to capture a university campus and a medical school:

> Increased opportunities for higher education in Omaha were strongly supported by the Club. In addition to backing the creation of the University of Nebraska at Omaha (then called the University of Omaha) in 1908, the Chamber also weighed in for an Omaha location for the University of Nebraska medical school. Lincoln and Omaha were at odds over location of the medical school and ended up taking the issue to the courts. When the long court battle was completed in 1912, the Club's executive committee agreed to split court costs with the university. The total was $257.[135]

Promotion: From Cruises to Celebrity Endorsement

Chances to snare educational institutions didn't come up every day. But the opportunity to tout one's community was always there. Promotion, often led by chambers of commerce, was constant.

Goodwill tours often opened up business in their wake. In June of 1910, 2,000 members of the Chicago Association of Commerce took a steamer, the *Theodore Roosevelt*, on a Great Lakes cruise. When they arrived in Milwaukee, they hosted 500 people of that city on their boat, including William George Bruce, the secretary of the local chamber.

The Denver Chamber of Commerce went all out in 1911 by arranging a big float parade for a visiting convention, with the floats showing the various products and attractions of the state. The chamber filmed the parade and had the short film shown at more than 6,500 movie theatres. Chamber President C.A Johnson claimed that the movie reached 50 million pairs of eyes in 90 days.[136]

Hawaii had an edge in promoting itself: a celebrity endorsement. Mark Twain had given a speech in New York in 1889 in which he briefly recalled his voyage to the islands in 1866 and the magic of the place. In 1908, the Honolulu Chamber's Hawaii Promotion Committee thanked the famous writer for his kind words by sending him a beautiful piece of custom-made furniture with the message "Aloha" on it. Twain's thank-you letter contained a phrase that the HPC subsequently used in much of its literature. He called Hawaii "the loveliest fleet of islands anchored in any ocean."[137]

Hawaii's exotic flora and fauna made it relatively easy to promote, even if the territory was hard to get to. The Honolulu Chamber's Hawaii Promotion Committee stumbled onto a bonanza when it set up an information bureau in Atlantic City and offered people pineapple juice. The interesting drink was a huge hit, sparking interest in the Pacific island territory and spurring the growth of the brand-new industry of pineapple juice bottling.[138] Chamber trustee James D. Dole had been tinkering for three years with ways to bottle the juice. In 1909, he finally made 2,000 trial bottles. Aided in part by the excitement in New Jersey, his Hawaiian Pineapple Products Company expected production of 2 million in the following year.[139]

A New Look at Local Government

Two new types of local public organization emerged after the turn of the century: commission government and city manager administration. Both embodied the idea that experts and expertise, rather than corrupt machine politics, should guide the life of towns and cities. Not surprisingly, both ideas became almost immediately popular with chambers of commerce, where members were anxious to see government run "like a business" and where skepticism of local governments was a time-honored tradition.

Commission government grew out of the Galveston hurricane disaster of 1900. So pressing were local needs, and so weak was what remained of the city administration, that the state legislature appointed a commission of five business people to run relief efforts and maintain order. Four of the commissioners each handled specific aspects of urban management while the fifth commissioner oversaw them. The process, immediately successful, drew attention both locally and nationally. In Galveston the system continued to operate, although the commissioners' jobs eventually were turned into elected positions.

Staunton, Virginia, initiated the city manager form of government in 1908. Under this system, the mayor and city council hired an expert in management who would mind the civic store efficiently. This simple way of uniting elected and appointed officials into a single system, with one person to blame if the street lights didn't work or the grass in the park turned brown, was immediately appealing. The city manager system began competing with the commission system in the minds of reformers.

Reformers, of course, typically were the business organizations. "Chambers of commerce almost always led in local efforts to make these changes," note Charles Glaab and Theodore Brown in *A History of Urban America*.[140] Chambers were the logical groups to implement these changes because they 1) stood outside of government operations (and hence were not tied to the civic status quo), 2) sought more efficient, businesslike government, and 3) frequently had enough standing and weight in their communities for their recommendations to be taken seriously by voters.

Hence, in hundreds of U.S. towns and cities, new, chamber-advocated governments sprang up. In some places, as in Sumter, S.C. in 1912, voters chose between commission government and the city manager system. There, the city manager plan, proposed by the brand-new chamber of commerce, was adopted.[141] In other communities, a sudden disaster prompted a change. A notable example was the Dayton, Ohio, flood in 1913, which encouraged voters to approve the city manager system that the Dayton Chamber of Commerce and its founder, John M. Patterson of the National Cash Register Company, were advocating.[142]

As in the case of so many other reforms, people eventually discovered that a new type of organization can't change human nature. Corruption and inefficiency managed to surface in both new forms of administration, and the commission form of government may have peaked in 1917 (when no fewer than 500 towns and cities had adopted it) and the city manager form in 1926, according to Glaab and Brown.[143] Still, one or both of these new forms, essentially brought to the nation by chambers of commerce and similar business organizations, remain in force in more than a thousand American communities.

Health

The Pure Food and Drug Act of 1906 had been the culmination of efforts by many chambers of commerce and other civic groups. Chambers had been urging better food and drug practices for decades, notably in many of the meetings of the National Board of Trade. For companies concerned about the reputation of their products, it was often seen as a good thing to have regulators clean up their industry and remove the bad apples.

It was, therefore, embarrassing that the first conviction under the 1906 act was against N. Harper, a drug manufacturer who happened to be president of the Washington, D.C., Chamber of Commerce. Harper's firm had created a headache remedy that could be fatal if too much of it was consumed. The patent medicine's ingredients included "anti-pyrine, acetanilide, caffeine, alcohol and other ingrediens [sic]." Harper was fined $500 for one offense and $200 for another connected with the incorrectly labeled product. President Roosevelt had personally urged a jail sentence for this first offense under the new act, but the judge demurred.[144]

Nonetheless, leading chambers continued to try to improve public health. The Boston Chamber's attempt to tackle the common cold is one example. The Honolulu Chamber of

Commerce had helped in rat exterminations and in preventing yellow fever.[145] The Pittsburgh Chamber of Commerce successfully advocated the creation of a water filtration plant that reduced typhoid deaths from 58 in one month to just eight in the same month of the following year.[146]

Some of the efforts to improve public health were out of genuine concern for people's welfare. But there was also the fear that outbreaks of disease would scare off investors and business partners. The Honolulu Chamber of Commerce disputed the "fallacy" that white people were in serious danger of getting leprosy in the territory, while the Atlanta Chamber of Commerce called for a conference on the hookworm disease, at least in part to remove the public relations black eye that the ailment was giving the South.[147]

Chambers looked into improving elementary and secondary education, cleaning up sewers and providing better water, and even – pursuing the pioneering reforms of the Cleveland Chamber of Commerce – vetting and supervising charitable giving. In an age of creative organizing, these business groups were hardly slackers in civic entrepreneurship. Indeed, their efforts even took them to the countryside.

Organizing Agriculture

C.L. Logan, the secretary of the Binghamton (N.Y.) Chamber of Commerce, began soon after the turn of the century to look into his city's agricultural hinterlands to find the key to growing his community. He was surprised to find that the rural area surrounding Binghamton had more people in 1865 than in 1895. And yet Binghamton's business depended to a great extent on the health of that rural area. How could the chamber help? How could it bring business methods and efficiency to farms?

It took five years to persuade chamber members to assemble a committee, which included chamber members and farmers, that could begin to tackle the problem. Part of the difficulty was uniting the efforts of city business people with the U.S. Department of Agriculture, the Delaware, Lackawanna & Western Railroad, and Cornell University's school of agriculture. For years, everything had been done piecemeal and it took Logan and the chamber to pull all the parties together.

The chamber created a new department within its structure, the Farm Bureau, funded one third by the chamber, one third by USDA, and one third by the railroad. The Farm Bureau came complete with a full mandate to improve agriculture in the Binghamton area through the various means at its disposal.[148]

On March 20, 1911, the first Farm Bureau employee, or "agent," Cornell agriculture graduate John Barron, began work in the Binghamton Chamber.[149] The idea almost immediately caught fire, as it seemed one of the first truly effective ways of uniting the considerable resources and expertise of the USDA and academia with local communities, including both individual farmers and business people. Soon the chambers in Cortland and Watertown had Farm Bureaus, too. By 1919 there was a national association of Farm Bureaus, and currently there are active Farm Bureaus in every state. These institutions gradually moved out of chambers and look on a life of their own, so that today, very few people on farms or in chambers realize that the original Farm Bureau was a part of the Binghamton Chamber.

Oklahoma City 1910: the new state capital

Hosting the State Capital

One night in 1910, the state seal of Oklahoma was spirited away in an automobile from the old capital of Guthrie to the new capital of Oklahoma City. The clandestine action symbolized the pathos of these two cities' struggle for state preeminence. Each had a chamber of commerce, and each had about 10,000 people in 1900. But the Oklahoma City Chamber was widely seen as more dynamic in attracting business and building up the city, and by 1910 Oklahoma City had many more people – about 65,205 people, while Guthrie had grown to just 11,654.

The Oklahoma City Chamber of Commerce pushed for a referendum on the state capital and engaged in a "very thorough and energetic campaign of the state" to appeal for capital status. On June 11, 1910, Oklahoma City won handily.[150] Such a feat was indeed a coup, as Oklahoma had nearly 1.7 million people in 1910, and so many people had to be persuaded to favor the brash newcomer against the more relaxed Guthrie.

For Sacramento, the problem was not getting the state capital but keeping it. In 1907, Berkeley began a campaign to grab the state government hub. To combat this effort, the Sacramento Chamber of Commerce held daily meetings. Nevertheless, the State Senate voted 30 to 9 in support of the idea, and House agreed by a vote of 58 to 19. Goaded by the local newspaper, the Sacramento Chamber went on the attack, pegging the cost of the move at $10 million. A statewide referendum in November 1908 brought total victory for Sacramento, with only three counties favoring Berkeley.[151]

Still, the Sacramento Chamber had to fight off similar attacks, including a continuing push to pry state offices from the capital. And there were other problems in maintaining the state's presence in town. In 1911, the incoming governor, Hiram Johnson, refused to move into the governor's mansion because of an infestation of bats. The outgoing official, James Gillett, had reported killing 11 of them in a single night. The Sacramento Chamber took up the challenge and campaigned for a new governor's mansion.[152]

Women and Chambers of Commerce in the Early 20th Century[153]

Women became more involved in chambers of commerce with the new century – not simply as an "annex" as in the San Diego Chamber in the 1890s. Women began to serve as members, speakers, even secretaries. One of the first known members of an American chamber of commerce was Emma Gillett, who was a member of the Washington Board of Trade around the turn of the century.[154] The Des Moines Commercial Club admitted two women members in 1907.[155] Some others chambers admitting women shortly afterward included those in Walla Walla, Wash. (1913), Raleigh (1917), and Jackson, Mich. (1917).[156] Other groups, including the Los Angeles Chamber of Commerce, had women on chamber committees.

Jane Addams, the famous social reformer and founder of Hull House, was made an honorary member of the Chicago Association of Commerce in 1910. This seems to have been a spontaneous, and unanimous, action of members after she gave a speech. But it wasn't clear that rules permitted women to be members. CAC President Homer Stillwell "was somewhat perplexed over the situation and admitted that the proceeding might be irregular to some extent, but would not admit that the rules were more important than the membership of Miss Addams."[157]

Addams also spoke to the Detroit Board of Commerce, where she was introduced as "a splendid type of the American woman." There the topic was women's suffrage.[158] That subject, soon to be a hot one in many cities and states, came before the San Francisco Chamber of Commerce as well. Its board in 1909 was given "full power to act" on a request to support a state constitutional amendment for equal suffrage, but the idea was tabled.[159] Chambers usually reflected the mores of their times, and the news certainly wasn't good for the cause of women's rights. Indeed, the Cincinnati Chamber of Commerce's board decided in 1910 to bar women from acting as traders on the Exchange.[160]

Women's status was higher in the West, including in some of the chambers there. It's possible that Fannie Reese Pugh was the first woman secretary of a local chamber of commerce in the United States. Pugh served her first chamber in 1909, when she handled the job in Yuma, Arizona, without a salary. She combined the local commercial club and chamber, raising membership from 15 to 120. Then she moved to Hearne, Texas, starting the chamber in 1914 and successfully running it until her retirement in 1923.[161]

Pugh was not alone; Texas was a step ahead of most other states in women's involvement in chambers of commerce. In 1910, A.W. Funkhouser was secretary of the chamber in Gainesville, apparently the first woman to have such a position in Texas.[162] (Pugh at this time was serving in Arizona.) By 1911 in Beaumont, the oil boom town, there was a civic committee of the chamber composed of eight men and eight women.[163]

Funkhouser and Pugh were active not only in their own chambers. Funkhouser was elected secretary of the Texas chamber executives' institute (education program) in 1910.[164] By 1915, Fannie Pugh, now in Hearne, was attempting to host a Texas chamber secretaries' meeting. She had difficulty, however, apparently running into some unwritten good ol' boy rules:

> Following the example of the National Association of Commercial Secretaries, the Texas commercial executives, at the Dallas convention in 1915, decided that they would not expect the future host cities to provide expensive free entertainment. Taking them at their word, Mrs. Fannie Pugh, the only women [*sic*] secretary in the state, invited them to host their next annual convention at Hearne and offered them a free possum hunt. The convention, nevertheless, went to Houston which offered free boat rides and an excursion to the bathing beach at Galveston.[165]

The women chamber secretaries in the West sometimes ran into issues, but so did those in the Midwest. The chamber in Columbus, Ind., hired Elizabeth Tirtel as its secretary in 1913. Two years later, however, it hired a man, John Northway, who immediately outranked her as "executive secretary." She nevertheless remained there for 32 years.[166]

Soon there were special chambers of commerce for women. In St. Louis a Woman's Chamber of Commerce began in 1913 and was still in operation six years later, handling projects such as the "Americanization" of immigrants.[167] Flint, Michigan, had a women's chamber in 1919, although it was involved primarily in horticultural work, much like the Annex in San Diego many years earlier.[168] Roanoke had an active women's chamber that was affiliated with the men's business organization.[169]

There were also national chambers for female executives. In fact, one of them, the Women's Chamber of Commerce, became affiliated with the U.S. Chamber, and its president, Sophia Delavan, spoke at the U.S. Chamber's "War Convention" in Atlantic City on September 18-21, 1917. Delavan was the head of the largest manufacturer of wigs for dolls, with 300 employees, and spoke about her experience breaking a strike and innovating to get the most out of female employees.[170]

Another group, the Woman's Chamber of Commerce, Inc., National and International, involved a number of women over a half dozen years but was dominated by one outspoken individual, Kathrine Clemmons Gould. She addressed several groups, including the U.S. Congress, and freely expressed strong opinions on the world of work and on male-dominated industry. Her organization focused, in particular, on the places where industry impinged on females: "For instance, for years the women have been tortured by the mandates of men who manufacture their clothes, of men who torture their feet with hideous shoes."[171] She also tackled issues such as job discrimination against Jewish and Catholic girls.[172]

Gould was a member of both the U.S. Chamber and the New York Merchants' Association, and her involvement with these groups points out the growing trend, even before the 19th Amendment, for chambers of commerce to open up to women members.

And as we have already seen, women began to be increasingly involved in chamber staff work, not only as stenographers but in key administrative roles and even as secretaries. At the NACOS meeting in 1918, E.M. McMahon, general secretary of the St. Paul Association, spoke in favor of there being women secretaries. Indeed, the NACOS discussion brought out that there were several women successfully running chambers around the country.[173]

Organizing the Organizations and the Beginnings of a Profession

So much was happening among chambers of commerce, and there were so many of them, that it's not surprising that they began meeting one another with greater regularity. There was much to learn from one another. New groups of them began forming and meeting.

One of the first state organizations for chamber secretaries (as opposed to for chambers as a whole) was formed in Texas in 1906. Oklahoma had a similar group in 1909 and Michigan in 1912.[174] And almost simultaneously, groups began forming across state lines. In October 1906, 25 secretaries from three states (New York, Pennsylvania, and New Jersey) met in Binghamton as the Inter-State Association of Chamber Executives, later the American Association of Commercial Executives.[175] In 1907, the Southern Commercial Secretaries' Association came together.[176] And in 1909 the Central Association of Commerce Secretaries formed in Cincinnati.[177] Still another active group at this time was the Associated Chambers of Commerce of the Pacific Coast. Soon these organizations and others would be coalescing into broader movements.

By the first decade of the twentieth century, many chambers had a professional secretary. In 1909, within a 100-mile radius of Dallas, there were 61 paid chamber leaders. It's perhaps not surprising that Texas hosted what may have been the first "institute" program for training chamber executives. In Fort Worth on August 4, 1909, an expert from Chicago on city-building, Elmer Batterson of the *Dry Goods Reporter*, began instructing Texas chamber staff members on how to do their jobs better.[178]

These chambers were tiny operations compared to the great enterprises of their day. But some of the business organizations, especially in the bigger cities, had enough money to complement the efforts of their often highly committed volunteers. In 1912, the Chicago Association of Commerce had a budget of $220,000, the Boston Chamber of Commerce $112,000, and the New York Merchants' Association $75,000.[179] Managing these organizations, and promoting their political and civic agendas, was becoming not only a significant job, but for many, a profession. In a couple of years, these full-time professionals would have their own national organization.

A Changed World

Isidor Straus was the co-owner of Macy's (with his brother Nathan) and an active member of the New York Chamber of Commerce. He had briefly served as the civic organization's vice president. Although he had always chosen to ride on German ships, in April 1912 he had made an exception and returned from Europe on a White Star luxury steamer. The passenger roster included three other members of the New York Chamber: John Jacob Astor, Benjamin Guggenheim, and John Thayer.[180]

Just before midnight on April 14, 1912, the ship hit an iceberg. The *Titanic* began taking on water and the crew began loading people into lifeboats, although there were not enough of them for all 2,223 people aboard ship. Like many couples on the boat, Isidor and his wife Ida discussed what to do next. A contemporary weekly then reported on what then happened:

> Colonel Gracie heard them discussing the matter between themselves, and agreeing that if they must die they would die together. So when the officers urged Mrs. Straus to enter the lifeboat she refused to leave her husband. "We have lived together all these years," said she, "and I will not leave you now." No persuasion could move her. Then, says a survivor, Mr. Stengel, the officers tried to make an exception in favor of Mr. Straus. "We told him," says Mr. Stengel, "that no one objected to an old gentleman like him going in the boat. But he said he would not leave till the other men did."[181]

The two Strauses died on April 15, and became the subject of "hundreds of poems" and even appeared in movies such as James Cameron's *The Titanic*. Their brave act appeared to many, in retrospect, to signify the nobility and grace of a passing age. Indeed, Isidor and Ida Straus showed they were, as per the New York Chamber's 1768 motto, "Not born for ourselves alone."

The *Titanic* took down only four members of the chamber, but there were other casualties during this period, primarily due to old age. The loss of four-time President Joseph Edward Simmons was painful. Chamber Secretary Sereno Pratt noted of his late boss, "In his final delirium he imagined he was presiding over a meeting of this body."[182] Other losses in these years included not only Secretary George Wilson, but also such leading members and officers as Gustav Schwab, Morris Jesup, and John S. Kennedy. Moreover, J. Pierpont Morgan, who had silently supported the chamber for years, missed his first chamber annual dinner in 30 years in November 1912, thanks to "indisposition,"[183] and he would die the following year.

While many old timers passed away, there was no guarantee that they would be replaced by equally talented young business people. The New York Merchants' Association was re-markably successful at capturing the energy of youthful and middle-aged boosters. But there was another, far stronger challenge to the New York Chamber.

Exactly one week after Isidor Straus lost his life in the North Atlantic, the New York Chamber of Commerce suddenly became the second most important commercial organi-zation in the United States. On April 22, 1912, the Chamber of Commerce of the United States met for the first time. Finally there had emerged a group that could command talent and resources from the whole country. As this national organization grew in strength, even the great and storied New York Chamber would be put, to some extent, in its lengthening shadow.

The Birth of the U.S. Chamber

The U.S. Chamber of Commerce took a long time to be born. One of the early supporters of the concept was a Connecticut business man and one of the lesser known framers of the Constitution, Pelatiah Webster. In 1783, Webster proposed "a chamber of commerce, composed of members from all trading towns in the states."[184] His proposal didn't make the Constitution, but the idea would frequently come up again.

The National Board of Trade, from its founding in 1868, had attempted to be a chamber of commerce for the whole country, but it lacked clout and representation. By 1911, it had only 52 organizational members, and not a single chamber west of Galveston except Honolulu. It was also weak in the South. Moreover, some of the most dynamic chambers of commerce in the nation at the time – such as the leading business groups in New York, Atlanta, Los Angeles, and Chicago - were not involved.[185] Nonetheless, the NBoT's very ex-istence, coupled with its annual issuance of resolutions, kept the idea of a powerful national chamber alive.

Through most of the 19th century and into the 20th, the New York Chamber of Commerce was the strongest chamber in the country. Theodore Roosevelt had called it the country's leading commercial body; others joined the chorus. Wisconsin's ex-Senator John Spooner got a laugh when he addressed the New York Chamber's annual banquet in 1907: "Mr. President and Gentlemen of the Chamber of Commerce of the United States."[186] At a New York Chamber banquet two years later, New York Senator Elihu Root said, "The Chamber of Commerce of the State of New York is not merely a Chamber of Commerce of the State, but it is a Chamber of Commerce of the Nation."[187]

Or was it? Among those in the audience for Senator Root's talk was Charles Nagel, the U.S. Secretary of Commerce and Labor under President Taft, along with George Cortelyou, a New York Chamber member who had been the first Secretary of Commerce and Labor. Both knew that the Commerce Department needed a true national chamber with which to interact; otherwise, it was simply a group of office holders theorizing about the needs of business. But in this regard, the New York Chamber fell short. It could not forever substitute for an organization that covered the whole country. The New York Chamber was, ultimately, "just" the New York Chamber.

Indeed, as we have seen, when John Kasson had championed the idea of a U.S. Department of Commerce at the New York Chamber in 1901, he had also proposed its mirror image and interfacing partner, a U.S. chamber of commerce. It would be hard to have one public organization for business without a private one with which it could interact. Not surprisingly, then, soon after the department's founding, two successive secretaries of the Department of Commerce and Labor would call for a national business organization.

On December 5, 1907, U.S. Secretary of Commerce Oscar Straus addressed the first meeting of a group he had called into being, the National Council of Commerce, which consisted of about 30 individuals from leading chambers of commerce, boards of trade, and trade associations. President Theodore Roosevelt also spoke to the delegates, emphasizing the importance of closer relations between the Department of Commerce and Labor and American business. The chairman of the group was Gustav Schwab, an active member of the New York Chamber of Commerce.[188]

While there were plans to expand this organization to make it truly representative of the entire country, the task wasn't seen as urgent. And with only a few months until the end of President Roosevelt's second term, the group didn't have a powerful boost from the administration that might have sustained it. When William Howard Taft took office in 1909, he and his Secretary of Commerce and Labor, Charles Nagel, took a different approach.

Nagel clearly was a man who meant business. In St. Louis in 1900, sworn in as a deputy sheriff and dressed in a Rough Rider-style uniform, Nagel was involved in confrontations with workers in a streetcar strike. His company of lawmen was among those that participated in a crackdown that resulted in the death of four workers. Nagel was proud of putting down the disturbance. He later noted, "I went to court when they were called for trial and personally saw them sent to the work house."[189]

The new secretary was tough but also a realist. He listened to leaders from the Boston Chamber of Commerce, who told him in 1910 that they hadn't had much luck when they tried to get other organizations to join a larger and reorganized National Board of Trade. The other business organizations "were unwilling to do this [join a reformed NBoT], but were willing to become members of a new organization, if one of an effective and representative character were founded."[190] Thus clearly there was a market for a brand-new, more powerful business organization.

What about the other national group, Oscar Straus's National Council of Commerce? Nagel attended a couple of its meetings and found it too small. He suggested to its members that they expand it radically, and they enthusiastically agreed.[191]

The impetus for change was echoed in the heartland, where the Chicago Association of Commerce strongly approved of the idea. Indeed, the CAC leaders had considered starting a national organization on their own, but demurred when they considered it might not have enough support if it were promoted from a single city.[192] Moreover, Nagel had called a meeting in St. Louis in 1911 where the response to the idea was equally strong.[193] And at a gathering of chamber secretaries, Nagel again found that the concept was popular.[194]

In December 1911, President Taft told Congress that a national chamber of commerce was needed to advance American interests and put business in better touch with government. The response was favorable. Taft sent 2,000 invitation letters to chambers and other business organizations throughout the country for a meeting to be held on April 22-23, 1912.

At the conference, President Taft and Secretary Nagel addressed the group of more than 600 people coming from 392 commercial organizations.[195] These delegates elected 25 directors. Harry A. Wheeler, vice president of Union Trust Company of Chicago and former president of the Chicago Association of Commerce, was elected temporary chair. Wheeler was a likeable and able man. His performance at the meeting convinced the group that he should stay at the helm, and thus he was made the first permanent president of the new organization, the Chamber of Commerce of the United States of America.

The U.S. Chamber, as it soon came to be known informally, would represent both local chambers of commerce and trade associations (business groups aimed at specific market sectors, such as printing or auto manufacturing). And individuals could join, too. Attempting to shield the new organization from the pitfalls of the NBoT and the National Council, the founders did all they could to make it an open, representative organization. Moreover, the directors immediately contributed their own funds to finance its rapid membership growth.[196]

Within just 18 months, the group would have 500 organizational members – roughly 10 times the size of the NBoT in 1912 – and by 1920 the group would have a budget of $1.33 million, or roughly 200 times the budget size of the NBoT in 1912.[197] Not surprisingly, the National Board of Trade, along with the National Council of Commerce, closed up shop at the formation of the U.S. Chamber. They weren't needed any more.

Organizing for Peace and War

1913-1920

Woodrow Wilson's Presidential election victory in November of 1912 was a harbinger of change for the country and for its chambers of commerce. To have a self-described progressive as the nation's leader meant challenges for business. At the same time, his idealism fell in neatly with the civic spirit that had awakened in chambers of commerce.

The Wilson years were, more than any other period, when local chambers of commerce expressed a strong sense of mission and their role in society. It wasn't just about protecting the interests of business. It was about making cities better, about enlisting volunteer business talent for the struggle to improve urban – and rural – life. The spirit of activist chambers spread across the nation, aided not only by a favorable national climate for progressive change, but by an increasingly well-organized network of professional support for chamber executives and their members.

Local Chambers Go National

The heavy attendance at the initial meeting of the U.S. Chamber of Commerce in April of 1912 was a good sign that business organizations across the country could effectively combine their efforts. The group steadily expanded during the following years. Its referenda on a variety of topics, with the largest organizations getting 10 votes and the smallest one vote, enabled local business associations to feel they had a voice that could catch the ears of even the President.

But the U.S. Chamber, despite its influence, wasn't set up to fulfill all the needs of the people running the nearly 3,000 local chambers of commerce in the United States. First, the board members of the U.S. Chamber were typically volunteers from businesses, not paid employees of local chambers. Second, the U.S. Chamber included non-chamber categories of members – not only individuals, but also trade associations representing specific industries, and therefore with needs and interests much different than those of general-business organizations in towns and cities. Third, the U.S. Chamber by definition handled national topics and thus was not sharply focused on the water filtration issues in Sacramento or the depth of the water in the Port of Houston.

Somehow, the paid secretaries of local chambers of commerce needed to find their own way to interact with their counterparts across the country. They wished to obtain means to help fund their chambers and to learn how to do their jobs better. Indeed, they had been meeting together for years in various local, state, and regional settings. All they needed was to expand the network to a national one.

The directors of two large sectional groups, the East Coast-concentrated American Association of Commercial Executives and the Midwestern-based Central Association of Commercial Secretaries, engaged in several conversations about merger. At the U.S. Chamber of Commerce meeting in February 1914, there were enough directors present from each group to have a quorum. They discussed consolidation and, after some concerns were addressed, the decision was unanimous to combine the two organizations into one.[1]

Thanks to some last-minute cancellations of conference plans for other cities, the two groups met jointly in Cincinnati in September 28-30, 1914. Together they formed the National Association of Commercial Organization Secretaries (NACOS). This group was active from the beginning, having a steadily increasing membership and well-documented annual meetings and other activities. Its name would change in 1948 to the American Chamber of Commerce Executives and in 2014 to the Association of Chamber of Commerce Executives. The first president of NACOS was S. Cristy Mead, the secretary of the New York Merchants' Association.[2]

The local-chamber network and resources expanded in August 1915 when the U.S. Chamber of Commerce opened a service to help them, the Organization Service Bureau (OSB). The manager of that office, Colvin Brown, worked with NACOS to make sure the OSB served chamber needs and didn't interfere with what NACOS was already doing. NACOS executives weren't shy, from the earliest days, in asking for help and resources from the U.S. Chamber, which had funding more than an order of magnitude greater than what NACOS could collect from its chamber-secretary members.

The Average Chamber Executive

In the coming decade and more, NACOS proved equal to the task of helping its members see what their colleagues were doing in the field. NACOS and many of its members followed the Progressive Era practice of surveys, surveys, and more surveys. As a result, we have a pretty good understanding of the kinds of chamber organizations that were prevalent at the time and the kinds of people who ran them. One chamber executive, John Northway from the Columbus, Ind., Chamber of Commerce, provided an interesting composite sketch of the average chamber secretary in 1919.[3]

Working from 177 questionnaires returned out of 300 that he sent out, Northway discovered that the average chamber secretary, a 37-year-old man, had been on the job for about five years. He didn't exercise. He started work each morning at 8:30 am and had lunch at about noon, preferably combining the lunch with some committee activities or other chamber function. He left work for dinner but, three nights out of the week, returned to the office to handle additional jobs. (The chamber executives from the larger cities, however, because of their commute times, did not return to the office in the evening.)

This chamber secretary had a private office, usually with an open door. When the phone rang, a stenographer or private operator would take the call, but nine times out of ten, it would be for the secretary. Most secretaries, Northway said, would take these calls. The chamber president (the volunteer who headed the chamber and to whom the paid secretary reported) called, on average, daily, although for some secretaries it was two or three times a week.

Chamber staff sizes varied from one to 78 (the number at the New York Merchants' Association). Usually there was one board meeting a month, but there were also many committee meetings – so many that much of the chamber secretary's time was spent attending them. When not doing that, he might be on the phone with a reporter, a task that few chamber executives shirked. He was likely to provide confidential information to one or more reporters, but rarely allowed his name to be used, even for on-the-record stories. (It was considered better to have volunteers in that role.)

Northway didn't dwell on this, but chambers at this time frequently employed specialists in the sales of chamber memberships. In fact, Northway's chamber had such a person on staff for a few months in 1915. This young man, Harland Sanders, later moved to Kentucky and started his famous fried chicken business.[4]

The membership salesperson who chickened out:
Col. Sanders in his kitchen (1930s)

Salaries of local chamber chief executives around 1919 ranged from about $1,500 to $12,000, with most falling in the $2,400 to $3,600 range. (A $3,000 salary in 1919 adjusted for inflation would be about $40,560 in 2014.) These pay rates "compare favorably with the earnings of other professional classes such as physicians, dentists and attorneys, and the trend of secretarial salaries is steadily upwards," said a contemporary expert.[5] Clearly, society valued these civic engineers. Apparently more than one of them bragged about his ability to raise the population of his communities – surely a tantalizing prospect to any hiring committee of local business people.[6]

Chamber budgets also were substantial. Northway mentioned the budgets of a number of large chambers in his study. Some of the bigger ones included the New York Merchants' Association ($295,000), the Detroit Board of Trade ($250,000), and the Seattle Chamber of Commerce ($190,000).[7]

While these budgets are not as large as those of chambers in those cities today – a 1919 budget of $100,000 would be the equivalent in purchasing power to $1.352 million in 2014 – they were considerable given the smaller economy and organizations of the time. Chambers of commerce had arrived, and their staff and the public knew it. Many of these organizations were fully empowered, both in financial resources and in the support of volunteers and the community, to effect significant local change.

Taking a Closer Look at Chambers of Commerce as Institutions

One measure of the growing reach and importance of these organizations was in what was being written about them. As early as 1900, former chamber secretary Charles Dwight Willard described his organization's exploits of the preceding dozen years in *A History of the Chamber of Commerce of Los Angeles, California.*[8] In 1918, Joseph Bucklin Bishop came out with a history of the great New York Chamber, *A Chronicle of One Hundred and Fifty Years.*[9] The former chamber was one of the most dynamic in the nation, while the latter had achieved more in the past than any other. (A special copy of the Bishop book was provided to King George V; the king commanded his personal secretary to thank the chamber for the book, with its "exquisite binding," and said the volume would be placed "among the treasures of the King's library at Windsor Castle."[10]) Moreover, many other chambers were involved in this writing and publishing phenomenon. NACOS was gathering and publishing the proceedings of its annual meetings beginning in 1914, and in 1920 issued a 467-page edition of its members' best papers, *Commercial Organizations: Their Function, Operation and Service.*[11]

But there was a unique writing project in the period as well – the only nearly book-length, single-author, extensively researched treatment of the chamber movement in the United States for any of the preceding 150 years, and indeed for nearly a century afterward.[12] This was Kenneth Sturges's *American Chambers of Commerce*, published in 1915, an extended essay he wrote as part of a Williams College competition.[13] Sturges carefully assembled the available sources of the time and painted a picture of a powerful movement that was culminating in progressive chambers such as the most admired one in the country, the Cleveland Chamber of Commerce. Drawing on writings of Ryerson Ritchie and on personal interviews, Sturges showed how this chamber, and others like it, were transforming American civic life.

Sturges made the most of his sources – even including the president of Williams College, Harry Augustus Garfield.[14] Garfield knew something about the topic of chambers. He had been the president of the Cleveland Chamber in 1898 and had subsequently led the effort, strongly advocated by the chamber, to improve the U.S. consular service.[15]

Another of Sturges's sources was Paul Cherington, a Harvard University professor. Cherington was a true believer in chambers; indeed, he would set up a course of instruction at Harvard for future chamber executives. Cherington announced the Harvard Business School project in May 1913, just four months after President Taft said at a U.S. Chamber banquet, "You will have to have a school from which the new Chambers of Commerce can draw their secretaries, who will train the new membership in the way in which the organization can be built up, and give them a practical knowledge of how they can do what they are organized to do."[16] Other universities, from Dartmouth to Michigan and the University of Chicago, also began teaching young men about these exciting local institutions that seemed to be on the leading edge of progressive policy.

In this charged atmosphere, there were still other resources for chambers of commerce: magazines that spread the word about their civic achievements. These included the U.S. Chamber's publication, *Nation's Business*, as well as *National Municipal Review, Town Development*, and *The American City.*[17] The latter two publications had consulting staff who would help chambers raise money via membership drives. *The American City* also offered a two-week summer-school course for chamber executives; it had as many as 90 students in 1917.[18]

Funding: Grappling with a Perennial Concern

While chambers had gathered a valuable group of admirers, analysts, and advisors, they still faced the persistent problem of money. No matter how much interest they stirred up, these business organizations constantly had to seek paying members. And even in the Progressive Era, it wasn't easy to get everyone on board.

A NACOS survey in 1915 showed that the leading concern of local business organizations, especially the small ones, was "financing the chamber."[19] This primarily revolved around getting and keeping members. Fortunately, in this period the renewal rate for members was relatively high – about 92 percent.[20] But with few non-dues sources of income, a high renewal rate did not necessarily lead to high living.

One way to broaden support for chambers, coming under increasing scrutiny at this time, was getting more money from the larger members. For example, in Philadelphia, the department store magnate John Wanamaker paid for each of his department heads to join the chamber.[21] Other chambers found similar multiple-membership supporters, although it was argued that it would be more useful and efficient to skip inactive individuals and instead simply ask for a larger contribution from their big-company employers.

The concept of "sustaining members" – companies that paid extra, in view of both their ability to pay and the greater value they received through the activities of the chamber – gradually took hold. In 1914, the president-elect of the Los Angeles Chamber of Commerce, Louis Cole, drew attention to the phenomenon, noting its success in such cities as Chicago, New Orleans, and Seattle. "Gentlemen, give Frank Wiggins the money and I will guarantee that he will make every dollar he receives do more for the benefit of our city and the advancement of its interests than could ten dollars expended by anyone else or in any other manner," said Cole, drawing applause.[22]

The most impressive marketer of enhanced membership was the U.S. Chamber of Commerce. This organization from the beginning was set up to be representative of all commercial groups and of individual business people. With that wide field open to it, the U.S. Chamber – unlike the National Board of Trade before it – was not confined to the limited budgets of local chambers of commerce. To capitalize on its diverse base of supporters, the U.S. Chamber set up a new category of membership, "associate," with no cap on its contributions. In the first year, that category brought in $370,000, and in the next year (fiscal 1920) $610,000 – nearly half of the U.S. Chamber's budget in that year.[23]

Many local chambers also held recruitment drives. The go-go chambers in California often set the pace in such events. In September 1917, despite there being a war on, the Sacramento Chamber of Commerce launched a massive membership drive that even asked high school students to recruit their parents to the chamber. Getting into the spirit of things, H.E. Yardley, a local mortician, cryptically offered free caskets for those who refused to join the chamber. The final tally for the Sacramento drive was 2,112 new members.[24]

Junior Chambers of Commerce

Before the First World War a number of chambers of commerce began developing programs for younger people – usually boys or young men. One of the first, in Little Rock, Ark., was originally called the "Young Men's Good Government Club" and was aimed at helping elect reform candidates in the municipal elections in late 1911. This group changed its name to the "Young Men's Chamber of Commerce" and was closely affiliated with the "senior" chamber. Membership was limited to young men aged 21 to 31. By late 1914 five other Arkansas cities had similar groups, and one of the Little Rock group's members considered taking the concept national.[25]

Many of the organizations had the name "Junior Chamber of Commerce," a relatively new term.[26] Indeed, it's possible this term was first popularized in the United States in July 1912, when a short story by Helen Christine Barrett called "How Poughkeepsie's Boys Made Good" appeared in *Pictorial Review*. This story was described as giving a fictional "account of a unique association of boys, a Junior Chamber of Commerce, the first in America and perhaps in the world."[27] This Junior Chamber concept was timely: another young males' group, the Boy Scouts of America, was founded only four years earlier, in 1908.

Junior Chambers of Commerce were organized, beginning in 1912, in such communities as San Jose, Sacramento, and Rome, N.Y.[28] Although these organizations were for high school boys, young working men's groups proliferated, and some soon would appropriate the "Junior" name. Like the Arkansas young men's groups, the similar organizations in other places were usually set up within – or in conjunction with – the local mainstream chamber of commerce. The young men in these new associations often wanted to socialize together and many did not have the connections, the years in business, or the patience to break into the inner circle of the regular chamber. Having a special organization or subgroup for these young people quickly became popular.

The Boston Chamber of Commerce, for example, set up the Under Forty Division in 1913.[29] The Grand Rapids, Mich., Association had a Junior Chamber of Commerce, and Arkansas City, Kan., a Junior Commercial Club, by 1914; Knoxville followed in 1915 with a Junior Board of Commerce.[30] In 1920, the Indianapolis Chamber of Commerce organized a special committee and unveiled ambitious plans for a Junior Chamber of Commerce to accommodate local young business people.[31]

St. Louis was the scene of a particularly notable development. In 1915, a 23 year old man, Henry Giessenbrier Jr., formed a group of 32 young people there, called the Young Men's Progressive Civic Association (YMPCA). The following year, the incoming chamber president in St. Louis, a steel company CEO named C.H. Howard, took a special interest in the young men's group and renamed it the Junior Citizen Council. (Howard also changed the mainstream chamber's name from the Business Men's League to the St. Louis Chamber of Commerce.)

The Junior Citizen Council was aimed at boys and men from the ages of 18 to 28. By 1918, the young men's group had migrated to the St. Louis Chamber and was called the Junior Chamber of Commerce. It had no fewer than 700 members, paying $6 per year in dues.[32] Only two years later, the junior and senior chambers in St. Louis, together with other groups, fostered the creation of a national organization, soon to be called the United States Junior Chamber of Commerce. This association, which in subsequent decades would gain hundreds of American affiliates, helped start Junior Chamber International in 1944, which, in turn, has grown significantly and is now in more than 100 countries.[33]

A Boat in the Sky

Grown men could occasionally be boys and could be interested in technical novelties that pointed to an exciting future. One young man, Tony Jannus, learned how to fly and quickly became known as an acrobatic daredevil. He soon came in contact with a man who had the means to make some flying dreams come true.

In 1913, the 40-year-old Julius Barnes of Duluth, Minn., decided to take up the flying hobby. He was then already active in the Duluth Chamber and was the world's leading wheat exporter. But he wanted more. He decided to purchase a Benoist airplane, a vehicle with a large hull that to some resembled a flying boat.

His banker wouldn't let him fly the plane, so he hired another man, Bill Jones, to learn how to take it up in the air. It was the well-known Tony Jannus, however, who gave Jones his flight lessons. Before Barnes knew it, Jannus was asking permission to take the airplane to Florida to set up a "flying service." Barnes consented.[34]

Jannus's reputation preceded him. He flew the first plane from which a parachutist jumped. And he always seemed to have beautiful women around him. It was said that his plane's sparkplugs often failed after he took up a pretty passenger, delaying his return with her while he allegedly fixed the malfunction.

It was a Jacksonville businessman, Percival Fansler, who heard about Jannus's flying exploits and wrote to Tom Benoist, the manufacturer whose planes Jannus flew. Fansler believed it was possible to set up an airline in Florida with regularly scheduled flights. Benoist was interested. Here was a way to sell more planes and open up a new market.

Fansler sought investors in Jacksonville without success. Then Tampa business people turned him down. Finally he approached St. Petersburg. There he met Maj. Lew B. Brown, the owner of the *St. Petersburg Independent*. Through Brown, Fansler met L.A. Whitney, the secretary-manager of the St. Petersburg Board of Trade.[35]

Whitney was concerned about safety, but Fansler pointed out that airplanes were becoming safer and that aviation was turning into an industry. Convinced, Whitney pledged $1,200 for the project, provided that Fansler could match it with others' investments. Whitney then introduced Fansler to a real estate developer, Noel Mitchell, who promised $1,000 and then got 11 investors to put up $100 each. This was enough to guarantee the start of air service. The Board of Trade's Whitney, then, both directly and through his introduction to Mitchell, brought the service to life.[36]

On January 1, 1914, Jannus took off from St. Petersburg with his first passenger, Abe Pheil, the former mayor of the city. Pheil had paid $400 at auction for the privilege of being the first passenger. Three thousand people, including Will Rogers, who happened to be in town, saw them off. Twenty-three minutes later, they landed in Tampa, where nearly as many people greeted them. The St. Petersburg-Tampa Airboat Line was in operation for all to see, and world's first regularly scheduled airplane service had begun.[37]

Whitney's wife flew across on January 8, becoming the first woman to fly on a regularly scheduled airplane. She said the experience was "as enjoyable as being rocked to sleep in your mother's arms."[38] But it was difficult to keep the service going on just $5 per one-way trip. The Airboat Line needed money for gas, maintenance, salaries, and capital costs. Finally, on March 31, 1914, the line closed down, having carried more than 1,000 passengers.[39]

Like some other pioneering chamber transportation projects – the *Savannah* steamship across the Atlantic in 1819, Charleston's railroad in the 1830s – the air service was just slightly ahead of its time. And unfortunately Jannus didn't live long enough to see the full flowering of the aircraft industry; while he was training Russian pilots during World War I, on October 12, 1916, his Curtiss H-7 aircraft had engine trouble and plunged into the Black Sea, killing him and two Russians. (Apparently the weather was bad and he had taken to the air under protest.)[40] But, with his chamber funding, he had started something – regular air service – that would one day carry millions of people with a degree of safety unimaginable in the early years of flying.

A War Footing

By 1913, Europe's troubling arms race, together with its periodic diplomatic crises, convinced a number of people in the United States that a major war was likely to break out on the Continent at some point. Such sentiments, however, were not high on the list of concerns of American chambers of commerce. After all, there had been no full-scale, all-out European conflict since the battle of Waterloo in 1815. And organizations of merchants were partial to the view that the growth of international commerce would make it less appealing, and more difficult, for nations to go to war.

The Los Angeles Chamber of Commerce, however, as it did in so many other areas of endeavor, kept an eye out for future military needs. Chamber officials praised their much-loved offspring, the port, as ideal for Uncle Sam, especially after the anticipated completion of the Panama Canal in 1914. The Navy could be a prime anchor tenant for the port, which had recently consumed so much federal investment. The Los Angeles Chamber lovingly recalled Navy Secretary Josephus Daniels's words: "In the past the fleets have visited the Pacific Coast; when the canal is opened the ships will come to stay."[41] The city's oil production, both encouraged and touted by the chamber, would be critical to supply the Navy in the Pacific.

Not leaving much to chance, the Los Angeles Chamber enthusiastically hosted Secretary Daniels during his visit to the city in July 1913. Nearly 3,000 chamber members were present for a smoker in honor of the dignitary, himself a former community booster and leader of the Raleigh Chamber of Commerce. Secretary Daniels was shown not just the harbor but also the city and suburbs.[42] Similar hospitality was shown to U.S. Secretary of War L. M. Garrison, Major General Leonard Wood, and other Army dignitaries on their visit – including to the ambitious Undersecretary of the Navy, Franklin Delano Roosevelt.[43] By the war's outbreak in Europe, all the key U.S. Army and Navy officials had been made aware of the military advantages of Los Angeles and its harbor.

When Great Britain declared war on Germany on August 4, 1914, American businesses and their organizations were nearly as confused as their government. The American economy was quick to feel the pain of interrupted trade, however. Cotton prices plummeted and southern chambers plaintively urged people to "buy a bale of cotton" to aid their stricken communities. African-American southerners began to move north in increasing numbers. Chambers entertained visitors, and held instructional sessions on, the wonders of trade with just about anywhere but Western Europe – Latin America, China, Japan, Africa, and even the relatively tranquil Rumania.

Chamber leaders were gripped by sometimes conflicting sentiments – a desire to stay out of the war and a desire to prepare for it (preferably with the maximum amount of military spending for their communities). The German U-boat sinking of the *Lusitania* on May 7, 1915, killing 1,198 civilians including more than 120 Americans, turned public sentiment against Germany and brought the war home to many in the United States. The U.S. Chamber, however, sent out a peace-oriented referendum in November 1915.[44]

Although most Americans did not want to fight, they were anxious to be ready for a fight if it came, and the country's chambers were among the groups leading the preparedness movement. To be sure, the country's military was tiny by the standards of Europe. Joseph Choate, the honorary member of the New York Chamber and former U.S. ambassador to Great Britain, made this clear at a special meeting on preparedness at the New York Chamber on March 22, 1916. He got a laugh when he commented that not only were our armed forces tiny, but "it is taking pretty much all of our available and movable army to capture and suppress a single Mexican bandit."[45] (At this time, General Pershing was in hot pursuit of Pancho Villa.)

The U.S. Chamber pushed hard for an increase in military spending. By May of 1916, the national chamber was reporting an 89 percent positive response to a referendum urging preparedness for war. President Wilson was skeptical: "Very well, now, we are going to apply the acid test to these gentlemen, and the acid test is this: Will they give the young men in their employment freedom to volunteer for this thing?"[46]

The chamber in Portland, Maine, went a good deal beyond preparedness parades and resolutions. It worked with one of its members – the famous Arctic explorer (and honorary New York Chamber member) Rear Admiral Peary – to fashion a plan for a coastal air patrol to keep eyes open for German U-boats and other hostile craft. The chamber raised $10,000 for the project and proudly reported that "thousands" of newspapers had mentioned its air defense project, which had received telegrams of support from President Wilson, Navy Secretary Daniels, and War Secretary Garrison.[47]

Preparedness meant many things to many chambers of commerce. For the chamber in El Paso, it meant being ready to combat incursions of lawless elements from Mexico, thanks to the political instability there. In 1916, the chamber ordered four machine guns and organized a rifle club of 400 men who practiced at nearby Fort Bliss.[48] They appear not to have had an opportunity to exercise their skills in combat, however, at least in North America.

The Dam That Led to Many Others

In the Tennessee Valley region, an opportunity arose that was tailor-made for chambers of commerce. If it entered the war, the country was going to need nitrates for explosives. These could be produced in many places, and indeed the Army had already selected Pulaski, Virginia, as the site for a proposed plant. But the Muscle Shoals rapids on the Tennessee had a critical advantage: they were a "twofer," with the potential to provide not only nitrates but enormous quantities of electric power – more than that of Niagara Falls. Moreover, nitrates were also used to make fertilizer, which would be tremendously valuable to the farms of the heavily agricultural region.

The Nashville Commercial Club jumped on the Muscle Shoals idea, and in July 1915 it helped form the Muscle Shoals Association. Will Manier, the secretary of the Commercial Club, doubled as the secretary of the association. The MSA called together support from all the affected states and produced an imposing document, *America's Gibraltar: Muscle Shoals – A Brief for the Establishment of our National Nitrate Plant at Muscle Shoals on the Tennessee River*. This book, of course, was forwarded straight to the War Department. Of the long list of groups endorsing Muscle Shoals, shown near the beginning of the book, most were local chambers and merchants' associations.[49]

President Wilson, faced with competing expert opinions on the site for the nitrate plant, chose Muscle Shoals. Apparently the potential for hydroelectric power swayed him.[50] But the water-power opportunity related as much to future economic development as to present defense capabilities. It's possible, as some have alleged, that the outpouring of political support, much of it from chambers of commerce, had some influence on this southern President. Without doubt, the Commercial Club-boosted project turned out to have an economic importance that long outlasted the war: Muscle Shoals became one of the inspirations for, and the kernel of, the vast Tennessee Valley Authority project, launched under President Franklin Roosevelt.

The War Effort

On April 6, 1917, Congress declared war on Germany. Now, ready or not, the United States plunged into hostilities. Or rather, it plunged further into preparing for hostilities.

The essential problem was that the United States was embroiled in total war – while being 3,000 to 6,000 miles away from the primary scene of conflict. Ultimately the nation sent two million troops to Europe, but the remaining 101 million Americans had to support the daunting logistical and financial task of getting and keeping the men "over there." More war work happened in the United States than on the fields of Flanders, and local chambers of commerce were intimately involved.

Raising Money for the Troops

An important part of the home-front work was financial. The country needed to pay for the massive war effort primarily by either one of two methods: taxes or borrowing. Too heavy a tax burden could cripple the economy and strike a devastating blow to the country's ability to wage war. The government, then, selected a plan to pay for 40 percent of the war effort through taxation and 60 percent via borrowing.

To enhance borrowing capacity, the national government pushed for the sale of war savings bonds ("Liberty Loans" or "Liberty Bonds") and other instruments. A series of four Liberty Loan campaigns raised a total of $17 billion for the war effort, a staggering amount at the time, equal to about 20 times the federal budget in 1913. These bonds were offered at below-market interest, and had to be sold with appeals to buyers' patriotism.

The federal government did not have the manpower to sell all these instruments. But it needed some groups, quickly, to help out, even if they had no experience since the Civil War in raising money for combat. To paraphrase what Donald Rumsfeld said many decades later, "You go to war with the organizations you have."

Chambers of commerce were among the main community sales directors for these efforts. Referring to Liberty Bond and Red Cross fund drives, Rochester Chamber Secretary Howard Strong wrote in August 1917, "The commercial organization [chamber] usually has been responsible for these efforts."[51] Chambers often bragged in their annual reports over how much they did and how their communities oversubscribed their quotas. At the NACOS meeting where the "average" chamber secretary was described, he was declared active in the war fundraising effort: "During the war he led the Liberty and Victory Loan drives; he was mixed up in every kind of war and patriotic work and usually he put over the Red Cross campaigns."[52]

Liberty Loans certainly weren't the only activity, as the "average" secretary's tasks indicated. Indeed, the plethora of fundraising projects was confusing, as a Detroit expert related to a NACOS meeting:

> In Detroit we had the seven war camp activities: the Red Cross, the campaign for local organizations, and we also had a Belgian Baby fund, two Liberty Loan campaigns, and a War Savings Stamp campaign.[53]

One of the major advances in fundraising at this time was the War Chest, an effort that combined many charities into a single fundraising campaign. This innovation was not completely new; the Cleveland Chamber, in particular, had been refining the vetting of charities since 1900. And in 1913 the Cleveland Chamber introduced a concept borrowed from Denver clergymen, federated giving, into modern civic life with its Cleveland Federation for Charity and Philanthropy.[54] Under this plan, a company or an individual could write a single check to be spread among a basket of preapproved charities, or could make specifications of a preferred charity or charities. This saved business people and others time in evaluating charities and in writing checks. So captivating was this idea at the time that young author Kenneth Sturges called it "the greatest step in municipal history."[55]

By 1919 there were 20 such civic (non-war related) federated giving organizations in the United States. But the War Chest phenomenon, even though it began only with World War I, sped up the combined-donations idea phenomenally, reaching upwards of 500 communities by the end of the war.[56] Chambers of commerce were closely involved in many of these, helping to morph them after the war into Community Chests, which, in turn, would lead to today's United Way programs.

Oversight by the chamber and other civic-minded watchdogs was important. There was plenty of chicanery in fundraising then, as now. Indeed, a French canvasser seems to have taken the "war chest" idea literally: "there came to most of the War Chest cities last June the woman who had some large and prominent decoration attached to her bosom." She had a female partner wearing similar attractive decorations on her chest, and while they captivated many a male onlooker, astute questioning exposed them as frauds.[57]

Managing the Home Front

Chambers were also engaged in many home-front activities other than fundraising. These included leading drives for "Victory Gardens" to grow more food and free up supplies for the troops. There were plenty of these gardens: an estimated three million were planted in the United States in 1917, and more in 1918.[58]

The Santa Rosa Chamber, urged on by local storeowner Max Rosenberg, pushed for war gardens as a way to fight the high cost of living. The chamber also proposed a Luther Burbank Creations Garden, named after the city's most famous resident and the world's best known horticulturalist, who would later be named the "Honorary President" of the chamber.[59] The Raleigh Chamber did more than most: it "started six hundred and fifty-seven gardens among the school children of Raleigh."[60] Youngstown, Ohio, was in the same league, with a paid chamber worker supervising the activities of 600 garden volunteers; the chamber also paid for preparing and fertilizing the gardens.[61] The chamber in Tiffin, Ohio, too, hired a young man for the effort, gave him a Ford, and sent him to work. It was estimated that the chamber-led project "practically took the population of Seneca County off the market for the entire year's supply of vegetables."[62]

Business organizations also helped with food conservation. The Boston chamber proudly reported that New England led the nation in the saving of food, with 9.4 million pounds of beef (not to mention huge quantities of many other food items) saved over five months by hotels, restaurants, and clubs alone. Much of this was accomplished by a chamber member who was the Massachusetts Food Administrator and head of the Massachusetts Committee on Public Safety, a group started by the Boston Chamber.[63] Meanwhile, the San Francisco Chamber praised the advantages of whale meat.[64] Of the 60-person committee selected by Herbert Hoover for the national food conservation program, more than 20 were chamber secretaries.[65]

Getting a Fair Share of Military Spending

Chambers' efforts to get more military business for their members served a double purpose: to improve the war effort and to help their local economies. Some chambers later reported that they were contacted daily by federal departments with needs connected with the war effort. Often these requests were for industrial surveys and fact-finding. Washington officials did not have the time or the knowledge to ascertain where to obtain many of the thousands of products needed to keep an army in the field or a warship on the water.

The Boston Chamber of Commerce was more active than most. It was designated in charge of one of the War Industries Board's regions for industrial support of the war. The chamber sent out daily bulletins on procurement and helped vital suppliers get the appropriate classifications so that they could receive priority or restricted materials.[66]

The revived St. Louis Chamber created a manufacturers' group to be prepared for government contracts. By war's end that group had secured $300 million in military procurement. The chamber also managed to prevent the Quartermaster's Depot from leaving town, which had been the Army's plan. The St. Louis Depot was buying $250 million worth of products annually, of which about $75 million was from local suppliers.[67]

Army business came up suddenly and the early bird got the worm. St. Louis Chamber Secretary Paul Bunn gave an example of quick action by the chamber-organized manufacturers' group. Hearing of a need for textile work, the group "made a list of every factory in town possessing a power sewing machine, and within a few days five thousand machines were working on $8,000,000 worth of merchandise."[68]

The Indianapolis Chamber created the "Indianapolis Plan" for procurement, one that apparently was much imitated by other chambers, and that included representation in Washington.[69] The Columbus, Ohio, Chamber also retained a representative in Washington[70]. Houston, Los Angeles, New York – all these and more did what they could to get what they considered a fair share of military business.

The war effort included direct help or advice to the military. Chambers encouraged enlistment; the Cincinnati organization, for example, claimed to have been the first chamber to have opened a U.S. Naval Recruiting Station.[71] The Adjutant General of New York State,

Charles Sherrill, enlisted the state's chambers to provide volunteers to ensure that the armories in their area were being run in a businesslike manner.[72]

The New York Chamber of Commerce was involved in the war effort in many ways, including the hosting of the British War Commission on May 12, 1917, just five weeks after the United States entered the war. This was the largest meeting ever held by the chamber up to that time, with nearly 1,000 members present. Included in the large British delegation were Principal Secretary of Foreign Affairs Arthur Balfour and Bank of England Governor Lord Cunliffe of Headley. The occasion was mostly ceremonial but outlined the deep Anglo-American ties that the chamber had been fostering in most of the years since its founding under King George III. Moreover, the visit was an indication of how much Britain depended on not only the American armed forces but on the industrial might and financial resources of the world's richest nation.[73]

Pound for pound, few chambers could match the Pittsburgh Chamber of Commerce for its involvement in the war effort. Years later, a president of the chamber noted that the organization held 3,100 meetings in 1917 alone. It was estimated that the Pittsburgh region, he said, accounted for 35 to 40 percent of the war material used by the Allies in Europe.[74]

Wooden Ships

The New York Chamber had one very specific suggestion on the conduct of the war. In line with the organization's traditional interest in maritime affairs, the chamber had a study done on the depredations of German U-boats. The study indicated that the wooden ships advocated by some Navy proponents were, literally, going to be dead in the water: any slow ship was at risk of sinking by U-boat attack, and wooden ships were unusually slow. A noted chart produced by the chamber showed that of ships that had speeds of five knots or lower, and encountered submarine attack, 100 percent were sunk. At 16 knots, the odds improved dramatically: only 25 percent of the faster (steel) ships were sunk.[75]

The chamber study fell right into a white-hot controversy between two determined adversaries: General George Washington Goethals, the builder of the Panama Canal and now the general manager of the Emergency Fleet Corporation (overseer of the nation's merchant marine), and William Denman, a lawyer who was president of the EFC. Denman subscribed to what was even then seen as a crackpot scheme to suddenly build a lot of wooden boats to overcome the U-boat menace by quickly flooding the ocean with a great deal of shipping tonnage. Goethals, an engineer and a realist, wanted steel ships. He angered Denman at one point by telling the American Iron and Steel Institute that, as a contemporary paraphrased it, "birds were still nesting in the trees which were to be used for this phantom fleet."[76]

The New York Chamber's study pretended not to weigh in on the wooden ship vs. steel ship controversy, instead focusing just on speed. To anyone with common sense, however, it was clear that the chamber's research was turning the wooden-ship proponents' arguments to splinters. "It is better to build 200 boats at a speed that will enable them to go over and come back again than 500 or 1,000 that won't get through," said Outerbridge on July 19, 1917, releasing the report. The New York Chamber urged the public to push the military for deployment of fast ships.[77]

General Goethals resigned as general manager of the EFC the day after Outerbridge's statement. Goethals was upset at having his authority split with Denman, who still insisted on his wooden-headed scheme. Denman – whose public reputation was, compared to Goethals's, like that of a toy boat next to a battleship - resigned simultaneously. Some viewed the double resignation as a vindication of Goethals's steel-ship propensities; for others, the real problem was divided authority; neither man had the full mandate to carry out his wishes.[78]

The consensus of history, and indeed of most of contemporaries, was that Goethals's views on steel v. wood were correct. His reputation was vindicated in many ways, including by his being appointed as Acting Quartermaster General in December 1917. His resignation from the EFC had been a statement of principle that he would not participate in a wooden-ship scheme that would cost many lives.

E.H. Outerbridge and the New York Chamber remained staunch allies and friends of General Goethals. The Panama Canal veteran already had been elected an honorary member of the New York Chamber on April 5, 1917.[79] The chamber was also helping push New York and New Jersey toward a joint Port Authority, of which Outerbridge would be the first executive director and Goethals the first consulting engineer. Today New York Harbor features a Goethals Bridge and, near, it, another span called the Outerbridge Crossing.

Goethals Bridge

In any case, the New York Chamber had weighed in on a major wartime controversy and chose what we now know to be the right side. The chamber, famous for its stance on gold, picked steel. But did the chamber's position make a difference? Perhaps somewhat, but not too much: in October 1917, of 1,039 ships being built by the Emergency Fleet Corporation, 353 were still wooden.[80]

Military Bases

Many of the nation's base sites were chosen during World War I, and in the rush and confusion of those times, the armed services often depended on chambers of commerce to help select where, and how, to locate the troops and equipment. Chambers, of course, had every incentive to attract the maximum amount of federal activity to their areas. A military base had the potential for being a long-term economic driver for the community.

Atlanta's Camp Gordon is one example of a chamber's involvement in base selection. General Leonard Wood visited the area and asked the Atlanta Chamber to get options on several parcels of about a thousand acres each so that the Army could choose one of them. The chamber did so and the Army picked a site about 13 miles out of town, where, unfortunately, there was no water access. The Army officials indicated that if the land had no water supply, they would recommend another site potentially outside the area to the Secretary of War. And so the chamber raised $200,000 to lay the water main and Atlanta got the base.[81]

General Wood also visited Charlotte, N.C., looking for a camp site for 60,000 soldiers. This was more people than lived in Charlotte, and clearly would be a huge boon to the economy. But several other cities, including Fayetteville, N.C., were competing. The Charlotte Chamber spent a nail-biting 11 days on its campaign, from July 4 to 15, 1917, with each day presenting new challenges. The chamber sent two separate delegations to Washington, called on all its contacts for help, promised the area would not be unfriendly toward the many Catholic soldiers coming from the North, pledged $75,000 for a water main, and added acreage to the 2,500 it initially proposed. Finally Charlotte won Camp Nathanael Greene, gaining even a bigger economic benefit than expected. But in a consolation effort, Charlotte then helped Fayetteville win a smaller camp, which eventually grew into the massive Fort Bragg.[82]

Kelly Field in San Antonio, the leading air force base in the nation at the time, was "in a sense the favored child of the San Antonio Chamber of Commerce," according to a military publication after the war. The chamber assembled most of the land for the base from local cotton fields, presented the deal in Washington in June of 1917, and got approval the following month. The haste of the military was so great that it contracted for the chamber to manage the fields at cost. This was a highly unusual arrangement, but one that ended up saving Uncle Sam $5,000.[83]

There was room for expansion at Kelly Field, but British and French pilots were worried about collisions. Consequently, the San Antonio Chamber found more land further away and offered it to the military. This new site became Brooks Field and the chamber managed the property as it did Kelly Field.[84]

As in San Antonio, so in Houston. In the Texas port city, the chamber of commerce handled "every detail, from the leasing of the land to the purchasing of supplies," at Fort Logan. The chamber also found the land and managed the lease for Ellington Field, an air base. The chamber did this not only for patriotic reasons: the two projects resulted in "the expenditure of many thousands of dollars by the government, of which the merchants and business men of Houston have been benefited, and Houston has received her share of advertising."[85]

And so it went, in dozens of communities. It often took lobbying to get a base. The Kalamazoo Chamber pushed hard for a military facility in the area; soon a facility named after one of the military's most famous losers, Camp Custer, emerged near Battle Creek (becoming Fort Custer in 1940).[86] A delegation from Columbus, Georgia, pushed the Army for months to get Camp Benning (later Fort Benning).[87] The Denver Chamber of Commerce, which had successfully lobbied in 1887 for what became Fort Logan, repeated the coup in 1917, purchasing, and later donating, the land for what eventually became Fitzsimons Army Medical Center.[88] Dallas's chamber directors helped bring both Camp Dick and Love Aviation Camp (later the civilian airport, Love Field) in 1917.[89]

The Indianapolis Chamber of Commerce came across some useful wartime intelligence on a chance to provide training for soldiers:

> In February 1918 our office got a 'tip' to the effect that the Government was going to request colleges and technical schools to train drafted men in various trades. We immediately offered to found and maintain a school for the special purpose of training automobile mechanics. The Government sent representatives to confer with us, and finally decided as an experiment to allow us to train five hundred men. The experiment was so successful that we were asked on two occasions to enlarge our school and give training in additional lines. Eventually we had

signed contracts for training approximately 30,000 men, making our school the largest of its kind in the United States.[90]

The facility ultimately brought about $1.5 million in spending to Indianapolis. It was, however, not without problems. A drunken cook served "very bad food," the postwar influenza epidemic killed 56 and sickened 1,500, and an officer stole government property and hid it in his home in Cincinnati.[91]

Chambers, not surprisingly, were all over the military spending that was erupting with the war. And it wasn't just training, materials procurement, or the military camps and airfields. Business organizations were also involved in the moving of troops. The Boston Chamber, for example, wanted the city to be designated a port of embarkation for the war and prepared an extensive report that helped win it the business. The chamber then got General Goethals (now back in the Army as acting quartermaster general) to agree to build a $25 million warehouse, with Boston Chamber members involved in the project.[92]

But Boston and Philadelphia still weren't getting their fair share of business, according to the Philadelphia Board of Trade (BoT). New York's harbor was congested and expensive but swimming in business. There was surely discrimination going on:

> We note as a singular condition that Philadelphia and Boston alone, of all the principal ports in the country, have been unrepresented on the Shipping Control Committee of the U.S. Shipping Board – notwithstanding that such representation has been earnestly urged by these cities – and that by a remarkable coincidence neither of these ports has received what is believed to be its proper allotment of Government overseas freight.[93]

The BoT went further, lapsing into redundancy in its attempt to make sense of the excuses for the mysteriously reduced market share for Philadelphia:

> It has been the belief of many of us that these explanations have not been explained, and that the influences of hidden and perhaps sinister character lay behind the camouflage of this alleged elucidation of the problem.[94]

At one point, attempting to explain the "obscure subterranean purposes" undermining Philadelphia, the BoT cited the view "in some quarters" that the railroads were responsible for some of it, but backed off to say that "we have no means of ascertaining" it.[95] Clearly, tensions were high. The BoT members were furious, for example, that eight or 10 ships were diverted from Philadelphia to other ports; finally, when the *Haverford*, a returning troop ship, was to be shifted to New York, the board of trade exploded in protest and got the ship reassigned to the City of Brotherly Love.[96]

Coal Stoppage

Chambers' frustration with shipping and the railroads was intense. Their anger at one man in the government, however, approached apoplexy. In January of 1918, the U.S. Fuel Administrator demanded that for a week, coal shipments to businesses were to be suspended so that the military could be sure to get the needed supplies. A coal shortage had menaced the country, whose industry was operating at levels never before experienced. But a diversion of coal would shut down factories and other establishments, including those making military supplies. The one-week suspension plan seemed absurd, particularly to those who knew that coal sat on various rail sidings in the fabulously congested rail system. It was a drastic step that meant unfilled orders, workers without wages, and people shivering in cold apartments.

The New York Chamber's E.H. Outerbridge thundered, "This order gives the greatest aid and comfort to the enemy and the greatest dismay to our allies that any step by Washington could give."[97] Ralph Bauer, chairman of the Lynn, Mass., Board of Trade, protested against the federal request "for our people to put in five days working for the Kaiser."[98] The angry reactions poured in to Washington, not only from chambers of commerce but from labor unions and from individual business people.

Who was that masked man? What individual, commissar-like, was using the blunt tool of a week's fuel interruption to keep the war machine running? It wasn't a career bureaucrat. In fact, it was a past president of the Cleveland Chamber of Commerce - a man who had negotiated leases with John D. Rockefeller, who knew business inside and out, and who indeed had been the godfather to Kenneth Sturges's study of American chambers of commerce – Harry Augustus Garfield himself.

Fuel Administrator Garfield, as noted earlier, a friend of Woodrow Wilson, managed to keep his job. Indeed, he had defenders. There was a war on, after all. The controversy was soon forgotten as the combat news recaptured the headlines, the winter subsided, and the coal returned into factory bins.

War's End

The oldest chamber in the United States was the first to get the news of the end of World War I. Peace was announced at a New York Chamber meeting on November 7, 1918. Spontaneous cheering broke out.[99] Unfortunately, the report was a mistake and the war was still on; the armistice was actually signed four days later.

Winding things down from the great conflict wasn't easy. In particular, many business people worried about the effect of the sudden cancellation of Army and Navy munitions and supplies contracts. The Boston Chamber and other groups urged that the federal government reduce its orders gradually in order not to leave many firms suddenly stranded with raw materials, inventory, and excess employees. The federal government ended up agreeing to a gradual phasing down of war production.[100]

With so many servicemen coming home, chambers had another task: finding jobs for them. The Boston Chamber created a Committee of One Hundred, each of whom was pledged to find work for 10 men. The committee then was enlarged to 300. By May 15, 1919, the committee had placed 1,480 veterans; this "Boston system" was imitated in many other communities.[101]

Labor Unrest

During the Wilson years (1913-1921), the nation experienced an upsurge of labor unrest. Rapid industrial growth and rising aspirations and group consciousness among workers led to a series of strikes across the nation. Two of these strikes appear to have had an impact not only on their local chamber, but on who would become a future President of the United

States. Several of the work stoppages left deep scars on the social fabric of their communities and their chambers.

One of the largest strikes of 1913 began shortly before New Year's Day. On December 27, 1912, 100,000 garment workers went on strike in New York City. The Arbitration Committee of New York Chamber of Commerce immediately tried to mediate the strike, but talks broke off after a week. According to the chamber, however, the final settlement eight weeks later was substantially what had been proposed on the last day of the talks.[102]

From the standpoint of business, chambers were logical mediators for strikes. Not beholden to any one company, these organizations could take a broader view of the rights and wrongs of a situation. As the Boston Chamber put it, there was great value in "fair-minded mediation by a strong, representative body of business men, considerate of both sides and, therefore, giving reason of the confidence of both."[103] Sometimes chamber intervention worked, as in the New England telephone strike that was averted in 1913, or in the actual strike by "the girls" that the Boston Chamber helped conclude in 1918.[104]

Plenty of chamber efforts at mediation flopped, however. When chamber intervention failed, it often had to do not only with the positions of the two opposing sides but with workers' inherent suspicion of business organizations professing to take their interests to heart. This suspicion of the chamber would become apparent in yet another, and much higher profile, Boston strike, the police strike of 1919.

Many chambers of commerce were not shy about siding against labor. In November 1913 in Indianapolis, during a violence-tinged streetcar workers' strike, 31 police were accused of refusing to board street cars to protect replacement workers operating the cars. Mayor Samuel Shank backed the police, saying they would be risking their lives to climb aboard. The Indianapolis Chamber of Commerce threatened to file impeachment proceedings against the mayor for such conduct.[105] After it appeared there would be more labor troubles, Shank resigned, complaining mainly of "the criticism that has been heaped on me by the Safety Committee of the Chamber of Commerce."[106]

Labor-management confrontations could be extremely acrimonious. It didn't get much worse than in the village of Ludlow, Colorado, in April of 1914, when 22 people, many of them women and children, were killed by a National Guard assault against a camp of striking coal miners and their families in the eponymous Ludlow Massacre. The news electrified the nation, although "the [coal] operators and their friends, members of the Denver Chamber of Commerce," were accused of attempting to muzzle the Denver press.[107]

After the strike was terminated by the United Mine Workers in December 1914, John D. Rockefeller, the absentee owner of the main coal mine in the area, fired key executives of his management company and visited the Ludlow-Trinidad area, winning some friends for his apparent compassion.[108] In February 1915 the Trinidad Chamber of Commerce telegraphed the oil magnate, saying he "could do a great work for mankind by helping to relieve the distress of this community, including others besides former employees of the Colorado Fuel and Iron Company." Rockefeller indeed promised to assist these afflicted groups.[109]

John D. Rockefeller, Sr.

Rockefeller was to give $100,000, much of which was used to build roads, thereby improving the area and providing employment to jobless people at the same time. The Trinidad Chamber ended up owning and managing a 90-acre park donated by Rockefeller's coal company and made accessible by the roads program. Ironically, given what the victims were doing at Ludlow, the park was offered for camping.[110]

The Campaign for Law and Order

Beginning in late 1915, not long after the popular Panama-Pacific International Exposition had advertised San Francisco's commercial potential to the world, the city's docks were threatened with closure by longshoremen's strikes and persistent violence. Businessmen were worried and angry. In May 1916 the San Francisco Chamber of Commerce elected a new and activist slate of officers, including the president, Frederick J. Koster.

Koster, measuring 6 feet 2 inches tall and wearing size 12 shoes ("built like a fighter," said a magazine caption), was a barrel maker.[111] Although generous with his own employees, he was worried about union activities and believed strongly in the "open shop," meaning a workplace in which no union could compel an unwilling worker to join the union. What really disturbed him was the violence and radical activities that seemed to him to be a part of the union movement. A steady stream of labor-related beatings and harassment was pouring from the docks, despite the chamber's public protests and appeals to Mayor James Rolph Jr.

2,000 meet and establish the Law and Order Committee of the San Francisco Chamber of Commerce

Reacting to the violence, in a room packed with 2,000 people, the chamber set up a Law and Order Committee on July 10, 1916. Koster was the chair. Within five minutes after formation the group had $200,000 in pledges.[112]

Less than two weeks later, on July 22, 1915, San Francisco, like many other communities, held a Preparedness Day Parade. Unions, for whatever reason, had been excluded from the list of participating organizations, and some labor advocates urged a boycott. But a crowd of 50,000 was there to watch. A mile into the march, a bomb exploded, killing 10 and injuring 40.[113] Horror was nearly universal, matched by white-hot fury among chamber leaders and members, who suspected the bomb was the work of labor agitators.

Four days later, the Law and Order Committee held a meeting, this time with 6,000 people. The group was infused with a sense that San Francisco had been in this boat before. As Edward Hurlbut wrote in the *San Francisco Call* the next day:

They sat with us last night at the Auditorium, the brooding shades of the Vigilantes.

The high resolve that consecrated their work sixty years ago, recrudescent, spoke from the lips of the younger generation.

Grim, stern, patriotic, the sons of the sires of 1856 pledged themselves to carry on in sacred trust the fair name of a great city that these men of an elder time cleansed of stain and dishonor and passed along to us unsullied and glorious, a golden escutcheon without blotch.[114]

Koster proposed, and was urged to set up, a Committee of One Hundred, hearkening back to the chamber-linked Vigilance Committee of 1856. The new group would be peppered with famous, established businessmen of the port city, as well as some parvenu players, including a chamber board member named A.P. Giannini, whose Bank of Italy catered to local immigrants and working class people, and later would be called the Bank of America.[115]

The Law and Order Committee fought ferociously on all fronts – seeking the culprits for the bombing with reward money and fighting unions, strikes, and the closed shop at every turn. So galvanizing was the struggle that the chamber held, from August 29 to September 1, a membership drive using telephone operators. The result was a phenomenal increase in membership, from 2,400 to 6,313.[116] This made it, said the organization, the largest chamber in the nation. Indeed, the drive may have been the most successful chamber membership push in the history of voluntary chambers of commerce anywhere.

Yet in all the feverish struggles, something was overlooked. The chamber had moved on from merely decrying violence to embracing division. Few people supported beatings on the wharfs, but lots of intelligent people favored the idea of unions, including closed-shop unions. An all-out push for the open shop was for many thousands of San Franciscans a reach too far. And many of the strong-arm tactics of the Law and Order Committee, including trying to enlist the clergy on its side and setting up what was probably an illegal trial before Mayor Rolph in its unsuccessful attempt to remove a political opponent on the Board of Election Commissioners,[117] were low on most people's ethics meter. It seemed that this neo-vigilantism was getting out of hand.

Amid this thunderstorm of righteous anger and frantic activity, an incident occurred that may have changed American history. The Republican candidate for the Presidency, Charles Evans Hughes, had a one-day campaign swing through California that included a stop in San Francisco on August 19. He let himself be persuaded to eat at the Commercial Club, which, following the Law and Order Committee's campaign, insisted on having an "Open Shop" plaque in its window. Union waiters refused to serve under these circumstances, and the publicity was not only statewide, but national.

Hughes's move, among other gaffes, including a famous failure to meet with California's governor, Hiram Johnson, hurt him in this vital state. In fact, he lost the Presidential vote in California by only 3,775 votes. Had he won California, he would have had enough electoral votes to become President.

San Francisco, which went for Wilson by 15,000 votes, clearly made the difference. It's quite likely, according to author Steven C. Levi, that 3,775 votes and more were lost at that fateful Commercial Club lunch, where Candidate Hughes identified himself – simply by appearing in a restaurant with an "open shop" sign – with the strident views, questionable tactics, and white-hot anti-closed shop campaign of the Law and Order Committee. Any Progressive-minded voter in northern California, and there were many of them, would be concerned by such a dalliance with hardline Republicanism.

Hughes believed he lost California because he failed to meet Progressive Governor Hiram Johnson when their paths crossed in southern California. But Hughes, who had a politically tone-deaf ear in this state, is not the most credible reviewer of the political landscape there. Steven Levi's thesis, that Hughes lost California and the Presidency because of that ill-fated lunch at the Commercial Club, is just as plausible.[118]

The Law and Order Committee continued to operate for another three years, but with increasing acrimony and decreasing public support and credibility. Although the organization was never directly tied to what, in retrospect, appears to have been a frame-up of the two men accused of the Preparedness Day bombing (labor organizers Tom Mooney and Warren Billings), many suspected it of involvement. Finally, in August of 1919, the chamber dissolved its controversial committee.[119]

Across the Nation

Much of the country was having difficulties grappling with labor unrest, although mostly not to the extent of San Francisco's. The Clayton Antitrust Act of 1914 strengthened the hand of workers by exempting unions and farm organizations from the provisions of the Act. At the same time, the Act tightened the screws on companies, making it more difficult for firms to combine into trusts or otherwise cooperate.

Chambers emphatically did not like the provision in the Act exempting unions and farm organizations. In fact, the U.S. Chamber's referendum on the topic found 99 percent opposed to the exemption.[120] (This united opposition did not result in the removal of the exemption, however, which even today ruffles the feathers of business people and their organizations.) But rarely were chambers this much in synch in their approaches to labor questions.

Even in the San Francisco Bay Area, chamber-labor relations differed. In 1916, the same year in which the San Francisco Chamber set up its fire-breathing Law and Order Committee, the Oakland Chamber of Commerce established its Common Weal Committee. This group, with five labor representatives and five employers, successfully brought an end to several labor disputes. Perhaps with a sympathetic if not patronizing glance across the bay, the Oakland Chamber's Eugene Bowles wrote in 1919, "Employer and employee were too inclined to circle around each other like a couple of snarling terriers. Now they pull together for the upbuilding of the community."[121]

Yet the spirit of the times, especially in the turbulent atmosphere after the troops came home from the European war, was less than pacific in many cities. Boston already had faced many labor crises, several of them handled smoothly by the chamber. In 1919, a dispute arose that the chamber couldn't manage.

The Boston Police Strike

The Boston Chamber, ever since its renewal under the leadership of Ryerson Ritchie, had taken a positive, civic-minded approach to the welfare of the city. Trying to fight corruption and improve the moral tone of local politics, the chamber had created the Good Government Association (GGA). The notoriously sleazy Mayor James Michael Curley merrily called this group the Goo-Goos.[122]

The GGA pushed for an alternative to Mayor Curley, and ended up successfully placing a nonentity named Andrew James Peters in the city's top job in 1917. Peters's political ineptitude, unfortunately, would help turn a serious labor dispute into national news.

Boston's police felt they were underpaid and overworked, and by some measures they were – although their salaries compared favorably with those of the average employee of the time. Police Commissioner Edwin Curtis warned his patrolmen not to form a union, but they wished to affiliate with the American Federation of Labor (AFL), which put them on a collision course with the city. The Boston Chamber of Commerce strongly supported Curtis. Indeed, an advertisement for "Able-Bodied Men" willing to protect city property asked them to report to the Chamber of Commerce Building.[123] Union organizers quickly denounced the chamber's serving as "the recruiting station for strike-breaking police."[124]

Trying to avoid a strike, Mayor Peters turned to an individual who was considered the most public-spirited of business people, James Jackson Storrow, who had been a founder of the revived Boston Chamber and was also involved in many other civic activities. In 1910, he had reorganized and headed General Motors, and then returned to the town he loved. He ran the chamber-created Massachusetts Committee on Public Safety during the war. He gave to many local causes. Storrow was as trusted a man as the business community could offer Boston.[125]

Unfortunately, Storrow's blue-ribbon committee failed to find common ground between the city and the police. Although most groups, including the Boston Chamber,[126] supported the committee's plan, Commissioner Curtis rejected the compromise. Meanwhile, eager recruits, including brawny ex-Harvard athletes, continued to sign up at the Chamber of Commerce Building, ready to take a stand for public order if called on.

They got their chance on September 9, 1919, when most of the police walked off the job. Before long the city erupted in riots, and the remaining police and the chamber recruits were unable to control the crowds. People broke store windows and looted openly, fighting back at anyone who stood in their way.

Ultimately Governor Calvin Coolidge had to call in the state militia to restore order. It turned out the physical damage wasn't as bad as feared – a third of a million dollars - and the human toll, while serious, was not catastrophic: eight killed, 21 seriously wounded, and 50 or more injured.[127] But most of the public, both in Boston and outside it, was furious at the police for walking off the job and leaving the city to the mercy of criminals. Coolidge was adamant that the striking police should not be allowed to return to work under any circumstances. This man of few words wrote a string of them that would make him famous: "There is no right to strike against the public safety by anybody, anywhere, any time."

The Boston Chamber's role in the crisis, ultimately, was ineffective. The mayor whom the chamber had helped into office was useless in the affair; the chamber couldn't persuade Commissioner Curtis to compromise; and the hundreds of young men recruited at the Chamber of Commerce Building had not been numerous enough to turn the tide of the riots. But the striking police, inadvertently, had made business's point more effectively than a business organization ever could.

The police had proven that they were needed, and that they should never be permitted to strike again. There were no police strikes in the entire United States in the ensuing decades. Meanwhile, Governor Coolidge had been propelled into the national limelight. Eventually this man would become President, thanks largely to his role in fixing what the chamber couldn't.

And so, paradoxically, the Boston Chamber got exactly what it wanted: a local and national political climate that increasingly favored civic calm, or "normalcy" in another U.S. President's famous phrase. The city of Boston, and the country, would be made safe for commerce. With a little civic order, it was amazing what economic feats the country would be able to achieve.

Civil Rights and Civil Unrest

Labor troubles and the war weren't the only concerns during the Wilson era. Racism, religious prejudice, and xenophobia were never far from view. Chambers of commerce were involved in working through these issues and, from a modern perspective, had a mixed record, although their country's was mixed, too - and the chambers may have come out slightly better than their nation as a whole.

In 1915, a Jewish factory supervisor, Leo Frank, was accused of the murder of a young white factory girl in Marietta, Georgia, just outside Atlanta. He was jailed for the killing and sentenced to die, but the governor commuted his sentence to life imprisonment, as there were clearly holes in the case. Shortly thereafter, however, a mob extracted him from jail and lynched him.

Much of Atlanta was horrified, as was the nation. The Atlanta Chamber of Commerce condemned the killing; not only was the lynching wrong, but it had a catastrophic impact on economic development in Georgia. An estimated half of the 3,000 Jewish people in the state moved out,[128] and suddenly there was one more reason for northern manufacturers to think twice about opening a plant in Atlanta.

Indeed, the waspish journalist H.L. Mencken would assert in 1920 that "the Leo Frank affair was no isolated phenomenon." He wrote:

> Georgia is at once the home of the cotton-mill sweater and of the most noisy and vapid sort of chamber of commerce, of the Methodist parson turned Savonarola and of the lynching bee.[129]

Yet clearly the Atlanta Chamber wanted no part of any extralegal proceedings – or for that matter, persecution of Jews. Indeed, after the Frank incident, a Jewish businessman who had been active in the chamber, Victor Kriegshaber, was elected its president. While this reflected his hard work, "it was also a way for the business community to placate the Jewish community in the wake of Leo Frank's lynching earlier that year."[130]

Racial tension increased in many parts of the nation during and after World War I. The hungry factories of the North needed workers from the South, and hundreds of thousands of blacks moved north to get jobs and to escape oppressive Jim Crow laws. Meanwhile, black soldiers moved through the country and into Europe, seeing new ways of life and realizing that the racial environment back home wasn't something that existed everywhere.

The Riot in East St. Louis

In East St. Louis, Illinois, tensions were high in mid-1917 as war production soared and the city attracted migrants from other regions, including blacks from the Deep South. At one firm, the Aluminum Ore Company, many white workers had been discharged because of their union affiliation, and most were replaced by blacks. On May 28, after a trade union group met Mayor Fred Mollman complaining about black in-migration, a mob of 3,000 whites began beating up blacks. Attacks continued sporadically the next day and subsided as six companies of National Guardsmen arrived in town.[131]

Things were quiet in June, but nothing was done to defuse the tension. On July 2, as rumors circulated of blacks attacking whites, a white riot ensued. By its end, between 40 and 200 people were dead, most of them African-American. Some were lynched, others shot, still others burned in the fires set by the rioters. This riot is believed to have cost more African-American lives than any other in U.S. history.

The event, of course, was a disaster for the local economy. Many African-Americans fled the community. The East St. Louis Chamber of Commerce issued a resolution demanding reorganization of the police and fire departments. It also called for blacks to return to the city and promised them protection of life and property; without their labor, the local factories would lose production. The rail yards of East St. Louis, which supplied transportation for the people and goods of the entire metro area, also needed their laborers back, according to the traffic manager of the St. Louis Chamber.[132]

The East St. Louis and St. Louis chambers found the riot to be a catastrophe. They wanted and needed these black workers. Who was responsible for the disaster?

Indeed, at a meeting in Carnegie Hall to celebrate the new Russian democracy, the AFL's Samuel Gompers implicitly laid the blame for the East St. Louis riot on the people (presumably factory owners) who had "lured" blacks from the Deep South to come to Illinois to work, thereby destabilizing conditions for the whites. Gompers said, drawing on a reference to the East St. Louis Chamber to garner support for his argument, "I can tell you that not only labor men but a member of the Chamber of Commerce of East St. Louis warned the men engaged in luring negroes from the South that they were to be used in undermining the conditions of the laborer in East St. Louis."

Gompers went on: "The luring of these colored men to East St. Louis is on a par with the behavior of the brutal, reactionary, and tyrannous forces that existed in Old Russia."

Gompers's dais-mate, Theodore Roosevelt, listened to Gompers a bit longer, and then asked to talk. He exploded, shaking his fist close to Gompers's cheek and said there was no excuse for murder. "I will go to any extreme necessary to bring justice to the laboring man to insure him his economic place, but when there is murder I'll put it down and I'll never surrender!"[133]

The crowd went wild during the altercation, but the obvious emotion on all sides shows how, in many people's minds, the East St. Louis riot was caused by labor friction. And was this, indeed, a job of evil "lurers" who brought blacks north? Weren't blacks capable of making such decisions themselves? And was it wrong to bring blacks north? If so, were there "good" people, as implied by Gompers, who tried to counteract the luring?

After the riot, the Black Nationalist Marcus Garvey saw a different kind of conspiracy – an "anti-luring" conspiracy. In a speech on July 8, he accused East St. Louis Mayor Fred Mollman of working with the New Orleans Board of Trade and Louisiana politicians to try to stop the migration of blacks north. Louisiana farms and businesses needed their black labor and didn't want it flowing north. Mollman indeed may have done as Garvey accused him: it appears he did meet with the New Orleans Board of Trade and discuss this topic, and perhaps he did make blacks feel unwelcome in East St. Louis, as Garvey argued.[134] But that doesn't directly implicate Mollman in the killing and destruction. It does, however, provide one more indication of how great the stakes were on all sides: the massive migration of blacks from South to North intensified pressures on society, on labor, on business, and on chambers of commerce.

Facing the Great Migration

Business organizations in the South, after Henry Grady especially, became focused on attracting people and business from the North. But as we have seen, all the while they witnessed a massive example of reverse economic development - in the form of an outflow of blacks to better work and better lives in the North. It wasn't just the New Orleans Board of Trade that attempted to put a stopper in the drain. The departure of so many workers caused many in the South to want to improve conditions for local blacks.

One of the more high-profile activities in this regard was carried out by the Memphis Chamber of Commerce beginning in 1917. There, George James, the chairman of the industrial welfare committee, studied the conditions of African-Americans and spoke on "the causes and the means to check the exodus of negroes from the South."[135] His committee launched a fundraising campaign to improve the lot of local blacks. The committee aimed to make Memphis the "best negro city in the South" and asked employers to contribute $2 per worker, with another $1 per man "to be raised by the negroes themselves." The money was to be used for such items as an orphanage, playgrounds, and vocational education.[136]

The chamber in nearby Greenville, Mississippi, a self-styled progressive city with an active chamber, launched a similar program in 1920 and gave credit to the Memphis Chamber for its three years' work in this area. The Greenville Chamber placed an ad in the Memphis *Commercial Appeal* that included this statement:

> We, the undersigned citizens of Greenville and Washington County, Mississippi, hold it to be self-evident that the racial contentment, prosperity, and progress of the laboring classes of any country or community are essential factors in the permanent prosperity and progress of such country or community as a whole.
>
> This is just as true where the bulk of such laboring population are Negroes as it is where they are white.[137]

Greenville became famous for its liberal approach to civil rights and for its crusading editor (and chamber member) Hodding Carter. Although the city was ahead of its time, in 1920 it still expressed genteel prejudice, offering, to give a patient hearing to the suggestions of "any respectable Negro of this community."[138]

The Nashville Chamber of Commerce fought a local injustice against blacks. There, the police made a weekly roundup of African-Americans and took them to court, "where they were always found guilty of whatever charge was assessed against them." They were invariably fined. As a result of the chamber's angry protests, a lawyer was assigned to the court to defend all African-Americans who were brought in.[139]

Other chambers, too, tried to better the lot of blacks in the South, in part to keep them from migrating to the North. The secretary of the white chamber in Gastonia, N.C., reported the creation of the Negro Business Men's League there in 1917, a group of "over 100 members, all old and reliable negroes of Gastonia." One of the League's goals was to develop industry and jobs that would "keep them in the South."[140]

Things were far from perfect in the North, however. Race riots broke out in many northern cities just after World War I. After one occurred in Omaha, in which a black rape suspect was lynched and the reformist mayor, Ed Smith, was strung up and almost killed, soldiers came in to restore order. The chamber offered sympathy to the mayor and drew up plans to prevent such occurrences in the future.[141]

Conditions for blacks in northern cities were seldom comfortable. Chambers occasionally took up their cause. The Detroit Board of Commerce's magazine, the *Detroiter*, criticized "rapacious" landlords as well as the practice of housing discrimination against blacks.[142]

Americanization

Following World War I, a wave of xenophobia swept the United States, powered in part by a desire to retire from the continuing troubles in Europe, in part by the public's confusion over its large immigrant population, and in part by the bloody Russian Revolution and civil war. The resulting Red Scare and Palmer raids were a blot on American civil liberties that many in the public, and in chambers of commerce, did not oppose.

A frequent chamber response to the postwar isolationist mood, however, was relatively harmless. It was the advocacy of "Americanization" programs for immigrants, such as the teaching of English and civics. These Americanization programs, which had been in existence for some time, had perhaps a nativist inspiration – after all, their name implied that the immigrants weren't fully American – but they did some good, too, helping a number of immigrants speed their climb up the economic ladder.

The era also witnessed a revival of ill feeling against Mormons. The Salt Lake Commercial Club, which had, with some difficulty, managed to help keep its local Mormon and "gentile" (non-Mormon) communities at peace, fought this upsurge of prejudice. In 1919, the club sent a group of non-Mormon business people, together with one church elder, to a Christian conference in Pittsburgh. These people tried to address the audience but were booed down.

The club responded by producing a pamphlet called "Anti-Mormon Slanders Denied," which debunked such myths as a report from England that "this very minute the church elders have twelve hundred girls ready for shipment to Utah." The Salt Lake Commercial Club noted that three quarters of its members were non-Mormon and that these members could attest that such wild rumors were completely unfounded.[143]

Peaceful Pursuits in Turbulent Times

Life went on even as concerns over the war, labor, and social change continued. And chambers of commerce pursued their traditional interests in education, economic development, infrastructure, and civic life. These busy organizations, while tackling the Germans and the American Federation of Labor, also attempted to make their communities just a little better than the one down the road.

Chambers continued to have a fascination with fairs and expositions, although the First World War dampened some of the enthusiasm. Two high-profile fairs took place in 1915 in California, both of them initially announced at their local chamber and heavily supported by that chamber.

In San Francisco, the Panama-Pacific International Exposition was anticipated with great excitement after San Francisco Chamber President James McNab first broached the idea.[144] His predecessor as chamber president, Charles C. Moore, was tapped to be the president of the exposition.

Despite the onset of war in Europe in 1914, the fair was a great success, attracting more than 18 million visitors and making a profit. The event featured a working Ford automobile factory that produced 18 vehicles a day. Another high-tech highlight was the first transcontinental phone call, between expo chief Moore and President Woodrow Wilson.[145]

The Panama-Pacific International Exposition was the biggest event held to date in the West and was – in part because it championed progress, a concept that would come into question with the great destructive wars and genocides of the 20th century - "the last of the classic world's fairs."[146] One of San Francisco's best-known landmarks, the Palace of Fine Arts, was originally built for the exposition. (While it fell into disrepair later, it was rebuilt in the 1960s.) All in all, the exposition was a source of lasting pride both for San Francisco and for its chamber.

The San Diego Chamber of Commerce had wanted to win the international fair that San Francisco obtained. San Diego proponents, however, persuaded both the San Francisco authorities and Congress to permit the city to hold a smaller fair, the Panama California Exposition. The chamber accentuated the regional, Spanish character to its celebration and the buildings. The city experienced a boom even before the fair came:

> As the building of the exposition gained great progress by 1913, [Chamber President] Davidson claimed the Chamber had "waved a magic wand over the city and inaugurated a period of permanent growth, which, while as rapid as any attending the 'boom days' of other places, is strikingly substantial and enduring."[147]

The population grew from under 40,000 in 1910 to about 70,000 at the time of the fair. And the event itself turned out to be a hit, with 2 million visitors in 1915 and a beautified City Park (whose name was changed to Balboa Park) as a lasting monument.

Education

Chambers took increasing interest in primary and secondary education during the Progressive Era, aiming for community betterment and, in some cases, inspired by the pathbreaking clerk training programs of the London Chamber of Commerce. But in big cities, reform often took the angle of removing education from the control of political machines and putting it into the hands of the experts. In an uncanny echo of modern times, business organizations tried to measure the output of the schools and to figure out ways to improve the "product."

In 1916, for example, the San Francisco Chamber performed a study showing that centralizing and professionalizing reforms were needed for the school system.[148] But the superintendent and others objected. The debate continued. Among the opposition's complaints was that not allowing school board members to take salaries would remove people of modest means from the board.[149] The chamber's reforms appeared to many to be a rich people's takeover of the schools.

One critic said the whole reform effort "was conceived, born, and nursed in the Chamber of Commerce conspiracy" and that as soon as the chamber took over the school board, it would hire "an Eastern, imported, high-salaried 'superintendent'" who would force teachers to "wear the Chamber of Commerce collar."[150] Nevertheless, the chamber and its progressive allies ultimately won the battle of public opinion. While the amendment that included these reforms failed to pass in 1918, it finally succeeded two years later.[151]

In New York, the struggle was just as messy. The New York Chamber released a report in 1917 that lambasted the school system for, among other things, being unable to get rid of teachers:

> It now takes twenty-four of the forty-six members of the Board of Education to dismiss a teacher after a protracted trial and if, with the custom above cited, is added personal sympathy and political influence in favor of a delinquent, it is not surprising that, in a force of 20,000 teachers, few if any have been dismissed for inefficiency during the past ten years.[152]

The report was fiercely critical. At one point, the paper quoted an anonymous principal saying that of his 400 graduates, not one was competent to "fill the lowest clerical job in a banking house."[153]

What followed was a textbook lesson in the disciplining of chambers of commerce. The press "viciously attacked" the study, complained Howard C. Smith, the chamber's education committee chair.[154] Ultimately, the chamber didn't have the heart to fight back. A critic noted that the chamber seemed to be politically tone deaf on some issues, citing the example of a new state constitution, which the chamber had championed but which the voters had overwhelmingly rejected.[155]

So the New York Chamber gave in. Moving the education establishment in the great city was much more difficult than advising the government on U-boat defense or meeting with the British War Commission or the Prince of Wales.

In this period, despite occasional acrimony, there was a good deal of interest in bringing business and education together. Shortly after World War I, NACOS joined with public school superintendents to create the National Committee for Chamber of Commerce Co-operation with the Public Schools (NCCCCPS). This group consisted of chamber secretaries and school superintendents from 30 cities. NCCCCPS, with the help of the American City Bureau, conducted surveys of schools in cities with 8,000 or more people in order to find out what more needed to be done in K-12 education.[156]

Not surprisingly, NCCCCPS found lots of weaknesses, and its results were widely disseminated. Teacher salaries had not kept up with inflation after World War I[157]; kindergartens needed more money[158]; of 295 cities, only 22 had tenure for teachers[159]; of every 100 children who were in school at age nine, only 36 were still in school at age 16[160]; buildings needed repair; and so on. The upshot of this study was a lesson that would be repeatedly taught in future decades: the schools needed more money.

In post-secondary education, chambers continued their pursuit of colleges as economic development plums. The ever-energetic Atlanta Chamber of Commerce helped raise $260,000 to revive the dormant Oglethorpe University, a Presbyterian school, in 1913.[161] In El Paso, the chamber of commerce put together $50,000 to attract the Texas School of Mines (today the University of Texas at El Paso) in 1914.[162] In Evansville, Ind., the chamber learned of a disastrous fire at the Methodist Moores Hill College and reached out to attract the school. After more twists and turns than a mountain road, including a cliff-hanging chamber-led fundraising campaign for $500,000, Evansville got its college in 1919.[163]

A Boost to Growth

"The hurrah circus style fellow, who shouted himself hoarse for his town, has practically disappeared from the scene."[164] Thus solemnly spoke William George Bruce, secretary of the chamber in Milwaukee, while delivering a paper on the history of NACOS at a meeting in 1918. How wrong Bruce was. As chamber executives attempted to add dignity to their profession, they preferred not to think about its promotional side. But when many of the delegates went home from NACOS conventions, they were banging the marketing drums with the usual fervor.

No one did it better, or with more conviction, than Frank Wiggins and his friends and directors at the Los Angeles Chamber of Commerce. Wiggins's outgoing president, Arthur Kinney, while addressing the annual banquet of the chamber in 1914, recited this poem about his ambitious city:

Los Angeles Will Be Great

Los Angeles will be great! She e'er has been
A temple to the strength of unity.
Our city's greatness has been well deserved,
Well earned has been her fame; her fitness for
Supremacy long demonstrated by
Her leadership in all those things that call
For vim, for patriotic enterprise,
For optimism, pluck and loyalty;
Her wondrous growth has been the proud reward
Of steadfast faith and tireless energy.

Los Angeles will be great! Her people dream
Fond dreams of greater destiny to come,
With hopes exalted, energies unflagged;
With purpose high, to cherished ideals pledged,
With past unsullied and with future sure,
They strive for every human betterment;
They recognize the vision of the world,
And realized will be each radiant dream.
Los Angeles will be great! Our city proud,
Is loved by all who live within her gates.
With hearts begetting progress unsurpassed,
With spirit of heroic mold sublime,
They will, in splendor, through the flight of years
Go conquering. Los Angeles will be great![165]

Even if its poetry was not great, Los Angeles would be heard. The chamber took brass bands and back-slapping goodwill delegations to neighboring communities. One such trip carried "five solid trainloads of Los Angeles Glad-Handers."[166] In the same year (1913-14), the chamber distributed 2.5 million pieces of literature promoting the metropolis.[167]

It was not just Los Angeles. For example, the goodwill and trade delegations were exceedingly common. Even longer "trade extension trips" took place in great numbers. A NACOS study in 1917 found 75 chambers reporting that they took week-long trips of 1,000 to 2,000 miles.[168]

Despite high-toned chambers' objections to "factory-grabbing," the process of aggressively seeking new employers continued. The Buffalo Chamber of Commerce was proud of its record: "The population of Buffalo will be increased by 10,000 because of four ads in the *Saturday Evening Post*," it crowed. Apparently those four ads had brought in 18 factories employing 3,200 people, with a combined investment of $3 million.[169]

The Cincinnati Chamber emphasized the critical, central location of the community. It provided one of the early examples of "concentric circle" marketing – drawing circles on a map to show how many people were close by. The Cincinnati map indicated, for example, that within 500 miles there were 43 million people.[170]

Chambers continued to exhibit energy and occasional creativity in their methods of raising money for economic development and other civic purposes. In Middletown, Ohio, the chamber set a record for per-capita civic fundraising: $40. In a community of 25,000 people, the chamber found 9,000 donors providing a total of $1,030,000.[171]

At the Scranton Board of Trade, members were acutely aware that the rich seams of anthracite coal nearby would not last forever. The BoT had been seeking new industry for some time but in 1913 created a financial instrument to help this process along. The group sold $100,000 worth of bonds for development, and then, in 1914, began a scheme to raise $1 million in bonds in 10 days in order to "Make Scranton Grow." That campaign, which was reported in many newspapers across the nation, ended up bringing in $1.144 million in eight days. The following year, bolstered with this money, the BoT was able to create the Scranton Industrial Development Company to help fund new ventures for the community.[172]

In 1916 a chamber executive named Porter Whaley told his Texas colleagues of a new concept in chamber financing. His chamber had become tax-supported and was called the Amarillo Board of City Development. Some Texas chambers saw this move as counterproductive, with the chamber losing its independence from, and therefore the credibility to criticize, the local government. Other Texas chambers adopted the model on the premise that if economic development and business attraction was benefiting everyone in the community, then everyone should pay. Ultimately, the model shifted so that many Texas chambers would raise money from members and be relatively independent, while at the same time sequestering their economic development work and performing it under contract to the city.[173]

Solar-Powered Economic Development

Another part of the country was quietly preparing its own economic revolution: south Florida. And one man would light the fuse, a born booster by the name of E.G. Sewell. Sewell grew up in semi-wild Kissimmee, Fla., where people hunted the wolf packs that attacked their cattle. In 1896, hearing that John D. Rockefeller associate Henry Flagler was building a railroad to a place called "Miami," Sewell moved there.

He arrived in a place that boasted just two families. As a later chronicler reported, "Seminoles paddled in with skins and egret plumes from the fearsome Everglades, which were described as 'deadlier than African jungles.'" But the Flagler railroad brought many workers and Sewell sold them shoes. By 1911, the town had grown enough that people raised enough money to bring the Wright Brothers to town to show off their aircraft.

Henry Flagler died in 1913, leaving the town with a hotel and a railroad and not much else. The following year, Sewell came up with his big idea. He read a newspaper article that indicated Americans would not be able to travel to Europe for vacations because of the war. Europe's loss was Miami's gain, he realized. Sewell passed the hat among Miami's 7,500 residents and in two weeks raised $3,000 for tourism promotion – "Miami's first booster fund."

The promotion succeeded beyond his expectations. The town was swamped with 5,000 tourists that winter. In the same year, 1915, Sewell was elected president of the Miami Chamber of Commerce. From this chamber perch, Sewell went on to one triumph after another, bringing hordes of tourists to the land of egrets.[174]

Sewell's secret of economic development success was not minerals or water power or rich soil or skilled workers. In fact, his success wasn't really local. He was staking everything on a flickering ball of fire 93 million miles away. The chamber filled the trains with sacks of literature featuring photos of scantily clad women acquiring tans. Often it was the same trains that would return in winter, bearing thousands of people from the North and Midwest, Flagler's and Sewell's children, coming in from the cold.

The Back Country

By this period, most chambers had split off from their grain-trading operations.[175] But the hinterlands of chambers of commerce were fertile fields, literally, for economic development activity. In 1914, when asked their leading accomplishments of the previous year, the most common type of achievement they cited was in building up agriculture.[176]

The chamber-initiated Farm Bureau momentum gathered steam during the Wilson years but was only one of many examples of chamber-agriculture ties. At the NACOS meeting in 1916, U.S. Agriculture Secretary David Houston indicated some of the reasons that business organizations might want to work with the farm movement, including the importance of the "back country" to city economies, farming's status as the largest industry in the country, and the Agriculture Department's big budget ($36 million).[177]

And many chambers beyond the Farm Bureau hotbed in upstate New York realized the value of agriculture. The Memphis Chamber, for example, raised $90,000 in 1919 for a three-year program to support the farm business in its region.[178] St. Louis garnered $75,000 for similar activity, while a Texas town boosted its purchasing power in three years from $7,400 to $75,000 by following suggestions from the Houston Chamber of Commerce.[179]

One of the key values of a focus on the hinterlands was in the promotion of that perennial favorite of chambers of commerce: getting governments to spend money on infrastructure. There were huge amounts of federal and state money available for good roads – and many of these roads went through farming regions. And then there were dams. . .

Dams to Help Those Poor Farmers

We have already seen how the potential for fertilizer and hydroelectric power production for southern farms was one of the points used to support arguments in favor of the Muscle Shoals dam and nitrate plant. Similarly, in the Wilson years, the Los Angeles Chamber of

Commerce began expressing an unusual degree of interest in "flood control" on behalf of the farmers in the path of the Colorado River. This concern for far-off farmers was unusual, to say the least: the chamber certainly had shown no similar concern for the farmers of the Owens Valley. (There, beginning in November 1913, the chamber-advocated Los Angeles Aqueduct slowly drained out the water from the once-lush valley.)

Why was the LA Chamber so worried about the poor Imperial Valley farmers? First, these struggling toilers represented what could become a rich hinterland, albeit a somewhat distant one. But more importantly, helping them with Colorado River floods also would mean damming the river, harnessing both the water's power and the water itself. This would represent a great shot of H2O, as well as a massive jolt of hydroelectric power, for Los Angeles.

Getting federal or even state money for the purpose of grabbing water to grow Los Angeles was not a politically saleable idea. But controlling floods that swept across state and even national borders, inundating helpless farmers – that was a job for Uncle Sam. Hence it was under the politically correct title of "Colorado River Regulation" that the chamber's 1914 annual report made clear some of its designs on this hinterland:

> Second in importance to none of the projects fathered by our Chamber and having as their object the development and progress of our Southwestern empire, is the plan for conserving the flood waters of the Colorado River by means of a system of immense dams and reservoirs.

"Conserving the flood waters" expressed the politically correct approach perfectly. The pristine Colorado snowmelt was not being seized; its unwelcome, excess, flood waters were being kept and used for good. And then, what a "back country" this would be:

> Contiguous to this river are one million acres of the richest soil which, when watered by our American Nile, will be made most highly productive. Thus will be doubled the present cultivated area of Southern California, and thus will be doubled the tributary domain of Los Angeles. Here in this mighty Colorado basin, through the splendid years to come, will be the stupendous field of action of the dreamers of great dreams and those who make them become realities – those sturdy men of toil who never fail to conquer – the empire builders of the west, whom all civilization delights to honor.[180]

Yes, it was an exciting project, making the desert bloom with conserved water and swirling currents of federal dollars. And that wasn't all. The project, eventually to become the Hoover Dam, would offer a delicious drink of water for Los Angeles.

There was another chamber with a true passion for its hinterland: the Spokane Chamber of Commerce in Washington state. Ever since a group in Spokane had organized the first chamber there in 1887, which in turn had put on a "Fruit Fair," agriculture had been an obsession for business in the area.[181] In 1910 this chamber achieved a national spotlight, and the praise of Teddy Roosevelt, when it had published the report of a Country Life Commission that had been suppressed under the Taft Administration.[182]

The Spokane Chamber also hosted a national Country Life convention; created a national apple show, potato show, and countless other conferences and events; and led visits throughout the wide agricultural region that was called the Inland Empire. In 1919, moreover, the chamber obtained $100,000 from the state legislature for the first survey of the Columbia Basin. The following year, the chamber organized the Northwest Reclamation Congress.[183] In the Twenties, these efforts would be reinforced and would lead to another massive water control project.

A New Kind of Transportation Initiative

War may be hell, but for chambers of commerce, it was a hell fully paved and dredged. Business organizations can't be stopped from moving mud or asphalt or performing cargo cult-like dances for airplanes.[184] The traditional chamber fetish for transportation infrastructure continued during the Wilson years, with a massive boost from World War I spending. Countless harbors, from Houston's to Manhattan's, were improved with federal aid. And military bases often included airfields, some of which would have peacetime uses.

For transportation infrastructure, perhaps the greatest long-term accomplishment in this period came out of the New York Chamber of Commerce: the creation of the New York-New Jersey Port Authority. The idea germinated within the chamber for some time, and by the end of the war the plans were coming to fruition, aided by allies such as the New York Merchants' Association and most other business groups (other than the New York Board of Trade and Transportation[185]). The concept was astonishingly ambitious: to remove the basic transportation approach of the nation's largest metropolis from the politics of two jealous states and one proud city.

Calvin Tomkins had brought up some of the basic issues at a chamber meeting on February 3, 1916. Ironically, a man who would later oppose the idea of a port authority was now setting it in motion. In the paper he delivered on the topic, Tomkins wrote that "we seem to have overlooked the fact that the city exists because of the port, and that the Port of New York and New Jersey is the greatest and most badly organized commercial and manufacturing seaport of the world."[186] People knew what needed to be done, but weren't doing it.

One of the problems was simply connecting railroads to the port in an efficient way. As things stood in early 1916, the system was close to breakdown: "For many months, a terminal congestion amounting at times to a freight embargo has existed in New York." There had to be a unified organization to deal with all the carriers and nine railroad terminal systems to make sense out of the chaos. Tomkins recommended that a study be conducted on the problem; the savings from better management would surely recoup its costs.[187]

Tomkins's timing, in retrospect, was close to perfect. The freight and shipping requirements of the war had ratcheted up pressure on the port. But the U.S. had not entered the war yet at the time of his talk, and so that pressure – and hence the realization that something needed to be done – would massively increase just as studies were being conducted. Moreover, there's nothing like a great war to demonstrate what people can do when they set their minds to something. World War I would show Americans and New Yorkers how concentrated authority could cut through German trenches and perhaps New York bureaucracy as well.

Then, there was New Jersey. The State of New Jersey lit a fuse in mid-1916: It applied to the Interstate Commerce Commission (ICC) for freight rates cheaper than those available to New York City. It was one thing for Boston or Philadelphia to pull a stunt like that. Those cities could never compete with New York's location and Erie Canal connection. But New Jersey? This could be war.

And so it was that the New York Chamber took the unusual step of hiring a special counsel, Julius Henry Cohen, to uphold the chamber's (and New York's) interests in the matter. The chamber noted that the New Jersey plot had been cooking for some time, and involved not only its legislature but its civic and commercial organizations. The petition was filed, moreover, in June, when the New York Chamber was adjourned and the New York press and other organizations were on less than high alert.[188]

Although it had been on summer recess, the New York Chamber was the first New York group to hire a special counsel on this matter. The chamber then contacted New York Governor Charles Whitman, who agreed to take on Cohen for the state as well. And the chamber alerted the City of New York, which hired its own legal expert. So imposing were the forces arrayed against the New Jersey side that "the New Jersey petitioners themselves realized the case was more important than they thought," and they asked the ICC for a delay, but it was too late.[189]

Unwittingly, the New Jersey side had made a case for the unified management of the port. As William Prendergast, comptroller of the city of New York, pointed out at a chamber meeting on March 1, 1917, the two sides of the harbor were intimately connected and really inseparable. The port area was 771 miles long, of which 193 miles were in New Jersey.[190] The newly elected governor of New Jersey, Walter Edge, addressed the same meeting with a message of peace and underlined his sincerity by reminded the audience that he had proposed a tunnel under the Hudson linking New Jersey and New York.[191]

Indeed, as a result of the March 1 meeting, Governor Edge proposed the creation of a Port and Harbor Development Commission. His legislature and New York Governor Whitman both agreed, and as a result, a joint New York-New Jersey commission was formed.[192] As if to underline the correctness of this approach, on January 22, 1918, the ICC ruled in favor of New York in the rate case, requiring the two states to work together on transportation needs. New York's Governor Whitman wired Chamber President Outerbridge the next day, saying that "the State is under deep obligation to the Chamber of Commerce."[193]

Cooperation went further: the two states joined in a special War Board to coordinate the progress of the harbor during the massive congestion of the final months of World War I. General Goethals served as consulting engineer, and Irving Bush as the chief executive officer. This War Board provided precisely the kind of unified command structure that, all realized, could be used in times of peace as well.

By April 4, 1918, the outlines of the program were becoming clear, with funding expected from both New York and New Jersey to complete studies of the harbor. Irving Bush summarized the history of the port effort and said, "the New York and New Jersey Port Commission is really a child of this Chamber, conceived in its council rooms," and then emerging directly out of Governor Edge's talk at the chamber only 13 months later.[194]

On December 19, 1918, the chamber held a special meeting on the port, including both Governors Whitman and Edge. Harbor Development Commission counsel Julius Henry Cohen noted that hundreds of millions of dollars were needed for the port, and that the states of New York and New Jersey were not prepared to provide this, but that a separate entity such as a port authority could provide it. If granted the ability to borrow, the port organization could draw on money that would be repaid from revenues from some of the richest and most powerful companies in the nation. Other speakers supported the port concept.[195] On February 6, 1919, the chamber unanimously passed resolutions in favor of the treaty to create a New York – New Jersey Port Authority.[196]

It wouldn't be till 1921 that the entity would begin operation, but the New York Chamber had set the process in motion. The first president of the New York – New Jersey Port Authority would be former Chamber President E.H. Outerbridge. In the ensuing years, the Port Authority would handle many massive transportation building projects, including JFK and LaGuardia airports and the George Washington Bridge, and the maintenance of one of the busiest transportation hubs in the world.[197]

Babes, Booze, and Babbitt

1921-1929

In the late summer of 1920, the Businessmen's League of Atlantic City, N.J., faced a problem. The hotels on the Boardwalk were doing well, but the second-tier hotels a few blocks from the action lost a lot of business after Labor Day. The town needed an event to attract people.

The chamber's leadership decided to put on a week of events after Labor Day, the Fall Frolic. On September 25, 1920, the collection of activities and contests began. The most popular event turned out to be a parade of rolling chairs along the Boardwalk – with attractive young women sitting in the chairs. For the following year, a newspaperman suggested holding a beauty contest with entrants from a variety of cities. The winner would be crowned as the "Golden Mermaid."

On June 8, 1921, 100,000 people crowded onto the Boardwalk to see the show. A 16-year-old girl from Washington, D.C., Margaret Gorman, claimed the prize of a free weekend in Atlantic City. In later years, she would be acclaimed as the first Miss America.

The famous pageant would do much for (and perhaps to) Atlantic City over the years, but without doubt, it expressed the spirit of what we now call the Roaring Twenties. Many chambers of commerce embraced the irrational exuberance of the times, even as they loosened their starched collars to get into occasional political fights. What was going on in these unsettled years?

S. Cristy Mead, speaking at a NACOS meeting in Washington in 1924, didn't like what was happening. He said:

Margaret Gorman, the first Miss America, 1921

> When we observe that activities ranging all the way from baby shows, horse racing and stock promotions to efforts to regulate all phases of community life, including politics, have been pursued by chambers of commerce, it

becomes evident that a reconsideration of basic principles and a return to fundamentals in the chamber of commerce movement is both desirable and necessary.[1]

Mead's point of view was understandable and was shared by others. There may have been decades when chambers accomplished more than they did in the Twenties. Still, America's local business organizations did manage to do a great deal in these raucous years, while contributing to arguably the most colorful decade of their history.

Party Time

Surely chambers weren't really holding baby shows, were they? Well, actually, they were. Indeed, when the secretary of the Atlantic City Chamber of Commerce (formerly the Businessmen's League) on September 8, 1925, rolled into town on a train that was carrying 62 beauty contestants, he kicked things off with a prettiest baby contest.[2] Not to be outdone, the chamber in Ocean City, N.J. held a contest involving 15 divisions of floats and lasting 2½ hours, with the heat causing several women to faint. Among the prizes was one for "Fattest Baby," obtained by Gladys Ritter, who weighed 52 pounds.[3] Other such parades and contests went on at non-resort locations from White Plains, N.Y. to Takoma Park, Md.

Many of these chamber celebrations were little more than excuses to have a party (and, in a more practical sense, to bring people to town and spend money). Some were large, such as Bronx Kiddies Day, an athletic celebration for up to 250,000 youngsters put on by the Bronx Chamber of Commerce.[4] Even bigger were some of the celebrations of the Coney Island Chamber of Commerce, including a 1925 Easter fashion parade with 600,000 to 800,000 people, apparently the largest crowd in New York since World War I.[5]

Decorum was not necessarily required. No doubt S. Cristy Mead would not have approved of the Trenton Chamber of Commerce's entertainment program in which Lieutenant Alvan Starr parachuted out of a tethered blimp into a diving pool, from which he emerged, smiling, for photographers.[6] The Rockville, Md., Chamber of Commerce announced plans for a contest of bathing beauties to be judged by two clergymen and a prominent church worker (all members of the chamber, of course).[7]

Indeed, commercial organizations occasionally gave short shrift to religious formalities. In an attempt to bring shoppers downtown, during the mid-1920s the Hollywood Chamber of Commerce began a Christmas event with not much connection to anything Biblical: it featured fake snow and chimneys, live reindeer, and a parade in which the famous Hollywood Boulevard's name was changed to "Santa Claus Lane."[8] This parade would continue, with only a brief interruption in World War II, all the way to 2007, with many a

Actress Lili Damita poses with Col. Harry Baine on the sleigh, but the actress who took the inaugural 1928 ride down Santa Claus Lane was Jeanette Loff.

famous star participating, including Gene Autry, who in 1946 co-wrote a song based on his experience, *Here Comes Santa Claus* ("right down Santa Claus Lane").

During the Twenties, many festivals emerged that focused on local agricultural items, history, or folklore. The public wasn't too fastidious about whether Hope really was the epicenter of watermelon husbandry or Punxsutawney had a magical groundhog. The main question: was the festival fun and different? And often it was.

In the mid-1920s, the Hope, Ark., Chamber of Commerce began offering slices of cold watermelon to the passengers of trains passing through town. It set up a watermelon day that included a Watermelon Queen and attracted about 20,000 people. The festival was discontinued in about 1931 because of economic conditions but was revived in 1975 and is a major economic driver for the community today. About 50,000 people come during the four-day festival, which continues to be managed by the local chamber of commerce.[9] After favorite son Bill Clinton, the festival remains perhaps Hope's leading claim to fame.

For Winchester, Virginia in 1924, it was a different agricultural product that interested the chamber of commerce. The chamber began the Shenandoah Apple Blossom Festival, complete with the usual parade and beauty pageant. Surprisingly, thanks to notices in newspapers in Washington, Baltimore, and Philadelphia, the event drew 30,000 people in the first year.[10] By the end of the decade the celebration was involving as many as 100,000 people, including a parade of 10,000. The festival continued to attract avid newspaper coverage, including in the Washington, D.C. area, where 30 northern Virginia high schools participated in the parade in 1929.[11]

Probably the success of the Shenandoah Apple Blossom Festival inspired the creation of the Cherry Blossom Festival in nearby Washington, D.C. The Washington Chamber of Commerce proposed such a cherry festival in 1929. Committee chair Isaac Gans said excitedly about the proposed event, "It would attract more people from every part of the country than do similar festivals in other cities, and would be the best way I know of to boost Washington."[12] He predicted 250,000 visitors, but would be wrong. When the chamber finally began the festival in 1934, it pulled in 500,000 visitors.[13]

Further down the Appalachians, a man came into Asheville, N.C. in 1927 complaining that no one played the old-time music anymore. The townspeople encouraged him to bring some of it into Asheville.

> So he got his neighbors from South Turkey and Rabbit Ham. Then he went back into the mountains to homes where he stayed all night and swapped tunes and ballads. He got the old-time fiddlers, the banjo pickers, the mouth harp players and the buck dancers.[14]

The old man, Bascom Lamar Lunsford, brought his entourage to the Rhododendron Festival that the Asheville Chamber of Commerce was holding. In the very first year, it started a trend that swept the Southeast and later the world: a group called the Soco Gap Square Dancers introduced a step that today is called "clogging."[15]

The Rhododendron Festival attracted 5,000 people in the first year, which was considered a great success. But much of that success was due to Lunsford's show, which split off two years later to form its own July event in Asheville, the Mountain Dance and Folk Festival.

That event continues today, the nation's longest-running folk festival, with dozens of imitators around the country.

Some time after 1927, when the Punxsutawney Chamber of Commerce was founded, this organization began helping look after the February 2 Groundhog Day observances. Those observances, in which people watch to see if a groundhog sees his shadow (and if he does, there are six more weeks of bad weather), were brought over by immigrants from Europe in the previous century or two. Germans watched badgers watching their shadows, while British watched hedgehogs. Groundhogs, being common in much of North America, were the hibernating animal of choice for many communities in the United States, including Punxsutawney.[16]

Even in the earlier days, Punxsutawney's celebration seemed to attract more attention than most, perhaps due in part to its initial mention in the local paper in 1886. But it was not a large celebration and, given that no money was charged for it, there was a value to having an organization such as the chamber of commerce to sustain and grow the activity. The Punxsutawney Chamber of Commerce officially ran the event until sometime in the late 1960s, when the Groundhog Club – still a part of the chamber – got more of a separate identity and acquired a board of directors.[17]

The Serious Business of Sports

The Twenties saw the emergence of sports as mass entertainment and as a driver of tourism and business. Not surprisingly, chambers of commerce wanted a piece of the action for their communities. And often they got it.

Boxing matches caught the interest of many local business organizations. Fight promoter Tex Rickard routinely played cities and chambers off against one another to get the best deal for his mega-matches. In April of 1921, he visited Jersey City to test the waters for a fight between Jack Dempsey and George Carpentier. After the visit, "wreathed in smiles," he praised the chamber and said that "not since I have been in the promotional game have I met a more enthusiastic body of men than in Jersey City." But he indicated he was still on the lookout for alternative sites.[18]

Jack Dempsey and George Carpentier before their fight
(July 2, 1921) in Jersey City, N.J.

The canny producer ended up taking the chamber's offer, and on July 2, 91,000 people saw the bout in Jersey City. Dempsey won in 10 rounds. The fight brought the first million-dollar gate in boxing history and, for the first time ever, was broadcast by radio, blow by blow.

In 1927, Rickard was on the lookout for a site for another big fight, a rematch between Gene Tunney and Jack Dempsey. He was to visit the "Chicago Chamber of Commerce" (probably the Chicago Association of Commerce) to bargain for holding the event in that city, although others preferred New York.[19] Chicago won out and raked in the first $2 million gate for a boxing match. The two fighters didn't disappoint. Tunney won a unanimous decision despite his having been on the canvas for 14 seconds in the famous "Long Count."

The Miami Beach Chamber of Commerce also didn't want to miss out on the action. It worked with co-promoters Jack Dempsey and William Carey to arrange a bout between heavyweights Jack Sharkey and Young Stribling. In the "greatest fistic affair the South has ever experienced," Sharkey won on a decision on February 27, 1929. But the venue in Miami Beach was disappointing (narrow aisles, etc.) and so the Miami – not Miami Beach - Chamber of Commerce signed a deal with Carey for fights to be held in Miami over the next five years.[20]

Florida became the nation's unofficial playground in the 1920s, and the Daytona Beach Chamber of Commerce did all it could to be in the center of the action. In the summer of 1925, citizens of three area communities (Daytona Beach, Seabreeze, and Ormond-Daytona Beach) formed what a newspaper described as the "second largest chamber of commerce in the world on a proportionate basis with a membership of nearly 7,000."[21] Given that there were only 25,000 people in the area, this was certainly an accomplishment. On August 9, 1925, citizens voted to consolidate the three areas into one city, Daytona Beach, a decision that took effect on January 1, 1926.[22]

To celebrate the new year and the consolidation, the chamber arranged a massive revival of auto racing along the beach, which had not seen such activity for 20 years, when the auto enthusiasts had included such luminaries as Henry Ford and W.K. Vanderbilt. The chamber also raised $100,000 for a winter sports program. The chamber soon had a "racing division" and in succeeding years made announcements of spectacular racing events. The community already had plenty of sports raw material – not just a 30-mile speedway along the beach, but a group of baseball stars who wintered there, including Walter Johnson, Mickey Cochrane, and Fred Merkle.[23]

Even more than auto racing, baseball was the national pastime in the 1920s, and chambers were not far from the action. Former star pitcher Christy Mathewson recognized the spirit. As president of the Boston Braves, he joined the Boston Chamber of Commerce and said this chamber should support the Braves the way the St. Louis Chamber supported the local teams.[24]

The St. Louis Chamber certainly took a strong interest in its teams, the Browns and the Cardinals. Always concerned about competition, St. Louis Chamber President F.W.A. Vesper issued a protest to Baseball Commissioner Kenesaw Mountain Landis and others when the powerful New York Yankees bought two players (Joe Dugan and Elmer Smith) from the Boston Braves in mid-season in 1922. Decades before George Steinbrenner's big-spending ways, Vesper wrote that "baseball has reached a point where the pocketbook and not the clubs or the players become the deciding factors."[25]

But this was only a minor irritant. The St. Louis Chamber got truly fired up when the manager of the St. Louis Cardinals, the immortal Rogers Hornsby, was traded to the New York Giants. The chamber once again complained to Commissioner Landis, who didn't block the deal. St. Louis Cardinals President Sam Breadon, however, angrily quit the chamber after its meddling.[26]

Ty Cobb was not the kindest or gentlest of baseball players, but he was beloved in his home town of Augusta, Georgia. After Cobb was tainted by late-breaking accusations of a connection with the Black Sox game-fixing scandal, he came home to wide acclaim, including a suggestion by Chamber Secretary L.S. Arrington that he become mayor. "No, boys, I'm a baseball player, not a politician," Cobb replied.[27] Cobb later helped the chamber bring the New York Giants to Augusta for spring training.[28]

Chambers were involved in all sorts of other sports activities, from swimming to horse racing to sailing, tennis, and football. And so perhaps it's not surprising that they showed interest in that ultimate "variety pack" of sports, the Olympics. Julian Reiss, president of the Lake Placid (NY) Chamber of Commerce, proudly announced in 1928 that his organization had raised $50,000 in guarantee money for the holding of the Winter Olympics in the rustic location.[29] Lake Placid won the events for 1932.

For Los Angeles's unsuccessful 1924 bid for the Olympics, and its successful 1932 bid, a group called the Community Development Association (CDA) was put together. *Los Angeles Times* publisher Harry Chandler proposed the group, which was headed by William May Garland, a longtime, active member of the Los Angeles Chamber of Commerce and also president of the California Chamber of Commerce.[30] The CDA did most of the heavy lifting for the bid, but the Los Angeles Chamber of Commerce remained busy in many ways: promoting publicity for the event, supporting the building of the Los Angeles Coliseum, and appointing a committee on parks that helped lay the groundwork for a city worthy of the Olympics.

Indeed, the relationship between the CDA and the Los Angeles Chamber of Commerce was exceedingly close. "Many CDA members had been or would soon become board members of the Los Angeles Chamber of Commerce," noted one student of the games.[31] The chamber's executive board was treated to a closed-door meeting with the CDA leadership two weeks before the Games, and afterward "the Chamber's president had nothing but praise for the Committee's work".[32] The chamber's leadership also had a private tour of the Olympic Village.

Some separation between the two organizations, however, was useful. For example, the United States Olympic Committee (USOC) president, Avery Brundage, asked the chamber to police the use of the Olympics logo because one of the CDA chiefs was using the Olympics connection to advance his bakery business.[33]

The chamber even did its best to erase a huge embarrassment for the city in 1926, as plans were being laid for the 1932 Olympics bid. Noted evangelist and spiritualist Aimee Semple McPherson mysteriously disappeared for five weeks after a swim at Ocean Park Beach, north of Venice Beach. She surfaced, alive and well, in Agua Prieta, Sonora, right across the border from Douglas, Arizona, claiming she had been kidnapped. Although her story was flimsy, she had many passionate followers and the idea that she had been kidnapped hurt the image of Los Angeles on the eve of the Olympics bid. Indeed, when she returned to Los Angeles, 50,000 people were there to greet her.

The chamber pressured the district attorney to investigate McPherson's disappearance.[34] Her already shaky story was weakened further by the investigation and the public was soon treated to stories alleging a "love nest" with her friend Kenneth Ormisten, who had rented a room under an alias. Although the criminal charges eventually were dropped, McPherson's reputation never recovered. She should have understood the lesson: When they sully the image of Los Angeles, even those with mighty spiritual powers should fear the wrath of the Los Angeles Chamber of Commerce!

Chambers in the Culture

Chambers, then, were becoming ensconced in festivals, sports events, and other aspects of American life and culture. It's not surprising that they could not escape the attention of authors in the Roaring Twenties. And no one described them with more satiric glee than Sinclair Lewis.

The author hit the big time with his 1920 book slamming small-town culture, *Main Street*. The novel's mythical town of Gopher Prairie – not unlike the town Lewis grew up in, he said later (Sauk Centre, Minn.) - was a steaming cauldron of gossip, stunted lives, and stunted minds. The bleak atmosphere lifts slightly toward the end of the book when Lewis introduces Jim Blausser, the glad-handing booster. Blausser addresses the local commercial club with such remarks as:

> They say we can't make Gopher Prairie, God bless her! just as big as Minneapolis or St. Paul or Duluth. But lemme tell you right here and now that there ain't a town under the blue canopy of heaven that's got a better chance to take a running jump and go scooting right up into the two-hundred-thousand class than little old G.P.![35]

Blausser's unintentionally comic booster lingo, and the transparently lame attempts to make Gopher Prairie a great metropolis by sending out a band with the baseball team, make enjoyable reading. Lewis seemed to realize he was onto something. Like a producer who makes new TV series based on a popular character of a previous series, Lewis spun off the Blausser character into a whole world of boosters for his next, smash hit.

Babbitt, published in 1922, was an indictment of mainstream business mores so dramatic that the word "Babbitt" quickly entered the lexicon. The word connoted conformist, middlebrow, grasping, city-boosting businessmen. While *Babbitt* isn't considered great literature, it is devastating caricature. Even today, business people are wary of being taken for a "Babbitt." One measure of the contemporary success of Sinclair's salvo is the great number of grimacing references to Babbitt in that essential handbook of business people of this period, the U.S. Chamber's *Nation's Business*.

As a mindless joiner and booster, George F. Babbitt was clearly a good argument *against* chambers of commerce. His thinking was muddled, as Lewis wickedly showed in describing the businessman's attitude toward unions:

> A good labor union is of value because it keeps out radical unions, which would destroy property. No one ought to be forced to join a union, however. All labor organizers who try to force men to join a union should be hanged. In fact, just between ourselves, there oughtn't to be any unions at all; and as it's the best way of fighting the unions, every business man ought to belong to an employer's association and to the Chamber of Commerce. In union there is strength. So any selfish hog who doesn't join the Chamber of Commerce ought to be forced to.[36]

One man appreciated the Babbitt satire more than most: the "Sage of Baltimore," H.L. Mencken. This gnarled cynic knew Babbitt was real:

> The fellow simply drips with human juices. Every one of his joints is movable in all directions. Real freckles are upon his neck and real sweat stands out upon his forehead. I have personally known him since my earliest days as a newspaper reporter, back in the last century. I have heard him make speeches such as Cicero never dreamed of at banquets of the Chamber of Commerce. I have seen him marching in parades. I have observed him advancing upon his Presbyterian tabernacle of a Sunday morning, his somewhat stoutish lady upon his arm. I have seen him crank his Buick.[37]

Sinclair Lewis and H.L. Mencken may have been the joint Knockers-in-Chief of the boosters and chamber members, but they had disciples. Another chamber critic was William Henry McMasters. In a brief essay, "On Chambers of Commerce," he tried to take them apart. "Nothing can stop a Chamber of Commerce that has consolidated a few times with other bodies of a like uselessness," he wrote. He concluded:

> So, if you would save your city, join your Chamber of Commerce. The joke is on you, true enough, but what's the harm? The Secretary and his Assistant have to be paid in order to keep all the membership cards up to date so that visitors can be told that "The Bolleweville Chamber of Commerce is now the largest in America east of the Connecticut River."[38]

While Lewis, Mencken, and McMasters had an issue or two with being involved with a chamber of commerce, others were more sympathetic. The "Sage of Emporia," Kansas newspaperman William Allen White, saw chambers as making business people something more than they might otherwise be. White riffed:

> The Chamber of Commerce modifies the innate cussedness of the average selfish, hardboiled, picayunish, penny pinching, narrow-gauged human porker, lifts up his snout, makes him see farther than his home, his business and his personal interest, and starts him rooting for his community.[39]

Perhaps White damned with faint praise, but at least there was praise. Another well-known writer of the period, Damon Runyan, was yet more positive about the civic spirit of the era of which chambers were such a notable part. The Scranton Chamber of Commerce (and then *Nation's Business*) quoted Runyan as follows:

> I hold that every city has (or has not) what I might call sporting blood. I mean to say its citizens either believe in its future, or they don't believe in it.
>
> In the first case they manifest their belief by betting their good money on their city, by putting it into real estate and home industries, by spreading their currency in development projects.
>
> In the second case they keep their money in their pockets, or hide it under the rock of extreme caution or conservatism. They wouldn't bet a nickel that the sun is going to shine over their town.

You undoubtedly know of cities well populated by these careful souls, and it is a 6 to 5 bet that their cities have not moved up an inch in many years, but are still laboring far back in the ruck of progress.[40]

Many chamber members were extremely proud of their institutions. Said Edwin Gibbs, president of the Cincinnati Chamber of Commerce:

I would not care to live in a city that had no church; nor in a city that had no court house; nor in a city that had no Chamber of Commerce; for as a church stands for righteousness, and a court house stands for the maintenance of law and order, so does a Chamber of Commerce stand for community progress.[41]

The Preferred Organization of Presidents

The Twenties saw a remarkable string of Republican, apparently pro-business Presidents, all of whom were comfortable with local chambers of commerce, and weren't averse to praising them publicly. This reinforcement from on high surely bolstered the position of chambers in society. Said Warren Harding, shortly before he was inaugurated as President in March 1921:

If I were to disassociate myself from the newspaper business, I assume I would be attracted to a Chamber of Commerce because business is the life blood of material existence, and no community is worth while unless it is very alert to business progress and greater commercial development.

He went on:

I know something of the inspiring work which is done by the live secretaries of the Chambers of Commerce throughout the country. They are ever pushing forward with such zeal that they take a great community of business men with them.[42]

President Calvin Coolidge (center) with members of the Brooklyn Chamber of Commerce

Harding's successor, Calvin Coolidge, not only worked with chambers, but entertained 500 NACOS chamber secretaries in the White House.[43] The dour President met various other chamber groups at the White House, including delegations from Tulsa and Brooklyn. Moreover, he gave an address to the U.S. Chamber in 1924 and to the New York Chamber in 1925. Although he never said precisely that "the business of America is business,"[44] this was a business-friendly

President. He kept his own counsel, however, and certainly was able to stand up to business organizations. Coolidge condemned the U.S. Chamber's proposed $400 million tax cut in 1927 as "absurd."[45]

Herbert Hoover worked closely with chambers for a good part of his professional life, including when he raised funds for Belgian relief during World War I. In 1921 he wrote, "Anyone who has watched the development of our cities must be impressed by the effective and constructive service rendered by their Chambers of Commerce."[46] For a time he was a business associate of Julius Barnes, probably the leading U.S. Chamber of Commerce figure of the 1920s.[47] Hoover praised the U.S. Chamber, wrote for *Nation's Business*, and turned almost immediately to the U.S. Chamber when the economy fell crashing down in October 1929. And like his two predecessors, he received local chamber groups in the White House, including the Boston Chamber of Commerce, which presented him with a 25-pound codfish.[48]

The three Presidents, who were in office for most of the decade, were believers in the idea of chambers of commerce. Their favorable attitude no doubt affected the public's perception of these institutions. Chambers had reached into everything from the highest office in the nation to the parades of babies.

Movie Culture
Hollywood, too, was riding on the national train of thought and culture, thanks to earlier chamber efforts to attract the movie industry to southern California. People, especially would-be actors, began flooding into the area, hoping to become movie stars. The Los Angeles Chamber of Commerce called together a conference to "consider ways and means of shutting off the flood of screen-struck boys and girls who were swarming into that city by every train."[49] Actress Mary Pickford addressed a crowd of 20,000 in Los Angeles on the topic. She urged girls to think twice before coming, and if they did come, to "Take mother along; you'll need her."[50]

The brouhaha led comedian Mack Sennett to come up with a movie on the topic of the ingénue coming to Hollywood, *The Extra Girl.*[51] Mabel Normand starred in the 1923 silent film about a girl coming to southern California with stars in her eyes. She didn't find success in the movies but realized that true love and happiness came from the people she knew back home.

There was power in this new medium, and it wasn't always a power for the good of chambers or their communities. The St. Petersburg Chamber of Commerce tried to stop Florida screenings of a Warner Brothers movie called *Foot-loose Widows*. The 1926 film includes a scene in which two women masquerading as wealthy widows, having failed in their attempt to snare a man, depart their hotel. One says to the other, "Well, like everything else in Florida, we're bust. I tried to get you to go to California."[52]

Some chambers created short moving pictures to get the word out about themselves. The St. Louis Chamber of Commerce was one of them. Early in the 1920s it put out a film about the advantages of its area, *The Spirit of St. Louis*. The film was a flop, not getting into as many theaters as the chamber's leaders had hoped, but the name would come in handy later.[53]

When Things Were Up in the Air
Perhaps nothing in the Twenties thrilled the public, and chambers of commerce, as much as flight. Balloons, dirigibles (also known as zeppelins), and airplanes were a constant

source of excitement and interest. People, of course, had always dreamed of flight, and heavier-than-air motored, flying vehicles had been around since the Wright Brothers in 1903. Moreover, the St. Petersburg Chamber and the glamorous Tony Jannus had set up commercial flights in 1914. Yet it wasn't until the 1920s that the full possibilities of the air became clear in most people's minds: for long-distance travel, for the carrying of mail and even passengers, and – crucially for local chambers of commerce – for the development and growth of cities.

Balloons caught the attention of members of the Indianapolis Chamber of Commerce. This chamber sponsored a balloon distance flying competition in July of 1923. The winning entrant, Army Lieutenant R.M. Olmstead, took his "bag" for 500 miles. The runner-up, H.E. Honeywell in the *St. Louis*, had a harrowing ride as he was blown to Canada, and then back to U.S. airspace and toward Lake Erie, where he landed in the dark on a 150 foot cliff near the edge of the water.[54] But the balloon of Navy Lieutenants L.J. Roth and T.B. Null had a worse fate. It crashed into Lake Erie, where Lieutenant Roth's body was found on July 9.[55]

Crossing the Atlantic

In 1919, a New York hotelier, Raymond Orteig, offered a $25,000 prize for the first airplane to cross the Atlantic, either travelling from Paris to New York or vice versa. The prize stirred up some interest in the cash-hungry, high-tech world of airplane flight, but no one was able to make the trip. The technology of fixed-wing flight had not advanced far enough yet. Orteig renewed the offer in 1924, and this time it got the attention of many fliers and their backers. The industry and much of the public focused on the challenge of crossing the Atlantic in an airplane.

Charles Levine, a member of the Brooklyn Chamber of Commerce and chairman of the Columbia Aircraft Corporation, was determined to back the first plane to make the trip. He offered $15,000 in prize money for his fliers if they were successful.

As Levine proceeded with his project, the Brooklyn Chamber of Commerce stepped in. This chamber was an extraordinarily large and active organization under its beloved and philanthropic president, Ralph Jonas. On April 23, 1927, the Brooklyn Chamber proposed to pay the $15,000 prize money itself and to make this a public project. Levine accepted out of "civic pride." Moreover, he remained the head of the group that would promote the flight attempt, the New York to Paris Nonstop Committee. All members of the committee were also members of the Brooklyn Chamber.[56]

The plane, created by the famed aircraft designer Giuseppe M. Bellanca, was clearly capable of the trip. It had recently set a world record for time in the air – 51 hours, which was more than enough time to cross the Atlantic. All that was needed was a crew and final touches for the voyage.

As the Bellanca was readied for flight, Levine decided he wanted to pilot the plane, not the man he had selected, Lloyd Bertaud, who angrily got an injunction to stop the flight. Bertaud's injunction was thrown out of court. This was soon after the judge heard the case at 10:00 am on May 20, 1927.[57]

But at 6:00 am on the same morning, a young man on another chamber-backed expedition had taken off from New York, heading to Paris. Charles Lindbergh piloted the *Spirit of St. Louis* from Long Island all the way to Le Bourget Field in Paris. His exploit won him not only the Orteig Prize but just about every kind of acclaim that an individual could receive in that or any other era. Lindbergh was mobbed by French crowds and went on to a triumphal tour of the United States, feted in city after city, often being hosted by chambers of commerce.

Brooklyn's Bellanca plane belatedly took off on June 4, 1927. The words "Auspices of the Brooklyn Chamber of Commerce" were proudly painted on its fuselage. The phrase "New York-Paris" also had been included, but now the "Paris" was painted over.[58]

With Lindbergh having "done" France, Germany would be the new destination: the Brooklyn Chamber had agreed to a $15,000 prize if the plane could cross the Atlantic and eventually make it to Berlin. Clarence Chamberlin would be the pilot, but he had trouble getting a navigator. Finally Charles Levine asked to tag along, and Chamberlin consented. As Chamberlin said years later, "After all, he owned the plane and was putting up the money." But both agreed not to tell Levine's wife, who didn't want him to go. Levine and Chamberlin took off without telling her; when she later found out, she fainted.[59]

The plane had some engine trouble over Newfoundland, and Chamberlin wanted to return. Levine refused. "And meet my wife?" he said.

The Brooklyn Chamber's civic project hurtled across the Atlantic, landing successfully in Germany. Levine thus became the first passenger taken across the ocean in an airplane. Chamberlin and Levine couldn't find Berlin at first; their map apparently had been blown out the window. But they ended up landing nearby and then made it to the German capital, to great acclaim.[60]

After this, Levine's life and career developed some new wrinkles. He went on a triumphal procession through Europe, meeting a glamorous woman called the "Queen of Diamonds." He promised to fly her across the Atlantic, but problems came up. When the flight was called off, the French pilot who was to have the job was supposed to receive a cancellation fee of $4,000. The French aviator secured an injunction preventing the plane from leaving France. But Levine, who had no idea how to land a plane, managed to steal into the Bellanca, take it aloft, and grind it to a bumpy landing in England. He eventually made it back to the States; he even spent time in a federal prison in the Thirties.[61]

Charles Lindbergh, the winner of the Orteig Prize, had a story of his own. For him and the St. Louis Chamber of Commerce, the transatlantic flight was, at least in the short run, a bonanza. If the project's aim was to make St. Louis well known, it certainly succeeded.

Lindbergh's Story

In the mid-Twenties, the young flier had decided that he could compete for the $25,000 Orteig Prize for transatlantic flight. There was only one problem: He didn't own a plane that could make the trip. After some research, he found that he might be able to buy one for $15,000. But he only had just over $2,000 in savings.

He knew a number of people in St. Louis, where he had been making flights to deliver air mail. Lindbergh resolved to "lay my Paris project before every businessman in St. Louis I can get an appointment with." One of the people he had met was a broker named Harry Knight, who was also the head of the St. Louis Flying Club.

Lindbergh met Knight and discussed the idea. As Lindbergh recounted it later:

Knight suddenly swings around in his chair, and picks up the telephone.

"Get me Harold Bixby at the State National Bank," he says --- "Bix, how about coming over here for a few minutes? --- sure you can --- okay --- in my office."

"He's only a block up the street," Knight tells me after hanging up, "—Fourth and Locust. You know he's president of the Chamber of Commerce."

Bixby came over and began asking questions. Soon he was discussing the money:

"You said you already have some money lined up. Who's in the project with you?"

"Yes sir. I can put in two thousand dollars myself. Major Lambert has promised to put in a thousand. Earl Thompson and Bill Robertson say they'll take part, but I haven't talked to them about amounts."

Bixby questioned why Lindbergh wanted a single-engine plane instead of a three-engine one. Lindbergh explained his reasoning and Bixby concluded:

"You let us think about this for a day or two, and talk to some of our friends. If you're going to make the flight, we've got to get started right away. Come down and see me next Wednesday. How about ten a.m., right at my office?"

"Any time at all. I'll be there at ten."

I can hardly believe what I'm hearing. I hoped, at most, to get a pledge for another thousand dollars. I never dreamed of finding anyone with sufficient interest to suggest taking over the entire financial burden.

Lindbergh had to fly to Chicago and, despite bad weather, returned to St. Louis in time for the meeting:

"Slim [Lindbergh's nickname], you've sold us on this proposition of yours," he [Bixby] says. "It's a tough job you're taking on, but we've talked it over and we're with you. From now on you'd better leave the financial end to us."

Lindbergh left the meeting feeling terrific. The toughest part of his job, finding the money, was to be taken care of by Bixby, the president of the chamber, and his friends.

Not long afterward, Lindbergh met Bixby at his office to pick up the check. Bixby said:

"What would you think of naming it The Spirit of St. Louis?"

Bixby's question strikes vaguely through my ears. I'm staring at the shredded and color-stained figures on a slip of paper in my hand – FIFTEEN THOUSAND DOLLARS. This slip can be traded for the Wright-Bellanca [an airplane he was considering for the trip], and this slip is mine – "Pay to the order of Charles A. Lindbergh" it says on the back.

The Spirit of St. Louis - - - it's a good name. "All right, let's call it the Spirit of St. Louis." My eyes go back to the check. "I didn't know you were going to make this out to me personally," I say.

Bixby laughs. "Well Slim, Harry and I decided that if we couldn't trust you with a check, we ought not to take part in this project at all."[62]

Charles Lindbergh

Thus Harold Bixby, the president of the St. Louis Chamber of Commerce, financed the most famous airplane flight in history. And he furnished the name as well, at least in Lindbergh's recollection (although, in fact, that name had been used once before for a chamber film). As we have noted, the chamber-backed plane beat its Brooklyn rival – also chamber-backed – to international acclaim. And St. Louis, just about as much as any city ever could, put itself on the map.

Lowell Thomas would later call Bixby, for his sponsorship and naming of the plane, "just about the most envied Chamber of Commerce president of all time."[63] The St. Louis bank president did indeed become well known for his achievement.[64] And his chamber capitalized on the plane's success in one important way: working to create an aircraft industry for the Midwestern community. On February 15, 1928, several months after the successful flight to Paris, Lindbergh spoke at a luncheon in his honor at the chamber, saying St. Louis – already with two airplane factories – ought to become the hub of the airline and air manufacturing business in the central United States. "It is within the reach of this city to become as great a center aeronautically as Detroit is in the automobile industry," said the famous flier to a community that loved him perhaps more than any other.[65]

Possibly a few in the audience knew how the St. Louis Chamber had once fought Abe Lincoln and the newfangled transportation innovation that was crossing the Mississippi, railroads. Chicago had jumped on that advance; was it now St. Louis's opportunity to seize the future? Determinedly, the chamber grabbed the baton handed over by Lindbergh. In 1928 the city passed a $2 million bond issue that would make their airport "second to none" in the United States.[66] In July of the same year, the chamber took 125 St. Louis citizens to Paris "with a view to popularizing their home city as an air center." The French were thrilled to be visited by a city named after a French king, although most of them didn't know, as the Associated Press snarkily reported, that "the St. Louis telephone directory contains many more names of over-the-Rhine origin than of French."[67]

An Air of Excitement

Lindbergh visited countless chambers of commerce as he returned to national acclaim, and chambers' excitement with flight only increased. The trajectory from the chamber to the air could be short indeed. Herbert O. Fisher joined the Indianapolis Chamber in early 1927 as an office boy. One of his first jobs was to pick a site for the local airport. His selection was adopted by the city. Fisher was bitten by the air bug, later becoming chief test pilot for Curtiss-Wright. During World War II, he pioneered the flights across "the hump," the Himalayan air supply route for the allied forces in China fighting the Japanese. He flew 96 missions, many of them believed to be too hazardous for airplanes. Credited with saving hundreds of lives, in 1945 he became the first living civilian pilot to win the Army Air Medal.[68]

Even the national association of chamber executives, NACOS, became involved. In mid-1927 it embarked on the "NACOS Good Will Flight of the States," covering 10,000 miles and visiting 131 cities in the United States and Canada aboard a Loening Amphibian seaplane. Twice a day the aircraft landed and NACOS President Walter Lochner addressed chamber audiences on the commercial potential of flight.[69] Two years later, NACOS sponsored an aviation luncheon at a U.S. Chamber meeting; one speaker was Amelia Earhart and another was "Miss Elinor Smith, the holder of the endurance record for women, who flew aloft for 26 hours while reading 'Tom Sawyer.'"[70]

Even as late as 1931, the excitement hadn't worn off. The Little Rock Chamber arranged the backing for a locally made airplane in a major race. The machine, the "Little Rocket," won first place, gaining the $15,000 first prize, various lap prizes, and lots of publicity for the city of its birth.[71]

Becoming a stop on an air mail route was a highly prized civic plum, coveted by chambers of commerce. The Toledo Chamber raised $257,000 to open an airport that would be a stop on the Transcontinental Air Mail line.[72] The Chamber of Commerce of Muskegon, Mich., on learning it would be a stop on an air mail line to Chicago, celebrated by sending the largest air mail letter ever dispatched to U.S. Postmaster Harry New. The letter was 8 feet 6 inches long by 6 feet wide.[73]

It wasn't enough to get a stop on an air mail route, however. It was also important to keep enough mail going to convince the authorities that the city or town merited a stop. For the Oklahoma City Chamber of Commerce, creating this volume required some ingenuity. Indeed, chamber Assistant Manager Stanley Draper occasionally mailed bricks in order meet the air mail weight quota. Even after he got caught, he continued this practice, albeit anonymously.[74]

All this work in the air industry brought chambers in close touch with companies that would become well known to the public. In Dallas, the chamber became involved in almost every aspect of the airport, including building the terminal and hangar for a small firm that eventually would become American Airlines.[75] In Detroit, the Board of Commerce handled many aviation activities and its leading volunteer for the air activities, William Mara, helped start Stinson Aircraft Company and then Northwest Airways (forerunner of today's Northwest Airlines).[76] The Salt Lake Chamber of Commerce and Commercial Club helped set up Western Express (later Western Airlines).[77]

A Haven for the Man From the Sky

The speaker at the Cleveland Chamber of Commerce was emphatic. There would be one airplane for every 1,000 people in Cleveland "in a very short time," said Anthony H. G. Fokker, the Dutch aviation expert. And the United States as a whole, with its great distances, was a promising location for the new industry.[78]

With more and more planes going aloft, it was important for them to have a place to come down. Chambers of commerce had done much to site airports for the armed forces during World War I, but most of their work came in the Twenties. Hundreds of cities and towns, often at the instigation of their local chamber of commerce, cleared land for landings. "Even the smallest of airports with a minimum equipment [*sic*] will provide a haven for the man from the sky," noted *Nation's Business*.[79] This was a project almost any chamber could take up.

Even as the air-happy St. Louis Chamber of Commerce was calling for an air show in 1923, the Denver Chamber of Commerce had begun raising money for land for a city airport, Lowry Aviation Field (later Stapleton Municipal Airport). The securing of the field for Denver was the chamber's outstanding achievement of 1924, the organization reported.[80] In Dayton, the chamber worked with the U.S. Army Air Service on the 1926 groundbreaking for Wright Field, now known as "Area B" for Wright Patterson Air Force Base.[81] The same chamber, in 1928, planned a "monster civic celebration" of the 25th anniversary of the Wright Brothers' first flight – complete with native son Orville Wright, who was still alive.[82]

New Jersey acted quickly to get more airports. In April of 1928, New Jersey Governor A. Harry Moore signed into law a bill that had been championed by the Bergen County Chamber of Commerce, allowing communities to issue bonds for municipal airports.[83]

Soon airports were popping up all over the state: Atlantic City's chamber worked to get one ready in time for the summer season of 1929, while Cape May's chamber leased 99 acres for its own airport.[84] This was only a part of the activity: every single county in the state had an airport (and some more than one) within a year of the bill's passage.[85]

Capturing some of the reflected glamour of the industry, Trenton's Walter Lochner offhandedly name-dropped to his colleagues at a NACOS conference, "I was talking with Amelia Earhart only last week when she was in Trenton. . ."[86]

The activity continued through the next decade. The New York City-based Aeronautical Chamber of Commerce reported in 1933 that there were aviation committees at nearly 500 chambers of commerce.[87] These years in the Twenties and early Thirties, when planes were better known for glamour than for dropping bombs, were the golden age both of aviation and of chamber involvement in the skies.

Three Projects

In the Twenties, as in most previous decades, chambers of commerce were intimately involved in public works projects. Three of them stood out, in magnitude and in their ability to capture the public's imagination: the Golden Gate Bridge, the Boulder (later Hoover) Dam, and the Grand Coulee Dam. Although not much dirt was moved on any of these projects by 1929, the groundwork was laid in public opinion. When the activist New Deal program began under President Franklin Roosevelt, the federal government implemented all three ideas. Local chamber activists who may not have voted for Roosevelt found him and his administration to be powerful supporters of the bold plans that their chambers and others had championed.

The Dreamers of Santa Rosa

The Sonoma County banker Frank Doyle, president of the Santa Rosa Chamber of Commerce, had called the meeting in the chamber's assembly room. On January 13, 1923, about 200 business people and civic leaders from San Francisco, Marin County, and Sonoma

County gathered to discuss the wild idea of building a new bridge that no private company was willing to finance. These serious men, the kinds of sober business dreamers that Nathaniel Hawthorne had written about 70 years previously, wanted to erect a structure to carry traffic from San Francisco to Marin County, over the cold, turbulent, and shark-filled waters at the mouth of the San Francisco Bay.

A reporter at the *San Francisco Bulletin,* James Wilkins, had crystallized the idea in 1916: "The vast Bay region will never be complete without a bridge across the Golden Gate," he wrote.[88] Wilkins spoke throughout the region about the idea and gradually drew enough support for a look at the feasibility of building a structure. Joseph Strauss came up with a workable design, but money was lacking.

With private builders shunning the risky venture – after all, there weren't many people living in Marin and Sonoma counties who might pay tolls on a bridge - the only alternative seemed to be public financing. The areas that might benefit from the bridge would need to band together to create a large district authority that could bear much of the cost of the undertaking. Such an organization also would remove the project from the often corrupt machinations of local politicians, making it palatable to conservative business people.[89] In this way it was similar to the New York Chamber-led creation, 3,000 miles away, of the New York-New Jersey Port Authority (although that organization was empowered to build many bridges, not just one).

Frank Doyle and his chamber played a catalytic role in garnering the public support needed to move the ambitious idea to reality. At the 1923 meeting, Doyle tasked his chamber with the job of moving the project forward. He himself became head of the new Bridging the Golden Gate Association. Six months later, Santa Rosa Chamber representatives attended a meeting of the San Francisco Board of Supervisors on the topic, and got the Sonoma County Board of Supervisors to attend as well. By 1925, the Santa Rosa Chamber was in charge of circulating petitions for the creation of the Golden Gate Bridge District. The little chamber was busily building the support for the big bridge.[90] Much of the additional support came from other chambers, from San Francisco all the way to Sacramento.

There were lots of twists and turns before construction began on the great bridge in 1933, and before it was completed in 1937. But many of the key steps in advancing the proj-

Construction on the Golden Gate Bridge

ect were made in the early Twenties, and Doyle's key role is uncontested. He is known as the Father of the Golden Gate Bridge. The portion of Highway 101 in San Francisco leading up to the Golden Gate Bridge is called Doyle Drive. He cut the chain to open the span to traffic. Despite this acclaim, in 1940 he said that "the bridge would never have been built if it had not been for the work of the Santa Rosa Chamber of Commerce."[91]

The Boulder Dam

On October 22, 1921, a double-sized headline ran in the *Las Vegas Age*:

LAS VEGAS-BOULDER CANYON DAM RECEIVES ENTHUSIASTIC SUPPORT:
THE CHAMBER OF COMMERCE HAS ROUSING MEETING
AS PRELUDE TO THEIR BIG DRIVE[92]

Like the leaders of the Los Angeles Chamber of Commerce, the organizers of the Las Vegas Chamber of Commerce in Nevada desperately wanted to harness the water and power of the Colorado River. C.P. Squires, the publisher of the *Las Vegas Age*, sometimes called "the father of Las Vegas," was a founding member of the chamber and a rabid supporter of the idea of a great dam.

Just as in Los Angeles, in Las Vegas the chamber support of the dam idea predated the First World War. Squires, in his history of the chamber, recalled the initial 1911 speech of the chamber's first president, James G. Givens: "He touched upon all the vital elements which might contribute to the growth of Las Vegas, except the Boulder Dam, an omission which, at that time was rather annoying to me, but which I forgave on the ground that he had been here but a few months."[93]

Damming the powerful Colorado River was an audacious idea requiring public money and political support. In this way it resembled the Golden Gate Bridge project. Both enterprises would likely have happened eventually, but for the local chambers of commerce, "eventually" was too risky. In each case, chambers did what they could to keep the political pressure behind their dream. Historian Kevin Wehr described the activism of chambers and allied groups for the Boulder Dam: "This vibrant civil society boosted the dam and canal project, keeping the idea alive in the face of congressional and elite opposition".[94]

The Las Vegas Chamber, like the Los Angeles Chamber, had a high-profile committee devoted to the dam enterprise. Many other chambers, from San Francisco to Phoenix to El Centro, were also supporting the creation of this massive Colorado River project. The secretary of one chamber, the Fullerton Chamber of Commerce, protested when a fake wire was printed in the *Los Angeles Times* indicating falsely that his chamber opposed the dam.[95]

Republican Congressman Phil Swing, who represented seven California counties from Riverside and San Bernardino to the border with Arizona, was the coauthor of the Swing-Johnson Bill promoting the dam and made pro-dam speeches at receptive audiences in several chambers of commerce.[96] Swing, later known as the "Father of Boulder Dam," knew chambers well: he had been a director of the El Centro Chamber of Commerce early in his career.[97] Chambers also were an important part of the Boulder Dam Association, which Swing founded in 1923.[98]

During the Twenties, the Los Angeles Chamber of Commerce continued to be a particularly strong proponent of harnessing the Colorado River, as it had been for many years already. It organized "booster groups" and George Clements, manager of its agricultural department, wrote a guest editorial favoring the dam in the *Los Angeles Times* (whose publisher at the time opposed the Swing-Johnson Bill).[99] The chamber sent speakers to chambers and other service groups throughout the Imperial Valley to promote the dam and the resulting irrigation program.[100] Without doubt, the dam could change the future of this city, and indeed of the entire Southwest.[101]

The Los Angeles Chamber drove on to the very end. In 1928, as the final push for the Boulder Dam legislation went on, city officials in Los Angeles began handing out a leaflet called "One Way to Help." The short flyer ended with an appeal for action:

Your help is urgently needed in securing the adoption of this Bill. The Los Angeles Chamber of Commerce has pointed out one way in which you may render aid. Here it is:

Write or telegraph today to your friends, relatives and former business associates in other parts of the United States. Give them the facts about Boulder Dam. Urge them, in turn, to communicate immediately with their Senators and Congressmen to the end that these members of Congress actively may support the pending Boulder Dam Bill.

Help secure Boulder Dam legislation at this session of Congress![102]

When the Swing-Johnson Bill's passage was announced on December 21, 1928, Las Vegas "went wild" and land prices skyrocketed.[103] The dam project, the largest construction job since the Panama Canal, began in 1931. Chambers celebrated the great undertaking for which so many had pushed so hard.

One person, some people believed, deserved special credit for the achievement. Herbert Hoover had strongly favored the Boulder Dam project. Among many other activities, such as negotiating a seven-state pact on the use of the Colorado River waters, he had written a pro-dam article for *Nation's Business,* "Conquering the American Nile." The Colorado was "one of the greatest unappropriated assets of the nation," he told the U.S. Chamber's readers, in unapologetically businesslike terms.[104]

Business organizations very much liked both Hoover and the dam he helped erect. It's not surprising, then, that the Salt Lake Chamber of Commerce urged that the name of the dam be changed from Boulder to Hoover.[105] Others agreed, including Hoover's old friend Ray Lyman Wilbur, who as Secretary of the Interior made the name change in 1930.[106]

Hoover Dam under construction, 1932

There would be skirmishing over who deserved credit for making possible what was perhaps the most ambitious and far-reaching reclamation project in American history. People would argue over whether Hoover, or California Senator Hiram Johnson, or Phil Swing, or even Franklin Roosevelt (whose administration was in power during most of the period of construction) was the key individual. And of course there were the Six Companies building the dam, the thousands of workers, 100 of whom died on the job, and the taxpayers who underwrote the project.

Obscured by this large crowd of actors, and others, were the chambers of commerce, which had kept the political pot boiling, especially in the early years. The chambers didn't ask for credit for the project, and they didn't get much. This was fine; it was the dam that mattered.

A Concrete Idea

Far away from the Nevada desert, the Spokane Chamber of Commerce showed a deep interest in its hinterlands and in the growth of its farming community. During the Twenties, that interest became an obsession, as the chamber pursued the biggest project in its history: the creation of a great dam on the Grand Coulee that would irrigate as much as 1.8 million acres and supply massive amounts of cheap electricity.

Attorney William Clapp came up with the idea of a dam on the Grand Coulee in the Columbia River Basin in Washington. He brought it up at a gathering of friends in Ephrata, Wash. in 1917. (A coulee is a steep ravine.) The first public mention of the concept was in the *Wenatchee Herald* on July 18, 1918, and it almost immediately captured the public's imagination.[107]

The nearest major community to Grand Coulee was Spokane, 86 miles away. Given the booster spirit of the Spokane Chamber and its decades-old interest in the surrounding countryside, it was only a matter of time before it became involved. Indeed, an active member of the chamber, Arthur D. Jones,[108] had already made "a close study of the Columbia basin project" by March of 1919. At that time Acting Governor Louis F. Hart appointed him to the five-member Columbia Basin Survey Commission.[109] The legislature empowered the commission to spend $100,000 exploring the potential of the region.

Over the next decade, the primary force attempting to move the needle of public opinion in favor of the dam was the Spokane Chamber of Commerce. The organization that the chamber founded in 1923, the Columbia Basin Irrigation League (CBIL), promoted the project.[110] Roy R. Gill, who was president of the chamber in 1922-1923, became the first chairman of the CBIL's executive board. He continued, either with CBIL or with the Basin Committee of the Spokane Chamber, to be one of the key figures in moving the dam project forward.

The Spokane-based dam boosters seem to have focused their strategy on three interconnected tactics: promoting studies of the project, spreading the word about the positive findings of the studies, and encouraging leading figures and potential supporters to visit the area. The visits were critical: without garnering support from outside the state of Washington, the dam was doomed. Among those enticed to see the project were General George Goethals, the Panama Canal builder and honorary New York Chamber member; Herbert Hoover; Elwood Mead, who headed the Bureau of Reclamation, and for whom Lake Mead is named;[111] and a group of Congressmen who saw the area in 1927, accompanied by no fewer than 150 local friends and supporters of a Columbia Basin project.[112]

During the 1927 visit of the Congressmen, Roy Gill made reference to the numerous studies of the irrigation and electric power potential of the area. He summarized the reports of four engineering boards over eight years, and the report of the "special commission" in 1925 that examined eight previous reports. The experts favored the project.[113] The special commission's members included the famed Elwood Mead as well as Assistant Secretary of the Interior John H. Edwards. Surely the idea was a worthy one if men such as these favored it.

As with any big idea, there were debates and disagreements. One was between the "pumpers" and the "ditchers." The pumpers favored a big dam to irrigate lots of territory. The ditchers preferred a relatively inexpensive canal for limited irrigation. The Spokane Chamber and the CBIL were on the pumper side, which ultimately prevailed.

Originally the Seattle Chamber of Commerce opposed the Columbia Basin project, perhaps influenced by its power-company members that fiercely opposed the cheap, subsidized electricity that the dam one day would provide. But this was about more than the electric companies, and by 1926 the Seattle Chamber was on board with the Spokane Chamber.[114] Spokane's hinterland was Seattle's, too: if uncountable acres of scrubland were turned into rich farmland, those farms would add greatly to the wealth of the state and its leading metropolis.

The Grange organization in Washington also first opposed the Columbia Basin irrigation idea. After all, at a time when farm prices were depressed and food overabundant, what was the point of spending money to irrigate many more acres? But by 1929, this organization, too, came around, apparently because of the lure of the cheap electricity that a major reclamation program would be sure to generate.[115]

Through all the ups and downs and disagreements of the Twenties, the Spokane Chamber and the CBIL kept up the pressure, jumping on anything favorable indicated by the swarm of studies. The upshot of perhaps the most important study, called the "308 Report," was that a dam offered enormous potential for electric power and irrigation. Major John Butler of the U.S. Army Corps of Engineers reported that the Columbia River offered "the greatest system for water power to be found anywhere in the United States."[116] This, of course, was "heaven for boosters," grist for the mill of the chamber and the CBIL.[117]

But while the dam's supporters had excellent documentation for the power production and irrigation potential of the project, they hadn't proven the need for the structure. Who in that sparsely populated region was going to use all that power? Who required more farmland at a time of weak demand for agricultural goods?

It took the Great Depression, as Columbia River historian Richard White has noted, to turn the big idea into a workable idea. The vast electric power unleashed by the river, and by the Grand Coulee Dam, could improve living standards. For "a society desperately seeking transformation," the dam offered a solution to wrenching economic dislocation and despair.[118] The same Roosevelt Administration that completed the Hoover Dam, authorized construction of the Golden Gate Bridge, and launched the Tennessee Valley Authority, saw the value

Grand Coulee Dam

of the Grand Coulee Dam proposal. Construction began in 1933 and was completed in 1942.

The resulting project on the Grand Coulee was enormous. The dam is the largest concrete structure in the world, containing nearly 12 million cubic yards of concrete, three times as much as the Hoover Dam.[119] It is also the largest hydroelectric power producing facility in the United States.

Like the Golden Gate Bridge and Hoover Dam projects, the Grand Coulee Dam was conceived before the 1920s and built largely in the 1930s. But just as these engineering marvels couldn't be built overnight, neither could they work their way into public opinion and public purpose overnight. It took the Spokane Chamber and the CBIL, and their growing group of allies, just about the entire decade of the Twenties to help spin the web of support and information needed to make the dam a compelling idea for the nation.

Beyond the Big Three

The nation's chambers went far beyond these three glamor projects (Hoover Dam, Grand Coulee Dam, and the Golden Gate Bridge) in their advocacy for ambitious building projects during the Twenties. Sometimes the ideas were too ambitious: the Reno Chamber of Commerce pushed the concept of steam pipes a few inches beneath 16 miles of a highway across the Sierras. The pipes would melt the snow that clogged the road in winter. The plan was to have boilers four miles apart, fueled by burning wood from the plentiful trees in the area. Two men, the chamber said, could handle the job of maintaining the system. The chamber was even toying with a slogan: "Steam-heated highways for hot Winter tourists."[120] Fortunately, not every chamber idea would come to pass.

The building of new roads, bridges, and dams was a national effort with plenty of chamber involvement and advocacy. In Fort Worth, serious flooding in 1922 led the chamber to push successfully for two large dams on the Trinity River, creating Eagle Mountain Lake and Bridgeport Lake.[121] In Mobile, the chamber formed a company that successfully built a 10-mile series of bridges and causeways linking the city to Baldwin County.[122] In Quincy, Illinois, people had been talking about a trans-Mississippi bridge to Missouri for 50 years, but in 1929 the Association of Commerce arranged for the sale of $250,000 in bonds that served as the down payment on a $1.5 million span.[123]

The Pittsburgh Chamber of Commerce also had infrastructure in its DNA. It rarely found a part of the Ohio River that didn't seem appropriate for a dam. As noted in its 50-year history in 1924, in 1874 there was practically no improvement on the Ohio River system. With a large helping hand from the chamber's advocacy, by 1924, there were 37 dams, 11 others under construction, and plans for four more had been prepared.[124]

A Bridge Too Near

And so it went. In Camden, N.J., business organizations, including a powerful new Camden County Chamber of Commerce, had a hand in the projection of the first bridge across the Delaware River below Trenton.[125] The Camden Bridge (now known as the Benjamin Franklin Bridge) was the spearhead of the ambitious "Greater Camden" movement, an attempt for the bustling city to break out of its confines along a five-mile strip along the river and unite with the county, while also garnering national recognition and acclaim.

Things didn't work out as planned. The bridge, built from 1922 to 1926, was a phenomenal financial success, despite its high cost. But it turned the axis of Camden commercial activity from north-south to east-west, permanently altering the character of the community and helping make the city more of a transit point than a destination.[126] For various other reasons, the consensus for a city-county combination collapsed. Meanwhile, the bridge's success sparked a flurry of projects to build other spans across the Delaware, including one strongly advocated by the Wilmington Chamber of Commerce at a point where the river was wider.[127]

Finally, many years later, the Walt Whitman Bridge would be the *coup de grace*, according to one critic, Alan Karcher. That bridge was the additional transportation improvement that connected, but also paradoxically isolated, the once-great city.[128] Camden was, literally, bypassed by the progress it had stimulated. At least according to Karcher, the upshot of the Greater Camden movement, and of its exciting and successful bridges, was ultimately a lesser Camden.

Usually, however, these transportation projects improved communities' prospects. Building out infrastructure was a project important enough for any community, any chamber, and any elected official. One aspiring young politician in the Midwest found his local chamber to be an ally in the effort to pass a bond issue for improving the county's roads. Harry S Truman worked with the large and energetic Kansas City Chamber of Commerce on a successful $10 million bond issue for Jackson County roads, which passed in 1928. The young Truman was a good friend of the chamber's most dynamic leader of this period, Lou Holland.[129]

Chambers of commerce continued to pay attention not only to specific projects, but to the wider scope of city planning. Indeed, they were more heavily involved in planning than ever. The U.S. Chamber's Civic Development Department reported that "out of 402 plans proposed for comprehensive city planning, thorofare [sic] plans and park proposals, chambers are responsible for 221."[130]

Transportation Authorities

Such ambitious projects were drawn up in the 1920s that often equally ambitious means were needed to finance them. There was a proliferation of quasi-public entities handling transportation and other issues (such as municipal water). Chambers frequently advocated these apparently efficient, specialized organizations. The New York – New Jersey Port Authority was perhaps the best known among them, but there were many others, including the multi-county organization that the Santa Rosa Chamber was cobbling together to support the Golden Gate Bridge project, not to mention the Savannah Port Authority, which the Savannah Chamber of Commerce ushered into existence in 1925.[131]

Indeed, it took a chamber-devised multi-county transportation authority to pierce the Continental Divide and open up western Colorado to development. The high mountain barrier 50 miles west of Denver made it difficult to operate profitable rail lines between Salt Lake City and Denver. One man, David Moffat, had dedicated his fortune and a good part of his life to making the rail connection work, but he ultimately failed.

In 1922, however, the Denver Chamber of Commerce led the effort to create a five-county consortium, the Moffat Tunnel Improvement District, to raise funds to bore a six-mile tunnel under the mountains. Challenges to the taxing district's legitimacy went all the way to the U.S. Supreme Court, which ruled in favor of the tunnel projectors. With that ruling, work could begin.

The Moffat Tunnel, partially completed in 1927 and fully operational a few years later, required the removal of three billion pounds of rock with 2.5 million pounds of dynamite. It cut 175 miles off the winding rail route to Salt Lake City and made the trains virtually immune to the snow blockages that used to close the rail line for 30 to 60 days each winter. Two million acres of public land in western Colorado land now lay open for potential development.[132]

Transportation authorities, then, often could get things done that otherwise might have been almost impossible without them. It wasn't just in raising money; it was in efficient decision making. Frequently equipped with dedicated sources of funding such as bridge tolls or port fees, these quasi-public entities could develop a surprising amount of independence from local political leaders. The new entities could simply do things that others only talked about.

Moffat Tunnel, 1928

Indeed, for many of the chamber reformers pushing for them, independence was practically the whole idea. And nowhere was some sort of knife-through-the-butter transportation approach of more apparent value than in the massively complicated political and urban environment in New York City. Inspired by the New York – New Jersey Port Authority example, many people in New York, including a member of the Albany Chamber of Commerce better known as Governor Al Smith, became interested in a sort of "domestic" port authority that could build bridges and tunnels between boroughs without the red tape and corruption that had traditionally plagued so many public works in Gotham.

New York City area chambers of commerce were particular proponents of the new Bridge and Tunnel Authority. Among those petitioning City Hall for this institution on March 19, 1928, were representatives from the chambers or boards of trade of Long Island, the Bronx, Brooklyn, Harlem, Queens, Staten Island, and the Rockaways.[133] The institution they desired did not begin to emerge until 1933, when the Triborough Bridge Authority was formed to complete that span. This organization later would become the vehicle by which the ultimate results-getting infrastructure expert, Robert Moses, would transform a good deal of the landscape of New York City and its surroundings.

Great Smoky Mountains National Park

The proliferating automobiles on the nation's roads made tourism an increasingly important source of revenue – and a good reason to open up new wilderness parks, which business organizations played a role in creating. A good example of their activity was in the creation of Great Smoky Mountains National Park.

Willis P. Davis, manager of the Knoxville Iron Company, and his wife Anna were touring the West in 1923. Upon their return, she asked her husband, "Why can't we have a national park in the Great Smokies?"[134]

He loved the idea. Willis Davis shared the idea with staff and others at the Knoxville Chamber of Commerce, of which he was a director. The assistant manager of the chamber, Carlos C. Campbell, commented on Davis's enthusiasm for the idea:

During those conferences I was often irritated because I had to listen to him "rave" – and that is what I then felt it amounted to – about the superlative beauty of the Great Smokies and the national park that we were to have there. I tried to be courteous.[135]

Yet Willis Davis wouldn't stop, nor would his wife, and the idea slowly began to catch on. He suggested the Knoxville Chamber take on the job, but the chamber's manager at the time demurred; actually the man, E.N. Farris, was sick and soon would die. The early torchbearer of the concept, therefore, became the Knoxville Automobile Club – which had exactly the same board as the chamber but with a different and more flexible manager, Russell Hanlon. (Hanlon said, because of the identical boards of the two organizations, he often found it difficult to tell which organization was meeting.)[136]

Subsequently, the park's would-be creators faced one challenge after another. These are amply chronicled by Farris's successor as manager of the Knoxville Chamber, Carlos Campbell, in his *Birth of a National Park*. Campbell gives credit to all but himself, but it's clear from his knowledge of virtually every aspect of the birth of the park that Campbell and his chamber were intimately involved. Moreover, at critical stages the chamber took a front-seat role, as when it raised $5,000 to take Tennessee legislators to see the park site and when, in 1926, it took a train of nearly 200 Knoxville and other East Tennessee proponents on a park-promoting trip to Florida.[137]

Not all of the chamber's activities worked completely smoothly. It hosted a group of 50 scientists that examined the park site, climbing Mt. Le Conte on New Year's Eve of 1927. The temperature dropped from 40 degrees Fahrenheit to -20 within 24 hours. A bucket of water 10 feet from their cabin's blazing fireplace froze solid. Said one scientist, "This will be a wonderful memory, but I'll be darned glad when it *is* a memory."[138]

No stone was left unturned. The famous Scopes monkey trial was happening in nearby Dayton, Tenn., and the park's boosters invited the eminent attorneys Clarence Darrow and William Jennings Bryan to see the Great Smokies (on separate visits). Bryan agreed to come. He then took an afternoon nap but did not wake up from it; newspapers reported that his last act was agreeing to come visit the park.[139] The Knoxville Chamber sent an "enormous" floral arrangement to his funeral.[140]

Taking a look at the Great Smokies, 1931

Across the mountains, the Asheville Chamber of Commerce pushed for the park as well, and contributed the final $35,000 to North Carolina's goal of raising $500,000 for the project.[141] Yet there were always more problems in this most complicated of endeavors, with more than 6,000 landowners to be compensated and all sorts of opposition, and there was always more money needed to complete the concept. It would take a large gift from John D. Rockefeller Jr. and support from the administration of President Franklin D. Roosevelt to complete the launching of the park in 1934.

On many occasions, the park project moved almost fell off the proverbial cliff. Hundreds of people, many of them chamber members, kept the vehicle somehow on the road on the many hairpin turns of the effort. Without the steady support of the Knoxville Chamber of Commerce (and no doubt some key assists from the Asheville Chamber), it's hard to see how the park could have survived its many close calls with the bottom of the ravine. As Campbell describes at the beginning of his book, "One of our persistent tendencies, perhaps, is that of taking things for granted." The Great Smoky Mountains National Park, Campbell wrote, "did not just happen."[142]

Social Change and Racial Friction

The xenophobia expressed in the Red Scare after World War I morphed into other activities during the Twenties, including a successful push to restrict immigration, legislation preventing Japanese-Americans from owning farmland in California, and, most pointedly, a resurgence of the Ku Klux Klan. Chambers of commerce dealt with all of these phenomena, not always willingly. Chambers' behavior varied from place to place, of course, and did not often rise far above the standards of the society in which they operated. But in a number of cases, these institutions showed the colors that would emerge more clearly during the civil rights movement of the Fifties and Sixties: a dislike of extremism and of activities that would hurt business and the reputation of their communities.

Unfortunately, in one community the chamber of commerce did as much to exacerbate as to calm race relations. The Tulsa Chamber of Commerce for years had been closely connected with one of the leading entrepreneurs in the community, hotel owner W. Tate Brady, and Brady had a mean streak.

In many ways, Brady and the chamber were natural partners. He loved to boost Tulsa, and indeed had participated in the early trip, complete with a brass band and fellow Oklahoman Will Rogers, to sing the praises of the community.[143] Brady is said to have coined the phrase "Tulsa spirit," which became the name of the Tulsa Chamber's publication.[144]

Tulsa's descent into violence began during World War I. As a part of the national Council of Defense program, the Tulsa Chamber of Commerce became charged with the task of upholding the "U.S. spirit," so to speak:

> Its members were asked to report any seditious activities, including statements of dissent, acts of industrial sabotage, or "slackerism" (the refusal to participate in work or war). In Tulsa, this essentially put business leaders in charge of finding and reporting anything or anyone they found threatening to the war effort.[145]

The organization most feared and hated by patriot watchdogs in Tulsa was the radical International Workers of the World (IWW). In November 1917, seventeen alleged IWW members were arrested on trumped-up charges in Tulsa and then spirited away by vigilantes. The 17 men's backs were whipped until covered in blood, then coated in boiling tar, and finally decorated with feathers. All those presiding at the torture session except two, reporter Glenn Condon and his wife, were wearing black sheets. The two men considered the ringleaders of the violence were the local police chief and Tate Brady.[146]

The December 1917 issue of the chamber's *Tulsa Spirit* declared with chilling sarcasm:

> The Tulsa social event of November to attract the most national attention was the coming out

party of the ᴋnights of Liberty with about seventeen I.W.W. in the receiving line. As is usual in such social functions, a pleasant time was not had by some of those fortunate enough to be present.

The year 1918 brought further tension, including lynchings, throughout Oklahoma. Meanwhile, the Tulsa Chamber and Tate Brady helped raise $100,000 to bring a convention to town: the Sons of Confederate Veterans. This group was headed by Nathan Bedford Forrest II, a KKK official and the namesake and grandson of the Confederate cavalry leader who was the first Grand Wizard of the KKK.[147]

Simmering tensions exploded in Tulsa on Memorial Day of 1921, when a young black man was accused of assaulting a white girl, although in unusual circumstances. (Both were supposed to be working in a building where the incident allegedly occurred, but this was a holiday.) A riot broke out the next day, May 31. The disturbance almost completely destroyed the black section of Tulsa, Greenwood, and resulted in dozens of deaths and hundreds of injuries. It was one of the worst racial disturbances in American history.

Tate Brady and other white men volunteered for guard duty that night. It's doubtful he was a typical night watchman:

> During his watch, Brady reported "five dead negroes." One victim had been dragged behind a car through the business district, a rope tied around his neck.[148]

When the smoke cleared, Brady was appointed to the Tulsa Real Estate Exchange Commission, which was created by the Tulsa Chamber of Commerce to examine the damage. The commission said $1.5 million of property had been destroyed, and it recommended relocating blacks to an area further away, where they would be more clearly separated from whites. The Oklahoma Supreme Court quashed this idea and Greenwood's blacks were able to rebuild, although without any compensation for their damages.[149]

After this, Brady's luck ran out. The Ku Klux Klan, of which he was a member, grew in strength in Tulsa and throughout the state, but this caused only problems. Its robed arms reached into politics and infuriated many Oklahomans. A new governor, John C. Walton, took a strong stand against the Klan and put Tulsa briefly under martial law in 1923. (Brady himself said he quit the KKK in 1922 because he didn't like being told for whom to vote.) Meanwhile, Brady's wealth had seriously declined. Then, in the spring of 1925, his son John Davis Brady died in a car accident in Virginia. Tate Brady, the former exemplar of Tulsa spirit, then killed himself on August 29, 1925, with a shot to the head.[150]

And so the violent man did violence to himself. But what about the Tulsa Chamber? Although the organization had denounced the mayhem of the 1921 riot, and promised to help the blacks in Greenwood rebuild, it raised no money to do so and refused the aid of outsiders, saying this was a Tulsa affair.[151] The chamber-backed Exchange Commission, in turn, unsuccessfully attempted to appropriate Greenwood for the white community. Although Tulsa Chamber President H.O. McClure spoke out against the KKK in 1923, it was too little, too late. His chamber had mistreated the black citizens of Greenwood at just about every turn.[152]

In the Capital City

In the state capital of Oklahoma City, things were not a great deal more settled than in Tulsa. The Klan had disturbed the peace and terrorized some citizens, and the governor was incensed. In fact, at one point Governor Walton had had machine guns set up on the roof of the Oklahoma County Courthouse.[153] But Walton was over-reaching in the eyes of many people and politicians.

The Oklahoma City Chamber of Commerce opposed the governor's martial law declaration, considering it to be grandstanding. Stanley Draper, the chamber's assistant manager, wrote an editorial against the governor's excessive zeal.[154] In November, Walton was impeached from office because of his various misdeeds, including his illegal suspension of *habeas corpus* in Tulsa County.

While many were relieved to see Walton go, they also found the Klan to be a plague on the community and cheered its demise in the mid-1920s. Stanley Draper was anxious to see Oklahoma's reputation restored. He also had deeper feelings on race than most people knew.

Once when he was a boy in coastal North Carolina, Draper walked home with his father and by chance saw a black man being brutally lynched. The experience so horrified the young Draper that he had sleeping problems, and occasional nightmares, for the rest of his life. His neck felt cold when he went to sleep and so he wore scarves to keep it warm. Once, near the end of his life when he was in the hospital, an accommodating nurse brought him a scarf. He screamed, however, because the scarf reminded him of the lynching and because he didn't think it could protect his neck. It was black.[155]

"This Klan Business"

Despite the example of the Tulsa Chamber while it was influenced by Tate Brady, most local business organizations in the nation were neither instigators of, nor fans of, the rise of the Ku Klux Klan in the Twenties. Burning crosses engendered fear and hatred, which were not emotions conducive to doing business. If chambers were the public face of business, this needed at least to be a welcoming face, not a sheeted one. But how to reconcile civic spirit and friendliness with the ascendant power of the KKK was not easy.

One insightful man caught the spirit of the contradiction. In his first attempt at being a newspaper columnist, Franklin D. Roosevelt wrote in 1928:

> Three years ago I was the guest of honor at a Chamber of Commerce banquet in a small city in Georgia. It was a community of almost pure Scotch and English Protestant ancestry. I sat on the right of the Mayor of the town and on the other side of me sat the Secretary of the Chamber of Commerce, a young man born in Italy and a Roman Catholic. Just beyond sat a Jew who was a member of the Executive Committee.
>
> I turned to the Mayor and asked him if the Ku Klux Klan was strong in the city. He said, "Yes, very." (It has since then nearly died out.) Then I asked if most of the members belonged to the Klan, and again he said, "Yes."
>
> Then I said, "If that is so, why is it that the Secretary is a Catholic and that a Jew is on the Executive Committee?"

He turned to me utterly surprised and said, "Why, Mr. Roosevelt, we know these men. They are intimate friends of ours, we respect and like them. You know this Klan business doesn't apply to people you know."[156]

Several southern chambers of commerce began to show relatively tolerant colors during the Twenties. The Atlanta Chamber of Commerce had minimized the casualties of a race riot in that city in 1906.[157] But its leaders also had called for better race relations and had been shaken by that violence, as well as the disastrous lynching of Leo Frank in 1915, and seemed determined to improve the image of their city.

One sign of progress was that in 1920, the National Association for the Advancement of Colored People (NAACP) made Atlanta the site of its first convention to be held in the South. The chamber was a key player in the improvement of race relations, as one commentator has noted:

> By the 1920s, the Chamber of Commerce in Atlanta had begun to turn vague rhetoric on interracial harmony and respect into reality. Paul Norcross, the group's president in 1924, explained that the business community was obliged to participate in interracial cooperation because it was "a matter of equity, a matter of right, a matter of justice."[158]

Another business organization attempting to improve race relations was the Birmingham, Ala., Chamber of Commerce. The chamber fought a 1923 measure to segregate the city's streetcars, which, however, was unanimously passed by the Birmingham City Commission. The chamber, with the Alabama Bar Association, also publicly denounced the Ku Klux Klan, but unfortunately these efforts to limit the Klan's influence were "almost totally ineffective."[159]

For most chambers of commerce, lynching was bad in just about every way – in breaking the law, in the cruelty and injustice of the punishment, and in the bad reputation it gave the community. Little Rock, which had the largest KKK chapter in the nation in 1926, was convulsed by an unruly mob that lynched a man on May 5, 1927. The Little Rock Chamber of Commerce denounced the lynching and the crowd's behavior, as well as the inaction of the sheriff, and called for a grand jury to investigate the crime.[160] Similarly, after a black mechanic, Amanuel McCallum, was taken from his home and hanged from a pine tree at the end of December, 1928, the Hattiesburg, Miss., Chamber of Commerce called a public meeting and requested an immediate grand jury investigation.[161]

Chambers' opposing the Klan and favoring better race relations took many forms in many places. In Indianapolis, at a time when 30 percent of the white males in the state were KKK members, the chamber championed the building of a well-equipped Negro high school and successfully attacked Klan proposals to create racial zones in the city as, among other things, needlessly expensive.[162] The Memphis Chamber continued to try to improve the lot of local blacks in order to deter them from migrating north; similar programs were carried out by chambers in Nashville, Albany (Ga.), and Savannah.[163]

Chambers would oppose the Klan for many reasons, but especially when their members felt the KKK was interfering with the life of their communities. The chamber in Mt. Rainier, Md., angrily protested after the Klan stopped the graduation exercises of a local school because a Catholic priest had been chosen to give the invocation and benediction.[164] But even though the Klan began declining after about 1925, it remained well entrenched in many places. In September 1929, the Fairfax County (Va.) Fair lasted four days: the first was designated "Children's Day," the second "Chamber of Commerce Day," the third "Grange Day," and the fourth – "Ku Klux Klan Day." Half the proceeds for that final day were to go to the local KKK chapter.[165]

Nativism and Anti-Semitism

The Klan wasn't the only group that frowned on those who weren't white and Protestant. Congress overwhelmingly passed the Immigration Act of 1924, a popular measure that greatly reduced immigration from southern and eastern Europe and from nonwhite regions such as Japan and China. There were further measures passed by such states as California and Washington that tightened the restrictions on "alien" land ownership. These laws were aimed particularly at Japanese farmers.

Most western chambers had not supported the original alien land laws.[166] Once these were upheld by the Supreme Court in 1923, however, there was a need to find "white farmers" to continue working on lands being vacated by as many as 30,000 Japanese cultivators on 500,000 acres of prime land. The Stockton Chamber of Commerce, with its key location in the fertile San Joaquin Valley, was "a leader in the movement to obtain white farmers," *The New York Times* noted.[167]

In 1925 there was a poignant reminder that some key leaders supported better treatment of Japanese immigrants and indeed wanted better relations with all of East Asia. Judge Thomas Burke, a founding member and the secretary of the Seattle Chamber of Commerce in 1882 – the man who had protected Chinese immigrants during riots and was almost hanged for it in 1886 – was asked to give remarks to the trustees of the Carnegie Endowment for International Peace. Deploring U.S. exclusion of Japanese immigrants, he spoke passionately for "good manners and kindly courtesy" with our Asian neighbors. He became so passionate, indeed, that he had a stroke and died in the arms of Columbia University President Nicholas Murray Butler.[168] This "man who built Seattle,"[169] who served as the chamber's president in 1914-15 and was perhaps the most respected man in the Pacific Northwest,[170] finally gave his life to the cause of tolerance of Asian immigrants, a cause for which he almost lost that life nearly 40 years earlier.

In the nativist and xenophobic currents that circulated in American society in the 1920s, anti-Semitism flowed, too. Chambers of commerce, unfortunately, were not immune to it. Carey McWilliams mentioned three examples of it in on a single page of his book, *A Mask for Privilege: Anti-Semitism in America*:

> In August 1922, the Sharon, Connecticut, Chamber of Commerce distributed a leaflet requesting property owners not to sell to Jews. A bulletin of the Philadelphia Chamber of Commerce advocated specific restrictions against "the Hebrew element" ... The secretary of the Chamber of Commerce in St. Petersburg, Florida, announced that the time had come to make St. Petersburg "a 100% American Gentile city."[171]

Crime Time

The Volstead Act, passed in 1919, inaugurated Prohibition and engendered, at least in those who continued to drink alcohol, a spirit of casual lawbreaking. Looser social mores and criminals with a huge new source of cash presented problems to law enforcement. And of course there were plenty of bad deeds done that were unconnected to booze. Chambers, whether willingly or not, were drawn into the issues of crime and punishment during the roaring decade.

In the boom years of the mid-Twenties, real estate sales soared in Florida. There was no shortage of shady operators taking advantage of gullible buyers. The Atlantic City Chamber of Commerce even investigated Florida firms that took pictures of choice real estate in Atlantic City and passed them off as being in Florida.[172] But in Florida itself, chambers got even more serious.

There, the excesses of dishonest salespeople were beginning to blacken the reputation of the state. The Florida State Chamber of Commerce enlisted the 176 commercial bodies in the state to join it in a push to oust the shady operators. Cooperating organizations included the National Better Business Bureau and the Associated Advertising Clubs of the World.[173]

The first foray of the campaign was a six-week investigation, leading to indictments aimed at an unscrupulous real estate operator who was, among other things, selling underwater real estate. His name was Charles Ponzi. He was out on bail from Massachusetts,

Charles Ponzi on the job.

where he was appealing charges against him for his "investment" activities there. In Florida, in just two years, he managed with his dishonest dealings to turn $10 into $5.3 million in illusory paper profits.[174] He was sentenced to a year in prison and appealed the charge. Among other things, he said he was trying to gain money to repay those he had defrauded in Massachusetts – a sort of Ponzi scheme of restitution.[175] He got out on bail, and travelled to Tampa, where he attempted to flee the country in disguise. He was caught and ended up serving a lengthy prison term in Massachusetts.[176]

There was plenty of crime to go around. In New York, the Chinese Chamber of Commerce tried to mediate in the "Tong War" between the Hip Sing and On Leong groups, both of them with some criminal connections, to no avail.[177] In Canton – Canton, Ohio, that is – the local chamber led the opposition to a criminal syndicate called "The Jungle" that had murdered anti-corruption *Canton Daily News* publisher Don Mellett.[178] Ultimately four men, including the Canton police chief at the time, were sentenced to life imprisonment for the murder.[179]

Prohibition had created an enormous criminal industry of bootlegging, leading to one issue after another for chambers of commerce. The Atlantic City Chamber of Commerce passed out handbills warning of the dangers of "hooch" – "It's bad dope" – while also urging visitors to check on the cover charges not only of bars, but of the girls who might sidle up to patrons.[180] The Miami Chamber of Commerce protested to Secretary of the Treasury Mellon regarding Customs officials' "indiscriminate firing on boats" suspected of alcohol smuggling. A wealthy man's yacht had been sunk by "Federal prohibition forces."[181] Meanwhile, in the nation's capital, the Washington Chamber of Commerce denounced the high-speed "flying squads" of Prohibition agents chasing rum-runners around town, causing greater danger for civilians than it was worth for the capture of small-time criminals.[182]

Sometimes the Prohibition issues were brought even closer to home. Officials of the Hoboken Chamber of Commerce were incensed when their shipboard dinner of 400 people was raided after a tip that booze would be provided as a souvenir. (Perhaps because of another tip, hardly any liquor was found on the guests.[183]) In a separate incident, Irving Austin, the organizer of the Port Chester, N.Y., Chamber of Commerce, was convicted of participating in a rum-running ring and was sentenced to federal prison for a year and a day and a fine of $5,000.[184]

Stock Promotion

As Charles Ponzi knew, the line between criminal activity and promoting investments wasn't completely clear in the Twenties. Many chambers of commerce were caught up in the excitement of the period and helped local entrepreneurs market their company shares to the public. Often the ending to these stories wasn't happy. *Nation's Business* even ran a two-part series on a fictional promoter, Bolivar Tips, who got a local chamber's endorsement for a bogus investment scheme and then defrauded the community.[185] Meanwhile, in the nonfiction world, the Memphis Chamber of Commerce backed the stock of Piggly Wiggly grocery stores, only to see the shares collapse, complete with a closed-door scene with the entrepreneur, Clarence Saunders, who emerged from the room with "his face bruised and collar torn."[186]

Another chamber-connected venture in Memphis worked out better, however. The story began in Texas. The San Antonio Chamber of Commerce initiated by early 1928 a novel program called the "Welcome Wagon." This buy-local activity involved an official greeter, Mrs. T.E. Everitt, who would take a basket of San Antonio goods to the homes of newly arrived residents. The items included free movie tickets, an ice pick and coupons for 100 pounds of ice, a pail of lard, bread and cake, a sack of flour, a map of the city, and so on. Local merchants said they got an appreciable increase in business from this program.[187]

Thomas W. Briggs, a Memphis newspaper advertising and promotion expert – perhaps having seen the Welcome Wagon article in *The New York Times* in April – bought the rights to the program from "two Texas youths" and was officially using the Welcome Wagon name in July of the same year.[188] He became a wealthy man and "Welcome Wagon" a tremendous success. Later the company's headquarters moved from Memphis to New York.

"There is no God but Advertising, and Atlanta is his Prophet"

If society shook off many of its traditional restraints in the 1920s, so did chambers of commerce. We've seen it already in promotions of airplanes, boxing, and Piggly Wiggly. It was also true in the broader sphere of economic development. Ryerson Ritchie and the strengthen-the-community-first philosophy, the build-the-city-and-they-will-come point of view, were largely forgotten in the scramble to get more businesses and tourists to town. All this was especially true in the South, including Florida, and in parts of the Midwest and West. In a period of growth people wanted to sell their communities to the nation and the world.

Many chambers brought their communities attention by taking delegations to other cities. This had gone on before but the pace stepped up in the 1920s. Tulsa, which had had just that exploratory foray in 1905 and a bigger one in 1908, took another big swing in 1926 and still another in 1929. The 1926 trip, occurring only five years after the race riot and three years after the governor had declared martial law, included visits to New York Governor Al Smith and President Calvin Coolidge, a brass band, as many as 150 participants, and stops in 26 cities.[189]

The Boston Chamber of Commerce took such a goodwill trip to the South and West in 1929. This 12,000-mile, 22-city "land cruise" brought the group into contact with many chambers of commerce in these regions. E.C. Johnson, vice president of the Boston Chamber, said afterwards that he had noticed something about those business organizations. He indicated that "many of the chambers of commerce visited seemed to have stronger financial support than similar bodies in New England and to be more appreciated by the communities they served."[190]

Books could be written about that observation, which some might say still rings true. Certainly the southern and western communities that had rapid population or business growth, or perceived themselves to have the potential for it, were likely to rally around expansion-oriented chambers of commerce. Those anxious to recruit more businesses tended to look kindly on business organizations, and especially on their own chamber of commerce if it encouraged growth.

The wonder child of growth in the 1920s was Florida. While Ponzi was selling underwater land, others were selling parcels above ground – lots of them. The Florida real estate boom (and bust, and then slow recovery) was the talk of the decade. Better automobiles, better roads, and a booming economy enabled hordes of tourists and potential home buyers to visit the sunny state.

Florida business organizations had a hand in the growth of their state. Chambers such as those in Miami and West Palm Beach raised money to support advertising efforts in the north. In Jacksonville, the chamber organized a group of 100 boosters called "Believers in Jacksonville" who paid $25 per month each to promote the city.[191]

Everyone in Florida was involved in PR. In Sarasota, the folksy chamber secretary Willis Powell ("Some men will not pay $1 a year to support a commercial organization but will cheerfully hand over $100 for a hunting dog") spun glorious but credible tales of growth. People were coming to the state not only for its sunshine but for its moonshine, he noted. He informed *Nation's Business* readers that Sarasota had 3,500 people in June of 1924 – and 10,000 by December![192]

But the Floridian chambers also had to fight off bad publicity. We have already seen the St. Petersburg Chamber's reaction to *Foot-loose Widows*. Moreover, a negative article about the state in *The New York Times* elicited several angry chamber rebuttals, along with at least one threat. Powell's successor at the Sarasota Chamber, General Secretary W.B. Estes, told the *Times* that "we will, at least, be on the lookout for your advertising and editorial representatives."[193]

The Miami Chamber of Commerce also objected to the *Times* article, but was even more exercised about false rumors being spread about disease in Miami – to deter tourists from visiting, so that they would stay in northern parts of the state. To stop the rumors, the chamber placed ads in newspapers in the offending cities (Jacksonville, St. Augustine, Daytona, St. Petersburg, and Tampa). The ads noted the state's law against spreading rumors of epidemics and offered a $500 reward for those catching the disease deceivers.[194]

People in other states occasionally felt sympathy for Florida – and chambers contributed to the relief of Miami after the great hurricane of September 1926 – but a more common emotion was envy. The president of a chamber along the Pacific slope was quoted as telling his members:

> In the southeastern corner of this great nation is a State smaller than we, and, speaking comparatively, poor in the mineral, agricultural and resort riches in which we abound. Yet, to that small State are rushing hundreds of thousands of men, women and children from across this great land.[195]

It was time for the West to stand up and shout out its message, he said. Indeed, West Coast chambers promptly put together a $400,000 advertising war chest, with an eventual goal of $3 million, to bring some attention back to the Pacific.[196]

An even more portentous reaction emerged from Atlanta. The city's business people not only envied Florida – some of them trying their luck in business there – but also were concerned by the collapse in cotton prices and the rise of the boll weevil. And there was a deeper rooted, continuing envy of the cities of the North, with their higher living standards and technological and commercial sophistication. How could this out-of-the-ashes Civil War city fight its way out of these constraints?

The answer emerged in August of 1925, when Atlanta Chamber President W.R.C. Smith, a publisher, announced an advertising campaign called Forward Atlanta. This effort would show the world, and especially the North, the advantages of this southern metropolis. The aim was to attract companies to come to Atlanta.[197]

The goal was $250,000. Fundraising began on October 6, resulting in pledges of $85,000 that day. By October 10, chamber volunteers had scooped up an extraordinary $668,000 in commitments. With this impressive war chest, the chamber began placing ads. The first appeared in the *Saturday Evening Post* on February 20, 1926. Soon the promotional pieces were appearing in *Forbes*, *Fortune*, trade magazines, and other publications. The ad choices were made by a senior team of Atlanta executives who knew the kinds of things their counterparts in other cities were looking for.[198]

The campaign was a smash hit:

> In 1926 alone, Atlanta added 169 new firms with nearly 5,000 jobs, prompting the Chamber to extend the campaign for an extra three years. By the campaign's end, 762 firms totaling 20,000 jobs had come to town, although it is unclear how many actually came as a direct result of Forward Atlanta.[199]

The newcomers included Chevrolet and Nabisco. In the excitement, local businesses expanded, too, and the Atlanta Chamber and the allied Junior Chamber of Commerce worked with Mayor Hartsfield on his harebrained scheme to turn Candler Field into a leading airport. Forward Atlanta didn't do all these things, but it did a great deal and somehow focused local business people and the community on the idea of growth, of the "Atlanta spirit." Just as chamber leader Asa Candler had successfully bottled refreshment with his appealing Coca-Cola drink, so Forward Atlanta bottled the Atlanta spirit and exported it to the world. A Junior Chamber of Commerce volunteer at the time, Duncan Peek, reminisced later about Forward Atlanta: "That was the beginning, in my estimation, of Atlanta becoming a great city."[200]

Perhaps influenced by the Atlanta example, the Dallas Chamber formed Industrial Dallas Inc., a separate business recruitment organization, in late 1928. In its first year the group raised $500,000 for advertisements in such publications as *The Saturday Evening Post* and *Nation's Business*. These ads generated 186 serious prospects for the area, blunting the impact of the Great Depression that was to come.[201]

Somehow, however, it was Atlanta that captured the limelight. Even before Forward Atlanta, the Georgia city was famous for its publicity machine. It was in 1924 when Gerald W. Johnson, while criticizing the Babbittry of his native Greensboro and other southern cities, issued his often-quoted dictum: "There is no God but Advertising, and Atlanta is his prophet."[202]

The campaign ran through 1929 and with the advent of the Great Depression it was not renewed in 1930. But there was something singular about this project, something worth repeating. The fizzy Atlanta spirit needed a bottle, needed some structure to capture and export the value of the overachieving southern metropolis. And so the multiyear community promotion/advertising campaign would return to Atlanta in the early Sixties, as ambitious as before, and copied by communities not only in the South but across much of the rest of the nation.

Blocking and Tackling

Advertising was the glamorous forward pass of the economic development game at the time. There was also the exhausting blocking and tackling of finding industrial prospects and persuading them to come to town. More and more specialized economic development organizations grew up to handle this work, which was related to, but different from, the everyday run of chamber activities. Chambers from Los Angeles to Buffalo to Atlanta set up industrial bureaus or departments to help recruit factories more scientifically. In Galveston, the chamber raised $100,000 to form an industrial finance company, technically separate from the chamber but housed in it and staffed by it.[203] A study in 1926 found that in 100 different cities of 10,000 or more people, there were specific organizations "to stimulate industrial growth."[204]

There was a bit more science involved in recruiting than there was in past decades, but the science was nevertheless far from perfect. An industrial site location expert from DuPont who had selected spots for 60 different factories complained to a NACOS conference that he felt chamber secretaries weren't applying themselves effectively. "Sometimes they remind me of Airdale terriers – a superabundance of energy illogically applied," he said. Chamber executives would assume he wanted things he didn't, drop his company's name when it wasn't appropriate, or assume their town was obviously the right location, even though it might lack critical factors such as proximity to markets or raw materials.[205]

Then as now, industrial recruiting was a numbers game with its full share not only of triumphs but of pitfalls. In 1921 the Justice Department uncovered a massive fraud ring that had taken in, among others, the Commercial Club of Centralia, Ill. The club had put up $50,000 to attract a factory that had never been built.[206]

Indeed, for every gazelle firm that a chamber might bag, there were dozens of dogs and cats. In 1927 the Sycamore, Ill., Chamber of Commerce reported its results from following up on 45 leads during the previous year, with a hope of getting one or two of them:

> Eight of the concerns investigated desired to sell stock in our community totaling $755,000; nine concerns were seeking financial aid; nine leads were unresponsive to our correspondence; ten leads proved to be concerns which had no intention of moving at that time; seven inquiries were followed up to the point where it was revealed that the concerns were either not substantial, wanted inducements of some nature, or required from 60 to 90 percent female labor. At the present time we are negotiating with two prospects considered good and are exerting all effort to close with at least one of them during 1927.[207]

Tourism Development

The town of Bradford, Pennsylvania, had a problem. While its industrial strengths were well publicized, it was losing hold of its consumers. The Bradford Board of Commerce's publication noted plaintively:

> On holidays and Sundays hundreds of automobiles go out of town. This is significant. Why do they do it?

This wonderful new machine, the car, was taking business out of town. People were voting with their tires. What if the board could reverse the situation?

> What would it mean if a thousand autos filled with pleasure seekers poured into Bradford the eve of a holiday? What new hotels would we need to care for them! What an instant reflex upon all our markets, our shops and our theaters. How many thousand people would come to Bradford during the summer to avoid the extreme heat of the cities if they knew of our climate and beautiful natural scenery?

The rhapsodizing writer was correct. The rapidly emerging, mobile consumer culture of the Twenties provided great business opportunities. Tourists and shoppers were important and needed to be attracted. Unfortunately, the Bradford Board of Commerce's publication, the provider of these forward-looking sentiments, had some work to do of its own. The newsletter's consumer-unfriendly name was *Oil Sand*.[208]

Even if every chamber didn't get tourism right, quite a few got things moving. Chambers from many communities, ranging from Coney Island to Okmulgee, Oklahoma, put up financing for hotels. Numerous business organizations promoted special events to attract visitors. Florida chambers, and the always resourceful Los Angeles and Honolulu chambers, did plenty to advertise and publicize their charms.

Salt Lake City, too, demonstrated success. For its ad campaigns in the Twenties, the Salt Lake Chamber consciously drew inspiration from Fischer Harris, its tourism-minded secretary from 1902 until his untimely death in 1909. Harris had come up with the slogan, "See

America First."[209] The chamber raised its advertising budget (some for tourism, some for industrial recruitment) from $9,000 in 1920 to $75,000 in 1924.[210] Tourism exploded: while just 50,000 people visited Utah in 1921, five years later the total was 427,000.[211]

Florida's chambers promoted tourism with an ingenuity few could match. But with Miami and Miami Beach catching most of the headlines, the St. Petersburg Board of Trade had an uphill battle for attention. Its publicity guru, John Lodwick, never met a gimmick he didn't like. Once he colluded with Mayor Frank Pulver to create the St. Petersburg Purity League, in which a woman complained of the skimpy bathing suits on Spa Beach. Soon more bogus complaints surfaced, so Lodwick and Pulver brought police to the beaches and began measuring women's bathing suits to prove they were not too revealing. Of course, the newspapers loved it, snapping pictures and sending the story across the country. St. Petersburg got more visitors.[212]

But as *Oil Sand* had plaintively noted, tourism dollars went into town, and also out. Chambers of commerce began in the Twenties a serious effort to take members on trips, not only within the United States, but overseas. The foreign trips, like the domestic ones, often combined business with pleasure. The San Francisco Chamber was perhaps the most ambitious of all: it took 150 people on a three-month, 19,000-mile cruise in 1921. The group visited Honolulu, Yokohama, Kobe, Shanghai, Hong Kong, Singapore, Saigon, Batavia (Jakarta), and Manila.[213] Quite a few other chambers took excursions to the Caribbean.

Education Efforts During the Twenties

It was a chamber secretary who got the children excited in each of the eight grades in the public schools in Asbury, N.J. "We've found a way to make them study," said Thomas Burley. The chamber executive had obtained baseballs signed by Babe Ruth and Lou Gehrig and was offering them to the top scholar in each grade.[214]

In a decade better known for play than for study, many chambers of commerce nevertheless retained the interest in primary and secondary education that they had begun to show since the turn of the century. The U.S. Chamber set up an education service within its Civic Development Department and distributed pamphlets to "thousands of Chambers of Commerce and other business organizations."[215] The head of that service, William Mather Lewis, echoed the perennial concern of business that it inherited the results of the work of the schools. He complained – as would his descendants in the chamber world for many decades afterward – about the dropout rate: "Out of every one hundred pupils who enter the public schools, only fifteen get through high school and fewer than three finish college."[216]

Many chambers set up education committees. Sometimes their work involved supporting bond issues for the public schools. The Los Angeles Chamber, for example, helped the public schools win a $17.4 million bond issue in 1922. Its efforts were multifaceted, including connecting the schools (which weren't allowed to spend any money on such campaigns) to private financial support and encouraging local companies to give their workers time off to vote (presumably in favor of the bond appeal). The measure won by a 15 to 1 margin.[217]

The training of potential employees always interested chambers of commerce. The Indianapolis Chamber, after finding through surveys that half of the city's labor force of 70,000 was unskilled, encouraged vocational counseling in the schools and other reform measures.[218] In 1929 the chamber in Savannah, Georgia, began talking with the city's board of education regarding the need for better trained workers in Georgia. As a result, the board set up the Opportunity School, the first technical education school in Savannah.[219] (That institution evolved into Savannah Technical College, which today has about 4,000 students.)

Junior colleges, the two-year post-secondary institution that had been invented in Joliet, Ill., in 1901, spread to other places, often with chamber encouragement. In 1921 the Marysville, Calif., Chamber of Commerce began pushing for such a college, and seven years later it got its wish.[220] In 1929 the Santa Rosa Chamber provided half the land need to set up a junior college named after the community's favorite son, Luther Burbank Memorial Junior College.[221] In the same year, the Springfield, Ill., Chamber of Commerce helped to create Springfield Junior College.[222] These early firecrackers of chamber involvement in junior and community colleges, however, were merely the prelude to an explosion in future years.

Obtaining Colleges: Study Hall or Fraternity Food Fight?

Business organizations coveted higher education for their communities during the 1920s. Rapidly developing Texas provided a good illustration of the lengths that chambers would go to make sure their city or town, and not the town down the road, got the school. West Texas was the site of one high-profile contest.

Apart from the School of Mines in El Paso, which the local chamber had enticed to town in 1914, there wasn't much in the way of advanced education in West Texas in the early 20th century. The inventive Amarillo Chamber Secretary Porter Whaley came up with the idea of asking the state to put an agricultural and mechanical arts college in the western part of the state.[223] The West Texas Association (soon to change its name to the West Texas Chamber of Commerce) supported a bill to put a branch of Texas A&M into the region. Pleading poor state finances, Texas Governor Pat Neff vetoed the bill. This sparked a furor, with some urging that West Texas secede from the state.[224] (One authority, however, argues that Neff really wanted the college and vetoed the bill in order to get more money for it in a future bill.[225])

The governor did support a similar bill in 1923. Neff signed the legislation, authorizing $1 million for the new institution, with a gold pen supplied by the West Texas Chamber of Commerce.[226] Subsequently, 37 towns began to compete for the new technological college. But this bill had been introduced by Lubbock's state senator, William Harrison Bledsoe, and apparently had provisions that gave Lubbock the inside track.[227] Even so, competition was intense.

The Lubbock Chamber of Commerce put a great deal of work into its proposal. Finally it sent a delegation to Austin to hand-deliver the document. The little town won its bid. The chamber then managed a celebratory barbecue on August 28, 1923 for 30,000 people[228] – a remarkable turnout, given that the town's population in 1920 was only 4,051. A local historian, Lawrence Graves, considered the chamber's role in securing Texas Tech the most important accomplishment in its history.[229] (Today, Texas Tech has about 30,000 students.)

West Texas's success in attracting such a major institution caught the interest of the rest of the state. To capture the potential of similar regional organizing, the East Texas Chamber of Commerce was founded in 1923, and although it lost momentum at first, was reestablished with a bang in 1926 and would go on with great energy for more than 60 years. The South Texas Chamber of Commerce was created in 1926 and immediately set to work on higher education.

The only upper-level school south of San Antonio was the South Texas State Teachers College in Kingsville. Chamber leaders wanted to see the school upgraded to a Texas Tech-style school for mechanical and agricultural science. A bill was introduced and passed the legislature but was vetoed by Governor Dan Moody because of a lack of funds.[230] The general manager of the South Texas Chamber of Commerce, Colonel Dan Leeman, made a request that was almost impossible to refuse: "Give us the college and we will operate under the old budget."[231]

The governor acquiesced, and the Teachers College became the Texas College of Arts and Industries. Leeman was severely criticized for settling for an institution with one quarter of the funding of Texas Tech, but he was able to encourage the legislature to provide greater backing for the Kingsville institution in 1931.[232] The school is now known as Texas A&M University-Kingsville and has about 6,200 students.

There was a good deal of ferment in the higher education world in Tennessee. The Memphis Chamber of Commerce, which had an active education committee, helped its city attract West Tennessee State Normal School in 1925. (This ultimately became the University of Memphis, which today has about 20,000 students.) In the same year, the chamber had a hand in attracting Southwestern Presbyterian University (SPU) from Clarksville.[233] (That university's descendant, Rhodes College, remains in Memphis and has about 1,700 students.)

The Clarksville, Tenn., Chamber of Commerce, however, did not take this lying down. It had had a committee, apparently unsuccessful, to keep good relations with SPU. But when the university decamped, the chamber managed to get a state normal school established in the emptied facilities in 1927.[234] (The descendant of that school, Austin Peay State University, has 10,000 students.)

At least one chamber played a double role: trying to steal a university from elsewhere and fighting off a theft attempt on its own higher education institution. In 1923 the Little Rock Chamber of Commerce advocated the relocation of the University of Arkansas from Fayetteville to Little Rock, but the effort failed.[235] Subsequently the chamber had a win, fighting successfully to keep in town what is now called the University of Arkansas Medical School.[236]

The Brooklyn Chamber had lost the battle to be first in the air across the Atlantic, but it had a consolation prize. Ralph Jonas, who had founded the Brooklyn Chamber in 1918, was still its president in 1927 when he proudly presided at the opening of Long Island University. Jonas and the chamber had been much involved in launching the private institution. In 1926 Jonas had pledged $1 million to LIU if the rest of community would come up with the remaining $9 million necessary for the school.[237] The coed, nonsectarian university took up temporary quarters in the Brooklyn Chamber of Commerce building.[238] (Today LIU has about 24,000 students.)[239]

The Birth of Institute

What about a school for the chamber executives themselves? As previously noted, President Taft had called for such an institution back in 1913.[240] Chamber executives, too, believed that they needed a place for instruction. Indeed, the American City Bureau, a New York City organization that helped chambers acquire members, had been running a summer school for chamber staff for a few years.

NACOS National School for Commercial and Trade Organization Executives
students and faculty at Northwestern University in 1927.

In early 1921 the National Association of Commercial Organization Secretaries began setting up its own school for secretaries. The two-week program first took place in July of that year at Northwestern University in Evanston, Ill. The president of the school was S. Cristy Mead, the secretary of the New York Merchants' Association and founding NACOS president.[241]

Tuition at the two-week school was $30 in the first year, which represented only about half the cost of instruction. The U.S. Chamber, whose board in April 1921 had formally endorsed the idea of education for chamber executives, agreed to add its financial support to that of NACOS for the school. Students' daily expenses for room and board were estimated not to exceed $2.50 each.[242]

The following year the school took on as students not just chamber executives but trade association officials.[243] The program that today is universally known among chamber executives as "Institute" (formally the Institute for Organization Management, provided by the U.S. Chamber of Commerce) had been fully launched. Faced with the united front of the U.S. Chamber and NACOS, the American City Bureau withdrew from the chamber-education field.[244] Other programs, however, would appear from time to time, such as a community leadership summer program at Stanford in 1923 that captured the "active interest" of the California Association of Commercial Secretaries.[245]

The Evolving Idea of the Chamber of Commerce

Arguably, each generation gets the chambers of commerce it deserves. These voluntary organizations take on the coloration of their times. In the Twenties, the chamber movement was dynamic, creative, reckless, and sometimes silly.

Each generation, also, tends either to strive for some "new" chamber of commerce that it wants to have, or, thinking it has found the answers, starts to denounce or speak patronizingly of the "old" kind of chamber – or, sometimes, to do a little of both. NYMA and NACOS leader S. Cristy Mead believed that his generation – starting with him, it appears – had revolutionized chambers by imbuing them with the goal of bettering the community. When Mead got started in 1897, he reminisced 32 years later, "Chambers in that day were mostly organizations that indulged in academic discussions and passed resolutions with no teeth in them." But Mighty Mouse was on the way: "Then came the Merchants' Association of New York."[246]

Whether we date the reform from Ryerson Ritchie's arrival in Cleveland in 1893 or S. Cristy Mead's coming aboard the new Merchants' Association of New York in 1897, something significant had come to chambers with the Progressive ethos: a sort of democratized, professional, energetic version of community spirit. Such spirit had existed before, but it was not as well organized or as broadly based. Something new really had come to the chamber movement.

In the Twenties, as Mead complained, things changed. Chambers got into all kinds of activities. Many of them supported the community and catered to its needs, but others were more acquisitive in spirit, seeking to grab business opportunities, tourists, or factories. What was new was not that chambers had a commercial bent, but that they behaved with fewer restraints, not unlike the society around them.

During the Twenties, everyone's idea of the old-fashioned chamber was embodied in the New York Chamber of Commerce. This group was self-consciously retro. As early as 1913, it had barely placed in a New York Bureau of Municipal Research poll that queried 23 leading chambers on the civic effectiveness of other chambers. In responses totaled over two categories of effectiveness, the Cleveland Chamber got 38 votes, Chicago Association of Commerce 32, Boston 30, Detroit 17, the New York Merchants' Association 12, and, far down the list, the New York Chamber had just one vote.[247]

Such a poor showing was unfair for the chamber that broke ground on the New York subway system and helped start the Federal Reserve Bank. But there was something about the chamber that was almost out of touch, and it became increasingly so in the Twenties. Perhaps it was in its leadership structure: just about unique among contemporary chambers of commerce, the New York Chamber lacked a governing board of directors.[248] The institution also had only a skeleton staff, thereby permitting its members at times to appear uninformed on the issues they argued, or caught up in silly causes – amateurs in a civic world becoming dominated by professionals.

Even the chamber's lighting system was archaic, if charming, dating from the early days of electrification. The Great Hall's 900 lamps, originally installed in 1902, required special dimmers to keep them from burning out. Defending the system, Executive Vice President Charles Gwynne said, "After 160 years of life we feel we are entitled to our traditions."[249] The chamber was indeed showing signs of age. In 1926, three statues on the chamber's façade were removed because of low-quality marble that had been used in their construction. The decaying marble was "like sugar" and pieces were falling off, endangering passers-by.[250]

Not just chambers aged; their leaders did also. John D. Rockefeller, Sr., a longtime member of the New York Chamber, was the oldest living member of the Cleveland Chamber when he sent it greetings on its 75th anniversary in 1923.[251] Rockefeller had joined the Ohio port city's chamber in 1870, the same year he founded a small firm there called Standard Oil Company. Another great leader of business, Frank Wiggins, the growth wizard of the Los Angeles Chamber, would die in 1924. He received some favorable notices, but not all the recognition that he deserved.[252]

If the New York Chamber and a few of its leaders were old, and the great Wiggins was gone, what was new? The chamber attracting by far the most notice was, not surprisingly, the Chamber of Commerce of the United States. The U.S. Chamber had grown from a staff of four in 1912 to 300 in 1922.[253] Its magazine, *Nation's Business*, built up a circulation of more than 250,000. The organization was the premier business group in a business-oriented decade. Naturally, many local and state chambers looked up to it, participated in its referenda, and conferred with its experts on transportation, education, and other subjects.

A New Profession in a Complex and Changing Society

The trend toward professionalizing chamber management grew during the decade. Executive education efforts helped, such as the NACOS-U.S. chamber school for secretaries. And as part of the modernizing trend, the title "secretary" began to go out of style in favor of others, such as "manager" or "vice president" or the even more impressive "executive vice president."

But there was no question about who was the ultimate boss, even at the ultramodern U.S. Chamber. There, the directors in 1926 rewrote the bylaws in order to reduce the power of the top full-time staff person, vice president Elliot Goodwin. He resigned. The directors had asserted their power. All agreed, however, that Goodwin had been responsible for much of the remarkable growth of the organization during his 15-year tenure.[254]

The trend toward increasing professionalism went along with the growing complexity of commercial and civic life. "My Town Has Too Many Organizations" was the title of one wryly insightful article of the period. The author, W.O. Saunders, a newspaper publisher in Elizabeth City, N.C., complained:

> We have a Chamber of Commerce and a Merchants Bureau; a Rotary Club and a Kiwanis Club; a Shrine Club, an Elk's Club, a Community Club, and a Country Club.

> We have Masons – Royal Arch, Knights Templar, Commandery, Scottish Rite, and brick; Pythians, Odd Fellows, Red Men, Junior Order, United American Mechanics, Woodmen (two brands) and what have you.

And he was just warming up; he claimed there were at least 40 different groups in the white part of town, and even more, proportionately, in the black part of town. Saunders concluded that Elizabeth City had "too many organizations and not enough organization."[255]

But of course, chamber executives were charged with getting things done in this environment, however complicated it might be. This ecosystem included the relatively new lunch clubs such as Rotary and Kiwanis.[256] Some saw these groups as rivals because their luncheon events and causes drew people away from chamber events and projects. Others saw them as complementary to the chamber.[257] Either way, these networking and philanthropic groups were now a part of the civic furniture.

Many times, the growth in the number of organizations in town was partly the fault of the chamber. It was common practice then, as now, for business organizations to spin off activities that required special skills or that didn't precisely fit the mission or the ordinary program of work of the chamber. Then, as now, there were critics of the spinoff strategy: little would be left of the chamber if it gave up tourism, recruitment of industry, and various other functions.[258]

The state-chamber phenomenon spread during the decade. New state chambers popped up in Maryland, Virginia, Wisconsin, Florida, Missouri, and elsewhere. (Florida's organization had begun life in 1916 as the Florida Cattle Tick Eradication Committee. By 1925 it had morphed into the state chamber.[259]) The state groups even had an organization: the National Association of State Chambers of Commerce, which was founded in 1924.[260]

A Pennsylvania State Chamber study in 1926 found 25 state chambers and five regional chambers.[261] One chamber executive noted that by 1929, only two of the major industrial states were without state chambers: New York and Michigan.[262]

Women took on a more noticeable role in chambers of commerce, as they did in society when they won the vote in 1920. As the Omaha Chamber of Commerce created a women's division, it was noted that 80 percent of the country's chambers of commerce had begun admitting women as members.[263] One woman, Eva Terwilleger, was elected president of the Port Jervis, N.Y., Chamber of Commerce; she was believed to be the first woman in the nation to hold the top voluntary post at a local chamber made up of men and women.[264] But not all was progress: in 1924, the Washington, D.C., Board of Trade barred women from membership, even though they had been members in the past.[265]

The Stock Market Crash

On November 13, 1929, an associate found R.M. Searle, a former president of the Rochester (NY) Chamber of Commerce, dead on his bathroom floor. Searle had killed himself with gas, which was one of his company's products: he headed Rochester Gas and Electric Corp. Searle, an inventor and a former office boy for Thomas Edison, had lost $1.2 million in the stock market crash.[266]

Less than three weeks earlier, the storm had hit. On Monday, October 28, 1929, the Dow Jones Industrial Average plunged by 13 percent, a record at the time. The following day, prices fell another 12 percent. Although it was unclear to many at the time, the opening act of the Great Depression had begun.

Like most Americans, the members of local and state chambers of commerce were unsure of what to do in the wake of the disaster. For many, including President Hoover himself, the answer to the business problem of the stock-market crash ought to come from business people. The U.S. Chamber of Commerce, as the most prominent business organization in the land, thus appeared suddenly in the national spotlight.

Merle Thorpe, the editor of *Nation's Business*, gave a nationwide NBC radio address on November 9 that was reassuring. "Today no factory has closed down; no bank has failed," he said. The basic economy was "more completely divorced than ever" from the ups and downs of the stock market.[267]

Calm before the storm: NACOS dinner at its annual meeting for 1929, held in Milwaukee on October 20-23.

Two weeks later, Thorpe introduced U.S. Chamber President Julius Barnes to the national NBC audience. Barnes called for "collective common sense." Business could solve the admittedly vexing economic problems without "government compulsion." Barnes asked people to avoid spreading rumors, such as the one that Macy's had laid off half its 12,000 employees. In fact, the firm had increased its staff by more than 200, Barnes said.[268]

President Hoover appointed Barnes to assemble a blue-ribbon group of business leaders to grapple with the economic downturn. These industrial chiefs, in turn, had submitted their reports at the White House. Many of these executives were not only members of the U.S. Chamber but of their local business organizations. Herbert Hoover turned to his trusted chamber friends and colleagues to get answers to the nation's perplexing economic problems.

Business, however, did not have the answers. At the economy plunged toward ruin, companies considered such ideas as the switch to a 13-month calendar. The same day that Barnes's talk was reported, a *New York Times* writer described this movement, which had received strong support from the chambers of commerce and associations making up the U.S. Chamber. Under this concept, there would be a new month, Sol, inserted in the calendar, probably between June and July, and each month would then have 28 days. A holiday would account for the 365th day of the year. In the U.S. Chamber's referendum on the calendar topic, the proposition that an international conference be held on calendar revision won 1,783 votes for and only 1,082 against. Yet the average person knew that the calendar revision idea was silly.[269]

If business organizations were not omniscient, perhaps they could make mistakes on things other than calendars. The U.S. Chamber and most of its members had not seriously opposed the harshly protectionist legislation, already passed by the House in May of 1929, that would become the Smoot-Hawley tariff. Many businessmen favored the legislation. Some people, however, feared that the tariff bill had spooked the stock market, causing or contributing to the crash.[270] (Senator Reed Smoot, of course, was convinced of the wisdom of protectionism, just as he had been when arguing its merits 41 years earlier at the Provo Chamber of Commerce.)

On December 5, 1929, President Hoover gave a speech at the U.S. Chamber of Commerce, just across Lafayette Square from the White House. He had asked his old friend Julius Barnes to assemble a group of several hundred business people to discuss how to fix the economy. Hoover said to the executives:

> You represent the business of the United States, undertaking through your own voluntary action to contribute something very definite to the advancement of stability and progress in our economic life.
>
> This is a far cry from the arbitrary and dog-eat-dog attitude of the business world of some 30 or 40 years ago.

Hoover was appealing to the spirit of the modern chamber movement, of business people cooperating for the common good. Could voluntary business organizations, led by the U.S. Chamber, help the nation in this time of crisis? Never before, and perhaps never again, would an American President depend upon chambers of commerce for so much.

Fear Itself

1930-1940

The Politics of Pain

As 1930 dawned, people wanted to believe that the stock market crash was an anomaly and that things were getting back to normal. Surely things would turn around. With a pro-business president and Congress, not to mention a powerful and supportive U.S. Chamber of Commerce, the nation, it appeared, had the leadership to steer the ship.

No one wanted good news more than the leaders of the U.S. Chamber. On January 9, the organization cited a number of positive indicators, including "strikingly optimistic reports" from the National Association of Commercial Organization Secretaries.[1] The following month, the U.S. Chamber forecast that things would be better in 60 days. Some industries were in excellent shape. Iron and steel orders totaled 175,365 tons in January, up from just 45,000 tons in the like month in 1928.[2]

A few good statistics, however, couldn't erase the underlying slump. The economic miasma continued over the succeeding months. Yet people wanted to be optimistic. President Hoover told his friends at the U.S. Chamber at its annual dinner on May 1, 1930, that things were going to be all right. And the key to recovery would be bringing together coalitions of the willing: organizations such as chambers of commerce. The President declared: "I do believe that our experience shows that we can produce helpful and wholesome effects in our economic system by voluntary cooperation through the great associations of business, industry, labor, and agriculture, both nationally and locally."[3]

Hoover, however, was unable to generate effective voluntary action. Without much really happening at the national level in combating the Depression, local chambers sought relief. The Philadelphia Chamber of Commerce tried something on October 20: a four-week "Buy Now" campaign, featuring prices lower than any seen since 1913. The project attracted lots of buyers, not to mention telegrams of interest from all over the country. U.S. Vice President Charles Curtis and Pennsylvania Governor John Fisher praised the idea. Other chambers attempted their own "Buy Now" campaigns. But the effect of such measures was fleeting.

Was it simply confidence that the nation needed? E.E. Shumaker, president of RCA Victor Company, told the Merchants' Association of New York that "there is nothing really wrong with business today except fear of the future."[4] (Shumaker thus anticipated Franklin Delano Roosevelt's comment in his first inaugural address, "The only thing we have to fear is fear itself".) And that fear persisted.

Local chambers found themselves involved in efforts to help the unemployed. Late in 1930, the Manhattan Chamber of Commerce put aside its civic work to focus solely on helping the jobless.[5] Around the same time, the Los Angeles Chamber of Commerce urged that a "work test" be applied, after discovering that many people who asked for food would not take jobs that were offered to them.[6]

As President Hoover reached the midpoint in his four-year term, many business leaders were unwilling to ask him for radical measures to fix the economy. The downturn, while steep, had only lasted for a year and a half. When the U.S. Chamber queried its member organizations whether a special session of Congress might help jump-start the economy, it received only 20 positive responses out of 250.[7]

Still the hard times continued. These began to affect more and more banks, jeopardizing the savings of businesses and workers alike. Early in 1931, in Quincy, Illinois, the Association of Commerce took action after two of the town's seven banks failed. The group brought together 100 business people who signed a statement that business conditions in the community were stable. The document was printed in the evening paper on the Saturday on which the second bank closed. The business people's action restored confidence. For the remaining five banks, business had returned to normal by Tuesday.[8] The chamber's action had worked, although just in the nick of time.

At the federal level, as usual, not much was happening. On May 4, 1931, President Hoover gave a talk to the International Chamber of Commerce meeting in Washington. Oddly, he blamed the arms race for the continuing Depression. (Will Rogers commented mordantly, "Why, the only people drawing salary now is the army and navy. What does he want to do, put them among the unemployed?"[9]) A few months later, Secretary of War Patrick Hurley told the New York Chamber of Commerce that Hoover was leaning toward a tax increase to plug the nation's deficit – a tactic then seen as good Main Street business practice, although today (and even later in the Depression) the move would be regarded as a disastrous inhibition of business activity at the very time a stimulus was needed.[10]

The U.S. Chamber seemed to have few better ideas. In June of 1931 it formed 20 committees to look into solutions for the downturn, but commentator C.F. Hughes expressed the views of many when he criticized the national chamber's stance as essentially "letting things work themselves out"[11] or a "faith cure."[12] The U.S. Chamber advocated as little interference with business as possible, and "local as opposed to national efforts to find jobs for the unemployed."[13]

President Hoover, with a continuing attraction to the organization that had essentially the same laissez-faire economic ideas as his, appointed the U.S. Chamber's founding president, Harry Wheeler, to head a national relief organization. Wheeler's committee promptly discovered and reported that the United States had great economic strength and resources.[14] More than ever, the President and the U.S. Chamber were becoming tied up with the ideas and policies – or lack of them – that were failing to stop the Depression.

As the election year of 1932 arrived, the nation's banking system showed increasing signs of stress. Many people didn't trust their banks and removed their deposits for safekeeping at home. Such actions not only imperiled banks but removed money from circulation, further weakening the economy.

Local chambers tried tactics of their own to boost their economies and currency flow. In Tenino, Washington (pop. 1,100), the local bank had closed, along with all but one bank in the county. Yet life had to go on. So in December of 1931, the local chamber of commerce issued wooden coins, guaranteed by prominent citizens. These were in denominations of 25 cents, 50 cents, $1, $5, and $10. They were made from the local spruce trees. Ultimately there was about $6,500 worth of this currency in town.

They would take a wooden nickel: the Tenino Chamber's wooden currency

The Tenino experiment captured the attention of the public far beyond the Pacific Northwest. The story was featured in news articles and newsreels and even was brought up in Congress. The chamber won out in the end. It only had to redeem $30 worth of the $6,500 in wooden currency; people kept the rest of the coins as souvenirs. With the proceeds, the chamber was able to buy the building and fixtures of the shuttered Citizens Bank. Thus on January 1, 1933, Tenino had a bank again and could convert from its wooden standard back to the gold standard.[15]

Tenino's chamber of commerce was not alone in fighting for its community's commercial life. Many business groups around the nation did what they could to keep their banks afloat or otherwise to avert panic. In Urbana, Illinois, the Association of Commerce successfully fought panicked bank withdrawals by issuing "confidence cards," signed by depositors who said they would not take out their money until "this present period of hysteria has fully subsided." A "Secret Committee of 300" was organized to combat whispering campaigns against the banks. The Urbana plan worked, inspiring nearby Aurora to similar bank-saving action.[16]

The chamber in Curwensville, Pennsylvania, marshaled community spirit and resolve and resurrected its failed bank on March 1, 1932. Apparently this was the first bank in the entire East to be saved in this way. The chamber's secretary, J. Thomas Dale, sent a letter to President Hoover asking for him to acknowledge Curwensville's efforts. Hoover, pleased to see a success in his efforts to fight "hoarding," obliged enthusiastically.[17]

Chambers tried all kinds of things to dramatize the importance of keeping currency moving. In Findlay, Ohio, the chamber and local newspapers found a dollar bill that had been unspent for 26 years, tagged it, and traced its circulation around town.[18] In Mount Sterling, Kentucky, the chamber of commerce president had a giant check, measuring 3 ½ feet long by 18 inches wide, created and followed its progress through town. The $10 check was spent 41 times during a single business day, representing $410 in transactions.[19]

Chambers were doing what they could, as was the Hoover Administration, but it wasn't enough. Some chambers proposed tax cuts because people and businesses had less money available for local government. Trying to activate the housing market, the chamber in Chatham, N.Y. offered free home sites for those willing to build on them.[20] Taking a different tack, the California Chamber of Commerce endorsed the idea of a five-hour workday. Why? This way two people could be employed in the place of one, while still providing enough money for each of the two workers to live on. The system had been tried in San Francisco and seemed to be working.[21]

But the economy only got worse. Even as business conditions deteriorated further, the umbilical connection between President Hoover and the U.S. Chamber remained intact. On June 23, 1932, the former president of the U.S. Chamber, Silas Strawn, paid a formal call at the White House to introduce his successor, Henry Harriman, to President Hoover.[22] It was important, both sides no doubt felt, to keep business and government working closely together at such a critical time.

The summer of 1932 brought a strange display of misery and anger to Washington, involving unemployed ex-military men. A "Bonus Expeditionary Force" (BEF) of 17,000 World War I veterans, family members, and others went to Washington seeking early payment of their military service certificates, not due until 1945. Hoover refused. He had the group roughly ejected from the capital city by the imperious General Douglas MacArthur, creating a terrible image for Hoover's leadership and contributing to his loss in the November election.

Hoover's position against the BEF had some local-chamber support, however. About 2,500 remnants of the BEF retreated to Johnstown, Pa. at the end of July 1932. There the populist Mayor Eddie McCloskey had invited them to regroup. The Johnstown Chamber's secretary, Harry Hesselbein, wired the state police for help in combating the "khaki shirts," but the police were powerless because of the official invitation from the mayor. McCloskey, meanwhile, lambasted the chamber. "Why, what right has the Chamber of Commerce to kick about bringing the veterans here? They've done more harm to this town than anything since the Johnstown flood."[23] But just a few days later the mayor persuaded his guests to leave, offering free food and transportation out of town. Allegedly he had faced an "ultimatum" from locals not willing to host this low-budget convention indefinitely.[24]

There was a growing sense that the old ways of handling economic problems just were not working. At least one chamber of commerce executive looked inward for the blame for the economic disaster facing the country. In a paper delivered to the National Organization of Commercial Organization Secretaries, Charles Ketchum of the Greensboro, N.C., Chamber said: "Summed up, here is the indictment – We did not anticipate the situation and were not prepared to meet it." Shouldn't chambers of commerce, of all organizations, have figured out how to prevent massive unemployment, rather than have had to run around with band-aids after the problem hit?[25]

By November 1932, most of the nation's voters were fed up with the failed policies of the Hoover Administration. New York's Democratic governor, Franklin Delano Roosevelt, crushed Hoover in the presidential election, winning 57.4 percent of the popular vote and capturing 472 electoral votes against Hoover's 59. The public wanted change, and change it would get.

A New Deal

Franklin Delano Roosevelt was inaugurated on March 4, 1933, taking over an economy that was in crisis, with an epidemic of bank failures and unemployment at 25 percent. In his inaugural address, he told the nation that "the only thing we have to fear is fear itself." And he blamed the nation's troubles on "unscrupulous money changers" whose "incompetence" had wreaked havoc on the people of the United States. This attitude did not bode well for the business organizations that had been cooperating with President Hoover.

One chamber, however, reported a boom in local output. The Bergen County, N.J., Chamber of Commerce announced that production of paper board and boxes had increased by 20 percent. It wasn't, however, thanks to a recovering national economy but to the "jig-saw puzzle craze which has swept the country."[26]

FDR was creating a jigsaw puzzle in government. Among the many new agencies that the Roosevelt Administration established was one that would have a sweeping impact on chambers of commerce: the National Recovery Administration (NRA). This bureau of Rube Goldbergian complexity, born from the National Industrial Recovery Act (NIRA), aimed to raise wages and improve business practices, on the one hand, while encouraging the public to patronize the complying businesses, on the other.

Initially headed by a manager of limited ability, General Hugh S. Johnson, the NRA attempted to suspend many of the laws of economics, and contravened restraint-of-trade law in the United States. (Ultra-right leaning Leonard Read of the Los Angeles Chamber would later call the NRA, exaggerating, "fascism, pure and simple.")[27] In just about any other period of American history, the NRA would have been considered a near disaster. But in the greater disaster of the Depression, the NRA's failure was merely a misstep for the Roosevelt Administration and a black eye for cooperating business organizations. Its advances on behalf of labor would make it popular among many voters, even if it was a problem for many businesses.

Present at the creation of the NRA was none other than Henry Harriman, the president of the U.S. Chamber of Commerce. Harriman, considered a liberal in the business crowd, was willing to work with FDR in the all-important effort to fight the slump. In turn, Roosevelt needed voluntary business cooperation so as not to have to take over all the reins of the ailing economy.

The essential bargain between Harriman and the Roosevelt Administration was that business, led by a committee formed by the U.S. Chamber, would police itself to avoid undue competition and ruinous price cuts, while the federal government would impose various labor-related and other regulations. Businesses that complied with the new regime would receive the "Blue Eagle," an NRA badge of approval that could be publicly displayed to attract consumers.

In July of 1933, General Johnson kicked off the NRA by means of telegrams to the presidents of chambers of commerce in every community with more than 10,000 people. Said Johnson to the chamber leaders:

> Will you take the initiative immediately in organizing a campaign committee in your community, to be composed of the Mayor, the official heads of the Chamber of Commerce, Clearing House Association, Rotary, Kiwanis, Lions, retail merchants, Federation of Labor, advertising

club, Federation of Women's Clubs, welfare societies, ministerial association, real estate association and any other civic organization which in your judgment is representative of an important element in the economic life of your community?[28]

The committees, typically led by the chamber president or secretary, were to begin the program of education and enlistment of companies into the Blue Eagle club. Thus local chambers were called on to lead the charge in their communities in the most ambitious jobs and economic program of the Roosevelt Administration. Some chambers were paid for their work on behalf of the program.[29] The Roosevelt administration predicted that the NRA would spark the creation of six million jobs by Labor Day.

It didn't live up to expectations; chamber reactions were mixed, with perhaps a few more being positive rather than negative, but not by much.[30] Instead of six million jobs, the programs created quite a few problems. The difficulties began almost immediately. Early in August, the chamber in Kansas City reported various types of cheating on NRA rules, including companies that discharged some workers so that they could raise the wages of others.[31] Similar allegations of cheating arose in Cleveland, where the chamber issued a "friendly warning" to local businesses to comply with the Blue Eagle pledge or face "serious consequences."[32] Hyman Kaplan, the secretary of the chamber in Chelsea, Mass., summoned 35 beauty parlor operators and told them to raise wages of their workers or face enforcement of the NRA by local police. They complied.[33] In Salt Lake City, where the chamber tried to make barbers stick with a price for haircuts of 50 cents, eggs were thrown at the chamber offices.[34]

As with many government programs, there were unintended consequences galore. In Annapolis, Md., the Blue Eagle strengthened the blue laws (restrictions on selling items on Sunday). In the past, local police had winked at violations of blue laws, but with the NRA requiring a level playing field for all competitors, enforcement increased.[35] Meanwhile, across the state in Hagerstown, the chamber faced complaints from two local furniture makers who said their production season lasted only five months, and if limited to just one daily shift as mandated by the NRA codes, they couldn't make a profit.[36]

Only Santa Claus could escape the NRA. The Columbia, S.C. Chamber of Commerce asked if Santa was bound by the NRA codes. Johnson instructed the chamber by telegram:

Ask Santa Claus to assure all the good children of the United States (and the bad children too) that the activities of the dear old Christmas saint are subject to no limitations this year because of codes.

What we are trying to do is to enlist the entire American nation under a code of "peace on earth, good will to men," under which Santa Claus has been operating for close upon 2,000 years.[37]

Here was benevolent government at work. But woe betide the critics of the Roosevelt Administration. After John Fisher, president of the Pittsburgh Chamber of Commerce (and former governor of Pennsylvania), made remarks at a private dinner against the monetary policy of the federal government, Johnson called Fisher "disloyal" and requested, and received, Fisher's resignation as head of the local NRA committee.[38]

In May of 1934, upon hearing of U.S. Chamber criticism of the NRA, Johnson announced that critics wanted to "scuttle the whole recovery program, make the Blue Eagle walk the plank, hoist the Jolly Roger on the ship of state, and sail back to the good old piracy that brought the crash of 1929."[39]

Roosevelt removed the buffoonish Johnson from his post in September of 1934, and in June of 1935, the U.S. Supreme Court declared the National Industrial Recovery Act unconstitutional on the grounds that it promoted the restraint of trade. This flagship program of the New Deal had consumed untold energies of the local chambers, which had recruited many hundreds of thousands of businesses to the Blue Eagle. This effort had been wasted, it appeared. But the New Deal had yet more challenges for chambers of commerce, and these began before the NRA perished.

The Roadrunner

The essential problem for national business organizations in the first two terms of the Roosevelt Administration was Roosevelt himself. The U.S. Chamber of Commerce, in particular, was identified with what appeared to be the failed policies of Herbert Hoover, whereas Roosevelt, rightly or wrongly, was the face that the public turned to for new ideas. And FDR was a remarkably skilled politician.

Roosevelt was more than a match for any of those who faced him from across Lafayette Square in the U.S. Chamber headquarters. However angry the businessmen of America might be at the seemingly socialistic turn of the federal government, however cleverly they plotted against FDR, they almost never caught the President. Like the Roadrunner in the well-known cartoons of later years, the President kept getting away, while the U.S. Chamber's carefully laid explosive charges usually blew up on its side of the Frenchman's square.

It was, however, the New York Chamber of Commerce that precipitated the first major break between business organizations and the President. The occasion was Roosevelt's decision to go off the gold standard in June of 1933. This move, which would allow the federal government to inflate the currency to combat the Depression, was anathema to the chamber of commerce that had proudly fought for a stable currency and for gold during a good part of its history since 1768.

On November 3, 1933, the New York Chamber approved a resolution condemning the departure from the gold standard.[40] Then, encouraged by an outpouring of congratulatory messages from across the country, the chamber announced on November 14 that it would take its campaign national.[41] Only a few days later, the U.S. Chamber of Commerce took up the cause, calling for a return to the gold standard and "complete avoidance of monetary experimentation, greenbackism and fiat money."[42]

Coincident with the U.S. Chamber announcement, President Roosevelt addressed a group in Savannah, Georgia, with a deliciously savage attack on the New York Chamber's (and now the U.S. Chamber's) initiative:

> It has been remarked of late by certain modern Tories that those who today are in charge of your national Government are guilty of great experimentation. And they are right. If I read my history correctly, the same suggestion was used when Englishmen, two centuries ago, protesting in vain against intolerable conditions at home, founded new colonies in the American

wilderness as an experiment. And the same suggestion was used during the period in 1776 when the Washingtons, the Adamses, the Bullocks and other people of that time conducted another experiment.[43]

The "Tories" remark stung, and was particularly germane to the Anglophile New York Chamber, so proud of its having been chartered under George III. Roosevelt had wrapped himself in the American flag and had impugned the patriotism of his corporate opponents. A seemingly innocuous historical analogy – after all, there weren't many remaining tensions over the Revolutionary War - deftly tarred and feathered the New York Chamber and, thanks to the U.S. Chamber's support of its position, the national chamber as well. But Roosevelt was just getting warmed up.

As the U.S. Chamber met in Washington in May of 1934, the humorist Will Rogers pointed out another chink in the armor of this organization. Its members were dependent on their government. Rogers recalled that at the previous year's meeting, which he had attended as the guest of Reconstruction Finance Corporation head Jesse Jones, he and Jones had seen a number of leading magnates address the assembly regarding the need to "keep government out of business." As each man spoke, Jones wrote down on Rogers' menu card how much that person had borrowed from the RFC, an arm of the federal government. "I got that menu card yet," Rogers wrote.[44]

Thus Roosevelt was grappling with opponents who had weaknesses. He also didn't fully sympathize with business people and with chambers of commerce. In September of 1934, the President went sailing near Providence, R.I., and turned down an invitation to address the Block Island Chamber of Commerce. Upon hearing, however, that 50 Boy Scouts were gathered on the island, he changed his mind and stopped there to talk to the boys.[45] Later in his presidency, he recalled his advice on travel to a young man from New York "who thought he knew it all": "Don't talk to your banking friends or your Chamber of Commerce friends, but specialize on the gasoline station man, the small restaurant keeper and the farmers you meet by the wayside and your fellow automobile travelers."[46] In this era of the New Deal, chamber officials were faced with a national leader who didn't particularly like them.

The feeling was mutual. As FDR was sailing near Block Island and avoiding the chamber there, Wile E. Coyote, in the form of the directors of the U.S. Chamber of Commerce, was plotting to trap the President. The chamber's directors went public on September 25, 1934 with five complaints about the activities of the federal government and, more pointedly, six questions for President Roosevelt to answer:

1. When and how is it proposed to balance the Federal budget?
2. Is it the intention of the Administration further to reduce the value of the dollar; and if so, then to what figure and what shall be the content of the dollar so reduced?
3. Will the Administration at the earliest opportune moment collaborate with the other nations in an effort to agree upon a plan for the international stabilization of exchange?
4. Will the efforts of the Administration be directed toward recovery by the encouragement of business initiative, with a minimum of Government interference and control and will it discontinue its activities in competition with private enterprise?

5. What is the Administration's policy toward agriculture?

6. Is it the policy of the Administration to continue the construction and development of public works not now needed?[47]

These sharp questions from openly hostile political opponents might put another politician on the defensive. But FDR tried a different approach.

The President deftly refused to answer the queries, saying that it would set a bad precedent for him to answer one set of questions from one organization; he would then have to answer questions from the hundreds of other organizations in Washington that had their own agendas to pursue. After thus effectively demoting the U.S. Chamber from its presumed role as the foremost of all the nongovernmental organizations in Washington, the President then made fun of its entrapment plans. He said the questions reminded him of the tale of the lawyer demanding a "yes" or "no" answer of someone on the witness stand: "Have you stopped beating your wife?"[48]

Not only the President's "spanking," as one commentator called it, but the Democrats' strong gains at the polls in November 1934, caused the U.S. Chamber to pull in its horns. It began to seek to cooperate with the President, seeing him   shield against the more extreme groups in his party.[49] But this cooperation was only t   n April 30, 1935, at the opening of the annual meeting of the U.S. Chamber, sp   peaker attacked the New Deal and its socialistic tendencies. FDR responded   ng a notice of greeting to the delegates. Secretary of Commerce Daniel Roper   ate meeting of allegedly sympathetic business people, some of whom later comp   that the Roosevelt Administration had exaggerated their support for the New Deal.

The renewed hardline stance of the U.S. Chamber came in part because the "liberal" Henry Harriman had finished his three years at the helm of the organization, and a businessman more representative of the organization, Harper Sibley, was taking over. Sibley, who knew Roosevelt from their Groton and Harvard days, was personally friendly to the President but just as antagonistic to the New Deal as were most of the U.S. Chamber's members. Sibley supported the resolutions of the chamber, which lambasted five of the key proposed programs of the Roosevelt Administration, for banking, the National Recovery Administration, utilities holding companies, social security, and transportation.[50]

Roosevelt, however, retained his popularity. The President, moreover, criticized the U.S. Chamber's resolutions for their lack of concern for the poor, the elderly, and the unemployed. He recalled how as governor, after the Triangle Shirtwaist Factory fire that had killed 150 to 200 women, he had asked for a factory inspection law. Even though most business organizations opposed the law, the public overwhelmingly favored it, and it passed and was implemented successfully. Business needed to be reined in sometimes, and it needed to offer positive solutions to pressing problems. Of the U.S. Chamber's demands he said, "You can search their resolutions from beginning to end, and you won't find one single reference to the seriousness of the unemployment situation or to remedies for it."[51]

A Sense of Shock

From the nasty U.S. Chamber-FDR fight in early May 1935 through the election in November 1936, there was a growing sense of shock in the business community of just how far government was moving to the left politically. The expansion of the federal leviathan was "beyond comprehension," mourned Merle Thorpe of *Nation's Business*, in an editorial entitled "Our Vanishing Freedom."[52] The Wagner Act safeguarding rights to form unions, strike, and engage in collective bargaining, the giant tax increase in August of 1935, federal investment in public power projects, and the institution of Social Security, among other measures, were a cause of mourning. Roosevelt's overwhelming victory over Republican Presidential candidate Alf Landon in November 1936 (FDR garnered 60.8 percent of the popular vote and won 523 electoral votes to just eight for Landon) capped off a repudiation of just about everything the U.S. Chamber and its allies stood for.

Out of East Texas came a small sign of how bad things were getting. The secretary of a chamber of commerce was fired for criticizing a Works Progress Administration program as "worthless and useless." His town's name, ironically, was Liberty.[53]

The leaders of the U.S. Chamber took on a bitter, intransigent public stance that appeared out of step to the majority in the country, but was certainly true to free-market principles, they thought. Even the business people's caustic tone was attacked. "We have earned the hatred of entrenched greed," FDR told Congress.[54]

Exacerbating the pain were the defections from and dissenters within the U.S. Chamber. Local chambers and national associations dropped out of the business group, or refused to support its policies, when they sensed it was in their best interest to side with the winning federal team. One of FDR's smaller supporters was the chamber in Warm Springs, Georgia, where the President frequently visited to convalesce and to strengthen his polio-weakened legs.[55] And the chamber in Monterey, Calif., dropped out of the U.S. Chamber during the spat with FDR in early May, 1935, claiming that the U.S. Chamber was "unrepresentative of the feelings of the smaller chambers throughout the country."[56] Also in California, the Sacramento Chamber of Commerce's directors refused to vote in a 1936 U.S. Chamber referendum on the New Deal. "Remembering the furor caused by participation in a previous vote, they decided to ignore it," noted a chamber history.[57]

It was in the territory of the government-subsidized Tennessee Valley Authority where many chambers, understandably, refused to damn their dams or their federal financiers. The chamber in Colbert County, Alabama, held a Tennessee Valley Appreciation Day on July 4, 1935, drawing 30,000 people including two governors, as well as a note of encouragement from President Roosevelt.[58] In November 1935, this chamber dropped out of the U.S. Chamber and urged others to do the same, citing the examples of the chambers in Columbia, S.C., and Knoxville, Tenn.[59] Another November 1935 dropout from the national business organization was the chamber in Tupelo, Miss., while the chamber in Bristol, Tenn., refused to vote in a U.S. Chamber referendum on the New Deal in the same month.[60]

Getting Worse?

After FDR's smashing election victory in November 1936, some business executives could be excused for thinking, "How much worse could things get?" At which point, in late December of 1936, a fledging union called the United Auto Workers began a sit-down strike centered at General Motors plants in Flint, Michigan. President Roosevelt refused to break up the massive strike, although he did apparently ask his old friend Harper Sibley to intervene personally. (U.S. Chamber President Sibley asked GM President Alfred P. Sloan to meet with union negotiator John L. Lewis, the head of the Congress of Industrial Organizations, but he was rebuffed.[61]) GM ended up settling with the UAW and recognizing the union, a move that enabled the labor organization to grow at lightning speed.

The U.S. Chamber went on record, not surprisingly, against sit-down strikes. It wasn't the only business organization perplexed by the newly explosive power of the labor movement. The New York Chamber proposed that unions be treated as corporations, subject to the same laws and regulations faced by corporations.[62] This, of course, would permit companies to sue labor unions that seized corporate property, as in Flint, or that engaged in fraudulent elections. The idea went nowhere.

In Excelsior Springs, Mo., the chamber of commerce's director of amusements, Harold Hulen, had a more personal response to the trouble in Flint. He conducted a "sit-down strike for love." He chained himself to a radiator near the apartment of Frances Hurlbut, hoping she would accept his marriage proposal. Sitting on a rubber cushion and playing one-handed solitaire, he waited. Finally, she agreed, first informally and then by radio from New York.[63] The stunt received national publicity for the chamber and for Excelsior Springs – which was his intention all along, according to a contemporary gossip columnist.[64]

In this period of labor tension, local chambers of commerce tended to lean against labor union organizing. Now, however, federal law under the NRA gave additional protection to workers. Occasionally, there were well-publicized examples of chambers acting as peacemakers in labor disputes. At other times, however, chambers could and did play rough. For example, an agricultural strike around Salinas was unusually bitter, reported the chamber secretary, Fred McCargar (a man who would prove to be equally combative toward a different group in World War II):

> Everything we did was known by the strikers within fifteen minutes, but neither did the strikers do anything that was not known to us within fifteen minutes. We had fifteen under-cover agents working all the time, and I guess they had as many.

The strike was finally resolved, but "it was very hard on the Salinas merchants," McCargar recalled to his peers in NACOS.[65]

Roosevelt's record of smashing victories over the business lobby faltered at the beginning of his second term. In early 1937, incensed that the Supreme Court had deemed the NRA unconstitutional and concerned its justices would try to derail his entire New Deal program, FDR counterattacked. He attempted to "pack" the Court with supporters, growing it from nine to 15 justices. This move attracted white-hot opposition, with business groups among those in the lead.

On behalf of the U.S. Chamber, Harper Sibley denounced the President's plan in February of 1937, urging other business groups to do the same.[66] The New York Chamber, in its largest meeting since the devaluation of the dollar, voted on March 4, 1937 to denounce the court-packing plan.[67] In July it went national with an appeal to stop the President. "Not since the days of Paul Revere has there been such a call to arms!" shouted the chamber's report on the bill. "Shall we surrender the safeguards of the Constitution?"[68]

By this time, however, Roosevelt was already beaten. On July 22, 1937, the Senate voted by 70 to 22 to take out critical language from the bill and send it back to committee. FDR backed down from the plan.

The President was sour and sullen in defeat – not unlike the groups he usually trounced. At a talk on Roanoke Island in August, he noted Lord Macaulay's favorable description of Britain's aristocracy and said, "Almost, methinks, I am reading not from Macaulay but from a resolution of the United States Chamber of Commerce, the Liberty League, the National Association of Manufacturers or the editorials written at the behest of some well-known newspaper proprietors." He followed up by saying, "we cannot go along with the Tory insistence that salvation lies in the vesting power in the hands of a select class, and that if America does not come to that system America will perish."[69]

But on most issues other than court packing, the country continued to support the President, and his natural good cheer returned. Halfway through his second term, he skewered chambers of commerce over their home-town spending bias. Hypothetically addressing a typical businessman who complained to him about federal spending, Roosevelt said, "You believe with the United States Chamber of Commerce that Federal spending on public works should cease – except in your home town."[70]

In an apparent response to FDR's challenge, less than two weeks later U.S. Chamber President Gibson Carey sent a letter out to local chambers urging them to restrain their requests for federal help.[71] He went further in October 1939, issuing a more detailed letter, noting the enormous tax increases of the previous 10 years – an 85 percent increase in federal taxes and a 45 percent increase in state and local taxes. In 1938 the average person's income was $479 and taxes were $113, as compared with income of $633 in 1928 and taxes of $79. Things were going in the wrong direction. If chambers wanted to reduce government's growth rate, they should stop asking for federal aid for things not affecting the general public welfare and should refuse government grants that didn't fit this category.[72]

In this, as in so many things during the Depression, the U.S. Chamber was pushing a stone uphill. Back in the Grant Administration, every chamber had been accused of seeking government help in "dredging some local sand-bank."[73] Business organizations in America would not drop pork from their public affairs diets. Indeed, they would continue to participate eagerly in the making of the legislative sausages for their bridges, roads, post offices, and other amenities.

It was a difficult decade for everyone. Even the representatives of "entrenched greed" felt the pain. Especially during FDR's first two terms, it was as if the country not only fell off the gold standard, but off the free-market wagon. Labor strife had mushroomed. Government was acting like Robin Hood, taking from the rich and giving to everyone else. Where would this end? In a newspaper article on New Year's Day in 1940, U.S. Chamber President Gibson Carey spoke for many business people when he described government's massive expansion in the 1930s as a "crime."[74]

The Idea of a Chamber When Business is Bad

On August 20, 1938, a lone representative of the chamber in Laredo, Texas, sat in the Mexico City office of Ignacio Garcia Tellez, Mexico's Secretary of the Interior. Philip Kazen recounted to the minister how many things American communities had done to improve cross-border business. He asked the secretary if it would be possible to remove a sign in

Nuevo Laredo warning Mexicans not to buy American products when they crossed the border to Texas.

Secretary Garcia listened carefully. Before Kazen had left his office, the government official had sent a telegram to Nuevo Laredo ordering that the sign be taken down. The lone Texan's chamber initiative had succeeded.[75]

The Mexican incident shows how, as long as there is business, however limited, there can be a need for business organizations. Local chambers of commerce continued to function during the Depression, although in most cases with significantly reduced funding. Even in the worst of times, some people had a sense that without their local chamber, things might be even worse.

Cheyenne Frontier Days in better days (1910)

It didn't take long for the Depression to sink its teeth into the budgets of local chambers of commerce. At the Cheyenne (Wyo.) Chamber of Commerce's annual dinner in 1930 the signs were already there: 127 members had paid their dues and 169 had not. Revenues from the chamber's cash cow, the Frontier Days celebration, were down, too.[76] Two years later, the Alexandria (Va.) Chamber of Commerce sued 30 members for nonpayment of dues, getting judgments on about half of them.[77]

The Washington Board of Trade's leadership examined a 1934 study showing that chambers had lost about 39 percent of their pre-Depression membership levels. But there were still strong chambers. The leading local organization in this study was the Chicago Association of Commerce, with 4,500 members, followed by the Washington group with more than 3,000.[78]

The Washington Board of Trade and the Washington Chamber of Commerce had a distinct advantage: Uncle Sam. The growth of the federal government meant plenty of business for the nation's capital. In 1934 the BoT and the Washington Chamber of Commerce merged, and before long the combined organization had more than 4,000 members. The organization reported its major meetings averaged 1,600 attendees, about 1,000 more than comparable chambers elsewhere in the nation.[79]

Los Angeles was another success story. This city's chamber benefited from its long history of boosting the city, and in particular of its promotion of the movie industry, of the Hoover Dam, of the seaport, and of the aircraft industry. All four enterprises gathered strength as the decade progressed, while the city's population rose from 1.2 million in 1930 to 1.5 million in 1940. The chamber was bragging by 1938 that it had become the largest in the country, with 10,000 members and 180 employees.[80]

Overall, the trial of the Depression was harrowing for chambers as much as for any other groups within the United States. The Southern Chamber Executives Association found itself in 1933 with \$44.08 in the bank and almost closed up shop. A NACOS study of the revenues of 16 larger chambers found these organizations rode a roller-coaster: if combined revenues were expressed as 100 in 1926, they soared to 127 in 1929, shrank to 67 in 1932, and clawed their way back to 96 in 1937.[81]

Membership sales and retention, never an easy matter for voluntary associations, became more difficult during the Depression. Chamber executives exchanged ideas for new members that included everything from sitting past-due members at the head table at banquets to sending attractive women to pick up overdue checks. NACOS spent a great deal of time tracking the behavior of national chain stores, reporting approvingly that the best of them all in chamber membership was Sears, which was a member of the chamber in 94 percent of the 324 communities in which it operated.[82]

Some kept a cool head in the greatest economic crisis in the history of the Republic. NACOS closed the chambers' Institute in 1932 and 1933 but brought it back in 1934. NACOS's president, C. M. Anderson (Memphis Chamber), argued, "We need not run after strange gods. The fundamental purpose of the Chamber of Commerce has not changed."[83] Later at the same 1935 NACOS meeting, the chamber general manager in hard-hit Birmingham, Ala., L.E. Foster, said that "there has not been a Chamber of Commerce of any consequence in the country that has closed its doors and folded up."[84]

While chamber managers somehow held on, it was indeed a wretched decade for business, and chambers of commerce struggled to make ends meet and to help their communities. The Richmond, Va., Chamber of Commerce fielded an offer of a self-described "attractive American girl 25 years old" from Ashby, Mass., who offered to marry a man willing to pay her mortgage and fix up her house.[85]

Trying to put a more positive spin on things, the quirky Chamber of Commerce and Civics of the Oranges and Maplewood held a "jubilation parade," featuring 2,000 onlookers, to end the Depression. The group fashioned a straw man called Old Man Depression, shot him, hanged him, and burned him. Chamber secretary Edmund Williamson then made a speech and pronounced the Depression over.[86] Unfortunately it was 1933, and the old man still had some life in him.

Even today we picture distraught people in the Thirties trying to sell apples or pencils on the street to make a living. Chambers of commerce, in defending their store-owning members, sometimes fought against these forlorn individuals. The Washington Chamber of Commerce attempted to remove a peanut and popcorn vendor from in front of the White House, claiming he obstructed traffic. But President Roosevelt intervened and saved the man's job.[87]

In New York, the West Side Association of Commerce attempted to rid the midtown area of peddlers. It managed to get police to round up 28 of the miscreants. The head of the chamber, James Danahy, stood his ground before a judge who was unhappy with the chamber's picking on these unfortunate individuals.

"We ask you to do your duty," Mr. Danahy said to the judge.

"Don't try to tell me what my duty is!" Magistrate Ford commanded. "I'm not going to be told my duty by a paid officer of a retailers' group."

"It is not a retailers' group," Mr. Danahy said icily. "It is a chamber of commerce."

The judge said he could not sleep if he put these poor men in jail or fined them, and he let them go, to the court's applause.[88]

Yet in the fiery crucible of the Depression, the idea of the chamber of commerce was not burned away. It remained powerful, both for its representation of people coming together to solve problems (the chamber) and for its calling in its very name for what the country longed for (commerce). Everyone wanted the prosperity for which these organizations still desperately searched.

In Florida, where chambers of commerce had witnessed so much growth in the Twenties, the spirit remained alive. In Miami, Mayor E.G. Sewell, who had been a fixture at the chamber even before riding on a Wright Brothers airplane wing to promote the city on its 15th birthday in 1911, bragged how his city had willed itself to grow from two families in 1896 to 160,000 in 1939.[89] People could still come together to transform their communities.

On Florida's west coast, the chamber spirit was just as full of life. Editorialized the *Sarasota Herald-Tribune*, "a city may be known by the kind of a Chamber of Commerce it has."[90] And in St. Petersburg, Mayor John Smith came out in support of the membership drive of the local chamber of commerce. He was asked, why have a chamber at all?

> Well, why have churches? Or schools? Or railroads? Why not lie along the wayside why other communities march past?
>
> It might have been possible to rest a while some years ago, but not any more. Business competition is far too keen among individuals and communities. Today, if ever, every community has vital need for an organization such as the St. Petersburg Chamber of Commerce, that will watch over the interests of its citizens. The individual citizen, however gifted, can by himself accomplish little.
>
> As a means of stimulating interest and producing concerted action, I know of no body so effectively organized as the St. Petersburg Chamber of Commerce.
>
> Some view the history of chambers of commerce in America as one of the proudest moments in the history of this country, and I happen to agree with them. The effect of these organizations upon American citizenship and civilization have been beyond measure.
>
> Why have a chamber of commerce, indeed![91]

Some Things Are Hard to Change

If chambers of commerce were still important, then perhaps they could take on one of the most perplexing problems of the 1930s: the weather. The ecological catastrophe of the Dust Bowl, not to mention other major and minor disruptions, exacerbated the problems of the Depression. And chambers couldn't help getting involved.

The Alexandria, Va. Chamber of Commerce had recruited a hotshot manager from Petersburg in 1930, Dan Hollenga. This can-do executive quickly tackled the drought afflicting the Washington area. He sent a telegram to nearby President Hoover to implore "divine aid for rain."[92] This government relations program apparently failed, perhaps because of its double-deckered complexity, appealing to two higher authorities at once.

As a backup, Hollenga got a plane ready to seed the clouds, but it hadn't got off the ground when some showers sprinkled Washington on August 27, 1930. "Don't blame us for it," said a woman at the chamber to a reporter. "Our airplane hasn't been off the ground. Furthermore, it's not raining in Alexandria. When we need rain we'll make our own, thank you."[93]

The aviation committee of the Atlantic City Chamber of Commerce teamed up with the local Aero Club for another aerial end run around the weather. The idea was for a plane that would get above the clouds so that people could sunbathe, nude, catching more rays than they would get for hours baking on the beaches below. This weather enhancing idea, however, didn't take off.[94]

The Kansas City Chamber of Commerce protested, apparently futilely, when the Weather Bureau (that child of the Cincinnati Chamber of Commerce telegraph program from years ago) moved its temperature reading instruments. The new location was on the ground. The chamber wanted the readings taken as before, from the top of a building that was 161 feet tall. Up on that civic roof, when a ground reading would show a temperature of 110, the thermometer would only show 108 degrees.[95]

The Dust Bowl was indeed the weather story of the decade, and it wasn't a good one. The Perryton, Texas, chamber of commerce took determined action against the weather. It asked other chambers and civic groups in the Texas Panhandle to protest against the waste of natural gas at stripping plants. The chamber's leaders believed that the gas blocked rain. Engineers, however, laughed at the idea.[96]

Another Texas Panhandle town, Dalhart, was right in the middle of the ecological and weather disaster of the Dust Bowl. The Dalhart Chamber of Commerce hired an explosives expert, Tex Thornton, to shoot rockets at the sky to bring precipitation, and after several days about a tenth of an inch of snow came down – but snow also fell in other places where no rockets rose.[97]

Then its image-conscious members became incensed when a painting, *Drouth Survivors* by Alexandre Hogue, showed the Dust Bowl at its worst: "two dead cows face-planted into a drift, the top of a leafless tree buried by dust, a tractor half-smothered by sand, a fence drifted." The chamber put up $50 to buy the painting in Dallas in order to take it back to Dalhart and publicly burn it. But it cost $2,000, so the chamber representative came home empty-handed.[98]

The Dalhart Chamber's director and leading booster, John McCarty, had formed the Last Man Club, taking pledges from Dalhart residents not to leave their beloved, dust-covered town, no matter what. But perhaps one too many disasters hit this unhappy town. A grasshopper plague ensued. McCarty got a job in Amarillo. The chamber's leading spirit gave up the ghost, leaving a town with a sense of betrayal that somehow stumbled through a few more years of dry and dusty pain.[99] Indeed, the once farm-filled, lush lands of the Dust Bowl never fully recovered from the disaster. There were some things that even an enthusiastic chamber of commerce manager couldn't fix.

Scarcity and How to Cope With It

Generally speaking, in Depression or out of it, when chamber executives see two units of government, they will express a preference for one. The State Chamber of Commerce in

Oklahoma proposed dropping 20 counties, reducing the total in the state from 77 to 57.[100] The Annapolis, Md. chamber asked for eight counties instead of 23, arguing that the automobile made it possible to run larger counties efficiently.[101] Unfortunately, perhaps, just about the only thing more difficult to get rid of than a government program is a government itself. Today, Maryland still has 23 counties, while Oklahoma still has 77.

Many chambers worked to reduce public expenditures or improve efficiencies, however. In 1932, the Omaha Chamber of Commerce, facing a mushrooming of public expenditures, started a taxpayers' group that, among other things, managed to reduce the city's bonded debt by $5 million within a few years.[102] Also in 1932, the Kansas City Chamber of Commerce worked on an efficiency initiative for county government that member and supporter Harry S Truman claimed would save $500,000.[103] Chambers were constantly urging their local governments to watch the purse strings.

But chambers do not live on tax and spending reductions alone. These organizations could not abandon their inherently optimistic efforts to promote their communities.[104] Such promotion didn't have to cost much money, and sometimes it brought tangible results.

Spreading the Word and Attracting Visitors

The Fredericksburg, Va., Chamber of Commerce had one vital publicity element to work with, even in times of depression: a remarkable history. One appealing item was the local dog auction, known as the Fredericksburg Dog Mart, which had occurred off and on over the years and began in 1698. The Dog Mart had been revived by the chamber in 1929 as a publicity stunt and continued well into the Depression, attracting visitors from near and far. By 1937, there were 1,000 dogs in town for the event, some to be sold and some for an associated dog show whose chief judge was the great former Major League pitcher Walter Johnson. But this was the Depression, and many people offered up their dogs not because they wanted to sell them, but because they needed the money or simply couldn't afford to keep their pets. As Fido and Rover went off to other homes, their former owners wept, no doubt calling into some question the value of this promotional event.[105]

But the chamber had a more successful project also involving the rifle-armed Johnson. This was to get him to throw a silver dollar across the Rappahannock River, near where George Washington was said to have done this, on the 200th anniversary of Washington's birth in 1736. For one thing, this would test whether the legend could be true or not.

So on February 22, 1936, the Big Train took a specially engraved dollar from a chamber representative, wound up, and fired it across the partly frozen river. He made the 272-foot throw, cheering a crowd of 11,000 people and millions more who read about the feat in the newspapers. Others tried to repeat the task, mostly unsuccessfully, although General Amos Fries managed to hit a golf ball across the river.[106]

There was plenty of additional publicity milked from the event, including a special gift from the Salt Lake Chamber of Commerce. Secretary Gus Backman sent three disks of pure Utah mined silver to Ben Pitts, the secretary of the Fredericksburg Chamber. The Utah disks would "go much farther" than the alloyed metal supplied by the U.S. Mint, Backman noted.[107] Meanwhile, local experts dug up interesting items on George Washington's past, including an apparently true story of his swimming in the river and some women stealing his clothes, one of whom got ten lashes for the deed.[108]

Rivers were civic assets worth exploiting – and protecting. Harold Colee, president of the Florida State Chamber of Commerce, heard some negative feedback about his state's waterways and gave a firm reply: "Florida rivers are not nasty, muddy streams infested with alligators that are a constant menace to cruisers," he announced, somewhat reassuringly.[109] Further west, the chamber in Newport, Ark., allegedly to prove a local river monster was *not* a publicity stunt, hired a former Navy diver to look for the beast in a 60-foot-deep eddy of the Arkansas River. Armed with an eight-foot harpoon and scuba gear, Charles Brown searched and searched, garnering worldwide attention, but found nothing but a log and a catfish. A barnstorming flyer offered rides overhead to peer into the water, while someone had set up a dance floor on the river bank so that people could dance until Brown emerged with, or perhaps inside, the mythical monster.[110]

Stars, of course were excellent for publicity. But hell hath no fury like a home town scorned. Actor Dick Powell incurred the wrath of several Arkansas chambers, especially that of Little Rock, when he was reported to have said, "I'm just a poor Arkansas razorback, but six years of civilization have fixed me up."[111] The Green Bay Chamber expressed equal displeasure after the Packers' 250-pound tackle (large for those days), Cal Hubbard, the inventor of the "Hubbard Squash" block, was traded to the New York Giants and said, according to a sportswriter, that Green Bay was a "just a whistle stop in the wilderness" and a "tank town."[112]

The chambers in Southern California treasured their film-star assets and made the most of them. The Beverly Hills Chamber of Commerce teamed up with Will Rogers to get a post-office grant and with Mary Pickford to launch a "Christmas Nights" holiday decoration program.[113] The Hollywood Chamber of Commerce voted Betty Grable the title of "America's Ideal Girl" in 1937. And the Hollywood Chamber created the first Hollywood Civic Award in 1940 to honor those who did most to promote a positive image for movieland. The first winner was a London-born comedian who had just co-starred with Bing Crosby in *The Road to Singapore*: Bob Hope.

Tourism Promotion

Tourism promotion, with or without stars and stunts, was a key element of local economic development in the 1930s. Despite the Depression, some people had money to travel, and everyone wanted to be on its receiving end. Chambers of commerce were at the forefront of efforts to attract visitors. Publicity and promotional stunts were part of the activity, but there was much more. The hotel bed tax hadn't been invented yet, but through a variety of funding mechanisms, some chambers, such as those in New York, Honolulu, and St. Petersburg, managed to generate significant revenues for travel promotion.

Most major organizations continued to hold conventions during the Depression, and chambers of commerce were anxious to attract them. The competition was intense. But the race didn't always go to the best financed or prepared organizations. An executive of the Chicago Association of Commerce recounted how his group had planned just about everything to win a convention of a women's organization – even going so far as printing fans for the attendees of the previous year's event printed with "Chicago 1938." The bid appeared to be in the bag.

Then Chicago finished its case. Up came a lonely woman from Kansas City. We shall call her Mrs. Jones. She didn't have her convention manager with her – she didn't have fifty women from the state working for her. She came up there and said: "Girls, I am coming to you today with a lump in my throat. Of course you know my president is home dying, but let me read this letter." Half way through the letter – the woman fainted. She was revived, came back and finished reading her letter. She added: "God knows, girls, if you will give Kansas City that Convention, it may prolong the life of my president for a year.

She stole the show: Kansas City, 51; Chicago, 9 votes.[114]

Still, money talked. By 1940, the St. Petersburg Chamber of Commerce was spending $200,000 per year on tourism development. Its efforts were exemplified in its extensive welcome to visitors, which included a bouquet of flowers and newspaper interviews for the first visitor to town after September 1 of each year. More than 60,000 tourists were meticulously registered when they visited the chamber. They were also furnished with maps and all sorts of tourist literature.[115]

Not every U.S. chamber was so sophisticated, however. In one Alaskan community the welcoming system was decidedly different:

Juneau, the capital and largest city, does not have a Chamber of Commerce delegation to meet distinguished arrivals. The official greeter for the city, so attested by a handsome, gold-plated collar, is a rheumy-eyed, unbelievably scrawny old white dog named Patsy Ann. Stone-deaf, Patsy Ann's ears are attuned only to the vibrations of a steamboat whistle. Then she lopes to the wharf to howl in F minor beneath the galley porthole and blink a watery greeting to the throng crowding down the gangplank.[116]

So, at a time when McDonald's outlets and Marriott Courtyard hotels were not sprinkled across a homogenized American landscape, there were many genuine differences between communities. Chambers of commerce were there to exploit them. Finding a town or city's special attraction, for example, was a big deal.

The deaths of famous people, much like when the Richmond Chamber sought Jefferson Davis's remains, provided opportunity to some chambers of commerce. When Deadwood Dick Clarke died in 1930, the Deadwood, S.D. chamber immediately planned to build a monument to the dime novel hero and icon of the Old West and the Black Hills. But somehow it never got around to the job until four years later, when tourists complained they couldn't find the dead Deadwood Dick. So the chamber put up a plaque marking the spot.[117] But of course, the "real" Deadwood Dick was a fictional character. So the chamber's plaque for Deadwood Dick Clarke actually marked a fake grave for a fake celebrity.[118] Welcome, tourists!

Thomas Edison had been unusually close to the Chamber of Commerce and Civics of Maplewood and the Oranges and Maplewood in New Jersey. So perhaps it was no surprise that his 1931 memorial services in Orange, although conducted in a church, were held under the chamber's auspices.[119] A few days after his death, the chamber and Mrs. Edison announced plans for a massive monument for him, a $10 million edifice featuring a "huge tower, surmounted by an ever-burning light to serve the entire metropolitan area as an aviation beacon."[120] A tower was built, but the top was a stone image of a light bulb, not a live one.[121] Edison's light was out.

When Will Rogers died in a plane crash in 1935, the towns of Oologah and Claremore fought over which one would get to build a memorial for him. J.B. Wise, president of the Oologah Chamber of Commerce, opined bitterly that his town's plans were "coolly ignored" by a committee in Oklahoma City, while the larger town of Claremore was favored:

> We don't believe that Claremore must be allowed the exclusive right of selecting the site of the memorial in view of the wishes of the Rogers family.[122]

Claremore won.

The Dayton Chamber of Commerce's aviation committee had had a pet project that ended up as one of the more enduring local-interest items of the decade: the Wright Brothers Memorial, dedicated in August 1940, with 69-year-old Orville Wright in attendance.[123] It was perhaps ironic that the monument would appear just as airplanes began to show the world the kind of military havoc they could wreak. Dayton received a huge economic boost from the Wright Brothers' heritage, but this was not so much in the form of tourism to the memorial as in the booming Wright Field (today known as Wright-Patterson Air Force Base), which, as noted previously, the chamber had a hand in creating years earlier.

Hundreds of communities and their chambers of commerce worked on building up local attractions for visitors. The sights weren't all for the squeamish. The chamber in Americus, Ga., recalled to the nation how a group of involuntary visitors had spent time nearby during the Civil War at the infamous Andersonville prison; many of them were permanent visitors, still resting in its cemetery.[124] The Dodge City Chamber of Commerce, with other local groups, wanted a historical marker to show their community's role in the destruction of Great Plains wildlife. They pointed out that Dodge City had once proudly hosted a stack of buffalo bones that was ¼ mile long, 60 feet high, and 50 feet wide.[125]

A heritage, real or fake, could be marketable. A 10-foot-tall stone-carved "petrified" cave man, the "Cardiff Giant," was almost a byword for deception. (Apparently when P.T. Barnum attempted to copy this fake item in wax, the Cardiff Giant's promoter exclaimed, "There's a sucker born every minute," a saying since misattributed to Barnum himself.) Yet the chamber in Fort Dodge, Iowa, insisted that the statue rightly belonged to that town, where its gypsum originally had been mined.[126] Business people in Syracuse, N.Y., where the hoax had come to full flower, wanted the statue back, but in 1947 it made its way to Cooperstown, N.Y., where it still resides in the Farmer's Museum.[127]

An Image Rising Out of Clay

Speaking of giants, a great iron figure was stirring on the red clay hills of Alabama. It was the Roman god, Vulcan. The leaders of the Birmingham Chamber of Commerce had decided to breathe new life into him, clean and polish him, and throw him up to the sky.

It wasn't a lame idea to recall that metal monster, recently lying in pieces on the Alabama State Fairgrounds, and revive him, Frankenstein-like. Yes, this was a Roman god in Bible country, but he was local too, a piece of southern-fried metal that had

Vulcan above Birmingham

been extracted from the very place, Red Mountain, where he would have his second coming. He was the god of smelting, the shaper and caster and cleanser of hot ores. This bearded booster, the son not of Zeus but of the old Commercial Club, soon stood on a 124-foot-tall pedestal erected by the Works Progress Administration. The chamber, the Kiwanis Club, and other local groups had pushed for this spirited revival and marked his 1939 dedication with a pageant starring a young man named George Seibels, who 30 years later would become Birmingham's mayor.[128] The city and chamber, in staging this revival, had created both a tourist attraction and an enduring symbol of their community.

There were giants in other hills. The Sturgis, S.D. Chamber of Commerce had been looking for a tourist attraction. It agreed to put up money for a local motorcycle race in 1938. That was the year the statues on Mt. Rushmore, about 50 miles away, were completed. The following year, the motorcycle event went all the way to the four stone-faced dead Presidents. It was a hit with riders and tourists alike. Not to beat a dead hearse, but perhaps it was because these real politicians were deader than another South Dakota attraction, Deadwood Dick. In any case, the motorcycle event continued, with a short interruption during World War II, to the present day, when it involves more than 500,000 people and is one of the largest motorcycle rallies in the world.[129]

If Vulcan, the Cardiff Giant, or the Rushmore megaliths could arise and go to the refrigerator for a bite to eat, they might take a look at the site of the world's largest concrete building project. Wenatchee, Wash., a stone's throw from the Grand Coulee Dam, had a chamber that wanted to draw attention and hence tourists. And so the Wenatchee Chamber created the world's largest apple pie. It was ten feet across and 20 inches thick and required a special oven for its baking and tractors to remove it.[130]

Tourism was on the minds of the members of the Las Vegas Chamber of Commerce in 1940. Like chambers in countless other cities, the Las Vegas Chamber sought hotels for out-of-town visitors. Two leading chamber members, James Cashman and Robert Griffith, and possibly other chamber representatives, invited California hotel man Thomas Hull to explore the opportunities in town. They wanted him to put one of his El Rancho hotels in the city. They suggested that if he included gambling on the premises, he would make a profit.

El Rancho Hotel, Las Vegas

Hull did all they asked except for one thing. He put the hotel on a strip of land by the highway outside the city. Hull realized the importance of automobile traffic for his hotel, not to mention the tax benefits of being outside city limits. And he also saw the value of incorporating gambling inside his little resort, keeping the money and the visitors to himself. He would soon add the innovations of showgirls and Hollywood-style entertainment. Thus Hull, instigated by the Las Vegas Chamber of Commerce, simultaneously invented the Strip, the modern resort gaming industry, and a great new field of enterprise for the desert community.[131]

Bad for Business

There wasn't much money in the 1930s, but there were lots of people who wanted it. And some of them were not picky about how they obtained it. For these people, the wooden currency from the chamber in Tenino, Washington, wasn't good enough. Some of the nation's most colorful and/or notorious criminals practiced their trades in this period, including John Dillinger, Baby Face Nelson, Pretty Boy Floyd, Machine Gun Kelly, and Bonnie and Clyde. One man, however, stood out even in this star-studded crowd.

In a decade rocked with crime, it was a beer wholesaler who topped the criminal charts. Al Capone made Chicago famous, but for all the wrong reasons. He projected an appalling image of his city and its business climate. And anything bad for business sparked the ire of Chicago's chamber of commerce. Soon he and the local chamber would cross paths.

The Untouchables, the memoir of Eliot Ness written with Oscar Fraley, begins:

> Cigar smoke hung in a heavy blue haze over the long polished table. Ash trays piled high betrayed the inner emotions of the little group as it listened to a tall, spare man with a thin, square-jawed face.

> They had every right to be tense and at least subconsciously apprehensive, I thought. For they were the "Secret Six," known more formally as the Citizens Committee for the Prevention and Punishment of Crime, a special committee of the Chicago Association of Commerce.

The book tells us more:

> The speaker was Robert Isham Randolph, chairman of the Secret Six. His voice rasped as he declared:

> "Chicago has the most corrupt and degenerate municipal administration that ever cursed a city – a politico-criminal alliance formed between a civil administration and a gun-covered underworld for the exploitation of the citizenry."

> His knuckles rapped loudly against the table.

> "There is no business, not an industry, in Chicago that is not paying tribute, directly or indirectly, to racketeers and gangsters. I know you gentlemen agree that we must spend any amount of money necessary to put these hoodlums where they belong."

> I felt a tremendous admiration for Randolph as the meeting ended.[132]

Ness, a prohibition agent with the Department of Justice, had been brought to the meeting by his brother-in-law, Alexander Jamie. Jamie had been employed by the Chicago Association of Commerce and its "Secret Six" committee to dig up incriminating material on Capone and his associates. Here was a chamber of commerce getting into law enforcement – a white-collar group of amateur police, a modern-day version of the fed-up businessmen-vigilantes of San Francisco.

The Untouchables, unfortunately perhaps, is largely fiction, an imaginative riff by Oscar Fraley on a more modest 21-page typescript written by Ness.[133] But the opening of the book accurately portrays at least the way Randolph saw himself: as a crusading businessman and chamber leader who was determined to put an end to the career of the nation's most famous crook. After all, Randolph's chamber had once started a committee that led to the creation of the Federal Reserve Bank; surely it could start a committee that would shut down the Bank of Capone.

A Look Backward

To take a close look at the CAC's involvement in the struggle against Capone, we must take a brief step backward in time. Chicago business people had long had an interest in keeping their great city safe for capitalism. We have seen how the members of the Chicago Board of Trade and the Commercial Club of Chicago opposed the disruptive and occasionally violent radicalism of the Haymarket era. After World War I, it was the relatively new and much larger, more broad-based organization, the Chicago Association of Commerce (CAC), that frequently lent its weight to the fight against crime.

In 1919, the CAC set up the Chicago Crime Commission (CCC), an organization that later would play an important role in the Capone struggle. Crime was never in short supply: during the commission's first year it faced the famous Black Sox scandal and the throwing of the World Series. The CCC was involved in all sorts of activities, including the collection of accurate crime statistics. The CCC's first operating director, Henry Barrett Chamberlin, said in 1920, "The Commission is not a vigilance organization for the purpose of apprehending offenders. It is a business organization that helps criminal justice officials to secure the necessary tools to work with. In addition, it monitors agencies charged with law enforcement."[134]

The same year that Chamberlin described the CCC's role in crime fighting, a young man from Brooklyn arrived in Chicago to work for a crime boss named Johnny Torrio. Alphonse Capone, with a winning smile that masked a streak of violence and cunning, proved adept at his trade, whose prospects had suddenly expanded with the enactment of Prohibition in the previous year. Capone's opportunities improved even more on May 11, 1920, when Torrio's business partner, Big Jim Colosimo, was gunned down by an unknown hit man. Torrio became the leading organized crime figure in Chicago.[135]

Capone's career took off. In 1923, when reform mayor William Dever won election, small-time criminals turned to the Torrio-Capone organization for help.[136] The criminal syndicate moved its headquarters to the suburb of Cicero, while continuing to bribe anyone necessary to keep the beer, wine, and liquor flowing in Chicago. In 1925, Capone's boss was wounded in a drive-by shooting by a submachine gun. Torrio recovered, but seems to have seen this attack as a summons to early retirement. He left town on vacation, putting Capone in charge, and never took back control.

Greater Chicago's organized crime world looked increasingly disorganized and anarchic. Shootings by Thompson submachine guns frequently brought down innocent victims, disrupted commercial activity, and were a public relations disaster for a community that was becoming famous for crime. A killing on April 27, 1926, set off alarm bells. In an attempt to move in on Capone's turf, Myles and "Klondike" Bill O'Donnell drove up to Cicero's Pony Inn and emptied more than 100 rounds of machine gun fire.

One of the three men killed turned out to be William McSwiggin, an assistant state's attorney. Public officials, even if they were on the take, were off limits. McSwiggin's boss deputized 300 police to find Capone, who protested his innocence by saying he liked the young man and used his services. "I paid McSwiggin. I paid him plenty and I got what I was paying for," Capone said.[137] Capone was jailed overnight but drove away blithely after prosecutors admitted they had no evidence linking him to the crime.

In February of 1926, two months before the McSwiggin killing, a Chicago businessman and civic leader, Charles Dawes, publicly called for an investigation into the corrupt judicial system of greater Chicago and of the inept work of the state prosecutor's office.[138] That Charles Dawes happened also to be the vice president of the United States lent *gravitas* to his message, and the April shootings only confirmed his opinions. He and his brother, banker Rufus Dawes, assembled a group of Chicago businessmen who agreed to work to get special prosecutors in from Washington to pursue local criminals.[139] Rounding up these businessmen wasn't difficult – Rufus was president of the Commercial Club of Chicago, while his cousin, William Dawes, was president of the Chicago Association of Commerce.

A business-government alliance was slowly forming to oppose the bootleggers. Two years after Vice President Dawes' anti-crime speech, the CAC-founded Chicago Crime Commission took an important step. Its president, Frank Loesch, asked Charles Dawes to lead the attack against Capone and friends. Although moved by the appeal, Dawes felt that personally leading a campaign aimed for the benefit of his home town would compromise the vice presidency. He managed, however, to persuade President Coolidge to authorize the U.S. Bureau of Internal Revenue to look into Al Capone's income taxes.[140] On October 28, 1928, the long arm of Uncle Sam came reaching into Al Capone's pockets.

While the anti-crime forces were gathering strength in Chicago and in Washington, the pro-crime contingent was as busy as ever. On St. Valentine's Day in 1929, a black Cadillac pulled up to S.M.C. Cartage Co. on North Clark Street, where a group of the men connected with a Capone rival, George "Bugs" Moran, were gathered. The four men from the Cadillac, two of them dressed as policemen, got the seven Moran associates lined up against a wall and sprayed them with Tommy gun and shotgun fire. The assailants quickly left. All the victims died, although one of them, Frank Gusenberg, lingered for a short while. When police asked who had attacked him, he famously said, "Nobody shot me."

Of course, those bullets had come from somewhere. Capone was the logical suspect as the person behind the plot, although he was in Miami Beach with ironclad alibis. Even though it wasn't clear who had committed the crime, the deed shocked not only Chicago, but the entire nation. The day after the killings, officials from the incoming Hoover administration promised 400 more Prohibition agents and $2.5 million to enforce Prohibition nationwide.[141] The following month, CCC head Frank Loesch brought a group of Chicago businessmen to Washington to meet the new President. They urged Hoover to continue the fight against the criminal syndicates in Chicago. The engineer-President promised to "get Capone."[142]

The Chicago Association of Commerce, too, was stirred to action by the crime. It pledged a $50,000 reward for information leading to the St. Valentine's Day killers. Other individuals and organizations in Chicago matched the amount, for a total of $100,000.[143] The identity of at least three of the four assailants, however, is still a matter of debate. "Bugs" Moran nevertheless vowed revenge against those he suspected, and apparently had three Capone men brutally assassinated. Other murders followed.

Only one man seems to have been tied to the crime scene with real evidence. Police later found two Thompson submachine guns in a cache of weapons in the home of Fred "Killer" Burke. The new science of forensics, thanks to a lab funded in part by some of the leading members of the Chicago Association of Commerce, enabled the authorities to determine that the Tommy guns were used in the St. Valentine's Day shootings.[144] Burke, however, was sentenced to life behind bars for a different slaying and died in prison in 1940.[145]

Prison was in the cards for both Al Capone and his brother Ralph. Al was arrested on a weapons charge in Philadelphia on May 16, 1929; he would not be released from the state penitentiary until 10 months later. Ralph was arrested for income tax evasion on October 9. But the Capone machine, and indeed organized crime in Chicago, continued to operate even with both men temporarily out of commission.

On February 5, 1930, a nonunion workforce was on the job at the construction site of the Lying-In Hospital on 59th Street. A black sedan pulled up. One of the workers, hired just two days before, suddenly ran around the car. He stepped on the running board, pulled out a gun, and fired six shots at construction superintendent Philip Meagher. Two bullets hit Meagher in the chest, two passed through his hat, and the last two lodged in the building behind him.[146]

The tough construction superintendent would survive the shooting, but this wasn't clear that evening. Meagher's boss, Harrison Barnard, head of the H.B. Barnard Construction Co., was shocked. This was not a case of gangsters killing gangsters. This was an incursion by crooks into legitimate business.

According to family lore, Barnard's wife Elizabeth was furious at the killing and worried about her family.[147] She insisted that her husband do something. And the next day, he did.

Barnard ignored the Chicago Crime Commission, believing this group did not have the gumption to go directly after the perpetrators.[148] Instead he went downtown to the CCC's parent, the activist Chicago Association of Commerce, and met with its president, Col. Robert Isham Randolph. Randolph was just as tough

Harrison Barnard

as Meagher and Barnard. He was a World War I veteran and a civil engineer of some accomplishment. His engineer father had reversed the flow of the Chicago River, helping the city flush its sewage down the Mississippi. Although the younger Randolph had worked on sewage disposal as well, he would soon become better known for helping remove a different kind of human waste from the city. Barnard found an individual who would take up the role of a kind of 1930s white-collar Batman, attempting to rid this lakeside metropolis of its criminal element.[149]

Barnard's company, H.B. Barnard Construction Co., was a member of the Chicago Association of Commerce. He argued to Randolph that his firm's dues should be used to deal with a significant problem like this one. The gangs could simply not be permitted to move into legitimate business. Three quarters of the contractors in Chicago were members of the CAC; surely these firms would appreciate a member service such as tackling Al Capone and his ilk. Barnard also put up $5,000 of his own money to reward those with information on who shot his employee.[150]

Col. Randolph and others met with State's Attorney John Swanson and Police Commissioner William Russell. Swanson had an interesting idea. He noted that public employees such as police were easily found and intimidated or bribed by the underworld. Swanson said, as Randolph recalled later:

> If you want to be helpful I suggest that you organize a real secret service, in which the operatives are not known to any one but the director, perhaps not even known to one another. If you can supply these men with money enough to run with the wolf pack and buy information from the jackals who trail the pack you can get the kind of evidence we need to secure convictions.[151]

Robert Isham Randolph

As early as February 8, 1930, Randolph formed a committee to fight Capone and other such criminals. There were six members in addition to him, it was reported. (Later, the total number including Randolph would be said to be six.) Their identity was to be kept secret.[152]

Also in early February, Randolph held a lunch at the Mid-Day Club including many of the leading business people of the city.[153] One person said he wasn't that concerned about gangsters killing one another; why not wait until "they kill one of us"? Randolph responded that, as the man out in front on the issue, he wasn't especially inclined to wait for the bullet, and he didn't think the questioner was offering himself as a sacrifice. Then utilities magnate Samuel Insull broke the ice:

> I think things are bad enough and I have very special means for knowing how bad they are. I think you are proceeding along the right lines. I haven't time to stay here and talk about it, but you may put me down for 10 percent of any amount you want to raise.[154]

The group took up pledges and raised more than $200,000 that day. (Randolph later said the total had reached $1 million, but may have been exaggerating the amount in order to intimidate his criminal foes.[155]) Among the 803 donors was Sears chief Julius Rosenwald. The business leaders of Chicago were preparing to take on the best known American criminal of their era, along with whomever else they could catch through their covert operations.

The newspapers and the public were interested in this gang-fighting project. But the official name of the CAC committee on crime, as we have seen, was not an attention getter: the Citizens Committee for the Prevention and Punishment of Crime. When Randolph refused to name the members of this committee (other than himself), a *Chicago Tribune* reporter, James Doherty, came up with a better name: "The Secret Six."

Who were these six? The question has been much debated, but these three were clearly involved: Randolph himself (the only publicly acknowledged member), Sears President Julius Rosenwald, and utilities baron Samuel Insull. The other three are the subject of some debate. Names that have been suggested include Frank Loesch, president of the Chicago Crime Commission; George Paddock, a stockbroker and member of the CCC; and Edward Gore, an accountant and CCC activist. Other possible candidates include the aggrieved and angry Harrison Barnard.[156]

The pace of activity against Capone quickly picked up after the Secret Six became involved. Randolph got federal permission – apparently from President Hoover himself – to get Alexander Jamie a leave of absence from his position as chief special agent of the Department of Justice for the district.[157] Jamie eagerly accepted the assignment but no doubt lent a hand from time to time to his eager brother-in-law, Eliot Ness. The bright young Ness, somewhat impulsive for a University of Chicago Ph.D., began specializing in the low-brow, high-publicity activity of busting up breweries and beer warehouses.

Prohibition agent Ness turned out to be great for the headlines, although not so important in the mechanics of gathering information on Capone. A newspaperman dubbed Ness's men "The Untouchables" because of their alleged imperviousness to bribery. His raids brought a great deal of attention to the anti-Capone cause.

Publicity clearly had a value. Two U.S. Presidents would not have put their prestige on the line for a project that didn't interest voters. Whether these crusaders were federal officers or corporate amateurs, local authorities would cooperate with the crime fighters, if these new forces captured newspaper headlines and seemed to be getting a jump on those who had the hops.

Another publicity break came via the Chicago Crime Commission. Although the CCC did not have the CAC's penchant for direct action, both President Frank Loesch and Operating Director Henry Chamberlin had journalism backgrounds. They had a feel for what interested the papers. The CCC put together a list of 28 of the leading bad guys in greater Chicago, with a short description of each. Chamberlin offered it to the press, mentioning in passing to "Secret Six" coiner James Doherty that these 28 were "public enemies."[158] Even the CCC executives were impressed when the *Chicago Tribune's* giant headline on April 24, 1930, read, "LIST 28 AS PUBLIC ENEMIES."

The term "public enemy" now became firmly lodged in the lexicon, and also became the name of a movie, starring James Cagney and Jean Harlow, the following year. Even more than the "Secret Six," the idea of a public enemies list was intriguing and focused people's minds on the names of these miscreants. What terrible deeds had they done to deserve placement on the list? Al Capone, of course, was "public enemy number one." Later, the FBI would appropriate the idea and create a widely read list of its most wanted criminals.

The Chicago Association of Commerce's group of six continued its work. Alexander Jamie, the brother-in-law of Eliot Ness and chief of operations for the Secret Six, hired a number of investigators and spent large amounts of money buying information from informants. The CAC's sextet even funded the establishment of an illegal speakeasy on Thirtieth Street, the Garage Café, where their men could gather gang intelligence.

Indeed, the Secret Six's investigating methods were not models of Sunday school behavior. Randolph indicated in 1932 that "we resort to all sorts of devious and extra-legal methods of securing information. Dictaphones, telephones, deception, simulation, all the arts and artifices of the spy are freely used."[159]

It was amazing what money could buy. Randolph wrote in 1932 that there was no honor among thieves:

"Thirty pieces of silver" was the price of the Crucifixion. The current market price of betrayal ranges between a "C" note ($100) or a Grand ($1,000). We buy this kind of information at the market and pay for it C.O.D. Sometimes we buy bad information, but we never buy a gold brick from the same man twice. If they want to continue to do business with us the information must prove up under our investigation. It usually does.[160]

Money could buy information and it could also buy murder. Randolph bragged to a group of Northwestern University students that he knew exactly the price of a hit. "I could have any man I designated killed for $200 or $300. I could have President Scott [Walter Dill Scott, president of Northwestern] put on the spot but it would probably cost a few hundred dollars extra."[161]

Of course, it was the criminals who were actually ordering hits, and prime candidates for murder were promising witnesses for the prosecution. One of the key activities of the Secret Six was protecting people who were willing to testify against Capone and other public enemies. In this period, there wasn't an official witness protection program capable of sequestering individuals for long periods. The Secret Six had the funds to remove people safely from the area until time for their testimony.

A vital witness against Capone and others in his organization was Fred Ries, an accountant for the Capone organization. Ries would testify about the earnings of gambling houses and of his relationship to Al and his associates. The Secret Six paid for Ries to take an all-expenses-paid trip to South America (accompanied by federal agents, financed with $10,000 from the Secret Six) before he appeared at Capone's trial for tax evasion.[162]

Capone was well aware of the wide-ranging activities of the Secret Six and their investigators and appeared to respect both the group's financial strength and its ability to cut legal corners. It's as if he faced a racketeer who was his equal or better. That curious respect is evident from Colonel Randolph's record of a bizarre face-to-face meeting between Al and the capo of the Secret Six in February of 1931. By this time, Al's empire was under severe strain from the forces of justice.

Colonel Randolph, according to his scrapbook (such collections of mementos were common in the period), received a call from an associate of Al Capone's, Jake Guzik, who told Randolph that Capone would like to see him. Packing his pistol, Randolph drove to the Lexington Hotel, where Capone did business. After being escorted up a freight elevator and passing different gang members, the Colonel was ushered in to meet the most feared criminal of his day. Capone came from behind his desk and greeted Randolph.

"Hell, Colonel, I'd know you anywhere – you look just like your picture."

Randolph smiled, "Hell, Al, I'd have never recognized you – you are much bigger than you appear to be in photographs."

Randolph took off his coat and handed him the .45-caliber pistol that he carried for protection.

Capone placed it on a chair.

"May I use your telephone? You see, your name has been used to frighten women and children for so long that Mrs. Randolph is worried about me; she knows of my visit. I would like to call her and tell her everything is o.k."

Al responded, "Women are like that."

When Randolph came back, Capone served him a beer and asked, "Colonel, what are you trying to do to me?"

"Put you out of business."

"Why do you want to do that?"

"We want to clean up Chicago, put a stop to these killings and gang rule here."

"Colonel, I don't understand you. You knock over my breweries, bust up my booze rackets, raid my gambling houses, tap my telephone wires, but yet you're not a reformer, not a 'dry.' Just what are you after?"

And before Randolph could answer, Capone continued, "Listen, Colonel, you're putting me out of business. Even with beer selling at $55 a barrel, we didn't make a nickel last week. You know what will happen if you put me out of business? I have 185 men on my personal payroll, and I pay them from $300 to $400 a week each. They're all ex-convicts and gunmen, but they are respectable businessmen now, just as respectable as the people who buy my stuff and gamble in my places. They know the beer, booze, and gambling rackets – and they're old rackets, rackets that sent them to the can. If you put me out of business, I'll turn every one of those 185 respectable ex-convicts loose on Chicago."

"Well, Al, to speak frankly, we are determined to put you out of business. We are burned up about the reputation you have given Chicago."

"Say, Colonel, I'm burned up about that, too. Chicago's bad reputation is bad for my business. It keeps the tourists out of town. I'll tell you what I'll do: If the Secret Six will lay off my beer, booze, and gambling rackets, I'll police this town for you – I'll clean it up so there won't be a stickup or a murder in Cook County. I'll give you my hand on it."

Randolph refused to go along, but he did drink another glass of beer.

Capone asked, "Say, Colonel, what do you think about the mayoral election? Should I come out for Cermak or ride along with Thompson?"

"I think you'd better stick with 'Big Bill.'"

Randolph put on his coat and hat, and Capone handed him back his pistol saying, "So even respectable people carry those things?"

Then Al shook Randolph's hand and said, "No hard feelings?"

Randolph replied, "No hard feelings."[163]

Capone's tone in this conversation with Randolph, admitting he (Capone) wasn't making any money thanks to the Secret Six, foreshadowed his demise. In an interview published just a few months later, on July 30, 1931, he lamented, "The Secret Six has licked the rackets.

Not having a good day

Al Capone sent to prison

They've licked me. They've made it so there's no money in the game anymore."[164]

Brought to trial, Capone almost escaped conviction by bribing the jury, but the clever judge switched juries at the last minute. The beer baron was convicted for tax evasion on October 17, 1931. He was released from prison in 1939, but a case of syphilis had affected his brain and prevented him from ever resuming a criminal career, or indeed any career. He died in 1947.

How much credit should the Chicago Association of Commerce take for its role in tackling Capone? It was clearly heavily involved, and got plenty of notice at the time. A Chicago Crime Commission member once said, however, "The Secret Six accomplished nothing in the purification of Chicago."[165]

Against the CCC critic, who wasn't and isn't alone, there are several responses. One is simply the volume of activity handled by the Secret Six, according to Alexander Jamie. The group was involved with 595 cases, aiding in 55 convictions with sentences totaling 428 years.[166] Most of the specific deeds of the Secret Six remain a secret, but clearly the protection of key witnesses was important, while providing funds to federal prosecutors (if illegal today) surely didn't hurt the overall effort. Prosecutor George Johnson, moreover, said he doubted whether he could have convicted the top 10 members of Capone's organization without the help of the Secret Six.[167] On top of that, we have Capone's statement that he was "licked" by the Six.

If success has many fathers, so did the downfall of Al Capone. Author Jonathan Eig, who came across a trove of the papers of George Johnson, credits this U.S. district attorney with the key role in the takedown. Then there is gangster Eddie O'Hare, who apparently reported the jury bribery attempt, thereby enabling Judge Wilkerson to make a clever jury switch that, in retrospect, saved the day. Eddie would be murdered for his cooperation, and would be remembered more for his gangster past than his near-final good deed. Later, his son Butch would die a hero in the skies above the Pacific during World War II, cleansing the family name so thoroughly that it was given to Chicago's great airport.

Eliot Ness in the Thirties got plenty of credit for shaking up the Capone empire, and got even more when the semi-fictional *The Untouchables* came out in 1957, not to mention when the movie of the same name, starring the actor Kevin Costner, appeared in 1987. By virtually every modern expert's estimation, Ness's role was exaggerated enormously, then and now. But Ness, too, gave some credit to Randolph and the Secret Six, who after all employed his brother-in-law and former boss Jamie. As for the CCC – it took on many tasks of crime fighting in Chicago, and especially in shining a harsh public light on the dark deeds of the lakeside criminals and in encouraging Vice President Dawes and later President Hoover to get Capone.

All these groups and others – honest cops and investigators, members of the jury, even the underworld informants who gave tips on the doings of Capone's gang – were a part of the occasionally unholy alliance bringing down Capone. But the story isn't complete without the chamber, the Chicago Association of Commerce, an organization that was all over the effort. It created both the Chicago Crime Commission and the Secret Six. It helped throw out corrupt Mayor "Big Bill" Thompson and brought in the more honest Anton Cermak. It bankrolled the forensics lab and the activities of federal prosecutors. It supported Judge Wilkerson and it was part of the delegations that visited Washington to encourage federal assistance. In short, the CAC was on the case.

Of course, the CAC and its Secret Six were made up of human beings, not immortal crime fighters. The Secret Six's three most powerful members – Randolph, Insull, and Rosenwald – soon faded from the limelight. Rosenwald died in 1932. Insull's utilities empire collapsed and he was tried (although acquitted) for mail fraud, embezzlement, and bankruptcy law violations. He died, penniless, in the Paris Metro in 1938.

CAC President Randolph and the Secret Six as an institution would be cut down a few rungs. The Six got into a nasty fight with State's Attorney John Swanson in August 1932 over what seems to have been a case of the suspicious wiretapping of one another. And in December of 1932, William Kuhn, a defendant in an extortion case, was acquitted of wrongdoing and was awarded $30,000 for wrongful arrest and persecution in a case pushed by the Secret Six. The CAC closed down its crime committee and its famous Secret Six in 1933.[168]

Randolph, who had betrayed with various comments that he wasn't above skirting the law to get his man, found himself in trouble for some of his actions during the Capone chase. It was revealed, for example, that he received a salary of $12,000 per year for his Secret Six leadership, even while the sanitary district was paying him an equal amount for engineering work. But Randolph remained a public figure in Chicago, more respected than reviled. He was made the director of operations for the 1933-34 Chicago World's Fair.

And so ended one of the highest profile chamber projects of all time. The Chicago Association of Commerce had rolled up its sleeves for a well-publicized brawl with the top criminal of the era. At the end of several rounds, the CAC had wobbled, but still stood, while Capone was down for the count.

The Missing Baby

Chicago had no monopoly on crime. Some cities followed the lead of its Secret Six in taking up private cudgels against public enemies. After a prominent chain store operator, Michael Katz, was kidnapped in Kansas City, the Kansas City Chamber of Commerce formed a secret committee of five to combat the problem. (Katz had obtained his freedom by paying ransom of $100,000, and authorities were unable to find his abductors.)[169]

Indeed, by 1932 there seemed to be a wave of kidnapping in the Midwest. In St. Louis,

Chamber President Walter Weisenburger campaigned for a law against kidnapping people and taking them across state lines. One of the alleged leaders of a kidnapping ring was a St. Louisian, Charles "Buster" Brown, who was being held by authorities in New York. Bills to make kidnapping a federal crime had been introduced by Senator Roscoe Patterson (R-Mo.) and Representative John Cochran (D-Mo.).

Weisenburger and Secret Six chief Robert Isham Randolph testified to the House Post Office Committee about the problem during the final days of February 1932. Randolph took out a piece of rope and said it came from a kidnapper who wrote that he would "strangle Dorothy" if the mother did not "come through." A lawman spoke of kidnappers starving and beating their victims and lowering them into lakes or throwing them into lime vats.[170]

As if on cue, on March 1, 1932, at 10:00 pm, nursemaid Betty Gow found her little charge, Charles Lindbergh, Jr., missing from his crib in New Jersey. The son of the famous pilot of the *Spirit of St. Louis* had been kidnapped. Police soon found parts of a ladder nearby; the baby clearly had been taken.

The crime quickly became the talk of the nation. As time went by and the baby wasn't found, panic turned to outrage. The kidnapping laws that the Missouri congressmen had proposed were incorporated into the Federal Kidnapping Act that passed Congress on June 22, 1932. The Act became popularly known as the Lindbergh Law.

The baby's abductor, Bruno Hauptmann, was finally found two years later; the baby had been killed in a fall from the ladder that Hauptmann had so carefully constructed. Hauptmann was executed in an electric chair on April 3, 1936.[171]

Charismatic Criminals

The Thirties certainly saw a colorful cast of criminals, practically straight out of Superman or Batman comic books. And for every famous criminal, there were many people who fantasized about bringing him or her to justice. Lots of people imagined being, like Colonel Randolph's associates at the Secret Six, somebody who figuratively pulled off his tie and put aside his day job to take on a secret identity and fight crime.

Chicago's Secret Six had chamber imitators, including the Secret Five in Kansas City, formed, as we have seen, by the local chamber in June 1930 after a kidnapping, and the Secret Seven in Cleveland, formed by its chamber in 1935 (just a year after Eliot Ness was transferred to Cleveland, where he later became head of the police). There was even a 1931 movie – not a particularly good one - called *The Secret Six*, very loosely based on the real Six. MGM's film featured a number of wooden performances, but a young actor named Clark Gable stole the show with an impressive portrayal of a crusading newspaperman.[172]

The crime battles of the early Thirties played out in interesting ways. The Department of Justice turned the island of Alcatraz into a site for a maximum security prison, despite a formal complaint filed by the San Francisco Chamber of Commerce,[173] and transferred Al Capone there as a very public warning against criminals. Perhaps had the chamber's leaders understood how this island would make the city even more famous, and would turn the island one day into a major tourist attraction, they might have encouraged Uncle Sam to put really bad guys on the shark-patrolled rock even sooner.

Cleveland went hog wild over the Secret Six and the Capone takedown. Cleveland's Secret Seven, however, went after its own set of villains. The chamber's Secret Seven provided a lengthy report "warning Cleveland citizens that reds and intellectual pinks are everywhere in our midst, engaged in deep, dark, menacing plots to overthrow the Government."[174]

The criminals kept busily at their craft. Indeed, the Atlantic City Chamber of Commerce, which had brought the Miss America Pageant to the world the previous decade, began the Thirties grappling with a corrupt city administration that tolerated gangs practicing "white slavery." The chamber attempted to rid its city of the criminal-coddling Mayor Anthony Ruffu, but it took a crash with a train to take out the politician, who was then found to have a substantial estate. (Ruffu was driving, celebrating after a "not guilty" verdict on four of 14 criminal charges against him. The passengers included two unidentified women.)[175]

Race, Immigrants, and Society

The Thirties in the United States certainly were marked by social and labor tensions, but not so much by the extremes of KKK activity and xenophobia that had been prominent in the years after World War I. Still, there were plenty of examples of negative racial and social attitudes. Most of the South was segregated with the aid of Jim Crow legislation, while the North and West were host to plenty of ill racial feeling of their own.

Chambers of commerce had a mixed record on race and related social issues. Peace among racial groups was important, as when, in Honolulu, the chamber attempted to defuse anti-Japanese sentiment after Japanese-Americans were accused of raping a white officer's wife in 1931.[176] On the other hand, if bringing the races together might be disruptive, a chamber might take a stance favoring separation of the races. In Fredericksburg, Virginia, for example, the chamber and other local groups protested futilely about the transfer of a "colored" Civilian Conservation Corps detachment to the area in 1934.[177]

The New York Chamber of Commerce, historically progressive on immigration issues, took an unfortunate turn in Thirties. In 1931, the group came out for the fingerprinting and registration of aliens.[178] Then in 1934, as Hitler was persecuting Jews in Germany, the New York Chamber issued a report on immigration control that singled out Jews and the need to make sure the United States made a careful check on who was admitted to its shores. The report was issued by a eugenics "expert" from the Carnegie Endowment, Dr. Harry H. Laughlin. Specifically mentioning the Nazi restrictions on Jews and American attempts to admit them across the Atlantic, Laughlin said Jews without the proper genetic background should be excluded.[179]

It's hard to imagine a chamber activity more destructive to its own historic reputation. While the New York Chamber's move did not singlehandedly shut America's doors to the flow of Jews from Hitler's Europe, it surely gave encouragement to the exclusionist, nativist, and anti-Semitic spirit that kept Jews bottled up with their persecutors across the ocean. The New York Chamber's issuance and defense of the report was, at minimum, a public relations debacle of the first order.

Bernard Deutsch, president of the Board of Aldermen and of the American Jewish Congress, led a protest meeting of 1,500 people against the report and the New York Chamber. "Dr. Laughlin's 'purification of race' theory is as dangerous and spurious as the purified Aryan race theories advanced by the Nazis, to which it bears suspicious resemblance," he said. "His singling out of the Jews for mention as a particular race group to be barred from general admission to the United States, despite the condescending tribute to so-called 'superior' Jews, is a knavish, deliberate slur upon the whole Jewish people, which differs only from the Nazi brand in that it is couched in more polite language."[180]

Deutsch, of course, was not alone in his outrage. Rabbi Stephen Wise called the New York Chamber "The Chamber of Stuffed Shirts."[181] The organization that had proudly counted Jacob Schiff, Felix Warburg, Isidor Straus, and so many other leading Jewish businessmen as its members, had not simply insulted the Jewish people; it had put them in danger.

The Harlem Compact

Black-white relations in New York might have been better than in the South, but they still left much to be desired. In Harlem, tensions rose as the population of about 300,000 blacks patronized stores almost exclusively managed by 10,000 white employees. Here, the potential for boycotts, if not even violence, persuaded the Uptown Chamber of Commerce to take action.[182] The compact it negotiated with local African-Americans in 1938 was a remarkable step in American race relations.

It took four months for the Uptown Chamber (representing such stores as Kresge, Woolworth, and W.T. Grant) to negotiate a deal with the Greater New York Coordinating Committee for Employment, a group representing 200 African-American organizations. The lead negotiator for the black community was a charismatic 29-year-old activist named Adam Clayton Powell Jr. Under the deal, one third of the white-collar jobs in the Harlem stores would be reserved for blacks, with the replacements coming in gradually as white workers left their jobs through attrition. The black workers would not be discriminated against once hired. And the GNYCC agreed that blacks in the community would not boycott stores, even those that didn't sign the agreement, before an arbitration committee had had the opportunity to evaluate charges of discrimination.[183]

Even at the time, participants and observers regarded the event as historic. They saw it potentially as a model for other cities and other parts of New York. It was a concrete example of an anti-discrimination program.

The precedent was not only a general one, but a specific one involving chambers of commerce. While the Harlem Compact, as it was called, would not be precisely replicated elsewhere, the concept of having African-American groups negotiate with the chamber representatives of white retailers would become common in the 1960s. The civil rights movement, both in 1938 and in 1968, would be intimately connected with a type of institution that first appeared in New York in 1768.

Women in Chambers of Commerce

Women clung to their toehold in the male-dominated world of chambers of commerce during the Depression. It was in this period that NACOS was first addressed by one of its female members. Mabel Dugan, executive vice president of the chamber in Middletown, Conn., talked in 1932 about how the role of women had evolved in the United States from the sole option of marriage to an increasing number of choices, but still limited to "ladylike" options such as dressmaking until the advent of the vote. Before suffrage, the typical woman "still fainted at a moment's notice and beat her wings against a cage!"[184]

By the Thirties, however, women represented a sizeable proportion of the workforce. Indeed, 173 of them were executives of chambers of commerce, Dugan noted. Women owned

41 percent of the nation's stock. Shouldn't chambers of commerce cater to this resource, and admit women not in bureaus or divisions, but "on a parity" as full members? It's not a question of whether a woman should be out of the home, said Dugan. "She has already left the home!"[185]

Buffalo Gals Don't You Come Out Tonight

Man does not live by bread lines alone. Even in the Depression, people wanted to have fun. Chambers of commerce did their best to play along, most of the time.

Early in the decade, the Silver Creek Chamber of Commerce held a banquet at the local Presbyterian Church Hall, where two scantily clad girls from Buffalo sang, "Kiss Me, Sweetheart, Kiss Me." The spectacle infuriated Rev. Joseph Lindsay, who called the chamber members who had arranged the affair "fools draped in lace." He told his congregation: "What that organization needs is a funeral oration." Chamber President Joseph Slack said no harm was done and he did not apologize.[186]

Other chambers took a more conservative stance on fashion. "Of late there has been an entire change of attitude of what constitutes modesty," noted the Chamber of Commerce of the Rockaways. People were wearing all sorts of things on the beach and in town. The chamber explained where it drew the line: "We are objecting to men walking in our residential and business sections without top shirts and in many cases merely wearing trunks, and we are objecting to women walking through our business and residential sections in rubber bathing suits with halters." But the chamber was willing to tolerate the new fad of shorts.[187] Meanwhile, the Coney Island Chamber of Commerce expressed strong opposition to men bathing without wearing shirts.[188]

THE BODY TABOO:

ITS ORIGIN,
EFFECT, AND MODERN DENIAL

BY
ELTON RAYMOND SHAW, M.A.

OVER TWO MILLION HOMES
HAVE OUR PUBLICATIONS

SHAW PUBLISHING COMPANY
WASHINGTON, D. C.

Elton Shaw, chamber executive and nudism champion

And then there was Elton Shaw. A former field secretary for the U.S. Chamber of Commerce in Michigan, in 1935 he was executive secretary of the newly formed Michigan State Chamber of Commerce. But in 1936 he was also elected president of the International Nudists Association. The following year he published a book on nudism: *The Body Taboo: Its Origin, Effect, and Modern Denial.*[189]

Most chambers of commerce favored measures that eased the restrictions, commonly known as "blue laws," against selling things on Sundays. And many were involved in secularizing other holy days, from Christmas to Easter. In these areas the chambers occasionally ran into clerical opposition.

Easter celebrations, including the buying of nice clothes, sending of telegrams and greeting cards, and highlighting the Easter bunny, were commercial, shameful, and a "travesty," according to the report of a committee of the Castle Heights Methodist Episcopal Church in New York's Westchester County. Part of the problem, noted the report, was that many people were struggling in the weak economy and encouraging people to buy clothes would only embarrass those who couldn't afford them.

But Wells Wise, secretary of the White Plains Chamber of Commerce, begged to differ. He called the committee's report "ridiculous" and argued that spring was a natural time for people to buy clothes, with or without Easter. Wise went on to say that "the Easter bunny is second only to Santa in the traditions of the people."[190] Let history remember this American chamber's defense of the religion-challenged rabbit.

Sports, Festivals, and Fairs

Chambers also promoted sports activities during this time. The Los Angeles Olympics, so strongly supported by the Los Angeles Chamber and related civic groups, went off well in 1932, as did the chamber-boosted winter Olympics in Lake Placid. Elsewhere, the occasional chamber put up a bid in order to attract a boxing match, while Sun Belt cities and their chambers performed the usual exertions to get Major League Baseball teams to host spring training in their communities.

John Ganzel, the Orlando Chamber's "one-man baseball committee," according to columnist Shirley Povich, was good at attracting teams to town. He promised Washington Nationals owner Clark Griffith – for whom Ganzel had played in Washington from 1903 to 1905 - $3,500 to secure the Nats in Orlando for the 1937 spring training season. This was the same amount paid the previous year.[191] Ganzel's genius for the game had been exhibited many years earlier, when he had recommended a young left-handed pitcher to the Baltimore Orioles. Babe Ruth's career took off soon afterward.[192]

Horseshoes were among the sports played in Florida in winter. The St. Petersburg Chamber of Commerce had routinely supplied the U-shaped footwear to the winter pitching tournament. Once, however, a stranger entered the competition, insisting on bringing his own horseshoes. But after his first pitches had yielded six ringers and four leaners, the tournament organizers investigated. Sure enough, the shoes were magnetized.[193]

Lots of chambers of commerce had sports committees, but few could top Augusta, Georgia in the fame of their committee chair. It was Ty Cobb, arguably the meanest man in baseball, but beloved in his home town. In 1931 he helped the chamber promote horse and dog shows and a southeastern golf tournament, while facing a well-publicized divorce suit from his wife on grounds of cruelty.[194]

The Washington Chamber of Commerce was about to launch the first Cherry Blossom festival in 1930 when a mini-scandal broke out. Did the chamber, indeed, plan to invite geisha girls to dance at the event? Missionaries in Tokyo heard about the plan and went ballistic. A bemused *Washington Post* reporter noted, "From what the missionaries have had to say, it seems that a geisha girl would do far more damage in an American city than a flapper, a gold digger or a chorus girl – or all three put together." Chamber Secretary Dorsey Hyde quickly noted that no geishas had been invited yet, and that the chamber would first consult with the State Department on the propriety of the request.[195] The question became moot when the festival was cancelled because of economic conditions.

The Cherry Blossom Festival, on its successful, apparently geisha-free launch in 1934, drew an amazing half million people.

Rockingham, Va., also sponsored its own chamber-supported festival. There were about 350,000 turkeys raised in Rockingham County, making it by some accounts the "turkey capital of the world." The idea of a turkey festival magically came to Russell Shultz, secretary

Senate Majority Leader Alben Barkley crowns Peggy Townsend Cherry Blossom Queen on March 31, 1939.

of the Harrisonburg-Rockingham Chamber of Commerce. The festival exploded in 1939 but lasted only two more years, cut off by the distraction of World War II. The event had its own excitement, however: in the first year, turkeys were thrown out of the top floor of the First National Bank Building, and people risked life and limb trying to catch the falling animals. (This was probably a more exciting pastime than the elaborate Turkeyrama Pageant, another part of the many-featured festival.) The Society for the Prevention of Cruelty to Animals, unsurprisingly, frowned on this flinging of birds that were bred for heft rather than for waft. And so in future years the obvious solution was implemented: tossing the turkeys out of a blimp, but with parachutes.[196]

Geishas and parachuting turkeys weren't invited to the Franklin County Fair in Tullahoma, Tenn. Rattlesnakes, however, were welcome. The local chamber of commerce encouraged people to bring dead rattlesnakes to the event in lieu of tickets. Chamber leaders believed that the area's reputation for having lots of rattlesnakes was hurting tourism.[197]

Of course, most big-city chambers looked for events with less of a rural flavor. The Dallas Chamber of Commerce was active in the city's successful bid to win the Texas Centennial Exposition in 1936. The chamber helped get a $3 million bond issue passed that built museums and other structures in Fair Park.[198] The event drew more than 6 million visitors, including FDR, and helped Dallas escape much of the Depression.

The era of the great World's Fairs wasn't quite over yet; perhaps it was television that would finally put the nail in the coffin of most of these giant expositions. The chambers in both San Francisco and New York were behind big fairs planned for the end of the decade. Their timing was atrocious, with a world war beginning in 1939, but of course no one knew that in the middle of the decade.

Originally, San Francisco's fair was to be a celebration of the two great bridges (Golden Gate and Bay bridges) that local chambers had been so active in promoting. The fair, while getting into financial difficulties, drew about 15 million people and left as a memento the 49-mile scenic drive for tourists that still exists today.

A group of individuals coming up with the New York World's Fair idea took it to George McAneny, head of the Regional Plan Association.[199] McAneny happened also to be an active member of the New York Chamber of Commerce, and informally he had had discussions with fellow member Percy Straus and other business people on how to revive the local economy. The men concluded that a fair would create construction jobs and bring outside investment and tourism to the city.

McAneny brought the plan to Mayor Fiorello LaGuardia, who embraced it. LaGuardia addressed the New York Chamber of Commerce on the plan just two weeks later, which pledged its support and put a committee together to back up the plan.[200] Indeed, the entire city rallied around the event, which brought about 44 million visitors over its two seasons (1939 and 1940).

Trying to Move Local Economies Forward

It was April 7, 1930. The Jersey City Chamber of Commerce, which had hosted the first radio-broadcast boxing match (the Dempsey-Carpentier bout won by Dempsey) just nine years earlier, had a new high-tech experiment going: America's "first television and radio sound theatre." Teaming up with Jenkins Radiovisor, the chamber managed to get TV outlets in 50 places around town to receive a feeble broadcast of a program. The session was opened by Mayor Frank Hague and included other notables such as vacuum tube inventor Lee de Forest.

Television experiments had been going on in various labs. This was one of its first truly public demonstrations of the power of this medium. By "first television and radio sound theatre," the promoters seem to have meant not the television audience – which was scattered all over town - but the simultaneous public broadcast of sound and accompanying visual images. Unfortunately for the locals, something similar had been demonstrated in London just a week earlier, but this was still a first for the United States.[201]

The experiment showed once again how chambers of commerce have been attracted to new technologies, from railroads to undersea cables to telegraphs and airplanes. Even in the Depression, progress inched forward on many fronts. Poignantly, in retrospect, the word "forward" came into vogue with chambers after the stock market crash of 1929. Copying the "Forward Atlanta" campaign's name, with Forward Alexandria, Forward Lawrence, etc., chambers in Alexandria, Washington, D.C., Fort Worth, Lawrence, Kansas, and no doubt elsewhere started their own ambitious campaigns to grow their chambers and their local economies, with limited success given the times they were operating in. The Atlanta Chamber dropped its Forward Atlanta campaign after the crash, and most chambers were more involved in trying to keep local business alive that in pursuing new dreams.

"It is plain that for the time being at least the go-getters and Babbitts are subdued," wrote Kyle Crichton in *Scribners* in 1932. He recounted the experience of a mythical western town called Beanville that since its successful Liberty Bond fundraising in World War I had engaged in one money-losing civic project after another, from a western fair to participation in the Atlantic City beauty pageant to a veteran's hospital to a tourist hotel that was a stock scam. Yet the credulous folk of Beanville, while reeling from the Depression, still wanted to be "put on the map" and were cautiously open to the idea of sustaining some of these dubious economic development opportunities.[202]

In some ways the Depression encouraged civic spirit. Adversity brought people together. Willard Hammer wrote an article for *Nation's Business* called "In Union There is Strength" (something of an amusing title for this anti-union magazine), drawing a distinction between how economic development used to happen haphazardly and how there was a better way. Before the Depression, he suggested, chambers worked to "lure smokestacks to their towns." After slightly changing course after the stock market crash, chambers appeared to be coming back to this losing game.

A different approach involving cooperation and organic growth was on display in North Carolina. The community of High Point, Hammer wrote, had thoughtfully built on the work of groups of leading business people. The town had developed a powerful cluster of furniture makers and hosiery manufacturers and had seen stability in jobs (with unemployment rising only because of people moving to the area in hopes of getting jobs).

"Over and over in the history of High Point's growth occurs the phrase, 'a group of leading citizens,'" Hammer wrote. It wasn't planning by the government, or even planning by the chamber as an institution, but planning by business people who had a civic purpose intertwined with their commercial interests. This organic growth, now supported by the chamber that had been organized relatively late in the process (in 1919), had created the prosperity of High Point.[203] Here was a model for planning of the free-market sort, of enlightened individualism and concern for the group – not too far from what Ryerson Ritchie had inculcated in the chambers in Cleveland, Detroit, Boston, and San Francisco during the Progressive Era. It was a spirit less of "y'all come" than of "let's build a community where all of us, and newcomers, will be proud to live."

Boosterism was on the run even in California, where Frank Wiggins had raised it to such high art. It had been ruined by none other than the Joads and their ilk, the Okies and other impoverished job seekers who were making life so difficult for the natives of the Golden State. One man, formerly a chamber of commerce executive, warned growers not to publish figures about their high production of oranges and other crops. "Why, that's simply asking half of Oklahoma to move in here and take over," he said.[204]

Those who can't boost, teach. This appeared to be a cynic's lesson from the Depression. Chambers that had bragged about production and sunshine, but for various reasons felt they couldn't do that anymore, began professing their interest in the facts and in a scientific approach to things. In Los Angeles, the ghost of Frank Wiggins put on a Ryerson Ritchie or S. Cristy Mead mask.

Somehow the LA Chamber even managed to impress a writer for the astringent *American Mercury*, James Cain, who clearly despised what he considered the typical chamber of commerce:

> The average American chamber of commerce, in my experience with it, is a noisy, tiresome, and exceedingly childish booster affair, with no maturer idea of its function than to bring as many factories to town as possible, in order that merchants will have more customers, realtors more prospects for their lots, and property more benefit from the unearned increment. That, and a running wrangle with the Interstate Commerce Commission, carried on by the traffic department, over some freight differential enjoyed by a nearby city, is about the extent of its activity.[205]

But oh, the Los Angeles Chamber – now there was a real chamber. This organization, "which with its affiliates pretty much controls the commercial development of the region," was a cut above:

> It is not content to get a new factory, although it has got plenty of these in the last few years. It has been forced to do what most Chambers of Commerce do not do: undertake an exhaustive

study of the possibilities of the region, that takes into account the needs of the population as a whole, and that is much broader than the leather-bound "presentation" got up for some particular manufacturer.[206]

This powerful chamber had discarded its old weapons, its piles of oranges and walnuts and grapefruits, and taken up the typewriter. It had progressed from the furrows of the plow to the furrows of the brow. It was still practicing economic development, and clearly still impressing writers, but in a method that was much different from the ways of its youth. Like a number of other chambers of commerce, and ahead of most of them, this chamber was becoming more scientific and professional. And yet . . . the urge to sell the community aggressively never really disappeared from most chambers, including the one that Frank Wiggins once ran with his team of oranges.

Jackrabbits and Jackhammers

The Phoenix Chamber of Commerce and its predecessor, the Phoenix Board of Trade, had done a few things over the years since the latter group emerged in 1888, even if the sleepy Arizona town was not much of an economic force in its early days. The Arizona capital had a population of just 48,000 in 1930. During the Depression, however, some of the local business people woke the town up from its reverie.

These Phoenician business people thought their town could be more than a sunswept crossroads plugging the four Cs (cotton, cattle, copper, and climate). Beginning in the late 30s, they pushed the Phoenix Chamber toward becoming a business recruitment organization. Among other reforms, they founded a "special honor fraternity" within the chamber. It was called the Royal Order of the Thunderbirds, and its members, in their 30s and 40s, worked hard to attract and entertain visiting CEOs. One of the first and most enthusiastic of the Thunderbirds was a man who would be a mover and shaker in the chamber, and then in politics, for years to come: Barry Goldwater.[207]

As a modern commentator (one not particularly fond of these union-averse, New Deal-bashing conservatives) would write, "There was nothing inevitable about the town's spectacular growth."[208] These hard-charging business people not only brought newcomers to Phoenix, but they built a culture and a political worldview that favored constant expansion, seldom turning down a federal subsidy but highly averse to impediments to increasing business activity. Lawyer Frank Snell, the Bimson brothers of Valley National Bank, Barry Goldwater, Harry Rosenzweig, and their chamber colleagues would create a sort of Venice in the sand, a sunny merchant city ruled by commerce as much as by mayors or governors or Presidents.

In future years, much as happened in Venice centuries earlier, these merchants would actually become the government, or at least a notable part of it. Chamber activists would become mayors of Phoenix, Maricopa County commissioners, Arizona legislators and governors, a U.S. Senator and Presidential candidate (Goldwater), a U.S. attorney general (Richard Kleindeinst), and two U.S. Supreme Court Justices (William Rehnquist and Sandra Day O'Connor). These were believers in small government who wanted to be a big part of it.

And they had something to show for their chamber's advocacy and fiery commitment to business expansion and recruitment. Although chamber power was weakened during and after the 1970s, Phoenix and the surrounding areas continued to ride the growth pony that Goldwater and his friends had set on its course in the late 1930s. Yes, air conditioning helped, but most of the key elements of growth had been put in place before this innovation was widespread.[209] The key element was unflagging promotion of new business and attempts to create tax, infrastructure, and regulatory systems that would please potential newcomers. By 2013, the booster-built community had become the fifth largest city in the nation.[210]

Balance Agriculture with Industry

During the Depression the South fostered a new kind of public financing for economic development, one that would create a lure stronger than the TVA: state-sanctioned industrial development bonds. It began with a businessman, Hugh Lawson White, who saw the lumber companies leave his town of Columbia, Miss., after they had harvested the wood, taking the potential of jobs and money with them. This was in 1929. White was mayor of the city. He was determined not to let Columbia die.[211]

White encouraged the creation of the Marion County Chamber of Commerce as a vehicle for finding industry. The chamber, remarkably energetic from the beginning, helped secure a small textile mill and canning factory.[212] Then he obtained the help of an industrial relocation consultant from Chicago, Felix Fantus, to find bigger game. Fantus came up with Reliance Manufacturing Company, which agreed to pump $1 million in payroll into the community over 10 years if the city of Columbia would come up with $85,000 to pay for the building of the factory.

This was standard practice of the time – indeed, precisely the kind of "bonus" for relocation (always in return for some sort of promise from the manufacturer) that was condemned by chamber after chamber, and practiced by chamber after chamber.

Then came White's next twist – approaching not just the bigwigs in the chamber, but the entire community for support. He declared a two-hour holiday and brought the townspeople together to hear the proposition and decide what to do. The support for the idea was overwhelming, and people from all walks of life signed promissory notes for small or large parts of the $85,000 obligation.

Even at this stage, the idea wasn't particularly new. Chambers in the past, often with the encouragement of local political authorities, had passed the hat to the community to bring Project X or Y to town – the railroad depot, the university, the scissors manufacturer. This process was perhaps less common in Mississippi, however, a state short on both industry and chambers of commerce in this period.

But White was determined to go one step further – to take the Columbia process statewide. Helped by the euphoria created by Reliance's rapid growth, he successfully ran for governor of Mississippi in 1935, with his primary campaign theme being his program to "Balance Agriculture with Industry" (BAWI). For the statewide rollout, he got legislation passed in 1936 that empowered the state to permit local authorities to raise bonds for buying land and building factories. A state commission would also vet the proposals from the many companies seeking support from this high-class, state-sponsored version of the old "bonus" system.

It worked. The commission evaluated no fewer than 3,800 proposals, selecting only 60 of them, and then issued just 21 certificates. These resulted finally in 12 plants, many of them textile facilities, locating in various parts of Mississippi. The impact was remarkable. A 1944 Federal Reserve Bank of Atlanta study found that the factories' payrolls increased from $1.4 million in 1939 to $17.9 million in 1942, all from the sale of public bonds of only $980,500. The BAWI idea soon had imitators in the South and elsewhere, although most of its impact would be seen after World War II.

BAWI, in one sense, was one more Depression Era intrusion of public organizations into private enterprise. But as in so many other cases, there were plentiful roles for chambers of commerce. Indeed, in subsequent years, chambers and their industrial development affiliates would be the leading private organizations behind the creation of publicly bonded industrial parks and other government-assisted factory expansion and relocation vehicles.

White had done chambers a favor: he had virtually automated the bonus-giving process, making it possible to give out many more awards of support to relocating businesses, and he had arranged it so that the money wouldn't come from chamber members themselves (except as they were taxpayers). White saw what FDR already knew: that chamber members frequently put aside their free-market principles when there was an opportunity to use other people's money to fund their favorite projects. With the public money came public rules and controls, of course, but also private benefits.

The tricky part with BAWI was its popularity. This, too, would become more clearly apparent after World War II. When just about everyone had a BAWI equivalent (some sort of government-guaranteed incentive system for relocating and expanding companies), of what comparative advantage was this mechanism? The debate would continue long after the New Deal grew old.

Education Efforts in the Thirties

In October 1930, *Nation's Business* featured an article called "How Chambers Help Schools," written by a school superintendent, Samuel Engle Burr. Burr's article pleasantly described a U.S. Chamber report on what 204 chambers of commerce were doing with their local schools. And Burr suggested that there were two potential views of school finance by local businesses and chambers: 1) schools were a drain on the treasury that should be minimized so as to keep taxes low, or 2) schools were a source of value to the community that should be cultivated and supported. Burr said that fortunately, most chambers appeared to be embracing "the broad point of view."[213]

By 1933, the U.S. Chamber was advocating the "narrow" point of view, urging reduced spending on schools (in line with reduced budgets everywhere), lower teacher salaries, and increased class sizes. This was making some educators angry. Columbia University's John Dewey criticized the U.S. Chamber for pushing local chambers to cut teacher salaries and he castigated such parsimonious groups as the "hired Hessians of big financial interests."[214]

Of course, it was never quite as simple as the evil chambers against the sainted educators. Many chambers desperately wanted institutions of higher education, and would make the most of local resources to house them. In 1933, when the Tampa Bay Hotel went bankrupt, the chamber successfully worked to have the Tampa Junior College relocate there, where it would become the University of Tampa.[215] The fundamentalist Bob Jones College ran into financial trouble in Florida and was induced to move north by the chamber in Cleveland, Tennessee, which raised $7,500 for the institution in a single afternoon.[216]

Many local chambers favored more spending on education, especially if it came from the state's coffers. California chambers pushed, for example, for the upgrading of normal schools and junior colleges to four-year status, angering the University of California trustees in Berkeley and Los Angeles, who saw their centralizing influence weakened by the centrifugal tendencies of the local chambers in other communities. While it might not be orderly to spread out the state's higher education resources, it was popular. Chambers of commerce had no trouble enlisting local politicians and voters to support the idea of having a full-fledged state-supported university in town.[217]

Indeed, the psychology of school upgrading was powerful. A reporter described a visit by big-city business people to an interior California city where a two-year institution existed.

"Would you like to see the university?" asked the local Chamber of Commerce official acting as a guide.

"University? I didn't know you had one here. What university is it?"

"Why, the university of _____," replied the guide, supplying the name of his home town. An item in the local promoters' program of faith without works was to establish the habit of calling the two-year college "the university."[218]

This process of incremental educational aggrandizement would prove to be a nearly universal phenomenon, certainly not confined to California. A town without a community college would move heaven and earth to get one. And when it had one, it wanted to turn that community college into a four-year institution. Then, perhaps, it would be time to push for a medical school or other graduate programs. And in many cases, it would be a chamber of commerce behind this inexorable pressure for increased outside funding for a local resource.

Dictators Lite

The increasing power and involvement of government in everyday life in the Thirties had its drawbacks. Westbrook Pegler, a popular, conservative newspaper columnist, put his finger on a phenomenon that became prominent during the decade: self-important, dictatorial mayors and other political figures who claimed credit for just about everything. The result, he said, was a diminution of the power of the local chambers of commerce. The old power structure wasn't perfect, but the new one was unusually grating. Pegler named John Hylan, the mayor of New York from 1918 to 1925, as the original culprit. As Pegler put it:

The first signs of dictatorship that I ever saw in this country occurred during the reign of Mayor John F. Hylan, although they were not recognized as such at the time and Mussolini then was a no-account Italian journalist who smelled of garlic and was always wanting his rights. I suppose the old chamber of commerce spirit and the dictatorship of the merchants and manufacturers in many of our towns had been fascism long before that, but I am speaking of the vulgar, outward signs. We were accustomed to the chamber of commerce spirit and the vigorous enthusiasm of the business interests, and but a few Socialists accepted their influence as a natural sort of thing in the Republic.

But as soon as Mr. Hylan was elected he began to 24-sheet himself around our town in a manner which suggested that he was dictator of New York and responsible for all the benefits which the taxpayers were buying for themselves. If the city built a bridge or paved a street, Mr. Hylan would put up a great big sign describing the project, and winding up with "John F. Hylan, Mayor."[219]

Pegler thus recounts how a particularly powerful or self-promoting leader such as Hylan can squeeze out chamber influence. The greater influence and prominence of government in the 1930s was both a cause and an effect of the spreading of the Hylan spirit, with men from FDR to Robert Moses to Huey Long exercising extraordinary powers, doing many significant things, and frequently taking extra helpings of credit. Much of this was reflected in the built environment, as Pegler indicated was the case in Hylan's time. Bridges, roads, and dams were typically government projects and the politicians and their appointees got the scissors at ribbon-cutting time. Yet the merchants couldn't be counted out. They may not have held the shears, but they continued to leave fingerprints on public projects all over the nation, sometimes as the originators or early prime movers of projects, sometimes as key supporters of the politicians and bureaucrats who got the funds.

One of the main roles for chambers of commerce in building projects was to draw attention to a problem or need and call for a strong hand to fix that problem. The prototype for this activity had been the New York Chamber's pioneering, when faced with rate competition from New Jersey, in the creation of the Port Authority of New York and New Jersey. That Authority, as we have seen, represented a new kind of government agency, one that could cut through the red tape and really get things done in a businesslike way.

In the Thirties and beyond, business groups and others called for similar types of dynamic "authorities." Roosevelt was known to admire the efficiency of the Port Authority and to have based the Tennessee Valley Authority largely on its model. In New York, the multitasking administrator Robert Moses would become almost a one-man authority himself, a kind of dictator lite. Yet Moses, and others like him who asked for significant public resources for major projects, could not operate without a base of political support. That support often came, especially at the early, critical stages of activity, from chambers of commerce.

The One-Man Chamber of Commerce

The master builder of New York state, as well as the wizard of its legislative process, was indeed the remarkable Robert Moses. Building on his relationship with Governor Al Smith, and on his understanding of how things worked in Albany and in the mayor's office in New York, Moses was able to transform much of the landscape of the city and the state. In a complex environment where major changes seemed almost impossible to effect, he built parks, parkways, highways, housing projects, and bridges.

While the New York Chamber of Commerce had cut through red tape to start creating the city's subway system, and had helped set up the red-tape-cutting entity known as the

Port Authority, so Moses took the scissors and electrified them. He sliced through obstacles on dozens of difficult projects, often on time and under budget. Working with a variety of different organizations, he did more to transform the look of greater New York than any other individual in the 20th century. And in most of his work, he had the support of chambers of commerce.

The Triborough Bridge

One of the building blocks to the success of this builder was the Triborough Bridge. This massive undertaking, completed in 1936, linked Manhattan with the neighboring boroughs of Queens and the Bronx. Like so many public works, it was conceived before the Depression and completed with federal funds under FDR's administration.

A local Republican politician named Frank Bowers was credited with the basic idea, although it was considered a wild one:

> To many people in the early 1920s the idea of a bridge three and one half miles in total length, leaping Hell Gate, Ward's Island, Little Hell Gate, Randall's Island, the Bronx Kills and the Harlem River, seemed utopian and fantastic.[220]

After Bowers's concept, which included an automobile as well as a rail span, was initially rejected, he got the Harlem Chamber of Commerce to champion it.[221] And as we have seen earlier, a group of chambers, including the Harlem Chamber, advocated the Bridge and Tunnel Authority that was created in 1928 (and soon became known as the Triborough Bridge Authority, or TBA). This authority began construction on the Triborough Bridge, however, just as the stock market crashed in 1929. The financial crisis caused work to be suspended.

Building the Triborough Bridge was an obvious win for the Democrats during the 1930s. The bridge, in the most heavily populated part of the United States, would relieve congestion, garner millions of dollars in tolls, and provide thousands of jobs. The FDR administration committed $37 million of the $62 million project, making it possible. But, with the federal funding committed, who would finish the job and help run the Triborough Bridge Authority?

The man of the hour was clearly Robert Moses. As the pioneering creator of the park system for the state of New York, he had built a string of parks and parkways, notably in Long Island, that had won votes for his boss at the time (Governor Al Smith) and brought him the undying friendship of just about every civic organization, including chambers of commerce, on Long Island. On January 18, 1934, the Long Island Chamber of Commerce led six other civic groups in a love-fest for Moses as he took over the job of Park Commissioner of New York City.

This lunch of 400 people clearly had a theme other than simply praising a man taking a new job. It was to promote him for *another* job, that of one of three commissioners of the Triborough Bridge Authority. Former governor Al Smith, the lead speaker at the lunch, praised Moses for his ability to handle more than one job at once. And F. Ray Howe, the president of the Queensboro Chamber of Commerce, provided legal advice a good deal beyond the normal purview of a chamber volunteer. Howe said that the Park Consolidation

Bill gave the mayor the authority to appoint Moses to another job, such as that of running the Triborough Bridge Authority. And Howe said things at the TBA weren't going well and could use Moses's help.[222]

Sure enough, Mayor LaGuardia appointed Moses to the Triborough Bridge Authority, a position that was to provide a base of power (and toll collections) that would keep Moses operating for many years to come. FDR had never liked Moses and tried to remove him from his TBA post, but Moses was able to hang on, thanks in part to an outpouring of support from chambers of commerce. The New York Chamber of Commerce gathered up 147 civic groups, many of them other chambers, in a successful effort to support Moses for the job and oppose FDR and the Public Works Administration chief, Harold Ickes.[223]

The local chambers of commerce may have thought of Moses as something of a dictator, but he was their dictator – most of the time. When he didn't get their support, he could be fierce. In April 1935, George Mand, president of the Bronx Chamber of Commerce, made public his letter to Mayor LaGuardia complaining about the disgraceful condition of the parks in the Bronx, which had been torn up for construction and then held up because of a temporary shortage of federal funds.

Moses responded after reporters told him of the letter:

> Mr. Mand is another Daniel come to judgment. His suggestion of concentrating on one project at a time is so preposterous as to require no extended reply. It is impossible to employ 33,000 people on park work relief on any such basis, not to speak of the 75,000 we shall probably have before the Summer is over as the Federal Government withdraws from home relief. No doubt Mr. Mand would have them all on home relief or doing Swedish exercises in Bronx Park.
>
> If Mr. Mand has something constructive to contribute, we shall all be glad to hear it. In the absence of any program he is simply another irresponsible mud-thrower. . . The only thing that surprises me about Mand's statement is that any reputable organization will lend its name to it.[224]

In tough times, New York certainly had a tough man to get the work done.

As New York building went, so went the nation. Project after project that was conceived or promoted in the 1920s or earlier, often by local chambers of commerce, went into high gear with federal funding in the 1930s. We have already mentioned how the Golden Gate Bridge, the Hoover Dam, and the Grand Coulee Dam were to rise with FDR's help, just like the Triborough Bridge. The San Francisco Chamber also pushed for $75 million for the San Francisco Bay Bridge.[225] The original request for Reconstruction Finance Corp. money went to President Hoover but the bridge was completed in 1936, six months before the Golden Gate Bridge was finished.

Chambers of commerce in the Chesapeake Bay region wanted a bridge, too. Paul Titsworth, president of the Kent County, Md., Chamber of Commerce, said in 1930 that "no stone will be left unturned" to get a $10 million span between the Eastern Shore and the mainland.[226] In this case, the stones remained in place for nearly two decades, although the Maryland General Assembly approved the idea in 1938.

A project heading from Maryland to Virginia, the George Washington Memorial Parkway, was approved by the National Capital Park and Planning Commission and strongly supported by the Arlington, Va., Chamber of Commerce. The chamber's Hugh Kirby secured the Virginia State Chamber's support and scheduled a visit to 100 counties to tout the project, in conjunction with the commission.[227] Further west, Virginia chambers that had been active in the creation of the Shenandoah National Park pressed for rapid completion of, and worked with property owners along, the Skyline Drive.[228] This roadway wound through the mountains toward the Smoky Mountains National Park (another chamber-influenced park, as we have seen).

Not every public works project involved building things skyward. Some things went down, including harbor floors. The Boston Chamber had been pushing for a deeper channel almost since it began in the 18th century. In the Thirties, a federal official informed the Boston Chamber of Commerce that the port would be excavated five more feet to a depth of 40 feet.[229]

The chamber obsession with public works and transportation was not immune to critical attention. Early in the Thirties, a noted intellectual, Charles Beard, took a sideswipe at chambers in his controversial and much commented on article, "The Myth of Rugged American Individualism." Said Beard about chambers' propensities for transportation projects and public funding of them: "There is not a single Chamber of Commerce on any Buck Creek in America that will not cheer until tonsils are cracked any proposal to make said creek navigable." Beard went on, "An interesting enterprise for the United States Chamber of Commerce would be to discover a single piece of pork in a hundred years that has not been approved by local businessmen as beneficiaries."[230]

Slums

Slums were another project that required government intervention. New York's East Side Chamber of Commerce became an early champion for the idea that slums were a blight on the city and should be cleared up, and the chamber embarked on the first step of slum removal: verbal condemnation. Establishing a consensus that a slum was a problem area was the intellectual foundation for the "improvements" to come.

Orrin Lester, the chairman of the East Side Chamber's board of directors and vice president of the Bowery Savings Bank, issued a statement in 1931 asserting there was consensus: "Everybody is agreed that improved housing is the major need of this section, as it is of every depleted area, but outside of a very few actual demonstrations of improved housing, and a great deal of talk, housing, like every other need on the lower east side, is standing still." He noted that 232,000 people had left the area in the 1920s. Clearly this was an emergency calling for government intervention and for a master plan. Otherwise, builders and lenders would not be able to perform the necessary, large-scale reconstruction, a project that could take decades.[231]

The program of slum clearance had roots not so much in popular demand for better housing as in business's demand for government-supported real estate development opportunities. This insight is certainly not a new one. Jane Jacobs's 1961 diatribe against the city planning at mid-century, *The Death and Life of Great American Cities*, consistently shows how urban renewal programs were driven by the projects of builders and lenders more than by those of residents. This pattern existed in the 1930s, with the East Side Chamber one of the main culprits.

Chambers, however, have never been welfare or social service agencies. The East Side Chamber, while emphasizing the weaknesses of low-income communities, also found positive ways to excite interest in improving the area's housing. Its publication, the *East Side Chamber News*, featured an article by economist Richard Ely describing the area as a "new frontier." The lower prices in the area offered returns as great as did the cheap land in the "old frontier." Redevelopment was a bonanza:

> The clearing of the forest of wretched buildings between Christie and Forsyth Streets, from Houston to Canal, and the widening of Allen Street are as the opening of new land to settlers. The proposed creation of additional parks and playgrounds and the improvement of the waterfront also will give prospect of a rejuvenation that will be as the building of a new city.[232]

It was a captivating vision. The East Side Chamber, including its dynamic secretary, Joseph Platzker, continued to advocate slum clearance later in the Thirties. Platzker said $500 million in federal money would fix the housing problem on the Lower East Side; he was a realist, however, and indicated he would be satisfied with a mere 10 percent of that amount.[233] In fact, the city would get 5 percent of Platzker's target; in April 1934, Mayor Fiorello LaGuardia proudly told a meeting of 10,000 people, presided over by the former president of the East Side Chamber, that his administration had secured $25 million in housing funding from the federal government.[234]

There was a lot of federal money for this popular work. There was even a perverse civic pride about slums on the East Side. This was "the district where American slums were born and bred," wrote an approving *New York Times* reporter while following Platzker on his rounds.[235] First in the nation in slums, and first in slum clearance.

A Road with No Red Lights

Pittsburgh had made itself the nation's capital of steel production, an industrial center of the first order. But this mountain-ringed community also specialized in the movement of people and freight. The western outpost of the "Keystone State" had been a natural transportation hub from the days when Conestoga wagons headed to Ohio via Pittsburgh and, later, when the Pennsylvania Railroad used the city as a footing for its dominant stance over the nation's transportation system.

Perhaps, then, it was natural that the Pittsburgh Chamber's Committee on Highways and Bridges would jump on an October 1933 speech by Public Works Administration Chief Harold Ickes regarding the building of a transcontinental superhighway. Ickes said the National Planning Board should hurry up and design such a project, as $400 million of public works money had been allocated for road building.[236] It was a political necessity to spend that money quickly so as to create jobs.

The Pittsburgh Chamber, alone among the nation's business groups and public entities, immediately grasped the significance of Ickes's idea. Of course, plenty of others had imagined a speedy route across the country.[237] Ickes's agency, however, had the money. Even though the Pittsburgh Chamber (along with countless chambers nationwide) questioned the wisdom of the left-leaning tendencies of the FDR administration, it pushed for a partnership with the federal government. The Pittsburgh Chamber's members wanted to see the superhighway idea realized in their back yard.

On December 14, 1933, the Pittsburgh Chamber met to discuss transportation and other issues.[238] The chamber approved the recommendations of its bridge and highway committee both for a note to Administrator Ickes asking "that serious, early consideration be given to the building of at least one super highway extending across the country" and for a suggestion to the Pennsylvania Department of Highways and Bridges that slow lanes be introduced on certain mountain roads so that cars going at normal speeds could pass trucks and other slow-moving vehicles.[239] These double requests for faster auto transportation soon would be combined into the first segment of what would one day become the Interstate Highway System.

The chamber sent notices of its idea far and wide, including to politicians and the President. Edward Snodgrass Jr., vice chair of the highways and bridges committee, wrote an article about the idea, "Trans-Continental Highway Needed," that was liberally distributed after publication in *Greater Pittsburgh* in November 1934. The article began with the stake-in-the-ground editor's note that "the Pittsburgh Chamber of Commerce was the first organization to urge the construction of a safe, high speed highway from the Atlantic to the Pacific, which was suggested by Hon. Harold L. Ickes, Federal Administrator of Public Works, in an address on National Planning."[240]

By March of 1935, the Pittburgh Chamber's board was considering paying up to $500 to send a lobbyist to Washington to "further the construction of a transcontinental super-highway."[241] Surveying of an old railroad route between Harrisburg and Pittsburgh began the same year. And so did the publicity for the Ickes-chamber partnership. For example, on November 10, *The New York Times* ran a feature article, "A Super-Highway for America," that talked about the Pittsburgh Chamber's pioneering role and its connection with Harold Ickes, now Secretary of the Interior.

What was unique about this highway? *Times* author Reginald Cleveland described it:

> The road which the Pittsburgh body is advocating would stretch from ocean to ocean without a single intersection at grade. It would have high-speed lanes, separated from low-speed lanes, in each direction. It would provide, in a central curbing, for power, light, telephone and water services. . . A study of other road, tunnel and bridge enterprises put into operation in recent years has convinced the advocates of the highway that its cost could readily be met by tolls which would be cheerfully paid.

The author quoted Edward Snodgrass regarding another feature of the proposed road, that it:

> should run from the neighborhood of New York to the neighborhood of San Francisco without touching any major city directly. This would avoid the necessity of condemning any very high-priced land.

Every ten miles or so, there would be on and off ramps.[242]

In short, the Pittsburgh Chamber's concept as described publicly in 1935 was remarkably similar to how superhighways and modern toll roads operate: multilane freeways without traffic lights, often paid for by tolls, with on and off ramps spaced a few miles apart, avoiding direct passage through cities, with services for motorists spread along the route, with fast motorists able to pass slow ones, and with the grade on the roadway as level as possible.

Ickes was happy to cooperate with the band of burghers from Pittsburgh. Here was his conception rapidly moving toward reality. On July 30, 1938, Secretary Ickes announced that the federal government would provide a total of $58 million for a modern turnpike between Pittsburgh and Harrisburg, a 162-mile route featuring seven tunnels and many other engineering challenges. Of the federal money, $32 million would be a loan to the Pennsylvania Turnpike Commission, which would pay it back with the money from motorists' tolls.[243]

By late 1940 the road had been completed. It turned out to be the hit that the chamber had hoped, cutting three hours off the trip from Harrisburg to Pittsburgh and having no more than a 3 percent grade in road level.[244] In the first three weeks of operation, 197,164 motorists crowded on to the ultramodern highway, paying average tolls of 86 cents each, in aggregate beating the early projections of toll revenue by $12,000.[245]

It was clear that the superhighway concept worked, at least in this part of the United States, and chambers of commerce and other groups began proposing additional legs to the route. Ultimately the massive Pennsylvania Turnpike (which still terms itself "America's First Superhighway") would result from this project, the original model and building block for the Interstate Highway System that was formally begun under President Eisenhower in 1956. Had World War II not intervened, it's almost certain that the Pittsburgh Chamber-Ickes collaboration would have spread across the country sooner.

Coping with Chaos Overseas

The Great Depression brought misery to the United States and exacerbated an already difficult world political situation. The challenges were enormous and chambers of commerce, from the smallest local organizations to the U.S. Chamber and the American committee in the International Chamber of Commerce (ICC), had limited ability to make things better. These organizations would have trouble with FDR; how could they cope with Hitler? And Hitler, unfortunately, was only one of the challenges.

President Hoover's muddled speech to the International Chamber of Commerce in May of 1931, which essentially blamed foreigners for prolonging (if not causing) the Depression, was only one in a series of failed opportunities to stoke the engine of international economic growth and cooperation. ICC delegates went home disappointed. The international arms race, decried by Hoover, continued, as did waves of protectionism after the tsunami of America's own Smoot-Hawley tariff. There were also the financial repercussions from the reparations that Germany was still being forced to pay, and from the debts that other European powers, notably France and Great Britain, owed the United States.

Which American business people and chamber leaders were prepared to guide the country through the international waters? First, perhaps, there was Edward Filene, the retailer who was the leading champion of the "bargain basement" and who had been the American most responsible for the creation of the ICC in 1919. He was the very first member of the

ICC.[246] But the left-of-center Filene was unhappy with traditional business organizations. The chambers he helped found – the revitalized Boston Chamber of Commerce, the U.S. Chamber of Commerce, and the International Chamber of Commerce – had a habit of disappointing him, wrote his perceptive friend, Lincoln Steffens.[247] Indeed, Filene's idealism would lead him to an embrace of the cooperative movement and credit unions and to resign publicly from the U.S. Chamber in 1936.

Thomas Watson, the president of International Business Machines (IBM), was also deeply committed to the International Chamber of Commerce. This energetic entrepreneur, once an itinerant peddler of sewing machines, had learned modern business at the feet of another tough master, John H. Patterson. (Patterson was the founder of National Cash Register and the moving force behind the creation of the Dayton Chamber of Commerce.) Watson followed the civic orientation of his mentor, becoming active in the American committee of the International Chamber of Commerce beginning in 1923,[248] and serving as president of the Merchants' Association of New York from 1931 to 1934.[249]

Watson hated war. He apparently coined the phrase, "World peace through world trade."[250] And like some other optimists in a decade not made for them, he looked for every silver lining in a multitude of dark clouds. His almost misty-eyed focus on avoiding war was shared by many of his contemporaries, including a large proportion of the members of the ICC, and would be something of a constant during a turbulent decade.

During the 1930s, as in the 1920s, the communist regime of the Soviet Union was a destabilizing factor and a source of much concern among chamber executives. The Soviets had some sympathizers in the United States, where capitalism was having its own trials. Indeed, Filene's friend Steffens had famously written in 1919, during his visit to Russia, "I have seen the future, and it works." But not everyone felt this way. In August of 1931, Frank Noxon, president of the chamber of commerce in Alexandria, Va., returned from a visit to Russia and said the country was doomed because economic incentives were lacking, while Stalin was spending money "like an inebriated sailor."[251]

Hitler Comes to Power

Soon there was another major source of instability in Europe. On January 4, 1933, the leader of the Nazi Party, Adolf Hitler, met with German ex-chancellor Franz von Papen. The linking of these two men was a key stepping stone in Hitler's rise to power. The man who made this critical connection, Baron Kurt von Schroeder, soon was rewarded with various key positions, including the presidency of the Cologne Chamber of Commerce. On January 30, thanks to Papen's promises that he could control Hitler, German President Paul von Hindenburg named Hitler the chancellor of Germany.

The storm of Nazi anti-Semitism broke almost immediately, despite denials from German authorities. Jewish chamber and other business leaders were replaced by "Aryans." Nazi repression became a fact of life with which foreign business people and their chambers of commerce had to deal.

Berlin hosted the Olympics in 1936. Some things were relatively normal about the event. American chambers of commerce cheered on their local athletes, as usual. The Fulton, Missouri, chamber aided one athlete who was short of funds: Helen Stephens, aka the "Fulton flash."[252] The Los Angeles Chamber, moreover, sent the Germans a sample house from the

Olympic Village that it had created for the 1932 Olympics. The Germans took the plans and did the Angelenos one better, making far more elaborate homes for the contending stars.[253]

The Nazis wanted to see their Aryan athletes win. One of the African-American track and field stars, however, Jesse Owens, confounded Hitler by winning four gold medals and besting blond Germans in the process. When he returned to Columbus, Ohio, he was given a huge welcome by Governor Martin Davey, Arthur Evans of the Columbus Chamber of Commerce, and others. The Junior Chamber of Commerce gave Owens's wife a chest of silverware. Owens told the crowd:

> I had a grand time, but the competition was really stiff, especially that Lutz Long, the German, in the broad jump. I'd jump 25 feet and 8 inches, then Hitler would give Long a look and he would jump 25 feet and 8 inches. I'd jump 25 feet and 10 inches and Hitler would give Long another look. Then he'd equal my jump again. The last time I was luckier.[254]

It was one thing to confront the Nazis on the playing fields, and quite another to deal with them in business organizations. In late June of 1937, Berlin hosted the annual meeting of the International Chamber of Commerce. Thomas Watson, who had headed the American committee of the ICC since 1933, sailed over to the meeting, along with the U.S. Chamber's ex-president Silas Strawn and other American business and chamber leaders.

At the opening of the ICC meeting, with 1,500 delegates attending, Hitler sat in a box and enthusiastically applauded as Reich Commissar Hermann Goering gave an angry speech about Germany's right to an army and access to raw materials. Another speaker, Minister of Economics Dr. Hjalmar Horace Greeley Schact, gave an intimidating speech about Germany's ability to create synthetics to counter the West's control of raw materials. Later, the atmosphere improved as propaganda minister Joseph Goebbels and his wife entertained the visiting businessmen at a garden party.

As *Life* magazine reported, German hospitality was "repeatedly spoiled by political sour notes," but Watson did not join in the carping against the Hitler regime.[255] He was elected president of the ICC. And he steadfastly accommodated his hosts. Watson was offered and accepted the Merit Cross of the German Eagle with Star, a decoration that Hitler's government had created two months earlier. He also raised his arm in the Hitler salute (or, according to one account, raised it but then caught himself and retracted it) – a gesture that some but not all the Western delegates also made in deference to the host country.[256]

Why was Watson so appeasing to Hitler, whose regime even then had become a byword for brutality? His son Tom Watson Jr. wrote later, "Dad's optimism blinded him to what was going on in Germany" and added that "Dad believed his German businessman friends, who assured him they had Hitler in check." The ICC president even had a private meeting with Hitler, who "fooled him completely," his son later reported. The elder Watson praised Hitler's sincerity to reporters and quoted the German leader as saying, "There will be no war. No country wants war, and no country can afford it."[257]

Unfortunately, the story isn't quite as simple as the optimistic Watson being fooled by a devious Hitler. Thomas Watson Sr.'s IBM kept its European subsidiaries well supplied with the technology and punch cards that would enable them, under Hitler's sway, to keep the Axis trains and war machine running on time. The high-tech firm's cards kept track of

Clockwise: Adolf Hitler, left, with Thomas Watson seated to Hitler's left; International Chamber of Commerce and IBM President Thomas Watson addresses the ICC in Berlin; Hitler and colleagues in a box seat overlooking the ICC conference, with Hermann Goering to Hitler's left; conference audience with ICC and swastika banners adjacent and U.S. flag in place of honor.

racial and religious classifications that sent millions of Jews and others to their deaths. An IBM punch-card machine holds a place of dishonor in the Holocaust Museum in Washington, D.C.

The story is recounted in much detail in Edwin Black's *IBM and the Holocaust*. While Black's book does not directly tie Watson or his U.S. associates to knowledge of the Holocaust, the degree of last-minute punch-card cooperation with the Axis Powers that the book demonstrates is remarkable. What does customer service mean when one's customer is the Nazi High Command?

Tom Watson was America's leading corporate internationalist up to the very start of World War II. He arguably strengthened Hitler's international position in this period:

> Watson never spoke a word of criticism against his customer Nazi Germany. But more than that, he worked to breach the gorge of isolation surrounding the Reich. One of his main venues was the International Chamber of Commerce and its U.S. affiliate, the United States Chamber of Commerce.[258]

As late as June 1939, at the International Chamber of Commerce Congress in Copenhagen, and even later in 1940, Watson was still currying favor with the Nazis, asking the countries of the world to be sure to be fair in their division of natural resources (so that Germany could have its share).[259] But after the Nazis invaded Holland, Watson finally returned his medal to Hitler, although first unsuccessfully trying to get the U.S. government to make him do so. Had he been able to return the medal under State Department compulsion, he could presumably have preserved his relationship with the Nazi government.[260]

More Troubles at Home

Despite Watson's frequent statements of optimism, the latter 1930s brought more and more bad news. On June 10, 1938, David Kirschbaum, a retired manufacturer who was a director of the Philadelphia Chamber of Commerce and chairman of its traffic committee, hanged himself from a door jamb with a dog chain. He had been upset over growing anti-Semitism.[261]

Oddly, sparked by local chamber leaders as noted earlier, both New York and San Francisco hosted World's Fairs in 1939 and 1940. These events created an eerie counterpoise to international events. Sometimes the results were comical, as when a mummy was shipped to the wrong fair.[262] Sometimes the results were sad, as when the Czecho-Slovak Chamber of Commerce announced it would continue to build its pavilion at the New York World's Fair, even though Hitler had overrun Czechoslovakia.[263]

American business groups overseas often were islands of enterprise in troubled seas. The American Chamber of Commerce in Berlin had been the place where, in 1933, U.S. Ambassador William Dodd had given a prophetic and controversial speech warning of the dangers of rule by half-educated autocrats.[264] Relatively open conversations were still possible there, even by ordinary U.S. business people, later in the 1930s.

The American-Russian Chamber of Commerce in Moscow, however, was not as well shielded from local authorities. Its secretary, Tatiana Sofiano, was arrested on November 21, 1937, without any description of the charges. Her husband, an engineer, had been arrested a year previously and exiled, while his brother and her brother also were arrested in separate actions.[265] That chamber finally closed in 1940, unable to resist the paranoia (and perhaps especially the anti-foreign paranoia) of Joseph Stalin and his lieutenants.[266]

It was Hitler's foreign aggression, however, more than Stalin's mostly domestic terror, that filled Europeans with fear. The Germans remilitarized the Rhineland in 1936, took over Czechoslovakia's Sudetenland in October 1938, and finally invaded Poland in September 1939, sparking a broader European war. Hitler's forces charged into France in May 1940 and defeated its armies with surprising speed, almost capturing a scrambled collection of French and British troops at Dunkirk.

Through all of these disturbing events, many American chamber leaders called for avoiding European entanglements and war. In the summer of 1940, John F. Kennedy, son of U.S. Ambassador to Great Britain Joseph Kennedy, came out with a book called *Why England Slept*, a description of how British appeasement had made Hitler's rise possible. Kennedy cited American mistakes as well, including resolutions by the U.S. Chamber calling for staying out of European conflicts.[267]

Indeed, the U.S. Chamber's pro-neutrality position – fueled by the opinions of rank-and-file members at local chambers of commerce across the nation – remained steady. A few days after the Germans invaded France, Chamber President James Kemper declared that entering a European war would bankrupt the United States.[268] He repeated his opposition six months later, in December of 1940, in a talk to the Merchants' Association of New York.[269]

There were countercurrents, both at the U.S. Chamber and elsewhere. Some of these impulses toward war were prompted by British pleas for help. In April of 1940, Britain's ambassador to the United States, Lord Lothian, told the St. Louis Chamber of Commerce that Hitler's ruthlessness threatened a new Dark Age. Quoting Theodore Roosevelt, he said, "We stand at Armageddon, and we battle for the Lord."[270] In June of 1940, the Anglophile New York Chamber of Commerce reversed an earlier position and urged that the American economy switch to a "war footing."[271] As we will see elsewhere, many chambers of commerce began to push for a share of growing federal military expenditures while the country prepared itself for war in case it did come to the United States.

Not every chamber impulse in the conflict was disinterested, by any means. The chamber in Lynn, Massachusetts, a shoe manufacturing center, found a silver lining in the dark cloud of German aggression. The German takeover of Czechoslovakia meant that trade agreements with the former nation were invalid and that low-priced shoe imports from Czechoslovakia would no longer be permitted, said the chamber's industrial secretary, Arthur Lalime.[272]

New York City also stood to benefit from the European war. When the Nazis captured Paris, the capital of the world fashion industry fell with it. This was an opportunity for New York, according to the optimists at the New York Chamber of Commerce. Such a chance to capture the fashion industry didn't come up every day, said the chamber in a report urging Mayor LaGuardia to take the baton and run:

> No city in the world is better qualified than New York to assume the heirship to the position of style arbiter which Paris held almost without interruption for 400 years.[273]

Mayor LaGuardia was extremely supportive of the idea. Paris, however, would bounce back to fashion leadership in the decades after the war ended.

Gearing Up for War

As the 1930s drew to a close, so did the Great Depression. The economic engine that seemed to be pulling the train out of despond was not the ingenuity of FDR's Brain Trust or the animal spirits of American enterprise, but something entirely different. It was fear itself, laced with anger, that shook the country out of the slump. Concern about the intentions of the tyrants of Berlin and Rome and Tokyo, and about their depredations against neighboring countries, prompted the United States to begin a massive military buildup and consequent explosion of hiring in countless communities.

Local chambers of commerce, as before World War I, eagerly sought to win the new military business. Some were prompted by desire for economic growth, some by envy of the growth of nearby communities, some by both. Few wanted this opportunity to pass them by.

In Oklahoma City, from which many people had emigrated during the Depression, even more were starting to leave for the military bases and associated factories on either coast. Chamber CEO Stanley Draper wanted to stanch the flow and take advantage of the community's strategic spot in the midsection of the country. He would later quote Shakespeare's Julius Caesar: "There is a tide in the affairs of men, which, taken at the flood, leads on to fortune." Draper bolstered the Oklahoma City's representation in Washington and soon won a plum: the Army Air Corps announced in September 1940 that it would locate a squadron at Will Rogers Field. The chamber manager created the Industries Foundation of Oklahoma

City to fund the purchase of land and construction for federal facilities, and by December 1940 had acquired 1,219 acres next to the airport, enough for a full-fledged bomber base. Draper was just getting started.[274]

The chamber in Tulsa was just as busy. The organization prepared a 138-page report on the community's suitability for aircraft and other military goods production. Chamber CEO Russell Rhodes took this report to Washington and chamber and city officials lobbied hard for opportunities. In December 1940 they won an enormous deal: a bomber production plant to be erected for the government by Douglas Aircraft Company. The factory eventually would employ 14,000 to 17,000 people.[275]

All over the country, chamber officials looked into their rolodexes for contacts. In 1934, Gus Backman, the manager of the chamber in Salt Lake City, together with his wife Nancy, befriended a pilot named Hank Arnold, who came to the city to handle air mail service. As a chamber history later recounted, "Mrs. Backman had young Arnold out to dinner frequently at their home, taught him to rhumba, and listened to his problems."[276] Although Arnold did not become famous for either his dancing or his problems, he became a rising star in the Army Air Corps. Just a few years later, as Henry H. (Hap) Arnold, chief of the Army Air Corps, he would repay those dancing lessons many times over.

The St. Louis Chamber, which was one of the leaders in attracting military business during World War I, was no slouch in the Second World War. In mid-1940, Chamber President Thomas Dysart, together with local Federal Reserve Bank President William McChesney Martin, began a census of the local manufacturers to determine what equipment they had and for what military purposes it might be used. This report ran into five volumes that, stacked together, were eight inches tall. It took inventory of every local tool bigger than a wrench.[277]

The chamber sent the study to 1,100 major defense contractors across the nation. This extensive homework gave the chamber a six-month lead over most rival organizations and helped the St. Louis economy tremendously. Contracts came in quickly; eventually the area boasted 420 manufacturers with direct contracts with the government and another 2,000 companies that were subcontractors.[278] St. Louis would have $230 million in defense business in March 1941 and $800 million in February 1942.[279]

The Philadelphia Chamber of Commerce was another early participant in the military business. In 1939 it established a Committee of Defense that helped secure $1 billion in war contracts by the following year.[280] The Jacksonville Chamber of Commerce, moreover, had formed a Military Base Committee that helped win support to turn the old Camp Joseph E. Johnston into Naval Air Station Jacksonville.[281] Dallas also won a Naval Air Station; its chamber was involved in so many defense activities that the *Dallas Journal* wrote in December 1940 that "Dallas should feel an everlasting pride in its Chamber" for what it had brought to town.[282]

Yet was all this chamber activity doing the nation any good? Or was the country thereby allowing a few energetic localities to reshape the national military agenda according to their economic needs and desires? Congressman Paul Shafer, a member of the House's Military Affairs Committee, took a 25,000-mile trip to various bases around the country and was appalled at the extravagant requests for funding of all sorts of things, from swimming pools and athletic fields, that had little to do with the direct needs of national security.

Some of these [funding] requests were made in formal compilations by commanding officers of the various forts. The greater number, however, were proffered by chambers of commerce, real estate dealers, and other earnest citizens apparently convinced that the way to protect America's coasts is to spend millions to boost trade in their particular areas. It is amazing how many spots in this country have the perfect climate and surroundings for an army post, and are also, by a fortunate coincidence, perfectly located from a strategic and tactical standpoint. Any chamber of commerce, anywhere in the country, can show you just such a site.[283]

Shafer angrily described how the Bisbee, Ariz., Chamber of Commerce asked $4 million of new money for Fort Huachuca, which was ideally placed to protect us from the menacing armies of . . . Mexico. And he decried the chambers downriver from Washington that advocated funding for local forts, not because they had any military value (most were outdated before the Civil War), but because they housed the remains of some military hero or other. The Cheyenne Chamber of Commerce praised Fort Francis E. Warren as a candidate for expansion, not because of its strategic value but for its amenities for soldiers and their families, and asked for another $3 million. Marvelous Marin, Inc., the county chamber based in San Rafael, had a grab bag of expensive requests to the military, including the waiving of tolls on the Golden Gate Bridge. And there were other equally embarrassing examples of locals' grabs for national funds.[284]

Shafer wasn't the only critic of the local efforts to make hay out of war concerns. U.S. Purchasing Coordinator Donald Nelson put it in a way that must have been comical to anyone except perhaps the chambers of commerce that heard his remarks read at the 1940 NACOS convention:

Among the hundreds upon hundreds of those who have petitioned us for new plants or facilities, only one did not request that the plant or facility by located in his home town. He was worried that it might be a [gun]powder plant and so he urged that it be located not in his area but in the next town.[285]

Shafer and Nelson had a good point, but the locals had something on their side as well. The sometimes inefficient bases in some places added to the political and business support for the war effort – local pride and, yes, greed combining to provide momentum for the most productive and dazzling display of military-industrial might that the world had ever seen up to that point. America's amazing productive capacity would be cited by friend and foe alike as one of the main reasons that the Allies won the war. And that capacity was based on local effort, motivation, and ingenuity as much as on national initiative. As for inefficiencies – the national government would have some examples to offer that might make even Marvelous Marin blush.

Chambers in many cases weren't asking for completely new projects, but for improvements on bases and ports and airfields for which they had successfully advocated in World War I or even earlier. A prime example of a chamber's long-term fixation on a military asset was Hawaii's Pearl Harbor. The Honolulu Chamber of Commerce, which had done so much to lock Hawaii into the American orbit in the first place, and which had pioneered in the development of Pearl Harbor even before World War I, took a particular interest in Asia-Pacific security matters.

On September 14, 1940, U.S. Navy Secretary Frank Knox addressed a luncheon at the Honolulu Chamber of Commerce. "We are living in ugly times, when force, and force alone, can give safety and security," he said. Knox had reviewed the Pacific fleet and was greatly impressed, while resolving to do even more to strengthen the Hawaiian base. Later in the day he told a reporter, "I am determined to do all I can to make the Pearl Harbor base the most formidable and impregnable bulwark of the American defenses in the Pacific area."[286]

Local Chambers in a Global War

1941–1945

I n the early months of 1941, the nation paused uncomfortably in the no man's land between war and peace. Hitler's armies had conquered much of continental Europe and were preparing for more. The British were hanging on gamely but only with the help of submarine-threatened supplies from their North American cousins.

Most Americans did not want to see their nation go to war against Hitler, but they did want to be prepared for the worst. The hurried buildup of the armed forces continued, and was going well in many respects, noted General George Marshall, Chief of Staff of the Army, to a Senate committee on April 22. The Army boasted 1.25 million men under arms with "the highest morale I've ever seen," he said.

But some things weren't going as fast as he desired. After three months – half the time allotted for the whole job - the Army had selected only seven of 28 training sites for its new recruits. The requirements were considerable, as was the space needed for these new cantonments.

"I think I've become personally unpopular with practically every Chamber of Commerce in the United States," he said, "as a result of the problems which arise when we seek, as we have to, to displace people from the large areas required."[1] World War II was a bigger war than World War I and required bigger training camps. Guns were more powerful and shot further than in World War I, the new tanks tore up land liberally, and the "triangular" structure of Marshall's divisions needed extra room to operate.[2]

Despite the difficulties, Marshall and his lieutenants pushed ahead, with local chambers of commerce greasing the wheels and tank treads of progress. He told the U.S. Chamber, "This is a war of smokestacks as well as of men."[3] The massive wealth of the country needed to be Marshalled, so to speak, for the war effort, providing a nearly insuperable advantage over the country's opponents – much as the nation's industrial might had aided in victories in other great wars, such as the Civil War and World War I.

Where soldiers and war-making capacity was concentrated, space was at a premium. An extreme example was Fort Bragg, N.C., which housed 5,000 soldiers on June 1, 1940, and was scheduled to have 63,000 12 months later. By February of 1941, I.M. Richardson, the secretary of the chamber of commerce in Fayetteville, had helped 1,000 officers and their families to find homes. He and the chamber weren't paid for this. Rents had risen 25 to 35 percent and many families had doubled up in homes to free up housing for newcomers.[4]

The Fayetteville Chamber's tasks were difficult, but not unique. One chamber executive, Albert Stowe of Alexandria, Louisiana, politely refused to answer a survey by NACOS. He explained his refusal by saying, "I am simply up against the practical job of working with 472,000 troops that are coming now and during the next several weeks for the biggest peace-time maneuvers in American history."[5] Stowe may have had himself to blame for the influx: at the beginning of 1940 he had reported to NACOS that the coming troops were the results of several years' effort by his chamber to attract military investment.[6]

By the middle of 1941, more than 700 chambers of commerce had defense committees, handling everything from the manufacture of armaments to finding homes for soldiers.[7] Indeed, the job description was never completely clear. For example, the Eugene, Ore., Chamber of Commerce helped Private Chuck Green find a local girl he had met while on leave at Fort Lewis. He had really liked the girl but couldn't remember her name. She might have been "Alice." As Green described her to the administrative assistant at the chamber, she said, "Wow." Somehow with this information the chamber found the girl, Alice Heinke, who promised to write to Green, her now very public private.[8]

Even in what we now know was the early stage of mobilization for a massive war effort, there were great contrasts between how things were done in peacetime and what was needed for war. The secretary of the Meadville, Pa., Chamber of Commerce, C.W. Williams, described how a local machine tool maker produced a big boring machine that could hollow out large naval guns. A British purchasing agent asked the price and was told it was normally $8,000, but the 32-person firm was busy and any additional orders would be priced at $14,000 each. Not much later, the company's owner received a call requesting 150 machines at $14,000 each. The owner hung up the phone and fainted. "He couldn't make 150 between now and Gabriel's trumpet call," Williams said.[9]

Selling arms and supplies to the government was a giant business and a complex one. Many chambers did all they could to help their members wend their way through the bureaucracy in Washington, D.C. or in military bases scattered around the country. The Chicago Assocation of Commerce reported that in a single year it had trained 10,000 local business executives in the ins and outs of government procurement.[10]

The rapidly growing production volumes and military expenditures made a mark upon the country – literally. In August 1941, for the first time, the map of the United States in *Nation's Business* was completely white, meaning that every state and region was doing more business than it was the year before.[11] For most people and most chambers barely out of the Great Depression, the good things about growth far outweighed the bad. Earlier in 1941, the Los Angeles Chamber of Commerce had been fielding complaints about private aircraft being crowded out of the area's airports by military planes; by July, the chamber was reporting that local aircraft makers were hiring a phenomenal 5,000 people per month to build even more military airplanes.[12] Growth caused inconveniences of all kinds – but it still looked a lot better than Depression-era stagnation.

This was a time of surprises, many of them on foreign shores. Earl Browder, the general secretary of the Communist Party of the United States, had said in 1939 that the chances of a Nazi-Soviet alliance were about as likely as Browder's election "as president of the Chamber of Commerce of the United States."[13] That same year, Molotov and Ribbentrop had signed such a nonaggression pact, shocking a lot of people including Browder.

But Stalin was not laughing at an even bigger surprise that occurred on June 22, 1941. Early on that morning, in a terrifying reversal of the Molotov-Ribbentrop Pact, 4 million Nazi troops mobilized and crossed the border into the Soviet Union. Hitler had double-crossed his erstwhile Communist allies.

And all of a sudden, things were looking brighter in beleaguered Britain and in the United States as well. Four days after the invasion began, Colonel Josiah Wedgwood, a Labor Party leader and Member of Parliament, addressed the British Empire Chamber of Commerce in New York. Hearing of the attack was the greatest joy of his life, he said. He thought there was a good chance the Russians would win a guerrilla war against Hitler. And he hoped that afterward, the United States would shoulder some of the responsibilities of keeping the peace in Europe.[14]

Meanwhile, the nation's capital was in near chaos. Washington needed some rational way to organize its mounting efforts against Nazism. Military personnel and their civilian support staff were scattered among 17 different buildings in the District of Columbia. This disorganized real estate fostered disorganized administration – which surely would only get worse as more workers crowded into the nation's capital. It was clear that the nation's armed forces needed a very large building or set of buildings to accommodate lots of workers – about 40,000 of them.

Where to put it? The District of Columbia was the first choice of many. But this could cause congestion. Moreover, as the president of the Arlington Chamber of Commerce, E.L. Usilton, said, buying a site in the District could cost up to $100 million. "Why not use land already owned by the Government?" he asked. Of course, Usilton thought the best place for the building would be on federal property in Arlington.[15] There was plenty of opposition, but soon Usilton and his allies, mostly because of the merits of their case and not because of political arm-twisting, would get their way. The Pentagon – a massive house for living defense workers - would rise from the dust not too far from where thousands of dead military heroes lay.

Staying Out of War

Despite all this activity, the United States still was not at war. And this was as it should be, according to many if not most Americans, and to quite a few chamber executives. Business organizations had a marked tendency to be conservative about government projects, including those megaprojects known as wars.

Formally constituted chambers of commerce had been in existence in America for 173 years by 1941. And during that long period they had frequently exhibited an aversion to war. A brief reexamination of key points in their history will illuminate their basic, although not complete, predilection toward peace.

In the years just before the Revolutionary War, the New York Chamber took no clear stand for or against revolution, and most of its members ended up on the Loyalist side.

The Charleston Chamber was formed not to dump British tea in the ocean, but to get it safely ashore. In 1795, the New York and Boston chambers gave a critical boost to President Washington's attempts to keep peace with Britain via the ratification of the Jay Treaty.

Just before the Civil War, the New York Chamber circulated a peace petition that was interpreted by posterity and by many contemporaries as a blatant attempt to placate the South and undermine the authority of the incoming President, Abraham Lincoln.

During the Venezuela crisis of 1895-6, the New York Chamber publicly called for international arbitration of the dispute at a time when President Cleveland had rattled the sabers of war. The New York Chamber's successful 1896 foray into peace-making was criticized at the time by some as bordering on treason – and this when it wasn't public knowledge that the New York Chamber was acting in collusion with, and indeed at the request of, the London Chamber of Commerce.

Sereno Pratt, secretary of the New York Chamber from 1908 to 1915, wrote extensively on how chambers of commerce were a force for peace. The U.S. Chamber sent a large delegation to the League to Enforce Peace that was created in 1915.[16] Fully 96 percent of the American chambers polled supported the peace-oriented League of Nations in 1918.[17] And U.S. chambers took the lead in establishing the International Chamber of Commerce in 1919, an organization with a mandate for creating peace through commerce. A later publication chronicling the ICC would be entitled *Merchants of Peace*.

Chambers' long history of commercial arbitration – some of it formal and much of it informal – figured into their push for peaceful negotiations among nations. Perhaps it was all based on a simple instinct to minimize risk and damages and get on with business. Some chamber executives, notably in the New York Chamber, consciously viewed international peace efforts as an outgrowth of their tinier struggles, through arbitration, to keep business disputes from erupting into costly litigation. IBM's Tom Watson would say during the middle of World War II, "If the principles of arbitration had been fully understood, appreciated and put into practice, the war which is not being waged would not have occurred."[18]

In the prelude to World War II, the process of reaching toward peace continued, sometimes to an extent that today we find distasteful or even disastrous. We have seen how ICC President Tom Watson not only accepted a medal from Hitler but helped give the Nazi leader international respectability and did a great deal of business with his regime, aiding its war and extermination machines.

We may even skip ahead to the civil rights era, beyond the immediate scope of this book, to see the chamber peace instincts continue to be in play. In dozens if not hundreds of communities in the South, chambers of commerce took on the job of tamping down racial tensions and attempting an accommodation with integration. This was not, in most cases, simply out of a pioneering enchantment with the idea of equality between blacks and whites, but perhaps primarily out of a desire to comply with federal law and to see business continue and grow, without disruption and without a public black eye to the community. When Martin Luther King Jr. defended an agreement that integrated much of downtown Atlanta, he was referring to an arbitration effort that involved, on businesses' side, Ivan Allen Jr., the president of the Atlanta Chamber of Commerce. Business works best where there is peace, both at home and abroad. And so for chambers of commerce, peace was usually the preferred option.

Thus, from anecdotal evidence and from logic, we can sense and perhaps understand a common chamber propensity toward peace, over a span of many decades. There were, of course, in a country that would one day have thousands of chambers, plenty of exceptions. During the leadup to the War of 1812, there were many belligerent screams of pain coming from coastal chambers of commerce, whose members' sailors and ships were being seized by the British navy. And lots of chambers before World War I militated for "preparedness" – not the same as agitating for war, but for some a step in that direction.

Furthermore, once war was declared, chambers of commerce traditionally were hotbeds of activity. Especially in the largest conflicts – the Civil War and World War I - U.S. chambers of commerce went to significant lengths to help bring about victory. The spirit of local boosterism and pride could quickly translate to a powerful will to win at the national level.

Still, there is a clear message from the history of American chambers that these organizations were not always the first into a fight. Intuitively, it's not surprising. Business people have more financial assets at risk than most of their compatriots. Like any good investors, they hesitate to risk their capital for uncertain returns. There are plenty of better investment options than those large, expensive, tax-friendly, unpredictable federal projects teeming with bullets and billets.

As political organizations with a basic leaning or propensity toward peace, chambers had played a significant role in the shaping of American foreign policy. The simple act of chamber (and broader business) support for the Jay Treaty in 1795 may have saved the fragile Union from the destruction or partition that could have resulted from war with Britain for the second time in two decades. Walter Russell Mead has shown in *Special Providence: American Foreign Policy and How It Changed the World* how contending factions in American democracy have quietly guided the country toward an international orientation that has been basically successful, enabling the country to grow to become a vast continental power and the richest nation on earth.[19] Chambers of commerce are only one set of institutions in a very rich American foreign-policy mix, but they have played a role over the years, not always on the front pages, but sometimes significant in the formation of national opinion on international strategy.

The idea that chambers have had a predominately peaceful orientation (at least before major wars break out) is perhaps strengthened and partly explained by academic findings that show that countries that trade together extensively are the least likely to fight one another – even less likely than democracies are to fight one another. The example of World War I, when most of the belligerent countries traded extensively with one another before the war, is the exception rather than the rule. An excellent summary of these academic findings and their implications can be found in Steven Pinker's *The Better Angels of Our Nature: Why Violence Has Declined*. Tom Watson, despite his frightening lapses of ethics and morality, was not completely off base with his motto of "world peace through world trade."

If U.S. chambers of commerce have had a tendency, whether slight or large, to favor peace, that looks good to us today in most cases. After all, most of us prefer peace to war, most of the time. But in the case of "just" wars, or those we today view as just, then opposition to them appears in hindsight to be misguided. It can even appear to be cowardly (much as we view British Prime Minister Neville Chamberlain's policy of appeasement of Hitler).

The U.S. Chamber took a position on war with Hitler that today doesn't look either courageous or wise. Nevertheless, the chamber's position was not far from the mainstream opinion of the time, and well within the peace-seeking tradition of many American chambers of commerce. Let's go back to our story and see some of the U.S. Chamber's activities in the pivotal year of 1941.

The New New Deal

The New Deal had never been a favorite among most chambers of commerce, and by the end of the Thirties, it still wasn't clear to many people that President Roosevelt's economic policies had done any good. Indeed, plenty of people shared U.S. Chamber President Gibson Carey's verdict that the government aggrandizement under FDR had been a "crime." But FDR's political skills had far outmatched those of his opponents (although to be sure he had, after all, kept the banks open). Many business executives and chamber officials felt tricked and cheated into the adoption of an alien economic system, one that was bad for the country and that had proven its ineffectiveness.

But like a clever magician, Roosevelt seemed to have come up with a new New Deal to distract attention from the failure of the old. This new project was support for Great Britain in its struggle against Hitler. And, economically speaking, there was no doubt that this policy boosted activity, at least in the short run. FDR's opponents worried about the long-run implications of increasing government debt for investments that were, by definition, unproductive. Exploding shells and long-range bombers were meant to destroy economic activity, not to create it. And there was that minor additional matter of stopping a German war machine that appeared to be more powerful and effective than any military organization in history.

Kemper argued this point of view to the Chicago Association of Commerce in early January 1941. Dictatorships, he said, are essentially formed as receivers for countries that have gone bankrupt. The United States seemed to be hurtling in this direction as it spent wildly to build up its military. The country should take "a good long look at the ultimate obligation, realizing that, win or lose, we still might lose."

In Kemper's view, this was a war that, literally, we could not afford. But we were getting tricked into it: "As I see it, the gravest peril we face is that the government, with the support of minority groups, may move so closely to the brink of war that events over which we have no control then may take charge of matters and force us into the struggle." Kemper praised the America First movement, whose most famous spokesperson was Charles Lindbergh. This group sternly opposed the pro-British policies that threatened to embroil the United States in war.[20] The U.S. Chamber leadership also opposed Lend-Lease, America's lifeline of military and other aid to Britain, unless it was strictly nonmilitary and controlled by Congress – conditions that would denude it of any value to the beleaguered islanders besieged by Hitler.

Merle Thorpe, the editor of *Nation's Business*, expressed the U.S. Chamber's antiwar stance with the occasional rhetorical flourish:

> Let us have this, then, from our leaders. Do they indeed think that America is in danger of foreign invasion? Do they see the Luftwaffe and Panzer divisions running over Boston, Cleveland, Memphis and Minneapolis? We cannot go to war today because bombing planes of 1960 may be able to cross the ocean in six hours.[21]

In April 1941 he opined, not very robustly, "Those who strive to hold America back from the pit of war are not cravens."[22] And yet it was fear itself that appeared to undermine his arguments and those of others in the isolationist camp. The confidence of President Roosevelt, and his sympathy for Hitler's victims, contrasted embarrassingly with Thorpe's hand-wringing appeals such as:

> And yet we fear – fear deeply, and for more than our lives. We fear the destruction of the American way of life.[23]

Thorpe's strident nay-saying would even continue after Pearl Harbor, when he became an alliterative nabob of negativism: "It is possible, if not probable, that the proud and profligate American republic may lose."[24]

In a sense, the bleak messages of the *Nation's Business* editorials were the culmination of 10 years of opposition. Their tone was reminiscent of the sour, pinch-mouthed profile of Hoover's hangdog Presidential campaign in 1932. This outlook wasn't a winning strategy, either for economic downturn or European war or for domestic political struggles. In retrospect, the leadership coup that would transform the U.S. Chamber in 1942 was overdue. The nation's leading business organization would adopt a positive approach in many things, including toward the great war that the chamber had so ardently tried to avoid.

Clinging to Normalcy

War may have been impending for the United States in the first 11 months of 1941, but no one knew it for certain. And so for many local chambers, life went on as best it could, with a few adjustments to the growing sense of international menace. Domestic concerns remained a leading part of the American chambers' agendas.

For the chamber in Sacramento, fighting off others' attempts to siphon off government work was a continuing challenge. Monterey attempted unsuccessfully to get the state capital moved to its shoreline community, while up the coast, San Francisco managed to finagle many state government offices that the Sacramento Chamber would prefer to see in the state capital.[25] And still further up the state, the chamber in tiny Yreka engaged in a quixotic attempt to create a new state out of northern California and southern Oregon.[26]

The powerful Merchants' Association of New York, that steady ally to the oldest chamber of them all (the New York Chamber of Commerce), underwent a couple of important changes. Its top paid official, S. Cristy Mead, also the founding president of the National Association of Commercial Organization Secretaries, stepped down in 1941 after 44 years at the helm of the merchants' group.[27] And months afterward the Merchants' Association, which actually claimed to represent 68 different lines of business, changed its name to the broader moniker of the Commerce and Industry Association of New York.[28]

With the uptick in economic activity, chambers found it easier to sign up new members. No doubt as a result, a new organization was created to help spread best practices among the specialists who recruited members. It was called the National Association of Membership Directors.[29]

Hundreds of chambers had fought, and were still fighting, to get the defense contracts and training camps that almost guaranteed full employment. But there was another area that chambers still could affect, and that they had been involved with for many decades: tourism.

Much of the activity, as always, occurred in communities near the water. The chamber in Long Beach, Washington, to publicize its clam-baking event, created the world's largest frying pan, 14.6 feet in diameter. Local girls skated on butter to kick off the cooking of the world's largest clam fritter.[30]

Other tourist-friendly festivals continued, including the Miss America Pageant in Atlantic City. The chamber's secretary, Thomas Husselton, dressed as King Neptune in a suit of clam shells and imitation seaweed as he announced the chamber's beauty contest. "Gosh, I'm roasting in this suit," he confided later. (It was 96 degrees in the shade.)[31] Sadly, not every shore was welcoming. Many beaches were segregated according to race. And the chamber in Lake Geneva, Illinois, advertised its attractive community and lake shore, but only "to a Gentile clientele."

Chamber tourism promotion was not without controversy. In Brighton Beach, New York, the chamber had promoted rules prohibiting individuals from providing space in their homes to allow visitors to change in and out of bathing suits. (This took away business from the city's licensed bath houses.) One of the first violators caught under the new rules was none other than the wife of Joseph Gerowitz, the chamber's vice president. She called the enforcement a "frame up."[32]

Inland, an emerging tourism success story was in Las Vegas. There, the chamber's persuasion of Thomas Hull to set up a gambling hotel had worked out well. The hotel opened on April 3, 1941 to lots of activity. Indeed, business was so good that the project caught the eye of another entrepreneur, Ben Siegel. "Bugsy" and his mob friends soon would be transforming the landscape of the city with their own gambling resort investments.[33] (Bugsy would even promote his Flamingo Hotel project at the chamber in 1946.[34])

Show business was always of interest to local chambers. It had become common practice for studios to promote "premiere junkets" in which movie stars would come to the scene of films on the day of their release.[35] A famous example was MGM's star-studded premiere of *Gone with the Wind* in Atlanta in 1939. Chambers were often involved in paying the travel expenses for these demanding stars. One such community was Lawrence, Kansas, whose chamber sponsored the Lawrence premiere of the movie *Dark Command,* which premiered in Lawrence in April 1940.[36] One chamber didn't have to find out-of-town star power: the radio personality Fibber McGee was known on the airwaves as head of the imaginary Wistful Vista Chamber of Commerce. But in 1941 he was also elected president of a real one, in Encino, Calif.[37]

At the NACOS annual meeting in mid-October 1941 in Los Angeles, movie-maker Louis B. Mayer introduced many stars to the appreciative audience. In a short concluding speech, he noted that in one thing without question, the United States was tops. "We are supreme in movie-making and we will not have it any other way," he said. The Germans and others were way behind us at least in this area.[38]

Somehow, despite the threat of Hitler's armies and submarines in and around Europe, people kept their eyes on the needs of the Pacific theater as well. The Honolulu Chamber of Commerce listened to Hawaiian Department Commander of the Army Gen. Walter Short announce in April 1941 that the territory needed to prepare for war and to have an "organization of doctors and nurses to care for injured and wounded."[39] And Secretary of the Navy Frank Knox told the Providence Chamber of Commerce on November 11, "The only thing we can be sure of is that the Pacific, no less than the Atlantic, calls for instant readiness for defense."[40]

Meanwhile, further south in the Pacific theater, the Hollywood Chamber of Commerce continued its famous Christmas parade down "Santa Claus Lane." It was Bob Hope who led the parade in 1941: he sat on an old nag that clumped aimlessly down Hollywood Boulevard. A huge sign that Hope had placed in front of the beleaguered broomtail read, "Bing Crosby's Fastest Racehorse."[41] The date was December 6.

Pearl Harbor

John Hamilton, secretary of the Honolulu Chamber of Commerce, heard the announcement of an impending attack by Japanese airplanes but could hardly believe it. He quickly went outside and saw 10 planes approaching. -

> There were three impressions which passed through my mind. The first was that it cannot be an enemy attack, the second, if it is an enemy attack it will just be too bad for the enemy, and the third was the final truth when the news of the damage done was made known. **This last and final impression was pressed home some two hours after the attack when a call came over the radio to report to my office in town. The call had to do with the need for more blood donors to save the lives of the wounded of the Army, the Navy, and defense workers.**[42]

The chamber's Public Health Committee had set up a blood bank in early 1941 and put the blood in cold storage in November, just a month before the bombing. The largest blood bank in the territory at the time, it was of critical importance as the tolls of wounded mounted. It was credited with saving scores of lives.

But more blood was needed. Fortunately, the chamber had the names of its hundreds of donors. It rounded them up and all of them save one (a bedridden patient) gave again.[43]

The attack was indeed devastating. It killed 2,402 Americans and wounded 1,282 others while sending four battleships to the bottom. The shock was complete. Clearly, despite all its warnings about the Pacific theater, the U.S. military was unprepared. At least the chamber's blood bank worked.

The attack suddenly solved the question of whether the United States should become a combatant nation. President Roosevelt, calling December 7 "a date which will live in infamy," urged a declaration of war on Japan, with which Congress complied by a vote of 82 to 0 in the Senate and 338 to 1 in the House.[44] Hitler then threw in his lot with Imperial Japan, declaring war on the United States on December 11. Now it was truly a second world war.

Businesses and their organizations quickly pledged their support. Two thousand telegrams arrived at U.S. Chamber headquarters on December 8 alone.[45] Chamber President A.W. Hawkes said his group favored "all necessary sacrifices" to win the war, including, when possible, 24-hour, seven-day-a-week production.[46] This would prove to be yet another conflict in which the nation's industrial might would help determine the fate of distant armies and navies.

Shock and Awful

The surprise attack on Hawaii caused many people, naturally, to wonder what would come next. Would there be an invasion of the West Coast or sabotage of the country's industries? Authorities raided the offices of Japanese-connected organizations, including the Japanese Chamber of Commerce in San Francisco and New York. If there was a fifth column in the United States, including among Japanese-Americans, the authorities wanted to unearth it.

Interestingly, and reassuringly to most of us today, the atmosphere on the West Coast (where many anticipated the next attack would take place) was initially calm toward its 117,000 Japanese-Americans. Newspaper articles were overwhelmingly positive and affirming these people's loyalty to the United States. Things began to change in January, however. Then the movement toward evacuation of Japanese-Americans happened with stunning rapidity: President Roosevelt signed the order for internment in the middle of February, 1942. What happened to cause such a sudden public policy change?

Even today, it's disputed as to what were the primary reasons for the evacuation. Morton Grodzins, a Ph.D. student at the University of California at Berkeley, wrote a dissertation on the evacuation order that placed most of the blame on civic groups, including chambers of commerce, which raised an outcry against the Japanese-Americans and influenced politicians to push for evacuation. He later published a polemical book on the topic, *Americans Betrayed: Politics and the Japanese Evacuation.*[47]

Grodzins's research had been part of a large project, the Japanese American Evacuation and Resettlement Study (JERS), handled out of U.C. Berkeley. His supervisors there, by some accounts angry at his unapproved solo attack on those responsible for the evacuation, attempted to stop him from publishing and subsequently three scholars issued a book that aimed at refuting his findings: *Prejudice, War and the Constitution: Causes and Consequences of the Evacuation of the Japanese Americans in World War II.*[48] These authors disputed many of Grodzins's claims and essentially concluded that the evacuation decision was based on widely shared racial bias that worked its way into a faulty decision by the military.

Part of the reason for the controversy was that things happened so quickly, often in conversations that were not recorded, so that in hindsight no one can point to exactly what led to what. The authors of *Prejudice, War and the Constitution* could see no evidence that the military was influenced significantly by civilian activity. Yet there are grounds for being skeptical of these authors' belief. A lot was happening behind the scenes in December 1941 and early 1942. And one of the primary orchestrators of that activity was the Los Angeles Chamber of Commerce.

The Los Angeles Chamber of Commerce was the first organization to call publicly for controls on the activities of Japanese-Americans on the West Coast. The agricultural committee of the chamber – a curious subgroup, perhaps, to be dealing with a purely military issue - recommended on December 22, 1941, that Japanese-Americans in the area be placed "under absolute federal control."[49]

Just four days later, a representative of the Los Angeles Chamber visited Allen W. Gullion, the War Department's Provost Marshal General, asking for the military authorities to gather up all the Japanese in greater Los Angeles. Gullion was nonplussed. When Gullion spoke with General John DeWitt, Commander of the Western Defense Command, on the same day, both generals were scratching their heads. DeWitt said (and Gullion agreed with him) in a routinely recorded telephone conversation:

> I thought that thing out to my satisfaction. . . . If we go ahead and arrest the 93,000 Japanese, native born and foreign born [in California], we are going to have an awful job on our hands and are very liable to alienate the loyal Japanese from disloyal . . . I'm very doubtful that it would be common sense procedure to try and intern or to intern 117,000 Japanese in this [West Coast] theater. . . . I told the governors of all the states that those people should be watched better if they were watched by the police and people of the community in which they live and have been living for years . . . and then inform the F.B.I. or the military authorities of any suspicious action so we could take necessary steps to handle it . . . rather than try to intern all those people, men, women, and children, and hold them under military control and under guard. I don't think it's a sensible thing to do. . . . I'd rather go along the way we are now. . . . rather than attempt any such wholesale internment. . . . An American citizen, after all, is an American citizen. And while they may not all be loyal, I think we can weed the disloyal out of the loyal and lock them up if necessary.[50]

General DeWitt, a dithering but important figure in these events, soon changed his mind about evacuation. By mid-January, as the public uproar to put away the Japanese-Americans grew, so did his concerns about their potential danger to the United States war effort. Was this because of acts of sabotage? Not exactly. In fact, as he told Provost Marshal Gullion on January 24, nothing had happened. But that was the problem! "The fact that nothing has happened so far is . . . more or less ominous," he told Gullion. This indicated, he said, that "there is control being exercised and when we have it it will be on a mass basis."[51]

In this irrational moment, then, the lack of evidence became evidence. And pressures mounted. On January 28, the Roberts Report on the Pearl Harbor attack was released, claiming that local subversion in Hawaii contributed to the success of the Japanese attack. (Its findings were later debunked.) Pressures grew from angry civic groups and politicians. On January 29, James Ingebretsen, the Washington representative of the Los Angeles Chamber, invited California congressmen to the office of the Speaker of the House for a discussion regarding Japanese evacuation. After lunch, Ingebretsen drew up a resolution for the congressmen to consider.

General John DeWitt

The paper was a "detailed set of policy recommendations" urging evacuation of Japanese-Americans on the West Coast.[52] The congressmen approved it enthusiastically and endorsed the identical document the following day in their own meeting, to which the only non-congressman permitted was Ingebretsen. The report became known as Costello's, even though Ingebretsen had written it, after consulting his boss Leonard Read, the general manager of the Los Angeles Chamber of Commerce.[53] The Costello resolution's recommendations were not far from the evacuation policy set forth in Executive Order 9066, signed by President Roosevelt on February 19, 1942, over the objections of J. Edgar Hoover and others.

Clearly the Los Angeles Chamber of Commerce was involved in the efforts to push for evacuation of the Japanese-Americans. But involvement is one thing; causation is another. General DeWitt and his military colleagues initially were skeptical of the idea of interning Japanese-Americans. Was DeWitt influenced by the clamor from civic groups, including (but certainly not limited to) chambers of commerce, in the final decision for internment? Here, it is instructive to see what two of the Los Angeles Chamber executives thought, in interviews with Morton Grodzins.

Although Grodzins probably was not aware of this fact, Chamber Managing Director Leonard Read was a libertarian – just about the last person one would expect to try to lock up more than 100,000 innocent people. Read was a confident man, Grodzins wrote: "Read is the picture of a successful executive. Slim, youngish looking, rapid talking, piercing gaze, etc. He is also damn intelligent."[54]

The 1943 interview notes by Grodzins show that Read was a man not a bit ashamed of his role in the internment. But Read convincingly debunked the idea (pursued by Grodzins in his 1949 book) that greed was the motive for internment. Said Read to Grodzins:

> I took a great deal of effort to help to get the Japanese off the coast in 1942 and I've spent a good deal of time keeping them off the coast in 43. But I think the Japanese were good for the economy of California before they were removed and I think they will be good for the economy of the state when they come back. I will certainly not oppose their return after the war. I will fight hard to keep them away during the war, not for any economic reasons but solely because I am afraid of the consequences to both our military and industrial installations and to the Japanese themselves. The Japanese produced good products at low cost. They supplied real competition and competition made America what it is today. I would be the last person in the world to want to remove such competition. America lives on it.[55]

Read's views on Japanese-American enterprise (apart from his conviction that they needed to be temporarily removed from their enterprises) fit well into his libertarian point of view. His familiarity with Washington, however, and his clear pride on how well he and his team could work the system, strayed significantly from libertarian orthodoxy:

> We have a good office in Washington. If we get interested in a problem, the Washington office first calls in our own Los Angeles representatives, then we can expand from there, to the Southern California people, the whole California delegation and, in the extreme incident, to the delegations from all the West Coast States. We usually can get what we want. We do a terrific amount of work behind the scenes, filter it to the right place and let the Congressmen themselves take credit for it. We do the work, they do the talking. We don't get the publicity and don't want it. If we got too much publicity, the Congressmen would have to keep away. There's nothing evil about the relationship. It's businesslike and it works. On the Japanese business, we got the Congressmen together not only prior to evacuation in order to get the movement underway, but also more recently to protest any move to let the Japanese come back to the Coast.[56]

Read talked at some length about his efforts to keep the Japanese-Americans in the camps in 1943, despite a move to let some of them return to the Coast. Apparently the Los Angeles

Chamber's work succeeded. Assistant Defense Secretary John McCloy privately admitted to a Berkeley professor that the pressure from the Congressional delegation and other West Coast groups caused him to "back down."[57]

Thus the Los Angeles Chamber had some clout on this issue in Washington. Certainly this was the opinion of James Ingebretsen, its Washington representative. Grodzins described him thus: "Ingebretsen is a youngish man, obviously proud of his position, and vain about the close personal relationships he maintains with the congressmen and senators of California."

Grodzins continued:

> Ingebretsen said that the Chamber of Commerce had deliberately kept in the background because "We frequently accomplish measures for the public good more easily by remaining anonymous."

Ingebretsen said:

> 1 - He had conferred with Congressman Costello before the January 30th meeting and had assisted Costello in drawing up the resolution adopted at that meeting.

> 2- He had gone to several luncheon meetings that the Congressmen held before January 30th at which the Japanese problem was discussed and at which "various representatives and various writers" had urged evacuation. One of these writers, he is certain, was one of the authors of "Mutiny on the Bounty." Several newspaper columnists also spoke.

> 3- He was the only person, other than the congressmen themselves, who was allowed to be present at many of the meetings that were held. He assisted in drawing up the resolution and in formulating the policy recommended to the President. "All . . . told, I was a very useful person to have around because I was well acquainted with the problem both on the coast and in Washington and enjoyed the confidence of the congressional representatives as well as groups from the Pacific coast."

> 4- There was no organization of various chambers of commerce. "It was not necessary to organize. We saw very early that the thing could be carried."[58]

Read and Ingebretsen were extraordinarily confident men. Clearly, they believed their chamber had an impact in Washington. One thing that helped was their close tie with Congressman John Costello. Indeed, after Costello lost his reelection bid in 1944, he became the new Washington representative of the Los Angeles Chamber.[59]

In this attempt to influence national policy, the Los Angeles Chamber had taken a strong stand. It had tried, and, on the face of it at least, succeeded in sparking two changes in U.S. policy on Japanese-Americans: first, to encourage the internment of these people, and then, to keep them interned. The number of civic organizations supporting this activity was significant (although not nearly as massive as Grodzins suggests). Many were chambers of commerce. But none of them played the government as skillfully as those two antigovernment insiders, Read and Ingebretsen, and their colleagues at the LA Chamber.

Did these chamber activities, however, cause General DeWitt to change his mind on the Japanese threat? It's hard to say. That the chamber made at least one direct attempt to influence the military decision, via the December 26 meeting with Provost Marshal Gullion, is beyond dispute. Would the chamber, which had unsurpassed access to the California congressional delegation on the evacuation issue, and which authored the Costello resolution, have abstained from similar efforts to influence the true decision-maker, General DeWitt? That is doubtful. Read and Ingebretsen had access to many people, including to one of DeWitt's superiors, Assistant Secretary of War John McCloy. These two chamber men were as proud of their ability to influence decision-makers as they were anxious not to be seen calling the shots.

In sync with the behind-the-scenes modus operandi of Read and Ingebretsen, after World War II the Los Angeles Chamber of Commerce escaped significant scrutiny for its role in the internment of the Japanese-Americans. Grodzins, while uncovering critical information, was involved in a wide-ranging study and was clearly fascinated by the upsurge of public opinion against Japanese-Americans and how that opinion, in his view, affected public policy. He was acting more as a big-picture scholar, albeit a polemical one, than as a detective in a whodunit. His intellectual opponents on the Japanese-American internment issue accused Grodzins, with some justice, of assessing villains of evacuation that "vary from chapter to chapter" of his book, and lumped him also into the unscientific camp of "students of liberal persuasion."[60]

And so the LA Chamber's role was camouflaged in a wider, inflammatory account of how hysteria and greed put the Japanese-Americans behind barbed wire.[61] Even Read and Ingebretsen's names were thinly disguised, as Larson and Draper, respectively, so that letters and other evidence from them could be used without specific permission. And well before Grodzins's book came out, both men had left the LA Chamber's employment. Arguably, another factor was at work in 1949: the country was in a pugnacious mood again, facing the dangers of communism, and the man and woman in the street had no great desire for extended hand-wringing over the loss of some people's constitutional freedoms years earlier, in the shadow of a surprise attack on U.S. soil.

Grodzins's intellectual opponents seem to have missed the mark on the LA Chamber, too. So anxious to rebut Grodzins, the authors of *Prejudice, War and the Constitution* failed to see that all civic groups are not the same, and that just because they have scant evidence of a certain action or actions does not mean nothing happened. As a result of many factors, DeWitt's mind changed, and Read and Ingebretsen may have had a slight hand – or sleight of hand - in this metamorphosis.

Seldom, however, did the Los Angeles Chamber act alone. In 1942, there were plenty of people with motives to dislodge Japanese-Americans from their lucrative farms and businesses. The manager of the Grower-Shipper Vegetable Association told the *Saturday Evening Post,* "We're charged with wanting to get rid of the Japs for selfish reasons. We might as well be honest. We do. It's a question of whether the white man lives on the Pacific Coast or the brown man."[62] But this intemperate comment, often re-quoted by others, was made by a man from Salinas, California, a community that was in shock. The Salinas Tank Force had been captured on the Bataan Peninsula in the Philippines and many of its young men were suffering and dying on the infamous Bataan Death March. The Salinas Chamber of

Commerce, as we shall see, would later fiercely oppose the return of Japanese-Americans to the area. It was probably misplaced anger more than greed that caused the bitter and frequently racist remarks coming out of the Central Valley of California.

As Grodzins's critics would point out, for every civic group that called for removal of the Japanese-Americans, there were several that didn't. We may never know precisely what role public opinion in general, and civic-group activism in particular, played in the internment decision. Certainly the Los Angeles Chamber of Commerce was only one of many such groups and it, alone, could not have caused such a radical policy change to take place.

Still - what if the chambers of commerce in California and elsewhere that were vocally in favor of internment had, instead, been equally vocal in opposition to internment? On numerous occasions in the past, the Los Angeles Chamber and other West Coast chambers had exercised a calming or restraining influence on the sometimes virulent anti-Japanese or Chinese passions that occasionally flared in the area. It is conceivable that the Los Angeles Chamber and others, if they had reversed course and argued vociferously against separation and internment, might have prevented the evacuation of Japanese-Americans. After all, local chambers in the West exercised considerable influence and had the ear of their members of Congress and even, occasionally, the military. We will never know the answer to that "what if" question – but we do know that in fact, the Los Angeles Chamber of Commerce was just about as involved in the national internment deliberations as a local chamber could be.

The Barbed-Wire Libertarian

The Los Angeles Chamber of Commerce was unusual in its early and extended advocacy of evacuation of Japanese-Americans. And indeed, during the Second World War, this was something of an unusual chamber. From 1939 to 1945, its general manager, Leonard Read, was one of the more colorful and interesting executives of any business organization. To a great extent, the chamber's activities reflected his strong personal enthusiasms and his powerful, although sometimes puzzling, streak of libertarianism.

Read had some experience with hardship early in life. He grew up in Michigan in a happy home, but his father died when he was 11 years old. He joined the Army's Signal Corps in World War I and almost lost his life when the ship taking him to Europe was torpedoed. He saved himself by restraining his impulse to jump into the icy waters and may have been the last man off the ship; about 200 drowned. Read managed to get onto a leaky lifeboat with 30 others and was picked up three hours later by an Irish trawler.[63]

After the war, he started a wholesale fruit and produce business but it foundered under ferocious pressure from retail chain stores. Indeed, the struggle occasionally turned violent and cost the life of a friend of his. Like many Midwesterners with dreams, from Frank Wiggins to Walt Disney, Read picked up and moved to the sunny promised land of California.[64]

Soon after arriving in northern California, the gregarious young man discovered chambers of commerce and fell in love with them. He became the secretary of the ailing Burlingame Chamber of Commerce in early 1927 and his success then brought him to the larger Palo Alto Chamber in 1928. There he managed the chamber as a local favorite son, Herbert Hoover, won the Presidency. Read organized a 16-car railroad train to carry 700 California business people to attend Hoover's inauguration, which caught the attention of the U.S.

Chamber of Commerce. In 1931, Read became the assistant manager of the Western Region of the U.S. Chamber.[65]

At the U.S. Chamber, he got to know many more business people across the state. One such person was W.C. Mullendore, the executive vice president of Southern California Edison. Mullendore, a conservative who was deeply upset at the inroads of the New Deal on American liberty and enterprise, had a conversation with Read in 1933 that changed Read's life. During that meeting, Mullendore convinced Read that the New Deal was a sham and that only complete devotion to the cause of free markets and limited government could take the country out of its funk.

Thereafter, Read followed the guiding principles of libertarianism and he remained close to Mullendore. Both of them realized that the average person in California, or for that matter the United States, wasn't ready for their radical doctrine. But perhaps people could be taught to see the principles of economic and political freedom.

Read, who had missed out on college because he lacked money at the time and was in a rush to get established, was a great believer in education. For 11 years he managed the U.S. Chamber's Western School for Commercial Organization Secretaries. Moreover, he wrote a book published in 1937, *The Romance of Reality*, which outlined his conviction that people should be taught about freedom and that political warfare wasn't the answer to turning back the tide of creeping government involvement in the economy.[66]

Leonard Read

The book brought him attention and his next job: general manager of the Los Angeles Chamber of Commerce in 1939, one of the top chamber jobs in the nation. Here was a bully pulpit from which to spread the free-market gospel. And he did so, sharpening the focus of the organization on the basic principles of economic freedom.

At least, he tried to. But the chamber also had to deal with the real world, which in 1939 was about as troubling as it could be. Before he knew it, in 1940 Read's chamber set up an office in Washington, D.C. to try to obtain more government contracts. Read and his colleagues feared that because so much of the Southern California economic activity was handled by small business, these companies would miss out on the phenomenal amounts of procurement that were coming in the rush to supply the British and strengthen the U.S. military.[67]

Here was a red-hot, antigovernment libertarian seeking more federal government contracts for his members. Surely the contradiction must have occurred to him (and he did cite the difficulty of promoting libertarian work as a chamber executive when he changed jobs in 1945[68]). Then, to top it off, in 1941-43 Read's chamber was one of the organizations in the forefront of the effort to take away the civil liberties of innocent Japanese-Americans on the West Coast.

His comments to Morton Grodzins appear to indicate a lack of racism, but it's not certain he was being entirely forthcoming or consistent in his beliefs. One of Read's letters to the West Coast Congressional delegation begins with a pun on "race":

Gentlemen: This war, more than any other, is a <u>race</u> to make things![69]

Racism, of course, was common in this era, and especially after Pearl Harbor. Read certainly tolerated racism in others. A Harvard professor whom Read revered and praised to NACOS chamber executives, Thomas Nixon Carver, wrote a pamphlet for the chamber in 1945 that included such nuggets as: "No one who studies the subject seriously will dispute the fact that, until Asiatics were excluded, we were in danger of being inundated by millions of oriental coolies."[70]

Read wasn't alone in his arguably peculiar application of libertarian ideas to American political life. He brought all sorts of libertarians to LA Chamber gatherings, including the economist Ludwig von Mises, with whom he would form a lifelong association, and Ayn Rand, with whom he was friends for a time, including when she rocketed to fame with her novel *The Fountainhead* in 1943. Read also found an ideological soul mate in his good friend, the attorney James Ingebretsen, who for a time, as we have seen, ran the Washington office.

Read's Los Angeles Chamber was so attention-getting and active that it attracted the eyes of the U.S. Department of Justice. In November of 1941, the month before Pearl Harbor, U.S. Attorney General Francis Biddle asked J. Edgar Hoover to set a wiretap on the chamber. The wiretap was placed under the standard of "persons suspected of subversive activities" although the chamber had "no record of espionage at this time."[71] We don't know what the wiretap uncovered, if anything. It's certainly ironic, however, that this chamber, which was about to call for the violation of the Constitutional rights of tens of thousands of Japanese-American citizens on grounds of subversion, was apparently suspected of subversion itself.[72]

During World War II, Read's chamber had a well-deserved reputation for right-of-center, if not far-right, politics. Read's chamber was a harbinger of a powerful brand of Los Angeles area conservatism that, among other things, would put two presidents in the White House over the next four decades and rock the political life of the nation. In short, Read was onto something.

In 1946, Read would form the first conservative think tank, called the Foundation for Economic Education, and propagandize for liberty without any limiting requirements of running a local chamber of commerce. The American Enterprise Institute, the Heritage Foundation, the Cato Institute, and many others would follow after him – not sharing all of his beliefs, but leaning toward the right, as he did.

And in the Fifties and beyond, sometimes with his friends Mullendore and Ingebretsen, Read would explore not just the free market but the free spirit. All three became entranced with the idea of finding the inner strengths of the soul. All three would dabble in LSD (although Read and Ingebretsen each claimed to have done it only once). Theirs was a pioneering brand of individualism that was aimed at expanding others' minds.

Indeed, these LA Chamber leaders' actions anticipated much that happened thereafter. For example, Ingebretsen's spiritual odyssey took him to Eastern mysticism as well as to LSD, and he founded a California spiritual retreat, the Academy of Creative Education (later called Koan of the Cross), that was a precursor to the freewheeling Esalen Institute.[73] And the threesome's proselytizing for limits on government, as suggested above, laid a good part of the political foundation for that southern California-nurtured conservative movement that became the Reagan Revolution.[74]

Did Read and Ingebretsen regret what they had done to the Japanese-Americans? They don't seem to have written about it, although both were handy with words and Read wrote a long string of books. The two men may have not have thought much about it. But Read's biographer, who wrote that he spoke out in favor of the Japanese-Americans' rights, probably didn't make that item up completely; likely Read either glossed over his role in the episode or he deliberately misled her. During the war, as noted above, both Read and Ingebretsen emphasized the importance of keeping their political actions out of the public eye.

Finally, in thinking about what Read and Ingebretsen did, or thought they did, to the Japanese-Americans, we should not immediately judge ourselves superior to them. Many mistakes have been made in the fog of war. Sixty years after Pearl Harbor, the United States was attacked by air once again. In the resulting confusion, U.S. troops invaded a country that, we now know, had absolutely nothing to do with the 9-11 attack, nor had any nuclear weapons, as U.S. authorities claimed. So after the shocks of both 1941 and 2001, Americans, perhaps looking to strike someone quickly in retribution, struck at the wrong people.

Let's Get It Done

While Leonard Read and his friends were turning the Los Angeles Chamber into a hotbed of can-do conservatism, something quite different was happening in Washington, D.C. The onset of war did not prevent a conflict of startling suddenness at the U.S. Chamber of Commerce. And the struggle related to the same thing that so bothered Read and Mullendore and Ingebretsen: the New Deal and big government.

We have seen how the U.S. Chamber had opposed just about every major FDR initiative since Henry Harriman stepped down from the presidency in 1935. This included resistance to domestic policies such as public power and employment projects and to the Supreme Court-packing attempt. It also included attacks on foreign activity such as Lend-Lease and other efforts to help the heroic and besieged people of Great Britain. Opposition had become practically a habit on H Street, but the delivery of the message wasn't winning hearts and minds. Continual negativity is the bane of many organizations holding minority points of view – perhaps especially of business organizations, which can easily be accused of greed when they attempt to stand up to increased taxes and regulations.

This negativity was hurting the chamber's image. The President himself had labeled groups such as the U.S. Chamber "Tories." And much of the electorate had loved it.

The LA Chamber's Leonard Read had neatly sidestepped the problem of constant, conservative nay-saying by focusing more on positive education for freedom.[75] He preferred not to engage in too much open hand-to-hand fighting over policy. But the U.S. Chamber's leadership did not have the luxury of passing over what had been happening, and was still happening, in Washington. It needed some authentic voice to grapple with the growing power of government and labor in American life, fueled by the Roosevelt Administration but ultimately because of decisions by the voters. Somehow the U.S. Chamber had to have a winning answer, an alternative message, to FDR and friends.

The storm broke at the annual meeting of the U.S. Chamber in Washington on April 27-30, 1942. Ironically, the meeting carried the title and theme, "Let's Get It Done."[76] The old guard tried to push through a contract to lock in John O'Leary for five more years (at a salary of $40,000) as general manager. O'Leary would represent more of the same old, naysaying policies. An almost spontaneous revolt took place, led by moderate Western-ers but soon joined in by many traditionalists as well. The reformers tabled the proposed contract and swept a surprisingly young man into the presidency of the organization: Eric Johnston. O'Leary would depart from the U.S. Chamber in July 1942 and be replaced by a more moderate and very popular man, Ralph Bradford, who had handled the interface with local chambers for the U.S. Chamber and previously was chief executive of the chamber in Corpus Christi, Texas.[77]

Boy Wonder of Business

Eric Johnston (originally "Johnson") was born in Washington, D.C., in late 1895. But he grew up in the state of Washington, where his family moved in 1905. The young man lived in "genteel penury." His father was a perpetually unsuccessful pharmacist. In 1911, when they lived in Spokane, his parents divorced. His mother subsequently changed their sur-name to "Johnston," very possibly out of anger; it is likely that Bertram Johnson did not provide the promised child support.[78]

Eric Johnston was a bayonet instructor for the Marines during World War I, then went to Russia and served in the American Expeditionary Force there. He was subsequently named a military attaché to the American legation in Peking (Beijing). Here he managed, on the side, to parlay $100 in military pay to $5,000 by speculating in Chinese currency. But he had to come home after complications from receiving a sharp blow on the head from a Chinese hoodlum.[79]

Like another chamber leader, Tom Watson of IBM, Eric Johnston early in his career earned a living selling items door to door. His products were vacuum cleaners, which he started offering shortly after his return to the United States in 1922. The good-looking, boyish, articulate young man seems to have won the business of quite a few housewives in the Northwest. (Many of the articles written about him later, especially those by women, include the word "handsome.")

He was a born salesperson and administrator. The vacuum cleaner company, headed by a man named Power Brown, soon became the Brown-Johnston Company, and Johnston bought out his partner by 1928. The business grew steadily, even during the Depression. Its value rose from about $20,000 in 1922 to $200,000 in 1941 and $1 million in 1945.[80] John-ston managed to take over and revive an ailing brick company during the Depression, too.

But Johnston also had a great interest in public life and politics, and became president of the Spokane Chamber of Commerce in 1931. During his two years at the helm of that business group, the self-confessed city booster frequently visited the U.S. Chamber in the "other Washington" and also secured approval for a $711,000 post office for Spokane and the Northwest headquarters for the Regional Agricultural Credit Corporation, a farm lending organization connected with the U.S. Farm Credit Administration.[81] The Spokane Chamber also championed, and was anticipating the benefits from, the giant, federally fi-nanced Grand Coulee Dam (built from 1933 to 1942). From the perspective of many in the Spokane Chamber, including Johnston, the federal government appeared more of a help than a hindrance to local business.

He was elected to be a director of the U.S. Chamber in 1934. In 1940 he made a last-minute run for the Republican nomination for the Senate in Washington, but only got 18 percent of the vote. He did, however, make further progress at the U.S. Chamber, winning election as a vice president in 1941 and then of course as the insurgent candidate for president in 1942.

Johnston essentially became the "war president" of the U.S. Chamber. He served four terms, ending in 1945, and received far more public recognition than any of his predecessors. In 1943 alone, U.S. newspapers carried 9,399 editorials about him.[82] He was more famous in this period than any business figure in the nation except perhaps the great industrialist and shipbuilder Henry Kaiser, and more in the public eye than Henry Ford himself.[83] He was occasionally compared to Wendell Willkie, another business-friendly moderate, who had come from nowhere to give FDR a scare in the Presidential race of 1940.

Soon after taking over his post at the U.S. Chamber, the son of the feckless pharmacist met the U.S. President. FDR was anathema to most of the U.S. Chamber's old guard, and none of its presidents had conferred with Roosevelt since 1937. To Johnston, the Democratic head of state was a potential partner. The two men came together for a half-hour session on May 22, 1942 that ballooned to 90 minutes. Roosevelt began the meeting with the wry remark, "Eric Johnston, how did they ever elect *yew* president of the U.S. Chamber?"[84]

In a striking Nixon-goes-to-China move, Johnston met each of the nation's two top labor leaders, Philip Murray of the Congress of Industrial Organizations (CIO) and William Green of the American Federation of Labor (AFL).[85] Surprisingly, Johnston got along with each of them. This led to a larger meeting on July 23, 1942 that included these three, President Roosevelt, and other top labor and chamber officials such as the AFL's George Meany, and William Witherow of the National Association of Manufacturers.[86]

The conference eventually would spark several positive developments, including Big Labor's pledge not to engage in strikes as long as the war lasted (although, of course, there were independent labor bosses such as the United Mine Workers' John L. Lewis who objected to this idea). Roosevelt was surprised and pleased by this labor-chamber amity. "Looks like the lions and the lambs were lying down together," he said. "Only I don't know which are the lions."[87]

Johnston believed in the "people's capitalism," in a third way between warring labor and management. There was food for everyone with an expanding economic pie. His was a captivating, fresh look at opportunity, not a hand-wringing diatribe against government. "Beaten paths are for beaten men," he said.[88] The press loved it. During the war years, the public got to hear plenty of optimism coming out of H Street. "We shall emerge from this devastating conflict with a new national soul," he proclaimed.[89]

The U.S. Chamber president even visited Russia during the war. He travelled thousands of miles and saw war plants in remote parts of the country. He met Communist Party General Secretary Joseph Stalin, regaling him with tales of the U.S. economy and comparing it to that of the Soviet Union. At one point Stalin said with a laugh, "I'm the capitalist; you're the Communist!"[90]

Here was the voice of labor-management cooperation, of free trade, of Democratic-Republican consensus on war fighting and postwar prosperity. After the long Depression, it was refreshing. Instead of crabby old men wielding sticks, here was a young man offering carrots. A *Life* magazine writer toward the end of the war concluded that "he has already fulfilled his destiny, which was to rescue a class – the class comprising the American business community – from despair and even from possible suicide."[91]

It wasn't a bad resume. But in American public life, as Johnston himself once said, it's three jumps from the master bedroom to the doghouse. Sadly, after the war Johnston's facility for compromise and business friendliness would besmirch his reputation, at least for proponents of civil liberties. In 1946 he became the president of the Motion Picture Producers and Distributors Association (subsequently the Motion Picture Association of America), which was beset by witch hunts for suspected communists in the entertainment industry. Censorship loomed – the horse-head-in-the-bed nightmare of every producer and movie mogul in Hollywood. Johnston attended a closed-door meeting of the industry in 1947 from which he emerged to announce the infamous blacklist of left-leaning writers and actors. This purported act of industry self-censorship ruined the careers of some of the best talent in Hollywood. The tactic took political pressure off the motion picture industry but left a black mark on the industry that lingers to this day.

President Truman (front and center) with War Mobilization and Reconversion Advisory Board; Eric Johnston is to his left.

Still, in the crisis of World War II, Johnston steered the U.S. Chamber toward a course that was remarkably forward-looking and positive. He anticipated the postwar consensus for moderate policies of government-business-labor cooperation, free trade, and economic expansion. As much as any person, this grinning booster was the sage of the coming business boom and the politics to go with it. Although they followed different gods, and occasionally stumbled badly on their paths, Eric Johnston and Leonard Read each were remarkably far-seeing prophets.

The War Comes Home

Of course, while domestic politics continued to percolate, there was still a fearsome war going on. And the panic that gripped the nation on December 7 continued to affect countless local groups. The fear that the Japanese would attack the mainland was real and palpable.

Several West Coast sporting events were cancelled after Pearl Harbor. Oregon State and Duke were scheduled to play in the Rose Bowl in Pasadena on New Year's Day.[92] The military authorities disapproved of the idea of holding such a huge event in a possible war zone. But they allowed the contest to go on at Duke. Durham Chamber Secretary Frank Pierson promised weather for the game "as fine as that advertised by California." He admitted, however, that at the big game with Pitt in 1938 "it was snowing like the devil – well, not exactly a deep snow – just sort of like a California mist." The chamber drummed up 2,000 homes that would accommodate guests, while the chamber in Pinehurst hosted the Oregon State team for lunch after the players had a golfing lesson.[93]

The East Coast wasn't immune from fears of war. At a local meeting held at the U.S. Chamber headquarters in Washington (which doubled as a sort of community center during the war), Chief Air-Raid Warden Clement Murphy said in February 1942 that people should expect to be bombed. "I believe we are going to die by the thousands on these streets within six months," he said. And the deaths would be literally hair-raising. There would be "hysterical people, people who would actually die from fear, standing up." He continued: "Very few people burn to death. They are scared to death."[94]

With experts like that, who needed enemies? Everyone, however, was learning and trying to adjust to the new round-the-clock war footing. And real enemies were there, too. In what they called the "Second Happy Time" (the first time being when the German U-boats operated before British developed effective countermeasures), German U-boat crews began attacking American shipping, with some of the most appalling results occurring near East Coast ports. There, the bright lights of the harbors silhouetted U.S. ships, making them easy targets.

To make things more difficult for the German sea wolves, the Army issued "dimout" regulations in the spring of 1942. This truly brought the war home to chambers of commerce along the coast. Tourism communities had to have the lights on to attract customers. Chamber members in places such as Atlantic City and Miami, and even on Broadway in New York, screamed in pain. The Greater Wildwood, N.J., Chamber of Commerce speculated that it was "over-dimming" compared with other communities, making the economic hit even worse than it had to be.[95]

Coney Island stood to lose millions in the darkness. Chamber President Charles Kean announced a possible solution in July of 1942: a $50,000 "dimout curtain," 18 feet tall and 14 blocks long, that would keep the light for the tourists but hide it from the Germans.[96] Then Parks Commissioner Robert Moses quashed the plan, noting several objections, including that the curtain would become a community drawing board: "Both sides would be used for art and literature of which 90 percent would be of the gutter type."[97]

Tourism ran into even more troubles as gasoline rationing took hold in 1942.[98] The country had plenty of gas, in fact, but needed to conserve the rubber that was used in tires after the Japanese had overrun the rubber plantations in Southeast Asia. And so the authorities strictly limited gas usage, constricting one of the great feeders of tourism growth since the early 1900s.

Business organizations did their best to cope with the restrictions. The Ocean City, Md., Chamber of Commerce advertised, "No Ration on Pleasure."[99] The Lake Placid Chamber, which had brought the Olympics there in the Twenties, cancelled the local bobsled run to conserve fuel and rubber.[100]

Some chambers, including those in New York, Atlantic City, and Ocean City, noted their location in the middle of great population centers, and hence their ability to hold onto tourists who might otherwise have gone to Florida or elsewhere.[101] The Sarasota Chamber of Commerce countered by insisting it could be reached by train and making it clear that no soldiers were staying in Sarasota.[102]

Soldiers frequently displaced tourists in other cities. Often the military would take over hotels for troops. This could go a long way to filling up hotel vacancies, but could cause other problems. Atlantic City Chamber President Alvin Poffenberger complained that the

Army had commandeered tourist hotels for two years but paid for only one.[103] The San Francisco Chamber protested that the Army was taking, without a preliminary hearing, four choice hotels with a total of 2,500 rooms, all for rehabilitation of wounded soldiers.[104] And the Daytona Beach Chamber felt it necessary to announce that, thanks to a change in military housing plans, there were still rooms available for tourists.[105]

Hosting American soldiers was good and bad. They boosted the economy but came with built-in drawbacks, as the British discovered during the buildup before D-Day (when they described the GIs as "overpaid, oversexed, and over here"). At a meeting at the U.S. Chamber, experts discussed the problem of girls living near bases becoming "khakiwacky."[106] In Phoenix, faced with an Army ban on visitation because the city permitted prostitution, the chamber ousted and replaced the city manager and police chief.[107]

Agnes Meyer, a journalist and wife of Eugene Meyer, the publisher of *The Washington Post*, visited several war-impacted communities and wrote about what she saw. One of the worst examples was Leesville, La., a town of 3,500 people that suddenly ballooned to 18,000 with the coming of soldiers to nearby Camp Polk. As she arrived in town for a lunch in her honor hosted by the Leesville Chamber of Commerce, the first person she encountered was a prostitute, wearing a negligee, walking down the highway. At lunch, one of her chamber hosts lied about how many bars and liquor stores were in town, greatly minimizing the number. The locals shamelessly overcharged those coming to town to visit soldiers; "hotels" were no more than shacks, often leaky and without plumbing.[108]

If many of the Leesville Chamber's members were profiteering from the overcrowding, other chambers were simply overwhelmed. Wilmington, N.C. found its population boomed from 33,000 in 1941 to 120,000 in 1943, although food rations were kept at the 1941 levels. As a result, everyone was hungry and restaurants were overcrowded but the portions were small. The Wilmington Chamber of Commerce advertised for more food service providers to come to town but got no takers; the providers feared they would have no food to serve.[109]

Other communities faced the opposite problem – a lack of people. In California, after the Japanese-Americans were removed, there was a serious shortage of labor for farms. The California State Chamber reported in mid-1942 that the state was in danger of missing its agricultural war production quotas because of the missing Japanese. While efforts were being made to bring in Mexicans and other labor, it was feared that this wouldn't be enough.[110]

Nevertheless, even in 1943, when the danger of Japanese invasion was clearly over, many chambers of commerce and other groups in California clamored to keep the internees from returning home. As noted earlier, the Los Angeles Chamber's Leonard Read discussed this in Washington with Assistant Secretary of War John McCloy, while Chamber President Frank Doherty added publicly, "I believe it is unadvisable – even from the standpoint of the Japanese – to allow them to come back."[111] In Salinas, Chamber Secretary Fred McCargar argued that his community, where the proportion of Japanese-Americans had been higher than anywhere else in California, should be considered a good judge of whether or not these people should be allowed to return to the West Coast. He announced a survey that showed 802 out of 803 leading community representatives in Salinas opposing the return of "loyal" Japanese. McCargar offered to send the results of the 14-page survey, complete with tabulations, to anyone who was interested.[112]

Hawaii, where the war had started, showed a remarkably different attitude toward its citizens of Japanese ancestry. The Chamber of Commerce of Honolulu assisted in the creation of the famous 442nd Combat Team. In January of 1943, chamber sent letters to employers asking them to release their Japanese-American employees who wished to join this unit. A total of 9,507 young men applied for enlistment, six times the quota, and 2,600 were picked by the Army.[113]

The chamber then joined Governor Ingram Stainback to give the soldiers an "aloha" sendoff on March 28 at the Iolani Palace grounds. Fifteen thousand cheering Hawaiians were there to say goodbye. The unit trained in Mississippi and Louisiana and was shipped off to Italy in the spring of 1944, where it remained till the end of the war. The 442nd, bolstered by another Japanese-American unit, the 100th Infantry Battalion (known as the "Purple Heart Batallion" because of the many battle wounds its soldiers received), would be termed the most decorated unit in U.S. military history.[114]

Soldier from the 442nd Infantry Regiment

Local pride and desire to make the newspapers did not disappear during a global war. The chamber in New Britain, Conn., sent a telegram to General MacArthur while his forces were fighting on an island in the Pacific. The telegram read: "New Britain, Conn., busy with war production, salute your attack on New Britain Island. We wish you and your boys speedy victory."[115]

The Show Must Go On

Even during wartime, people were interested in show business and actors. Sometimes chambers were a part of this national obsession, like it or not. In New York for the filming of *Lady Killer,* Charlie Chaplin remarked that eating clams on the West Coast is risky because "they're about ten days old." A reporter asked him what the chamber of commerce would say about that. "I'm not a member of the Chamber of Commerce so I don't care," he said.[116]

Also in New York, the Oklahoma City Chamber and one of the state's senators, Josh Lee, threw a party at the Stork Club for the cast of the hit Broadway show, *Oklahoma!* The publicity this musical gave the state was close to priceless. Cast members were given certificates making them honorary citizens of the state. "Senator, this certificate and 50 cents can get us a drink anywhere, right?" asked one of the dancers.

"Anywhere, except Oklahoma," replied Senator Lee. "It's a dry state."[117]

California chambers continued to get more than their fair share of publicity from show business. This was especially true in Los Angeles, where the chamber had first attracted the movie business in 1907. In October 1942, the LA Chamber signed up an actress to be the spokesperson for National Fire Prevention Week. It was Elyse Knox, a wartime pinup girl and Lon Chaney's costar in *The Mummy's Tomb.* Knox's title for the chamber's purposes was, of course, Flame Girl.[118]

Within the thicket of War Production Board rules and regulations for American industry was a $5,000 limit on the cost for materials in movie sets. This limit forced Alfred Hitchcock to use a real town, Santa Rosa, Calif., as his setting for his film *Shadow of a Doubt*. The local chamber of commerce helped rope off the entire community and provide free set materials for the famous director.

Santa Rosa Chamber Secretary Charles Dunwoody cut the deal with Hitchcock. This wasn't an easy sell to the community: in 1925 a "producer" had sold $25,000 worth of stock in a movie and then absconded from town. But Dunwoody and friends made the sale and Hitchcock forged ahead, even bringing in author Thornton Wilder. Dunwoody said Universal would pay the town $50,000 and that another $50,000 would come in from sales of tickets to people wanting to see the movie made. Hitchcock, for his part, announced that Santa Rosa was as fine a small town as his team could find in the West, just made "for murder by a babbling brook."[119]

On March 28, 1944, the Hollywood Chamber of Commerce hosted a meeting about a menace other than murder, fire, or dry states. It was about communism. This was one of the first gatherings of a new organization called the Motion Picture Alliance for the Preservation of American Ideals (MPA). The group was concerned about communist influence in the entertainment industry and later would contribute to the blacklisting of left-leaning actors and writers.

At this meeting, Gary Cooper spoke of "the luke-warm Americans who dally with sedition in the guise of being liberals" and recommended they study the Pledge of Alliance. Clark Gable, back from overseas duty, intoned: "It has been said that there are no atheists in foxholes. There were no Communists either in the foxholes where I was. The boys sit around and talk about home and what they want to find when they get back – and it's not communism."[120] Other prominent members of the group included, or soon would include, Cecil B. DeMille, Walt Disney, John Wayne, Ginger Rogers, Barbara Stanwyck, and Ronald Reagan.[121]

Full-Speed Production

To defeat the Axis Powers, the United States needed to make maximum use of its resources and its phenomenal productive power. This involved, first of all, an undeclared war on trees. The U.S. Chamber of Commerce printed 1 million copies of a 62-page directory of the federal agencies connected with the war effort. A blizzard of questionnaires emanated from the federal government, leading to protests by chambers and business people and, of course, hearings and reports, requiring still more paper. Chambers also took inventories of their available factory space and equipment and published the results.

As we have seen, the St. Louis Chamber of Commerce garnered many military orders thanks to its five-volume survey of local industrial capabilities. A good deal of that business was aeronautical, due to the goodwill and fame of Lindbergh's 1927 transatlantic trip. The chamber supported a bond issue for a massive airport, which attracted airplane industry companies to the area. One of the plants was a giant Curtiss-Wright facility. Confronted with a shortage of labor, by early 1942 the factory began a program to replace young men, who were being drafted by the armed services, with women and elderly workers. Women were being trained in such male-dominated skills as riveting. The St. Louis

Chamber encouraged other factories to follow Curtiss-Wright's lead, as this solution to the labor shortage relied on local workers and avoided the problem of bringing in lots of outside workers, an approach that caused housing shortages and other disruptions.[122]

The St. Louis Chamber was ahead of its time in backing the air industry and in war production – and the community gained greatly from both efforts. On August 1, 1943, however, the city's focus on airplane manufacturing resulted in tragedy. An Army plane towed a new glider 3,000 feet off the ground over a crowd of 4,000 onlookers. After the plane and glider had descended to about 1,000 feet, the glider disengaged.

Suddenly, perhaps because the wings could not bear the weight of the free-floating structure, one wing snapped, and then the other. The glider plummeted downward nose first, hitting Lambert Field near the runway by the Curtiss-Wright plant, and tossing debris and bodies up to 50 feet in the air. None of the 10 people aboard survived. One of them was Mayor William Dee Becker, and another was Chamber President Thomas Dysart.[123] The chamber that had bet on "Lucky Lindy" was a loser on this day, another victim of the great war that was killing millions around the world.

For most business people around the country, the explosion of activity was perhaps exhausting, but also exhilarating after the poverty-stricken Thirties. The South's extreme case of wartime transformation was Birmingham, Alabama, where unemployment or underemployment had reached a staggering 85 percent during the Depression. After 1942, factories were not only operating, but running three eight-hour shifts per day, seven days a week. A writer termed the city "the military arsenal of the South" – a fair statement given that Birmingham was producing more than 75 percent of the military ordnance in the entire region.[124]

The Birmingham Chamber sought both new defense contracts and the workers to fulfill them. Trying to attract a munitions plant in January of 1942, the organization surveyed the local labor market and found that most of the available workers were women. The labor shortage continued through most of the war. By 1944, however, as servicemen began coming home, the chamber devised the "Birmingham Service Plan" that placed at least 200 men in positions. The booming postwar economy apparently soon eliminated the need for this program, but it was widely admired and at one time 35 chambers were studying it.[125]

It was widely acknowledged in World War II, much as it is today, that it was difficult for small businesses to penetrate the recesses of the federal government to obtain military contracts. Chambers did much to help, holding meetings on federal procurement and organizing companies to make joint bids. One of the leaders in this tactic was the York Manufacturer's Association, which devised a widely copied method of breaking down production into bits and pieces (called the "York Plan") that could be farmed out to a variety of area factories, large and small.

War plants mushroomed across the country. Many were placed between the Appalachians and the Rockies in order to minimize the danger of attack by an invading force. Chambers of commerce in these areas did all they could to capture the business. Often the efforts were personal.

Gus Backman at the Salt Lake Chamber found the rhumba lessons his wife had given Hap Arnold would be handsomely rewarded. Arnold, now a five-star general and head of the Army Air Corps, arranged for Backman to meet with William Knudsen, the chairman of the Office of Production Management. The meeting eventually led to the building of a steel plant in Utah County, Geneva Steel, which was by far the largest war facility in the state. The massive plant required 10,000 workers for its construction and it produced, after opening in 1944, hundreds of thousands of tons of steel, mostly for West Coast shipyards.[126]

The Oklahoma City Chamber's Stanley Draper, who knew how to cut a corner when he had to, once was confronted with an embarrassing problem: a military inspector who had looked over the area for a massive air depot was arrested and jailed for public drunkenness. Draper worked with city officials to release the man and had his arrest record removed and sent back to the officer in Washington, where he had returned. Later, when, against the odds, Oklahoma City won the air depot project, Draper learned that the owners of pipelines under the land refused to identify themselves, bringing construction to a standstill. Draper got a shovel and an ax, fractured a pipe, and as the oil began to leak out, the owner quickly appeared. The other owners followed suit. Out of the vast construction site grew Tinker Air Force Base, which employed 15,000 civilians by October of 1943.[127]

Paying for the War

World War II was expensive - one of the key reasons that U.S. Chamber leaders and others had wanted to stay out of it. But once it began, financing it became everyone's problem. The trouble began even before Pearl Harbor, as the soaring costs of the defense buildup and aid to Great Britain threatened the nation's financial stability.

For this giant conflict, as it turned out, savings bonds would be a relatively small contributor. It became clear that taxes had to go up.

The U.S. Chamber of Commerce, in an attempt to slap away the covetous fingers of the Democrats from the wallets of the wealthy, had proposed a "withholding tax" of 3 percent on all wage earners in mid-August of 1941. The chamber's expert on tax policy, Ellsworth Alvord, argued that without such a tax, an unfair burden would fall on those in the upper income brackets.[128] Alvord was absolutely right that his proposal would shield the wealthy: it was essentially a low, flat tax and prevented the government from collecting the extra funds that the rich were capable of paying. Unpopular with Democrats and not ambitious enough to finance a great war, Alvord's proposal got nowhere.

Once the American battleships sat on the floor of Pearl Harbor, the stakes were entirely different. The massive national mobilization effort required scooping up all the tax money possible that would not interfere with industry's ability to finance its rapid expansion. Individuals, whose wages were rising and for whom there were plentiful jobs, were capable of paying more in taxes.

In the spring of 1942 President Roosevelt proposed a plan to cap earnings at $25,000, taking all the rest from top earners as tax revenue. This shocked most of the business community and chambers protested it. The move was a clear shift in the direction of socialism. A competing plan – a national sales tax of 10 percent that would affect every American – was proposed by the U.S. Chamber's Alvord.[129] This, too, failed to pass muster.

The winning approach for financing the war, and as it turned out for making possible a massive increase in federal spending over future decades, came from a creative thinker named Beardsley Ruml. He was chairman of the New York Federal Reserve and treasurer of Macy's. Ruml had noticed how Macy's employees had difficulty paying their past year's tax bill when they retired or went into the military. If only they had been able to pay a little of it with each paycheck during that year. . .

Ruml called this the "pay-as-you-go" plan. We, of course, call it "withholding." As noted above, the U.S. Chamber's Ellsworth Alvord had proposed a roughly similar plan to tax 3 percent of incomes "at the source," but its timing was poor (as the idea was introduced before Pearl Harbor) and the U.S. Chamber had little political standing in Washington at the time. There was much interest in the Treasury Department, too, in the far-from-novel concept of withholding.[130] As befitting his post at Macy's, however, Ruml had come up with a more popular plan. His proposal had a consumer-friendly name, was conceived specifically to help the average wage earner cope with his or her tax burden, and offered to eliminate a whole year's worth of back taxes.

People intuitively saw the benefits of Ruml's plan. Congress rejected the idea as proposed in mid-1942, however, primarily because of its provision for writing off 1942 taxes and starting fresh with the new levy system in 1943. Ruml believed that paying two years' taxes in one year (the back taxes for 1942 and the pay-as-you-go taxes for 1943) would be too burdensome.

How did chambers of commerce love the proposal? Let us count the ways: 1) It shared the tax burden with the less well-to-do; 2) It eliminated a year's taxes; 3) It was efficient to administer; 4) It was relatively painless, being taken out of each paycheck; and 5) It would go far toward funding a war that the nation simply had to win.

The New York Chamber of Commerce held a rare special meeting on September 10, 1942 to listen to Ruml. The more than 500 members present unanimously endorsed the idea and urged it on Congress.[131] The man from Macy's and the Federal Reserve – two institutions intimately connected with the New York Chamber – had been given a blessing by that often conservative, but occasionally deeply creative, chamber of commerce.

With support from many organizations, including chambers of commerce, and with a provision to ease the previous year's tax burden without eliminating it, Congress passed the Current Tax Payment Act of 1943, signed by President Roosevelt on June 9. Life thereafter would never be the same. Chambers of commerce were among the more enthusiastic supporters of a tax system that, by making the government's tax levies relatively painless for the average person, would help government expand amazingly in the succeeding decades, much like one of those giant balloons in the Macy's parade.

It's Tough to Make Predictions, Especially About the Future

At a surprisingly early stage during the war, chambers and communities began planning for the transition to a peacetime economy. In retrospect, we can see why the interest in planning was so strong. First, everyone wanted to do whatever was possible to avoid a return to a Depression-like economy. Second, people owed it to the soldiers to try to create for them a bright and promising home for them to return to. Third, planning was a contribution people could make to their nation that, while less exciting than firefights in the South Pacific or the Ardennes Forest, was still a patriotic and helpful task.

Planning was also in vogue. While New Deal programs had mixed success, there were plenty of very visible examples of modern, industrial-style projects that had involved attention to the minutest details and to step-by-step creation of major enterprises: hundreds of dams from the TVA to the Boulder and Grand Coulee projects; the Pennsylvania Turnpike and other road systems; the Golden Gate and other bridges; the massive retooling of industry for war; and the greatest single U.S. undertaking of the war, the invasion of Europe.

As early as January 1942 – just *one month* after Pearl Harbor – the Indianapolis Chamber of Commerce had set up a study on "postwar problems."[132] On February 2 the Pittsburgh Chamber of Commerce had a committee for postwar planning. Chamber President Frank Duggan said that if industry didn't plan for the future, "there will be a serious postwar depression."[133] By April of 1942, the Twentieth Century Fund found that there were at least 100 organizations engaged in postwar planning, including everything from the American Library Association to the U.S. Chamber of Commerce.[134] The Philadelphia Board of Trade and Chamber of Commerce announced a 10-point plan for postwar stability in June.[135]

In early August of 1942, the U.S. Chamber released one of many surveys it would make of the likely postwar buying habits of consumers.[136] The optimistic Eric Johnston had only been president of the chamber for a few months, but already his bullish outlook was being reflected in the output of the organization. And it would turn out that the U.S. Chamber was more prescient about the postwar boom than just about any other public organization.

The big push on planning, however, came from a different organization, founded in August 1942 at the request of U.S. Secretary of Commerce Jesse Jones. It was called the Committee for Economic Development (CED) and was created specifically to engage in planning for the postwar era. This blue-ribbon, high-profile group included the enthusiastic Johnston, whose chamber soon announced it would lead an effort of 1,700 local chambers in concert with the CED work. CED, befitting its roots as a government-created entity, was a model of public-private partnership and centrist politics.[137]

To some extent, CED was off track. The organization based its planning on the assumption that the war would end in 1947. A couple of well-planned bombs blew up that idea. CED President Paul Hoffman might have done better to plan for the future of his company and left the national work to others. His firm, Studebaker, wouldn't survive long after the war.[138]

Meanwhile, however, some things went right. The San Francisco Chamber of Commerce developed a widely imitated "work-pile plan" that involved companies figuring out what products and services they would immediately buy at the end of the war. The idea was to erase the dangerous gap – which became a chasm after World War I - between the war's end and the full adjustment to peacetime production.[139]

A number of the plans bruited about at this time became reality later. This was perhaps especially true in the high-growth West. Many western chambers, anxious not to lose the enormous influx of residents and business from the war – about 2 million people in California, Oregon, and Washington alone – announced efforts to make sure the growth was locked in. The Seattle Chamber proposed the creation of an organization to promote the Pacific Rim and said it strongly opposed "Eastern monopolies" buying up government-built plants in the West after the war and shutting them down.[140]

Seers envisioned a "Pacific era" after the war and argued that the West Coast could support not just 10-12 million people, but 40 million.[141] It didn't matter that some military jobs would disappear. A committee of the San Diego Chamber of Commerce wisely recommended that the Mission Bay area, teeming with military personnel, be developed for tourism after the war.[142] The chamber in Portland, Ore., where people hoped for a postwar "baby boom," was trying to persuade 80 companies to move to the area and found that 300 local firms intended to hire a total of 10,000 people after the war.[143]

Ultimately, the massive push to map out the country's economic future was a benefit to the nation. To plan that assiduously, people had to believe there *was* a future. It was the very idea of planning that was positive. As General Eisenhower said after D-Day, "Plans are nothing. Planning is everything."[144] Although nearly all the national experts lacked the optimism expressed by Eric Johnston and the U.S. Chamber's surveys, at the grassroots level and at many local chambers of commerce, people seemed to be confident. Perhaps they felt that if they could win the war, they could also win the peace.

The Education of a Nation

With ultimate victory in sight well before the end of the war, people had begun to think more about the future, not only with respect to generalized planning, but to education. Giving more and better schooling to the young was one more attack on the poverty of the Depression, still fresh in people's minds. Not surprisingly, it was the U.S. Chamber under the youthful and can-do Johnston that took a leadership role in promoting education.

In 1944, there were about 200 chambers around the nation that had committees connected with education. This number began to mushroom after public calls by the U.S. Chamber for better-educated workers. By 1948, the number of such committees had reached 1,157.[145]

The push began partly out of the need to repay the nation's ballooning war debts. In July of 1943, the U.S. Chamber's education committee chair Thomas Boushall said the United States would have to sustain its wartime GNP of about $120 billion per year in peacetime in order to pay back expected debts of $250 billion. Only better-educated workers, he said, could keep the economy running at such a high pitch after the end of the war.[146]

Snatching colleges and universities from other cities didn't take a break during the war, especially in Texas. One day after Pearl Harbor, the leaders of Waxahachie-based Trinity College accepted an offer of the San Antonio Chamber of Commerce to move to San Antonio.[147] This move allowed the financially strapped school an opportunity to regain its footing. Today Trinity University, with 2,500 undergraduates, remains in San Antonio, wealthier and stronger than it was in 1941.

The Houston Chamber of Commerce made a successful bid to move Baylor University's medical school out of Dallas, raising $500,000 on its own and adding more funds from the fortune of entrepreneur M.D. Anderson.[148] This project, along with a concomitant push for a cancer hospital and the Baylor dental school, led to the creation of an umbrella organization, the Texas Medical Center, in 1945.[149] This complex would grow dramatically in the postwar years.

Dallas's chamber did not sit still. Baylor's move could not be deterred, but the chamber managed to work with the Dallas Citizens Council to create a new medical school. It was called the Southwestern Medical Center and is now known as the University of Texas Southwestern Medical Center.[150] While not the size of its Houston counterpart (it admits a class of 325 medical students each year), the UT SMC can certainly boast quality: It has four Nobel laureates and was responsible for the world's first pediatric heart transplant.[151]

Just as the chambers in Houston and Dallas showed great interest in medical education in the early 1940s, so did the Birmingham, Ala., Chamber of Commerce. In 1943, the chamber took a leading role in the formation of a committee whose "sole mission was to ensure Birmingham's selection as the site of an expansion of the two-year Medical College of the University of Alabama into a four-year program."[152] Birmingham faced strong opposition from other cities in the state. But the committee raised $160,000, got land donated, and won the Medical College in 1944.[153]

This victory, major in itself, became the leading wedge of later efforts by the Birmingham Chamber of Commerce to expand the University of Alabama's offerings in the city. The result ultimately – with plenty of lobbying by the chamber in subsequent years – has become the University of Alabama at Birmingham, which today is the largest employer in the city and has about 17,000 students.

Toward the Finish Line

The war was nearing its close when Roosevelt, Churchill, and Stalin met at Yalta in the Crimea from February 4 to 11, 1945. FDR's health was rapidly deteriorating and could hardly escape notice. At one point in the deliberations, Roosevelt told a wandering story that, to some at least, evinced a decline in his mental faculties.[154] While trying to make an appeal to unity among the great powers, Roosevelt talked about different kinds of people getting along in the South. It was the story he had recounted years earlier as a columnist, concerning Georgia men who were members both of the chamber of commerce and the Ku Klux Klan, but who overlooked their prejudices against fellow chamber members who were Jews and Catholics.[155]

The President died on April 12, 1945, and was mourned by people all over the world. Vice President Harry Truman took the reins of the country. One of the first things he was told was of the existence of a strange new weapon, the atomic bomb, which was being readied secretly for possible use in Germany or, even more likely, Japan. Berlin fell in May, and most Americans prepared themselves for what they thought would be a long and costly campaign to invade the Japanese home islands.

Admiral Halsey's saddle

The Reno, Nev., Chamber of Commerce generated a firestorm of publicity from an idea it took from Admiral "Bull" Halsey. The pugnacious and opinionated admiral, something of a General Patton with gills, announced that when the Americans captured Tokyo, he wanted to ride down its streets on Emperor Hirohito's famous horse, Shirayuki.

The Reno Chamber declared that if the community reached its quota on its seventh war-bond drive, the chamber would commission a saddle for Admiral Halsey for that ride. The fundraising gimmick worked: Reno met its quota and a local saddle maker spent six weeks making a saddle expertly matched to the rear end of the vice admiral.[156]

The seat was ready in early August 1945. The beautiful, much-photographed equine recliner travelled far and wide, spending time in Marshall Field's in Chicago and then aboard the USS Missouri in time for the September 2 signing of the documents of the Japanese surrender. The ship created a special postcard for September 2, featuring, of course, a photo of the saddle.[157]

Admiral Halsey never rode Shirayuki. He did get on a horse in Tokyo, but it was a spontaneous affair with no time to get a special saddle. (Apparently, once aloft on the animal, he was petrified it would throw him off.)[158] After the firebombing of Tokyo and the atomic bombs at Hiroshima and Nagasaki, not to mention Japan's surrender, the idea of triumphantly riding the emperor's horse through the streets of Tokyo didn't seem as appropriate as it once did, at least to some commentators.[159] But the Reno Chamber had grabbed its seat at the table of history, pulling off one of the more original and successful chamber publicity stunts of the war.

John D. Rockefeller and the 40 Chambers

As the war moved toward what appeared to be its inevitable close, people thought about creating some organization that could avert future conflicts of such magnitude. President Roosevelt came up with the term "United Nations." The U.S. Chamber surveyed its members on the concept of a strong international organization to enforce peace and found the response overwhelmingly positive: 1,848 to 6.[160]

At Yalta, the three heads of state selected San Francisco as the site for the initial meeting to set up the United Nations. The leaders chose a West Coast city to emphasize the need to finish the Pacific War. The San Francisco Chamber did much to host the meeting; its president, Dr. Henry Grady, was a former assistant secretary of state and headed the committee to welcome the delegates.[161] One of the many chamber tasks in handling the visitors was the fight to get people and newspapers to stop using the shortened term for the City by the Bay, "Frisco."[162]

Dr. Grady also wanted San Francisco to be the permanent headquarters of the United Nations. Other chambers, however, also coveted this economic development prize. Offers poured in and in early December 1945, there were no fewer than 23 chambers in London making pitches for the headquarters site.[163] The Poughkeepsie, N.Y. chamber, headed by former Supreme Court Justice John E. Mack, had an inside track: It proposed FDR's Hyde Park estate as the ultimate site.[164] Philadelphia brought the endorsement of comedian W.C. Fields. The Black Hills of South Dakota termed themselves the "center of the universe."[165]

By late December there were 40 U.S. communities (most if not all with delegations led by and/or including chambers of commerce) hawking their civic wares in London. The daunting selection process was somewhat simplified when some European delegates, who had preferred that the organization be sited in Europe, expressed a preference for an East Coast location. And the South faced a major hurdle when an Indian delegate, Sir Ramaswami Mulidar, said the chosen site should provide the delegates of all races "absolute freedom of movement and thought."[166] So much for the Jim Crow states. The U.N. decision was briefly postponed.

The winner of the decision was not so much a chamber of commerce as a chamber leader. John D. Rockefeller, Jr. donated an $8.5 million, 17-acre piece of land in midtown Manhattan for the United Nations Organization site, and this clinched the deal for New York in December 1946. The Rockefellers had belonged to many organizations and contributed to many more over the years – but they had a special place in their heart for chambers of commerce. (At one time, the Rockefeller family set a record when it had members in the New York Chamber from three different generations.[167]) The Rockefeller millions trumped the appeals of the 40 chambers, and New York won one of the highest profile site location competitions of the century.

Coming Out of the War

Chambers of commerce had performed many different roles in the war and, as in previous wars, had greased the wheels of the nation's remarkable industrial machine. That machine, in turn, had flattened the country's foes as surely as had the boots of 12 million GIs. By keeping up the home front, these chambers had made a major contribution to the war.

There had been mistakes, of course. The Los Angeles Chamber of Commerce and others had clamored to put – and keep – West Coast Japanese-Americans behind barbed wire, violating the civil liberties of more than 100,000 people, impeding war production, and tying up valuable labor of both guards and guarded. And certainly in retrospect, the U.S. Chamber's feverish efforts to avoid war were misplaced and tied President Roosevelt's hands in helping the victims of Hitler. Finally, up to the very last legal minute and arguably beyond it, IBM's Tom Watson, one of the most prominent chamber volunteers in the nation, used his chamber diplomacy as a tool by which to strengthen his company's European business. That business gave material aid to the Nazis and to the Holocaust.

World War II also gave added force to major institutions other than local and state chambers of commerce. It took big organizations to fight big enemies. National trade associations, which the Depression and FDR's New Deal policies had brought into the limelight, became more critical than ever. These organizations helped industry remake itself for the war effort. The U.S. Chamber, too, as the umbrella organization for trade groups and local chambers, found new vitality and purpose in helping organize business for the great fight.

Many local chambers had less visibility than they had in the First World War. In part this was because the Second World War was longer for the United States and involved many more people. Government had grown far larger and plucked more men, and many women, into the military services. Quite a few chambers were short-handed during the war or simply closed down.[168] Many cancelled parades, annual dinners, and other activities. Other groups did what chambers had done in the previous war. National chain stores, for example, sold war bonds, while trade associations helped local plants retool.

But chambers often had plenty to do with bringing military bases to town or in facilitating their expansion. And they provided local services of all kinds, from finding housing for GIs to grouping small businesses together to obtain war contracts. Local life didn't disappear in an international war, even if it took a back seat to the great events on the newsreels.

One of the greatest impacts of local chambers, and of the U.S. Chamber, was in paving the way for a new, mostly positive national spirit in the postwar era. The "Let's Get It Done" slogan of the U.S. Chamber's 1942 meeting expressed the attitude of many people in the chamber movement. Pragmatism, not conservative ideology, was the watchword.

The accommodation of business with labor, the realization that big government and big labor and big business were here to stay, the embrace of free trade and open markets, the willingness to take on international responsibilities, the eye on youth and the importance of education, and the glorification of consumer culture – all these things were a part of the postwar national mood and consensus, and were presaged by the actions and words of many American chambers in World War II. Even a powerful countercurrent to the politically moderate spirit of the day – the steaming anger of Southern California libertarians, anti-Communists, and other aggrieved sun people of the right – could be found in some wartime chambers.

When Japan formally surrendered on September 2, 1945, Americans readied themselves for a new kind of economy and national spirit. And much of this involved a return to Main Street. The U.S. Chamber's Ralph Bradford saw such a trend:

> My concern is that we turn our gaze inward and homeward and away from Washington, that we return to the spirit of local independence and individual self-reliance that have made us great, that we rebuild and revivify and strengthen our local institutions and our local organizations that they may face the problems of the future upon the local basis – which finally is the basis of freedom and safety.[169]

At least as far-seeing as Ralph Bradford was the Asbury Park Chamber of Commerce, the same chamber that, during the 1920s, gave star students baseballs autographed by Babe Ruth and Lou Gehrig. Did the chamber realize the impact of all those GIs coming home with money in their pockets and dreams of their futures that had been postponed for so long? On December 18, 1945, this New Jersey chamber and the local mayor announced that they would revive an event that had been in abeyance since 1932, when the Depression had stymied it. In its heyday, the project had attracted as many as 150,000 viewers, and now with the end of the war, the time was ripe to revive it. This event celebrated not war, or even victory, but birth. It was the chamber's baby parade.[170]

Epilogue

1946-Today

he charismatic President had his chamber audience in his hands as he continued his short talk at the Hilton:

And I want to say a word about that pledge here in Fort Worth, which understands national defense and its importance to the security of the United States. During the days of the Indian War, this city was a fort. During the days of World War I, even before the United States got into the war, Royal Canadian Air Force pilots were training here. During the days of World War II, the great Liberator bombers, in which my brother flew with his co-pilot from this city, were produced here.

The first nonstop flight around the world took off and returned here, in a plane built in factories here. The first truly intercontinental bomber, the B-36, was produced here. The B-58, which is the finest weapons system in the world today, which has demonstrated most recently in flying from Tokyo to London, with an average speed of nearly 1,000 miles per hour, is a Fort Worth product.

The Iroquois helicopter from Fort Worth is a mainstay in our fight against the guerrillas in South Viet-Nam. The transportation of crews between our missile sites is done in planes produced here in Fort Worth. So wherever the confrontation may occur, and in the last 3 years it has occurred on at least three occasions, in Laos, Berlin, and Cuba, and it will again - wherever it occurs, the products of Fort Worth and the men of Fort Worth provide us with a sense of security.

And in the not too distant future a new Fort Worth product - and I am glad that there was a table separating Mr. Hicks and myself - a new Fort Worth product, the TFX Tactical Fighter Experimental - nobody knows what those words mean, but that is what they mean, Tactical Fighter Experimental - will serve the forces of freedom and will be the number one airplane in the world today. [1]

President John F. Kennedy was addressing the Fort Worth Chamber of Commerce. This President, trying to sound a positive note on the way to uniting the factious liberal and conservative wings of the Democratic Party in Texas, chose to hit this civic organization in the bull's eye: military spending. The 2,000 listeners were most appreciative. Most probably did not know that many of the military outlays he referred to had been anxiously pleaded for by this very chamber in the past. Praising local productive acumen, appealing to local pride, ticking off military

JFK with well-wishers in Fort Worth

spending projects in the area, linking them to national ideals and patriotism, this President knew how to win over a chamber audience. Without realizing it, JFK had been drawing on nearly two hundred years of local chamber tradition and experience.

It was John F. Kennedy's last speech. Shortly afterward, he flew to Dallas, where he and Jackie rode in an open car in a motorcade and he was assassinated by Lee Harvey Oswald Jr. His talk, like the chamber activities he unknowingly referred to, and the history and tradition behind them, was nearly forgotten in the sweep of urgent and pressing national affairs.

The Continuing Story

After World War II, chambers continued to find a way into the affairs of their communities and their society. In the postwar years, chambers of commerce did a good many things that people did not see, mesmerized as they were by the great events that no one could miss: the hydrogen bomb, Sputnik, Kennedy's assassination, social changes in the Sixties and Seventies, the oil embargo, Iranian hostage crisis, Reagan Revolution, 9-11, and, of course, the Kardashians.

This book's main narrative has stopped at 1945 as a rough halfway point in the achievements and history of American chambers of commerce. But so as not to leave the reader hanging, what follows is a very brief synopsis of what's gone on in recent years. This epilogue by necessity lacks both the objectivity and detail of the previous, lengthier story, but perhaps its relative brevity and recent history will provide compensating values.

After the second great war of the twentieth century, slowly but surely, the economy's impetus moved to the mind. Technologies and know-how supplanted bulk cargo. Lightweight microchips proved more valuable than tons of coal and steel. Services supplanted manufacturing and agriculture in the economy. In this new environment, education – almost always at least a tangential concern of chambers of commerce – became by 2014 more central to the concerns of local business and its organizations. Chambers continued to focus on transportation projects, which were as much in their DNA as ever, but the mind and the Internet were slowly beginning to take over roadbeds and riverbeds in chamber boardroom discussions.

At the same time, social and community concerns also drew more attention. This was never more in evidence than in the 1960s. The civil rights movement in particular relied upon a strong, moderate force of opinion in favor of peaceful integration. Chambers of commerce, in community after community, took on that role, often reluctantly. Yet because of that measured response, the chambers' actions in some cases were surprisingly effective.

Paradoxically, the federal government grew more powerful and less powerful in the post-war period. The role of Washington in funding all kinds of local programs and infrastructure rose after 1945 and began to recede with the 21st century. Social security, Medicare, and defense spending ate up much of the money gathered in Washington, leaving local chambers at a loss for sources of funding for their pet projects not only in transportation but in education and other areas. On top of this, the acrimonious partisan debates at the national level – in part due to the shrinking federal pie of discretionary money available to be sliced up - made it difficult to look to the nation's capital for answers. In this sense, the new century brought chambers of commerce back to their 18th and 19th century roots: they were forced to look more closely to their own communities for answers to local problems.

Overall, from 1946 to 2014, chambers of commerce managed to keep their seat at the table of the nation's history. As was typically the case in their own pasts, these chambers' role was little noticed at the time and soon forgotten. But they left a mark, physical and otherwise, on their country. A brief look at a few broad areas will provide a hint of some of the things they did.

Transportation

It was the advent of transatlantic commerce that spawned chambers of commerce as we more or less know them today, and the succeeding revolutions of railroads, automobiles, and air travel each generated, as we have seen, a whirlwind of chamber activity. While these primary revolutions had occurred by World War II, the buildout of the nation's airports and road and highway system was a huge task still to be confronted. This meant there was a great demand not just for these transportation improvements, but for the chambers to plan for and ask for them.

During the Fifties and beyond, with the building of the Interstate Highway System and massive suburbanization, chambers were busy with the roads. Some of them jumped into this work with alacrity. A good example is the Birmingham, Ala., Chamber of Commerce (today known as the Birmingham Business Alliance). This chamber had its weaknesses, honestly and fairly chronicled by journalist Mark Kelly in A Powerful Presence in 2008. But when it came to the roads, this business organization usually got the job done, as Kelly noted:

> It is no exaggeration to say that the Chamber has had some involvement in every major highway improvement that has taken place in Birmingham over the past sixty years and counting; most often, that involvement has been extensive and out front.[2]

Chambers of commerce were closely involved with many of the suburban arteries and county and state expressways that proliferated after 1945: Fairfax County Parkway in suburban Washington, the Garden State Parkway in New Jersey, and many of the freeways in southern California, thanks to the still pavement-happy Los Angeles Chamber of Commerce. Even the Hollywood Chamber got into the act, successfully lobbying for eight exits off the Hollywood Freeway instead of one.[3] To the north in what would become Silicon Valley, the Palo Alto Chamber used photos of bloody accidents to promote road improvements that would lead to the creation of the Bayshore Freeway.[4]

Elsewhere in the Sun Belt, the San Antonio Chamber of Commerce successfully pushed for such car carriers as the McAllister Freeway and the Northwest Freeway.[5] The Houston Chamber of Commerce was closely involved in the breakneck expansion of auto capacity there.[6]

Chambers also pushed for bridges. The Baltimore Chamber of Commerce had for decades advocated for the construction of the Chesapeake Bay Bridge, on which work began in 1949. The Sunshine Skyway Bridge from Manatee County to St. Petersburg, Florida, ranked #3 on the world's top 10 bridges by The Travel Channel, was completed in 1987 and originally advocated by local chambers, starting with the Bradenton Chamber of Commerce (now known as the Manatee Chamber of Commerce).

Mass transit continued to make limited progress in American cities, often with chamber assistance. The Greater Washington Board of Trade, which began studying other cities' subway systems in 1936 with a view to having one in the nation's capital, finally got its wish four decades later.[7] The Salt Lake Chamber pushed for and got the Transit Express light rail system beginning in 2001.

Airports grew in importance after World War II. Many of them were in place by 1946, but not all of them. The Atlanta Chamber of Commerce, later the Metro Atlanta Chamber, worked closely with the city's mayors to keep its vital airport among the leading ones in the nation, as it had done since the old days of Candler Field. The airport had been a chamber obsession since the 1920s. Indeed, there is a plausible argument, richly described in Mark Kelly's history of the chamber in Birmingham, that the Alabama city ceded its future to Atlanta by not keeping up with the Georgians' airport focus.

Atlanta and Birmingham had roughly equal populations after World War II. But the City of Birmingham wouldn't move its airport to a better location, thereby losing the hub business of a young firm that soon would be known by the name of Delta. That firm flew off to Atlanta. Had Birmingham's chamber been more influential at the time, it's possible it could have pushed for a better airport site and changed the course of southern civic history. The Atlanta airport, well known as the required stop for southerners on the way either to heaven or hell, became arguably the leading engine of growth for a community for which expansion was as popular as Georgia Tech or Coca-Cola. Today, Atlanta has four times Birmingham's population.[8]

Certainly, getting carriers could be as important as getting the airports themselves. The Greater Providence Chamber, after its members complained of sky-high air ticket costs, orchestrated a letter writing campaign to Southwest Airlines that resulted in 1996 in the low-cost carrier making stops in the local airport, its first destination in the North. The surge in traffic surprised everyone, leading to what would soon become known as the famous "Southwest effect" of drastically reduced airfares and additional business for the community because of the increased traffic.[9]

There were limits to infrastructure improvement. Environmental and political restrictions on building proliferated, and as the nation coalesced into a constellation of communities dominated by a relative handful of massive metropolitan areas, the cost of obtaining rights of way for roads and bridges and rail links increased dramatically. The Denver Chamber of Commerce began a push for a new airport in 1978; while the project was immense and controversial and ultimately judged by most to be a success sometime after its opening in 1995, it was only one chamber and one new airport – not, as in the 1920s or 1930s, hundreds of chambers and new airports.[10] It was the first major new airport in the country in 25 years.

Brand-new highway projects were a rarity. The Chamber of Commerce of Southwest Indiana, based in Evansville, spent several decades pushing for construction of the 143-mile segment of highway I-69 linking Evansville to Indianapolis. The first 65 miles of the highway, completed in 2012, comprised one of the last major new interstate highway segments to be built in the United States.

A massive plan to improve metropolitan Atlanta's road and transit systems, promoted by the Metro Atlanta Chamber, the Georgia Chamber, and other groups, failed badly at the polls in 2012, and was widely noted by other chambers and transportation industry figures. Fiscal conservatives, and voters generally, were suspicious of temporary tax increases for infrastructure. Would such improvements really reduce traffic congestion? Without large dollops of federal funding, the financing of big concrete-and-steel solutions was becoming a difficult proposition.

By 2014, much needed to be done in a creaky national transportation system, and the sums involved were enormous, but the return on investment was not so exciting when the cost of a new runway might equal that of five or 10 airports a few decades earlier, or when the addition of a new highway made only a negligible dent in the average person's perception of traffic conditions. There were plenty of improvements to be made on the margins with better road maintenance, bridge replacements, toll roads, telecommuting, and smart transportation systems. But by 2014, few people were joining local chambers of commerce so that their community would have better transportation access. Chambers and their members were awaiting – and no doubt some of them were fomenting – the next revolutions in movement.

Community Image and Promotion

In 1948, a windstorm blew down the "H" of the real estate sign "Hollywoodland." The sign hadn't been kept up since 1939. The city considered taking the sign down. The Hollywood Chamber of Commerce, however, promised to fix the weatherbeaten advertisement, dropping the "land" and sprucing up the letters. The result is perhaps the world's most famous sign, which the chamber has taken a few steps since to refurbish and protect. And in 1960, the same chamber initiated its "Walk of Fame" project, setting stars on Hollywood Boulevard and Vine Street to correspond with actors, singers, and other famous personages in entertainment. This became one of the world's best known tourism promotion and downtown development projects.[11] (The Hollywood Chamber got an extra taste of fame in 2013 when it turned down Kim Kardashian's application for a star on the grounds that she lacked talent.)

These chamber activities are emblematic of the kind of impact that an organized group of business people can have on the promotion of their community and its image. The projects are an indication that community promotion was far from dead in the post-World War II era. Americans had not become so sophisticated that they didn't want to attract tourists, shoppers, and more.

Festivals, fairs, and games remained fair game for chambers of commerce. The Chicago Association of Commerce staged a huge trade fair in 1959 that included a visit from Queen Elizabeth II and a bevy of ships from the U.S. Navy. The Seattle Chamber was involved in the World's Fair of 1962, memorable today because of the Space Needle that still serves as the city's leading landmark.[12] The San Antonio Chamber conceived of and played a major role in attracting the HemisFair in 1968[13], while, the following year, the president of the tiny chamber in Bethel, N.Y., with a grand total of four members, obtained the permit for a little gathering that would be known to the world thereafter as Woodstock.[14] There were thousands of other chamber-connected events, from the Mother Goose Parade in San Diego (begun in 1947 with an El Cajon Chamber contribution of $150, and today with hundreds of thousands of onlookers each year) to the Ostrich Festival in Chandler, Arizona (complete with ostrich chariot races), to the New Orleans Jazz & Heritage Festival.[15]

In sports, too, chambers continued to play a role, as they had for decades. When a Major League team decamped from one city to another, or a new franchise was created, there was a good chance that a chamber's fingerprints would be found on the locker room door. Although the major decisions were made by owners, aided in many cases by promises of tax abatements, chamber backing was a common lubricant of the deals. Leading companies (often chamber members) purchased luxury suites or otherwise supported the franchise, and without that support, such moves were difficult to contemplate.

The Olympic Games have also seen their share of chamber involvement. Such giant projects are hard to win and pull off without chamber assistance. The Los Angeles Chamber was connected with the effort to obtain the Olympics in 1984. The Metro Atlanta Chamber of Commerce (now the Metro Atlanta Chamber) was a major player in bringing the 1996 Centennial Olympics to Atlanta.

The Atlanta campaign to win the games began in 1987 as a nearly hopeless effort because Athens, Greece, where the modern Olympics originated in 1896, was also making a bid, and the Olympics had just been held in Los Angeles in 1984. The Atlanta public was uninterested. The sparkplug of the campaign and the man with an impossible dream, Billy Payne, a young real estate attorney, sought the help and support of the chamber and its business leadership, and a cooperative effort began.[16] It ended in success. Bringing the games and the world to the Deep South was a moment of historic significance that went far beyond sports and reached into the best traditions of the Atlanta Chamber and of its historic trade-promoting hero, Henry Grady.

In 2002, the Winter Olympics went to Salt Lake City, the chamber was a major part of the effort to win the games. Although the city's bid was tarnished by accusations of bribes of the International Olympic Committee judges, the chamber wasn't implicated in those, and it later gave its highest honor to Mitt Romney, who was brought in to clean up the mess created by the scandal.[17] Another person involved in the repair effort, Utah Senate President Lane Beattie, was named president of the Salt Lake Chamber in 2003.

Downtown Development

The massive suburbanization of the postwar era sapped many cities of residents and money. It took time for chambers and other groups to come up with cost-effective strategies to counter urban decay. Indeed, those efforts continue today. But the same kinds of chamber impulses that fueled the city planning work of Burnham, the Olmsteds, and others continued after 1945.

Sometimes it took a new organization to develop a new way to look at the city. In Pittsburgh, Richard King Mellon founded the Allegheny Conference on Community Development in 1945 to begin the process of cleaning up the smoky industrial city and beautifying the downtown area. Mellon and his colleagues in the business organization were highly successful, working in partnership with Mayor David Lawrence. Ultimately the Allegheny Conference absorbed the Pittsburgh Chamber and other local groups into a still larger and more broadly based organization.

In Baltimore, inspired by the work of the Allegheny Conference, visionary urban planner James Rouse saw a need for better public housing and a more beautiful downtown. He led the formation of a new business group in 1955, the Greater Baltimore Committee, whose success in various development projects ultimately resulted in its supplanting the local chamber as the leading business organization in town. (Today, the Greater Baltimore Committee is the de facto metro chamber of the city; the Metropolitan Baltimore Chamber of Commerce is defunct.) One of the projects that the Greater Baltimore Committee and Rouse pioneered was Baltimore's Inner Harbor, one of the most popular and successful postwar redevelopments of urban space in the nation.

Similar beautification and development projects went on, with varying degrees of success, in dozens of cities, often with the local chamber involved. In 1959, David Straus formed the Tourism Attraction Committee at the San Antonio Chamber to look at the potential of the Riverwalk area.[18] This bed of the San Antonio River was a somewhat scraggly park by day and a crime risk at night. Over the next few years, the chamber helped fund studies and support initiatives that led to the development of Spanish-style architecture by the river and a cleaned-up environment with more restaurants and shops. The modern Riverwalk was thus born, and given extra impetus by the HemisFair that the chamber also promoted in 1968.

One of the most interesting and closely watched downtown development projects grew out of the Oklahoma City Chamber of Commerce in 1993. Chamber leaders had been discouraged to hear that the reason United Airlines had decided not to choose their city as a maintenance hub was because living standards were better in Indianapolis, the chosen site. As a result, the chamber and city put together a program called Metropolitan Area Projects (MAPS) plan that would fund renovation or new construction of nearly a dozen different high-profile projects, from the Bricktown Canal to a downtown area.

A majority of voters (54 percent) approved a five-year, one-cent sales tax for the effort, and five years later, 68 percent approved an extension of funding to finish the projects and eliminate all debt on them.[19] Almost at a stroke, a chamber and its allies had transformed the look and feel of much of the city. Not every voter, nor every economist, would approve of this kind of taxpayer-funded urban regeneration effort. But the efficiency of the spending, which was carefully monitored throughout the process, disarmed some critics, while the sweeping nature of the changes impressed others. At least in this one case, a community could look at itself in the mirror, decide it wanted a completely new wardrobe, and go out and get it and put it on for the world to see. Some other chambers and their communities attempted similar projects; the Greater Des Moines Partnership, for example, abandoned its traditional focus on a single project at a time to begin looking at many at once.

The Civil Rights Era

One of the most wrenching, and ultimately positive, periods in the nation's history was the civil rights struggle. The 1954 U.S. Supreme Court decision in the case of *Brown v. Board of Education*, striking down school segregation, heralded the end of Jim Crow laws and racial segregation. Yet while integration was the law of the land, it would be implemented at different times and in different ways depending on the place. In many cases, chambers would be involved in the deliberations.

Commentators from widely differing points of view have noted how, in the South, it was business organizations that, in city after city, turned the tide of white public opinion to the side of compliance with federal law and in support of integration. These chambers were not comprised of inherently liberal people. Often the chambers' motive was simply to avoid a PR black eye. Certainly, it was difficult, on the one hand, to seek investment from the North while, on the other, the local police force was capturing headlines by beating up demonstrators who favored compliance with the law. As one anonymous person wrote to segregationist Alabama Governor George Wallace in 1963: "Stop these Yankee corporations from putting pressure on these third-rate Babbitts in these Chambers of Commerce to surrender to these Negroes."[20] Those "Babbitts" needed an environment in which blacks and whites, and the South and the North, could live together.

It wasn't just about the need for better PR for southern communities. As we have seen, there was some tradition in chambers, notably but not exclusively in the Atlanta Chamber, to seek reconciliation and peaceful relations among the races. Racial peace and legal compliance were important in and of themselves. They were in the spirit of community betterment that was a natural outgrowth of local business people banding together, from the "not born for ourselves alone" gangs of New York to Ryerson Ritchie's Goo-Goos of Boston, Cleveland, and assorted other cities, to Colonel Eli Lilly in Indianapolis and Thomas Burke in Seattle and Booker T. Washington in Tuskegee, not to mention leaders of many other chambers, North and South.

How chambers in the South handled the challenge of integration is a gripping story, and a bigger one than can be handled in a page or two of an epilogue. Of the dozens of individual examples from communities throughout the South, two, arguably, stand out: Atlanta and Birmingham, the same two cities that had shown such varying degrees of interest in promoting their airports.

Atlanta's chamber leadership tackled integration first, in part because the city and its chamber had a tradition of leadership on racial issues. Indeed, it was Ivan Allen Jr., the son of the manager of the chamber during its Forward Atlanta campaign of 1926-29, who was president of the chamber in 1961 when African-American demonstrators threatened a boycott of downtown businesses. Allen negotiated an integration agreement that would be defended by Martin Luther King, Jr., who said eloquently to a large, heavily African-American audience at Wheat Street Baptist Church, "If anyone breaks this contract, let it be the white man."[21]

One person was unhappy with the agreement. It was an Atlanta store owner named Lester Maddox. Maddox quit the Atlanta Chamber as a result.[22] He would later successfully run for governor brandishing ax handles of defiance to integration. In the long run, however, moderation prevailed. Ivan Allen Jr. subsequently was elected mayor of Atlanta.

In Birmingham, the chamber had not done much to help the city cope with, or accept, integration. At the same time, its leaders were beginning to see that their city's and region's reputation for poor race relations was getting in the way of business. Ill feeling was exacerbated by County Commissioner Eugene ("Bull") Connor, a proud member of the Ku Klux Klan.

The new chairman of the Birmingham Chamber of Commerce, Sid Smyer, had not been a fan of Connor's, and had begun taking steps to reform local government so that Connor would lose power, but there appeared little urgency to the task until one day in May of 1961. On that day, Smyer was at a meeting of the International Rotary Club in Tokyo. He opened a Tokyo newspaper and, on the front page, saw photographs of white men beating up blacks in the Birmingham bus station. The horrified reactions of Japanese who saw the same photos indicated to Smyer not only that Connor had to go, but that Birmingham race relations had to change.[23]

It took some time, but the Birmingham Chamber helped complete the changes that took power away from Connor and also made peaceful integration possible in Birmingham. But this was only after horrific church bombings and other violence shocked the city, the nation, and the world. The Birmingham Chamber finally did the right thing, if two or three years behind the schedule of these rapidly moving times.

This was indeed a lesson of the Sixties: business organizations could be a force for calm and reconciliation. James Cobb in his fascinating look at, among other topics, the integration process, *The Selling of the South*, notes that in the southern communities that adapted well, peacefully, and early to integration, typically there were strong business organizations pushing this agenda. Where the business-group leadership was lackluster or nonexistent, troubles arose.

A number of chambers, then, acquitted themselves reasonably well in one of the greatest social challenges in American history – not as liberals crusading for change, in most cases, but as moderates campaigning for peace and civil order. And the challenge continued in city after city throughout the South, and to a lesser extent, outside it. At a time of great social change, key local chambers played a significant role in helping their communities adjust to that change. In an environment tinged with anxiety, violence, and strident rhetoric, a little moderation could go a long way.

Economic Development

Plus ça change, plus c'est la même chose. For more than 100 years, almost everyone deplored a practice but a pretty high percentage engaged in it at the same time: providing incentives to bring business to town. Stores brought in customers with sales; cities and chambers brought them in with discounts, tax breaks, "bonuses," regulatory fixes, and other enticements. Such practices were elevated to state policy with the Balance Agriculture With Industry (BAWI) initiative in Mississippi, which was quickly copied by other states in the postwar era, with chambers of commerce the most frequent local partners of the states.

Gradually, as increasing tax money poured into the economic development business, more public-private partnerships emerged to handle the funds. Chambers of commerce could manage the activity, but this was not always politically feasible in some communities where 1) the public wasn't especially keen on business organizations working with taxpayers' funds, 2) the chamber was sharply critical of leading politicians, or 3) both. In many cases, the new public-private groups were started by chambers to keep the economic development ball rolling in a way compatible with the new public funding sources.

Removing chambers from economic-development leadership, however, had limits. It turned out that marketing entities with too public a focus didn't always have the staff incentives or orientation in place to do a good job selling the community. Sometimes, therefore, the job of promoting and attracting business came back to the chamber (or to a nonprofit marketing organization connected with the chamber). Indeed, as Association of Chamber of Commerce Executives President Mick Fleming has pointed out, there is something of a "grass is greener" phenomenon operating, in which for many communities, the economic development job has moved from the chamber to some other entity, and back, and out again, and back again, as people assume that the model they don't have is the one that works better.

There is something inherently unstable in a public effort to attract private business. When tax money is involved, so are politics, and this can sometimes lead to conflicting points of view among the public and private partners in a deal. Yet the same tax money can sometimes bring success when the right firm is recruited or retained in the right way. Many economic development funds have become mixtures of private and public monies – sometimes with the private money predominating so as to ensure chamber control, sometimes not.

Postwar economic development was not a model of Adam Smith invisible-hand purity, but it worked. Elizabeth Shermer describes with some clarity in *Sunbelt Capitalism: Phoenix and the Transformation of American Politics* how the allegedly free-market Phoenix Chamber boosters, including Barry Goldwater, worked extensively with government to create their high-growth hothouse. Like Chairman Deng Xiaoping in China, American communities and their chambers of commerce haven't cared greatly if the economic development cat is black or white, so long as it catches mice. And many a mouse was caught.

The postwar growth of the Sun Belt, not just of Phoenix, owes a good deal to the efforts of chambers of commerce in the South and West to attract business from the North and Midwest. Not only special business incentives, but also lower taxes and wages in the South and West, together with right-to-work laws often championed by local and state chambers, were a magnet for many northern firms. Much of the corporate migration, as many experts have recounted, was because of the success of southern and western chambers and other business organizations in their sales efforts and in shaping their communities' tax and regulatory structures to the desires of outside firms. The resulting movement, essentially a reverse Great Migration, was a process with winners and losers, to be sure. But without question, the shifting of tens of thousands of businesses, with the ultimate employment (after expansions in their new locations) of millions, changed the economic and population landscape of the entire United States.

Certainly, the availability of cheap and plentiful air conditioning helped in the move to the South. Yet man does not live by air alone. It wasn't just the indoor climate but, in the terminology of the times, the "business climate." It was the entrepreneurial feeling in the air, more than the temperature of the air, which mattered most. As the sociologist Rupert Vance said in 1955, well before air conditioning was widespread, "The dominant psychology in the South is no longer agrarian; it is Chamber of Commerce."[24]

Of course, the economic development game was not really about a renewed North-South civil war. This was a struggle among individual communities, taking place in all parts of the country. There were many ways to seek competitive advantage. One of the favorites was to find the community's industrial/economic strengths, sometimes known as "clusters," and build on them and trumpet them to the world.

In 1945, Houston had a world-famous cluster nearby: East Texas oil wells. Under perhaps the leading chamber executive of his generation, Marvin Hurley (serving first as manager of the industrial department and in the fifties and sixties as executive vice president), the chamber pushed into at least three new clusters. One was the obvious, but also extremely lucrative, field of petrochemicals: making products out of the black gold pouring out of those pipes. "Plastics," said the excited businessman in *The Graduate* to the nonplussed character played by Dustin Hoffman. In 1968 plastics may have seemed boring, if lucrative; in 1945, they were exciting to just about everyone in the business community of Houston, and helped fuel the continued rapid growth of Harris County.

Marvin Hurley, chamber manager in Houston and other cities

A second field, mirroring the growing importance of the mind in the modern economy, was the Texas Medical Center, as noted previously. The Houston Chamber, along with many local partners and allies (and aided especially by the M.D. Anderson Foundation and other donors), would continue to push this project with nearly single-minded devotion for seven decades. Now this complex is by far the largest of its kind in the world, with more than 100,000 employees.

Houston Ship Channel, 1939

A third was the Houston Ship Channel, that once snag-infested bayou that today is a key to Panama Canal traffic. Marvin Hurley and his chamber colleagues pushed the Humble Oil Company to develop its land there. Then he visited some Congressional and Senate offices for an innovative project that was a perfect fit, he and others thought, for that land.[25] This became, with the help of Vice President Lyndon Johnson[26]), the home of the Manned Space Center for the National Aeronautics and Space Administration. One chamber idea had led to another, and another. A vast array of associated space-related companies joined NASA in East Texas.

The Evolution of Silicon Valley

An even more remarkable cluster was taking shape in the West. There is a creation myth of Silicon Valley, in which Stanford engineering professor Frederick Terman got his students Bill Hewlett and Dave Packard to shake hands and make history. Except that there is much missing from that abbreviated tale.[27]

In electronic terms, there was a chamber substrate to much of what happened in the valley of youthful millionaires. Massive military spending (especially from the vast, technology-rich Moffett Field, a prize brought in with chamber help[28]), huge electronics "anchor tenants" from San Jose that served as the market for many high-tech startups (with many of the larger firms having been recruited by the San Jose Chamber or others nearby), hundreds of smaller electronics subcontractors enticed by California chambers from the East or elsewhere – all these helped build the expertise and labor pool of the magical business-incubating valley.

One of the key pieces to the puzzle was Russ Pettit, a young PR executive who joined the San Jose Chamber of Commerce staff in 1925 and would become its manager; he ultimately remained there for 40 years, pushing for growth every step of the way. Pettit would be honored by his chamber peers during his life and afterward; like the Houston Chamber's Marvin Hurley, he had a knack for moving an ambitious chamber agenda forward.

Pettit and his chamber had a hand in bringing some key businesses to San Jose at an early date, notably IBM in 1943. He knew the costs of advertising and promotion to a penny. Pettit had an almost Frank Wiggins-like joy in promotion and grasp of what moves a crowd.[29] The pro-development policies proclaimed by Pettit's chamber and the business community in general no doubt contributed (as was the case in other development-happy cities of this period) to the willingness of companies to move to the area.[30] In 1949, the chamber reported to *Nation's Business* that it had recruited 79 businesses since 1944 with an expected payroll of 6,000.[31] Many of these were electronics companies.

The chamber's work was aided by a new, pro-business city manager (Anthony "Dutch" Hamann) whom the chamber and other business groups got the city to bring on in 1950. Hamann was wildly pro-growth, working hand-in-hand with Pettit and others to bring ultimately hundreds of electronics companies to the area. San Jose had 95,000 people when Hamann took office in 1950 and 446,000 when he retired in 1970.[32] By the time he left office, a substantial number of voters had begun to oppose his pro-growth policies – but by then the southern end of the amazing valley had been stripped of prune and walnut orchards and fully planted with electronics – fruit that was still to ripen.

Other California chambers, too, were involved in ways big and small in the creation of this industrial Disneyland of the northern part of the state. It was at a Los Angeles Chamber of Commerce black-tie dinner in 1955, for example, where William Shockley became reacquainted with fellow Caltech associate Arnold Beckman. Months later, Beckman became the angel investor for Shockley's new high-tech firm, Shockley Semiconductor, which located in Mountain View and would soon put the silicon in Silicon Valley.[33]

Everybody, not just in the Santa Clara Valley, wanted an industrial identity. The Durham Chamber of Commerce termed its community the "City of Medicine"; the Albany, N.Y. chamber invented the "Tech Valley" moniker for its region; the Richardson, Tex., Chamber came up with the "Telecom Corridor"; and so on. Starting in the early 1980s, the Greater Austin Chamber of Commerce took the lead in transforming its community into a high-tech hotbed that some would call "Silicon Hills," "Silicon Gulch," or "Silicon Prairie."

Chambers of Education

In 1989, a Democratic state senator from Wisconsin, Annette Polly Williams, decided to lead an effort to pass a bill allowing children to use public money, in the form of vouchers, to attend the nonreligious school of their choice. (This program was later expanded to include religious schools.) At one point she addressed the board of the Metropolitan Milwaukee Association of Commerce (MMAC), the local metro chamber. MMAC, convinced by her arguments for better education for these students, became the primary institutional supporter of the idea for vouchers, which passed the legislature and went into effect in the 1990-1991 school year.

The program grew over the succeeding decades, but probably would have perished without MMAC's continued support. Voucher programs subsequently caught on in a few other communities, although not as many as opponents of the program feared. However, the existence of this arguably radical option for change helped make a much more moderate option – charter schools, which paid the same teacher salaries as the public schools did – a frequently chosen compromise for those seeking reform and greater choice within school systems.

The Milwaukee experiment, still controversial today, was essentially based on a critique of public schools. Historically, much public school reform has occurred from the outside – and frequently from chambers of commerce. A significant amount of the education reform movement in the United States today is still fueled by business advocates, including chambers, whose members seek employees with the skills needed to function effectively in the workplace.

In 1946, the push was not so much for education reform as for more education – fast. The GI Bill, of course, helped millions of veterans crowd into colleges and technical schools. But the real demand for education came when the veterans' baby-boom children sought education, at all levels. Chambers of commerce played a significant role in pushing for increased funding for schools in countless communities in the Fifties and Sixties to accommodate these young people, whether they wore coonskin caps, rat finks, mood rings, love beads, or other emblems of the creative class.

Two-year institutions of higher education had existed before World War II, but they exploded in numbers in the postwar years. In a particular two-decade period, their growth was extraordinary. From 1960 to 1979, enrollment in publicly supported two-year colleges soared by 930 percent, compared to "just" 220 percent for all of higher education.[34] These institutions had 392,000 students in 1960 and 4,057,000 in 1979. By 2007 total fall enrollment had risen further to 11.8 million.[35] Clearly, the two-year college had caught on in American society.

Chambers of commerce were among the biggest supporters of these institutions. Community colleges provide an engine for local economic growth and well-trained workers for local companies. Such schools also are magnets for economic development. As a former chamber member, U.S. President George W. Bush, said in 2004:

> There's nothing like the Chamber of Commerce being able to say, "We've got a fantastic community college system here. If you move your business here, the community college will make sure – will help train people for the jobs you need."[36]

While educators are usually the primary movers or catalysts in the creation of community colleges, chambers of commerce have been critical partners. One study indicated the depth of this support:

> Businesspeople – whether as individuals, firms, or organizations such as chambers of commerce – supported the establishment of 68% of the community colleges studied across the states of California, Illinois, New York, and Washington. And in nearly all of these cases their support was strong.[37]

Dallas provides an instructive example. In the early 1960s, Dallas had no community colleges; the nearest ones were 90 miles away. Students were commuting to far-off suburbs to take the courses they needed. As a result, local educational leaders felt something should be done. County schools superintendent L.A. Roberts wrote to the educational chair of the Dallas Chamber of Commerce suggesting his board's readiness to move forward with any "conservative" plan.[38] The Dallas Chamber came up with the idea of a district that now boasts 100,000 students[39] – perhaps not so "conservative" after all.

The Dallas Chamber of Commerce gathered together a blue-ribbon group of 22 leading local citizens, headed by R.L. (Bob) Thornton, Jr., who later became the district's first board chair.[40] Before long, in 1965, Dallas voters had approved a $41.5 million bond issue by a two-to-one margin.[41] One of the leading community college systems in the nation had been launched.

The Dallas effort, however massive in its ultimate impact, came from the work of a handful of people. The launch of the first school, El Centro, was infused with a sense of possibility and excitement.[42] One author argues that the success of the entire district project is a testimony to Margaret Mead's statement, "Never doubt that a small group of thoughtful citizens can change the world; indeed, it is the only thing that can."[43]

What may look to us like just another public building could be someone else's dream. Dave Cooley, the executive director of the Greenville, S.C., Chamber of Commerce, described what prompted his chamber to start technical schools in there in 1960: "The textile industry had the town by the throat and was choking it to death." Local people needed to have the skills to make a living some other way. These schools spread in the state and became the South Carolina technical college system, he noted.[44]

There are myriad examples of community colleges that chambers have been involved with in the postwar period. And there are other examples of post-secondary education, including a favorite chamber task, "promoting" two-year-colleges to four-year institutions. Medical schools, too, were prizes to attract, as always; very recently, the chambers in both El Paso and Spokane have managed to help win medical schools to go with their local universities.

Future education efforts by chambers of commerce are difficult to predict, but based on present activity, it's almost certain that some of the work will focus on encouraging schools and colleges to make students better prepared for an interactive, Internet-based working life. Perhaps this will mean, as some predict, more offering of short-term, highly marketable credentials such as certificates in operating certain kinds of popular cloud-based information tools. Chambers are unlikely to be the leading theorists of educational change. They may, however, be among the first to support successful pilot programs or to persuade local school boards to experiment to make their graduates more successful in the marketplace.

It's likely that chambers will continue to be drawn into educational policy discussions if for one reason only: schools need money and require outside support to back up their requests for it. Educators asking for more public money can sound self-serving. But when a relatively disinterested party such as a chamber of commerce – often with a reputation for hard business sense – speaks up for education and asks the voters or elected officials to say "yes," it can make all the difference. There are many school buildings today that owe a brick or two to the endorsement of the local chamber of commerce. Yet precisely because of the importance of the chamber's "vote" on such issues, it should be cast wisely and not automatically in either the "yes" or "no" column. Clearly, putting more money into education doesn't always improve education, a fact that business people are as likely to point out as anyone.

Ultimately, as Thomas Boushall of the U.S. Chamber noted in 1943, echoing comments of the influential Horace Mann a century earlier,[45] it's about incomes. Higher incomes are correlated with better education, a relationship that, if anything, appears to be getting stronger. If this is the case, chambers of commerce will not stray far from education, and may get a good deal more involved.

Government

In some examples above we have seen chambers interacting with government on transportation, education, and other issues. Chambers also exercised their traditional check on elected and bureaucratic power, and used their right to criticize public officials. Sometimes business organizations blew the whistle on what they perceived as corruption; more often it was for spending or taxing too much, or for wasting public funds.

In many cases, however, chambers were as much an ally of local government as an opponent. Chambers generally preferred one government over two or 20, when they had a choice, and this meant conferring more acreage and tax authority on that one government. Many municipalities expanded during the postwar era through annexations, often with the support of, if not at the instigation of, the local chamber. Tulsa and Oklahoma City underwent massive expansions as each attempted a sort of annexation one-upmanship.[46] San Jose's city manager, Dutch Hamann, who was first urged on the public scene by business organizations including the chamber, was just as anxious to grow.

Consolidation of city and county government, a sort of super-annexation, took place in a handful of cities, almost invariably with chamber support. Jacksonville, Florida, became the largest city in the United States through this method. The chamber was the leading force behind the consolidation of Duval County with the City of Jacksonville, according to Dave Cooley, who was the CEO of the chamber at the time (1967).[47] In Louisville, Kentucky, it took a charismatic mayor, Jerry Abramson, to put through consolidation, but he had the firm support of the chamber, which had been pushing for such a move for decades.

Conversely, the splitting of a city into two governments, while it might please a few citizens, was anathema to most local business organizations. Why double the number of public officials and taxing authorities? The Los Angeles Area Chamber of Commerce under CEO Rusty Hammer fought hard and successfully to keep Hollywood and the San Fernando Valley from their gnarly plan to secede from Los Angeles County in 2002.

Many cities got into fiscal trouble in the Sixties and thereafter, sometimes because of overspending on existing services, sometimes because of huge commitments of funds for pensions of city employees. Chambers of commerce routinely complained about spending problems but often did not have the power or influence to stop their cities' decline. Indeed, it was the New York Chamber's inability to solve the problems behind New York City's near bankruptcy in the mid-1970s that caused David Rockefeller to found the New York City Partnership in 1979. This organization, less a small-business advocacy group than a philanthropic and policy association of large-company CEOs, ultimately would absorb the once-great New York Chamber in 2002. At that time the New York Chamber had already given up its storied name, and was called the Chamber of Commerce and Industry.[48]

As the 21st century dawned, many chambers of commerce raised increasing concerns about the high pension obligations of city governments. Their stridency sometimes made them appear to be scolds, especially in the view of local politicians and union officials. But it was often chambers that were called on to advise cities when things went too far and when it was almost time to negotiate with the cities' creditors.

It was the Michigan Chamber of Commerce that lit a political fuse in 1990, which proceeded to explode two decades later. In the case of *Austin v Michigan Chamber of Commerce*, the business organization had challenged state restrictions on corporate financing of political campaigns, considering these to be in violation of Constitutional free-speech provisions. The chamber lost the case but won later when, in 2010, the verdict was overturned via the U.S. Supreme Court's ruling in *Citizens United v Federal Election Commission*.

The Supreme Court's *Citizens United* decision, which loosened restrictions on campaign contributions, opened up an era of free-spending political campaigns that arguably added an edge of harshness to American debates in the 21st century. At the same time, the free-for-all may have made races more competitive and certainly brought in plenty of out-of-town money to Congressional and other races. By empowering single-issue campaigns at the national level, the ruling may have, as an unintended consequence, weakened multiple-issue groups (such as chambers) operating at the local level.

The U.S. Chamber of Commerce, which had become a sleepy, overlooked force in Washington in the 70s and 80s, woke up suddenly in 1997 when the outspoken Tom Donohue took the helm. The organization quickly entered the lists on a wide variety of business issues and gave the name "chamber of commerce" a sharper edge in the public mind than it had had for years. Although local chambers of commerce were independent of the U.S. Chamber, many of them joined in its campaigns. Some of these were for centrist legislation on trade and immigration; others for causes targeting hot-button tax or union issues that some (but certainly not all) considered "far right." As was the case in the FDR years, some local chambers dropped out of the U.S. Chamber, complaining that its national aims conflicted with their local points of view.

Local chambers faced a novel group in the early 21st century that frequently opposed their agendas: the "Tea Party," or loosely organized groups of anti-tax activists. Chambers, as we have seen, weren't in great sympathy with the extremism of the original Boston Tea Party. In modern times, as earlier, chambers have been known to ask for a half-cent sales tax for this transportation improvement and a bond issue for that new school building. But for the Tea Party, which considers Americans greatly overtaxed as it is, any tax increase adds to an already unacceptable tax burden. Hence some chambers of commerce have found the most powerful political gales beating down on them not in the thunder and lightning from the left, but in the tempests of the Tea Party. Today when there's a troll under a bridge blocking its construction, often that wily monster is sipping a cup of tea.

Local chambers of commerce aren't invariably moderate: we've seen plenty of evidence of their going to the edges of public opinion on this issue or that. But as organizations rooted in place and unable to flee their communities, and as groups attempting to see that people get along well enough so that "business as usual" can continue to be conducted, chambers do tend to avoid extremes most of the time, at least on issues not directly affecting company finances. As such, they may become a force aiding the nation as it works to add more civility in public discourse. Indeed, not long ago the Denver Metro Chamber of Commerce made civility a goal of its public policy.

Cliff Dwellers

Walk into any of hundreds of chambers of commerce in the United States to see the photo galleries of past presidents or chairs on the walls, and you're likely to be struck by the faces of no one but white men up to sometime in the 1970s or 1980s. Some members of this wall-dwelling tribe may have been "young" – perhaps 40 or 45. But no matter how one examines the photographs or portraits, the idea is the same: this fraternity was hardly diverse. The face of business leadership was a white male one, generally speaking, until relatively recently.

The social changes of the 1960s gradually brought about shifts in corporate boardrooms that were, in turn, reflected in the membership of chambers of commerce, and then, even later, in the leadership of those chambers. The process of change continues, even if, to outsiders, it appears painfully slow. The leadership of the chamber of commerce in most cities and counties is a good deal whiter and perhaps more male than the membership of the nearest kindergarten. But things are transforming steadily, especially for women, who have become CEOs of many hundreds of chambers, including several of the largest in the land.[49]

The idea that only the most wealthy and powerful in the community must sit at, or hover near, the chamber's board meetings also has come in for a challenge. Society is more democratic today than it was in 1950. People do not want there to be a closed room anywhere in the county where their future is decided. In that sense, chambers of commerce have opened up, whether enthusiastically or not, to the world around them.

The imagined Dickensian business world of times past, which no one wants to bring back – everything from the counting-house to the high starched collars to the harsh discipline, poor working conditions, and long hours of laborers – is evoked indirectly by the old portrait gallery of the magnates of the New York Chamber of Commerce. The most imposing of these leadership portraits were gathered in the Great Hall of the New York Chamber's building before it was sold in 1989. The 1983 Eddie Murphy film *Trading Places* shows that Great Hall, the biggest room in a building called fictionally the "Heritage Club." It's clearly shown as a place of some other time, and not a very friendly one at that, and one that has an image, warranted or not, of snobbery and exclusivity.[50]

Thus it's no doubt a good thing that many chambers are perhaps less imposing as organizations than they once were. No one wants to be governed by the guy with the house on the hill. If chambers of commerce inspired only anxiety and reverence, they would not be effectively representing their business members today. Some things change for the better. At the same time, if chambers of commerce become so "nice" and friendly to the public that they don't stand for anything or accomplish anything, or exist nearly indistinguishably from a civic ensemble of other active groups, then they risk being ignored.

Internationalism and the Web

The chain stores that appeared to threaten local chambers of commerce in the 1920s, and the national and international forces that buffeted them in subsequent decades, haven't let up, with a few exceptions. Some chambers worried that they were made obsolete by the Great Depression, but all the main chambers survived the economic catastrophe, and they took note of that.[51] A chamber leader wondered rhetorically if chambers would be "among the expendables" in World War II, but they were not, just as he predicted: they found new jobs to do.[52] Since then, social changes and a host of other forces have blown across the civic landscape, obscuring local concerns and local chambers of commerce.

A relatively recent arrival, at least in the centuries-long history of chambers, has been the ubiquitous Internet. This protean new appendage to the human family, at times Big Brother and at other times a crazy uncle, now a friend and later an enemy and sometimes none of the above, has been viewed as an obliterator of local values. Nonetheless, the big moneymaker of the web is "local search," people's attempts to find businesses in their own communities. People are using the Internet, and mobile phone apps, to understand their own communities better.

All business is local. This is one of the insights of the Internet and of modern cell phone technology. Of the zillions of bits of information slung across the universe, a high percentage is about one's friends, one's community, or perhaps a handful of trusted web sites or organizations. Where can I get locally grown food? What's playing at the café down the street this Friday? Did you see the swim team video? What was the text that your daughter sent to my daughter? The Internet may be making us not less local, but more local.

If technology has not obliterated the local, what about local business? Here, too, it's hard to see the end of the world as we know it. Many Fortune 500 companies seek to give their firms a local look and to create local experiences. Companies, large and small, have no incentive to sweep Appleton, Wisconsin, or Hot Springs, Arkansas, off the map. It's much better to be considered a part of Appleton or Hot Springs than to be considered their Darth Vader. Even from a purely commercial standpoint, it's better to keep what's local than to try to stamp it out.

Community and Business

Local business is unlikely to disappear, even in the waves of internationalization and electronic commerce that are sweeping across every region. The same can be said of local government and decision making, which have been much put upon by the federal system over the years, but which persist, not only in the Constitution and in our imaginations, but in reality. It's still, perhaps more than ever despite our complaints about it, a free country.

If all these things remain with us – the idea of community and of local business and local government – then local business organizations will continue as well. With a few mortalities, and quite a few births, chambers of commerce have survived the past roughly 250 years in North America. And what will take them through another century or two?

Tomorrow's successful chambers, like today's, will require people who care simultaneously about two things: community and business. Chambers of commerce always have promoted the two values. Those who join chambers just to get business may be disappointed; those who join just to be a part of the community will lack some of the critical focus of these groups. But those who can look after the interests of business and keep an eye on the community will live in a world of creative possibility.

Community and business . . . living and making a living. The struggle of chambers is in many ways the struggle of people, of balancing the needs of consuming and producing. Beyond that, chambers, like people, seek to do something worth remembering: "We are not born for ourselves alone."

Chambers of commerce, indeed, are a lot like people. They operate with a mixture of motives. They aren't all good, and they aren't all bad. But when they get it right – really right, in a way that makes some significant and lasting change – their stories may, one day, live on beyond them and take off into the ages.

Appendix A

13 Reasons Why We Forget the Achievements of Local Chambers

1. Chambers tend to avoid taking credit for themselves. Ralph Waldo Emerson could have been speaking about them when he famously noted, "There is no limit to what can be accomplished if it doesn't matter who gets the credit." For best results, and for many reasons, chamber leaders tend to share the credit or even to step into the background behind their influential members or politicians. Chambers may therefore get a lot done, but not attract much notice to their role in the achievements.

2. Along with shared credit, chambers participate primarily in shared achievements. Chambers have few direct powers of their own; they don't throw people in jail or raise taxes. Therefore they must influence policy through other organizations and the government. But how does one evaluate a fractional share in something? Just like teachers, historians are averse to awarding partial credit. "The chamber was about 40 percent responsible for the new convention center" isn't a line that gets quoted in the New York Times Book Review or the Pulitzer judges' deliberations.

3. Chambers, although sometimes led by charismatic individuals, by definition are groups of people. We find groups harder to identify with or care about than specific individuals. Napoleon interests us more than the 600,000 men in his army outside Moscow.

4. Chambers start things but, by design, often don't finish them. When something new and different works, a chamber is as likely as not to turn it over to someone else, often another nonprofit organization, and to return to the core business of running a local chamber of commerce. Ten or 50 or 100 years down the road, few people, if any, remember who brought that new idea into the community or who kept it alive in its early stages.

5. "Rich boy makes good" or "rich boy does good" can make boring copy. Who cares if a group of privileged individuals in a chamber does something valuable? But actually, not every chamber member is rich (by a long shot), and not every rich person is a chamber member (by another long shot). Moreover, some chamber activities have been failures. But a busy journalist or historian may not have time to get past preconceived ideas of what constitutes the membership or the activities of chambers of commerce.

6.   The business of business people is business. Business people may be admired for their public spirit, but they are lionized for their success in making money and building enterprises. We tend to forget that people who have succeeded in one thing may succeed in another, and that one other thing, their work through a chamber of commerce, may on occasion be as enduring as, or more enduring than, what they accomplish for their own bank account.

7.   People assume that chamber achievement is inevitable and therefore not worth remembering. Of course chambers do a lot of things! If you put many of the most influential people in town into a room not just once, but several times a year, for a period of as much as one or even two centuries – and you multiply that times 500 or 5,000 communities – you are likely to end up with a few interesting achievements. The fallacy of this thought process is that it ignores any specifics. Some chambers do a lot with the people and resources they have, while others don't. Who succeeded, and why, and who didn't? Such explorations can uncover unexpected and useful information.

8.   Government agencies and nonprofit organizations have proliferated. In the past, chambers were one of a very few institutions that grappled with the key problems of civic life. Today there are hundreds of public agencies, private charities and other nonprofits, and local, state, and federal laws and regulations that tackle local issues, from the important to the almost insignificant. Chambers, including their sometimes glorious pasts, can get lost in the flood of activities and actors in the present.

9.   Local chambers are "just local." Where's the sweep of history and the path of armies? Where's the glamour of Main Street? What's the glory in changing a street-sign ordinance? And yet, as Tip O'Neill said, "All politics is local." Jerusalem, Florence, and Athens are local. From comparatively little places, big things can happen.

10. Local chambers aren't ideological. Sweeping ideas from the left or right often break up on the particular shores of communities and their chambers. These chambers tend to be pragmatic and, while many members may lean toward the right of the political center, are likely to veer wildly to the left when it comes to attracting federal or state money to their community. The ideological left, moreover, is suspicious of chambers because of their roots in local privilege, while the hard right is exasperated by chambers' willingness to campaign for a half-cent sales tax for transportation, a bond issue for education, or some other costly local cause. Hence these chamber organizations don't fit into any ideological box that's convenient shorthand for the public, academia, or the media.

11. Most chamber members are neither saints nor villains. Many of them care about money and profits and most of them aren't a bit ashamed of it. Yet chamber members do give of their time and money for things that do not yield immediate profit, and indeed that may never provide them an individual return on their investment.

12. Chambers of commerce depend to a significant extent on something that you can't touch. Do you believe in Atlanta? What is the "Atlanta spirit" or the "spirit of St. Louis"? These are essentially emotional bonds among people, some form of "spirit." We are accustomed to spiritualism in great matters of the soul or the religious community. And we are accustomed to belief in a "team spirit" that accomplishes small but measurable things against the odds, such as pushing a piece of pigskin past defenders the size of hogs. But what about spiritualism for one's community or for one's economy? This form of belief and togetherness can be, and has been, derided as insincere or misguided. Yet every form of spiritualism has found its critics. And civic or chamber spirit surely does exist. This intangible spirit is partly and sometimes largely responsible for a myriad of tangible creations, from roads and bridges to canals and auditoriums and public parks. Whether it's a "rah-rah" spirit or a buttoned-down, urbane, noblesse oblige-inspired caring for the community, it's still something immaterial but very real.

13. The U.S. Chamber of Commerce is seen as local chambers' leader. The U.S. Chamber was formed in 1912 through, in part, the efforts of many local chambers of commerce that wanted a national voice. They got that voice. An unintended consequence of that activity is that the local chambers are now seen by many in the public, incorrectly, as chapters commanded by the national chamber. Local chambers remain as individual, and as independent, as ever, but it's harder to see when newspapers report "the Chamber's" position. The U.S. Chamber has done important work, most of it centered around national politics and policies. It has a solid claim to its own place in American history over the past century. But local chambers, even after 1912, have continued to plug away at a host of issues and activities, and have no small list of achievements of their own.

Appendix B

Chamber Founding Dates

Founding Dates of Selected Local Chambers in the United States

Note: This list is not footnoted, nor is it complete. The author created it as an aid to his own research and is passing it on as a time-saver for readers and for those interested in further research.

1750-1800

New York, NY	1768	technically a state chamber but most activities were local
Charleston, SC	1773	re-formed in 1784
Boston, MA	1785	earlier, simpler groups, 1733, 1760; later chambers 1794, 1836, 1854
New Haven, CT	1794	revived 1872
Lexington, KY	1797	new chamber started in 1881
Hartford, CT	1799	new chamber started in 1888

1801-1850

Philadelphia, PA	1801	Board of Trade founded in 1833; absorbs chamber, 1845
Norfolk, VA	1801	revived 1858
Savannah, GA	1806	
New Orleans, LA	1806	re-formed in 1834
Meadville, PA	1807	
Baltimore, MD	1820	re-formed as Board of Trade in 1836; re-formed, 1849
Albany, NY	1823	or earlier; also in 1847; new organization in 1901
Pittsburgh, PA	1835	revived 1854
Mobile, AL	1836	
St. Louis, MO	1836	early traders' group in 1793
Wilmington, DE	1837	later Delaware State Chamber of Commerce
Galena, IL	1838	
Memphis, TN	1838	reestablished in 1860
Cincinnati, OH	1839	
Louisville, KY	1839	disbanded 1843; reorganized in 1862
Houston, TX	1840	
Matagorda, TX	1840	
Watertown, NY	1843	modern chamber, 1902
Apalachicola, FL	1843	possibly earlier

1801-1850, continued

Wheeling, WV	1843	"Virginia Board of Trade"; new chamber, 1966
Buffalo, NY	1844	
Columbus, GA	1845	
Galveston, TX	1845	apparently existed (without state charter) in 1841
Nashville, TN	1847	
Oswego, NY	1848	
Cleveland, OH	1848	
Chicago, IL	1848	(Board of Trade) (Chicago Assoc of Commerce, 1904)
Toledo, OH	1849	revived in 1895
San Francisco, CA	1850	
Honolulu, HI	1850	later CoC of Hawaii

1851-1900

Wilmington, NC	1853	
Portland, ME	1853	
Detroit, MI	1856	earlier organization in 1847; later in 1892, 1901
New Albany, IN	1857	possibly earlier
St. Paul, MN	1858	revived in 1867
Evansville, IN	1858	
Atlanta, GA	1859	
Denver, CO	1860	
Milwaukee, WI	1861	Chamber of Commerce (grain trading org) in 1858
Selma, AL	1861	
Macon, GA	1861	
Saginaw, MI	1862	
Troy, NY	1863	
Cairo, IL	1865	
Quincy, MA	1865	
Bay City, MI	1865	or earlier; new chamber, 1882
Bangor, ME	1865	or earlier (Mercantile Association); new org in 1872
Erie, PA	1865	or earlier
Kalamazoo, MI	1865	or earlier (Michigan Central Board of Trade)
Springfield, OH	1865	or earlier; reorganized 1869
Little Rock, AR	1866	
New Bern, NC	1866	new organization in 1899
Scranton, PA	1867	
Richmond, VA	1867	Board of Trade in 1854
Lincoln, NE	1867	
East St. Louis, IL	1867	
Salem, MA	1867	possibly earlier
Dubuque, IA	1868	
Newark, NJ	1868	

1851-1900, continued

Trenton, NJ	1868	
Providence, RI	1868	
Bath, ME	1868	or earlier
Burlington, IA	1868	or earlier
Peoria, IL	1868	or earlier (a Merchants' Exchange; Board of Trade in 1870)
Jackson, MI	1868	or earlier
Ogdensburgh, NY	1868	or earlier
Sandusky, OH	1868	or earlier
Madison, WI	1869	
Knoxville, TN	1869	
Portland, OR	1870	
San Diego, CA	1870	
Charlotte, NC	1870	
Lynchburg, VA	1870	
Leavenworth, KS	1870	or earlier
Chattanooga, TN	1870	or earlier
Portsmouth, OH	1870	or earlier
St. Joseph, MO	1871	or earlier
Washington, DC	1872	or earlier; predecessor of Gr. Washington Board of Trade
New London, CT	1872	or earlier
Burlington, VT	1872	or earlier; new org in 1889; another in 1910
Duluth, MN	1872	or earlier
Elgin, IL	1872	
Lancaster, PA	1872	
Worcester, MA	1873	reorganized in 1892
Montgomery, AL	1873	
Thurston Cty., WA	1873	
Paterson, NJ	1873	
Santa Barbara, CA	1873	
Dallas, TX	1874	Dallas Commercial Club in 1893; CoC in 1909
Bridgeport, CT	1874	
Erie, PA	1874	
Zanesville, OH	1874	or earlier
Walla Walla, WA	1875	
Tuscaloosa, AL	1875	
Minneapolis, MN	1876	
Austin, TX	1877	BoT; later became CoC
Greensboro, NC	1877	
Helena, MT	1877	BoT; in 1890, the chamber of commerce was founded
Lawrence, KS	1878	

1851-1900, continued

Astoria, OR	1878	or earlier
Muskegon, MI	1879	
Winona, MN	1879	
Dover, NH	1879	or earlier
Wichita, KS	1880	Commercial Club, 1897; new chamber, 1917
Topeka, KS	1880	
Fremont, NE	1880	
Vallejo, CA	1880	or earlier
Passaic, NJ	1880	
Reading, PA	1881	previous orgs in 1807 and 1870
Washington Cty., PA	1881	
Deadwood, SD	1881	
Cedar Rapids, IA	1881	
Iowa City, IA	1881	or earlier
Albert Lea, MN	1881	
Fort Worth, TX	1881	
Belleville, IL	1881	or earlier
Joliet, IL	1881	or earlier
Seattle, WA	1882	
Santa Fe, NM	1882	
Green Bay, WI	1883	
Petersburg, VA	1883	or earlier
Jacksonville, FL	1884	previous board of trade, 1867
Tacoma, WA	1884	
Columbus, OH	1884	
Tampa, FL	1885	
Boise, ID	1885	
Spokane, WA	1885	[current org founded in 1898]
New Bedford, MA	1885	
Fargo, ND	1885	or earlier
Terre Haute, IN	1885	or earlier
Winston-Salem, NC	1885	
San Jose, CA	1886	
Great Falls, MT	1886	
Rapid City, SD	1886	
Dodge City, KS	1886	board of trade; CoC founded in 1917
Pensacola, FL	1886	
Kansas City, MO	1887	previous chamber, 1856
Ogden, UT	1887	
Logan, UT	1887	or earlier
Rochester, NY	1887	
Salt Lake City, UT	1887	Utah BoT – 1879 or earlier; new chamber, 1902

1851-1900, continued

Grand Rapids, MI	1887	
Springfield, OH	1887	revived from 1868 organization
Ashtabula, OH	1887	
Lima, OH	1887	
Fort Smith, AR	1887	
Provo, UT	1887	
Bartow, FL	1887	
Findlay, OH	1887	
Muncie, IN	1887	
Eureka, CA	1887	or earlier
Anderson, SC	1887	or earlier; new chamber formed, 1902
Greenville, SC	1887	or earlier
Goldsboro, NC	1887	or earlier
Meridian, MS	1887	or earlier
Winona, MN	1887	or earlier
Mankato, MN	1887	or earlier
Brunswick, GA	1887	or earlier
Lewiston, ID	1887	[Lewiston Sun newspaper]
Phoenix, AZ	1888	
Raleigh, NC	1888	
Los Angeles, CA	1888	Board of Trade founded 1883; chamber existed in 1876
St. Albans, VT	1888	
Long Beach, CA	1888	
Pasadena, CA	1888	
Johnstown, PA	1888	
Fort Scott, KS	1888	or earlier
Jersey City, NJ	1888	
Catlettsburg, KY	1888	
Des Moines, IA	1888	
Syracuse, NY	1889	Board of Trade incorporated in 1878
Jackson, MS	1889	
Bradenton, FL	1889	reorganized in 1895, 1925, and 1962
Kearney, NE	1889	
Waterbury, CT	1889	
Oklahoma City, OK	1889	
Santa Ana, CA	1889	
Santa Cruz, CA	1889	
Sing Sing, NY	1889	
Elizabeth, NJ	1889	or earlier
Napa, CA	1889	
Indianapolis, IN	1890	earlier attempts in 1853, 1857, 1864 and 1870

1851-1900, continued

City	Year	Notes
Spencer, IA	1890	
Missoula, MT	1890	
Roanoke, VA	1890	
Springfield, MA	1890	
Montgomery, AL	1890	
Stamford, CT	1890	
Helena, AR	1890	or earlier
Hastings, NE	1890	or earlier
Gloversville, NY	1890	
Coatesville, PA	1890	
Flagstaff, AZ	1891	
Billings, MT	1891	
Conway, AR	1891	
Colorado Springs, CO	1892	
Beaufort, SC	1892	
Modesto, CA	1892	new chamber in 1912
Birmingham, AL	1892	
Williamsport, PA	1892	or earlier
Yonkers, NY	1893	
Tallahassee, FL	1893	or earlier
Hopkinsville, KY	1893	
Yakima, WA	1893	
Omaha, NE	1893	earlier organization in 1872
Tempe, AZ	1893	reorgs in 1896, 1908, 1912
Vicksburg, MS	1894	
Norwood, MA	1894	
Chester, PA	1894	or earlier
Keokuk, IA	1894	or earlier
Fullerton, CA	1894	
Huntsville, AL	1894	
San Antonio, TX	1894	earlier org. existed in 1872; also, Commercial Club in 1866
Danville, VA	1894	earlier org. existed in 1887
Staunton, VA	1894	or earlier
Bronx, NY	1894	new chamber in 1915
Sacramento, CA	1895	
Moline, IL	1895	
Medford, OR	1895	
Staten Island, NY	1895	
Tucson, AZ	1896	
Harlem, NY	1896	
Meriden, CT	1896	attempt at formation in 1887

1851-1900, continued

Asheville, NC	1898	
York, PA	1898	Board of Trade existed in 1892
Hawaii Island, HI	1898	
El Paso, TX	1899	earlier organization in 1873
Waco, TX	1899	
Fort Atkinson, WI	1899	
Fresno, CA	1899	or earlier
Port Arthur, TX	1899	
Marysville, CA	1900	
Charleston, WV	1900	BoT existed in 1889
Covina, CA	1900	
Woodland, CA	1900	
Champaign, IL	1900	

1901-1950

St. Petersburg, FL	1901	(earlier chamber in 1899)
Freeport, IL	1901	
Haverhill, MA	1901	
Eugene, OR	1902	
Glastonbury, CT	1902	
Enumclaw, WA	1902	
Columbia, SC	1902	(earlier Board of Trade was at Taxpayers Convention, 1871)
Newport News, VA	1903	
Tulsa, OK	1903	
Kalamazoo, MI	1903	
Paris, IL	1903	
Athens, GA	1903	
Lompoc, CA	1903	
Beaumont, TX	1903	
Albany, OR	1904	
Kalispell, MT	1904	
Rocky Mount, NC	1904	
Fort Collins, CO	1904	
Grand Forks, ND	1904	previous chamber existed in 1882
Hampton, VA	1904	
New Paltz, NY	1904	
Peterborough, NH	1904	
Kankakee, IL	1904	
Oakland, CA	1905	Board of Trade existed in 1892
Clarksville, TN	1905	Board of Trade existed in 1870
Berkeley, CA	1905	

1901-1950, continued

Davenport, IA	1905	earlier org existed in 1872
Corpus Christi, TX	1905	
Boulder, CO	1905	
Davis, CA	1905	
Jackson, TN	1905	
Alexandria, VA	1906	
Durham, NC	1906	
Santa Rosa, CA	1906	
Sapulpa, OK	1906	
Steamboat Spgs., CO	1906	
Cheyenne, WY	1907	BoT in 1868 or earlier; new one in 1897 started rodeo
Akron, OH	1907	
Dayton, OH	1907	commercial club existed in 1899
Greenville, NC	1907	
Miami, FL	1907	
Bremerton, WA	1907	
Augusta, GA	1907	board of trade existed in 1869
Poughkeepsie, NY	1907	board of trade existed in 1872
Binghamton, NY	1907	
Edmond, OK	1907	
Alexandria, MN	1907	
Elko, NV	1907	
Oshkosh, WI	1907	
Porterville, CA	1907	
Garden Grove, CA	1907	
Temple, TX	1907	
Newport Beach, CA	1907	
Abilene, TX	1908	
Kingsville, TX	1908	
Wichita Falls, TX	1908	
Monterey, CA	1908	
Natchez, MS	1908	
South Bend, IN	1909	
Mission San Jose, CA	1909	
Albany, GA	1910	Board of Trade existed in 1873
Elizabeth City, NC	1910	
Fort Lauderdale, FL	1910	
Prescott, AZ	1910	
St. Augustine, FL	1910	
New Brunswick, NJ	1910	earlier attempt in 1887
Rockford, IL	1910	
Salina, KS	1910	

1901-1950, continued

Shreveport, LA	1910	earlier org existed in 1872 (Board of Trade)
Winter Haven, FL	1910	
Palo Alto, CA	1910	
North Hollywood, CA	1910	called Lankershim Businessmen's Association at first
Las Vegas, NV	1911	predecessor organization founded in 1906
Van Nuys, CA	1911	
Fall River, MA	1911	BoT existed in 1875
Lakeland, FL	1911	
Lakewood, OH	1911	
Elizabeth, N	1911	BoT existed in 1879
Bangor, ME	1911	Board of Trade in 1872
Queens, NY	1911	
Manchester, NH	1911	Earlier org about 1890
Kinston, NC	1911	
Warsaw, IN	1911	
Chambersburg, PA	1911	
Peoria, IL	1911	
Pittsfield, MA	1911	
Hammond, IN	1912	
Wausau, WI	1912	
Carrollton, MO	1912	
Valdosta, GA	1912	
Apopka, FL	1912	
Sauk Valley, IL	1912	
Streator, IL	1912	
Pasco, WA	1912	
Pueblo, CO	1912	
Sumter, SC	1912	
Coeur d'Alene, ID	1912	predecessor organization formed in 1903
Canoga Park, CA	1912	
Hermosa Beach, CA	1912	
Pierre, SD	1912	
Battle Creek, MI	1912	
Lake Worth, FL	1912	
Bayonne, NJ	1912	
Rome, NY	1912	
Plattsburgh, NY	1912	
Chandler, AZ	1912	
Mesa, AZ	1912	
Denison, TX	1912	
Cache, UT	1912	
Somerset, PA	1912	Somerset, PA; Merchants' Association existed previously

1901-1950, continued

Frederick, MD	1912	first chamber chartered by the U.S. Chamber
West Palm Beach, FL	1913	
Orlando, FL	1913	
Gaston, NC	1913	
Owensboro, KY	1913	BoT incorporated in 1888
Kauai, HI	1913	
Brockton, MA	1913	precursor BoT founded in 1897
Lafayette, IN	1913	
Charlottesville, VA	1913	
Lubbock, TX	1913	
Indiana, PA	1913	
Harrisburg, PA	1913	BoT incorporated in 1886
Carlisle, PA	1913	
Canton, OH	1914	
Atlantic City, NJ	1914	
Bluffton, IN	1914	
Kokomo, IN	1914	
Whittier, CA	1914	
Corning, NY	1914	
Madison, WI	1914	
Sheboygan, WI	1914	
La Habra, CA	1914	
Novato, CA	1915	
Laredo, TX	1915	
Waukegan, IL	1915	
Bloomington, IN	1915	
Anchorage, AK	1915	
Cape May, NJ	1916	previous board of trade formed in 1878
San Angelo, TX	1916	
Watertown, SD	1916	
Kenosha, WI	1916	
Fredericksburg, VA	1916	
The Dalles, OR	1916	
Joplin, MO	1917	
Albuquerque, NM	1917	commercial club existed in 1897
Greenwich, CT	1917	
Laguna Beach, CA	1917	
Cape Girardeau, MO	1917	BoT existed in 1894
Elko, NV	1917	
Brooklyn, NY	1918	
Annapolis, MD	1918	
Spartanburg, SC	1918	BoT existed in 1887

1901-1950, continued

Michigan City, IN	1918	
Ennis, TX	1918	previous Commercial Club
Springfield, MO	1919	
New Braunfels, TX	1919	
Dothan, AL	1919	
Concord, NH	1919	
Chillicothe, OH	1919	
Glenwood Spgs., CO	1919	
Manhattan, NY	1920	
Gilbert, AZ	1920	
Casa Grande, AZ	1920	
San Rafael, CA	1920	
Golden, CO	1920	
Nacogdoches, TX	1920	
Jerome, AZ	1920	
Sanford, FL	1920	Sanford Commercial Club, 1900
Bakersfield, CA	1920	
State College, PA	1920	
Hollywood, CA	1921	to replace Hollywood Board of Trade
Lakeland, FL	1921	
Traverse City, MI	1921	
Evanston, IL	1921	
Sarasota, FL	1921	
Monroe, LA	1921	
Culver City, CA	1921	
Orange, CA	1921	
McPherson, MO	1921	
Miami Beach, FL	1921	
Gallatin, TN	1921	
Rogers, AR	1922	
Clearwater, FL	1922	
Milford, MA	1922	
Alamosa, CO	1923	
Lake Mary, FL	1923	
Winnetka, IL	1923	
Lodi, CA	1923	
Baton Rouge	1923	beginning of the modern chamber
Reidsville, NC	1923	
Beverly Hills, CA	1923	
Corpus Christi, TX	1924	
Ada, OK	1924	
Westminster, MD	1924	

1901-1950, continued

Orange, VA	1924	
Longview, WA	1924	
Gainesville, FL	1924	
Manhattan, KS	1925	
Hancock, MD	1925	
Santa Monica, CA	1925	
Uniontown, PA	1925	
Delray Beach, FL	1925	
Fairfax County, VA	1925	
Gaithersburg, MD	1926	
Amarillo, TX	1926	
Buckeye, AZ	1926	
Saratoga, CA	1926	earlier org started in 1887
Bend, OR	1926	
Long Island, NY	1926	
Shelbyville, KY	1926	
Arlington, VA	1927	
Encino, CA	1927	
Punxsutawney, PA	1927	
Naples, FL	1928	
Seat Pleasant, MD	1928	
Rockwall, TX	1929	
Madison, SD	1930	
Wickenburg, AZ	1931	
Hackensack, NJ	1933	
Nantucket Isl., MA	1934	
Conroe, TX	1934	
Manassas, VA	1935	
Columbus, NE	1935	
Danbury, CT	1936	
Brownsville, TX	1937	
Monterey Park, CA	1937	
Washington, DC	1938	D.C. Chamber of Commerce
Myrtle Beach, SC	1938	
Cortez, CO	1938	
Marathon, FL	1939	
Paducah, KY	1939	
Washington, MO	1939	
San Mateo, CA	1939	
Bethany, DE	1939	
Troy, OH	1939	
Front Royal, VA	1940	

1901-1950, continued

Strongsville, OH	1941
Palmdale, CA	1941
San Bruno, CA	1942
Cullman, AL	1943
Henderson, NV	1945
Arlington, TX	1945
Downington, PA	1945
Quantico, VA	1945
Richardson, TX	1946
Roseville, CA	1947
Goleta, CA	1947
Santa Clara, CA	1947
Falls Church, VA	1947
Glen Burnie, MD	1947
Danville, CA	1948
Zapata, TX	1948
Howell, MI	1949
Auburn, AL	1949
Lake Elsinore, CA	1949
Warner Robins, GA	1949

1951-2010

Paramus, NJ	1951	
Boca Raton, FL	1952	
Deerfield Beach, FL	1952	
Grapevine, TX	1952	
Brentwood, MO	1953	
Federal Way, WA	1953	
Waseca, MN	1953	
Euless, TX	1953	
Concord, MA	1953	
Chincoteague, VA	1954	
Castle Rock, CO	1954	
Albertville, AL	1955	
Rochester, MI	1955	
Parma, OH	1955	
Amherst, NY	1956	
Mesquite, TX	1956	
Mahwah, NJ	1957	
Rockville, MD	1957	earlier chamber founded 1925
Brandon, FL	1959	
Keizer, OR	1959	

1951-2010, continued

Princeton, NJ	1960
Bellevue, NE	1961
Clear Lake, TX	1962
Katy, TX	1962
Woodbridge, NJ	1964
Pearland, TX	1965
Thibodaux, LA	1966
Plainfield, IN	1967
Leesburg, VA	1968
Cocoa Beach, FL	1968
Barrington, IL	1969
Northern Ky, KY	1969
Lake Havasu City, AZ	1970
Middletown, DE	1972
Mason, MI	1972
North Pole, AK	1973
Wilsonville, OR	1973
Cedar Park, TX	1973
Crisfield, MD	1975
Chesterfield, MO	1976
Moncks Corner, SC	1977
Louisburg, NC	1977
Hoover, AL	1978
Green Valley, AZ	1979
Oviedo, FL	1982
Reston, VA	1982
Englewood, CO	1983
Gretna, NE	1984
Otay Mesa, CA	1987
Clarkston, MI	1988
Palm Bay, FL	1989
Chelmsford, MA	1990
Gas City, IN	1992
Holden, MA	1992
Ahwatukee, AZ	1994
Holladay, SC	2003
Brookfield, CT	2005
Linden, TN	2006
Lone Tree, CO	2006
Algonquin/ Lake in the Hills, IL	2008

Founding Dates of State Chambers[1]

Hawaii	1850	
Utah	1879	or earlier; new organization in 1929
California	1887	new one in 1921
Louisiana	1889	or earlier
Maine	1889	
Nevada	1890	
Massachusetts	1890	
Connecticut	1890	another group, 1899 (Conn. Business Men's Assn.)
New York	1891	NY State Board of Trade; Empire State CoC, 1926
Virginia	1892	re-formed in 1924
Ohio	1893	reorganized in 1924
New Jersey	1911	
New Hampshire	1913	re-formed in 1923
Georgia	1915	new organization, 1928
Pennsylvania	1916	
Illinois	1919	
Oregon	1919	
California	1921	began as California Development Association
Indiana	1922	
Missouri	1923	
Washington state	1923	
Kansas	1924	
Florida	1925	began as Florida Tick Eradication Committee, 1916
Mississippi	1925	began as Mississippi State Board of Development
Idaho	1925	
Oklahoma	1927	
South Dakota	1929	or earlier
Maryland	1929	organization "well under way" at this time
Wisconsin	1929	
Colorado	1929	called "Colorado Association"
North Dakota	1929	or earlier; called "Greater North Dakota Association"
Montana	1931	
Delaware	1935	[official name change from Wilmington CoC – 1942]
Michigan	1935	re-formed in 1959
West Virginia	1936	
Kentucky	1946	
Vermont	1957	

Founding Dates of Selected Minority Chambers

Colored Board of Trade, Macon, GA, 1881 [limited information; Woolf, 4]
Italian Chamber of Commerce, San Francisco, 1886
Italian Chamber of Commerce, New York, 1888
National Negro Business League, 1900 [founded by Booker T. Washington]
Honolulu Japanese Chamber of Commerce, 1900
Hawaii Chinese Chamber of Commerce, 1911
Nashville Negro Board of Trade, 1912
Japanese Chamber of Commerce, Los Angeles, 1916
Dallas Black Chamber, 1926
Colored Merchants' Association (Montgomery, AL), 1928
San Antonio Hispanic, 1929 (oldest Hispanic chamber in the country)
Atlanta Negro Chamber of Commerce, 1933 or earlier
Houston Citizens CoC (black), 1935
Negro Chamber of Commerce (Chicago), 1937
Alamo City Black Chamber of Commerce (originally Negro Chamber of Commerce), San Antonio, 1938
Chinese Chamber of Commerce (Phoenix), 1939
Hawaii Korean Chamber of Commerce, 1940
Merced County (CA) Hispanic Chamber of Commerce, 1947
Arizona Hispanic Chamber of Commerce, 1948
Honolulu Japanese Junior Chamber of Commerce, 1949
Hispanic Chamber of Commerce of Silicon Valley, 1955
Chinese Chamber of Commerce (Los Angeles), 1955
Greater Seattle Chinese Chamber of Commerce, 1963
Sand Springs (OK) Women's Chamber of Commerce, 1966
Korean American Chamber of Commerce (SF Bay Area), 1967
Sacramento Hispanic Chamber of Commerce, 1972
San Francisco Black Chamber of Commerce, 1973
Native Hawaiian Chamber of Commerce, 1974
Golden Gate Business Association, 1974 [first gay and lesbian coc in USA]
Greater Washington Hispanic Chamber of Commerce, 1976
Latin American Chamber of Commerce (Chicago), 1976
Hispanic Chamber of Commerce of Greater Kansas City, 1977
Houston Hispanic Chamber of Commerce, 1977
Denver Hispanic Chamber of Commerce, 1978
U.S. Hispanic Chamber of Commerce, 1979
San Diego's Gay and Lesbian Chamber of Commerce, 1979
Hispanic Chamber of Commerce of Metropolitan St. Louis, 1982
Capital City African American Chamber of Commerce (Austin, TX), 1982
North American Indian Chamber of Commerce (Tucson), 1983
Central California Hispanic Chamber of Commerce, 1983
Philippine Chamber of Commerce (Chicago), 1984

Founding Dates of Selected Minority Chambers, continued

Georgia Hispanic Chamber of Commerce, 1984
U.S. Pan Asian Chamber of Commerce, 1984
Kern County Hispanic Chamber of Commerce, 1985
Asian Chamber of Commerce (Las Vegas), 1986
Orange County Hispanic Chamber of Commerce (California), 1986
San Diego County Hispanic Chamber of Commerce, 1989
Michigan Hispanic Chamber of Commerce, 1989
Camden County (NJ) Hispanic Chamber of Commerce, 1990
Denver Gay and Lesbian Chamber of Commerce, 1992
Greek American Chamber of Commerce (New Jersey), 1992
San Diego Regional African American Chamber of Commerce, 1992
San Diego County Black Chamber of Commerce, 1992
Hispanic Chamber of Commerce (Orlando), 1993
National Black Chamber of Commerce, 1993
Southern Colorado Women's Chamber of Commerce, 1993
Madera Hispanic Chamber of Commerce, 1993
African American Chamber of Commerce of San Antonio, 1993
Atlanta Gay & Lesbian Chamber of Commerce, 1994
Hudson Valley (NY) Hispanic Chamber of Commerce, 1994
California Black Chamber of Commerce, 1994
Gulf Coast Latin Chamber of Commerce, 1994
Austin Asian Chamber of Commerce, 1995
Chicago Area Gay & Lesbian Chamber of Commerce, 1996
Birmingham Black Chamber of Commerce, 1997
Antelope Valley (CA) Hispanic Chamber of Commerce, 1997
Irving Hispanic Chamber of Commerce, 1998
Armenian American Chamber of Commerce (Southern California), 1999
Chattanooga African American Chamber of Commerce, 1999
Greater Tulsa Hispanic Chamber of Commerce, 1999
Jackson Madison County African American Chamber of Commerce, 1999
(Memphis area)
Colombian-American Chamber of Commerce (Atlanta), 1999
Virginia Hispanic Chamber of Commerce, 2000
U.S. Women's Chamber of Commerce, 2001
Indus Valley American Chamber of Commerce (Northern California), 2001
Baltimore Hispanic Chamber of Commerce, 2001
Nashville Area Hispanic Chamber of Commerce, 2001
Greater San Jose Hispanic Chamber of Commerce, 2002
Afghan-American Chamber of Commerce (Virginia), 2002
Florida Puerto Rican-Hispanic Chamber of Commerce, 2002
New Mexico Hispanic Chamber of Commerce, 2003
West Michigan Hispanic Chamber of Commerce, 2003

Founding Dates of Selected Minority Chambers, continued

California Turkish American Chamber of Commerce, 2004
Barstow Hispanic Chamber of Commerce, 2005
Rwanda-American Chamber of Commerce (Miami), 2005
International Gay and Lesbian Chamber of Commerce (Montreal), 2006
Tennessee Chinese Chamber of Commerce, 2007
American Muslim Chamber of Commerce, 2009

Gay and Lesbian chambers with founding dates:

http://www.nglcc.org/BIZ/community/miniprofiles

Founding Dates of Selected Local and Provincial Chambers in Canada

Halifax, NS	1750	
Quebec, QC	1776	re-formed 1809
St. John, NB	1819	
Montreal, QC	1822	
Kingston, ON	1841	
Toronto, ON	1845	
Hamilton, ON	1845	
Ottawa, ON	1857	
Victoria, BC	1863	
Charlottetown, PEI	1865	or earlier
London, ON	1865	or earlier
St. Catherine's, ON	1865	or earlier
Windsor, ON	1865	or earlier
Stratford, ON	1865	or earlier
Guelph, ON	1868	
St. Thomas, ON	1869	
Winnipeg, Manitoba	1873	
Prince Edward Island	1874	
Kitchener, ON	1886	
Vancouver, BC	1887	
Edmonton, Alberta	1889	
Niagara Falls, ON	1889	
Sault Ste. Marie, ON	1889	
Calgary, Alberta	1891	
St. John's, NL	1894	
Kelowna, BC	1906	
Prince George, BC	1911	
Burlington, ON	1947	
Oakville, ON	1949	

Founding Dates of Selected Other Foreign Chambers

Marseilles	1599	
Paris	1618	addressed by Samuel de Champlain in this year
Bruges	1667	based on Brokers Guild, 1293
Dunkirk	1700	
Bayonne, France	1726	
Denmark	1742	
Jersey	1767	
Guernsey	1768	reestablished in 1808
Florence	1770	
Liverpool	1774	
Manchester	1774	also 1793, 1820
Jamaica (Kingston)	1778	also 1785, 1839
Dublin	1783	
Belfast	1783	refounded 1802
Glasgow	1783	
Birmingham	1783	
Waterford	1787	refounded 1804
Cologne	1803	
Rotterdam	1803	
Cape Town	1804	
Limerick	1807	
Guernsey	1808	
Frankfurt on Main	1808	
Warsaw	1809	
Newcastle	1813	
Moscow	1813	Moscow Merchants' Society
Metz	1815	
Cork	1819	
Danzig (Gdansk)	1822	
Bristol	1823	
Barbados	1825	
Sydney	1825	
Dusseldorf	1831	
Calcutta	1834	
Rio de Janeiro	1834	
Lisbon	1834	
Madras	1836	
Bombay	1836	
Singapore	1837	
Penang	1837	
Ceylon	1839	
Adelaide	1839	

Founding Dates of Selected Other Foreign Chambers, continued

Munich	1843	
Vienna	1848	
Malta	1848	
Santo Domingo, DR	1848	
Liverpool	1850	
Mauritius	1850	
Bratislava	1850	
Pest (Budapest)	1850	
Melbourne	1851	
Southampton	1851	
Auckland	1856	
Durban	1856	
Karachi	1860	
Hong Kong	1861	
Leipzig	1862	
Dresden	1862	
Geneva	1865	
Yokohama	1866	first annual report published
Bucharest	1868	
Dakar	1870	
Zurich	1873	
Tokyo	1878	
Trinidad and Tobago	1879	
London	1882	earlier existence in 1782 to 1800
Istanbul	1882	
Damascus	1882	
Gibraltar	1882	
Seoul	1884	
Tunis	1885	
Izmir	1885	
Barcelona	1886	
Madrid	1887	
Perth	1890	
Johannesburg	1890	
Stockholm	1902	
Shanghai	1902	
Bath	1902	
Bermuda	1907	
Haifa	1910	
Macao	1913	
Helsinki	1917	
Tel Aviv	1919	

Founding Dates of Selected Other Foreign Chambers, continued

Alexandria, Egypt	1919
Cairo	1920
Amman	1923
Baghdad	1926
Tehran	1926
Aruba	1930
Bahrain	1939
Addis Ababa	1947
Dhaka	1956
Kuwait	1959
Qatar	1963
Cayman Islands	1965
Dubai	1965
Phnom Penh	1995

Miscellaneous

International Chamber of Commerce: 1919
Junior Chamber of Commerce: 1920
International Bureau of Chambers of Commerce (now World Chambers Federation): 1951
Eurochambres: 1958

Notes

Introduction

1 Nathaniel Hawthorne, *Mosses from an Old Manse* (New York: George P. Putnam, 1851), 163-4.

2 Study by Cortera Inc. for the American Chamber of Commerce Executives, February 2010. Ten different chambers' members in ten different states were studied to evaluate their credit ratings. See for example: "New Study Shows Chamber of Commerce Members Offer Safer Bet When it Comes to Business Credit Risk," Cortera Inc. press release, February 22, 2010.

Beginnings

1 William J. Bernstein, *A Splendid Exchange: How Trade Shaped the World* (New York: Grove Press, 2008), 23-24.

2 William J. Bernstein, *A Splendid Exchange: How Trade Shaped the World* (New York: Grove Press, 2008), 26.

3 Werner Keller, *The Bible as History*, Second Revised Edition (Barnes & Noble Books, 1995), 62.

4 William J. Bernstein, *A Splendid Exchange: How Trade Shaped the World* (New York: Grove Press, 2008), 27.

5 William J. Bernstein, *A Splendid Exchange: How Trade Shaped the World* (New York: Grove Press, 2008), 43-53.

6 William J. Bernstein, *A Splendid Exchange: How Trade Shaped the World* (New York: Grove Press, 2008), 8.

7 Charles Rockwell, *Sketches of Foreign Travel and Life at Sea* (Boston: Tappan and Dennet, 1842), Volume II, 219.

8 "I am a Jew, from Tarsus in Cilicia, a citizen of no mean city." Acts 21: 39.

9 Andries Van den Abele and Michael Catry, *Makelaars in handelaars: Van middeleeuwse nering del makelaars naar moderne kamer van koophandel in het XVIIde-eeuwse Brugge, met de list van de leden (1281-1795) en van de besturen (1340-1791)*, (Bruges, 1992), English summary, 170-2.

10 Hugh Chisholm, editor, "Trade Organizations," *Encyclopedia Britannica*, 11th Edition, Volume 27 (Cambridge, England: University Press, 1911), 137.

11 David Hackett Fischer, *Champlain's Dream* (New York: Simon and Schuster Paperbacks, 2008), 353-356.

12 Hugh Chisholm, editor, "Trade Organizations," *Encyclopedia Britannica*, 11th Edition, Volume 27 (Cambridge, England: University Press, 1911), 137.

13 Napoleon Bonaparte, letter to Joseph Fouché, minister of police, July 28, 1809, from: M. Leon Lecestre, Editor, *New Letters of Napoleon I, Omitted From the Edition Published Under the Auspices of Napoleon III* (New York: D. Appleton and Company, 1898), 140-1. Here is the quoted passage with more context: "We do not need any advice from the Chamber of Commerce. . . Some conversation with certain well-informed merchants may be useful, but the deliberations of the Chambers are invariably valueless, and have certain serious drawbacks." Earlier in the same letter, Napoleon writes: "I have received a farrago which you have sent me on the subject of the corn trade, and which is perfectly ridiculous. I do not know why you begin there. I wonder you did not begin by teaching me the alphabet. It is mere political economists' chatter. . . The chamber of commerce knows nothing at all, and only chatters theories. I beg you will not expose me to the annoyance of receiving such memoirs." Napoleon's cavalier attitude toward others' possessions no doubt failed to endear him to chambers and helps explain his low esteem for those institutions. When the emperor made a big deal of establishing a chamber in Amsterdam, a local merchant complained that, thanks to the ravages of French troops, "there was no need of a chamber, since a closet would hold all the commerce left them." This is from: Sir Walter Scott, *Life of Napoleon Bonaparte* (Paris: A. and W. Galignani, 1828), 506.

14 John Latimer, *The History of the Society of Merchant Venturers of the City of Bristol* (Bristol, U.K.: J.W. Arrowsmith, 1903), 2.

15 David Macpherson, *Annals of Commerce* (1805), as quoted by Cornelius Walford in the entry, "Chamber of Commerce," in *The Insurance Cyclopedia*, Volume 1 (New York: J.H. and C.M. Goodsell, 1871), 485. Macpherson states: "The King being desirous of consulting with judicious and prudent merchants concerning the establishment of the staple of wool in Flanders and other commercial matters, John of Cherleton, citizen of Lond. and mayor of the merchants of England, who was furnished by the King's council with a particular statement of the matters to be considered, together with two merchants chosen out of every city and burgh throughout the kingdom, were summoned to meet in Lond. in the Octaves of St. Hilary, in order to deliberate upon those matters (*Foedera*, vol. iii p. 740). This is, properly speaking, the earliest council of trade known in English history or record, as the merchants appear to have formed a board of themselves; whereas those summoned to Lincoln in the year 1315 seem to have been called only to give information and perhaps advice to the King's council or parliament."

16 John Latimer, *The History of the Society of Merchant Venturers of the City of Bristol* (Bristol, U.K.: J.W. Arrowsmith, 1903), 36-46. For the Cabot voyage, see for example: "About Us," The Society of Merchant Venturers, www.merchantventurers.com.

17 In later years, the Board of Trade's powers were diminished in the run-up to the American Revolution because George III did not want opposition. On a different matter, the Board of Trade is often confused with the U.S. and Canadian "boards of trade" that would emerge in the 19th century. These North American organizations shared the British council's name, but were far different in structure: these were mostly either local, voluntary chambers of commerce, agricultural commodity trading organizations, or both.)

18 Robert J. Bennett, *Local Business Voice: The History of Chambers of Commerce in Britain, Ireland, and Revolutionary America 1760-2011* (Oxford: Oxford University Press, 2011), 93-98. All the information in this paragraph comes from Bennett's excellent description of the intellectual origins of chambers in the English-speaking world.

19 Robert J. Bennett, *Local Business Voice: The History of Chambers of Commerce in Britain, Ireland, and Revolutionary America 1760-2011* (Oxford: Oxford University Press, 2011), 126.

20 Thomas Beamish Akins, *History of Halifax City* (Halifax, Nova Scotia, 1895), 27.

21 Thomas Beamish Akins, *History of Halifax City* (Halifax, Nova Scotia, 1895), 27.

22 Brian Cuthbertson, *Voices of Business: A History of Commerce in Halifax 1750-2000* (Halifax, Nova Scotia: Metropolitan Halifax Chamber of Commerce, 2000). According to this source, in 1786, a new, possibly short-lived, group was formed, the Halifax Marine Association, also "for the benefit of trade." Then, after peace with France in 1803 reduced the business of Halifax merchants, they came together in 1804 to form the Halifax Committee of Trade to "solicit His Majesty's Ministers for relief, and generally to watch over the interests of the trade and commercial concerns of this community." This group is the ancestor of today's Metropolitan Halifax Chamber of Commerce.

23 Ron Taylor, *A History of Chambers of Commerce in the United Kingdom, 1768-2007* (London: British Chambers of Commerce, 2007), 10.

24 Robert J. Bennett, *Local Business Voice: The History of Chambers of Commerce in Britain, Ireland, Revolutionary America 1760-2011* (Oxford: Oxford University Press, 2011), Chapter 5, "Diffusion."

25 Robert J. Bennett, *Local Business Voice: The History of Chambers of Commerce in Britain, Ireland, and Revolutionary America 1760-2011* (Oxford: Oxford University Press, 2011), 13, footnote 5. See also: Anna Plunkett-Cole, "Early Years of the Jersey Chamber of Commerce," This is Jersey Website:

http://www.thisisjersey.com/2008/11/27/early-years-of-the-jersey-chamber-of-commerce/

26 Robert J. Bennett, *Local Business Voice: The History of Chambers of Commerce in Britain, Ireland, and Revolutionary America 1760-2011* (Oxford: Oxford University Press, 2011), 14.

New Chambers in a New Nation (1768-1815)

1 John Austin Stevens Jr., *Colonial New York: Sketches Biographical and Historical 1768-1784* (New York: John F. Trow & Co., 1867), 62-63.

2 John Austin Stevens Jr., *Colonial Records of the New York Chamber of Commerce, 1768-1784* (New York: John F. Trow & Co., 1867), 313-314.

3 John Austin Stevens, *Sketches Biographical and Historical* (New York: John F. Trow & Co., 1867), 10-11.

4 Joseph Bucklin Bishop, *A Chronicle of 150 Years: The Chamber of Commerce of the State of New York 1768-1918* (New York: Charles Scribner's Sons, 1918), 2. For a copy of the charter, see: John Austin Stevens Jr., *Colonial Records of the New York Chamber of Commerce, 1768-1784* (New York: John F. Trow & Co., 1867), 89-97.

5 This critical point about chambers will be seen at several stages in this book – not only a tendency to avoid revolution but to avoid major wars in general. Regarding revolution, Robert Bennett makes substantially the same point. He says that "chambers have generally been bodies advocating reform rather than revolution." This is from: Robert J. Bennett, *Local Business Voice: The History of Chambers of Commerce in Britain, Ireland, and Revolutionary America 1760-2011* (Oxford: Oxford University Press, 2011), 71.

6 Arthur M. Schlesinger, *The Colonial Merchants and the American Revolution, 1763-1776* (New York: Columbia University Ph.D. Thesis, 1917), 295.

7 The newspaper, the *South-Carolina Gazette; And Country Journal* reported the above-quoted item and this on December 28, 1773. "John Savage, Esq.; is elected President, Miles Brewton, Esq; Vice-President, Deavid Deas, Esq; Treasurer, and Mr. John Hopton, Secretary, of the said Society."

8 A listing of the 1774 members of the Charleston Chamber of Commerce is available on Robert Bennett's Web site at Cambridge University: http://www.geog.cam.ac.uk/research/projects/chambersofcommerce/charleston.pdf

9 Arthur M. Schlesinger, *The Colonial Merchants and the American Revolution, 1763-1776* (New York: Columbia University Ph.D. Thesis, 1917), 298.

10 David Duncan Wallace, *The Life of Henry Laurens with a Sketch of the Life of Lieutenant-Colonel John Laurens* (New York: G.P. Putnam's Sons, The Knickerbocker Press, 1915), 175.

11 "History of the Charleston Chamber of Commerce," created by the Charleston Chamber of Commerce in 1973, 1. A bill of exchange is "essentially an order made by one person to another to pay money to a third person." (Wikipedia, "Bills of Exchange," under the article, "Negotiable Instruments.") Such documents were commonly used in trade transactions.

12 "History of the Charleston Chamber of Commerce," created by the Charleston Chamber of Commerce in 1973, 1.

13 John Austin Stevens Jr., *Colonial Records of the New York Chamber of Commerce, 1768-1784* (New York: John F. Trow & Co., 1867), 204.

14 John Austin Stevens Jr., *Colonial Records of the New York Chamber of Commerce, 1768-1784* (New York: John F. Trow & Co., 1867), 342.

Notes

15 Joseph Bucklin Bishop, *A Chronicle of 150 Years: The Chamber of Commerce of the State of New York 1768-1918* (New York: Charles Scribner's Sons, 1918), 26.

16 John Austin Stevens, *Sketches Biographical and Historical* (New York: John F. Trow & Co., 1867), 69-104. The arrest is mentioned on page 103.

17 Lorenzo Sabine, *Boston Board of Trade 1862, Eighth Annual Report of the Government, Presented to the Board at the Annual Meeting, on the 15th January, 1862* (Boston: Alfred Mudge & Son, 1862), 36.

18 John Austin Stevens Jr., *Colonial Records of the New York Chamber of Commerce, 1768-1784* (New York: John F. Trow & Co., 1867), 255.

19 John Austin Stevens Jr., *Colonial Records of the New York Chamber of Commerce, 1768-1784* (New York: John F. Trow & Co., 1867), 257.

20 John Austin Stevens Jr., *Colonial Records of the New York Chamber of Commerce, 1768-1784* (New York: John F. Trow & Co., 1867), 258-9.

21 John Austin Stevens Jr., *Colonial Records of the New York Chamber of Commerce, 1768-1784* (New York: John F. Trow & Co., 1867), 218, 224, 241, 348.

22 Joseph Bucklin Bishop, *A Chronicle of 150 Years: The Chamber of Commerce of the State of New York 1768-1918* (New York: Charles Scribner's Sons, 1918), 39-40.

23 Joseph Bucklin Bishop, *A Chronicle of 150 Years: The Chamber of Commerce of the State of New York 1768-1918* (New York: Charles Scribner's Sons, 1918), 41.

24 Joseph Bucklin Bishop, *A Chronicle of 150 Years: The Chamber of Commerce of the State of New York 1768-1918* (New York: Charles Scribner's Sons, 1918), 41.

25 Joseph Bucklin Bishop, *A Chronicle of 150 Years: The Chamber of Commerce of the State of New York 1768-1918* (New York: Charles Scribner's Sons, 1918), 42.

26 Charles King, *History of the New York Chamber of Commerce: With Notices of Some of Its Most Distinguished Members. An Anniversary Discourse, Delivered Before the New York Historical Society, November 21, 1848* (Ithaca, N.Y.: Cornell University Library digital edition, 1993), 414.

27 Douglas W. Bostick, *Sunken Plantations: The Santee Cooper Project* (Charleston, S.C.: The History Press, 2008), 12.

28 *A Journal of the Charleston Chamber of Commerce, Commencing 6, of February 1784*, 29-31.

29 *A Journal of the Charleston Chamber of Commerce, Commencing 6, of February 1784*, 31.

30 *A Journal of the Charleston Chamber of Commerce, Commencing 6, of February 1784*. Page numbering in the minutes has stopped at this point but the August 1, 1785 meeting report has some of the information, and the citizens' memorial is dated August 11, 1785.

31 *A Journal of the Charleston Chamber of Commerce, Commencing 6, of February 1784*, 16.

32 George C. Rogers, *Charleston in the Age of the Pinckneys* (Norman, Oklahoma: University of Oklahoma, 1969) 52, 85-6.

33 *A Journal of the Charleston Chamber of Commerce, Commencing 6, of February 1784*, from the minutes of the meeting on March 30, 1791.

34 Robert Bennett lists the members of this 1784 chamber on his Web site at Cambridge:

http://www.geog.cam.ac.uk/research/projects/chambersofcommerce/philadelphia.pdf

35 While this kind of organization was apparently new in the United States, it wasn't in Great Britain. The Society of the Encouragement of Arts, Manufactures, and Commerce was founded in London in 1754.

36 Robert Dalling, *The Story of Us Humans, From Atoms to Today's Civilization* (Lincoln, Nebraska: iUniverse Books, 2006), 402.

37 Robert Dalling, *The Story of Us Humans, From Atoms to Today's Civilization* (Lincoln, Nebraska: iUniverse Books, 2006), 402.

38 *A Journal of the Charleston Chamber of Commerce, Commencing 6, of February 1784*. Coxe's letter was reported in a meeting dated June 13, 1792.

39 But the addition of industry to the older activity of trading would cause some problems for chambers of commerce, as the mother country's example would show. In the same year – 1787 - that Samuel Slater was reading about the Pennsylvania Society's cash award, there was trouble in central England. Angry peasants were rioting and smashing up the machines that were powering Britain's nascent textile industry. (A later generation of these malcontents would be called Luddites.) After an incident on October 26, the Nottingham Chamber of Commerce offered a reward of 20 guineas "for the discovery of the offenders." [John Frost Sutton, *The Date-book of Remarkable and Memorable Events Connected with Nottingham and Its Neighborhood, 1750-1850* (London: Simpkin & Marshall, 1852), 169.] This wouldn't be the last time that chambers sided with management and order, and against labor, in this new activity of manufacturing.

40 Justin Winsor, Editor, *The Memorial History of Boston: Including Suffolk County, Massachusetts, 1630-1880* (Boston: Ticknor and Company, 1881), Volume IV, 212.

41 Justin Winsor, Editor, *The Memorial History of Boston: Including Suffolk County, Massachusetts, 1630-1880* (Boston: Ticknor and Company, 1881), Volume IV, 212-13.

42 Edward Warren, *The Life of John Warren, M.D.: Surgeon-General During the War of the Revolution; First Professor of Anatomy and Surgery in Harvard College; President of the Massachusetts Medical Society, Etc.* (Boston: Noyes, Holmes and Company, 1874), 377-9.

43 Floyd M. Shumway and Richard Hegel, "The First Century of the Greater New Haven Chamber of Commerce, 1794 – 1894," *Journal of The New Haven Colony Historical Society*, Volume 40, No. 2, Spring 1994, 3-4. The authors list the 26 members.

44 Floyd M. Shumway and Richard Hegel, "The First Century of the Greater New Haven Chamber of Commerce, 1794 – 1894," *Journal of The New Haven Colony Historical Society*, Volume 40, No. 2, Spring 1994, 3.

45 Rebecca Smith Lee, *Mary Austin Holley: A Biography* (Austin: University of Texas, 1962), 10.

46 Rebecca Smith Lee, *Mary Austin Holley: A Biography* (Austin: University of Texas, 1962), 10.

47 Joseph Bucklin Bishop, *A Chronicle of 150 Years: The Chamber of Commerce of the State of New York 1768-1918* (New York: Charles Scribner's Sons, 1918), 45-6.

48 Franklin Bowditch Dexter, *Biographical Sketches of the Graduates of Yale College with Annals of the College History* (New York: Henry Holt and Company, 1911), Volume V, June, 1792 – September, 1805, 20. Also: Rebecca Smith Lee, *Mary Austin Holley: A Biography* (Austin: University of Texas, 1962), 10.

49 Julius Goebel Jr. and Joseph H. Smith, editors, *The Law Practice of Alexander Hamilton: Documents and Commentary* (New York: Columbia University Press, 1981), Volume V, 30-31.

50 Joseph Bucklin Bishop, *A Chronicle of 150 Years: The Chamber of Commerce of the State of New York 1768-1918* (New York: Charles Scribner's Sons, 1918), 49. See also "Jay Treaty," Wikipedia. The full text of the treaty is available at such sources as www.earlyamerica.com.

51 Joseph Bucklin Bishop, *A Chronicle of 150 Years: The Chamber of Commerce of the State of New York 1768-1918* (New York: Charles Scribner's Sons, 1918), 48.

52 Ron Chernow, *Alexander Hamilton* (New York: Penguin Press, 2004), 482.

53 Letter from George Washington to Alexander Hamilton, July 29, 1795, from *The Works of Alexander Hamilton; Comprising His Correspondence, and His Political and Official Writings, Exclusive of The Federalist, Civil and Military* (New York: John F. Trow, 1851), Edited by John Hamilton, Volume VI, 25.

54 Sean Wilentz, *The Rise of American Democracy: Jefferson to Lincoln* (New York: W.W. Norton & Company, 2006), 67.

55 Letter from George Washington to Edmund Randolph, July 29, 1795, from *The Writings of George Washington; Being His Correspondence, Addresses, Messages, and Other Papers, Official and Private*, Volume XI, edited by Jared Sparks, (Boston: Ferdinand Andrews, 1839), 48.

56 Joseph Bucklin Bishop, *A Chronicle of 150 Years: The Chamber of Commerce of the State of New York 1768-1918* (New York: Charles Scribner's Sons, 1918), 47.

57 *The American Remembrancer; or, an Impartial Collection of Essays, Resolves, Speeches, &c. Relative, or Having Affinity, to the Treaty with Great Britain* (Philadelphia: Mathew Carey, August 20, 1795), 129-130.

58 Thomas Paine, "Letter to George Washington", July 30, 1796, from *The Writings of Thomas Paine*, Volume 3, 1791-1804, by Thomas Paine and edited by Moncure Daniel Conway (New York: G.P. Putnam's Sons, The Knickerbocker Press, 1895), 250-1.

59 Letter to James Monroe, September 6, 1795, from *The Works of Thomas Jefferson in Twelve Volumes*, Federal Edition, Volume VIII, by Thomas Jefferson, collected and edited by Paul Leicester Ford (New York: G.P. Putnam's Sons, The Knickerbocker Press, 1904), 188.

60 Letter to James Monroe, December 20, 1795, from *Letters and Other Writings of James Madison, Fourth President of the United States, in Four Volumes*, Volume II, 1794-1815 (Philadelphia: J.B. Lippincott & Co., 1865), 65.

61 Mentor, "State of Opinions on the Treaty," from the *Lancaster Journal*, published in *The American Remembrancer; or, an Impartial Collection of Essays, Resolves, Speeches, &c. Relative, or Having Affinity, to the Treaty with Great Britain*, Volume II (Philadelphia: Mathew Carey, October 10, 1795), 201.

62 Letter from Comfort Sands to Alexander Hamilton, April 27, 1795, from *The Papers of Alexander Hamilton*, edited by Harold C. Syrett, Volume XVIII, January-July 1795, (New York: Columbia University Press, 1973), 334.

63 Greg H. Williams, *The French Assault on American Shipping, 1793-1813: A History and Comprehensive Record of Merchant Marine Losses* (Jefferson, N.C.: McFarland & Company, Inc., 2009), 165.

64 Letter from Alexander Hamilton to Gouverneur Morris, February 27, 1802, from *The Works of Alexander Hamilton; Comprising His Correspondence, and His Political and Official Writings, Exclusive of The Federalist, Civil and Military* (New York: John F. Trow, 1851), edited by John Hamilton, Volume VI, 530. This is an interesting letter not only in reference to the possibility of Hamilton having induced the New York Chamber to support the Jay Treaty publicly in 1795. It also shows Hamilton's understanding of one of the unique abilities of chambers of commerce: to introduce political arguments that appear fair and disinterested. In the situation cited by Hamilton to Morris, if Hamilton had proposed legal reforms through the bar association, the lawyers could have been accused of self-interest. But if those same reforms were proposed by a chamber of commerce, the motives of the chamber would not be questioned. As Hamilton put it: "It appeared to me best because it saved our delicacy and because in the abstract I am not overfond of the precedent of the bar addressing Congress. But I did what I thought likely to do more good – I *induced* the Chamber of Commerce to send a memorial."

65 Letter from George Washington to Comfort Sands, August 20, 1795, from *Washington, George, 1732-1799. The Writings of George Washington from the Original Manuscript Scores*, Electronic Text Center, University of Virginia Library.

For the similar letter to Thomas Russell, see: Letter from George Washington to Thomas Russell, Esq., August 22, 1795, from *The American Remembrancer; or, an Impartial Collection of Essays, Resolves, Speeches, &c. Relative, or Having Affinity, to the Treaty with Great Britain*, Volume II (Philadelphia: Mathew Carey, October 10, 1795), 216. Here is the related paragraph from the Russell letter:

"While I regret the diversity of opinion which has been manifested on this occasion, it is a satisfaction to learn, that the commercial part of my fellow citizens, whose interests are thought to be most directly affected, so generally consider the treaty, as calculated, on the whole, to procure important advantages for our country."

66 Robert J. Bennett, *Local Business Voice: The History of Chambers of Commerce in Britain, Ireland, and Revolutionary America 1760-2011* (Oxford: Oxford University Press, 2011), 391-4.

Notes

67 Henry Adams, *The History of the United States*, as cited in: Joseph Bucklin Bishop, *A Chronicle of 150 Years: The Chamber of Commerce of the State of New York 1768-1918* (New York: Charles Scribner's Sons, 1918), 48.

68 James Neal Primm, *Lion of the Valley: St. Louis, Missouri, 1764-1980*, Third Edition (St. Louis: University of Missouri Press, 1998), 57.

69 Abraham Phineas Nasatir, editor, *Before Lewis and Clark: Documents Illustrating the History of the Missouri, 1785-1804*, Red River Books Edition (Norman, Oklahoma: University of Oklahoma Press, 2002), 217.

70 Commonwealth of Kentucky Record #31019, created July 4, 2009.

71 George Washington Ranck, *History of Lexington, Kentucky: Its Early Annals and Recent Progress* (Cincinnati, Ohio: Robert Clarke & Co., 1872), 202.

72 H.A. Ratterman, *Kentucky's German Pioneers: H.A. Ratterman's History*, translated and edited by Don Heinrich Tolzmann (Westminster, Maryland: Heritage Books, 2007), 40-41. Also: Albert Bernhardt Faust, *The German Element in the United States*, Volume 1, (Boston: Houghton Mifflin Company, 1909), 380.

73 William Elsey Connelley and Ellis Merton Coulter, *History of Kentucky* (Chicago: American Historical Society, 1922), Volume I, 486. The authors cite *The Mirror* in Washington, Mason County (September 30, 1797).

74 George Washington Ranck, *History of Lexington, Kentucky: Its Early Annals and Recent Progress* (Cincinnati, Ohio: Robert Clarke & Co., 1872), 202.

75 George Washington Ranck, *History of Lexington, Kentucky: Its Early Annals and Recent Progress* (Cincinnati, Ohio: Robert Clarke & Co., 1872), 202.

76 William Elsey Connelley and Ellis Merton Coulter, *History of Kentucky* (Chicago: American Historical Society, 1922), Volume I, 486. The authors cite *The Mirror* in Washington, Mason County (October 28, 1797).

77 Joseph Bucklin Bishop, *A Chronicle of 150 Years: The Chamber of Commerce of the State of New York 1768-1918* (New York: Charles Scribner's Sons, 1918), 50-1.

78 In 1799, a group of local merchants formed the Hartford Chamber of Commerce. Their secretary was John McCracken, who headed a local branch of a New York trading firm. McCracken, a 1792 graduate of Yale College, also helped start a local Episcopal church in 1796. At his trading house, he offered such products as "West India rum 7 shillings by the hogshead." See: Frank Andrews, *Hartford Business Directory* for the year 1799, Vineland, NJ 1910,

http://files.usgwarchives.net/ct/hartford/history/directories/business/hartford60gms.txt

McCracken and his colleagues apparently got the idea for their chamber from the New York Chamber of Commerce. The Hartford organization had a relatively short existence, from 1799 to 1804. The problem of apathy (or of a lack of things to do) may have explained the group's changing, in 1801, the frequency of its meetings from monthly to quarterly.

79 Letter from Thomas FitzSimons, president of the Philadelphia Chamber of Commerce, to the Secretary of the Navy, Benjamin Stoddert, on February 27, 1801, from *American State Papers. Documents, Legislative and Executive, of the Congress of the United States, From the First Session of the First to the Third Session of the Thirteenth Congress, Inclusive, Commencing March 13, 1789, and Ending March 3, 1815*, edited by Walter Lowrie and Matthew St. Clair Clarke, Volume II (Washington, D.C.: Gales and Seaton, 1832), 347.

80 Letter from Thomas FitzSimons, president of the Philadelphia Chamber of Commerce, to President Thomas Jefferson, on October 10, 1801, from *American State Papers. Documents, Legislative and Executive, of the Congress of the United States, From the First Session of the First to the Third Session of the Thirteenth Congress, Inclusive, Commencing March 13, 1789, and Ending March 3, 1815*, edited by Walter Lowrie and Matthew St. Clair Clarke, Volume II (Washington, D.C.: Gales and Seaton, 1832), 441.

81 *Journal of the Senate of the United States of America: Being the First Session of the Seventh Congress, Begun and Held at the City of Washington, December 7th, 1801* (Washington, D.C.: Printed by Way and Groff, 1801), January 25, 1802, 61.

82 "An Act to Empower the Board of Wardens," from *Laws of the Commonwealth of Pennsylvania, from the Seventh Day of December, 1802, to the Fourth Day of April, 1805*, Volume VII (Philadelphia: Printed by John Bioren, 1806), 488.

83 Extract from a memorial of the New Haven Chamber of Commerce, signed by President Henry Dagget on February 7, 1806, from *The Olive Branch: or, Faults on Both Sides, Federal and Democratic. A Serious Appeal on the Necessity of Mutual Forgiveness and Harmony*, by Mathew Carey, Seventh Edition (Philadelphia: Mathew Carey, December 20, 1815), 104.

84 Joseph Bucklin Bishop, *A Chronicle of 150 Years: The Chamber of Commerce of the State of New York 1768-1918* (New York: Charles Scribner's Sons, 1918), 182.

85 William S. Forrest, *Historical and Descriptive Sketches of Norfolk and Vicinity* (Philadelphia: Lindsay and Blakiston, 1853), 108-9.

86 Dr. R.A. Brock, *Virginia and Virginians. Eminent Virginians.*, Volume I (Richmond, Va.: H.H. Hardesty, 1888), 168.

87 "America," *The National Register*, No. 30, July 24, 1808, 470.

88 Walter Wilson Jennings, *The American Embargo 1807-1809: With Particular Reference to its Effect on Industry*, from *University of Iowa Studies in the Social Sciences*, edited by A.M. Schlesinger, Volume 8, No. 1 (Iowa City: University of Iowa, 1921), 95.

89 Walter Wilson Jennings, *The American Embargo 1807-1809: With Particular Reference to its Effect on Industry*, from *University of Iowa Studies in the Social Sciences*, edited by A.M. Schlesinger, Volume 8, No. 1 (Iowa City: University of Iowa, 1921), 99.

90 Savannah Area Chamber of Commerce Web site:

http://www.savannahchamber.com/about-the-chamber/history

91 Charles Gayarre, *History of Louisiana. American Domination.* (New York: F.F. Hansell & Bro., 1905), 165.

92 Charles Gayarre, *History of Louisiana. American Domination.* (New York: F.F. Hansell & Bro., 1905), 173.

93 George P. Oslin, *The Story of Telecommunications* (Mercer University Press, 1999), 4-6.

94 Jonathan Thomas Scharf and Thompson Wescott, *History of Philadelphia. 1609-1884.*, Volume 3 (Philadelphia: L.H. Everts & Co., 1884), 2128.

95 Jacob Newton Cardozo, *Reminiscences of Charleston* (Charleston, S.C.: Joseph Walker, 1866), 23.

The Challenges of Peacetime (1816-1836)

1 For the explanation of these and the private-law chambers, see the early chapter on "What is a Local Chamber of Commerce?"

2 Robert J. Bennett, *Local Business Voice: The History of Chambers of Commerce in Britain, Ireland, and Revolutionary America 1760-2011* (Oxford: Oxford University Press, 2011), 15.

3 "James Maury," The Athenaeum: http://www.theathenaeum.org.uk/notables/page11.html

4 Joseph Bucklin Bishop, *A Chronicle of 150 Years: The Chamber of Commerce of the State of New York 1768-1918* (New York: Charles Scribner's Sons, 1918), 52.

5 *Annual Report of the Chamber of Commerce of the State of New-York for the Year 1859-'60* (New York: John W. Amerman, Printer, 1860), 18.

6 "Notes for a History of Steam Navigation (continued from page 643, vol. iv.), III., 1809-1820, from *United Service: A Monthly Review of Military and Naval Affairs, Volume 5* (Philadelphia: L.R. Hamersley & Co., 1881), 118.

7 This publication has a list of the founding members of the Savannah Chamber of Commerce in December 1806: *Rules and Regulations of the Savannah Chamber of Commerce* (Savannah: Seymour and Woolhopter, 1807). For a list of investors in the steamship company, see: Frank O. Braynard, *S.S. Savannah, the Elegant Steam Ship* (Athens, Georgia: University of Savannah Press, 1963; paperback, 2008), 29-31. For a list of the four directors other than Scarbrough, see Braynard, 71. Even today, the chamber proudly cites this project as chamber-promoted. This steamship voyage presaged another city-promoting transatlantic first that was facilitated by a chamber 108 years later, the *Spirit of St. Louis* air crossing in 1927.

8 Frank O. Braynard, *S.S. Savannah: The Elegant Steamship* (Athens, Ga.: University of Georgia Press, 1963), 28.

9 "Notes for a History of Steam Navigation (continued from page 643, vol. iv.), III., 1809-1820, from *United Service: A Monthly Review of Military and Naval Affairs, Volume 5* (Philadelphia: L.R. Hamersley & Co., 1881), 118. Also: Edward J. Cashin, *Beloved Bethesda: A History of George Whitefield's Home for Boys, 1740-2000* (Macon, Georgia: Mercer University Press, 2001), 159, citing a book by Preston Russell and Barbara Hines, *Savannah: A History of Her People Since 1733* (Savannah, Georgia: Frederic C. Beil, 1992).

10 Senate proceedings record for January 12, 1820, from *Journal of the Senate of the United States of America, Being the First Session of the Sixteenth Congress*, begun December 6, 1819 (Washington, D.C.: Gales & Seaton, 1819), 95.

11 The notion of comparative advantage makes it possible to envision benefiting from broadly from trade – from imports as well as exports. If your country makes wine more efficiently than mine does, and mine makes wool more efficiently than yours does, then I'm better off not trying to make wine at all. Instead, I should concentrate on making all the wool that I can. I should import wine from you and ship you all the wool you are willing to buy from me.

12 Daniel Webster's involvement, and the train of events leading up to it, are clearly shown in this collection of evidence from a writer in 1838, who wishes to prove that Webster was a leader of free-trade forces in 1820. The reprinted *Daily Advertiser* article of September 2, 1820 shows that the precipitating event for the Boston merchants' initial meeting was an invitation from the Philadelphia Chamber of Commerce. And the quotes of Webster are but one piece of evidence that the Boston merchants found an effective champion. All this is from "Mr. Calhoun and Mr. Webster," from the *Boston Advocate*, reprinted in *Extra Globe*, Thursday, April 5, 1838 (Blair and Rives, Publishers), 20.

13 William Ogden Niles, "Chronicle," *Niles Weekly Register*, September 16, 1820, 48.

14 Robert Gilmor et. al., "Memorial of the Merchants and Traders of Baltimore to the President of the United States, and the Senate and House of Representatives of the United States of America, in Congress assembled," January 21, 1806, from *American State Papers. Documents, Legislative and Executive, of the Congress of the United States, from the First Session of the First to the Third Session of the Thirteenth Congress, Inclusive: Commencing March 3, 1789, and Ending March 3, 1815* (Washington: Gales & Seaton, 1832), edited by Walter Lowrie and Matthew St. Clair Clarke, Volume II, 750-756.

15 "1816-1860: The Second American Party System and the Tariff," from the Tax History Museum, published by Tax Analysts, a nonprofit organization:

http://www.tax.org/Museum/1816-1860.htm

16 "Memorial of the New-York Chamber of Commerce, to the Hon. the Senate and House of Representatives of the United States, in Congress Assembled; With Statements, Prepared by Order of the Chamber, to Show the Present Rate of Duties, and the Rate of Duties Proposed by the Tariff Bill, Now Before Congress. With Remarks, &c." (New York: Daniel Fanshaw, 1824).

17 One of Jacob's grandnephews was to be Benjamin Nathan Cardozo, the noted Supreme Court justice. See Andrew L. Kaufman, *Cardozo* (Cambridge, Mass.: Harvard University Press, 1998), Chapter One.

18 Jacob Newton Cardozo, *Reminiscences of Charleston* (Charleston, S.C.: Joseph Walker, 1866), 23.

19 Jacob Newton Cardozo, *Reminiscences of Charleston* (Charleston, S.C.: Joseph Walker, 1866), 23.

20 "Jacob N. Cardozo," from *The New American Cyclopaedia: A Popular Dictionary of General Knowledge*, edited by George Ripley and Charles Dana, Volume IV, Brownson-Chartres (New York: D. Appleton and Company, 1870), 427.

21 John Roscoe Turner, *The Ricardian Rent Theory in Early American Economics: A Dissertation Presented to the Faculty of Princeton University in Candidacy for the Degree of Doctor of Philosophy* (New York: The New York University Press, 1921), 75.

22 Jacob Newton Cardozo, *Reminiscences of Charleston* (Charleston, S.C.: Joseph Walker, 1866), 24.

Notes

23 Here is the wording from the letter from Charleston Chamber of Commerce President David Alexander to Joseph Johnson, Intendant of the City of Charleston, June 12, 1827, introducing a memorial to Congress on the Woollens Bill, from *Niles' Weekly Register,* June 30, 1827, 295:

Attentive as all chambers of commerce are bound to be in the interests of trade, it must not be understood, because the chamber of commerce have taken the lead in this business, that they, by any means, wish to dictate either to yourself or their fellow-citizens, what is proper to be done in opposition to the measure in question; they, however, conceive, that a general expression of the opinion of the citizens of Charleston at large, will have more weight throughout the state, in inducing the country towns and districts to take up the subject, than if it was confined to any particular association or public bodies in the city

The chamber, essentially, is admitting to the credit, or the blame, in sparking the entire Nullification Crisis. South Carolina politicians were only too happy to oblige to the call to raise the decibel level on this issue.

24 "Memorial to Congress," regarding the Woollens Bill, Charleston Chamber of Commerce, June 12, 1827, from *Niles' Weekly Register,* June 30, 1827, 298.

25 Cardozo had apparently run into financial problems after acquiring his newspaper, *Southern Patriot.* Hayne and others assisted him in 1825 by seeing that he kept a contract for "printing the laws." See "Applications, Recommendations, December 17, 1825," from *The Papers of Henry Clay: Secretary of State, 1825,* Volume 4, edited by James F. Hopkins (University of Kentucky, 1972), 922.

26 "Farmers and Manufacturers' Meeting," *Niles Weekly Register,* June 2, 1827, footnote on column 1, 239.

27 Curiously, even then, the confluence of waters at the Port of Charleston was called "Rebellion Roads."

28 John Steele Gordon, *An Empire of Wealth: The Epic History of American Economic Power* (New York: HarperCollins Publishers, 2004), 109.

29 Joseph Bucklin Bishop, *A Chronicle of 150 Years: The Chamber of Commerce of the State of New York 1768-1918* (New York: Charles Scribner's Sons, 1918), 55-6.

30 Remarks on the Delaware Breakwater in the Senate by Connecticut Senator Samuel Foot, March 19, 1828, from *Register of Debates in Congress, Comprising the Leading Incidents of the First Session of the Twentieth Congress,* Volume IV (Washington, D.C.: Gales & Seaton, 1828), 465.

31 Most of the information in this paragraph comes from "The Delaware Breakwater and Ice Breaker," which is found at this Web site: http://140.194.76.129/publications/misc/un16/c-3.pdf. It is unclear to the author which book this chapter is taken from, but the information appears reliable and jells with similar information from other sources.

32 John Steele Gordon, *An Empire of Wealth: The Epic History of American Economic Power* (New York: HarperCollins Publishers, 2004), 147-8.

33 The quotation is from Walter J. Fraser, *Charleston! Charleston!: The History of a Southern City* (Columbia, S.C.: University of South Carolina Press, 1989), 208. The information on the committee is from "The Charleston Chamber One Hundred Years Ago," Letter from Sidney S. Rittenberg, publicity secretary, Charleston Chamber of Commerce, from *The American City,* Volume 15, No. 2, August 1916, 168.

34 "The Charleston Chamber One Hundred Years Ago," Letter from Sidney S. Rittenberg, publicity secretary, Charleston Chamber of Commerce, from *The American City,* Volume 15, No. 2, August 1916, 168.

35 Walter J. Fraser, *Charleston! Charleston!: The History of a Southern City* (Columbia, S.C.: University of South Carolina Press, 1989), 208.

36 Michael Coker et al., "Charleston 101: Defining Moments That Shaped Our City," *Charleston Magazine,* February 2009. See www.charlestonmag.com. Item 26 is "Train Service Begins, 1830."

37 Joseph Bucklin Bishop, *A Chronicle of 150 Years: The Chamber of Commerce of the State of New York 1768-1918* (New York: Charles Scribner's Sons, 1918), 59-60. Also "Erie Railroad" from the Western New York Railroad Archive: http://wnyrails.org/railroads/erie/erie_home.htm

More information is available under "Erie Railroad" in Wikipedia.

38 "Memorial of the Philadelphia Chamber of Commerce," January 7, 1834, reprinted in *Hazard's Register of Pennsylvania,* edited by Samuel Hazard, Volume 13, January through June, 1834 (Philadelphia: William Geddes, printer, 1834), 60-62.

39 Ralston headed the chamber from 1820 to 1825, and in 1826 was succeeded by William Jones, according to the chamber's *Bicentennial History: 1801-2001,* compiled by Judith F. Kennedy (Philadelphia: Greater Philadelphia Chamber of Commerce and Kennedy Consulting, July 28, 2000), 31. He was also apparently president in 1830, with vice presidents Thomas Cope and Lewis Clapier, treasurer Robert Smith, and secretary John Vaughan, according to *Philadelphia in 1830-1: Or, a Brief Account of the Various Institutions and Public Objects in this Metropolis.* (Philadelphia: E.L. Carey and A. Hart, 1830), 95.

40 "Bank of the United States," report of stockholders' meeting, from *Niles' Weekly Register,* H. Niles, editor, September 6, 1834, Volume 47 (Baltimore: H. Niles, 1835),13.

41 James Parton, *Life of Andrew Jackson,* Volume III (New York: Mason Brothers, 1860), 550.

42 The destruction of the Second Bank of the United States was regarded widely by contemporaries and by succeeding generations of economists as contributing to the Panic of 1837. For an overview of the consensus views of the causes of the Panic, see the Wikipedia article on the topic. The lack of a central bank in the United States from 1832 through 1913 also has been seen by economists as a weakness that invited panics. Laurence Laughlin and other economists promoting the Federal Reserve concept argued that a national banking system would put financial panics behind us – an idea, however, that later experience, such as in 1929, would occasionally call into question. No system yet found on this earth appears able to banish financial uncertainty.

43 Alexis de Tocqueville, *Democracy in America,* quoted in *The Perfect Gift: The Philosophical Imagination in Poetry and Prose,* by Amy Kass (Bloomington, Indiana: Indiana University Press, 2002), 28.

44 "Biographical: Thomas P. Cope," *The American Merchant*, July 1858, 139.

45 For the 1824 debate, see for example the reference to "the memorials of Philip Tutchett and others" in the *Journal of the Senate of the United States*, February 27, 1824 (Washington, D.C.: Jones & Seaton, 1823), 202. In 1828, Pennsylvania support for the tariff was widespread.

46 John Thomas Scharf and Thompson Westcott, *History of Philadelphia: 1609-1884*, Volume III (Philadelphia: L.H. Everts & Co., 1884), 2342.

47 John Thomas Scharf and Thompson Westcott, *History of Philadelphia: 1609-1884*, Volume III (Philadelphia: L.H. Everts & Co., 1884), 2342.

48 Cope was aware of the juntos and of many of Franklin's other ideas. For example, when the teenaged Cope admitted he was awakened at night because of having cold feet in bed during the cold Philadelphia winter, Franklin told him how to avoid the problem: strip off his clothes before going to bed and stand there getting really cold, and then hop into bed, which, comparatively speaking, would be warm! For these and other insights from Cope, see: Eliza Cope Harrison, editor, *Philadelphia Merchant: The Diary of Thomas P. Cope, 1800-1851* (South Bend, Ind.: Gateway Editions, 1978). The cold feet incident is on page 405.

49 Lorenzo Sabine, Secretary, *Boston Board of Trade 1859: Fifth Annual Report of the Government*, presented to the board on January 20, 1859 (Boston: T.R. Marvin & Son, 1859), 20. In Canada, too, the Board of Trade name caught on, with some chambers and "committees of trade" switching their names to Board of Trade, and others (such as the Toronto Board of Trade and the Hamilton Board of Trade, both in 1845) being founded with that name.

50 The "board of trade" fad was the first of the chamber name manias to animate the country's business people. Others would follow, such as "Businessmen's League" and "Commercial Club" in the latter part of the 19th century, and "Partnership" and "Alliance" in the latter half of the 20th century. In a field dominated by voluntary activity and few rules, names and functions were not always clearly delineated. The nearest thing to standardization would come when the Chamber of Commerce of the United States was founded in 1912, after which most local business organizations gravitated back to that term.

51 *Fifty-First Annual Report of the Chamber of Commerce of the State of New York for the Year 1908-09* (New York: Press of the Chamber of Commerce, 1909), 4-7.

52 Edwin G. Burrows and Mike Wallace, *Gotham: A History of New York City to 1898* (Oxford: Oxford University Press, 1999), 559.

53 Edwin G. Burrows and Mike Wallace, *Gotham: A History of New York City to 1898* (Oxford: Oxford University Press, 1999), 560.

54 Lewis Tappan, *The Life of Arthur Tappan* (New York: Hurd & Houghton, 1870), 269. See also: Edwin G. Burrows and Mike Wallace, *Gotham: A History of New York City to 1898* (Oxford: Oxford University Press, 1999), 560. Note also: Bertram Wyatt-Brown, *Lewis Tappan and the Evangelical War Against Slavery* (Cleveland, Ohio: The Press of Case Western Reserve University, 1969), 156.

55 Hartmut Berghoff, "Civilizing Capitalism? The Beginnings of Credit Rating in the United States and Germany," *Bulletin of the GHI*, German Historical Institute, Fall 2009, 16.

It is Dangerous to Listen to Such Dreamers as These (1837-1860)

1 For St. Louis, see the chamber's memorial: "Memorial of the Chamber of Commerce of St. Louis, Missouri, Praying the Creation of a National Bank," September 11, 1837, addressed to the Senate and the House, reprinted in *Public Documents Printed by Order of the Senate of the United States, First Session of the Twenty-Fifth Congress* (Washington, D.C.: Blair and Rives, 1837), 105-6. For the New Orleans memorial: Ibid, 99-102. For New Orleans, see the short item regarding the chamber's memorial to the Senate, featured in *The Daily Pittsburgh Gazette*, Sept. 12, 1837, page 2, column 2.

2 For New York: Letter of a New York Chamber of Commerce committee to Secretary of the Treasury Levi Woodbury, August 28, 1837, reprinted in *Register of the Debates in Congress, Comprising the Leading Debates and Incidents of the First Session of the Twenty-fifth Congress* (Washington, D.C.: Gales and Seaton, 1837), Appendix, 31-32. For Boston: Ibid, 27-28. For New Orleans: Ibid, 28.

3 *Daily Pittsburgh Gazette*, June 2, 1837, page 2, column 3.

4 "James Gore King," *The National Cyclopaedia of American Biography*, Volume1 (New York: James T. White & Co., 1898), 498-99. King served as vice president of the chamber from 1841 to 1845. He served as president from June 1845 through May of 1847, and then again for the 1848-9 fiscal year, with Moses Grinnell serving in the 1847-48 fiscal year, according to the records of the New York Chamber of Commerce. (See for example its annual report of 1859-60, page 102.)

5 Nathaniel Hawthorne, *Mosses from an Old Manse* (New York: George P. Putnam, 1851), 163-4.

6 "Mouths of the Mississippi," from *The New York Times*, reprinted in *The Army and Navy Chronicle*, Volume V, From July 1 to December 31, 1837 (Washington, D.C.: B. Homans, 1837), 220-1.

7 Letter from Edward Tracy to the Congress of the United States, November 23, 1838, from *Public Documents Printed by Order of the Senate of the United States, Third Session of the Twenty-Fifth Congress*, Volume II (Washington: Blair and Rives, 1839), Appendix, 49.

8 For information on the founding of this chamber and background on Galena, this book is helpful: *The History of Jo Daviess County, Illinois* (Chicago: H.F. Kett & Co., 1878; no author listed). Founding information is on page 478. An example of a memorial to Congress on Mississippi River improvements is here: "Memorial of the Galena Chamber of Commerce, praying an appropriation for the improvement of the Mississippi River, at the Des Moines and Red Rock rapids, February 4, 1840," from *Public Documents Printed by Order of the Senate of the United States, during the First Session of the Twenty-Sixth Congress, begun December 2, 1839* (Washington, D.C.: Blair and Rives, 1840), Volume IV, 255-6.

9 Greater Memphis Chamber Web site, history section: http://www.memphischamber.com/The-Chamber/History.aspx

Notes

10 This 1837 source on Louisville notes: "A chamber of Commerce has existed for several years." William Gilman Lyford, *The Western Address Directory: Containing the Cards of Merchants, Manufacturers, and Other Business Men* (Baltimore: Joseph Robinson, 1837), 360.

11 Cincinnati USA Regional Chamber History, Part 1: 1839-1911: http://www. cincinnatichamber.com/cham_a.aspx?menu_id=146&id=6786

12 Elizabeth Brand Monroe, *The Wheeling Bridge Case: Its Significance in American Law and Technology* (Northeastern University Press, 1992). This book provides excellent background on the bridge, the Wheeling Board of Trade's involvement with it, and the controversy and Supreme Court case surrounding the project.

13 Adam B. Chambers, *Proceedings of the St. Louis Chamber of Commerce, In Relation to the Improvement of the Navigation of the Mississippi River, and Its Principal Tributaries and the St. Louis Harbor* (St. Louis, Mo.: Chambers & Knapp, 1842).

14 "The Houston Chamber of Commerce Celebrates its One Hundredth Anniversary: And Related Here is the Story of the Founding of This Organization," *Houston*, the magazine of the Houston Chamber of Commerce, April 1940.

15 Both the quotation and the fundraising information are from "The Formative Years (1840-1850)," in *Houston History, 174 Years of Historic Houston*, a Web site: http://www.houstonhistory.com/decades/history5a.htm

16 Bud Myers, "Chamber Active Force in Houston Since Days of First Stage Line," *Houston Press*, December 17, 1946.

17 Quoted by R.M. Farrar, "The Story of Buffalo Bayou and the Houston Ship Channel," November, 1926, page 5 of the chapter following the introduction. Farrar was the president of the Houston Chamber of Commerce and former member of the Port Commission. He was also president of Union National Bank and of Farrar Lumber Company.

18 All the information on the founding of the Buffalo Board of Trade, and the activities of Wilkeson, is taken from this source: Lloyd Graham and Frank Severance, *The First Hundred Years of the Buffalo Chamber of Commerce* (Buffalo, N.Y.: Foster & Stewart Publishing Corp., 1945). Heywood's background is described on pages 16-17 and his speech is on pages 21-24. The Buffalo Harbor Association's original efforts to improve the port are described in the initial chapter, on pages 1-15.

19 William Cronon, *Nature's Metropolis: Chicago and the Great West* (New York: W.W. Norton, 1992), 114.

20 William Cronon, *Nature's Metropolis: Chicago and the Great West* (New York: W.W. Norton, 1992), 114.

21 William Cronon, *Nature's Metropolis: Chicago and the Great West* (New York: W.W. Norton, 1992), 115.

22 William Cronon, *Nature's Metropolis: Chicago and the Great West* (New York: W.W. Norton, 1992), 115-6.

23 William Cronon, *Nature's Metropolis: Chicago and the Great West* (New York: W.W. Norton, 1992), 119.

24 William Cronon, *Nature's Metropolis: Chicago and the Great West* (New York: W.W. Norton, 1992), 120.

25 William George Bruce, editor, *History of Milwaukee, City and County* (Milwaukee: S.J. Clarke Publishing Company, 1922), 378-413. Chapter XXIV describes the Milwaukee Chamber of Commerce and Chamber XXV describes the Merchants' Association and its various names in the succeeding decades.

26 Thomas G. Thrum, "History of the Hudson's Bay Company's Agency in Honolulu," Eighteenth Annual Report of the Hawaiian Historical Society, for the Year 1910 (Honolulu: Paradise of the Pacific Print), 47.

27 "Address to the House of Representatives of the Hawaiian Kingdom, on the Inefficiencies of High Duties on Spirits, in Promoting Temperance, Morality and Revenue, and the Expediency of Lowering the Duties, in Conformity with the Strong Recommendations of the Chamber of Commerce of Honolulu," by Robert Crichton Wyllie, Esq., Minister of Foreign Relations, Honolulu, Oahu, 1851.

28 Chester W. Burks, *Annals of the Chamber of Commerce of San Francisco* (San Francisco: Neal Publishing Company, 1909), 2. Burks was the secretary of the San Francisco Chamber of Commerce in 1909 and indicated that he had come across a yellowed "bundle of documents" from the chamber that were from December 1850. The quotation about the disorder of San Francisco society is from those documents.

29 Thomas Stauffer, "A History of the San Francisco Chamber of Commerce, 1850-2000," from *San Francisco: From the Gold Rush to Cyberspace* by Charles A. Fracchia and Thomas Stauffer (San Francisco: San Francisco Chamber of Commerce and Marcoa Publishing Inc., 2000), 90.

30 "List of Officers from May, 1873 to May, 1874," *Annual Reports of the Chamber of Commerce of San Francisco, Submitted to a Meeting Holden May 13th, 1873* (San Francisco: Alta California Printing House, 1873), 2.

31 James A. B. Scherer, *"The Lion of the Vigilantes": William T. Coleman and the Life of Old San Francisco* (Indianapolis: The Bobbs-Merrill Company, 1939), 21-22.

32 James A. B. Scherer, *"The Lion of the Vigilantes": William T. Coleman and the Life of Old San Francisco* (Indianapolis: The Bobbs-Merrill Company, 1939), 27-28.

33 James A. B. Scherer, *"The Lion of the Vigilantes": William T. Coleman and the Life of Old San Francisco* (Indianapolis: The Bobbs-Merrill Company, 1939), 17.

34 James A. B. Scherer, *"The Lion of the Vigilantes": William T. Coleman and the Life of Old San Francisco* (Indianapolis: The Bobbs-Merrill Company, 1939), 35-37.

35 James A. B. Scherer, *"The Lion of the Vigilantes": William T. Coleman and the Life of Old San Francisco* (Indianapolis: The Bobbs-Merrill Company, 1939), 101-6.

36 James A. B. Scherer, *"The Lion of the Vigilantes": William T. Coleman and the Life of Old San Francisco* (Indianapolis: The Bobbs-Merrill Company, 1939), 109.

37 Mary Floyd Williams, *History of the San Francisco Vigilance Committee of 1851* (Berkeley, California: University of California Press, 1921), Footnote 2, 188. The text of the footnote is as follows: "Future Vigilantes formed more than one-third of the signers of an early call for a Chamber of Commerce (Alta 1849, Nov. 1 1/1)."

38 James A. B. Scherer, *"The Lion of the Vigilantes": William T. Coleman and the Life of Old San Francisco* (Indianapolis: The Bobbs-Merrill Company, 1939), 109.

39 Thomas Stauffer, "A History of the San Francisco Chamber of Commerce, 1850-2000," from *San Francisco: From the Gold Rush to Cyberspace* by Charles A. Fracchia and Thomas Stauffer (San Francisco: San Francisco Chamber of Commerce and Marcoa Publishing Inc., 2000), 92.

40 James A. B. Scherer, *"The Lion of the Vigilantes": William T. Coleman and the Life of Old San Francisco* (Indianapolis: The Bobbs-Merrill Company, 1939), 118-9.

41 James A. B. Scherer, *"The Lion of the Vigilantes": William T. Coleman and the Life of Old San Francisco* (Indianapolis: The Bobbs-Merrill Company, 1939), 121-6.

42 James A. B. Scherer, *"The Lion of the Vigilantes": William T. Coleman and the Life of Old San Francisco* (Indianapolis: The Bobbs-Merrill Company, 1939), 146.

43 So ingenious was one of his false-bottomed ballot boxes (with the bottom, of course, filled with bogus votes) that it was later displayed to the public. See: James A. B. Scherer, *"The Lion of the Vigilantes": William T. Coleman and the Life of Old San Francisco* (Indianapolis: The Bobbs-Merrill Company, 1939), 149-50.

44 James A. B. Scherer, *"The Lion of the Vigilantes": William T. Coleman and the Life of Old San Francisco* (Indianapolis: The Bobbs-Merrill Company, 1939), 152-6.

45 James A. B. Scherer, *"The Lion of the Vigilantes": William T. Coleman and the Life of Old San Francisco* (Indianapolis: The Bobbs-Merrill Company, 1939), 159-86.

46 William Tecumseh Sherman, *Memoirs* (New York: Penguin Classics, 2000), 116-127. The "orderly in the extreme" quote is on page 121.

47 "To Steamboat Masters and Owners" and "To the Chamber of Commerce," *New-Orleans Commercial Bulletin*, February 17, 1852, page 2, column 4.

48 Fred Irving Dayton, *Steamboat Days* (New York: Frederick A. Stokes, 1925), Chapter 4.

49 "Public Meeting," *The Louisiana Courier*, April 13, 1854, page one, column 4.

50 Untitled item, *The New York Times*, May 30, 1855, 8.

51 Untitled item, *The Daily True Delta*, December 18, 1858, page 2, column 4.

52 "Boston vs. New York," *American Railroad Journal*, March 13, 1847, 170. The article refers erroneously to the Pittsburg Chamber of Commerce, which did not exist at this time. The paper was delivered at the Pittsburg Board of Trade.

53 *Twenty-sixth Annual Report of the Philadelphia Board of Trade*, (Philadelphia: King & Baird Printers, 1859), 19.

54 *Twenty-sixth Annual Report of the Philadelphia Board of Trade*, (Philadelphia: King & Baird Printers, 1859).

55 "Mercantile Miscellanies: The Boston Board of Trade," *Hunt's Merchant Magazine and Commercial Review*, Volume 34, January-June 1856 (New York: Freeman Hunt, 1856), 261. The author of this article chides the New York Chamber of Commerce for not having a full-time secretary. Perhaps this criticism, and/or the larger rivalry with Boston, explains why the New York Chamber soon hired its own man, I. Smith Homans, to be a paid secretary. Homans joined the New York Chamber in 1858 and was hired in 1859, at the remarkably high salary (for the times) of $1,000, with a recommendation soon afterward that it be raised to $1,500. (See the New York Chamber's annual report for 1859-60, page 89.) George Wilson, moreover, who would become the secretary of the chamber in 1868, was on board as a clerk in 1858. The hiring of these professionals no doubt made it possible for the New York Chamber to begin publishing its remarkable series of annual reports, beginning for the year 1858-59.

56 Hamilton Andrews Hill, "Memoir of Isaac Chapman Bates," *The New-England Historical and Genealogical Register*, April 1877, 142-145. All the preceding information about Bates is taken from this source.

57 "The Great Pacific Railroad. New York Chamber of Commerce.", *The American Whig Review*, September 1849, 311-2.

58 "Resolutions of the Chamber of Commerce of New York, in favor of Whitney's plan for a railroad from Lake Michigan to the Pacific," August 7, 1849, presented to the Senate on December 24, 1849, *Index of Miscellaneous Documents Printed by Order of the Senate of the United States during the First Session of the Thirty-First Congress, 1849-50*, Volume I, (Washington: W.M. Belt, 1850), xxxix.

59 David Haward Bain, *Empire Express: Building the First Transcontinental Railroad* (New York: Viking Press, 1999), 43.

60 "Argument in the Rock Island Bridge Case," Daily Press of Chicago, September 24, 1857, from The Writings of Abraham Lincoln, Volume 2: http://www.classicreader.com/book/3331/101/.

61 Note these remarks by a native of Davenport, Iowa, in 1863: "The accident of the Effie Afton was the signal for the bursting forth of the long suppressed wrath of the citizens of St. Louis, who had from the commencement of the project placed every obstruction in the way of the erection of the bridge, and deemed it as the beginning of a series of similar structures over the Mississippi river at various points, tending to divert from St. Louis the commerce which formerly followed this natural highway from St. Paul Southward. At the instigation of the St. Louis Chamber of Commerce, the owners of the Effie Afton commenced a suit in Chicago against the Bridge Company for damages, to recover the value of the lost boat . . ." The source is: Willard Barrows, "History of Scott County, Iowa," from the *Annals of Iowa*, Volume 1, No. 4, October 1863, available on www.past2present.org.

62 "Argument in the Rock Island Bridge Case," Daily Press of Chicago, September 24, 1857, from The Writings of Abraham Lincoln, Volume 2: http://www.classicreader.com/book/3331/101/.

63 Willard Barrows, "History of Scott County, Iowa," from the *Annals of Iowa*, Volume 1, No. 4, October 1863, available on www.past2present.org.

64 C.C. Spalding, *Annals of the City of Kansas: Embracing Full Details of the Trade and Commerce of the Great Western Plains* (Kansas City: Van Horn and Abel's Printing House, 1858), 63.

65 Minutes of the Chamber of Commerce of Kansas City, January 7, 1879, 68. These are handwritten minutes from the first volume of the collected records of this chamber. The first entry, dated October 1, 1856, notes in its second article of incorporation: "The object of said Association shall be by organized and systematic effort to foster and advance the public interests of Kansas City, until she shall occupy that exalted position to which her superior natural advantages so justly entitle her, the great Commercial Emporium of the West."

66 Monroe Dodd, *Business and the Making of Kansas City* (Kansas City: Rockhill Books, 2012), 20-21.

67 "Effect of the Disturbances Upon Business. Appeal from the Merchants of Kansas. From the *St. Louis Globe Democrat*," *New York Daily Times*, February 28, 1856.

68 "Plate to Commodore Perry," *The New York Times*, December 15, 1855.

69 Joseph Bucklin Bishop, *A Chronicle of 150 Years: The Chamber of Commerce of the State of New York 1768-1918* (New York: Charles Scribner's Sons, 1918), 128.

70 "The New York Chamber of Commerce – the Merchants and the Atlantic Cable," *American and Commercial Advertiser*, August 24, 1858, page 1, column 5.

71 Joseph Bucklin Bishop, *A Chronicle of 150 Years: The Chamber of Commerce of the State of New York 1768-1918* (New York: Charles Scribner's Sons, 1918), 129.

72 A modern sleuth can easily check the math of these chamber calculators: two letters per ounce times 16 ounces equals 32 letters per pound, times 40 pounds in a sack equals 1,280 letters in a sack. Each rider has a sack, making a total of 2,560 letters in a day. With 365 days in a year, that's a total of exactly 934,400 letters.

73 "The Chamber of Commerce on the New Tariff, and Warehousing Bill and on the Overland Mails," *Daily Evening Bulletin* (San Francisco) Friday, June 1, 1860; Issue 47; column D.

74 "News of the World," *The Golden Era*, December 23, 1860, page 4, column 6.

75 "The Republican Convention," *The Huntingdon (PA) Globe*, May 23, 1860, page 2, column 2.

76 Richard N. Current, *The History of Wisconsin, Volume II. The Civil War Era, 1848-1873* (Madison: State Historical Society of Wisconsin, 1976), 293.

77 Benson J. Lossing, *Pictorial History of the Civil War*, Volume I (Philadelphia: George W. Childs, 1866), 206. Also: Thomas Prentice Kettell, *History of the Great Rebellion* (Hartford, Conn.: L. Stebbins, 1865), 55.

78 "Meeting of Prominent Citizens at the Chamber of Commerce," sidebar at end of an article entitled: "Congressional Proceedings," *The New York Times*, January 19, 1861, 1.

79 "Chamber of Commerce," *The New York Times*, February 8, 1861, 3.

80 Harold Holzer, "Pre Civil War Peace Conference," Weider History Group, www.historynet.com. This article was published online on November 8, 2010. It was originally published in *America's Civil War*, a magazine.

Coming Together and Coming Apart (1861-1865)

1 Sanborn, Alvan F., Editor, *Reminiscences of Richard Lathers: Sixty Years of a Busy Life in South Carolina, Massachusetts and New York* (New York: The Grafton Press, 1907), 167.

2 "Meeting at the Chamber of Commerce; A Public Meeting to be Held in Union-Square on Saturday," *New York Times*, April 18, 1861.

3 "New York is Constant," *New York Tribune*, July 16, 1862, from *Proceedings of the Mass Meeting of Loyal Citizens on Union Square, New-York, 15th Day of July, 1862*, John Austin Stevens, Secretary (New York: George F. Nesbit & Co., Printers, 1862), 116.

4 "Resolutions of the N.Y. Chamber of Commerce," April 20, 1861, reprinted from *The World*, in *The Rebellion Record: A Diary of American Events*, Volume I, edited by Frank Moore (New York: G.P. Putnam, 1861), 77.

5 "Resolutions of the N.Y. Chamber of Commerce," April 20, 1861, reprinted from *The World*, in *The Rebellion Record: A Diary of American Events*, Volume I, edited by Frank Moore (New York: G.P. Putnam, 1861), 78.

6 "Testimonial to the Captain and Crew of the Minnie Schiffer," *The New York Times*, October 19, 1860.

7 *Fourth Annual Report of the Chamber of Commerce of the State of New-York for the Year 1861-'62* (New York: John W. Amerman, Printer, 1862), 16. The man who suggested removing the portrait was G.W. Blunt. In October 1861, he moved that three members who had "absconded" should be removed from the chamber rolls. These were Isaac V. Fowler, Mansfield Lovell, and Gustavus W. Smith. (See p. 20 of the *Fourth Annual Report*.) Smith, a Kentuckian, joined the Confederacy and commanded the Army of Northern Virginia for one day after the fatal wounding of Joseph E. Johnston, until Jefferson Davis appointed Robert E. Lee as the permanent commander. Mansfield Lovell became a major general in the CSA Army but lost New Orleans to Yankee attack, and was severely criticized for it. Isaac Fowler ran out of town not because of the war, but because he was accused of embezzling money from his office as postmaster. These brief bios of all three absconders are taken from information in Wikipedia.

8 Frank Moore, editor, *The Rebellion Record: A Diary of American Events*, Volume I, (New York: G.P. Putnam, 1861), 96.

9 Phineas Camp Headley, *Massachusetts in the Rebellion* (Boston: Walker, Fuller and Co., 1866), 98.

10 "Letter from the President of the Chamber of Commerce of Charleston, S.C., to the Superintendent of the U.S. Coast Survey, requesting a tracing of the chart of Charleston harbor," June 18, 1851, from *Executive Documents Printed by Order of the Senate of the United States, During the First Session of the Thirty-Second Congress, 1851-2*, Vol. V (Washington, D.C.: A. Boyd Hamilton, 1852), 487.

11 "The First Confederate Flag," *The Confederate Veteran Magazine*, 1895 (Nashville, Tenn.: Blue and Gray Press, 1971), Volume 3, No. 10, October 1895, 315.

12 New York: "Harbor Defenses of New York," *New York Times*, September 14, 1861. Philadelphia: "The Philadelphia Board of Trade: Defences of Philadelphia," Resolutions on November 25, 1861, *The Merchants' Magazine and Commercial Review*, Volume 45, covering July-December 1861, 634. New York: William B. Dana, 1861.

13 "Condition of the Baltimore and Ohio Railroad: Necessity of Having it in Operation," *New York Times*, October 17, 1861.

14 *First Annual Statement of the Trade and Commerce of Memphis, for the Year Ending August 31, 1861: Reported to the Memphis Chamber of Commerce by Jno. S. Toof, Secretary* (Memphis: O'Neill & Parrish, Printers, 1861), 3.

15 Letter from Thomas Hunt and Jno. Toof of the Memphis Chamber of Commerce to CSA President Jefferson Davis, October 30, 1861, from *The War of the Rebellion: A Compilation of the Official Records of the Union and Confederate Armies* (Washington: Government Printing Office, 1898), Series I – Volume LII – in two parts; Part II – Confederate Correspondence, etc., 189.

16 Joni Woolf, *Sesquicentennial of the Macon Chamber of Commerce* (Macon, Georgia: Macon Chamber of Commerce, 2011), 1-2.

17 "A Vision of Southern Commerce," *The New York Times*, October 20, 1861.

18 Lorenzo Sabine, *Boston Board of Trade, 1862: Eighth Annual Report of the Government, Presented to the Board at the Annual Meeting, on the 15th January, 1862* (Boston: Alfred Mudge & Son, 1862), 25.

19 Lorenzo Sabine, *Boston Board of Trade, 1862: Eighth Annual Report of the Government, Presented to the Board at the Annual Meeting, on the 15th January, 1862* (Boston: Alfred Mudge & Son, 1862), 28.

20 "Loyalty in St. Louis Business Circles," *The New York Times*, January 13, 1862.

21 "Swearing the Rebels," *The New York Times*, February 5, 1862.

22 "The Western Department; Guerrillas Throughout Halleck's Department to Be Treated as Outlaws – Charities of New-York & Eastern Ladies, & etc. Up the Tennessee," *The New York Times*, March 23, 1862.

23 It is also known by its official CSA name of *CSS Virginia*.

24 *Fifth Annual Report of the Chamber of Commerce of the State of New-York for the Year 1862-'63* (New York: John W. Amerman, Printer, 1863), 18-19.

25 Dr. J.S. Newberry, *The U.S. Sanitary Commission in the Valley of the Mississippi During the War of the Rebellion, 1861-1866* (Cleveland: Fairbanks, Benedict & Co., Printers, 1871), 291-2.

26 "News from Washington; Bulletin from the War Department. Acknowledgment of Offers of Assistance for the Wounded in the Great Battle," *The New York Times*, April 12, 1862.

27 Telegraph from Secretary of the Treasury Salmon P. Chase to Cincinnati Chamber of Commerce President Joseph C. Butler, June 9, 1862, from *The Merchants' Magazine and Commercial Review*, edited by William B. Dana, Volume 47, June-December 1862 (New York: William B. Dana, Publisher, 1862), 73.

28 "News of the Day; The Rebellion," *The New York Times*, July 25, 1862.

29 "Affairs in Illinois.; The West Fairly Waked Up," *The New York Times*, July 31, 1862.

30 This engagement is also known as the Battle of Fair Oaks.

31 George H. Stowits, *History of the One Hundredth Regiment of New York State Volunteers* (Buffalo, N.Y.: Printing House of Matthews & Warren, 1870; courtesy of BiblioLife Reproduction Series), 62-64. Also Lloyd Graham and Frank Severance, *The First One Hundred Years of the Buffalo Chamber of Commerce* (Buffalo, N.Y.: Foster & Stewart Publishing Corp., 1945), 71-72.

32 Lloyd Graham and Frank Severance, *The First One Hundred Years of the Buffalo Chamber of Commerce* (Buffalo, N.Y.: Foster & Stewart Publishing Corp., 1945), 74.

33 Lloyd Graham and Frank Severance, *The First One Hundred Years of the Buffalo Chamber of Commerce* (Buffalo, N.Y.: Foster & Stewart Publishing Corp., 1945), 74-76.

34 Lloyd Graham and Frank Severance, *The First One Hundred Years of the Buffalo Chamber of Commerce* (Buffalo, N.Y.: Foster & Stewart Publishing Corp., 1945), 74-76.

35 *The Charleston Chamber of Commerce: List of Members, Arrears Lists, and Treasurer's Annual Statements, 1838-1863*, South Carolina Historical Society library, Charleston, S.C. After the ledger from February 9, 1863, there is one piece of paper with an identical message written twice by hand: "The annual meeting of this society will be held on Monday the 9th Feb. at PM [*sic*] at the Hall of the Bank of Charleston, when a statement of its affairs will be submitted and the usual elections held. [Signed] John Laurens, Sec. & Treas." There are no subsequent records until the reopening of the chamber after the war. Likely at the February 9 meeting, a decision was made to close the chamber for a while.

36 *Fifth Annual Report of the Chamber of Commerce of the State of New-York for the Year 1862-'63* (New York: John W. Amerman, Printer, 1863), 52.

37 The U.S. Ambassador to France, John Bigelow, wrote Abiel Low to say that the New York Chamber's tirades against the British aid to privateers had helped dissuade the French from following the British example. See: Gerald Kurland, *Seth Low: The Reformer in an Urban and Industrial Age* (Ardent Media, 1971), 17.

38 *Fifth Annual Report of the Chamber of Commerce of the State of New-York for the Year 1862-'63* (New York: John W. Amerman, Printer, 1863), 59.

39 *Fifth Annual Report of the Chamber of Commerce of the State of New-York for the Year 1862-'63* (New York: John W. Amerman, Printer, 1863), 16-17.

40 *Fifth Annual Report of the Chamber of Commerce of the State of New-York for the Year 1862-'63* (New York: John W. Amerman, Printer, 1863), 46.

41 "The New-York Chamber of Commerce and British Neutrality; from the London Times," *The New York Times*, November 20, 1862.

Notes

42 "What Has England to Do With This?" *The New York Times*, November 21, 1862.

43 Sanborn, Alvan F., Editor, *Reminiscences of Richard Lathers: Sixty Years of a Busy Life in South Carolina, Massachusetts and New York* (New York: The Grafton Press, 1907), 187.

44 Gideon Welles, *Diary of Gideon Welles, Secretary of the Navy Under Lincoln and Johnson*, Volume 1, 1861- March 1864 (Boston: Houghton Mifflin Company, 1911), 215.

45 "Letter from New York," March 12, from *The Era*, New Orleans, March 22, 1863, page 1, column 6.

46 "Local Intelligence; Chamber of Commerce," *The New York Times*, July 3, 1863.

47 Trenholm joined the chamber in 1840 and stayed in it faithfully as long as it operated. He was chosen as its second vice president in 1845 and became its first vice president in 1847 and its president in 1851 and 1852, with his final term ending in February 1853. Then in February 1855 he served on the Committee of Appeals, apparently as its head, until at least February 1862. His son William joined the chamber and served as a steward in the 1861-62 year. The only volunteer who seems to have been more active than George Alfred Trenholm during this period was A.O. Andrews, who served as president of the chamber from 1857 to 1869. The information on Trenholm's activities comes from the Charleston Chamber's records: *The Charleston Chamber of Commerce: List of Members, Arrears Lists, and Treasurer's Annual Statements, 1838-1863*, South Carolina Historical Society library, Charleston, S.C.

48 Royce Shingleton, *High Seas Confederate: The Life and Times of John Newland Maffitt* (Columbia, S.C.: University of South Carolina Press, 1994), 39.

49 Admiral Raphael Semmes, *Memoirs of Service Afloat, During the War Between the States* (Baltimore: Kelly, Piet & Co., 1869), 490.

50 Lorenzo Sabine, *Boston Board of Trade, 1865: Eleventh Annual Report of the Government, Presented to the Board at the Annual Meeting, on the 11th January, 1865* (Boston: Press of T.R. Marvin and Son, 1865), 37.

51 George H. Stowits, *History of the One Hundredth Regiment of New York State Volunteers* (Buffalo, N.Y.: Printing House of Matthews & Warren, 1870; courtesy of BiblioLife Reproduction Series), 132.

52 George H. Stowits, *History of the One Hundredth Regiment of New York State Volunteers* (Buffalo, N.Y.: Printing House of Matthews & Warren, 1870; courtesy of BiblioLife Reproduction Series), 119-121.

53 George H. Stowits, *History of the One Hundredth Regiment of New York State Volunteers* (Buffalo, N.Y.: Printing House of Matthews & Warren, 1870; courtesy of BiblioLife Reproduction Series), 141.

54 "Relief of Sufferers by the Riot," *The New York Times*, July 27, 1863.

55 James A. B. Scherer, *"The Lion of the Vigilantes": William T. Coleman and the Life of Old San Francisco* (Indianapolis: The Bobbs-Merrill Company, 1939), 240-3.

56 The Cincinnati Chamber of Commerce; The Oath of Allegiance," *The New York Times*, July 22, 1863.

57 "From the Mississippi; The Condition of Memphis Business," *The New York Times*, July 29, 1863.

58 *Illustrated Life, Campaigns and Public Services of Lieut. General Grant: The Hero of Fort Donelson! Vicksburg! Chattanooga! Petersburg! And Richmond! Also, Captor of General Lee's! General Johnston's! and other Rebel Armies* (Philadelphia: T. B. Peterson & Brothers, 1865),134.

59 Marshall N. Rich, *History of the Work of the Board of Trade of Portland, Maine* (Portland, Maine: Press of Ford & Rich, 1887), 21.

60 Lorenzo Sabine, *Boston Board of Trade, 1864: Tenth Annual Report of the Government, Presented to the Board at the Annual Meeting, on the 13th January, 1864* (Boston: Press of T.R. Marvin and Son, 1864), 37-42.

61 Milwaukee Chamber of Commerce, *Report*, 1862, 5, cited in Frederick Merk's *Economic History of Wisconsin During the Civil War Decade* (Madison, Wis., State Historical Society of Wisconsin, 1916), 224.

62 "Room for this Gold," *The Era* (New Orleans), February 23, 1864, 3.

63 Linus Pierpont Brockett and Mary C. Vaughan, *Woman's Work in the Civil War: A Record of Heroism, Patriotism and Patience* (Philadelphia: Zeigler, McCurdy & Co., 1867), 178-9.

64 Linus Pierpont Brockett and Mary C. Vaughan, *Woman's Work in the Civil War: A Record of Heroism, Patriotism and Patience* (Philadelphia: Zeigler, McCurdy & Co., 1867), 202.

65 Lloyd Graham and Frank H. Severance, *The First One Hundred Years of the Buffalo Chamber of Commerce* (Buffalo, N.Y.: Foster and Stewart Publishing Corp., 1945), 78.

66 Lloyd Graham and Frank H. Severance, *The First One Hundred Years of the Buffalo Chamber of Commerce* (Buffalo, N.Y.: Foster and Stewart Publishing Corp., 1945), 79.

67 George H. Stowits, *History of the One Hundredth Regiment of New York State Volunteers* (Buffalo, N.Y.: Printing House of Matthews & Warren, 1870; courtesy of BiblioLife Reproduction Series), 317.

68 Jacqueline Jones, *Saving Savannah: The City and the Civil War* (New York: Vintage Books, 2008), 207-8.

69 Charles Green, Secretary, Savannah Chamber of Commerce, letter to James Hunter, Collector of the Port and District of Savannah, December 7, 1842, from *Reports of the Secretary of the Treasury of the United States* (Washington, D.C.: Printed by John C. Rives, 1851), Volume IV, 592.

70 Charles Green, President, Savannah Chamber of Commerce, letter to Lord Lyons, January 19, 1865, from *Papers Relating to Foreign Affairs: Accompanying the Annual Message of the President to the First Session Thirty-Ninth Congress* (Washington, D.C.: Government Printing Office, 1866), Part II, 59.

71 See his letter supporting the Signal Corps: Letter to E.F. Bryan, April 5, 1876, from *Report of the Secretary of War; Being Part of the Message and Documents Communicated to the Two Houses of Congress at the Beginning of the Second Session of the Forty-Fourth Congress* (Washington, D.C.: Government Printing Office, 1876), Volume IV, 484.

72 "Congress," *The New York Times*, January 19,1865, regarding the Philadelphia Board of Trade's position. Also, from the same publication, "General News," January 20, 1865, regarding the Boston Board of Trade's position being described to the New York Chamber of Commerce.

73 Lawrence Meir Friedman and Harry N. Scheiber, editors, *American Law and the Constitutional Order: Historical Perspectives* (Cambridge, Mass.: Harvard College, 1978), 244-5.

74 Lloyd Graham and Frank H. Severance, *The First One Hundred Years of the Buffalo Chamber of Commerce* (Buffalo, N.Y.: Foster and Stewart Publishing Corp., 1945), 80.

Reconstruction and Renewal (1866-1876)

1 *Eighth Annual Report of the Chamber of Commerce of the State of New-York, for the year 1865-66* (New York: John W. Amerman, Printer, 1866), 17-19.

2 Speech of Joseph Aspinall, president of the Detroit Board of Trade, as reprinted in *Proceedings of the Commercial Convention, Held in Detroit, July 11th, 12th, 13th and 14th, 1865* (Detroit: Advertiser and Tribune Company Print, 1865), 11-12.

3 Hamilton Hill, *A Review of the Proceedings of the Detroit Convention* (Boston: J.H. Eastburn's Press, 1866), 3-4.

4 Speech of Joseph Aspinall, president of the Detroit Board of Trade, as reprinted in *Proceedings of the Commercial Convention, Held in Detroit, July 11th, 12th, 13th and 14th, 1865* (Detroit: Advertiser and Tribune Company Print, 1865), 9.

5 *Proceedings of the Commercial Convention, Held in Detroit, July 11th, 12th, 13th and 14th, 1865* (Detroit: Advertiser and Tribune Company Print, 1865), 44.

6 N.S. Benton, "The Canals of the State.; Statement of the President of the Detroit Board of Trade Corrected," letter published in *The New York Times*, August 21, 1865.

7 Letter to President Andrew Johnson from W.W. Totten and others from the Nashville Chamber of Commerce, May 22, 1865, from *The Papers of Andrew Johnson: May-August 1865*, Paul H. Bergeron, editor (University of Tennessee Press, 1989), 103.

8 "Meadville to Cincinnati by the Atlantic and Great Western," *The Railway News*, November 4, 1865, 487, column 2.

9 Ivan Allen Sr., *Atlanta from the Ashes* (Atlanta: Ruralist Press, 1928), 38.

10 W.H. Leahy, "Atlanta, City of the Present," *Town Development*, January 1914, 15.

11 Don Harrison Doyle, *New Men, New Cities, New South: Atlanta, Charleston, Nashville, Mobile, 1860-1910* (Chapel Hill, N.C.: University of North Carolina Press, 1990), 139.

12 *Minutes, Charleston Chamber of Commerce: 1866-1878*, handwritten manuscript, South Carolina Historical Society library, Charleston, S.C. Entry for February 13, 1866.

13 *Minutes, Charleston Chamber of Commerce: 1866-1878*, handwritten manuscript, South Carolina Historical Society library, Charleston, S.C. Entry for February 13, 1866.

14 *Minutes, Charleston Chamber of Commerce: 1866-1878*, handwritten manuscript, South Carolina Historical Society library, Charleston, S.C. Entry for March 12, 1866.

15 *Minutes, Charleston Chamber of Commerce: 1866-1878*, handwritten manuscript, South Carolina Historical Society library, Charleston, S.C. Entry for March 12, 1866.

16 *The Papers of Andrew Johnson: May-August 1865*, Paul H. Bergeron, editor (University of Tennessee Press, 1989), 193-4. Note the footnotes on 194 regarding Trenholm's incarceration, parole, and pardon.

17 Stanley Chapman, *Merchant Enterprise in Britain: From the Industrial Revolution to World War I* (Cambridge, U.K.: Cambridge University Press, 1992), 97-98.

18 Jerome Greene and Douglas Scott, *Finding Sand Creek: History, Archaeology, and the 1864 Massacre Site* (Norman, Oklahoma: University of Oklahoma Press, 2004), 7.

19 Anonymous, Summary of the Minutes of the Denver Board of Trade and the Denver Chamber of Commerce, 1867 to 1949, chapter entitled "1867 – 1884," page a.

20 Anonymous, Summary of the Minutes of the Denver Board of Trade and the Denver Chamber of Commerce, 1867 to 1949, chapter entitled "1867 – 1884," page b.

21 *Greater Scranton Chamber of Commerce, 1867 – 1967: 100 Years of Service* (Scranton, Pennsylvania: Greater Scranton Chamber of Commerce, 1967), 8-11. All of the information on Scranton here is taken from this source.

22 "The Pacific Railroad," *The New York Times*, May 13, 1869.

23 Hamilton Andrews Hill, Secretary, *Seventeenth Annual Report of the Boston Board of Trade, for the Year Ending January 11, 1871* (Boston: Barker, Cotter & Co., 1871), 98.

24 Hamilton Andrews Hill, Secretary, *Seventeenth Annual Report of the Boston Board of Trade, for the Year Ending January 11, 1871* (Boston: Barker, Cotter & Co., 1871), 106.

25 Hamilton Andrews Hill, Secretary, *Seventeenth Annual Report of the Boston Board of Trade, for the Year Ending January 11, 1871* (Boston: Barker, Cotter & Co., 1871), 109-110.

26 Hamilton Andrews Hill, Secretary, *Seventeenth Annual Report of the Boston Board of Trade, for the Year Ending January 11, 1871* (Boston: Barker, Cotter & Co., 1871), 132.

27 Hamilton Andrews Hill, Secretary, *Eighteenth Annual Report of the Boston Board of Trade, for the Year Ending January 10, 1872* (Boston: Barker, Cotter & Co., 1872), 32.

28 "The Goat Island Grant," a pamphlet on the proceedings of a mass meeting on March 16, 1872 (San Francisco: San Francisco Chamber of Commerce, 1872), 3-6.

29 "The Merchants Organizing Against Railway Autocracy," *The New York Times*, November 23, 1874.

30 H.T. Johns, Secretary, *Seventh Annual Report of the Saint Paul Chamber of Commerce* (St. Paul, Minn.: St. Paul Press Company, 1874), 4.

31 U.S. Bureau of the Census Records, Population of the 100 Largest Urban Places: 1870: http://www.census.gov/population/www/documentation/twps0027/tab10.txt

32 *Proceedings of the First Meeting of the National Board of Trade, Held in Philadelphia, June, 1868* (Boston: J.H. Eastburn's Press, 1868), 93-94.

33 *Proceedings of the First Meeting of the National Board of Trade, Held in Philadelphia, June, 1868* (Boston: J.H. Eastburn's Press, 1868), 47.

34 *Proceedings of the First Meeting of the National Board of Trade, Held in Philadelphia, June, 1868* (Boston: J.H. Eastburn's Press, 1868), 66.

35 *Proceedings of the First Meeting of the National Board of Trade, Held in Philadelphia, June, 1868* (Boston: J.H. Eastburn's Press, 1868), 86.

36 "The Merchants at Richmond," *The Galaxy*, January 1870, 130-1.

37 "Storms," *The American Cyclopedia: A Popular Dictionary of General Knowledge*, Volume 15, edited by George Ripley and Charles A. Dana (New York: D. Appleton and Company, 1883), 405. This article almost certainly is written by weather prediction pioneer Cleveland Abbe, as he refers to Abbe's activities as those of "this writer."

38 Cleveland Abbe, "Historical Notes on the Systems of Weather Telegraphy, and especially their Development in the United States," *The American Journal of Science and Arts*, edited by James B. Dana and B. Silliman, Third Series, Volume II, No. 7-12, July to December, 1871 (New Haven: Tuttle, Morehouse & Taylor, 1871), 85.

39 Cleveland Abbe, "Historical Notes on the Systems of Weather Telegraphy, and especially their Development in the United States," *The American Journal of Science and Arts*, edited by James B. Dana and B. Silliman, Third Series, Volume II, No. 7-12, July to December, 1871 (New Haven: Tuttle, Morehouse & Taylor, 1871), 86.

40 Cleveland Abbe, "Historical Notes on the Systems of Weather Telegraphy, and especially their Development in the United States," *The American Journal of Science and Arts*, edited by James B. Dana and B. Silliman, Third Series, Volume II, No. 7-12, July to December, 1871 (New Haven: Tuttle, Morehouse & Taylor, 1871), 87.

41 Cleveland Abbe, "Historical Notes on the Systems of Weather Telegraphy, and especially their Development in the United States," *The American Journal of Science and Arts*, edited by James B. Dana and B. Silliman, Third Series, Volume II, No. 7-12, July to December, 1871 (New Haven: Tuttle, Morehouse & Taylor, 1871), 87.

42 This saying, attributed to Mark Twain, apparently was actually first written by Twain's colleague Charles Dudley Warner. It first appeared in the *Hartford Courant* in 1897. See this source: Paul Boller and John George, *They Never Said It: A Book of Fake Quotes, Misquotes, & Misleading Attributions* (Oxford, U.K.: Oxford University Press, 1989), 124. Regarding the weather program itself: The Army Signal Office began producing weather reports based on the kind published initially by the Cincinnati Chamber. Many chambers of commerce were among the stations collecting the weather data. That federal service was transferred to the Agriculture Department in 1891 and today is known as the National Weather Service, a part of the National Oceanic and Atmospheric Administration.

43 A.T. Andreas, *History of Chicago*, Volume III (Chicago: A.T. Andreas Company, 1886), 295.

44 "The Chicago Fire," *The New York Times*, October 15, 1871.

45 A.T. Andreas, *History of Chicago*, Volume III (Chicago: A.T. Andreas Company, 1886), 296.

46 Charles Randolph, Secretary, Chicago Board of Trade, *Fourteenth Annual Report of the Trade and Commerce of Chicago, for the Year Ending December 31, 1871* (Chicago: Horton & Leonard, Printers, 1872), 8.

47 Charles Randolph, "The Year, Seen from the Board of Trade," *The Lakeside Monthly*, Volume VIII, July to December, 1872 (Chicago: The University Publishing Company, 1872), October 1872, 254.

48 Despite its courageous commitment to going ahead with the new building, the Board of Trade moved out in just over a decade. This was because its commercial operations outgrew the building – not out of dissatisfaction with anything other than the size of the original structure.

49 *Fourteenth Annual Report of the Corporation of the Chamber of Commerce, of the State of New-York, for the Year 1871-1872* (New-York: Press of the Chamber of Commerce, 1872), iii-iv.

50 *Report of the Chicago Relief and Aid Society of Disbursement of Contributions for the Sufferers by the Chicago Fire* (Chicago: Riverside Press, 1874), various pages.

51 The parallelism of reform efforts in the North and South, with the outsider groups of free blacks (South) and immigrants (North) as the subjects to be reformed, is made clear in this book: Heather Cox Richardson, *West from Appomattox: The Reconstruction of America after the Civil War* (New Haven: Yale University Press, 2007). A classic treatment of the topic, moreover, is: Robert H. Wiebe, *The Search for Order: 1877-1920* (New York: Hill and Wang, 1967).

52 Jean Edward Smith, *Grant* (New York: Simon & Schuster, 2001), 524-5.

53 *Proceedings of the Adjourned Meeting of the National Board of Trade, Held in Baltimore, January, 1874* (Chicago: Knight & Leonard, Printers, 1874), 160.

54 *Proceedings of the Adjourned Meeting of the National Board of Trade, Held in Baltimore, January, 1874* (Chicago: Knight & Leonard, Printers, 1874), 165.

55 *Proceedings of the Adjourned Meeting of the National Board of Trade, Held in Baltimore, January, 1874* (Chicago: Knight & Leonard, Printers, 1874), 170.

56 "Another Bid for Whitewash," *The New York Times*, August 5, 1871. See also the item from the August 9, 1871 edition of the *Times*, beginning, "It is reported that the Chamber of Commerce will refuse to step into the trap prepared for them by the Ring". Additional information is available in: John Bucklin Bishop, *The Chronicle of One Hundred & Fifty Years* (New York: Charles Scribner's Sons, 1918), 92-3.

57 John Bucklin Bishop, *The Chronicle of One Hundred & Fifty Years* (New York: Charles Scribner's Sons, 1918), 93.

58 "The General Order Business: The New Plan – Material Reduction of Rates Decided Upon – Some New Correspondence – Action of the Chamber of Commerce Awaited," *The New York Times*, February 28, 1872. Also "Reforms in the Customs: The Report of the Chamber of Commerce Committee," *The New York Times*, April 23, 1872.

59 "Newark Board of Trade – the Morris Canal," *The New York Times*, September 14, 1870.

60 *Third Annual Report to the Saint Paul Chamber of Commerce, By the Secretary, Ossian E. Dodge, for 1869* (St. Paul: Office of the Press Printing Company, 1870), 8.

61 "The District of Columbia: Meeting of Tax-Payers in Washington to Devise Measures of Protection," *The New York Times*, July 2, 1874.

62 There was certainly discontent throughout the South, as one would expect for any region on the losing end of a civil war. And the formation of the Ku Klux Klan was an attempt to circumvent or undermine the Yankee-imposed governments of the region. But scattered discontent and a white-sheeted guerrilla movement were not the same as a head-on, daylight political challenge to the legitimacy of the new establishment.

63 *Minutes, Charleston Chamber of Commerce: 1866-1878*, handwritten manuscript, South Carolina Historical Society library, Charleston, S.C. Entry for March 30, 1871.

64 Sanborn, Alvan F., Editor, *Reminiscences of Richard Lathers: Sixty Years of a Busy Life in South Carolina, Massachusetts and New York* (New York: The Grafton Press, 1907), 299.

65 *Testimony Taken by the Joint Select Committee to Inquire into the Condition of Affairs in the Late Insurrectionary States, Volume I: South Carolina* (Washington, D.C.: Government Printing Office, 1872), 474.

66 *Testimony Taken by the Joint Select Committee to Inquire into the Condition of Affairs in the Late Insurrectionary States, Volume I: South Carolina* (Washington, D.C.: Government Printing Office, 1872), 5.

67 "The Board of Trade," *The New York Times*, January 6, 1874.

68 *Sixteenth Annual Report of the Corporation of the Chamber of Commerce of New-York* (New York: Press of the Chamber of Commerce, 1874), 6.

69 "The New York Chamber of Commerce and Plans of Currency," *The Banker's Magazine and Statistical Register*, June 1875, from Volume 29 (New York: I. Smith Homans, 1874-5), 970-4.

70 "A Board of Trade for This City," *The New York Times*, September 20, 1874.

71 "The Board of Trade," *The New York Times*, October 14, 1875.

72 Quotation of John Bright, from *Proceedings of the Seventh Annual Meeting of the National Board of Trade, Held in Philadelphia, June 1875* (Chicago: Knight & Leonard, Printers, 1875), ii.

73 "Drift-Wood: Public Spirit," from *The Galaxy*, edited by William Conant Church and Mark Twain, April 1874, from Volume 17, January to June 1874 (New York: Sheldon & Company, 1874), 553.

74 "On Pork Packing Establishments," from the *Twentieth Annual Report of the Boston Board of Trade, January 1, 1874*, by Cornelius G. Attwood, Secretary and Superintendent (Boston: James F. Cotter & Co., Printers, 1874), 22-28.

75 Jack Claiborne, *Crown of the Queen City: The Charlotte Chamber from 1870 to 1999* (Charlotte: Charlotte Chamber of Commerce, 1999), 19.

76 "Seals in Alaska," from the *San Francisco Herald*, reprinted in *The New York Times*, March 27, 1869.

77 *Seventh Annual Report of the Saint Paul Chamber of Commerce for the Year Ending December 31, 1873*, by the Secretary, H.T. Johns (Saint Paul: St. Paul Press Company, 1874), 5-6. Here is the full list of the items brought to the chamber the previous year:

Erection of a new City Hall and Court House.

Union of St. Paul and Minneapolis.

Securing the permanent location of the State Fair in this City.

Location of Hamline University within this City.

Erection of fire-proof buildings for public records.

Erection of Elevator and warehouses for the wagon grain trade.

Securing of low freights.

Bridging the Mississippi at Minnehaha Falls.

Securing cheap fuel to our citizens.

Annexation of West St. Paul.

Transforming our bridge into a free bridge.

Examination of the building stone at Frontenac.

Regulation of freight-rates by law.

Establishment of a Buckskin Glove factory.

Amendment of the City Charter.

Improvement of the Mississippi River by the general government.

Peat.

Establishment of manufactures.

78 *Eighty-eighth Annual Report of the Philadelphia Board of Trade, Presented to the Association January 24, 1921* (Philadelphia: Philadelphia Board of Trade, 1921), 68.

79 "The American Centennial: Action of the Chamber of Commerce," *The New York Times*, December 24, 1873. All five members of the delegation (Welsh, Patterson, Shortridge, McKean, and Wetherill) had had or would soon have significant leadership roles in the Philadelphia Board of Trade.

80 "John Welsh," brief biography in *Universities and Their Sons: University of Pennsylvania*, editor-in-chief: General Joshua Lawrence Chamberlain (Boston: R. Herndon Company, 1901), 339.

81 "Centennial Exposition," Wikipedia.

82 Clarence L. Hodge and Peggy Ferris, *Building Honolulu: A Century of Community Service* (Honolulu: Chamber of Commerce of Honolulu, 1950), 15.

83 Jean Ingram Brookes, *International Rivalry in the Pacific Islands, 1800-1875* (Berkeley, California: University of California Press, 1941), 278.

84 *Annual Report of the Board of Health of the State of Louisiana to the General Assembly: 1875* (New Orleans: Printed at the Republican Office, 1876), 21.

85 *Annual Report of the Board of Health of the State of Louisiana to the General Assembly: 1875* (New Orleans: Printed at the Republican Office, 1876), 15.

86 *Annual Report of the Board of Health of the State of Louisiana to the General Assembly: 1875* (New Orleans: Printed at the Republican Office, 1876), 18.

87 *Annual Report of the Board of Health of the State of Louisiana to the General Assembly: 1875* (New Orleans: Printed at the Republican Office, 1876), 22.

88 *Annual Report of the Board of Health of the State of Louisiana to the General Assembly: 1875* (New Orleans: Printed at the Republican Office, 1876), 23.

89 C.B. White, M.D., "Disinfection in Yellow Fever as Practiced in New Orleans in the Years 1870 to 1876 Inclusive," a paper read on October 6, 1876, from *Public Health Reports and Papers*, Volume III, presented at the meetings of the American Public Health Association in the years 1875-6 (New York: Hurd and Houghton, 1877), 161.

90 C.M. Gidney, Benjamin Brooks, and Edwin Sheridan, *Santa Barbara, San Luis Obispo and Ventura Counties, California* (Chicago: The Lewis Publishing Company, 1917), Volume II, 565-6.

91 C.M. Gidney, Benjamin Brooks, and Edwin Sheridan, *Santa Barbara, San Luis Obispo and Ventura Counties, California* (Chicago: The Lewis Publishing Company, 1917), Volume II, 565-6.

92 *Seventh Annual Report of the Saint Paul Chamber of Commerce for the Year Ending December 31, 1873*, by the Secretary, H.T. Johns (Saint Paul: St. Paul Press Company, 1874), 5-6. See the list of items that were brought before the chamber. Hamline University is today in St. Paul. According to the university's Web site (history section), the plans to start building the university (relocated from Red Wing) were to begin in 1873, but economic conditions slowed the move down and the "doors finally opened" in 1880. Hamline today has about 2,000 undergraduate students and a total student population of about 5,000.

93 J.C. Power, *History of Springfield, Illinois: Its Attractions as a Home and Advantages for Business, Manufacturing, Etc., Published Under the Auspices of the Springfield Board of Trade* (Springfield: Illinois State Journal Print, 1871), 101.

94 "Southern Immigration: The Late Convention in New-Orleans – Fourteen States Represented," from the *New-Orleans Republican*, reprinted in *The New York Times*, March 11, 1876.

95 "Southern Immigration: The Late Convention in New-Orleans – Fourteen States Represented," from the *New-Orleans Republican*, reprinted in *The New York Times*, March 11, 1876.

Taming Disorder (1877-1886)

1 "Chamber of Commerce Dinner," *The New York Times*, May 7, 1877.

2 *Twentieth Annual Report of the Corporation of the Chamber of Commerce, of the State of New-York, for the Year 1877-78* (New-York: Press of the Chamber of Commerce, 1878), 6.

3 "A Merchants' Banquet," *The New York Times*, May 15, 1877.

4 James Green, *Death in the Haymarket: A Story of Chicago, the First Labor Movement, and the Bombing that Divided Gilded Age America* (New York: Random House, 2006), 183.

5 "The Railroad Strike: An Insurrection in Earnest," *The Bayonne Herald and Greenville Register*, July 28, 1877, page 2, column 3.

6 James M. Dennis, *Robert Koehler's The Strike: The Improbable Story of an Iconic 1886 Painting of Labor Protest* (Madison, Wisconsin: University of Wisconsin Press, 2011), 83.

7 This quotation and much of the material above on Parsons is from his pamphlet, "The Autobiography of Albert Parsons," published in 1887, and available on this link: http://law2.umkc.edu/faculty/projects/ftrials/haymarket/autobiography1.html

8 Richard Schneirov, "Chicago's Great Upheaval of 1877: Class Polarization and Democratic Politics," from *The Great Strikes of 1877*, edited by David O. Stowell (University of Illinois, 2008), 95.

9 Charles Randolph, Secretary, Chicago Board of Trade, *Twentieth Annual Report of the Trade and Commerce of Chicago, for the Year Ending December 31, 1877* (Chicago: Knight & Leonard, Printers, 1878), 11.

10 Charles Randolph, Secretary, Chicago Board of Trade, *Twentieth Annual Report of the Trade and Commerce of Chicago, for the Year Ending December 31, 1877* (Chicago: Knight & Leonard, Printers, 1878). The list of members begins on page 159. The list of board members is on page six.

11 In this, of course, it was not alone. Produce, meat, and grain trading were the main activities of scores of chambers, including those in Cincinnati, Boston, and Minneapolis.

12 J. Seymour Currey, *Chicago: Its History and Its Builders: A Century of Marvelous Growth* (Chicago: S.J. Clarke Publishing Company, 1912), Volume II, 306. For more details on the birth of the Commercial Club of Boston, see: Robert Batcheller, *The Commercial Club of Boston, Organized November 7, 1868: Constitution, Officers, Chronology, Retrospect* (Boston: Riverside Press, 1906), 59-60. The club originally was a committee of 40 men within the Boston Board of Trade that raised $11,000 for the first meeting of the National Board of Trade in Boston in early 1868. After the NBOT meeting, the committee decided to form the Commercial Club, raising its membership total to 50.

13 J. Seymour Currey, *Chicago: Its History and Its Builders: A Century of Marvelous Growth* (Chicago: S.J. Clarke Publishing Company, 1912), Volume II, 306.

14 Donald L. Miller, *City of the Century: The Epic of Chicago and the Making of America* (New York: Simon & Schuster, 1996), 233.

15 Secretary, Chicago Board of Trade, *Thirtieth Annual Report of the Trade and Commerce of Chicago, for the Year Ending December 31, 1887* (Chicago: Knight & Leonard Co., Printers, 1888), xxi.

16 *Origin, Growth and Usefulness of the Chicago Board of Trade: Its Leading Business Men, and Representative Business Men in Other Branches of Trade* (New York: Historical Publishing Co., 1885-6), 58.

17 "Fun in the Chicago Board of Trade," *The New York Times*, January 1, 1885. In 1883, as this article describes, the more decorous members suspended the annual practice of smashing bags of white flour to sully the black suits of the traders. The next year, 1884, the clerks erupted into merriment once again. With "the air full of produce and profanity," Secretary Stone tried to read the Board's election results but had to retreat after a bag of flour hit the railing near him. Ultimately things calmed down, and "the usual threats of disciplining the riotous members were made."

18 *Origin, Growth and Usefulness of the Chicago Board of Trade: Its Leading Business Men, and Representative Business Men in Other Branches of Trade* (New York: Historical Publishing Co., 1885-6), 59.

19 P.G. Smyth, "The World's Food Exchange: Sketches of Life and Character on the Chicago Board of Trade," *Donahoe's Magazine*, May 1905 issue, from Volume 53, January-June 1905 (Boston: Donahoe's Magazine Company, 1905), 499-500.

20 P.G. Smyth, "The World's Food Exchange: Sketches of Life and Character on the Chicago Board of Trade," *Donahoe's Magazine*, May 1905 issue, from Volume 53, January-June 1905 (Boston: Donahoe's Magazine Company, 1905), 501.

21 "Address of Samuel Fielden," from *The Famous Speeches of the Eight Chicago Anarchists in Court: When Asked if They Had Anything to Say Why Sentence of Death Should Not Be Passed on Them* (Chicago: Lucy Parsons, Publisher, 1910), 48.

22 Carl Smith, *Urban Disorder and the Shape of Belief: The Great Chicago Fire, The Haymarket Bomb and the Model Town of Pullman* (Chicago: University of Chicago Press, 1995), 115.

23 James Green, *Death in the Haymarket: A Story of Chicago, the First Labor Movement and the Bombing that Divided Gilded Age America* (New York: Anchor Books, 2006), 7.

24 George F. Stone, Secretary, Chicago Board of Trade, *Twenty-Ninth Annual Report of the Trade and Commerce of Chicago, for the Year Ending December 31, 1886* (Chicago: Knight & Leonard Co., Printers, 1887), xxi.

25 George F. Stone, Secretary, Chicago Board of Trade, *Twenty-Ninth Annual Report of the Trade and Commerce of Chicago, for the Year Ending December 31, 1886* (Chicago: Knight & Leonard Co., Printers, 1887), xxi.

26 James Green, *Death in the Haymarket: A Story of Chicago, the First Labor Movement and the Bombing that Divided Gilded Age America* (New York: Anchor Books, 2006), 213.

27 Interestingly, the term "kangaroo court" seems to have emerged in the gold mining territory of California in 1849, according to Wikipedia, and perhaps refers to the same types of Australian criminals whom the San Francisco vigilantes (and chamber members) went after.

28 James Green, *Death in the Haymarket: A Story of Chicago, the First Labor Movement and the Bombing that Divided Gilded Age America* (New York: Anchor Books, 2006), 259.

Notes

29 For Dodge City, see: Robert M. Wright, *Dodge City, The Cowboy Capital* (Dodge City, Kansas, 1913), 315. Copy was donated to the Ford County Historical Society in 2006 and is available at: http://www.skyways.org/orgs/fordco/wright/ . For Tombstone, see: Eric L. Clements, *After the Boom in Tombstone and Jerome, Arizona: Decline in Western Resource Towns* (Reno: University of Nevada Press, 2003), 236. Tombstone in earlier days is an interesting case. Wyatt Earp and his brothers and associates had won a famous victory over the "cowboys" at the Gunfight at the OK Corral in 1882. There wasn't a board of trade in Tombstone then, but Wyatt and his cronies leaned heavily on the businessmen in town for support during their storied attempt to maintain order. One of the local businessmen, George Parsons, kept a diary that illuminated much of the zaniness of Tombstone and occasionally described the interactions of the business elite with the lawmen. Parsons later would move to Los Angeles and become a prominent member of the Los Angeles Chamber of Commerce, for a time heading its mining committee, where he pushed through a program to erect signs pointing toward water along roads in the desert. See: "George W. Parsons," *The New York Times*, Associated Press, January 6, 1933, 17.

30 Johnny Hughes, *Famous Gamblers, Poker History, and Texas Stories* (Bloomington, Ind.: iUniverse Books, 2012), 112.

31 Elliott West, *The Saloon on the Rocky Mountain Mining Frontier* (Bison Books, 1996; University of Nebraska Press, 1979), 66.

32 Mary Franz, "The Real Men of Deadwood," *Wild West Magazine*, August 2006.

33 David A. Wolff, *Seth Bullock: Black Hills Lawman* (Pierre, S.D.: South Dakota Historical Society, 2009), 1788.

34 David A. Wolff, *Seth Bullock: Black Hills Lawman* (Pierre, S.D.: South Dakota Historical Society, 2009), 1790-91.

35 Mary Franz, "The Real Men of Deadwood," *Wild West Magazine*, August 2006.

36 Mary Franz, "The Real Men of Deadwood," *Wild West Magazine*, August 2006.

37 Theodore Henry Hittell, *History of California*, Volume IV (San Francisco: N.J. Stone and Company, 1897), 595.

38 In 1851 and 1856, Coleman had ignored San Francisco's lawful authorities, once personally taking two people from jail and having them hanged.

39 Hubert Howe Bancroft, *History of the Life of William T. Coleman: A Character Study* (San Francisco: The History Company, 1891), 352-3.

40 William T. Coleman's report of his activities in the 1877 disturbances, as reprinted in this source: Hubert Howe Bancroft, *History of the Life of William T. Coleman: A Character Study* (San Francisco: The History Company, 1891), 368.

41 Hubert Howe Bancroft, *History of the Life of William T. Coleman: A Character Study* (San Francisco: The History Company, 1891), 360.

42 Hubert Howe Bancroft, *History of the Life of William T. Coleman: A Character Study* (San Francisco: The History Company, 1891), 363.

43 Hubert Howe Bancroft, *History of the Life of William T. Coleman: A Character Study* (San Francisco: The History Company, 1891), 372.

44 *Thirty-Second Annual Report of the Chamber of Commerce, of the State of New-York, for the Year 1889-90* (New-York: Press of the Chamber of Commerce, 1890), 59.

45 Letter to His Excellency Grover Cleveland, President of the United States, from J.W. Sprague, president of the Tacoma Chamber of Commerce, November 3, 1885, as reprinted in *The Report of the Governor of Washington Territory to the Secretary of the Interior: 1886* (Washington: Government Printing Office, 1886), 31.

46 Telegram to Governor Watson Squires from Assistant U.S. Attorney C.H. Hanford, November 5, 1885, as reprinted in *The Report of the Governor of Washington Territory to the Secretary of the Interior: 1886* (Washington: Government Printing Office, 1886), 25.

47 Merle Thorpe, "Why They Cheered – 'He Built Seattle,'" *Nation's Business*, August 1925, 30.

48 *The Report of the Governor of Washington Territory to the Secretary of the Interior: 1886* (Washington: Government Printing Office, 1886), 4.

49 Fred H. Hackett, editor, *The Industries of San Francisco: Her Rank, Resources, Trade, Commerce & Manufactures* (San Francisco: Payot, Upham & Co., Publishers), 20.

50 "Redressing His Wounded Honor: Horsewhipping a Man on the Floor of the Cincinnati Chamber of Commerce," *The New York Times*, January 1, 1879.

51 "An Editor Who Shoots: A Politician Wants Satisfaction or Fight, and Gets the Last," *The Providence Morning Star*, October 15, 1882.

52 "An Editor Who Shoots: A Politician Wants Satisfaction or Fight, and Gets the Last," *The Providence Morning Star*, October 15, 1882.

53 Candice Millard, *Destiny of the Republic* (New York: Anchor Books, 2011), 295.

54 Candice Millard, *Destiny of the Republic* (New York: Anchor Books, 2011), 277.

55 Molly Caldwell Crosby, *The American Plague: The Untold Story of Yellow Fever, the Epidemic That Shaped Our History* (New York: Berkley Books, 2006), 40. This book provides an excellent look at the outbreak of the 1878 epidemic and also makes a brief reference (p. 37) to the involvement of the New Orleans Chamber of Commerce in helping ease quarantine restrictions.

56 Molly Caldwell Crosby, *The American Plague: The Untold Story of Yellow Fever, the Epidemic That Shaped Our History* (New York: Berkley Books, 2006), 54.

57 Molly Caldwell Crosby, *The American Plague: The Untold Story of Yellow Fever, the Epidemic That Shaped Our History* (New York: Berkley Books, 2006), 55.

58 Molly Caldwell Crosby, *The American Plague: The Untold Story of Yellow Fever, the Epidemic That Shaped Our History* (New York: Berkley Books, 2006), 87 and 93.

59 *Twenty-First Annual Report of the Corporation of the Chamber of Commerce, of the State of New-York, for the Year 1878-79* (New-York: Press of the Chamber of Commerce, 1878), 47.

60 "Help from New-York City. Meeting of Merchants and Bankers to Devise Means of Relief," *The New York Times*, August 24, 1878.

61 *Twenty-First Annual Report of the Corporation of the Chamber of Commerce, of the State of New-York, for the Year 1878-79* (New-York: Press of the Chamber of Commerce, 1878), xxvi.

62 Molly Caldwell Crosby, *The American Plague: The Untold Story of Yellow Fever, the Epidemic That Shaped Our History* (New York: Berkley Books, 2006), 103. Crosby cites the opinion of a Memphis historian, Gerald M. Capers.

63 Bob Holladay, "Leading Change: The Nashville Area Chamber of Commerce: A Historical Perspective on 150 Years of Providing Support for Nashville's Business and Removing Obstacles for Nashville's Progress," white paper, 1997, 3.

64 *Proceedings of the Tenth Annual Meeting of the National Board of Trade* (Boston: Tolman & White, Printers, 1880), 82-3.

65 This organization had added "and Transportation" to its name thanks to the pressing business issues involving primarily railroads but also canals.

66 "Railways and Senators: The Board of Trade Points Out Present Dangers," *The New York Times*, January 13, 1881.

67 Charles Randolph, Secretary, Chicago Board of Trade, *Twenty-Third Annual Report of the Trade and Commerce of Chicago, for the Year Ending December 31, 1880* (Chicago: Knight & Leonard, Printers, 1881), xxi.

68 "Freight Discrimination: New-York Merchants Protesting," *The New York Times*, January 31, 1878.

69 *Twenty-Second Annual Report of the Corporation of the Chamber of Commerce of the State of New-York, for the Year 1879-80* (New-York: Press of the Chamber of Commerce, 1880), 40.

70 "Hatch on Vanderbilt," *Chicago Daily Tribune*, October 17, 1882. Cited on this Web site: http://www.barrypopik.com/index.php/new_york_city/entry/the_public_be_damned_william_h_vanderbilt/

71 *Twenty-Second Annual Report of the Corporation of the Chamber of Commerce of the State of New-York, for the Year 1879-80* (New-York: Press of the Chamber of Commerce, 1880), 105.

72 Another defender of the railroads betrayed similar anger with the New York Chamber of Commerce. Responding to accusations of freight discrimination, William Shipman, counsel for the New York, Lake Erie & Western Railway Company, protested against "this wild and absurd raid of the Chamber of Commerce against the railroads of this State." This is from *Extracts Referring to the Subject of Differences in Railroad Transportation Charges Between Common Points West and the Seaboard Cities, Selected from the Official Report of the Proceedings of the Special Committee on Railroads Appointed by the New York State Assembly to Investigate Alleged Abuses in the Management of Railroads Chartered by the State of New York* (New York: Evening Post Job Printing Office, 1882), 322.

73 "The Problems of Trade: Last Day's Session of the National Board of Trade," *The New York Times*, December 13, 1879.

74 According to the Wikipedia article on Adirondack Park, the park is larger than the entire state of Vermont. It is also larger than these national parks combined: Yellowstone, Yosemite, Glacier, Grand Canyon, and Great Smoky Mountains.

75 *Save the Adirondack Forests and the Waterways of the State of New-York: Opinions of the Press* (New-York: Press of the Chamber of Commerce, 1883).

76 "Events in the Metropolis: Mountains Bare of Timber – The Changes in the Adirondack Forests in Twenty Years," *The New York Times*, December 25, 1883.

77 "The Adirondack Bills: The Chamber of Commerce Disappointed with the Legislature's Action," *The New York Times*, March 2, 1884.

78 "Watchful Care of State Forests: Board of Trade's Efforts for Their Preservation," *The New York Times*, November 15, 1894.

79 "Saint Paul Winter Carnival," Wikipedia, with citations to the St. Paul Winter Carnival Association records at the Minnesota Historical Society.

80 St. Paul Winter Carnival Web site, history section:

http://www.winter-carnival.com/about_us/history/

81 W.L. Trenholm, "The Centennial Address Before the Charleston Chamber of Commerce, 11th February 1884" (Charleston, S.C.: The News and Courier Book Presses, 1884), 23.

82 W.L. Trenholm, "The Centennial Address Before the Charleston Chamber of Commerce, 11th February 1884" (Charleston, S.C.: The News and Courier Book Presses, 1884), 24.

83 W.L. Trenholm, "The Centennial Address Before the Charleston Chamber of Commerce, 11th February 1884" (Charleston, S.C.: The News and Courier Book Presses, 1884), 25.

84 W.L. Trenholm, "The Centennial Address Before the Charleston Chamber of Commerce, 11th February 1884" (Charleston, S.C.: The News and Courier Book Presses, 1884), 31-32.

85 Other developments confirmed South Carolina's economic development problems. The Charleston Chamber hired a Yankee business booster, Jonathan Land, during the year of Trenholm's soon-to-be-famous speech, but Land's most memorable achievement seems to have been the production of a book touting the merits of the city. See: Walter J. Fraser, *Charleston! Charleston! The History of a Southern City* (Columbia, S.C.: University of South Carolina Press, 1989), 312. Then there was a devastating earthquake in 1886, after which the city received assistance from various chambers and other groups. See: "Organized to Give Aid: The Chamber of Commerce Preparing for Prompt Relief," *The New York Times*, September 7, 1886.

86 "Boasting of Puritan Sires – The Proudest Festival of New-England's Sons," *The New York Times*, December 23, 1886.

87 "The New South: As Shown by a Georgia Editor to New Englanders – High Tribute to Lincoln – The Way Mr. Grady Talked to the Yankees," *The Meriden Journal*, December 23, 1886.

88 "Henry Grady, 'The New South' Speech (December 22, 1886), Web Document: Primary Source," from History 367, the University of Puget Sound: http://www.anselm.edu/academic/history/hdubrulle/CivWar/text/documents/doc54.htm

89 "Henry Grady, 'The New South' Speech (December 22, 1886), Web Document: Primary Source," from History 367, the University of Puget Sound: http://www.anselm.edu/academic/history/hdubrulle/CivWar/text/documents/doc54.htm

Gathering Strength (1887-1900)

1 *Proceedings of the Twenty-First Annual Meeting of the National Board of Trade: Held in Louisville, October 1889* (Boston: "Washington Press," George E. Crosby & Co., Printers, 1890), 14. The meeting was actually the twentieth annual meeting, because one meeting was skipped. The report for the next year, correctly named, has the same title as this one.

2 *Proceedings of the Twenty-First Annual Meeting of the National Board of Trade: Held in New Orleans, December 1890* (Boston: "Washington Press," George E. Crosby & Co., Printers, 1891), 19.

3 *Proceedings of the Twenty-First Annual Meeting of the National Board of Trade: Held in New Orleans, December 1890* (Boston: "Washington Press," George E. Crosby & Co., Printers, 1891), 19.

4 *Proceedings of the Twenty-First Annual Meeting of the National Board of Trade: Held in New Orleans, December 1890* (Boston: "Washington Press," George E. Crosby & Co., Printers, 1891), 20.

5 "Some Would Stand Alone: Chamber of Commerce Somewhat Divided; Indifferent to Representation in the National Board of Trade," *The New York Times*, January 6, 1888.

6 *Thirty-fourth Annual Report of the Corporation of the Chamber of Commerce of the State of New-York for the Year 1891-92* (New-York: Press of the Chamber of Commerce, 1892), xvi.

7 All information comes from the annual reports of the New York Chamber of Commerce during this period from 1887 through 1892.

8 *Thirty-second Annual Report of the Corporation of the Chamber of Commerce of the State of New-York for the Year 1889-90* (New-York: Press of the Chamber of Commerce, 1890), 26-7 (invitations to both men), 79 (Sherman's acceptance, and 80 (Edison's acceptance).

9 *Thirty-fifth Annual Report of the Corporation of the Chamber of Commerce of the State of New-York for the Year 1892-93* (New-York: Press of the Chamber of Commerce, 1893), 63.

10 "Honors for Reid: The Chamber of Commerce Banquet Last Night," *The Morning Herald*, April 17, 1892.

11 *Annual Report of the Boston Chamber of Commerce, Compliments of Wm. Herbert Pearson, Secretary* (Boston: C.M. Barrows and Co., 1889), 3.

12 Letter from Cincinnati Chamber of Commerce Superintendent Sidney Maxwell to S.S. Guthrie of the Buffalo Board of Trade, December 12, 1888, reprinted in: *Annual Report of the Boston Chamber of Commerce, Compliments of Wm. Herbert Pearson, Secretary* (Boston: C.M. Barrows and Co., 1889), 4.

13 Letter from Cincinnati Chamber of Commerce Superintendent Sidney Maxwell to S.S. Guthrie of the Buffalo Board of Trade, December 12, 1888, reprinted in: *Annual Report of the Boston Chamber of Commerce, Compliments of Wm. Herbert Pearson, Secretary* (Boston: C.M. Barrows and Co., 1889), 4.

14 George and Miriam Geib, *Indianapolis First: A Commemorative History of the Indianapolis Chamber of Commerce and Local Business Community* (Indianapolis: Indianapolis Chamber of Commerce, 1990), 17.

15 Col. Eli Lilly, handwritten letter to William Fortune, September 21, 1892, photocopy of the original, Box 136, archives, Greater Indianapolis Chamber of Commerce.

16 "William Fortune," biographical article, reprinted from *Cyclopedia of American Biography* of the American Historical Society, Inc., Volume XXXIV, 1928. In Box 136, archives, Greater Indianapolis Chamber of Commerce. The exact wording of the CVB claim is as follows: "Notwithstanding, Mr. Fortune as executive director of the encampment, pronounced the best provided by a city to an encampment, at an expense of $63,000. He turned back to the city $42,000 of its appropriation, and proportionate parts of the contributions of others, and the Commercial Club retained enough of its refund to establish a permanent organization for the bringing of conventions to Indianapolis. This was the first permanently organized activity for the bringing of conventions to a city, an activity that few large cities are without today."

17 Don Woodward and Joel Campbell, *Common Ground: 100 Years of the Salt Lake Chamber* (Montgomery, Alabama: Community Communications Inc., 2003), 17.

18 *Proceedings of the Twenty-First Annual Meeting of the National Board of Trade: Held in Louisville, October 1889* (Boston: "Washington Press," George E. Crosby & Co., Printers, 1890). This was actually the twentieth annual meeting; a mistake was made on numbering. The four delegates to the meeting are mentioned on page two and their organization is formally admitted as a member on page 17. The four delegates were A.K. Miller, Leon Jastremski, L. O'Donnell, and J.C. Andrews.

19 *Proceedings of the Twenty-First Annual Meeting of the National Board of Trade: Held in New Orleans, December 1890* (Boston: "Washington Press," George E. Crosby & Co., Printers, 1891), 14.

20 "Semi-Annual Meeting of Portland Board of Trade," *Portland Board of Trade Journal*, April 1904, 480, first column.

21 "A New State Board of Trade," *The New York Times*, October 31, 1890.

22 The 1890 meetings of the organization are mentioned in an index of this book: *Report of the Librarian of the State Library for the Year Ending September 30, 1891* (Boston: Wright & Potter Printing Co., 1892), 61. The arrangements for what appears to have been the second annual meeting of the Connecticut State Board of Trade are described here: "Connecticut Commerce: Arrangements for the Meeting of the State Board of Trade," *The New York Times*, January 13, 1892.

23 *Report of the Chamber of Commerce of Richmond, Virginia, 1891-1893* (Richmond: J.W. Ferguson & Son, 1893), 92.

24 "Ohio Wants a State Board of Trade," *The New York Times*, May 13, 1893.

25 *History of the Organization of the Nevada State Board of Trade: Its Aims and Purposes, Constitution and Bylaws* (Nevada State Board of Trade, circa 1890), 4.

26 The Ogden and Salt Lake chambers were founded in April 1887, and the Provo chamber some time later in the year. Ogden was apparently first, as this chronicler proudly attests:

Ogden may justly boast that she organized the first Chamber of Commerce in Utah, and while it would not be fair to take a feather from the plume of the Salt Lake Board of Trade who have formed their Chamber and inaugurated their monuments, because the time and circumstances called their efforts forth, still is it [*sic*] true that Ogden was in the advance and that her southern neighbors – Salt Lake and Provo – had the example of the success of her commercial fusion on which to predicate the happy results and potency of their later organization and well arranged business movements.

This is from "Ogden City," *The Western Galaxy*, June 1888, Volume 1, No. 4, 443. However, the initial meeting for the Salt Lake Chamber occurred on April 2 (see *Common Ground*, page 18), so the scrupulous Ogden chronicler may be mistaken. And of course Salt Lake had its Board of Trade dating from 1879.

27 William Monroe Egan, *The Utah Industrialist*, Volume 1, December 1887 issue (Provo, Utah: The Utah Industrialist Co., 1888), 186.

28 Charles Hedges, compiler, *Speeches of Benjamin Harrison, Twenty-Third President of the United States* (New York: United States Book Company, 1892), 433.

29 Don Woodward and Joel Campbell, *Common Ground: 100 Years of the Salt Lake Chamber* (Montgomery, Alabama: Community Communications Inc., 2003), 18.

30 Don Woodward and Joel Campbell, *Common Ground: 100 Years of the Salt Lake Chamber* (Montgomery, Alabama: Community Communications Inc., 2003), 21-22.

31 Don Woodward and Joel Campbell, *Common Ground: 100 Years of the Salt Lake Chamber* (Montgomery, Alabama: Community Communications Inc., 2003), 23.

32 Don Woodward and Joel Campbell, *Common Ground: 100 Years of the Salt Lake Chamber* (Montgomery, Alabama: Community Communications Inc., 2003), 19. All the information about the rail car comes from this source.

33 Charles Dwight Willard, *History of the Los Angeles Chamber of Commerce* (Los Angeles: Kingsley-Barnes & Neuner Company, 1899), 65-67.

34 Charles Dwight Willard, *History of the Los Angeles Chamber of Commerce* (Los Angeles: Kingsley-Barnes & Neuner Company, 1899), 67.

35 Charles Dwight Willard, *History of the Los Angeles Chamber of Commerce* (Los Angeles: Kingsley-Barnes & Neuner Company, 1899), 152.

36 Charles Dwight Willard, *History of the Los Angeles Chamber of Commerce* (Los Angeles: Kingsley-Barnes & Neuner Company, 1899), 143.

37 Charles Dwight Willard, *History of the Los Angeles Chamber of Commerce* (Los Angeles: Kingsley-Barnes & Neuner Company, 1899), 152.

38 Charles Dwight Willard, *History of the Los Angeles Chamber of Commerce* (Los Angeles: Kingsley-Barnes & Neuner Company, 1899), 188.

39 Charles Dwight Willard, *History of the Los Angeles Chamber of Commerce* (Los Angeles: Kingsley-Barnes & Neuner Company, 1899), 151.

40 Charles Dwight Willard, *History of the Los Angeles Chamber of Commerce* (Los Angeles: Kingsley-Barnes & Neuner Company, 1899), 123. Also, Web site of the Los Angeles Area Chamber of Commerce.

41 "Ladies Annex," *The Great Southwest: A Monthly Journal of Horticulture*, September 1889, 10.

42 "Ladies' Annex: A Wonderful Growth and Much Good Work," *The Great Southwest: A Monthly Journal of Horticulture*, October 1889, 8. (This page of the magazine mistakenly shows "1886" but the other pages correctly show the date as 1889.)

43 "The Ladies' Annex: An Able Ally of the Chamber of Commerce," *The Great Southwest: A Monthly Journal of Horticulture*, January 1890, 3.

44 *Matthew Nye, "A Life Remembered: The Voice and Passions* of Feminist Writer and Community Activist Flora Kimball," California History, *September* 2010, page 3, www.Findarticles.com

45 Matthew Nye, "A Life Remembered: The Voice and Passions of Feminist Writer and Community Activist Flora Kimball," California History, September 2010, page 7, www.Findarticles.com

46 "An Address: Read Before the Annex, February 25 [or possibly 23 or 28; difficult to decipher], 1890 by Mrs. Carrie Williams," *The Great Southwest: A Monthly Journal of Horticulture*, March 1890, 14.

47 "The Park Tract Will Bloom," by R.H.Y., *The Great Southwest: A Monthly Journal of Horticulture*, February 1890, 8.

48 "Annex Meeting, October 24," *The Great Southwest: A Monthly Journal of Horticulture*, December 1890, 6.

49 "Report of Proceedings from the Year Ending June 9, 1892," from *Report of the Chamber of Commerce of Richmond, Virginia, 1891-93* (Richmond, Va.: J.W. Fergusson & Son, Printers, 1893), 54.

50 "Report of Proceedings from the Year Ending June 9, 1892," from *Report of the Chamber of Commerce of Richmond, Virginia, 1891-93* (Richmond, Va.: J.W. Fergusson & Son, Printers, 1893), 54-5.

51 "Annual Meeting of the Richmond Chamber of Commerce, June 8th, 1893," from *Report of the Chamber of Commerce of Richmond, Virginia, 1891-93* (Richmond, Va.: J.W. Fergusson & Son, Printers, 1893), 137.

Notes

52 "The Death of Windom: While Attending a Banquet at New York He Falls and Expires," *Spokane Daily Chronicle*, January 30, 1891. The article attributes his sudden death to "heart disease."

53 "William Tecumseh Sherman," Wikipedia.

54 Schiff's complete remarks, as recorded in the New York Chamber of Commerce's annual report, were as follows:

Mr. Chairman, I hesitated and was in doubt whether or not I should come to this meeting, for, as you are aware, I belong to that race which has suffered so terribly at the hands of the Czar's Government. What decided me to come was a suggestion made to me yesterday by one of the prominent members of this Chamber, one of the prime movers in this proposition to aid the Russian famine sufferers, who thought it might be good policy for the Hebrews to second this movement. I wish primarily to say that the Jew as a rule does not do charitable or philanthropic acts for the sake of good policy. If he helps the unfortunate, he does not ask him his nationality, race or creed, but aids him because he recognizes, even in the most miserable, the image of our Creator. The Hebrews, terribly as they have suffered through Russian persecution, sympathize with the famine-stricken Russian peasants, and so long as the fund now proposed to be raised is to be disbursed direct to the famine sufferers and is not to pass through the hands of the corrupt Russian officials, they will not fail to contribute. If, however, the funds received are to be transmitted through official Russian sources, we Jews will tightly close our pockets, for we know what Russian official corruption is, and we know that little of the fund would through such channels reach the famine sufferers. I take no stock in Russian friendship for the United States and our free government and institutions. If the Czar's Government has any love for the latter, why does it persecute and oppress its own children, banishing them either to Siberian prisons, or forcing them into exile to these United States? Let us aid, then, the perishing Russian people, and ignore the despotic Czar's Government, the very existence of which is a blot upon the civilization of this end of the nineteenth century.

These are from the following report: *Thirty-Fourth Annual Report of the Corporation of the Chamber of Commerce of the State of New-York, for the Year 1891-92* (New York: Press of the Chamber of Commerce, 1892), 99.

55 Jean Strouse, *Morgan: American Financier* (New York: HarperCollins, 2000), 547.

56 Letter to Lord Rothschild, April 4-5, 1904. From Cyrus Adler and Mortimer Schiff, *Jacob H. Schiff: His Life and Letters, Part 2* (Garden City, New York, 1929), 122.

57 *Thirty-Third Annual Report of the Corporation of the Chamber of Commerce of the State of New-York, for the Year 1890-91* (New York: Press of the Chamber of Commerce, 1891), Part II, 17.

58 "Fall of a Crown: Hawaii's Kingdom is a Thing of the Past; Annexation is the Cry," *The Washington Reporter*, January 31, 1893, 6, column 1.

59 "Hawaiian News: Talk of All Sorts Concerning Annexation," *Morning Missoulian*, February 1, 1893, 1.

60 In 1861, a total of 1,283 tons of sugar was shipped to the United States, according to this source: Clarence Hodge and Peggy Ferris, *Building Honolulu: A Century of Community Service* (Honolulu: Chamber of Commerce of Honolulu, 1950), 15, column 1. The figure of 120,000 tons exported to the United States, already cited, comes from this source: *Thirty-Third Annual Report of the Corporation of the Chamber of Commerce of the State of New-York, for the Year 1890-91* (New York: Press of the Chamber of Commerce, 1891), Part II, 17.

61 John Glessner's history of the Commercial Club of Chicago is quoted by this source: Josiah Seymour Currey, *Chicago: Its History and Builders, A Century of Marvelous Growth* (Chicago: Clarke Publishing Co., 1912), Volume II, 308.

62 Carl S. Smith, *The Plan of Chicago: Daniel Burnham and the Remaking of the American City* (Chicago: University of Chicago Press, 2006), 64.

63 John Bucklin Bishop, *A Chronicle of 150 Years: The Chamber of Commerce of the State of New York, 1768-1918* (New York: Charles Scribner's Sons, 1918), 116.

64 *Thirty-Sixth Annual Report of the Corporation of the Chamber of Commerce of the State of New-York for the Year 1893-94* (New York: Press of the Chamber of Commerce, 1894), 36.

65 *Thirty-Sixth Annual Report of the Corporation of the Chamber of Commerce of the State of New-York for the Year 1893-94* (New York: Press of the Chamber of Commerce, 1894), xiv.

66 The National Board of Trade had done something similar in 1891: a letter campaign to about 1,300 chambers of commerce urging the creation of a permanent Bureau of the Census. It received "several hundred" replies, resulting in an investigation of the idea by the Department of the Interior and a favorable report, and was incorporated in Senate Bill 690, which, however, never made it out of committee. That effort to create a permanent Census Bureau then ended, perhaps largely because of the death of its sponsor, Colonel John A. Price from Scranton. Most of this information comes from this source: Walter F. Willcox, "The Development of the American Census Office Since 1890," *Political Science Quarterly*, Volume 29 (New York: Ginn and Company, 1914), 441-444. Price himself describes the surveying effort and its early results in: *Proceedings of the Twenty-Second Annual Meeting of the National Board of Trade, Held in Washington, January 1892* (Boston: George E. Crosby & Co., 1892), 14-15.

67 This interesting private intervention to save the nation's economy is described well in this source, among many others: Ron Chernow, *The House of Morgan: An American Dynasty and the Rise of Modern Finance* (New York: Grove Press, 2001), 73-75.

68 Letter from President Grover Cleveland to New York Chamber President Alexander E. Orr on November 1, 1895, as quoted in "The Duty of the Nation: Secretary Carlisle on the Country's Financial Policy; The Chamber of Commerce Dinner," *The New York Times*, November 20, 1895.

69 *Thirty-Ninth Annual Report of the Corporation of the Chamber of Commerce of the State of New-York for the Year 1896-97* (New York: Press of the Chamber of Commerce, 1897), 31.

70 Most of the information here about the Presidential election results is from "United States Presidential Election, 1896," Wikipedia.

71 "No Rest for Mr. Hanna: Republican Chairman Busy from His Arrival," *The New York Times*, August 20, 1896.

72 *New York Tribune* article of November 18, 1896, as cited in *The Outlook: a Family Magazine*, Saturday, November 28, 1896, Volume 54, Number 22, 949.

73 *Thirty-Ninth Annual Report of the Corporation of the Chamber of Commerce of the State of New-York for the Year 1896-97* (New York: Press of the Chamber of Commerce, 1897), 86.

74 *Thirty-Ninth Annual Report of the Corporation of the Chamber of Commerce of the State of New-York for the Year 1896-97* (New York: Press of the Chamber of Commerce, 1897), 86.

75 *Report of the Monetary Commission of the Indianapolis Convention of Boards of Trade, Chambers of Commerce, Commercial Clubs, and Similar Bodies of the United States* (Chicago: the University of Chicago Press, 1898), 8.

76 *Forty-Second Annual Report of the Corporation of the Chamber of Commerce of the State of New-York for the Year 1899-1900* (New York: Press of the Chamber of Commerce, 1900), 134 and 143.

77 "Strong! Tammany Overwhelmed by a Plurality of About 50,000," *The New York Times*, November 7, 1894.

78 Sven Beckert, *The Monied Metropolis: New York City and the Consolidation of the American Bourgeoisie, 1850-1896* (Cambridge, U.K.: Cambridge University Press, 1993), 318.

79 "To Fight Quay Politics: The Better Element of Philadelphia Aroused at Last; Organized for Good Government," *The New York Times*, January 6, 1895.

80 *Annual Report of the Board of Trade of the City of La Crosse, Wis. For the Year 1895* (La Crosse, Wis.: Volksfreund Electric Print, 1896), 21.

81 "Bad Meat in Spokane: Chamber of Commerce May Call for a City Inspector," *Spokane Daily Chronicle*, August 31, 1899, 7.

82 Joseph Bucklin Bishop, *A Chronicle of One Hundred and Fifty Years: The Chamber of Commerce of the State of New York, 1768-1918* (New York: Charles Scribner's Sons, 1918), 106. See also: David C. Hammack, *Power and Society: Greater New York at the Turn of the Century* (New York: Russell Sage Foundation, 1982), 243.

83 *Forty-Second Annual Report of the Corporation of the Chamber of Commerce of the State of New-York for the Year 1899-1900* (New York: Press of the Chamber of Commerce, 1900), xvi.

84 *Fifth Annual Report of the Washington Board of Trade: November, 1895* (Washington, D.C.: National Publishing Company, 1895), 7. Unfortunately, despite additional years of advocacy, it was not till 1925 that funding for the bridge was authorized by Congress. Reportedly for want of that bridge, President Warren G. Harding was caught in a three-hour traffic jam to Arlington Cemetery. The funding materialized soon afterward.

85 Charles Dwight Willard, *A History of the Chamber of Commerce of Los Angeles, California: From its Foundation, September 1888, to the Year 1900* (Los Angeles: Kingsley-Barnes and Neuner Company, 1900), 169.

86 Roger Butterfield, "'Los Angeles is the Damnedest Place. . .', The City That Started with Nothing but Sunshine Now Expects to Become the Biggest in the World," *Life* magazine, November 22, 1943, 104.

87 Susan Smyer, "City of Houston Wastewater History," May 2008.

88 Web site on Houston's history: http://houstonhistory.com/decades/history5f.htm

This link covers the 1890s.

89 This quotation (without a date citation, but apparently occurring shortly before the disastrous hurricane of 1900) comes from the HoustonHistory.com Web site: http://houstonhistory.com/decades/history5f.htm

90 *Hand Book of the City of Atlanta: A Comprehensive View of the City's Commercial, Industrial and Residential Conditions* (Atlanta: Atlanta City Council and the Atlanta Chamber of Commerce, 1898), 107. This source cites a figure of $10 million for the investment in the Columbian Exposition, but elsewhere it's mentioned as $11 million.

91 *Hand Book of the City of Atlanta: A Comprehensive View of the City's Commercial, Industrial and Residential Conditions* (Atlanta: Atlanta City Council and the Atlanta Chamber of Commerce, 1898), 107-8.

92 Bobby Lawrence, *Tennessee Centennial: Nashville 1897* (Charleston, S.C.: Arcadia Publishing, 1998), 7.

93 "Louisiana Purchase Exposition," *The Annual Cyclopaedia and Register of Important Events During the Year: 1902* (New York: D. Appleton and Company, 1903), 362.

94 Charles Dwight Willard, *A History of the Chamber of Commerce of Los Angeles, California* (Los Angeles: Kingsley-Barnes & Neuner Company, 1899), 79-80.

95 William Deverell, Whitewashed Adobe: *The Rise of Los Angeles and the Remaking of its Mexican Past* (Berkeley, Calif.: University of California Press, 2005), 55.

96 Alvick A. Pearson, "The Tournament of Roses," *The Overland Monthly*, February 1907.

97 John Balser, "Pardners in Prosperity," *Cheyenne Business Monthly*, July 2009, 1. A source with wonderful photos of some of the early events is Chapter 10 ("Frontier Days") of this book: Nancy Weidel, *Images of America: Cheyenne, 1867-1917* (Charleston, S.C.: Arcadia Publishing, 2009).

98 "Klondike Miners Starving," *The New York Times*, November 6, 1897.

99 "Klondike Relief Movement: Portland to Give 100 Tons of Food, and is Waiting for Congress to Act," *The New York Times*, December 9, 1897.

100 "The Relief Preparations: Secretary Alger Actively Arranging for the Getting of Supplies to Starving Miners," *Dubuque Daily Herald*, December 23, 1897.

101 "Klondike Relief Useless: The Federal Government Abandons the Proposed Reindeer Expedition; No Danger of Starvation," *The New York Times*, March 2, 1898.

102 L.G. Kaufman, "Report of the Chamber of Commerce of Juneau, Alaska," from *Bulletin of the Department of Labor, Volume III – 1898*, edited by Carroll D. Wright, Commissioner (Washington: Government Printing Office, 1898), 419-425.

103 Eugene McElwaine, *The Truth About Alaska, the Golden Land of the Midnight Sun* (Chicago: Published by the Author, Regan Printing House, 1901), 222-226.

104 "Reports of Storms and Deaths at Cape Nome Are All Confirmed: Nome Chamber of Commerce and Army Officers Send Out Relief Parties," *The Seattle Times*, April 24, 1901, page 1, column 3.

105 Charles Dwight Willard, *A History of the Chamber of Commerce of Los Angeles, California: From its Foundation, September 1888, to the Year 1900* (Los Angeles: Kingsley-Barnes and Neuner Company, 1900), 148.

106 "President Cleveland's Message," his address to Congress on December 17, 1895, from *Collection of Pamphlets, 1885-1897*, edited by Burke Aaron Hinsdale. No publisher or publication date shown.

107 "National Honor and Self-Respect," *The New York Times*, December 20, 1895.

108 "National Honor and Self-Respect," *The New York Times*, December 20, 1895.

109 "Irish-American Press on 'England First,'" *The Literary Digest*, December 17, 1898, 711-12. The excerpts from *Irish World* have other juicy comments on the Anglophilia of the New York Chamber, even accusing it of opposing U.S. policy during the War of 1812 – which would have been difficult to do, given that the chamber was not operating then. But there is no doubt that this was a chamber with a long history of affection with Great Britain.

110 *Thirty-Ninth Annual Report of the Corporation of the Chamber of Commerce of the State of New-York for the Year 1896-97* (New York: Press of the Chamber of Commerce, 1897), 110.

111 *Forty-Second Annual Report of the Corporation of the Chamber of Commerce of the State of New-York for the Year 1899-1900* (New York: Press of the Chamber of Commerce, 1900), 11-12.

112 Joseph Bucklin Bishop, *A Chronicle of One Hundred and Fifty Years: The Chamber of Commerce of the State of New York, 1768-1918* (New York: Charles Scribner's Sons, 1918), 139.

113 Joseph Bucklin Bishop, *A Chronicle of One Hundred and Fifty Years: The Chamber of Commerce of the State of New York, 1768-1918* (New York: Charles Scribner's Sons, 1918), 140.

114 William Adams Brown, *Morris Ketchum Jesup: A Character Sketch* (New York: Charles Scribner's Sons, 1910), 126. This source repeats the remark of the toast and notes the "suggestive" title of the commemorative booklet on the London visit, "A Pledge of International Friendship." The writer goes on to say: "The manner in which the call [for the New York Chamber to intervene in the crisis] was responded to made a lasting impression, and it was the desire to mark their deep sense of the service rendered that prompted the Council of the London Chamber to invite the New York Chamber to pay a visit to London, which should still further strengthen the bonds of sympathy and of friendship which united the two Chambers."

115 It appears likely that the idea was, indeed, a British one. Just as Alexander Hamilton admitted he "induced" the New York Chamber on a measure regarding lawyers in 1802, and perhaps also in the case of the Jay Treaty, it appears from the toast that the New York Chamber was prompted and encouraged by the London Chamber to champion arbitration for the Venezuela dispute. Whether or not the idea was initiated by the London Chamber, it is clear that the two chambers colluded in this process. For example, note a remark by Sir Albert Rollit during the London Chamber's later visit to New York (of which he was the delegation head): "we shall never forget that arbitration, as the alternative to that which would have been a public crime, war between our two countries, was ultimately effected, in a very large measure, by the joint action of your Chamber and our own." This is from: *Forty-Fifth Annual Report of the Chamber of Commerce of the State of New York for the Year 1902-1903* (New York: Press of the Chamber of Commerce, 1903), 75. Rollit made a similar remark in a thank-you note after the British delegation's visit to New York: "The Chamber regards it as a happy circumstance that its correspondence with the New-York Chamber in connection with the Venezuelan incident some years ago brought the two nations closer together". This is from the same annual report, page 133.

116 David L. Lewis, *W.E.B. Du Bois: A Biography* (New York: Holt Paperbacks, 2009), 158-9.

117 David L. Lewis, *W.E.B. Du Bois: A Biography* (New York: Holt Paperbacks, 2009), 159.

118 Raymond Smock, *Booker T. Washington in Perspective: Essays of Louis R. Harlan* (University Press of Mississippi, 1988), 99.

119 Washington did, however, cite Du Bois's "The Negro in Business" from time to time. See: Raymond Smock, *Booker T. Washington in Perspective: Essays of Louis R. Harlan* (University Press of Mississippi, 1988), 99.

120 *Proceedings of the National Negro Business League: Its First Meeting, Held in Boston, Massachusetts, August 23 and 24, 1900* (Boston: J.R. Hamm, Publisher, 1901), 26.

121 "Trade with Italy," *The New York Times*, December 22, 1887.

122 The information on the New York organizations is taken primarily from this source: Edward A. Moseley, *List of National, State and Local Commercial Organizations; National, State and Local Agricultural Organizations; and Railway Associations* (Washington, D.C.: Interstate Commerce Commission, February 1898), 36, 39-41.

123 Edward A. Moseley, *List of National, State and Local Commercial Organizations; National, State and Local Agricultural Organizations; and Railway Associations* (Washington, D.C.: Interstate Commerce Commission, February 1898), 32-3. Here are the 17 in Montana:

Town	Organization
Big Timber	Commercial Club
Billings	Commercial Exchange
Bozeman	Board of Trade
Butte	Chamber of Commerce
Choteau	Commercial Club
Fort Benton	Board of Trade
Great Falls	Board of Trade

Hamilton	Ravalli County Board of Trade
Helena	Board of Trade
	Business Men's Association
Kalispell	Board of Trade
Lewistown	Board of Trade
Livingston	Park County Board of Trade
Miles City	Chamber of Commerce
	City Club
Missoula	Board of Trade
Red Lodge	Business Men's Club

124 Chauncey Depew, "Address Before the Detroit Chamber of Commerce, May 2, 1895," from *Orations, Addresses and Speeches of Chauncey M. Depew*, Volume II, edited by John Denison Champlin (New York: Privately Printed, 1910), 51.

125 A.E. Orr, "Commercial Organizations," *The Encyclopedia Americana*, edited by Franklin Converse Beach (New York: The Americana Company, 1904), volume 5.

A New Energy (1901-1912)

1 Roosevelt's interest in chambers was made manifest in one way: he joined one. In 1903, the President sent in a check to become a member of the Oyster Bay Board of Trade. This tiny organization, with 150 members, was located in Roosevelt's home town on Long Island. See: "President to Join a Board of Trade," *The New York Times*, March 24, 1903. Also "Rival Celebrations May Mar President's Reception," *The New York Times*, June 26, 1903.

2 Theodore Roosevelt, "Speech at the Chamber of Commerce Banquet," November 11, 1902, from *The Triumphant Life of Theodore Roosevelt: Citizen; Statesman; President*, by Shelby Cullom, William Loeb, George Perkins, et. al., edited by J. Martin Miller (Washington, D.C.: J. Martin Miller, 1905), 358.

3 *Forty-Third Annual Report of the Corporation of the Chamber of Commerce of the State of New-York, for the Year 1900-1901* (New York: Press of the Chamber of Commerce, 1901), 106.

4 *Forty-Third Annual Report of the Corporation of the Chamber of Commerce of the State of New-York, for the Year 1900-1901* (New York: Press of the Chamber of Commerce, 1901), 110.

5 "For the Pacific Cable: Chamber of Commerce Asks Government to Grant Facilities; Also Favors Creation of a Department of Commerce and Industries – Trade Relations with Canada," *The New York Times*, November 8, 1901. Also, including the distribution strategy: *Forty-Fourth Annual Report of the Corporation of the Chamber of Commerce of the State of New-York, for the Year 1901-1902* (New York: Press of the Chamber of Commerce, 1902), xviii.

6 *Fifty-Second Annual Report of the Chamber of Commerce of San Francisco, Submitted to a Meeting Held January 21, 1902* (San Francisco: Commercial Publishing Company, 1902), 65.

7 *Proceedings of the Thirty-Second Annual Meeting of the National Board of Trade, Held in Washington January, 1902* (Philadelphia: John McFetridge and Sons, 1902), vi, 199–201.

8 Theodore Roosevelt, "Desirability of a Secretary of Commerce and Labor," from the President's message to the opening of the first session of the fifty-seventh Congress, December 3, 1901, reprinted in *The Roosevelt Policy: Speeches, Letters and State Papers, relating to Corporate Wealth and Closely Allied Topics, of Theodore Roosevelt* (New York: The Current Literature Publishing Company, 1908), Volume One, 170-1.

9 Henry Barrett Learned, *The President's Cabinet: Studies in the Origin, Formation and Structure of an American Institution* (New Haven: Yale University Press, 1912), 357.

10 "Police in Battle Royal on Business Men's Outing," *Baltimore Morning Herald*, August 9, 1902.

11 "East Baltimore Business Men. Seventeenth Annual Banquet of the Association at Philanthropy Hall," *Baltimore American*, February 5, 1902, p. 11, column 2.

12 *Fifty-Second Annual Report of the Cincinnati Chamber of Commerce and Merchants' Exchange, for the Year Ending December 31, 1900* (Cincinnati: The Ohio Valley Company, Printers, 1901), 46.

13 *Fifty-Third Annual Report of the Cincinnati Chamber of Commerce and Merchants' Exchange, for the Year Ending December 31, 1901* (Cincinnati: The Ohio Valley Company, Printers, 1902), 45.

14 *Fifty-Fourth Annual Report of the Cincinnati Chamber of Commerce and Merchants' Exchange, for the Year Ending December 31, 1902* (Cincinnati: The Ohio Valley Company, Printers, 1903), 49.

15 "State Board of Trade: Official Programme of the Fourteenth Annual Meeting," *Meriden Daily Journal*, October 17, 1903.

16 "National Board of Trade: Officers Elected After a Warm Debate on Some Canal Propositions," *The New York Times*, January 21, 1904.

17 *Proceedings of the Thirty-Fourth Annual Meeting of the National Board of Trade, Held in Washington January, 1904* (Philadelphia: John R. McFetridge and Sons, 1904), 129.

18 *Fiftieth Annual Report of the Trade and Commerce of Milwaukee for the Year Ending December 31st, 1907, and Fiscal Year of the Chamber of Commerce Ending April 6th, 1908* (Milwaukee: Radtke Brothers and Kortsch Co, 1907), 46.

19 Mike Carlisle, "Roy Miller 'Loved His Corpus Christi'!", "I Love My Corpus Christi" blog, May 30, 2006, ilovemycc. blogspot.com. One of those rival communities, perhaps unfortunately for its chances, was named Rockport

Notes

20 "Clarence St. Elmo Holland," *The Handbook of Texas Online*, Texas State Historical Association, www.tshaonline.org.

21 Lynn Alperin, *History of the Gulf Intracoastal Waterway* (National Waterways Study, U.S. Army Engineer Water Resources Support Center, 1983), 4-5.

22 Lynn Alperin, *History of the Gulf Intracoastal Waterway* (National Waterways Study, U.S. Army Engineer Water Resources Support Center, 1983), 6.

23 Carl Blasig, *Building Texas* (Brownsville, Texas: Springman-King Company, 1963), 33.

24 Robert Caro's extraordinary multivolume biography on LBJ begins with *The Path to Power* (Volume I), in which the author makes clear Roy Miller's reputation as one of the leading cash-rich lobbyists in an ethics-challenged political environment. Miller, at this point working for Texas Gulf Sulphur, thus became a natural partner to LBJ in politics. Other volumes continue with the theme of Miller's corrupt influence (although LBJ comes off no better in morals in Caro's telling). Yet even a company man who plied legislators with drinks and women likely couldn't get an awful idea past the legislature. Miller appears to have used, like many of his contemporaries, the mother's milk of politics to help get some infrastructure projects and other work accomplished. In the case of the Intracoastal Waterway, few today would say that Miller's end was a bad one, even if his means were questionable. And without the support of other business people and business groups, notably chambers of commerce, his odds of success no doubt would have shrunk dramatically.

25 John Trotwood Moore, "A Remarkable Southerner," *Trotwood's Monthly*, July 1906, 572.

26 Henry Stonewall Herring, *History of The New Orleans Board of Trade Limited, 1880-1930, and Annual Report for Year 1929* (New Orleans: New Orleans Board of Trade, 1930), 40. Among many laudatory remarks here, Herring says of the November 30, 1892 convention, "This Congress was one of the most notable conventions of business men ever held in the South, and revived interest in the Isthmian Canal, which had been hanging fire for many years. The widespread interest compelled Congress to act, and it was this action that resulted materially in the Panama Canal."

27 Procter, the son of P&G founder William Procter, gave Ivory Soap its name. The idea for its name came when he was sitting in church. Previously it had simply been called "White Soap." See: www.thegreatideafinder.com.

28 Philippe Bunau-Varilla, *Panama: The Creation, Destruction, and Resurrection* (New York: McBride, Nast & Company), 173-4.

29 Philippe Bunau-Varilla, *Panama: The Creation, Destruction, and Resurrection* (New York: McBride, Nast & Company), 179.

30 Philippe Bunau-Varilla, *Panama: The Creation, Destruction, and Resurrection* (New York: McBride, Nast & Company), 192.

31 "125 Years of Big Ideas: 125th Annual Meeting & Luncheon of the Fort Worth Chamber of Commerce, Thursday, June 7, 2007," 9 (first page of the subsection, "Fort Worth History: 1882-2007).

32 J'Nell Pate, *North of the River: A Brief History of North Fort Worth* (Fort Worth: 1994), 23. For the BOT's involvement, see: "125 Years of Big Ideas: 125th Annual Meeting & Luncheon of the Fort Worth Chamber of Commerce, Thursday, June 7, 2007," 10 (second page of the subsection, "Fort Worth History: 1882-2007). See also: Clay Reynolds with Marie-Madeleine Schein, *A Hundred Years of Heroes: A History of the Southwestern Exposition and Livestock Show* (Fort Worth: Southwestern Exposition and Livestock Show, 1995), 33. And also: R.E. Cleburne, "The Fort Worth-Cleburne Interurban," from *Stone & Webster Public Service Journal*, Volume 11, July-December 1912 (Boston: Stone & Webster, 1912), 332.

33 "125 Years of Big Ideas: 125th Annual Meeting & Luncheon of the Fort Worth Chamber of Commerce, Thursday, June 7, 2007," 10 (second page of the subsection, "Fort Worth History: 1882-2007).

34 Carl Blasig, *Building Texas* (Brownsville, Texas: Springman-King Company, 1963), 50.

35 Frederick Judson Soule, *An American Village Community: A Sociological Study of Village Association* (New York: Columbia University Department of Political Science, Ph.D. Thesis, 1909), 14-15.

36 "History of Clarksville Chamber, Clarksville Area Chamber of Commerce Web site: http://www.clarksvillechamber.com/about/history-clarksville-chamber/

37 "A Visitor's Views: Gettysburg, Her Past and Future, as Seen by a Baltimorean," *The Star and Sentinel*, Gettysburg, PA, March 27, 1901, page 1, column 6.

38 *Fifty-Third Annual Report of the Cincinnati Chamber of Commerce and Merchants' Exchange, for the Year Ending December 31, 1901* (Cincinnati: The Ohio Valley Company, Printers, 1902), 49.

39 Clarence Hodge and Peggy Ferris, *Building Honolulu: A Century of Community Service* (Honolulu: Chamber of Commerce of Honolulu, 1950), 46, column 2.

40 "1904," Summary of the Minutes of the Denver Chamber of Commerce, 52. Manuscript copied from the original at the Metro Denver Chamber of Commerce.

41 Roger Kullenberg and Dave Hager, *Kalamazoo: Kalamazoo Regional Chamber Celebrating 100 Years/ 1903-2003* (Kalamazoo: Kalamazoo Regional Chamber, 2003), 19.

42 U.C. Davis University Library, Special Collections, "Previous Exhibits: Davisville 1905" description, http://www.lib.ucdavis.edu/dept/specol/exhibits/?item=davisville

43 James D. and Georgiana Wallis Kornwolf, *Architecture and Town Planning in Colonial North America*, Volume 2 (Baltimore: The Johns Hopkins University Press, 2002), 1014.

44 Angie Debo, *And Still the Waters Run: The Betrayal of the Five Civilized Tribes* (Princeton, N.J.: Princeton University Press, 1940, 1968), 136-9.

45 *The Tale of a Wonderful Land: Eastern Oklahoma, Formerly Indian Territory* (Muskogee, Okla.: Muskogee Commercial Club, 1910).

46 "Unique Effects of United Efforts," *Nation's Business*, September 23, 1912, 7.

47 *Will Rogers Weekly Articles: The Harding Coolidge Years*, Oklahoma State University Press, as quoted in: Bill Waller, *History of the Tulsa Metro Chamber* (Tulsa: Tulsa Metro Chamber, 2003), 5-6.

48 *Fifty-Sixth and Fifty-Seventh Annual Reports of the Chamber of Commerce of San Francisco, Submitted to Meetings Held January 16th, 1906 and January 15th, 1907* (San Francisco: Neal Publishing Company, 1907), 6.

49 *Fifty-Sixth and Fifty-Seventh Annual Reports of the Chamber of Commerce of San Francisco, Submitted to Meetings Held January 16th, 1906 and January 15th, 1907* (San Francisco: Neal Publishing Company, 1907), 5.

50 *Fifty-Sixth and Fifty-Seventh Annual Reports of the Chamber of Commerce of San Francisco, Submitted to Meetings Held January 16th, 1906 and January 15th, 1907* (San Francisco: Neal Publishing Company, 1907), 14, 19, and 111-112.

51 "100 Years of Achievement," history item on the Oakland Chamber of Commerce Web site: http://www.oaklandchamber.com/chamber_100years_first100.shtml

52 *Forty-Eighth Annual Report of the Corporation of the Chamber of Commerce of the State of New-York, for the Year 1905-1906* (New York: Press of the Chamber of Commerce, 1906), xxxviii.

53 Charles Dwight Willard, *The Herald's History of Los Angeles City* (Los Angeles: Kingsley-Barnes & Neuner Co., 1901), Appendix, vii-viii. This appendix covers the decade after 1901.

54 "1906 Earthquake: the Spin Begins," from Comstock House History and Restoration, www.comstockhouse. org. The commentary is followed by the reprint of an article from the *Santa Rosa Press Democrat*, dated September 7, 1906, and entitled, "Chamber of Commerce Sends Out Bulletin Regarding Santa Rosa's Progress." This Web page is at this address: http://comstockhousehistory.blogspot.com/2010/02/1906-earthquake-spin-begins.html

55 Daniel Osmer, "Education of Economics (Heroes of Finance)," column 1 (first page of article), August 2008, from The Associative Economics Café, www.aecafe.com. The full Web page is: http://www.theaecafe. com/fileadmin/aecafe/articles/Social_Science_Section_doyle_mackay_Daniel_O_2008.pdf

56 Albert Whitney, *Report of the Special Committee of the Board of Trustees of the Chamber of Commerce of San Francisco on Insurance Settlements Incident to the San Francisco Fire, Approved at a Meeting of the Board of Trustees on November 13, 1906* (San Francisco: Chamber of Commerce of San Francisco, 1906), 6.

57 Albert Whitney, *Report of the Special Committee of the Board of Trustees of the Chamber of Commerce of San Francisco on Insurance Settlements Incident to the San Francisco Fire, Approved at a Meeting of the Board of Trustees on November 13, 1906* (San Francisco: Chamber of Commerce of San Francisco, 1906), 14.

58 Albert Whitney, *Report of the Special Committee of the Board of Trustees of the Chamber of Commerce of San Francisco on Insurance Settlements Incident to the San Francisco Fire, Approved at a Meeting of the Board of Trustees on November 13, 1906* (San Francisco: Chamber of Commerce of San Francisco, 1906), 37.

59 *Fifty-First Annual Report of the Chamber of Commerce of the State of New York for the Year 1908-1909* (New York: Press of the Chamber of Commerce, 1909), xxxiii.

60 *Fifty-First Annual Report of the Chamber of Commerce of the State of New York for the Year 1908-1909* (New York: Press of the Chamber of Commerce, 1909), xviii.

61 *Fifty-First Annual Report of the Chamber of Commerce of the State of New York for the Year 1908-1909* (New York: Press of the Chamber of Commerce, 1909), 30.

62 *Fifty-First Annual Report of the Chamber of Commerce of the State of New York for the Year 1908-1909* (New York: Press of the Chamber of Commerce, 1909), 28.

63 "Chamber of Commerce Farewell to Old Quarters; President Jesup Reviews the Past - $10,800 Given to Secretary George Wilson," *The New York Times*, November 7, 1902.

64 *Fifty-First Annual Report of the Chamber of Commerce of the State of New York for the Year 1908-1909* (New York: Press of the Chamber of Commerce, 1909), 30.

65 *Fifty-First Annual Report of the Chamber of Commerce of the State of New York for the Year 1908-1909* (New York: Press of the Chamber of Commerce, 1909), 35, 37.

66 *Fifty-First Annual Report of the Chamber of Commerce of the State of New York for the Year 1908-1909* (New York: Press of the Chamber of Commerce, 1909), 31.

67 Frank Wiggins, "Advertising California," *Official Report of the Twenty-Eighth Fruit-Growers' Convention of the State of California, Held Under the Auspices of the State Horticultural Convention, at Los Angeles, Commencing Tuesday, May 5th, and Ending Friday, May 8th, 1903* (Sacramento: W.W. Shannon, Superintendent of State Printing, 1903), 117.

68 *Final Report of the California World's Fair Commission: Including a Description of All Exhibits from the State of California, Collected and Maintained Under Legislative Enactments, at the World's Columbian Exposition, Chicago, 1893* (Sacramento: State Office, A.J. Johnston, Supervisor of State Printing, 1894), 49.

69 Harry Ellington Brook, *The City and County of Los Angeles in Southern California* (Los Angeles: Los Angeles Chamber of Commerce, November 1907), 68.

70 Roger Butterfield, "'Los Angeles is the Damnedest Place. . .', The City That Started with Nothing but Sunshine Now Expects to Become the Biggest in the World," *Life Magazine*, November 22, 1943, 111. Many other secondary sources mention Selig's reading of the chamber of commerce brochure and of its sunny optimism regarding the 350 days of clear weather per year.

71 Eileen Bowser, *The Transformation of Cinema, 1907-1915* (Los Angeles: University of California Press, 1994), 162.

72 "The Pacific Coast," *American Shipping*, February 10, 1921, column 1.

73 Catherine Mulholland, *William Mulholland and the Rise of Los Angeles* (Los Angeles: University of California Press, 2002), 112.

74 Roger Butterfield, "'Los Angeles is the Damnedest Place. . .', The City That Started with Nothing but Sunshine Now Expects to Become the Biggest in the World," *Life* magazine, November 22, 1943, 104.

75 "Commercial Organization: An Address by Mr. Ryerson Ritchie, of Boston," *City Club Bulletin*, City Club of Philadelphia, March 3, 1910.

76 The relative population chart and other remarks are taken from: Ryerson Ritchie, "The Modern Chamber of Commerce," *National Municipal Review*, April 1912, 161-169. The full chart, including population figures, is on page 166.

77 Clarence Monroe Burton, William Stocking, and Gordon K. Miller, *The City of Detroit, Michigan, 1701-1922* (Detroit-Chicago: The S.J. Clarke Publishing Co., 1922), Volume I, 527.

78 "Ryerson Ritchie Resigns," *San Francisco Chamber of Commerce Journal*, March 1912, 12.

79 Samuel Peter Orth, *A History of Cleveland, Ohio: Biographical* (Chicago-Cleveland: The S.J. Clarke Publishing Co., 1910), Volume II, 39.

80 Clarence Monroe Burton, William Stocking, and Gordon K. Miller, *The City of Detroit, Michigan, 1701-1922* (Detroit-Chicago: The S.J. Clarke Publishing Co., 1922), Volume I, 527.

81 "Ryerson Ritchie to Resign: His Organization Work in the Chamber of Commerce Practically Completed," *Boston Evening Transcript*, October 15, 1909.

82 Thomas Stauffer, "A History of the San Francisco Chamber of Commerce, 1850-2000," within this book: Charles A. Fracchia and Thomas Stauffer, *San Francisco: From the Gold Rush to Cyberspace* (San Francisco: San Francisco Chamber of Commerce and Marcoa Publishing, 2000), 94.

83 *Report of the Boston Chamber of Commerce for 1909* (Boston: Boston Chamber of Commerce, 1910), 16. Also: *Report of the Boston Chamber of Commerce for 1910* (Boston: Boston Chamber of Commerce, 1911), 24.

84 Frederick C. Howe, "Cleveland's Education through its Chamber of Commerce," *The Outlook: A Weekly Newspaper*, Volume 83, May-August 1906, 748-9.

85 *Report of the Boston Chamber of Commerce for 1910* (Boston: Boston Chamber of Commerce, 1911), 54-55.

86 *Report of the Boston Chamber of Commerce for 1910* (Boston: Boston Chamber of Commerce, 1911), 59.

87 Ryerson Ritchie, "The Modern Chamber of Commerce," *National Municipal Review*, April 1912, 168.

88 *Members' Annual: Twenty-Eighth Year, Los Angeles Chamber of Commerce, March 1916* (Los Angeles: Los Angeles Chamber of Commerce, 1916), 88.

89 Tom Jackson, "Boost New York," from *Greater New York: The Bulletin of the Merchants' Association of New York*, November 25, 1912, p. 1, column 2.

90 "Greater City is Fully Aroused to Its Duty," *Greater New York: The Bulletin of the Merchants' Association of New York*, November 25, 1912, pp. 8-9.

91 *Forty-eighth Annual Report of the Corporation of the Chamber of Commerce of the State of New-York for the Year 1905-1906* (New York: Press of the Chamber of Commerce, 1906), 110-111.

92 *Forty-eighth Annual Report of the Corporation of the Chamber of Commerce of the State of New-York for the Year 1905-1906* (New York: Press of the Chamber of Commerce, 1906), 111.

93 *Forty-eighth Annual Report of the Corporation of the Chamber of Commerce of the State of New-York for the Year 1905-1906* (New York: Press of the Chamber of Commerce, 1906), 112.

94 *Forty-eighth Annual Report of the Corporation of the Chamber of Commerce of the State of New-York for the Year 1905-1906* (New York: Press of the Chamber of Commerce, 1906), 119.

95 *Forty-eighth Annual Report of the Corporation of the Chamber of Commerce of the State of New-York for the Year 1905-1906* (New York: Press of the Chamber of Commerce, 1906), 121.

96 *Forty-ninth Annual Report of the Corporation of the Chamber of Commerce of the State of New-York for the Year 1906-1907* (New York: Press of the Chamber of Commerce, 1907), 15-32.

97 *Sixtieth Annual Report of the Cleveland Chamber of Commerce* (Cleveland: Cleveland Chamber of Commerce, April 1908), 155.

98 William Howard Taft, "Speech at the Banquet, Boston Chamber of Commerce, Boston, Mass.," September 14, 1909, from *Presidential Addresses and State Papers of William Howard Taft from March 4, 1909, to March 4, 1910* (New York: Doubleday, Page & Company, 1910), Volume One, 186.

99 Gabriel Kolko, *The Triumph of Conservatism: a Reinterpretation of American History, 1900-1916* (New York: The Free Press, 1963), 186.

100 Harry A. Wheeler, "The National Citizens' League: A Movement for a Sound Banking System," from *The Federal Reserve System: Its Purpose and Work*, in *Annals of the American Academy of Political and Social Science*, January 1922, 27.

101 Gabriel Kolko, *The Triumph of Conservatism: a Reinterpretation of American History, 1900-1916* (New York: The Free Press, 1963), 186.

102 Harry A. Wheeler, "The National Citizens' League: A Movement for a Sound Banking System," from *The Federal Reserve System: Its Purpose and Work*, in *Annals of the American Academy of Political and Social Science*, January 1922, 27-28.

103 *Banking and Currency: Hearings Before the Committee on Banking and Currency, United States Senate, Sixty-Third Congress, First Session, on H.R. 7837 (S. 2639), a Bill to Provide for the Establishment of Federal Reserve Banks* (Washington: Government Printing Office, 1913), Volume II, 1811.

104 Jean Reith Schroedel, *Congress, the President, and Policymaking: A Historical Analysis* (Armonk, N.Y.: M.E. Sharpe, 1994), 71.

105 "Booming Mount Vernon," *The New York Times*, May 29, 1910.

106 *Fifty-Third Annual Report of the Corporation of the Chamber of Commerce of the State of New York for the Year 1910-1911* (New York: Press of the Chamber of Commerce, 1911), 75.

107 "Turn of the Century (1900-1910)," in *Houston History, 174 Years of Historic Houston,* a Web site: http://www.houstonhistory.com/decades/history5a.htm. One of the Houston financiers active in this project, Jesse Jones, would go on to play several key roles in the federal government, including that of U.S. Secretary of Commerce from 1940 to 1945.

108 "Remarks at the Banquet Tendered Him by the Chamber of Commerce at Los Angeles, Cal. (October 11, 1909)," from *Presidential Addresses and State Papers of William Howard Taft: from March 4, 1909 to March 4, 1910* (New York: Doubleday, Page & Company, 1910), Volume One, 345.

109 Burt A. Heinly, "Carrying Water Through a Desert: The Story of the Los Angeles Aqueduct," *National Geographic,* July 1910, 582.

110 Margaret Leslie Davis, *Rivers in the Desert: William Mulholland and the Inventing of Los Angeles* (e-reads book, 1999; original copyright, 1993), 101-2.

111 Carl Blasig, *Building Texas* (Brownsville, Texas: Springman-King Company, 1963), 82.

112 This information comes from a page of the Web site of the Abilene Chamber of Commerce that has been removed. The text of the removed page noted: "The problems have changed somewhat during the years. In 1912, the Chamber was plugging for more hitch racks in the town. In 1913, taking note of developments in the field of transportation, the 'Chamber appointed J. M. Radford, J. P. Wooten and George L. Minter, Sr., to investigate the possibilities of an 'auto road from Abilene to Fort Worth.'"

113 G. Grosvenor Dawe, "Commercial Organization in Good Roads Campaign," address to the American Road Congress, reprinted in *Nation's Business,* November 18, 1912, 6. Dawe noted specifically that the good roads and new road agitation was not coming from agricultural areas or farmers, but from towns (especially small towns) and cities, even though the farmers benefited from new and better roads.

114 George and Miriam Geib, *Indianapolis First: The Commemorative History of the Indianapolis Chamber of Commerce and the Local Business Community* (Indianapolis: Indianapolis Chamber of Commerce, 1990), 61.

115 Don Woodward and Joel Campbell, *Common Ground: 100 Years of the Salt Lake Chamber* (Montgomery, Alabama: Community Communications, 2003), 90.

116 Myrtle Shaw Lord, *A Sacramento Saga: Fifty Years of Achievement – Chamber of Commerce Leadership* (Sacramento: Sacramento Chamber of Commerce, 1946), 330.

117 "Prize for Atwood: Talk of One After Washington Commerce Chamber Refuses to Help," *The New York Times,* July 19, 1911.

118 Kevin Starr, "The Columbia Catastrophe and the California Experience," www.sfgate.com, February 9, 2003.

119 Lois Wille, *Forever Open, Clear, and Free: The Struggle for Chicago's Lakefront* (Chicago: University of Chicago Press, 1991), 85.

120 Carl Smith, *The Plan of Chicago: Daniel Burnham and the Remaking of the American City* (Chicago: University of Chicago Press, 2006), xv.

121 Lloyd Graham and Frank H. Severance, *The First Hundred Years of the Buffalo Chamber of Commerce* (Buffalo, N.Y.: Foster and Stewart Publishing Corp., 1945), 141.

122 "From the Field: Projects, Prospects and Problems of Commercial Organizations," *The Worcester Magazine,* July 1910, 203.

123 W.B. Moore, "Oklahoma City Unique in Nation: Wondrous Town Made in 23 Years," *Nation's Business,* October 21, 1912. The two firms also got a five-year tax holiday and a guarantee of free water. W.B. Moore was secretary of the chamber.

124 Lloyd Graham and Frank H. Severance, *The First Hundred Years of the Buffalo Chamber of Commerce* (Buffalo, N.Y.: Foster and Stewart Publishing Corp., 1945), 141.

125 "Kelly Drops Toledo Tire Project," *The Motor World,* March 24, 1910, 785.

126 *Report of the Boston Chamber of Commerce for 1911* (Boston: Boston Chamber of Commerce, 1912), 46.

127 "Roll of Honor: Special Finance Campaign Closes with $74,250.50 Subscribed by Public Spirited Business Men of Seattle," *New Seattle Chamber of Commerce Record,* November 1, 1912, p. 1.

128 "Roll of Honor," *New Seattle Chamber of Commerce Record,* November 15, 1912, p. 1.

129 Walter Littell, "Initiative Displayed in Ad-Club Work," *Printers' Ink,* November 16, 1911, 42.

130 Mary Jo Jackson Bratton, *East Carolina University: The Formative Years, 1907-1982* (Greenville, N.C.: East Carolina University Alumni Association, 1986), 24-37, 47.

131 Text from a Heritage Trails plaque in Fort Worth, Texas, sponsored by Texas Christian University. See also "New Historical Marker Celebrates TCU's 100-Year Partnership with Fort Worth," by Diane Smith, *Fort Worth Star-Telegram,* August 31, 2010.

132 Anne Harding, "90 Years of Building a Better Dallas: The History of the Greater Dallas Chamber, 1909 to the Present," 6. This is a 15-page paper made available by the Greater Dallas Chamber in 1999.

133 Emory University Web site: http://www.fm.emory.edu/PLAN/refounding1.html

See also: Ivan Allen, *Atlanta from the Ashes* (Atlanta: Ruralist Press, 1929), 74.

134 Greater Memphis Chamber of Commerce Web site, history section: http://www.memphischamber.com/The-Chamber/History.aspx

135 Louise Gilmore Donahue, *Pathways to Prosperity: A History of the Greater Omaha Chamber of Commerce* (Omaha: Greater Omaha Chamber of Commerce, 1993), 6.

136 "Denver's Big Moving Picture Campaign," by C.A. Johnson, *Printers' Ink,* October 12, 1911, 74-76.

Notes

137 Clarence Hodge and Peggy Ferris, *Building Honolulu: A Century of Community Service* (Honolulu: Hawaii Chamber of Commerce, 1950), 62.

138 *Annual Report of the Honolulu Chamber of Commerce for the Year Ending August 16th, 1910* (Honolulu: The Hawaiian Gazette Company Ltd., 1910), 27-28.

139 *Annual Report of the Honolulu Chamber of Commerce for the Year Ending August 16th, 1910* (Honolulu: The Hawaiian Gazette Company Ltd., 1910), 9-10.

140 Charles N. Glaab and A. Theodore Brown, *A History of Urban America* (London: The Macmillan Company, 1967), 217.

141 "The 'City Manager' Plan Adopted by Sumter, S.C.," *The American City*, July 1912, 38.

142 Charles N. Glaab and A. Theodore Brown, *A History of Urban America* (London: The Macmillan Company, 1967), 195-6. For the Dayton Chamber's involvement, see: Bonnie Langdon and Phillip Parker, *Dayton Area Chamber of Commerce* (New York: Newcomen Society of the United States, 1996), 9.

143 Charles N. Glaab and A. Theodore Brown, *A History of Urban America* (London: The Macmillan Company, 1967), 195-6.

144 "Fined for Violating the Pure Food Law," *The Deseret News*, April 16, 1908.

145 Re yellow fever: *Annual Report of the Honolulu Chamber of Commerce for the Year Ending August 21st, 1912* (Honolulu: Paradise of the Pacific, 1912), 17. Regarding rats, see: Clarence Hodge and Peggy Ferris, *Building Honolulu: A Century of Community Service* (Honolulu: Chamber of Commerce of Honolulu, 1950), 22, column 2.

146 Logan McKee, "Civic Work of the Pittsburgh Chamber of Commerce," *The American City*, July 1911, Vol. 5 No. 1, 12.

147 Newton Evans, "The Conference on the Hookworm Disease," *Life and Health*, March 1910, 149. Re leprosy in Honolulu: *Annual Report of the Honolulu Chamber of Commerce for the Year Ending August 21st, 1912* (Honolulu: Paradise of the Pacific, 1912), 17-18.

148 C.L. Logan, "City Trade Bodies and Agriculture," *Corn Exchange National Bank Corn Show and Agricultural Conference* (Philadelphia: December 4-6, 1913), 41. Here is the wording of the mandate: "The object is to undertake propaganda work in the agricultural district in the vicinity of Binghamton, N.Y.; to make an agricultural survey of the territory; study the farmer's problems, find their solution by a study of the practices of successful farmers; study the relations of types of farming to local conditions of soil, climate, markets, etc. To demonstrate systems of managements used by successful farmers in the district and conduct experiments with the farmers, educational work through the media of institutes, etc., advising with the farmers individually and otherwise as to the best methods, crops, cropping systems, stock, labor, tools and other equipment."

149 Most of the information on the Farm Bureau, including the March start date, comes from: C.L. Logan, "City Trade Bodies and Agriculture," *Corn Exchange National Bank Corn Show and Agricultural Conference* (Philadelphia: December 4-6, 1913), 38-43.

150 Several sources mention briefly the Oklahoma City Chamber's role in the campaign. One source is: Kenneth Sturges, *American Chambers of Commerce* (New York: Printed for Williams College by Moffat, Park and Co., 1915), 225.

151 Myrtle Shaw Lord, *A Sacramento Saga: Fifty Years of Achievement – Chamber of Commerce Leadership* (Sacramento: Sacramento Chamber of Commerce, 1946), 185-187.

152 Myrtle Shaw Lord, *A Sacramento Saga: Fifty Years of Achievement – Chamber of Commerce Leadership* (Sacramento: Sacramento Chamber of Commerce, 1946), 194.

153 For clarity's sake on the topic of women, this section includes items that could have been put in the following chapter, covering the years 1913-1920. This entire book is a shaky compromise of organization by chronology (the dominant form now, at least in the overall chapters, which have years attached to them), topic (infrastructure, politics, economic development, etc.), and geography. In the author's view, the big-picture focus on chronology helps tie the hundreds or indeed thousands of facts and examples to the major currents of American history.

154 Jessica I. Elfenbein in association with Howard Gillette, Jr. and William H. Becker, *Civics, Commerce, and Community: The History of the Greater Washington Board of Trade, 1889-1989* (Dubuque, IA: Kendall/Hunt Publishing Company, 1989), 2.

155 David Elbert, *Standing on the Shoulders of Giants* (Des Moines: Greater Des Moines Partnership, 2013), 45.

156 For Walla Walla: "Activities Along the 'Right of Way,'" *Town Development*, October 1913, 28, column 3. For Raleigh: "General," *Town Development*, September 1917, 27, column 1. For Jackson, MI: "Woman's Activities," *Town Development*, September 1917, 29, column 2.

157 "Trade Body Elects Woman: Jane Addams a Member of the Chicago Association of Commerce," *The New York Times*, April 22, 1910.

158 "Jane Addams Our Guest," *The Detroiter: Spokesman of Optimism,* October 1912, 33.

159 *Sixtieth Annual Report of the Chamber of Commerce of San Francisco, Adopted at a Meeting Held January 18th, 1910* (San Francisco: A. Carlisle & Co., 1910), 34, 36.

160 *Sixty-Second Annual Report of the Cincinnati Chamber of Commerce and Merchants' Exchange for the Year Ending December 31, 1910* (Cincinnati: Robert T. Morris Printing Company, 1911), 40.

161 "A Remarkable Career: Mrs. Fannie Reese Pugh, First woman chamber of commerce manager in the United States," Howard W. Rosser, editor, *The First Fifty Years: A History of the East Texas Chamber of Commerce* (Longview, Texas: *East Texas Magazine,* 1976), 92. Pugh died in 1936: "First Woman CoC Secretary Dies," *NACOS News,* February 1936, 3.

162 Carl Blasig, *Building Texas* (Brownsville, Texas: Springman-King Company, 1963), 95.

163 George A. Smith, "The Development of Beaumont, Texas," *The American City*, November 1911, 257.

164 Carl Blasig, *Building Texas: A History of the Commercial Organization Movement and its Impact on Texas Progress* (Brownsville, Texas: The Springman-King Company, 1963), 95.

165 Carl Blasig, *Building Texas: A History of the Commercial Organization Movement and its Impact on Texas Progress* (Brownsville, Texas: The Springman-King Company, 1963), 124.

166 Robert Marshall (1978), updated by Harry McCawley (1999), "A Brief History of the Columbus Area Chamber of Commerce," provided by the Columbus, Ind., Area Chamber of Commerce, 1.

167 For brief references to some of its Americanization work, see: *St. Louis Public Library Annual Report: May 1, 1913 to April 30, 1914* (St. Louis: St. Louis Public Library, July 1914), 65-66.

168 "Flint," *Michigan Manufacturer and Financial Record*, February 15, 1919, 38, column 1.

169 *Proceedings of the Fourth Annual Meeting of the National Association of Commercial Organization Secretaries*, November 1918, Rochester, N.Y. (Rochester, N.Y.: NACOS, 1918), 37.

170 "Sophia E. Delavan, Who changed her whole source of workers to meet her 'labor problem,'" *The Magazine of Business*, edited by A.W. Shaw, Volume 38, July to December 1920, September issue, 421-22, 447-49.

171 Kathrine Clemmons Gould, "Women in Trade Reconstruction," *The Forum*, October-November 1919 issue, 471-79.

172 "Statement of Mrs. Howard Gould [Kathrine Clemmons Gould], founder and president of the Woman's Chamber of Commerce of the United States of America," from hearings on the National Employment System, U.S. Senate Committee on Education and Labor, July 25, 1919, contained in *National Employment System: Hearings Before the Joint Committees on Labor, Congress of the United States, Sixty-Sixth Congress, First Session, on S. 688, A Bill to Provide for a National Employment System*, Part 1 (Washington: U.S. Government Printing Office, 1919), 641-664. Comments on Jewish and Catholic girls, and her interceding for them, are on page 643.

173 *Proceedings of the Fourth Annual Meeting of the National Association of Commercial Organization Secretaries*, November 1918, Rochester, N.Y. (Rochester, N.Y.: NACOS, 1918), 61.

174 Carl Blasig, *Building Texas* (Brownsville, Texas: Springman-King Company, 1963), 27, 34, 43.

175 William George Bruce, "The National Association of Commercial Organization Secretaries," *Commercial Organizations: Their Function, Operation and Service* (Milwaukee: The Bruce Publishing Company, 1920), 451.

176 "Chambers of Commerce," *History of Alabama and Dictionary of Alabama Biography*, by Thomas McAdory Owen (Chicago: The S.J. Clarke Publishing Company, 1921), Volume I, 229.

177 William George Bruce, "The National Association of Commercial Organization Secretaries," *Commercial Organizations: Their Function, Operation and Service* (Milwaukee: The Bruce Publishing Company, 1920), 452.

178 All this paragraph's material comes from this book: Carl Blasig, *Building Texas* (Brownsville, Texas: Springman-King Company, 1963), 46, 78.

179 "Enthusiasm the Key Note: The 'Get Together' Dinner Yields a Phalanx of Determined City Workers," from *Greater New York: The Bulletin of the Merchants' Association of New York*, November 18, 1912, p. 2, column 3.

180 *Fifty-fourth Annual Report of the Corporation of the Chamber of Commerce of New York for the Year 1911-1912* (New York: Press of the Chamber of Commerce, 1912), xxxi-xxxii.

181 *The Independent*, May 9, 1912, 1026.

182 *Fifty-third Annual Report of the Corporation of the Chamber of Commerce of New York for the Year 1910-1911* (New York: Press of the Chamber of Commerce, 1911), 50.

183 "Root Asks if Nation is Moving on Right: At Chamber of Commerce Dinner He Says Thousands Think the Chamber a Den of Thieves," *The New York Times*, November 22, 1912.

184 Hannis Taylor, *The Real Authorship of the Constitution of the United States Explained*, U.S. Senate Document No. 787, 62nd Congress, 2d Session (Washington: 1912), 35.

185 *Proceedings of the Forty-First Annual Meeting of the National Board of Trade, Held in Washington January, 1911* (Philadelphia: John R. McFetridge & Sons, 1911), xix-xx.

186 *Fiftieth Annual Report of the Corporation of the Chamber of Commerce of the State of New York for the Year 1907-1908* (New York: Press of the Chamber of Commerce, 1908), 47.

187 "Taft Rule Pleases Commerce Guests: Speakers at Chamber's 141st Dinner Praise Administration's Sympathy with Business," *The New York Times*, November 19, 1909.

188 "Straus Organizes Council. Will Promote Closer Relations Between Department and Business Men," *The New York Times*, December 6, 1907.

189 Carl Sandburg, "Fixing the Pay of Railroad Men – Third Article," from *International Socialist Review*, Volume 15, June 1915, 711-712.

190 *Report of the Boston Chamber of Commerce for 1910* (Boston: Boston Chamber of Commerce, 1911), 58.

191 Harwood Lawrence Childs, *Labor and Capital in National Politics* (Columbus, Ohio: The Ohio State University Press, 1930), 10.

192 Harwood Lawrence Childs, *Labor and Capital in National Politics* (Columbus, Ohio: The Ohio State University Press, 1930), 10.

193 Harwood Lawrence Childs, *Labor and Capital in National Politics* (Columbus, Ohio: The Ohio State University Press, 1930), 10-11.

194 "Two Years' Progress: The Second Annual Meeting of the Chamber of Commerce of the United States of America Reveals the Wonderful Growth and Invaluable Work of the Most Potent Commercial Organization in the World," *Town Development*, March 1914, 67, column 2.

195 Several sources mention that 600 or more people attended the meeting. This source indicates the number of 392 organizations represented: "Chamber of Commerce of the United States of America," *Commercial America*, published by the Philadelphia Commercial Museum, June 1912, 5.

196 "Two Years' Progress," *Town Development*, March 1914, 67, column 3.

197 The figure of 500 organizational members after 18 months comes from: "Two Years' Progress," *Town Development*, March 1914, 67, column 1. The 1920 budget figure, along with other interesting information on the U.S. Chamber's growth, comes from: Harwood Lawrence Childs, *Labor and Capital in National Politics* (Columbus, Ohio: The Ohio State University Press, 1930), 34.

Organizing for Peace and War (1913-1920)

1 "Secretaries Meeting at Washington," *Town Development*, March 1914, 69.

2 S. Cristy Mead is no known relation to the author of this book, Chris Mead.

3 John Northway, "The Secretary in Action," from *Proceedings: Fifth Annual Meeting of the National Association of Commercial Organization Secretaries*, October 27-29, 1919 (Worcester, MA: NACOS, 1919), 93-102. All the information from Northway's findings is taken from this paper by Northway.

4 Robert Marshall (1978), updated by Harry McCawley (1999), "A Brief History of the Columbus Area Chamber of Commerce," provided by the Columbus, Ind., Area Chamber of Commerce. The information about both Tirtel and Sanders is taken from this source.

5 Lucius E. Wilson, *Community Leadership: The New Profession* (New York: The American City Bureau, 1919), 3. Wilson was vice president of The American City Bureau.

6 We have already seen how Ryerson Ritchie considered his methods responsible for the rise in city populations. Frank Wiggins was, no doubt, responsible for much of the growth of Los Angeles, and probably because of that was offered, as we have also seen, three times the salary he was making in Los Angeles. But Wiggins, unlike Ritchie, didn't seem much inclined to brag about himself. Others may not have been so circumspect. S.P. Puffer, on moving from Charleston, West Virginia to the one in Florence, Alabama, was cited by the Florence paper as having been "largely instrumental in building that city from a place of ten thousand population to its present number of fifty thousand." (From "Offer Place as Secretary: Chamber of Commerce Unanimous in Opinion That Mr. Puffer is Right for the Place," *The Florence Times*, December 12, 1919, 1.)

7 Other budgets cited by Northway included those from chambers in: Los Angeles ($127,750), St. Paul ($122,700), and several cities including Salt Lake City at about the $100,000 mark. There were other large chambers that apparently did not respond to his 1919 survey. These included the San Francisco Chamber of Commerce ($250,000), the New York Chamber of Commerce ($130,000), and the U.S. Chamber of Commerce ($750,000). The 1919 figures from the latter three chambers come from: *Commercial and Industrial Organizations of the United States: Revised to November 1, 1919* (Washington: Government Printing Office, 1919), issued by the U.S. Department of Commerce's Bureau of Foreign and Domestic Commerce, Miscellaneous Series, No. 99.

8 Charles Dwight Willard, *A History of the Chamber of Commerce of Los Angeles, California, from its Foundation, September, 1888, to the Year 1900* (Los Angeles: Kingsley-Barnes & Neuner Company, 1899).

9 Joseph Bucklin Bishop, *A Chronicle of One Hundred and Fifty Years: The Chamber of Commerce of the State of New York, 1768-1918* (New York: Charles Scribner's Sons, 1918).

10 *Sixty-Second Annual Report of the Corporation of the Chamber of Commerce of the State of New York for the Year 1919-1920* (New York: Press of the Chamber of Commerce, 1920), 75.

11 William George Bruce, Editor, *Commercial Organizations: Their Functions, Operation and Service* (Milwaukee: The Bruce Publishing Company, 1920).

12 A rough word estimate by the author of this book gives the Sturges work about 45,000 words, slightly short of a standard modern book length of 60,000 words, and slightly less than one fourth the length of the perhaps excessive (at the time of the writing of this footnote) 208,000 words of *The Magicians of Main Street*. But only about the first third of the Sturges book recounts the history of American chambers; the rest is a description of what chambers were doing in the years immediately leading up to the study's publication in 1915.

13 Kenneth Montague Sturges, *American Chambers of Commerce* (New York: Moffat, Yard & Company, 1915). This book was printed on behalf of the department of political science at Williams College. The work won the David A. Wells Essay Prize for the year submitted.

14 Garfield, a son of the assassinated President James Garfield, had been a professor of political science at Princeton and was a good friend of Princeton's president, now the U. S. President, Woodrow Wilson.

15 "Senator Jones Defends the Fuel Administration," *The Mining Congress Journal*, April 1918, 139-40.

16 President Taft's Speech at Annual Banquet," *Nation's Business*, January 28, 1913, 1. (Taft also said in the same talk that "there is no town and no village too small that it does not have either a Board of Trade or a Chamber of Commerce.") Regarding the Harvard course, here is an announcement of it: "Harvard Announces Course for Commercial Secretaries," *Nation's Business*, May 15, 1913, 6.

17 Some of these magazines lasted for years. The first to disappear was *Town Development*, whose last volume was in 1918. *The American City* made it to the mid-1960s and *Nation's Business* until 1999. *The National Municipal Review* continues today under the name of *National Civic Review*.

18 Advertisement in *The American City*, June 1918 issue, 584.

19 J.P. Hardy, "The Problems of the Commercial Organization in the Town and Small City," from *Proceedings of the First Annual Meeting of the National Association of Commercial Organization Secretaries, St. Louis, September 27-29, 1915* (Minneapolis: NACOS, 1915), 87.

20 George Gillette, "Organization Costs and Results," from *Proceedings of the First Annual Meeting of the National Association of Commercial Organization Secretaries, St. Louis, September 27-29, 1915* (Minneapolis: NACOS, 1915), 173. Gillette refers to the "uncollected dues" average of 8.2 percent, which would translate to an average renewal rate (in today's U.S. terms) of 91.8 percent. This is a higher renewal percentage than that in the United States today – roughly 82 percent. There are many reasons for the modern decline in renewal rates, which will be addressed later in this book. The best analysis of chamber renewal rate fluctuations over time, by far, is in Robert Bennett's *Voice of Business*.

21 From remarks of Robert Beacham, secretary of the Merchants' and Manufacturers' Association of Baltimore, in the *Proceedings of the First Annual Meeting of the National Association of Commercial Organization Secretaries, St. Louis, September 27-29, 1915* (Minneapolis: NACOS, 1915), 181.

22 Remarks by outgoing President Louis Cole, at the annual dinner of the Los Angeles Chamber of Commerce on February 21, 1914. From *Los Angeles Chamber of Commerce Members' Annual: 1914* (Los Angeles: Los Angeles Chamber of Commerce, March 1914), 111-112.

23 Harwood Lawrence Childs, *Labor and Capital in National Politics* (Columbus, Ohio: The Ohio State University Press, 1930), 33-35. Note especially the chart on page 34.

24 Myrtle Shaw Lloyd, *A Sacramento Saga: Fifty Years of Achievement – Chamber of Commerce Leadership* (Sacramento: Sacramento Chamber of Commerce, 1946), 86-7.

25 Hugh D. Hart, "Young Men's Chamber of Commerce," *Nation's Business*, December 15, 1914, 16.

26 A brief Web search has uncovered very few uses of the term before about 1912. One earlier place where it did appear was dated 1907 – a volume in which an individual named E.J. Crosier was interrogated about his knowledge of a foreign city (Liege) and he began by replying, "If I must blow my own trumpet, I am the originator of the Junior Chamber of Commerce up in the North." This appears to be in the north of England, and Crosier describes it as a kind of debating society where he was going to discuss Liege. This is from: *Report of the Committee Appointed by the Board of Trade to Make Enquiries With Reference to the Participation of Great Britain in Great International Exhibitions* (London: Printed for His Majesty's Stationery Office by Wyman and Sons, 1907), 273, column 1.

27 "The Reader's Index," *The American Educational Review*, July 1912, 570, column 1, "Educational."

28 For Sacramento: Myrtle Shaw Lloyd, *A Sacramento Saga: Fifty Years of Achievement – Chamber of Commerce Leadership* (Sacramento: Sacramento Chamber of Commerce, 1946), 75. For San Jose: "Topic: Linking School Work with Business Enterprises; A. The San Jose Junior Chamber of Commerce," *Journal of Proceedings and Addresses of the Fifty-Third Annual Meeting and International Congress on Education Held at Oakland, California, August 16-27, 1915* (Ann Arbor: National Education Association, 1915), 903. For Rome, N.Y.: "'Safety First' in Precept and Policy," William A. Searle, *The American City*, September 1914, 229, column 3.

29 *Report of the Boston Chamber of Commerce for 1913* (Boston: Boston Chamber of Commerce, 1914), 44, 49, 61, etc.

30 "Achievements of Commercial Organizations," *Nation's Business*, January 15, 1914, 10. For Knoxville: "With the Organizations," *Nation's Business*, November 15, 1915, 22.

31 "Fred Mills Made 'General Sales Manager' of Indianapolis – Junior Chamber of Commerce Organized," *Advertising and Selling*, June 26, 1920, 39.

32 Paul Bunn, "Rebuilding an Organization," from *Proceedings of the Fourth Annual Meeting of the National Association of Commercial Organization Secretaries, November 1918, Rochester, N.Y.* (Rochester, N.Y.: NACOS, 1918), 75-76. The information in this paragraph about the St. Louis Chamber, about Howard's role in working with the Junior Chamber, and about the membership and dues of the Junior Chamber in 1918, is taken from Bunn's interesting paper on the rejuvenation of the St. Louis Chamber of Commerce.

33 Most of the U.S. Jaycees (U.S. Junior Chamber of Commerce) history items cited here (those not directly connected to the St. Louis Chamber of Commerce) can be found on many Jaycees Web sites, such as http://www.dubuquejaycees.org/about-2/history-of-the-jaycees/. These are likely to have been taken originally from Junior Chamber International.

34 Thomas Reilly, *Jannus, an American Flier* (Board of Regents of the State of Florida, 1997), 155.

35 Roger Clendening II, "Tony Jannus's New Year's Day Flight Made History," *St. Petersburg Times*, January 1, 1994, 6.

36 Will Michaels, *The Making of St. Petersburg* (Charleston, S.C.: The History Press, 2012), 91.

37 Will Michaels, *The Making of St. Petersburg* (Charleston, S.C.: The History Press, 2012), 91. See also: Thomas Reilly, *Jannus, an American Flier* (Board of Regents of the State of Florida, 1997), 130. Reilly points out that there was regularly scheduled air service previous to this – inaugurated in Germany on November 16, 1909. But this was a Zeppelin, lighter-than-air craft. The German firm, which landed thousands of passengers, was called Deutsche Luftschiffarts AG.

38 Thomas Reilly, *Jannus, an American Flier* (Board of Regents of the State of Florida, 1997), 147.

39 Thomas Reilly, *Jannus, an American Flier* (Board of Regents of the State of Florida, 1997), 157.

40 Thomas Reilly, *Jannus, an American Flier* (Board of Regents of the State of Florida, 1997), 188-192.

41 *The Members' Annual of the Los Angeles Chamber of Commerce, Twenty-Sixth Year, March 1914* (Los Angeles: Los Angeles Chamber of Commerce, 1914), 84.

42 *The Members' Annual of the Los Angeles Chamber of Commerce, Twenty-Sixth Year, March 1914* (Los Angeles: Los Angeles Chamber of Commerce, 1914), 33.

43 For the Army visit, see: *The Members' Annual of the Los Angeles Chamber of Commerce, Twenty-Sixth Year, March 1914* (Los Angeles: Los Angeles Chamber of Commerce, 1914), 33. For the visit of Franklin Delano Roosevelt, see: *Members Annual, Twenty-Seventh Year, March 1915* (Los Angeles: Los Angeles Chamber of Commerce, 1915), 41, 95.

44 "Business Men Start Anti-War Campaign: Chamber of Commerce of the United States Taking Referendum on Peace Methods," *The New York Times*, November 17, 1915.

Notes

45 *Fifty-Eighth Annual Report of the Corporation of the Chamber of Commerce of New York for the Year 1915-1916* (New York: Press of the Chamber of Commerce, 1916), 213.

46 For President Wilson's reaction to the preparedness referendum, see: "Wilson Replies to Criticisms of Peace League," *The New York Times*, May 31, 1916. A fuller description of the referendum and is results can be found here: "Business Men Urge Military Training: Chamber of Commerce of the United States Makes Its Referendum Vote Public," *The New York Times*, July 24, 1916.

47 Leonard Withington, "An Aeroplane Coast Patrol: Portland (Maine) Chamber Takes First Real Step in 'Preparedness' and Provides a Fund With Which to Make the Work Effective," *Town Development*, March 1916, 3.

48 "Obregon Hits Protocol: His Request That Americans Quit Mexico at Set Date Refused," *The New York Times*, May 10, 1916. (Item is near the very end of a fairly long article.)

49 *America's Gibraltar: Muscle Shoals – A Brief for the Establishment of our National Nitrate Plant at Muscle Shoals on the Tennessee River* (Nashville: Muscle Shoals Association, 1916), 8.

50 A brief and helpful discussion of the decision is available in the following: Harry E. Wallace, "The New Century," *Times Daily*, February 25, 1999, reprinted on this Web site: http://www.rootsweb.ancestry.com/~allauder/historyshoals7.htm

51 Howard Strong, "Leading the Way in War's Confusion," *Nation's Business*, August 1917, 28.

52 John Northway, "The Secretary in Action," from *Proceedings: Fifth Annual Meeting of the National Association of Commercial Organization Secretaries*, October 27-29, 1919 (Worcester, MA: NACOS, 1919), 101.

53 W.J. Norton, "The Application of the War Chest Principle to Local Social Agencies," from *Proceedings: Fifth Annual Meeting of the National Association of Commercial Organization Secretaries*, October 27-29, 1919 (Worcester, MA: NACOS, 1919), 177.

54 The original Denver plan emerged in 1887 but was a "victim of the silver panic" in 1893, according to one author. She notes that "by 1895 there were more than one hundred charity organization societies in the United States." Hence Cleveland's claim to be the originator is not sustainable. However, the chamber seems to have made advances in the businesslike vetting of charities and the unified raising of funds for them. For the Denver idea and its aftermath, see: Lynda Lee Adams-Chau, *The Professionals' Guide to Fund Raising, Corporate Giving, and Philanthropy* (Westwood, Conn.: Greenwood Publishing Group, 1988), 103-104.

55 Kenneth Montague Sturges, *American Chambers of Commerce* (New York: Moffat, Yard & Company, 1915), 153. It's interesting that Sturges maintained this enthusiasm for the concept throughout his career. After joining the Cleveland Chamber when he graduated from Williams College, he later became the director of the Cleveland Community Chest, the successor organization to the Cleveland Federation for Charity and Philanthropy, remaining there till he retired.

56 W.J. Norton, "The Application of the War Chest Principle to Local Social Agencies," from *Proceedings: Fifth Annual Meeting of the National Association of Commercial Organization Secretaries*, October 27-29, 1919 (Worcester, MA: NACOS, 1919), 179.

57 W.J. Norton, "The Application of the War Chest Principle to Local Social Agencies," from *Proceedings: Fifth Annual Meeting of the National Association of Commercial Organization Secretaries*, October 27-29, 1919 (Worcester, MA: NACOS, 1919), 178.

58 J.W.E. Lawrence, "Again, the War Garden," *Nation's Business*, April 1918, 21.

59 Gary Quackenbush, "A Century with the Chamber," *North Bay Business Journal*, September 18, 2006, 21.

60 "Our War Gardens," *Town Development*, September 1917, 24.

61 Howard Strong, "Leading the Way in War's Confusion," *Nation's Business*, August 1917, 28.

62 "Tiffin Goes to War," *Nation's Business*, March 1918, 44. This article provides a good overview of one chamber's involvement in the home front of the war.

63 *Report of the Boston Chamber of Commerce for 1917-18* (Boston: Boston Chamber of Commerce, 1918), 20.

64 "General," *Town Development*, September 1917, 27, column 2.

65 James McKibben, opening remarks for NACOS meeting, from *Proceedings: Third Annual Meeting of the National Association of Commercial Organization Secretaries*, Chicago, September 24-26, 1917 (Chicago: NACOS, 1917), 25-26.

66 *Report of the Boston Chamber of Commerce for 1918-19* (Boston: Boston Chamber of Commerce, 1919), 21-22.

67 Paul Bunn, "Rebuilding an Organization," from *Proceedings of the Fourth Annual Meeting of the National Association of Commercial Organization Secretaries*, November 1918, Rochester, N.Y. (Rochester, N.Y.: NACOS, 1918), 77.

68 Paul Bunn, "Rebuilding an Organization," from *Proceedings of the Fourth Annual Meeting of the National Association of Commercial Organization Secretaries*, November 1918, Rochester, N.Y. (Rochester, N.Y.: NACOS, 1918), 77.

69 George and Miriam Geib, *Indianapolis First: A Commemorative History of the Indianapolis Chamber of Commerce and the Local Business Community* (Indianapolis: Indianapolis Chamber of Commerce, 1990), 45, 47.

70 "Industrial," *Town Development*, September 1917, 28, column 2.

71 *Sixty-Ninth Annual Report of the Cincinnati Chamber of Commerce and Merchants' Exchange for the Year Ending December 31, 1917* (Cincinnati: The Robert T. Morris Printing Company, 1918), 11.

72 *Sixtieth Annual Report of the Corporation of the Chamber of Commerce of the State of New York for the Year 1917-1918* (New York: Press of the Chamber of Commerce, 1918), 131.

73 *Sixtieth Annual Report of the Corporation of the Chamber of Commerce of the State of New York for the Year 1917-1918* (New York: Press of the Chamber of Commerce, 1918), 29-46.

74 "What Is Expected of Chambers of Commerce in Our National Preparedness Program?", *NACOS News*, July 1940, 8. The chamber president in 1940 who was responsible for the remarks was Frank L. Duggan.

75 "20 Knot Ships Safe from Submarines," *American Marine Engineer*, August 1917, 7.

76 "Political Shipbuilding," *The Bellman*, June 19, 1917, 623.

77 "Say Speed Alone Can Beat U-Boats: Chamber of Commerce Produces Figures Showing That Slow Ships Rarely Escape," *The New York Times*, July 20, 1917.

78 "Hurley and Capps Start on Ship Work," *The New York Times*, July 26, 1917. The *Times* article indicates what appears to have been a genuine disagreement on wood vs. steel ships. On the other hand, divided authority was also a contributor to the double resignation, as shown in this contemporary article: "New Shipping Board Begins to Act," *The Marine Review*, September 1917, 306.

79 *Fifty-Ninth Annual Report of the Corporation of the Chamber of Commerce of the State of New York for the Year 1916-1917* (New York: Press of the Chamber of Commerce, 1917), 244.

80 "Goethals Dispute" and "Work Accomplished," *The Chicago Daily News Almanac and Year-Book for 1918*, edited by James Langland (Chicago: Chicago Daily News Company, 1918), 531.

81 Ivan Allen, *Atlanta from the Ashes* (Atlanta: Ruralist Press, 1929), 54.

82 Jack Claiborne, *Crown of the Queen City: The Charlotte Chamber from 1870 to 1999* (Charlotte: Charlotte Chamber of Commerce, 1999), 46-47.

83 Lt. Harry David Kroll, editor, *Kelly Field in the Great World War* (San Antonio: Press of San Antonio Printing Co., 1919), Second Edition, 24.

84 Lt. Harry David Kroll, editor, *Kelly Field in the Great World War* (San Antonio: Press of San Antonio Printing Co., 1919), Second Edition, 24.

85 "Chamber of Commerce Activities," *Houston's Part in the World War*, edited by Mrs. W.M. Baines (Houston: 1919), 151.

86 Roger Kullenberg and Dave Hager, *Kalamazoo: Kalamazoo Regional Chamber Celebrating 100 Years/ 1903-2003* (Kalamazoo: Kalamazoo Regional Chamber, 2003), 25.

87 *Greater Columbus Georgia Chamber of Commerce History Time Line*, under listing for 1917. This listing includes a mention of the names of two delegation members, Past Chamber Chair Albert F. Kunze and John Betjeman, an engineer at the Jordan Company.

88 History timeline from the Denver Metro Chamber of Commerce, provided about 2009. Both the 1887 and 1917 dates, and the other information shown regarding the two military facilities, are included in this timeline.

89 Anne Harding, "90 Years of Building a Better Dallas: The History of the Greater Dallas Chamber, 1909 to the Present," 3. This is a 15-page paper made available by the Greater Dallas Chamber in 1999.

90 "Final Report on The Indianapolis Chamber of Commerce U.S.A. Training Detachments: April 15, 1918 – January 1, 1919," Indianapolis Chamber of Commerce archives, Board of Directors minutes, 1919.

91 "Final Report on The Indianapolis Chamber of Commerce U.S.A. Training Detachments: April 15, 1918 – January 1, 1919," Indianapolis Chamber of Commerce archives, Board of Directors minutes, 1919.

92 *Report of the Boston Chamber of Commerce for 1917-1918* (Boston: Boston Chamber of Commerce, 1918), 27-28.

93 *Eighty-Sixth Annual Report of the Philadelphia Board of Trade, Presented to the Association January 27, 1919* (Philadelphia: Philadelphia Board of Trade, 1919), 75.

94 *Eighty-Sixth Annual Report of the Philadelphia Board of Trade, Presented to the Association January 27, 1919* (Philadelphia: Philadelphia Board of Trade, 1919), 74.

95 *Eighty-Sixth Annual Report of the Philadelphia Board of Trade, Presented to the Association January 27, 1919* (Philadelphia: Philadelphia Board of Trade, 1919), 76.

96 *Eighty-Sixth Annual Report of the Philadelphia Board of Trade, Presented to the Association January 27, 1919* (Philadelphia: Philadelphia Board of Trade, 1919), 76-77.

97 "City's Business Protests: Head of Commerce Chamber Calls Order "Aid to the Enemy," *The New York Times*, January 17, 1918.

98 "Country's Protests on Work Stoppage: Manufacturers, Trade Boards, and Labor Bodies Joined in Bombarding Congress," *The New York Times*, January 20, 1918.

99 *Sixty-First Annual Report of the Corporation of the Chamber of Commerce of the State of New York for the Year 1918-1919* (New York: Press of the Chamber of Commerce, 1919), xxvi-xxvii, 113.

100 *Report of the Boston Chamber of Commerce for 1918-1919* (Boston: Boston Chamber of Commerce, 1919), 20.

101 *Report of the Boston Chamber of Commerce for 1918-1919* (Boston: Boston Chamber of Commerce, 1919), 24.

102 *Fifty-Sixth Annual Report of the Corporation of the Chamber of Commerce of the State of New York for the Year 1913-1914* (New York: Press of the Chamber of Commerce, 1914), 15-16.

103 *Report of the Boston Chamber of Commerce for 1913* (Boston: Boston Chamber of Commerce, 1914), 24.

104 For the 1913 incident, see: *Report of the Boston Chamber of Commerce for 1913* (Boston: Boston Chamber of Commerce, 1914), 23-24.

105 "Mayor of Indianapolis Faces Impeachment Trial: Chamber of Commerce Expects to File Charges Tomorrow – Outgrowth of Street Car Strike," *The Evening Independent*, November 27, 1913, page 12, column 3.

106 "Mayor Shank Quits; Wallace at Helm," *The New York Times*, November 29, 1913.

107 "John D., Jr., Will Not Arbitrate Coal Strike: Tells Representative of Wilson He Is in No Position to Parley With Miners," *Pittsburgh Post-Gazette*, April 28, 1914, page 7, columns 1-2.

108 Philip Dray, *There is Power in a Union: The Epic Story of Labor in America* (New York: Doubleday, 2010), 347-8.

Notes

109 "Asks Rockefeller to Aid: Trinidad Appeals to Younger Oil Man to Widen Relief Work," *The New York Times*, February 27, 1915. Also: "Colorado Miners in Need: Destitute of Food, Clothing, and Fuel – Rockefeller, Jr., to Aid," *The New York Times*, February 28, 1915.

110 Franklin P. Wood, "Chamber of Commerce Owner and Manager of Public Camping Ground," *The American City*, November 1919, 483, 483.

111 J.R. Caldwell, "How They Did It," *System: The Magazine of Business*, April 1918, 561-562.

112 Steven C. Levi, *Committee of Vigilance: The San Francisco Chamber of Commerce Law and Order Committee, 1916-1919* (Jefferson, N.C.: McFarland & Company, 1983), 29-30.

113 Steven C. Levi, *Committee of Vigilance: The San Francisco Chamber of Commerce Law and Order Committee, 1916-1919* (Jefferson, N.C.: McFarland & Company, 1983), 41-44.

114 Edward H. Hurlbut, "Six Thousand Brave Bomb – Join Crime War," *San Francisco Call*, July 27, 1916, reprinted in: *Law and Order in San Francisco: A Beginning* (San Francisco: San Francisco Chamber of Commerce, 1916), 26.

115 Steven C. Levi, *Committee of Vigilance: The San Francisco Chamber of Commerce Law and Order Committee, 1916-1919* (Jefferson, N.C.: McFarland & Company, 1983), 131. This page provides a complete list of the 100. The top contributors to the Law and Order Committee, and the amounts they pledged, are listed on page 133.

116 *Law and Order in San Francisco: A Beginning* (San Francisco: San Francisco Chamber of Commerce, 1916), 37.

117 Steven C. Levi, *Committee of Vigilance: The San Francisco Chamber of Commerce Law and Order Committee, 1916-1919* (Jefferson, N.C.: McFarland & Company, 1983), 65-80.

118 Steven C. Levi, *Committee of Vigilance: The San Francisco Chamber of Commerce Law and Order Committee, 1916-1919* (Jefferson, N.C.: McFarland & Company, 1983), 54-64.

119 Steven C. Levi, *Committee of Vigilance: The San Francisco Chamber of Commerce Law and Order Committee, 1916-1919* (Jefferson, N.C.: McFarland & Company, 1983), 109.

120 "Fight Labor Exemption: U.S. Chamber of Commerce Has Referendum on Clayton Bill," *The New York Times*, June 12, 1914.

121 Eugene Bowles, "Labor Disputes Adjusted by Oakland Chamber's Common Weal Committee," *The American City*, December 1919, 577.

122 Francis Russell, *A City in Terror: Calvin Coolidge and the 1919 Boston Police Strike* (Boston: Beacon Press, 1975), 69.

123 Francis Russell, *A City in Terror: Calvin Coolidge and the 1919 Boston Police Strike* (Boston: Beacon Press, 1975), 89.

124 Francis Russell, *A City in Terror: Calvin Coolidge and the 1919 Boston Police Strike* (Boston: Beacon Press, 1975), 90.

125 Francis Russell, *A City in Terror: Calvin Coolidge and the 1919 Boston Police Strike* (Boston: Beacon Press, 1975), 94-95.

126 "Bay State Governor Firm: Says Wilson Suggestion Does Not Apply as Boston Police Quit Jobs," *The New York Times*, September 15, 1919.

127 Francis Russell, *A City in Terror: Calvin Coolidge and the 1919 Boston Police Strike* (Boston: Beacon Press, 1975), 170.

128 Athan Theoharis and John Cox, *The Boss: J. Edgar Hoover and the American Inquisition* (New York: Bantam Books, 1990), 50.

129 Henry Louis Mencken, *Prejudices: Second Series* (New York: Alfred A. Knopf, 1920), 141.

130 Glenn Feldman, editor, *Politics and Religion in the White South* (Lexington, Ky.: University of Kentucky, 2005), 43.

131 "Brutal 1917 East St. Louis (Ill.) White-on-Black Race-Riot Disaster: Worst in American History," Suburban Emergency Management Report, Biot #414, March 20, 2007: http://www.semp.us/publications/biot_reader.php?BiotID=414

132 "East St. Louis Business Men Seek Return of Negroes Who Fled City," *Dubuque Telegraph-Herald*, July 6, 1917. All the information in this paragraph comes from this article, although parts of it are substantiated in other sources.

133 "Roosevelt and Gompers Row at Russian Meeting: Colonel's Denunciation Turns Welcome to Envoys Into a Quarrel Over Race Riots," *The New York Times*, July 7, 1917.

134 Marcus Garvey, "The Conspiracy of the East St. Louis Riots," Speech on July 8, 1917, from *The American Experience* by PBS: http://www.pbs.org/wgbh/amex/garvey/filmmore/ps_riots.html

135 "Annual Meeting of the Southern Alluvial Land Association," *Mississippi Valley Magazine*, December 1919, 21.

136 "Plan to Make Memphis the 'Best Negro City,'" *Lumber (Manufacturers' Edition)*, October 20, 1919, 30.

137 "A Mississippi Message," *The Outlook*, January 21, 1920, 99.

138 "A Mississippi Message," *The Outlook*, January 21, 1920, 99.

139 "Defeating the Fee-Grabbers," *Association Men: The Official Magazine, North American Young Men's Christian Associations*, December 1920, 158.

140 "A Negro Business Men's League," *The American City*, June 1917, 633.

141 Louise Gilmore Donahue, *Pathways to Prosperity: A History of the Greater Omaha Chamber of Commerce* (Omaha: Greater Omaha Chamber of Commerce, 1993), 11.

142 "1914-1923 – The Great War and the Roaring '20s: The Detroit Board of Commerce is the 'Spokesman of Optimism' and a Hub of Activity," *The Detroiter*, June 2003.

143 Don Woodward and Joel Campbell, *Common Ground: 100 Years of the Salt Lake Chamber* (Montgomery, Alabama: Community Communications Inc., 2003), 39-40.

144 McNab was among those caught up in exposition fever. He became one of the fair's directors. Unfortunately, the strain seems to have been too much. He was stricken by apoplexy in early December of 1915, apparently very shortly after the exposition closed on December 4. He died the following March. This information is taken from: Frank Morton Todd, *The Story of the Exposition: Being the Official History of the International Celebration Held at San Francisco in 1915 to Commemorate the Discovery of the Pacific Ocean and the Construction of the Panama Canal* (New York: G.P. Putnam's Sons, The Knickerbocker Press, 1921), Volume Five, 367.

145 Frank Morton Todd, *The Story of the Exposition: Being the Official History of the International Celebration Held at San Francisco in 1915 to Commemorate the Discovery of the Pacific Ocean and the Construction of the Panama Canal* (New York: G.P. Putnam's Sons, The Knickerbocker Press, 1921), Volume Five, 313.

146 William Lipsky, Images of America: *San Francisco's Panama-Pacific International Exposition,* (San Francisco: Arcadia Publishing, 2005), 7.

147 Matthew F. Bokovoy, *The San Diego World's Fair and Southwestern Memory, 1880-1940* (University of New Mexico Press, 2005), 20.

148 David Tyack, *The One Best System: A History of American Urban Education* (Cambridge, Mass.: Harvard University Press, 1974), 123.

149 David Tyack, *The One Best System: A History of American Urban Education* (Cambridge, Mass.: Harvard University Press, 1974), 165.

150 David Tyack, *The One Best System: A History of American Urban Education* (Cambridge, Mass.: Harvard University Press, 1974), 165-6.

151 David Tyack, *The One Best System: A History of American Urban Education* (Cambridge, Mass.: Harvard University Press, 1974), 165.

152 "Preliminary Report on Commercial Education," *Bulletin of the Chamber of Commerce of the State of New York,* May 1917, 19.

153 *Sixtieth Annual Report of the Corporation of the Chamber of Commerce of the State of New York for the Year 1917-1918* (New York: Press of the Chamber of Commerce, 1918), 66.

154 *Sixtieth Annual Report of the Corporation of the Chamber of Commerce of the State of New York for the Year 1917-1918* (New York: Press of the Chamber of Commerce, 1918), 59.

155 *Sixtieth Annual Report of the Corporation of the Chamber of Commerce of the State of New York for the Year 1917-1918* (New York: Press of the Chamber of Commerce, 1918), 95-96.

156 Several sources refer to the NCCCCPS study, including: "Section Meetings," from *Monthly Record of Current Educational Publications,* September 1920, United States Department of the Interior, Bureau of Education (Washington: Government Printing Office, 1920), 120.

157 E.S. Evenden, "Teachers' Salary Schedules and Falling Prices," *The Journal of the New York State Teachers Association,* New York State Education Association, No. 8, Volume 8, January, 1922, Bound Volumes 7-8, 225.

158 Bertha Johnson, editor, *The Kindergarten-Primary Magazine,* Volume 33, No. 8, April 1921, 235.

159 Charles O. Williams, "Report of the Committee on Tenure," from *Addresses and Proceedings of the Fifty-Ninth Annual Meeting Held at Des Moines, Iowa, July 3-8, 1921,* Volume LIX (Washington, D.C.: National Education Association, Secretary's Office, 1921), 146.

160 "Department of School Libraries," *Public Libraries* (Chicago: Library Bureau, 1921), Volume 26, 351.

161 Ivan Allen, *Atlanta from the Ashes* (Atlanta: Ruralist Press, 1929), 64.

162 "Activities Along the 'Right of Way'," *Town Development Magazine,* July 1914, 92. Chamber's involvement confirmed by Richard Dayoub, president, Greater El Paso Chamber of Commerce, in an email dated September 1, 2010.

163 George Klinger, *We Face the Future Unafraid* (Evansville, Ind.: University of Evansville Press, 2003), 29-35.

164 William George Bruce, "The N.A.C.O.S.," from *Proceedings of the Fourth Annual Meeting of the National Association of Commercial Organization Secretaries,* November 1918, Rochester, N.Y. (Rochester, N.Y.: NACOS, 1918), 173.

165 Arthur Kinney, "Los Angeles Will Be Great," a poem reprinted in *The Members' Annual Report of the Los Angeles Chamber of Commerce, Twenty-Sixth Year* (Los Angeles: Los Angeles Chamber of Commerce, March 1914), 87.

166 *The Members' Annual Report of the Los Angeles Chamber of Commerce, Twenty-Sixth Year* (Los Angeles: Los Angeles Chamber of Commerce, March 1914), 103.

167 *The Members' Annual Report of the Los Angeles Chamber of Commerce, Twenty-Sixth Year* (Los Angeles: Los Angeles Chamber of Commerce, March 1914), 45.

168 Leroy M. Gibbs, "Trade Extension Trips – Methods and Results," *Proceedings, Third Annual Meeting of the National Association of Commercial Organization Secretaries, September 24-26, 1917* (Chicago: NACOS, 1917), 197.

169 Fred Drinkwater, "City Building on a Scientific Basis," *Board of Trade Journal* (Portland, Me.), May 1914, 11.

170 *Sixty-Fifth Annual Report of the Cincinnati Chamber of Commerce and Merchants' Exchange for the Year Ending December 31, 1913* (Cincinnati: Robert T. Morris Printing Company, 1914), 59.

171 "Million-Dollar Civic Fund Raised by Middletown Chamber," *The American City,* June 1920, 627.

172 *Greater Scranton Chamber of Commerce, 1867 – 1967: 100 Years of Service* (Scranton, Pennsylvania: Greater Scranton Chamber of Commerce, 1967), 21-22.

173 Carl Blasig, *Building Texas* (Brownsville, Texas: Springman-King Company, 1963), 127.

174 The information in these paragraphs on Sewell comes from this feature article: Gilbert Swan, "Miami's Success Story," *The Washington Post*, January 14, 1940, A8.

175 Grain trading and civic-minded chambers were not easily combined into a single organization. In Chicago, where the Board of Trade had invented modern grain trading, the Association of Commerce and Industry (which soon became known as the Chicago Association of Commerce) grew up as a separate organization beginning in 1904 and quickly established itself as a civic leader, while the BOT continued with its focus on grain and commodities. In Minneapolis, the Chamber of Commerce was a grain trading operation, much like the Chicago BOT. To fill the need for a more civic-focused group, a new organization, the Civic and Commerce Association, was founded in 1911. (See: "Firmly Founded Year-Old League Achieves Results: Minneapolis's Civic and Commerce Association Aids City Development," *Nation's Business*, December 16, 1912, 9. The new group was founded on December 11, 1911.) In Boston, the chamber's civic-minded leadership chafed at the grain traders' costing nearly 25 percent of the expenses while contributing 10 percent of the dues. (See *Report of the Boston Chamber of Commerce for 1917-18*, published by the chamber in 1918, page 41.) And in Cincinnati, the grain traders departed and the chamber's subsequent annual report gave a good summary of the situation around the country: "Thus, with the possible exception of but one or two organizations known as Chambers of Commerce, (such as that of Baltimore), but which, in fact are strictly Grain and Hay Exchanges, there remain but two Chambers of Commerce in the United States, (Boston and San Francisco) with grain exchanges in their organization." This is from *Seventieth Annual Report of the Cincinnati Chamber of Commerce and Merchants' Exchange for the Year Ending December 31, 1918* (Cincinnati: Robert T. Morris Printing Co., 1919), 25.

176 "Achievements of Commercial Organizations," *Nation's Business*, January 14, 1914. The article says: "More organizations speak of agricultural development as an achievement than any other form of activity during the year."

177 Address by David Houston, Secretary of Agriculture, from *Proceedings of the Second Annual Meeting of the National Association of Commercial Organization Secretaries, Cleveland, September 25-27, 1916* (Cleveland: NACOS, 1916), 66-74.

178 "$90,000 Fund for Farm Development Bureau of the Memphis Chamber of Commerce," *The American City*, September 1919, 273.

179 "Co-operation with the Farmer," group discussion at the NACOS Convention, from *Proceedings, Fifth Annual Meeting of the National Association for Commercial Organization Secretaries, Indianapolis, October 27-29, 1919* (Indianapolis: NACOS, 1919), 157.

180 *The Members' Annual Report of the Los Angeles Chamber of Commerce, Twenty-Sixth Year* (Los Angeles: Los Angeles Chamber of Commerce, March 1914), 79-80.

181 Not many chambers have an agricultural bureau that's more than a century old, but Spokane does. In 2010 the author received a Powerpoint document from Greater Spokane Inc. that has the information about the Fruit Fair and related achievements of the "Ag Bureau." The Powerpoint is entitled, *Greater Spokane Incorporated's Agricultural Bureau: "The Past, Present and Future" – 1890 to 2010 and beyond...*

182 The Country Life Commission's president, Henry Wallace, had been appointed by Teddy Roosevelt but the commission's report wasn't scheduled for release until 1909. It was probably suppressed by the conservative Taft Administration because of its populist leanings. For example, the report said of the typical farmer that "he usually stands practically alone against organized interests." (*Report of the Commission on Country Life with an Introduction by Theodore Roosevelt*, Reprinted by the Spokane Chamber of Commerce, 1910, page 19.) It advocated an enhanced federal role to protect the farmer. Interestingly, although Wallace died in 1916, his farm-advocacy legacy was carried on by his son, Henry C. Wallace, who became Secretary of Agriculture under President Warren Harding from 1921 until his (Henry C. Wallace's) death in 1924, and by his grandson, Henry A. Wallace, who served as vice president under President Franklin D. Roosevelt.

183 *Washington Centennial '89, Spokane Area Chamber of Commerce* (Spokane: Spokane Area Chamber of Commerce, 1989). See the page entitled: "Highlights: Chamber Chronological Chart." Both the $100,000 study and the National Reclamation Congress are mentioned here.

184 During World War II, it was reported that Polynesian islanders who were in primitive communities would occasionally see big planes land that were full of precious cargo. The islanders wanted these luxuries and so performed special dances that they hoped would cause more such magical birds to land. Chamber executives don't perform such dances, but many of them would move heaven and earth to get a major new airline or flight to town.

185 "City's Business Demands Improvement of Port," *Greater New York*, March 31, 1919, 15.

186 *Fifty-Eighth Annual Report of the Corporation of the Chamber of Commerce of the State of New York for the Year 1915-1916* (New York: Press of the Chamber of Commerce, 1916), 190.

187 *Fifty-Eighth Annual Report of the Corporation of the Chamber of Commerce of the State of New York for the Year 1915-1916* (New York: Press of the Chamber of Commerce, 1916), 190-1.

188 *Fifty-Ninth Annual Report of the Corporation of the Chamber of Commerce of the State of New York for the Year 1916-1917* (New York: Press of the Chamber of Commerce, 1917), 157.

189 *Fifty-Ninth Annual Report of the Corporation of the Chamber of Commerce of the State of New York for the Year 1916-1917* (New York: Press of the Chamber of Commerce, 1917), 158.

190 *Fifty-Ninth Annual Report of the Corporation of the Chamber of Commerce of the State of New York for the Year 1916-1917* (New York: Press of the Chamber of Commerce, 1917), 234.

191 *Fifty-Ninth Annual Report of the Corporation of the Chamber of Commerce of the State of New York for the Year 1916-1917* (New York: Press of the Chamber of Commerce, 1917), 230.

192 *Sixtieth Annual Report of the Corporation of the Chamber of Commerce of the State of New York for the Year 1917-1918* (New York: Press of the Chamber of Commerce, 1918), 166.

193 *Sixtieth Annual Report of the Corporation of the Chamber of Commerce of the State of New York for the Year 1917-1918* (New York: Press of the Chamber of Commerce, 1918), xxxi.

194 *Sixtieth Annual Report of the Corporation of the Chamber of Commerce of the State of New York for the Year 1917-1918* (New York: Press of the Chamber of Commerce, 1918), 245.

195 *Sixty-First Annual Report of the Corporation of the Chamber of Commerce of the State of New York for the Year 1918-1919* (New York: Press of the Chamber of Commerce, 1918), 142-162.

196 *Sixty-First Annual Report of the Corporation of the Chamber of Commerce of the State of New York for the Year 1918-1919* (New York: Press of the Chamber of Commerce, 1918), 199-204.

197 An excellent book-length source on the genesis and future career of the Port Authority is the following: Jameson W. Doig, *Empire on the Hudson: Entrepreneurial Vision and Political Power at the Port of New York Authority* (New York: Columbia University Press, 2001). This book, unlike so many of its kind that describe public works and transportation projects and politics, gives a good amount of attention to the chamber of commerce that, in this case as in so many others, had a lot to do with getting the ball rolling.

Babes, Booze, and Babbitt (1921-1929)

1 "President Greets 500 Secretaries in White House Call," *The Washington Post*, October 21, 1924, page 2.

2 "Atlantic City Greets Beauty Contestants: Sixty-Two Girls Arrive by Special Train – Pageant Opens with Baby Parade," *The New York Times*, September 9, 1925, page 10.

3 "Two Jersey Towns Hold Baby Parades," *The New York Times*, August 11, 1928, page 11.

4 "Bronx Kiddies' Day Postponed," *The New York Times*, August 28, 1927, page E10.

5 "Easter Jams Coney, No Room to Parade; Crush 5th Avenue: Police Unable to Force Land Through Boardwalk Crowd for Fashion Parade," *The New York Times*, April 13, 1925, page 1.

6 "Drops From Dirigible: Lt. Starr in Parachute at Trenton Lands in Diving Pool," *The New York Times*, August 9, 1928, page 12.

7 "Ministers Are Asked to Judge Bathing Girls," *The Washington Post*, July 4, 1927, page 7.

8 Wade Werner, "Screen Life in Hollywood," *The Washington Post*, December 23, 1928, page A3. See also: Karal Ann Marling, *Merry Christmas! Celebrating America's Greatest Holiday* (Harvard College, 2000), 254.

9 Hope-Hempstead County Chamber of Commerce Web site, www.hopechamberofcommerce.com/festival

10 "It's Time for Conventions – and for Festivals," *Kiplinger's Personal Finance*, May 1948, 44-46.

11 "30 Schools Placed in Bloom Parade," *The Washington Post*, April 18, 1929, page 2.

A number of other *Washington Post* articles in the 1920s cover the festival.

12 "Annual Cherry Bloom Fete Planned by Chamber Group," *The Washington Post*, April 13, 1929, page 1.

13 Jessica I. Elfenbein, in association with Howard Gillette, Jr. and William Becker, *Civics, Commerce and Community: The History of the Greater Washington Board of Trade, 1889-1989* (Dubuque, IA: Kendall/Hunt Publishing Company, 1989), page 26.

14 John Martin, "The Dance: Seasonal Matters," *The New York Times*, July 15, 1945, 22. The article quotes a "very attractive little booklet" from the Asheville Chamber, written by George Myers Stephens.

15 Ronald D. Cohen, *A History of Folk Music Festivals in the United States* (Lanham, MD: Scarecrow Press, 2008), 6.

16 Interview with Bill Cooper, former president of the Groundhog Club and former director of the chamber in Punxsutawney, July 2010.

17 Around the beginning of 2009, the Club became a separate, 501©3 organization, in large part to facilitate the receipt of grants and sponsorships, according to Marlene Lellock, the president of what is now known as the Punxsutawney Area Chamber of Commerce. Even today, however, the one full-time employee of the Groundhog Club works out of the chamber offices. The chamber, moreover, sells souvenirs that support, in part, a weeklong Groundhog Festival in a more tourist-friendly part of the year (the summer). This festival draws several thousand people, according to Lellock. Groundhog Day, with its weather authority named Punxsutawney Phil, has certainly put this town of 6,000 people on the map. Attendance doubled after the movie *Groundhog Day* came out in 1993. There are between 10,000 and 40,000 people who attend the February 2 event; the number depends on the day of the week that it falls on, the weather, and other factors. The chamber has been the key spokesperson for the event in the town and the world beyond. But on Gobbler's Knob, without question the boss (after Punxsutawney Phil himself, of course) is the Groundhog Club. Ex-chamber director and recent Groundhog Club President Bill Cooper, speaking for the club, says that over the years the chamber has been "our strongest advocate and supporter and enabler."

18 "Tex Tours Jersey City: Promoter of Big Bout Tours Many Sites, Smiles and is Silent," *The New York Times*, April 15, 1921, page 23.

19 "Tunney Held Cheaply by Flynn: 'We'll' Knock Gene Out, Says Manager of Dempsey. Prefers New York to Chicago as Scene of Title Bout," *The Washington Post*, July 26, 1927, page 11.

20 "Miami Beach Fight Drew $395,369 Gate," *The New York Times*, March 1, 1929, page 25.

21 "City Enlarged by Merger of Several Towns; Daytona Beach Now Ranks as One of Largest Cities in State," *Sarasota Herald*, January 3, 1926, section one, page 4.

22 "City Enlarged by Merger of Several Towns; Daytona Beach Now Ranks as One of Largest Cities in State," *Sarasota Herald*, January 3, 1926, section one, page 4.

23 "Program of Winter Sports at Daytona Beach Unequaled," *The Washington Post*, December 27, 1925, page FDN6.

24 "Matty Honored by Boston Chamber of Commerce," *The New York Times*, February 28, 1923, page 14.

25 "Decries Dugan Deal: St. Louis Chamber of Commerce Protests to Baseball Heads," *The New York Times* (from the Associated Press), July 26, 1922, 16.

26 "Hornsby to Offer Stock to Breadon," *The New York Times*, December 23, 1926, page 16.

27 "Augusta Wants Cobb for Mayor," *The New York Times*, December 25, 1926, page 8.

28 "25 Cities Offered Camps to Giants: Florida, Texas, Arizona and Coast Towns Made Bids Against Augusta, Ga.," *The New York Times*, November 30, 1927, page 18.

29 "Tennis a Lure to Adirondack Colony: Tourney at Saranac Inn on This Week – Olympic Prospects at Lake Placid," *The New York Times*, August 19, 1928, page 105.

30 Wilbur C. Rich, *The Economics and Politics of Sports Facilities* (Westport, CT: Quorum Books, 2000), 18; also John R. Short, *Global Metropolitan: Globalizing Cities in a Capitalist World* (New York: Routledge, 2004), 102.

31 Jeremy White, "The Los Angeles Way of Doing Things: The Olympic Village and the Practice of Boosterism in 1932," *Olympika: The International Journal of Olympic Studies*, Volume XI, 2002, 79-116; quotation on 82.

32 Jeremy White, "The Los Angeles Way of Doing Things: The Olympic Village and the Practice of Boosterism in 1932," *Olympika: The International Journal of Olympic Studies*, Volume XI, 2002, 79-116; 80.

33 Jeremy White, "The Los Angeles Way of Doing Things: The Olympic Village and the Practice of Boosterism in 1932," *Olympika: The International Journal of Olympic Studies*, Volume XI, 2002, 79-116; 88.

34 Richard Etulain, *Western Lives: A Biographical History of the American West* (University of New Mexico Press, 2004), 314.

35 Sinclair Lewis, *Main Street* (Project Gutenberg ebook, no. 543, www.gutenberg.org), Chapter XXXV, section III.

36 Sinclair Lewis, *Babbitt* (New York: Grosset & Dunlap, 1922), page 44.

37 Henry Louis Mencken, "Portrait of an American Citizen," from *H.L. Mencken's Smart Set Criticism*, edited by William H. Nolte (Washington, D.C.: Regnery Gateway, 1987), page 282.

38 William Henry McMasters, "On Chambers of Commerce," from *Originality and Other Essays* (Boston: The Four Seas Company, 1921), pages 67-71.

39 White's quotation can be found in various sources, including A.S. Dudley, "The Local Chamber and the Chain," *Nation's Business*, March 1928, page 82, column 3. It is also quoted in: Charles A. Glenday, "Glenday Sets Nashua Chamber's Goals," *Nashua (N.H.) Telegraph*, January 25, 1969, page A7. An earlier rendering of the quotation indicates White's comment was part of a book review of Sinclair Lewis's *Main Street* and another book. This comes from the *Omaha Chamber of Commerce Journal*, February 4, 1922, page 11:

In the beginning there was the Chamber of Commerce. Of old the Chamber of Commerce rented a room, subscribed for half a dozen daily papers, a dozen magazines, hired a steward to take care of the lockers when prohibition came to the States twenty years ago, and used the place as a resort of more or less guilty joy where a little poker, some chess and occasional checkers were played, a few bad cocktails were consumed and much idle time.

The Chamber of Commerce today in the American small town and in the American city is the leading exponent of altruism in the community. It is not a wide interurban altruism that the Chamber of Commerce fosters; it is Higginsville first. But it is for Higginsville all the time. The Chamber of Commerce modifies the innate cussedness of the average selfish, hard-boiled, picayunish, penny-pinching, narrow-gauged human porker, and lifts up his snout; makes him see further than his home, his business, and his personal interest, and sets him rooting for his community.

40 Robert Barnes, "News of Organized Business," *Nation's Business*, June 1926, page 120. Under the subheading, "Has Your City Sporting Blood?", Barnes cites the Runyan quotation from its reprinting in the *Scranton Chamber of Commerce Bulletin*.

41 *Seventy-Second Annual Report of the Cincinnati Chamber of Commerce and Merchants Exchange for the Year Ending December 30, 1920* (Cincinnati: Robert T. Morris Printing Company, 1921), 19.

42 "The Log of Organized Business," subheading "Mr. Harding Praises Chamber," *Nation's Business*, April 1921, page 60.

43 "President Greets 500 Secretaries in White House Call," *The Washington Post*, October 21, 1924, page 2.

44 What President Coolidge actually said, at a meeting of the American Society of Newspaper Editors in 1925, was, "After all, the chief business of the American people is business." He went on to say, "Of course the accumulation of wealth cannot be justified as the chief end of existence." This and more information is available in an essay by Cyndy Bittinger, "The Business of America is Business?", which is available on the Web site of the Calvin Coolidge Memorial Association.

45 "Chamber Tax Plan Angers President," *The New York Times*, November 26, 1927, page 1.

46 Herbert Hoover, "The Chamber of Commerce," *Nation's Business*, December 1921, page 46.

47 S.T. Williamson, "Morrow, Barnes – and Some Others: A Few Footnotes on Some Personalities Whose Names Have Appeared in the Headlines," *The New York Times*, December 22, 1929, page XX4.

48 "Bostonians Present Big Codfish to Hoover," *The New York Times*, April 25, 1929, page 23.

49 "On to Hollywood Movement Breeds Germ of an Idea," *The Washington Post*, March 16, 1924, page AA3.

50 "Hollywood Warns Film-Struck Girls; Chamber of Commerce Seeks to Stop Big Influx as Jobless Cause Social Problem," *The New York Times*, December 4, 1923, page 23.

51 "On to Hollywood Movement Breeds Germ of an Idea," *The Washington Post*, March 16, 1924, page AA3.

52 "Chamber Acts to Bar Movie: Alleged Slanderous Picture May Be Boycotted by State Group," *St. Petersburg Times*, July 30, 1926, Section One, page 11.

53 "Why Plane is Named 'Spirit of St. Louis,'" *The New York Times*, June 13, 1927, page 7.

54 "Balloon is Missing with Two Officers," *The New York Times*, July 7, 1923, page 1.

55 "Other Balloonists Met Dangers," *The New York Times*, July 10, 1923, page 3.

56 "Brooklyn is Backer of Bellanca Plane: Chamber of Commerce to Give $15,000 to Fliers if They Reach Paris," *The New York Times*, April 24, 1927, page 3.

57 One could write a book about Charles Levine and the squabbles with his pilots. For the disputes connected with the Bellanca's transatlantic flight, *The New York Times* is a good contemporary source, including this article: "Bertaud May Lose Post in Bellanca; Its Flight in Doubt: Levine Considers Ousting Him, Insists Hop Will Be Made with Chamberlin as Pilot," *The New York Times*, May 18, 1927, page 1. For another look at those problems, as well as a fascinating look at Levine's colorful character, see Clarence Chamberlin's 1965 recollection of the man and his escapades, in an interview with Bill Van Dusen: "Clarence D. Chamberlin Recalls Historic Flight, Explains Why Lindbergh Beat Levine Across the Atlantic," available from the Yiddish Radio Project on this Web site: http://yiddishradioproject.org/exhibits/levine/chamberlin.php3?pg=1. Yet another helpful source on Levine is the Wikipedia article about him.

58 "Words 'To Paris' Taken From Plane Before Hop," from the Associated Press, *The Washington Post*, June 5, 1927, page 4.

59 "Clarence D. Chamberlin Recalls Historic Flight, Explains Why Lindbergh Beat Levine Across the Atlantic," 1965, Yiddish Radio Project: http://yiddishradioproject.org/exhibits/levine/chamberlin.php3?pg=1

60 This information, including the quote from Levine about returning to his wife, comes from: "Clarence D. Chamberlin Recalls Historic Flight, Explains Why Lindbergh Beat Levine Across the Atlantic," 1965, Yiddish Radio Project: http://yiddishradioproject.org/exhibits/levine/chamberlin.php3?pg=1

61 "Clarence D. Chamberlin Recalls Historic Flight, Explains Why Lindbergh Beat Levine Across the Atlantic," 1965, Yiddish Radio Project: http://yiddishradioproject.org/exhibits/levine/chamberlin.php3?pg=1. See also the Wikipedia article on Charles Levine.

62 Lindbergh, Charles A., *The Spirit of St. Louis* (New York: Scribner, 1953), 58-61, 67, 74.

63 Lowell Thomas and Lowell Thomas Jr., *Famous First Flights That Changed History: Sixteen Dramatic Adventures* (Guilford, Connecticut: Lyons Press, 2004), 150.

64 Bixby was even portrayed in the 1957 Warner Brothers movie starring Jimmy Stewart as Lindbergh, *Spirit of St. Louis*. The chamber of commerce president was played by actor David Orrick McDearmon. The Billy Wilder-directed movie adds a few touches to an already dramatic story, including Lindbergh choking on a cigar as he presents his case to Bixby and others at the State National Bank.

65 "Conquest of Air Almost Complete, Lindbergh Holds: Only Sleet and Fog Are Yet to be Overcome, Aviator Tells Lunchers," *The Washington Post*, February 16, 1928, page 3.

66 "Aviation Advancement," *NACOS News*, June 25, 1937, 5.

67 "St. Louis Residents Welcomed in Paris," by the Associated Press, printed in *The Washington Post*, August 1, 1928, page 21.

68 "Former Chamber Man Given Exceptional Honor," *Indianapolis Business* (a newsletter published by the Indianapolis Chamber of Commerce), Volume III, Number 14, April 1945, 3. See also: Jerry Ashfield, "Biography of Herbert O. Fisher," received by the Indianapolis Chamber of Commerce on May 15, 1989, Box 136, archives, Indianapolis Chamber of Commerce.

69 "Good Will Air Tour Proves Great Success," *NACOS News*, July 1927, 1, 3.

70 "Aviation Program Big Success in Washington," *NACOS News*, May 1929, 5, 7.

71 "Backing a Winner," *NACOS News*, January 1931, 7.

72 "News of Organized Business," subheading "Chambers Open Airports," *Nation's Business*, May 1928, page 175.

73 "Largest Air Mail Letter Reaches Postmaster General," *The New York Times*, July 20, 1928, page 22.

74 James M. Smallwood, *Urban Builder: The Life and Times of Stanley Draper* (Norman, Oklahoma: University of Oklahoma Press, 1977), 58-60.

75 Anne Harding, "90 Years of Building a Better Dallas: The History of the Greater Dallas Chamber, 1909 to the Present," 3. This is a 15-page paper made available by the Greater Dallas Chamber in 1999. The paper indicates that Love Field was turned back to the chamber after World War I; the precise timing of the building of the hangar for what became American Airlines is not clear from this paper, although it appears from the context that it was in 1919 or in the early Twenties.

76 "1924-1933: From Boom to Gloom – the Detroit Board of Commerce is Active on the Air, at Sea and on the Ground," *The Detroiter*, June 2003.

77 Don Woodward and Joel Campbell, *Common Ground: 100 Years of the Salt Lake Chamber* (Montgomery, Alabama: Community Communications Inc., 2002), 68.

78 "Plane for Every 1,000 People in Cleveland, Fokker Predicts," *The New York Times*, January 30, 1924, page 21.

79 "News of Organized Business," subhead "Air Services Prove of Value to Business," *Nation's Business*, April 1928, page 152.

80 Anonymous, Summary of the Minutes of the Denver Board of Trade and the Denver Chamber of Commerce, 1867 to 1949, section entitled "1924," page 109.

81 Bonnie Langdon and Phillip Parker, *Dayton Area Chamber of Commerce* (New York: Newcomen Society of the United States, 1996), 10.

82 "To Celebrate Wrights' First Flight," *The New York Times*, June 24, 1928, page 20. The chamber made plenty of economic development hay out of the Wright Brothers in this period. It created 40,000 copies of a brochure, "The Shop That Became a Shrine," at a cost of just $1,000. Sending it to the newspapers, the chamber reaped "incalculable" publicity as many of the papers reprinted the Wright Brothers encomium as an article. See: Wayne G. Lee, Managing Director, Chamber of Commerce, Dayton, Ohio, "Advertising Problems of Chambers of Commerce," *Fifteenth Annual Meeting of the National Association of Commercial Organization Secretaries* (Milwaukee, Wis.: NACOS, October 21-23, 1929), 296-300.

83 "New Jersey Aims at Air Progress: Governor Moore Signs Bill Providing Issuance of Bonds for County Airports," *The New York Times*, April 15, 1928, page 125.

84 "Airport for Atlantic City: Municipal Field to Cost $150,000 to Be Ready for Summer Traffic," *The New York Times*, March 13, 1929, page 19. See also: "Jersey to Spend $2,000,000 on Its Airports This Spring," *The New York Times*, March 10, 1929, page 160.

Notes

85 "Jersey to Spend $2,000,000 on Its Airports This Spring," *The New York Times*, March 10, 1929, page 160.

86 Comment by Walter Lochner, Secretary, Trenton Chamber of Commerce, in "Development of Activities at Airport," *NACOS 16th Annual Meeting* (Tulsa, Okla.: NACOS, Octoer 19-22, 1930), 250.

87 "Chambers Aid Aviation," *Nation's Business*, October 1933, 43.

88 Louise Nelson Dible, *Paying the Toll: Local Power, Regional Politics, and the Golden Gate Bridge* (Philadelphia: University of Pennsylvania Press, 2009), 16.

89 Louise Nelson Dible, *Paying the Toll: Local Power, Regional Politics, and the Golden Gate Bridge* (Philadelphia: University of Pennsylvania Press, 2009), 23.

90 Gary Quackenbush, "A Century with the Chamber," *North Bay Business Journal*, September 18, 2006, 21.

91 Gary Quackenbush, "A Century with the Chamber," *North Bay Business Journal*, September 18, 2006, 26.

92 Kevin Wehr, *America's Fight Over Water: The Environmental and Political Effects of Large-Scale Water Systems* (New York: Routledge, an imprint of the Taylor & Francis Group, 2004), 75.

93 Charles P. Squires, "Early History of Las Vegas Nevada Chamber of Commerce," a 12-page typewritten manuscript from 1940 (UNLV Library, Call Number F 849 L35 5678 1940), page 2.

94 Kevin Wehr, *America's Fight Over Water: The Environmental and Political Effects of Large-Scale Water Systems* (New York: Routledge, an imprint of the Taylor & Francis Group, 2004), 75.

95 Kevin Wehr, *America's Fight Over Water: The Environmental and Political Effects of Large-Scale Water Systems* (New York: Routledge, an imprint of the Taylor & Francis Group, 2004), 96.

96 Beverley Bowen Moeller, *Phil Swing and Boulder Dam* (Berkeley: University of California Press, 1971).

97 Edgar F. Howe and Wilbur J. Hall, *The Story of the First Decade in Imperial Valley, California* (Imperial: Edgar F. Howe and Sons, 1910), 252.

98 Beverley Bowen Moeller, *Phil Swing and Boulder Dam* (Berkeley: University of California Press, 1971), 40.

99 Kevin Wehr, *America's Fight Over Water: The Environmental and Political Effects of Large-Scale Water Systems* (New York: Routledge, an imprint of the Taylor & Francis Group, 2004), 73.

100 Ronald C. Tobey, *Technology as Freedom: The New Deal and the Electrical Modernization of the American Home* (Berkeley, California: University of California Press, 1996), 82.

101 There is no doubt that the water and electricity from the dam greatly increased Los Angeles's ability to grow. It has even been suggested that the dam was so important to the city's expansion as a Pacific port and industrial center that, without it, the U.S. struggle against Japan in World War II would have lasted much longer because Los Angeles would not have been able to sustain the war effort on a sufficient scale. See Frank N. Magill, editor, *Great Events from History II: Science and Technology Series, Volume 3, 1931-1952* (Pasadena, California: Salem Press, 1991), 1078.

102 David P. Billington, Donald C. Jackson, and Martin V. Melosi, *The History of Large Federal Dams: Planning, Design, and Construction* (U.S. Department of the Interior, Bureau of Reclamation; U.S. Department of the Army, Corps of Engineers; and U.S. Department of the Interior, National Park Service, 2005), 167.

103 Thomas "Taj" Ainlay, Jr. and Judy Dixon Gabaldon, *Las Vegas: The Fabulous First Century* (Charleston, S.C.: Arcadia Publishing, 2003), 39.

104 Herbert Hoover, "Conquering an American Nile," *Nation's Business*, August 1922, 9-11.

105 "'Hoover' Name Urged for New Boulder Dam," *The Washington Post*, April 28, 1929, page M8.

106 The dam's name was changed to Hoover Dam in 1930, then back to Boulder Dam in 1933, and back to Hoover Dam in 1947.

107 L. Vaughan Downs, *The Mightiest of Them All: Memories of Grand Coulee Dam* (American Society of Civil Engineers, 1993), 19.

108 Arthur D. Jones was one of the key business and civic leaders of Spokane. He was involved with the Spokane Chamber in many ways over the years. In one unfortunate case in 1901, he was alerted to a stench in one of the apartments he owned at Temple Court. The smell was from the body of one of his tenants, Robert H. Greely, who had died of a heart attack some time earlier. Greely was the secretary of the Spokane Chamber. ("Found Dead in His Room: Robert H. Greely, Secretary of the Chamber of Commerce, a Victim of Heart Disease," *Spokane Daily Chronicle*, July 11, 1901, page 1.) In 1912, Jones led a fundraising session that yielded $27,607 for the chamber, which worked out to an impressive $1,000 per minute. ("Launch Campaign for Prosperity: At Banquet $27,607 is Subscribed in Promotion Fund," *The Spokesman-Review*, June 19, 1912, page 1, column 2.) Later Jones would serve the chamber in other roles, such as on its traffic committee.

109 "Good Appointments for Columbia Basin Project," *The Spokesman-Review*, March 11, 1919, page 4, column 2.

110 Kevin Wehr describes the CBIL, for example, as "the group of boosters working out of the Spokane Chamber of Commerce" that backed the 'pumping plan,'" or in other words the big-dam, major-irrigation alternative for Columbia Basin public works. He describes the extensive propaganda activities of the CBIL for the dam here: Kevin Wehr, *America's Fight Over Water: The Environmental and Political Effects of Large-Scale Water Systems* (New York: Routledge, an imprint of the Taylor & Francis Group, 2004), 126.

111 No known relation to the author, who has, however, gratefully waded in his namesake lake.

112 "Congressmen See Basin From Saddle Mountains," *Spokane Daily Chronicle*, August 17, 1927, page 1.

113 "Congressmen See Basin From Saddle Mountains," *Spokane Daily Chronicle*, August 17, 1927, page 1.

114 "Spokane and Seattle," *The Spokesman-Review*, January 16, 1922, page 3, column 1. See also: "Why They Are Against a Report by Goethals," *The Spokesman-Review*, January 22, 1922, page 3, column 1. The 1922 editorial imputes murky motives to the Seattle Chamber: "The hostility of the Seattle Chamber of Commerce to this inspiring project, upon which the legislature has expended $100,000, can not be reasonably accounted for on any other theory than that the Seattle chamber is manipulated by covert and powerful water power interests." But by 1926, the Seattle Chamber seems to have been testifying in favor of the project: "Cost of Project is $300,000,000: Jones Bill is First Step in Greatest Reclamation Project Ever Undertaken," *The Deseret News*, February 3, 1926, page 5, column 7. Also: "President Tells Spokane Delegation He Will Thoroughly Investigate All Angles of Irrigation Project," *Spokane Daily Chronicle*, August 30, 1927, page 1.

115 Kevin Wehr, *America's Fight Over Water: The Environmental and Political Effects of Large-Scale Water Systems* (New York: Routledge, an imprint of the Taylor & Francis Group, 2004), 73.

116 Richard White, *The Organic Machine: The Remaking of the Columbia River* (New York: Hill and Wang, 1995), 54-55.

117 Richard White, *The Organic Machine: The Remaking of the Columbia River* (New York: Hill and Wang, 1995), 55.

118 Richard White, *The Organic Machine: The Remaking of the Columbia River* (New York: Hill and Wang, 1995), 55.

119 "Grand Coulee Dam: History and Purpose," Northwest Power and Conservation Council, at this Web site: http://www.nwcouncil.org/history/grandcouleehistory.asp

120 "Hetch Hetchy Plan is Finally Adopted," *The New York Times*, May 13, 1928, page 48.

121 Deborah Light Sizemore, "The Common Thread," *Fort Worth* (magazine published by the Fort Worth Chamber of Commerce), March 1982, page 22.

122 *175: A History of Mobile's Progressive Business Advocate – Mobile Chamber of Commerce 1836-2011* (Mobile, Ala.: Mobile Area Chamber of Commerce, 2011), 6.

123 Willard Hammer, "News of Organized Business," subheading "A Chamber Sells Bonds," *Nation's Business*, April 1929, page 199.

124 *Fifty-Years [sic] of the Chamber of Commerce of Pittsburgh, 1874-1924* (Pittsburgh: Pittsburgh Chamber of Commerce, 1924), 30.

125 The structure of the Camden business organizations of this period is confusing, but it's clear they were powerful. Karcher says the business groups ranked after the Republican Party in influence: "The second most powerful institution was the Camden Board of Trade and its affiliates, composed for the most part of interlocking directorates, the Chamber of Commerce, and the Manufacturers' Club of Camden." See Alan J. Karcher, *New Jersey's Multiple Municipal Madness* (Piscataway, N.J.: Rutgers University Press, 1998), 158. The Camden County Chamber of Commerce apparently was organized in about 1920, when the the president of Victor Talking Machine Company, Eldridge Johnson, offered to put up $100,000 toward the building of a hotel that would include the chamber's offices. In this and further examples, author Jeffery Dorwart shows not only how the chamber had energetic directors, but how deeply it was involved in the bridge project and ancillary activities such as hospitality and tourism promotion. See Jeffery Dorwart, *Camden County, New Jersey: The Making of a Metropolitan Community, 1626-2000* (Camden, N.J.: Camden County, 2001), 122.

126 Alan J. Karcher, *New Jersey's Multiple Municipal Madness* (Piscataway, N.J.: Rutgers University Press, 1998), 160.

127 "Bridge Building in South Jersey: Success of Camden Span Has Stimulated Many Other Projects for Motor Traffic Over Delaware River," *The New York Times*, January 29, 1928, page 135.

128 Alan J. Karcher, *New Jersey's Multiple Municipal Madness* (Piscataway, N.J.: Rutgers University Press, 1998), 162.

129 Holland was president of the chamber from 1925 to 1927 and later would be its executive secretary. He and the chamber proved instrumental not only in helping pass the road bond issue but in building support for the airport and air service. For more on the Truman-Holland connection and the road bond issue, see: Alonzo L. Hamby, *Man of the People: A Life of Harry S Truman* (New York: Oxford University Press, 1995), 150.

130 "News of Organized Business," subheading "City Planning and Zoning Accomplishments," *Nation's Business*, June 1928, 138.

131 This organization has evolved into the Savannah Economic Development Authority (SEDA). "The Savannah Chamber created the Savannah Port Authority," says a short history of the chamber, published on its 200th anniversary in 2006. (This untitled paper is six pages long and provided in 2010 to the author by the Savannah Chamber. The quotation is from page 3.) A timeline issued in 2006 by the Savannah Chamber includes a 1925 achievement as "Savannah Port Authority created as a result of chamber pressure." See "200th Anniversary Chronology," Savannah Area Chamber of Commerce, page 1.

132 "Six-Mile Bore Named for David Moffat Under Continental Divide Between Utah and Colorado Cuts the Hours of Travel," *The New York Times*, March 13, 1927, page X16. All the information here about the tonnage of rock removed, etc. by Moffat Tunnel is taken from this article. An interesting sidelight is that when the project was further along, the Denver Chamber of Commerce submitted it in a NACOS competition for best chamber projects. It won sixth place, behind some other projects that today don't seem nearly as notable. For the NACOS competition and the writeup of this project, see: "Twenty-Five Best Service Ideas for 1932," *NACOS Annual Meeting: Readjustment, Reconstruction, Recovery* (Memphis, Tenn.: NACOS, October 23-26, 1932), 201-23. The Denver Chamber/Moffat project is on page 206. Unfortunately for historians, NACOS abandoned the best-project contest soon thereafter, citing not enough entries.

133 "City Asked to Back Bridge-Tunnel Bill: Civic Groups Urge Creation of Authority with Power to Link the Boroughs," *The New York Times*, March 20, 1928, page 16.

134 Carlos C. Campbell, *Birth of a National Park in the Great Smoky Mountains* (Knoxville: University of Tennessee Press, 1960; paperback edition, 1993), 13.

135 Carlos C. Campbell, *Birth of a National Park in the Great Smoky Mountains* (Knoxville: University of Tennessee Press, 1960; paperback edition, 1993), 14.

136 Carlos C. Campbell, *Birth of a National Park in the Great Smoky Mountains* (Knoxville: University of Tennessee Press, 1960; paperback edition, 1993), 17.

Notes

137 Carlos C. Campbell, *Birth of a National Park in the Great Smoky Mountains* (Knoxville: University of Tennessee Press, 1960; paperback edition, 1993), 32 and 41.

138 Carlos C. Campbell, *Birth of a National Park in the Great Smoky Mountains* (Knoxville: University of Tennessee Press, 1960; paperback edition, 1993), 43.

139 Carlos C. Campbell, *Birth of a National Park in the Great Smoky Mountains* (Knoxville: University of Tennessee Press, 1960; paperback edition, 1993), 41.

140 Paul R. Mallon, "Throng Greets Body of Bryan in Washington," *The Pittsburgh Press*, July 30, 1925, 1, 5.

141 Carlos C. Campbell, *Birth of a National Park in the Great Smoky Mountains* (Knoxville: University of Tennessee Press, 1960; paperback edition, 1993), 39.

142 Carlos C. Campbell, *Birth of a National Park in the Great Smoky Mountains* (Knoxville: University of Tennessee Press, 1960; paperback edition, 1993), xi. Incidentally, park fever spread up the Appalachians. The idea for one in the Shenandoah area in Virginia was not new. In 1915, Hugh E. Naylor, a businessman and secretary of the Front Royal/Riverton Board of Trade, proposed a national park in the nearby mountains. [See: John A. Conners, *Shenandoah National Park: An Interpretive Guide* (McDonald and Woodward Publishing Company, 1988), 92.] In February of 1925, the Virginia State Chamber of Commerce announced that it was consolidating business support for this new recreation area. [See: "Virginia Business Men Uniting for New Park: State Chamber of Commerce Moves to Consolidate Work of Other Bodies," *The Washington Post*, February 10, 1925, 2.] Just a year later, President Coolidge signed a bill authorizing the park. Virginia state government took over the park, although it continued to need the support of chambers and other civic groups to raise funds for purchase of privately owned lands within the park's grounds. [This brief opinion piece shows how business organizations were needed to build support for the Shenandoah park project, even though the State of Virginia had taken control of the effort to get the park off the ground: "Virginia's National Park," *The Washington Post*, January 19, 1928, 6.]

143 Lee Roy Chapman, "The Nightmare of Dreamland," This Land Press, originally published September 1, 2011.

144 The phrase "Tulsa spirit" is commonly used in Tulsa even today, including in the name of a women's soccer team. Tate Brady coined the term, according to several sources, including "The Nightmare of Dreamland."

145 Lee Roy Chapman, "The Nightmare of Dreamland," This Land Press, originally published September 1, 2011.

146 Lee Roy Chapman, "The Nightmare of Dreamland," This Land Press, originally published September 1, 2011.

147 Lee Roy Chapman, "The Nightmare of Dreamland," This Land Press, originally published September 1, 2011.

148 Lee Roy Chapman, "The Nightmare of Dreamland," This Land Press, originally published September 1, 2011.

149 Lee Roy Chapman, "The Nightmare of Dreamland," This Land Press, originally published September 1, 2011.

150 Lee Roy Chapman, "The Nightmare of Dreamland," This Land Press, originally published September 1, 2011.

151 Scott Ellsworth, *Death in a Promised Land: The Tulsa Race Riot of 1921* (Baton Rouge, La.: Louisiana State University Press, 1982), 82-85.

152 For an extensive explanation of the Tulsa Chamber's actions in the aftermath of the riot, see the bulk of the fourth chapter of Ellworth's book: Scott Ellsworth, *Death in the Promised Land: The Tulsa Race Riot of 1921* (Baton Rouge, La.: Louisiana State University Press, 1982), 71-94.

153 James M. Smallwood, *Urban Builder: The Life and Times of Stanley Draper* (Norman, Okla.: University of Oklahoma Press, 1977), 48.

154 James M. Smallwood, *Urban Builder: The Life and Times of Stanley Draper* (Norman, Okla.: University of Oklahoma Press, 1977), 49.

155 James M. Smallwood, *Urban Builder: The Life and Times of Stanley Draper* (Norman, Okla.: University of Oklahoma Press, 1977), 15-16.

156 "F.D. Roosevelt Turns Columnist: In Beacon Standard, He Comments for 'Neighbors' of Dutchess County," *The New York Times*, August 3, 1928, page 38.

157 After the 1906 riot, a public meeting was held at the chamber of commerce, presided over by Chamber President Sam Jones. [See: Rebecca Burns, *Rage in the Gate City: The Story of the 1906 Atlanta Race Riot* (Athens, Ga.: University of Georgia Press, 2009), 150.] The great majority of attendees were white, but among the handful of blacks in the room was the well-known author and civil rights advocate, W.E.B. DuBois. Atlanta's optimism, so foreign to DuBois's writings, was evident even in this meeting. Jones said something that was the precursor to the well-known "too busy to hate" slogan of another Atlanta leader: "Keep white and colored hard at work, and they'll have no time to stand around the street corners." [*Rage in the Gate City*,150] The leaders at the meeting condemned both the slow response of the police to the crisis and the rioters themselves. Many worried about "the better negroes" leaving town and the impact of the crisis on the image of Atlanta throughout the nation. A report on the riot was co-written by the secretary of the Atlanta Chamber of Commerce, Walter Cooper, and department store owner and chamber member George Muse. [*Rage in the Gate City*, 151] The chamber minimized the number of casualties, saying only 12 had been killed. [See: David Fort Godshalk, *Veiled Visions: The 1906 Atlanta Race Riot and the Reshaping of American Race Relations* (Chapel Hill, N.C.: University of North Carolina Press, 2005), 105.]

158 W. Fitzhugh Brundage, *Lynching in the New South: Georgia and Virginia, 1880-1930* (University of Illinois, paperback edition, 1993), 223.

159 Mark Kelly, *A Powerful Presence: The Birmingham Regional Chamber of Commerce and the History of Birmingham* (Birmingham, Ala.: Birmingham Regional Chamber of Commerce, 2008), 34.

160 "Lending a Helping Hand," a chapter in *Greater Little Rock Chamber of Commerce, 1867-2004*, Greater Little Rock Chamber of Commerce Web site:

http://www.littlerockchamber.com/CWT/EXTERNAL/WcPages/Membership/Lending_a_Helping_Hand.aspx

161 "Inquiry Into Another Lynching," Associated Press, *The Washington Post*, January 1, 1929, 2.

162 For the KKK membership and the high school information, see: Phillip M. Hoose, *Hoosiers: The Fabulous Basketball Life of Indiana* (Indianapolis: Guild Press, 2005), Second Edition, 145. For the item on racial zones, see: George and Miriam Geib, *Indianapolis First: A Commemorative History of the Indianapolis Chamber of Commerce and the Local Business Community* (Indianapolis: Indianapolis Chamber of Commerce, 1990), 67, 69.

163 Rose C. Feld, "Negro Problem Dooms South's Old Traditions: Whites Realize Future Prosperity, Industrially and on the Plantation, Depends Upon Putting Aside Prejudice and Meeting the Reasonable Demands of the Blacks," *The New York Times*, January 20, 1924, XX16.

164 "Mt. Rainier Chamber Resents Klan Action," *The Washington Post*, June 29, 1926, 2.

165 "Official Klan Day Scheduled at Fair: Night Riders Will Get Half of Proceeds at Fairfax County Event," *The Washington Post*, September 10, 1929, 2.

166 *Immigration: Hearings Before the Committee on Immigration and Naturalization, House of Representatives, Sixty-Seventh Congress, Seventh Session*, Serial 1-B (Washington: U.S. Government Printing Office, 1922), 424.

167 "Japanese Will Quit California Farms: More Than 30,000 Will Abandon Nearly 500,000 Acres of Richest Crop Lands," *The New York Times*, December 16, 1923, E1.

168 "Jurist Drops Dead Before Peace Board: Ex-Justice Burke Expires in Arms of Dr. Butler at Carnegie Endowment Meeting," *The New York Times*, December 5, 1925, 1.

169 Merle Thorpe, "Why They Cheered – 'He Built Seattle,'" *Nation's Business*, August 1925, 30.

170 "Jurist Drops Dead Before Peace Board: Ex-Justice Burke Expires in Arms of Dr. Butler at Carnegie Endowment Meeting," *The New York Times*, December 5, 1925, 1.

171 Carey McWilliams, *A Mask for Privilege: Anti-Semitism in America* (Rutgers, N.J.: Transaction Publishers, 1999; originally published by Little Brown & Co., Boston, in 1948), 37-38.

172 "Florida Realty Men Under Fire at Shore: Atlantic City Chamber of Commerce Investigates Alleged Misrepresentations," *The New York Times*, August 8, 1925, 4.

173 "To War on Swindlers in Florida Realty: National Business Groups Join for Campaign to Protect Public From Sharks," *The New York Times*, February 6, 1926, 8.

174 "Ponzi Sees Lawyer as Search Goes On: Indicted Land Promoter Talks to Newspaper Men Who Find Him in Jacksonville," *The New York Times*, February 10, 1926, 12.

175 "Ponzi Among 4 Indicted in Florida Land Sales: Charges Follow Investigation by Better Business Bureau Agent," Associated Press, *The Washington Post*, February 9, 1926, 1.

176 Curiously, there was another, albeit indirect, connection between chambers of commerce and Charles Ponzi. Ponzi had hired a publicity agent in Massachusetts – none other than William McMasters, the same man who wrote the anti-chamber essay (quoted earlier in this book), "On Chambers of Commerce." McMasters, when he learned how dishonest Ponzi was, reported him to his former employer, the magazine *Barron's*, leading to an expose and the beginning of the end for this ingenious swindler. For the McMasters information, see the Wikipedia article on Charles Ponzi.

177 "New Tong Murders: 500 Chinese Seized," *The New York Times*, September 19, 1925, 1.

178 "Canton's 'Jungle' Boasts Immunity: Underworld Envoys Declare Mellett Murder Won't Be Solved – Deride 'Clean-Up,'" *The New York Times*, July 28, 1926, 2.

179 "Don Mellett," Wikipedia.

180 "'Ware 'Hooch' and Hostess: Card Warns of Atlantic City Cabaret Perils," *The New York Times*, September 30, 1923, 11.

181 "Protest to Mellon Over Firing on Yacht," *The Washington Post*, November 23, 1924, 3.

182 "Protection of the Public," editorial, *The Washington Post*, November 19, 1925, 6. See also: "Chamber of Commerce Assails Auto Rum Chases," *The Washington Post*, November 4, 1925.

183 "400 Diners on Liner Searched for Liquor; Guests on Berlin Resent Dry Agents' Action," *The New York Times*, January 18, 1928, 52. Also: "Deny Ordering Raid on Hoboken Dinner: Officials Insist Regular Pier Guards Searched as Part of Routine 400 Aboard Liner," *The New York Times*, January 19, 1928, 13.

184 "Rich Rum-Runner Gets 2-Year Term: Wormser of Port Chester Ring Must Serve Long Sentence and Pay $10,000 Fine," *The New York Times*, January 15, 1927, 1.

185 J.R. Sprague, "A Civic Campaign," parts one and two. Part one: *Nation's Business*, January 1924, 52, 54. Part two: *Nation's Business*, February 1924, 44, 46.

186 "Memphis Men Suspend Piggly Stock Campaign: Saunders Involved in Physical Encounter in Meeting of Pool Members," *The Washington Post*, May 11, 1923, 1.

187 "San Antonio Has Plan to Hold Newcomers: Texas City's Official Greeter and 'Welcome Wagon' Helps to Keep Trade at Home," *The New York Times*, April 22, 1928, 54.

188 Briggs's company refers to July 1928 as the beginning date for the use of the name in various places such as Filing No. 538327 (filed on October 18, 1947) with the U.S. Patent Office. Briggs "bought the idea outright from two Texas youths" according to an item in *The Literary Digest*, Volume 123, Issues 1-13, January July 1927, 32.

189 "150 Oklahomans Visit Gov. Smith at Albany," *The New York Times*, May 12, 1926, 28. Also: "Tulsa Delegates Get Welcome Here: 'Educational Special Train' Heralds Oklahoma City as Cleanest in America," *The New York Times*, May 9, 1926, 8. For the visit to Washington and the meeting with Coolidge, see: "Police Stop Tulsa Boosters' Parade: Visitors are Entertained by Luncheon and Welcomed by Coolidge; Go to Baltimore," *The Washington Post*, May 7, 1926. The 1929 visit is described here: "138 Oklahomans Here on Tour of Big Cities," *The New York Times*, June 23, 1929, 2.

190 "Urges New England to Encourage Youth: Leader of 'Land Cruise' Tells Council That Young Men Push Business in South and West," *The New York Times,* June 9, 1929, 18.

191 "News of Organized Business," subhead "Jacksonville 'Believers' Advertise," *Nation's Business,* June 1925, 84.

192 Willis Powell, "Simply Staggering," *Nation's Business,* May 1925, 19-21. For the hunting dog quote and others like it, see: "The Log of Organized Business," *Nation's Business,* January 1921, 37.

193 "Threat to the Times," letter to the editor by W.B. Estes, *The New York Times,* January 11, 1927, 30.

194 "For the Defense of Miami," *Miami Daily Metropolis,* January 23, 1922, 6.

195 "Pacific Coast Wants Boom, Too: California, Oregon and Washington Communities Raise Campaign Fund of Millions To Bid for Eastern Favor," *The New York Times,* January 3, 1926, page XX8.

196 "Pacific Coast Wants Boom, Too: California, Oregon and Washington Communities Raise Campaign Fund of Millions To Bid for Eastern Favor," *The New York Times,* January 3, 1926, page XX8.

197 Clifford M. Kuhn, Harlon E. Joye, and E. Bernard West, *Living Atlanta: An Oral History of the City, 1914-1948* (Athens,Ga.: University of Georgia Press, 1990, 2005), 89-90.

198 Clifford M. Kuhn, Harlon E. Joye, and E. Bernard West, *Living Atlanta: An Oral History of the City, 1914-1948* (Athens,Ga.: University of Georgia Press, 1990, 2005), 90.

199 Clifford M. Kuhn, Harlon E. Joye, and E. Bernard West, *Living Atlanta: An Oral History of the City, 1914-1948* (Athens,Ga.: University of Georgia Press, 1990, 2005), 92.

200 Clifford M. Kuhn, Harlon E. Joye, and E. Bernard West, *Living Atlanta: An Oral History of the City, 1914-1948* (Athens,Ga.: University of Georgia Press, 1990, 2005), 93.

201 Anne Harding, "90 Years of Building a Better Dallas: The History of the Greater Dallas Chamber, 1909 to the Present," 5. This is a 15-page paper made available by the Greater Dallas Chamber in 1999.

202 Gerald W. Johnson, "Greensboro, Or What You Will," from *South-Watching: Selected Essays by Gerald W. Johnson* (Chapel Hill, N.C.: The University of North Carolina Press, 1983), 45. This essay first appeared in the *Reviewer* in April 1924.

203 "News of Organized Business," subhead "Fund of $100,000 for Industries," *Nation's Business,* November 1924, 86.

204 "News of Organized Business," subhead "Agencies for Industrial Growth," *Nation's Business,* April 1926, 124.

205 J.L. Warner, "Industrial Development as an Engineer Sees It," *Fourteenth Annual Meeting of the National Association of Commercial Organization Secretaries* (Nashville, Tenn.: NACOS, October 22-24, 1928), 300-12. Quote is on page 300.

206 "Get $2,265,000 in Chicago Swindle: Cleveland Department of Justice Agent Seizes Notes of Alleged Fraud Ring; French Letter Taken; It Refers to Centralia Contract for a Bonus Which Was Never Fulfilled," *The New York Times,* September 4, 1921, 14.

207 "News of Organized Business," subhead "Industrial Prospects," *Nation's Business,* November 1927, 135.

208 "News of Organized Business," subhead "The Play Side," *Nation's Business,* December 1923, 86.

209 Don Woodward and Joel Campbell, *Common Ground: 100 Years of the Salt Lake Chamber* (Montgomery, Alabama: Community Communications Inc., 2003), 35, 43.

210 Don Woodward and Joel Campbell, *Common Ground: 100 Years of the Salt Lake Chamber* (Montgomery, Alabama: Community Communications Inc., 2003), 35.

211 Don Woodward and Joel Campbell, *Common Ground: 100 Years of the Salt Lake Chamber* (Montgomery, Alabama: Community Communications Inc., 2003), 43.

212 Scott Taylor Hartzell, *St. Petersburg: An Oral History* (Charleston, S.C.: Arcadia Publishing, 2002), 57-8.

213 When the ship finally returned to San Francisco shortly after Christmas in 1921, three passengers weren't aboard. Judge Alexander Morrison had suddenly died in Singapore, so his wife and a friend came back with his body on another ship. Information on this cruise may be found in several issues of *San Francisco Business,* a weekly published by the San Francisco Chamber of Commerce. The October 7, 1921 issue, beginning on page 7, provides the itinerary and an extensive list of the passengers. The December 30, 1921 issue, beginning on page 5, mentions the judge's death and other interesting details of the now-completed voyage.

214 "Balls Signed by Ruth, Gehrig School Prizes," The Associated Press, *The Washington Post,* October 16, 1927, 24.

215 "Business and the Schools," *The Journal of the National Education Association,* November 1921, 153.

216 "Business and the Schools," *The Journal of the National Education Association,* November 1921, 153.

217 Susan M. Dorsey, "How Los Angeles Voted $17,400,000," *The Journal of the National Education Association,* Volume 11, September 1922, 273-4.

218 George and Miriam Geib, *Indianapolis First: A Commemorative History of the Indianapolis Chamber of Commerce and Local Business Community* (Indianapolis: Indianapolis Chamber of Commerce, 1990), 67.

219 "History of the Savannah Area Chamber of Commerce," six-page document published by the Savannah Area Chamber of Commerce on its 200th anniversary in 1906, 4.

220 "Yuba Sutter Chamber of Commerce History," Web site, Yuba Sutter Chamber of Commerce: http://www.yubasutterchamber.com/index.php?option=com_content&view=article&id=163&Itemid=167

221 Gary Quackenbush, "A Century with the Chamber," *North Bay Business Journal,* September 18, 2006, 24.

222 James Krohe Jr., *Shoulder to the Wheel: A Centennial History of the Greater Springfield Chamber of Commerce* (Springfield, Ill.: Greater Springfield Chamber of Commerce, 1976), 20.

223 Carl Blasig, *Building Texas* (Brownsville, Texas: Springman-King Company, 1963), 156.

224 "Legislator's Work Led to Tech," *Lubbock Avalanche-Journal*, February 8, 2009.

225 Carl Blasig, *Building Texas* (Brownsville, Texas: Springman-King Company, 1963), 156.

226 Carl Blasig, *Building Texas* (Brownsville, Texas: Springman-King Company, 1963), 157.

227 "Legislator's Work Led to Tech," *Lubbock Avalanche-Journal*, February 8, 2009.

228 Doug Hensley, "Landing Tech May Have Been Biggest Step in Lubbock's First 100 Years," citing book by Paul Carlson, *Lubbock Avalanche-Journal*, August 3, 2008.

229 Lawrence Graves, *Lubbock: From Town to City* (Lubbock: West Texas Museum Association, 1986), 62.

230 Carl Blasig, *Building Texas* (Brownsville, Texas: Springman-King Company, 1963), 170.

231 Carl Blasig, *Building Texas* (Brownsville, Texas: Springman-King Company, 1963), 170.

232 Carl Blasig, *Building Texas* (Brownsville, Texas: Springman-King Company, 1963), 170.

233 Greater Memphis Chamber of Commerce Web site, history section timeline, 1925 listings:

http://www.memphischamber.com/The-Chamber/History.aspx

234 "Austin Peay Relations," from "History of Clarksville Chamber," Clarksville Area Chamber of Commerce Web site:

http://www.clarksvillechamber.com/about/history-clarksville-chamber/

235 "Lending a Helping Hand," a chapter in *Greater Little Rock Chamber of Commerce, 1867-2004*, Greater Little Rock Chamber of Commerce Web site:

http://www.littlerockchamber.com/CWT/EXTERNAL/WcPages/Membership/Lending_a_Helping_Hand.aspx

236 "Lending a Helping Hand," a chapter in *Greater Little Rock Chamber of Commerce, 1867-2004*, Greater Little Rock Chamber of Commerce Web site:

http://www.littlerockchamber.com/CWT/EXTERNAL/WcPages/Membership/Lending_a_Helping_Hand.aspx

237 "Offers $1 Million to College Fund: Ralph Jonas Makes Conditional Gift for Endowed Institution in Brooklyn," *The New York Times*, January 22, 1926, 21.

238 "New University is Opened: Long Island Institution's Start is Marked by a Celebration," *The New York Times*, September 22, 1927, 15.

239 There was another interesting New York-connected education development in the 1920s. In 1924, Trinity College in Durham, N.C. became Duke University, thanks to Trinity's receiving a large portion of a $40 million charitable donation from James B. Duke, the cigarette and utilities magnate. The man who interested the Duke family in southern education was Dr. John Franklin Crowell, who had been the top paid staffer at the New York Chamber from 1915 to 1917. A few years before working at the chamber, from 1887 to 1893, Crowell had been the president of Trinity University.

240 President Taft's Speech at Annual Banquet," *Nation's Business*, January 28, 1913, 1.

241 "School to Open for Secretaries," *Greater New York: The Bulletin of the Merchants' Association of New York*, May 2, 1921, 9.

242 "National Chamber Aids New School for Secretaries: Joins National Association for Commercial Organization Secretaries in Underwriting the Expenses of Secretarial Training in Northwestern University," *Greater New York: The Bulletin of the Merchants' Association of New York*, July 4, 1921, 10.

243 "Commercial Secretaries Study Their Jobs," *Nation's Business*, October 1922, 54-56.

244 Scott Cutlip, *Fund Raising in the United States: Its Role in America's Philanthropy* (New Brunswick, N.J.: Transaction Publishing, 1990; an expanded book from the original, which was published by Rutgers University in 1965), 193.

245 "News of Organized Business," subhead "A Summer School at Stanford," *Nation's Business*, September 1923, 86.

246 S. Cristy Mead, "I Believe in My Work," *Nation's Business*, May 1929. The article is on pages 31, 33, 186, 188, and 190. The quoted items are on page 188. We can see from Mead's remarks that Ryerson Ritchie was not the only chamber executive of the era to have an ego.

247 Kenneth Montague Sturges, *American Chambers of Commerce* (New York: Moffat, Yard & Company, 1915), 259-261. Sturges reports the full results of the study's two questions, one essentially about the civic achievements of the chambers, and the other on their ability to bring out the civic spirit of members. If the scores on the two questions are combined, the results are as follows:

Cleveland	38 votes
Chicago	32
Boston	30
Detroit	17
New York Merchants' Association	12
Minneapolis	12
Kansas City	11
New Orleans	9
Rochester (probably NY)	9
Los Angeles	7

San Francisco	3
Seattle	3
Baltimore	2
St. Louis	2
Buffalo	2
Cincinnati	2
Portland (not specified if ME or OR)	1
Denver	1
Louisville	1
Newark	1
New York Chamber of Commerce	1
Philadelphia	1

One of the fascinating things about this tally is how well placed Ryerson Ritchie's alumni chambers are. Cleveland, Boston, Detroit, Kansas City, and San Francisco have a combined total of 99 votes – more than all the others, including the hundreds of chambers that got no votes, combined (98). Ritchie had a short list of friends, but cast a long shadow. Another interesting thing is how slighted the New York Chamber and Los Angeles Chamber are in this 1913 poll. Each of the two chambers, for different reasons, did not greatly capture the imagination of other chambers in the period, even though both chambers had had monumental achievements by this time.

248 James A. McKibben, *The Structure or Organization of a Chamber of Commerce* (Evanston, Ill.: National School for Commercial Secretaries, 1922), 15. See the asterisk at the bottom of the page. This 40-page booklet was the first in a series provided as text for the second gathering of this NACOS-U.S. Chamber project for the training of commercial secretaries, the school that today is the U.S. Chamber program known informally as "Institute." Here is a more extended description of the unique organizational structure of the Chamber of Commerce of New York State, provided by its president, James Brown, in a speech to NACOS in 1933:

I do not think there is a Chamber of Commerce or a Trade Association anywhere that works as we do. We have a president, 12 vice-presidents and an executive vice-president, various other officers, and an executive committee largely composed of chairmen of the standing committees, such as the committees on taxation, on finance and currency, on foreign commerce and the revenue, etc. Incidentally, 127 of our members, exclusive of the officers and secretaries, worked on our committees last year. But we have no board of directors. And no officer, not even the executive committee, can bind the Chamber. The committees propose but the body of the Chamber itself has the final say. This way may seem cumbersome and old-fashioned , but it makes for careful thinking and prevents snap judgment by a small body of men.

The source of the above quote is: James Brown, "Greeting," *NACOS 19th Annual Meeting: The Challenge to Organization Leadership* (New York: September 24-27, 1933), 134.

249 "1902 Light System Kept as Tradition: State Chamber of Commerce Spurns New Device That Would Change Great Hall," *The New York Times*, January 18, 1927, 35.

250 "Commerce Building Statues Removed: Crumbling of Marble Called a Public Danger – New Ones May be Made; Figures Only 23 Years Old; They Represented Clinton, Jay and Hamilton and Were of Heroic Size," *The New York Times*, September 22, 1926, 41.

251 "Rockefeller Greets Cleveland," *The New York Times*, July 8, 1923, 6.

252 The main monument to Frank Wiggins was the city he left behind him. But there was also a school named after him: Frank Wiggins Technical School, a large vocational school that the Los Angeles Chamber had helped set up, opened in 1927. It is now called Los Angeles Trade Tech. Moreover, a Liberty Ship built in 1943, *SS Frank Wiggins*, may have been named after the great chamber secretary. (See "List of Liberty Ships, A-F," Wikipedia.)

253 U.S. Chamber 100th Anniversary timeline: http://www.uschamber.com/about/100th-anniversary

254 "Goodwin Resigns From Business Body: Ends 15 Years' Work Building Up the United States Chamber of Commerce; Differed with Directors," *The New York Times*, October 20, 1926, 14.

255 W.O. Saunders, "My Town Has Too Many Organizations," *Nation's Business*, June 1928, 36-37.

256 The first Rotary club was founded in Chicago in 1905; Kiwanis began in 1915.

257 Willard Hammer, "News of Organized Business," subhead "Chambers and Lunch Clubs," *Nation's Business*, October 1929, 198.

258 Robert Barnes, "News of Organized Business," *Nation's Business*, January 1927, 110. Barnes decries the "centrifugal tendencies" of chambers and warns that if they continue to offload too many jobs, they will be reduced to "more or less impotent general interest bodies."

259 "Florida Chamber History," Florida Chamber of Commerce Web site: http://flcc.harvestmanager.net/mx/hm.asp?id=about_history

260 "National Association of State Chambers of Commerce Organized," *The American City*, Volume XXXI, July-December 1924, 599.

261 Robert Barnes, "News of Organized Business," subhead "The Work of State Chambers," *Nation's Business*, October 1926, 122.

262 George B. Chandler, Secretary, Ohio State Chamber, "The History and Present Status of State Chamber of Commerce Organization," *Fifteenth Annual Meeting of the National Association of Commercial Organization Secretaries* (Milwaukee, Wis.: NACOS, October 21-23, 1929), 76-82.

263 Louise Gilmore Donahue, *Pathways to Prosperity: A History of the Greater Omaha Chamber of Commerce* (Omaha: Greater Omaha Chamber of Commerce, 1993), 12.

264 "Woman Heads Chamber of Commerce," *The New York Times*, January 21, 1923, 8.

265 Jessica I. Elfenbein in association with Howard Gillette, Jr. and William H. Becker, *Civics, Commerce, and Community: The History of the Greater Washington Board of Trade, 1889-1989* (Dubuque, IA: Kendall/Hunt Publishing Company, 1989), 26.

266 "Commits Suicide over Stock Losses: R.M. Searle, Rochester Utility Man, Said to Have Dropped Nearly All of His Fortune," *The New York Times*, November 14, 1929, 2.

267 "Sees Trade Independent: Merle Thorpe Says Market's Fall Affects Industry Only a Little," *The New York Times*, November 10, 1929, 21.

268 "Barnes Assures Business Advance: Chamber Head, Disclosing Magnitude of Projects to Hoover, Hails Cooperation," *The New York Times*, November 24, 1929, 1.

269 James C. Young, "Simplified Calendar is Sought in Business: Vote of Chambers Favorable, But Undecisive; George Eastman Explains Advantages of the Thirteen Month Year," *The New York Times*, November 24, 1929, XX11. George Eastman, founder of Kodak, was the leading business proponent of the 13-month calendar. His chamber of commerce, in Rochester, N.Y. (the same chamber of which the unfortunate R.M. Searle had been president), took up the cause, as did the New York Chamber of Commerce and many others. Having 13 identical months appeared efficient but the problems involved in a calendar change were enormous, as the average person knew without much reflection.

270 There are almost as many opinions on the causes of the Great Depression as there are economists. But certainly one of the leading theories, promoted by Jude Wanniski and others, is that the stock market crash was prompted by anticipation of the ill effects of the Smoot-Hawley tariff legislation. The enactment of the legislation then confirmed investors' fears and locked in the disaster for years to come.

Fear Itself (1930-1940)

1 "Reports Business Nearing Normal," *The New York Times*, January 10, 1930, 27.

2 "Leaders Report Industrial Gains," *The New York Times*, February 8, 1930, 20.

3 "Text of Hoover's Speech Before Commerce Group," *The Washington Post*, May 2, 1930, 1.

4 "Find Business Ready to Move Forward," *The New York Times*, October 24, 1930, 1.

5 Willard Hammer, "News of Organized Business," subheading "Fighting Unemployment," *Nation's Business*, December 1930, 105.

6 Willard Hammer, "News of Organized Business," subheading "Chambers and Employment," *Nation's Business*, January 1931, 88.

7 "Trade Groups Score Extra-Session Plan," *The New York Times*, February 5, 1931, 3.

8 Willard Hammer, "News of Organized Business," subheading "Stabilizing Business," *Nation's Business*, February 1931, 103.

9 Will Rogers, "Mr. Rogers Discusses a Guess On How to End the Depression," *The New York Times*, May 6, 1931, 25.

10 "Hurley Predicts Increase in Taxes," *The Washington Post*, November 20, 1931, 1.

11 C.F. Hughes, "The Merchant's Point of View," *The New York Times*, August 9, 1931, 32.

12 C.F. Hughes, "The Merchant's Point of View," *The New York Times*, September 13, 1931, N18.

13 "Major Proposals for Help in the Depression as Outlined by Labor Unions and Employer Bodies," *The New York Times*, October 5, 1931, 14.

14 "Self-Contained America," *The Washington Post*, November 19, 1931, 6.

15 The Tenino experiment got a lot of attention. See for example, "Americana," subheading "Washington," from *The American Mercury*, July 1932, 313. Also: "Town Balks Crisis by Wooden Money," *The Washington Post*, UPI, February 21, 1932, M13. And: "Wooden Money Big Success, Town Back on Gold Basis," *The Washington Post*, Associated Press, January 1, 1933, M2.

16 "How Two Towns Saved Their Banks," *Nation's Business*, May 1932, 80-81.

17 "2,395 Communities Join Hoarding Fight," *The New York Times*, March 12, 1932, 5.

18 "To Spend Dollar Hoarded 26 Years," *The New York Times*, Associated Press, March 31, 1932, 23.

19 H.G. Hoffman, "10 Check Pays $410 Debts," Letter to the Editor, *The New York Times*, April 27, 1932, 16.

20 "Chatham (N.Y.) Offers 50 Home Sites Free," *The New York Times*, March 2, 1932, 35.

21 "Double 5-Hour Day Success on Coast," *The Washington Post*, January 31, 1932, R2.

22 "President of Chamber Calls at White House," *The Washington Post*, Associated Press, June 24, 1932, 1.

23 "Recruiting 'Khaki Shirts': Leaders Get Pledges of 2,500 to Join Political Party of the Jobless," *The New York Times*, July 31, 1932, 1.

24 F. Raymond Daniell, "Mayor Backs Up Waters," *The New York Times*, August 4, 1932, 1.

Notes

25 Charles Ketchum, "Unemployment Relief," *NACOS 18th Annual Meeting: Readjustment, Reconstruction, Recovery* (Memphis: NACOS, October 23-26, 1932), 128-36. The quote is on page 134. The response and discussion afterward shows that Ketchum's peers did not feel as responsible as Ketchum did for the Depression's unemployment problem.

26 "Rise in Jersey Paper Output is Laid to Jig-Saw Puzzles," *The New York Times*, March 5, 1933, N2.

27 Leonard E. Read, "Keynote Address: Our Battles on the Home Front," *NACOS Second War Conference: "Home Front Battles Of Chambers of Commerce* (Pittsburgh: NACOS, October 24-27, 1943), 44.

28 "Support Pledged for Blanket Code: Backing of Hundreds Spurs Start of Recovery Drive in Local Organizing," *The New York Times*, July 22, 1933, 1.

29 Gerrish Gassaway, Manager, Chamber of Commerce, Wilmington, Del., "Trends in the Field of Governmental Aid to Business Groups – Relationship of Local Chamber of Commerce," *NACOS 20th Annual Meeting: Trends in the Organization Field* (Cincinnati: NACOS, October 21-24, 1934), 115-25. On page 124, Arthur Dudley of the chamber in Sacramento, Calif., shows some clever ways that chambers in the West have managed to corral solid federal funding to cover overhead costs of carrying out programs such as the NRA.

30 An extensive compilation of reactions to the NRA is featured in the annual proceedings of the Southern Commercial Secretaries Association annual proceedings for the year 1934, 28.

31 "Violations of Code Charged to Stores," *The Washington Post*, Associated Press, August 4, 1933, 3.

32 "Clevelanders Are Warned on NRA Cheating," *The Washington Post*, Associated Press, August 3, 1933, 2.

33 "Enforces NRA Code: Chelsea (Mass.) Arbiter Uses Police Power for Pay Rise," *The New York Times*, August 13, 1933, 5.

34 Don Woodward and Joel Campbell, *Common Ground: 100 Years of the Salt Lake Chamber* (Montgomery, Alabama: Community Communications Inc., 2003), 82.

35 "New NRA Fair Business Code Tightens Annapolis Blue Law," *The Washington Post*, August 14, 1933, 3.

36 "Plants Oppose Furniture Code in Hagerstown," *The Washington Post*, October 16, 1933, 5.

37 "Santa Claus Unrestricted by Codes, Johnson Says," *The New York Times*, Associated Press, December 5, 1933, 2.

38 "NRA Head Out at Pittsburgh," *The Washington Post*, Associated Press, December 13, 1933, 5.

39 "Foes Plotting to Sink NRA, Says Johnson," *The Washington Post*, United Press, May 5, 1934, 1.

40 "Chamber Demands a Return to Gold to Aid in Recovery," *The New York Times*, November 4, 1933, 1.

41 "Trade Body Widens Sound Money Drive," *The New York Times*, November 15, 1933.

42 Franklyn Waltman Jr., "Business Men Attack Money Experiments; Rift Seen," *The Washington Post*, November 19, 1933, 1.

43 Franklin D. Roosevelt, Address Delivered at Savannah, Georgia, November 18, 1933, from The American Presidency Project: http://www.presidency.ucsb.edu/ws/index.php?pid=14558

44 Will Rogers, "Mr. Rogers Makes Public a Little Inside Stuff," *The New York Times*, May 3, 1934, 21.

45 Untitled item with a byline of Providence, R.I., *The New York Times*, September 17, 1934, 2.

46 "President Roosevelt's Talk to Forum," *The New York Times*, October 6, 1937, 14.

47 Franklyn Waltman Jr., "Chamber Asks Roosevelt Tell Future Course," *The Washington Post*, September 25, 1934, 4.

48 "President Ignores Policy Questions," *The New York Times*, September 27, 1934, 5.

49 Arthur Krock, "President is Supported as Check to Radicalism," *The New York Times*, November 18, 1934, E1.

50 "Spurns Major Policies: U.S. Chamber of Commerce in Uncompromising Mood," *Montreal Gazette*, May 3, 1935, 17.

51 Leon Dure Jr., "Business Leaders Ignore Human Side in Censure, President Says," *The Washington Post*, May 4, 1935, 1.

52 Merle Thorpe, "Our Vanishing Freedom," *Nation's Business*, September 1935, 13.

53 "Chamber of Commerce Ousts Critic of WPA," *The Washington Post*, Associated Press, March 18, 1936, X11.

54 "The News of the Week Passes in Brief Review: National Affairs – Friday Night Fireside," *The Washington Post*, January 5, 1936, B2.

55 The Warm Springs Chamber was one of the groups defending FDR against charges by Georgia Governor Eugene Talmadge: "Warm Springs Aims Attack at Talmadge," *The New York Times*, Associated Press, April 28, 1935, 24.

56 "One Chamber Withdraws: Monterey, Calif., Business Men Oppose Break with Roosevelt," *The New York Times*, Associated Press, May 4, 1935, 2.

57 Myrtle Shaw Lord, *A Sacramento Saga: Fifty Years of Achievement – Chamber of Commerce Leadership* (Sacramento: Sacramento Chamber of Commerce, 1946), 114.

58 "30,000 Witness Fete Honoring TVA's Program," *The Washington Post*, Associated Press, July 5, 1935, 4.

59 Untitled article, dateline Sheffield, Ala., *The New York Times*, Associated Press, November 15, 1935, 18.

60 For Tupelo, see: "Quits National Chamber," *The New York Times*, Associated Press, November 23, 1935, 2. For Bristol, see: "Bars Referendum on New Deal," *The New York Times*, Associated Press, November 21, 1935.

61 "Harper Sibley Fails to Move Alfred P. Sloan," *Palm Beach Daily News*, February 1, 1937, 1.

62 "Union Regulation by Law Is Asked," *The New York Times*, February 5, 1937, 13.

63 "Sit Down Love Strike Ended; Girl Says Yes," *Sarasota Herald*, Associated Press, February 7, 1937, 2.

64 Leonard Lyons, "The Post's New Yorker," *The Washington Post*, February 10, 1937, 18.

65 "Fred S. McCargar," remarks, *NACOS 22nd Annual Meeting: Readjustments to Meet Changing Conditions* (Omaha: NACOS, November 8-11, 1936), 109-11. The quote is on page 111.

66 "U.S. Chamber Attacks Court Reform Plan," *The Washington Post*, February 21, 1937, M4.

67 "County Bar Fights Court Reform Plan," *The New York Times*, March 5, 1937, 1.

68 "Chamber Rallying Public Over Court," *The New York Times*, July 20, 1937, 2.

69 "Text of President Roosevelt's Address at Virginia Dare Celebration on Roanoke Island," *The Washington Post*, August 19, 1937, 21.

70 Merryle Stanley Rukeyser, "Rukeyser Says: Local Groups Must Stop Cry for Federal Aid," *The Washington Post*, May 26, 1939, 32.

71 "Chambers Urged to Fight U.S. Spending," *The Washington Post*, June 4, 1939, 7.

72 "U.S. Chamber Urges Let-up in Local Aid," *The New York Times*, October 2, 1939, 15.

73 "Drift-Wood: Public Spirit," from *The Galaxy*, edited by William Conant Church and Mark Twain, April 1874, from Volume 17, January to June 1874 (New York: Sheldon & Company, 1874), 553.

74 "Ten Leaders Look Into the New Decade, Foresee Change and Progress for U.S.," *The Washington Post*, January 1, 1940, 3.

75 "Texas Business Man Prevails on Mexico To Remove Hostile Sign Near U.S. Border," *The New York Times*, August 21, 1938, 1.

76 Shirley E. Flynn and William Robert Dubois, *We've Worked Hard to Get Here: The First 100 Years of the Cheyenne Chamber of Commerce* (Cheyenne, Wyo.: Greater Cheyenne Chamber of Commerce, 2007), 31.

77 "Delinquent Group Sued by Chamber," *The Washington Post*, August 20, 1932, 5.

78 Jessica I. Elfenbein in association with Howard Gillette, Jr. and William H. Becker, *Civics, Commerce, and Community: The History of the Greater Washington Board of Trade, 1889-1989* (Dubuque, IA: Kendall/Hunt Publishing Company, 1989), 26.

79 Jessica I. Elfenbein in association with Howard Gillette, Jr. and William H. Becker, *Civics, Commerce, and Community: The History of the Greater Washington Board of Trade, 1889-1989* (Dubuque, IA: Kendall/Hunt Publishing Company, 1989), 26.

80 Elmer T. Peterson, "West Coast Business Upswing Encouraging," *The Washington Post*, April 24, 1938, B9.

81 "Aggregate Total Income: Chart No. 2," *NACOS 24th Annual Meeting: "The Present Day Job of the Chamber of Commerce,"* (New Orleans, La.: NACOS, October 23-26, 1938), 167.

82 Don E. Mowry, "Sears' Membership in Chambers of Commerce – 94.13%," *NACOS News*, March 1932, 5-6.

83 C.M. Anderson, "President's Address: 'What's Next'", *NACOS 21st Annual Meeting: What's Next* (Washington, D.C.: NACOS, October 20-23, 1935), 25-28. The quote is on page 27.

84 L.E. Foster, General Manager, Chamber of Commerce, Birmingham, Ala., "Keeping Our Work in Step With the Times," *NACOS 21st Annual Meeting: What's Next* (Washington, D.C.: NACOS, October 20-23, 1935), 106-112. The quote is on page 107.

85 "Who'll Pay Mortgage and Win Fair Bride?", *The Washington Post*, Associated Press, June 11, 1935, 9.

86 "Hail End of Depression," *The New York Times*, April 1, 1933, 6.

87 In this case, actually, the man had been peddling food since before the Depression. His job was allegedly saved by President Wilson years earlier: "Steve to Keep Right on Selling Goobers – President Says So!", *The Washington Post*, January 18, 1934, 1.

88 "War on Peddlers is Lost in Court," *The New York Times*, August 28, 1935, 19.

89 Gilbert Swan, "Miami's Success Story," *The Washington Post*, January 14, 1940, A8. See also: "E.G. Sewell Dies; Mayor of Miami," *The New York Times*, Associated Press, April 3, 1940, 29.

90 "Our Chamber of Commerce," *Sarasota Herald-Tribune*, November 14, 1940, 4.

91 "C. of C. Support Urged by Mayor in Public Plea," *The Evening Independent*, March 7, 1936, 2.

92 "Test Will Be Made for Artificial Rain," *The Washington Post*, August 6, 1930, 18.

93 "Alexandria Rainmakers Refuse Responsibility," *The Washington Post*, August 28, 1930, 2.

94 "Flying Sun Baths to Be Inaugurated," *The Washington Post*, November 11, 1934, S9.

95 "Kansas City is 'Too Hot'; Asks Thermometer Shift," *The New York Times*, Associated Press, August 11, 1934, 3.

96 "Say Gas Causes Drought," *The New York Times*, February 2, 1936, E4.

97 Timothy Egan, *The Worst Hard Time: The Untold Story of Those Who Survived the Great American Dust Bowl* (New York: Houghton Mifflin, 2006), 231.

98 Timothy Egan, *The Worst Hard Time: The Untold Story of Those Who Survived the Great American Dust Bowl* (New York: Houghton Mifflin, 2006), 282.

99 Timothy Egan, *The Worst Hard Time: The Untold Story of Those Who Survived the Great American Dust Bowl* (New York: Houghton Mifflin, 2006), 286.

100 "Too Many Governments," from the *Pittsburgh Press*, reprinted in "What is to Come? Press Surmises as to Probable Developments in Politics as a Result of the Election," *The Washington Post*, November 21, 1932, 6.

101 "Chamber Asks County Fusion for Maryland," *The Washington Post*, February 22, 1934, 10.

102 Walter L. Pierpoint, "When Taxpayers Are Organized," *Nation's Business*, October 1938, 15, 96.

103 Alonzo L. Hamby, *Man of the People: A Life of Harry S Truman* (New York: Oxford University Press, 1995), 155.

Notes

104 A NACOS study published at the convention in 1931 showed that of 211 communities reporting to a survey, 207 of them had publicity and advertising handled by chambers of commerce. See: Harry Bell, Chairman, "Report – Centralization of Activities Committee," *NACOS 17th Annual Meeting: Organization Responsibilities* (Toledo: NACOS, October 18-21, 1931), 50-53.

105 "Dog Sellers Weep at Virginia Mart," *The New York Times*, October 15, 1937, 25. See also: George Berner, "Just Dogs," *The Washington Post*, September 27, 1936, R19.

106 Wilbur Jennings, "Dunn's Dollar is Short in Rappannahnock Test, So His Secretary Throws One Across River," *The Washington Post*, February 28, 1936, 20.

107 "Silver Discs Rushed for 'Big Train's' Toss," *The Washington Post*, Associated Press, February 20, 1936, 4.

108 "Virginians Flunk Washington's Feat," *The New York Times*, Associated Press, February 21, 1936, 19.

109 "Florida Rivers are Defended by State Chamber's President," *The Washington Post*, November 9, 1936, F5.

110 Among the many references to this anti-publicity-stunt publicity stunt, see: "Holiday Crowds Pay to Watch Diver Hunt Arkansas Monster," *The Washington Post*, Associated Press, July 23, 1937, 1.

111 Douglas Churchill, "Unquiet on the Western Front," *The New York Times*, August 2, 1936, X3.

112 John Kieran, "Sports of the Times," *The New York Times*, November 22, 1936, S2.

113 "History of the Chamber," Web site of the Beverly Hills Chamber of Commerce: http://www.beverlyhillschamber.com/general.asp?id=590

114 William J. Hennessy, manager, bureau of conventions, Chicago Association of Commerce, "The Chamber and the Convention Bureau" (Buffalo: NACOS, October 24-27, 1937), 167-172. The quote is on page 170.

115 "Registration Books to Open on Wednesday," *St. Petersburg Times*, August 29, 1937, 8.

116 Calvin White, "Alaska, Where Life is Merry," *The New York Times*, May 30, 1937, 134.

117 For the chamber's ambitious plans, see: "Deadwood Dick's Tomb to Be on Mountain," *The New York Times*, May 7, 1930, 27. For what it actually seems to have done and when, see: "Deadwood Dick's Grave at Last to be Marked," *The New York Times*, March 23, 1934, 28. The 1934 article mistakenly calls the man Carver instead of his real name, Clarke.

118 Richard W. Slatta, "Deadwood Dick," *The Mythical West: An Encyclopedia of Legend, Lore, and Popular Culture* (Santa Barbara, Calif.: ABC-Clio Inc., 2001), 119-20.

119 "Oranges Have Memorial Service," *The New York Times*, November 2, 1931, 18.

120 "Mrs. Edison Approves Plan for Memorial," *The Washington Post*, United Press, November 11, 1931, 5.

121 The finally completed tower was built for only $134,200, not $10 million, but was and is still impressive. See: http://www.menloparkmuseum.org/commemorative-history

122 "Clash Over Will Rogers," *The New York Times*, Associated Press, September 8, 1935, 37.

123 *What Dreams We Have: The Wright Brothers and Their Home Town of Dayton, Ohio*, Chapter 12, National Parks Service Web site:

http://www.nps.gov/history/history/online_books/daav/chap12.htm

See also: Bonnie Langdon and Phillip Parker, *Dayton Area Chamber of Commerce* (New York: Newcomen Society of the United States, 1996), 12.

124 "Cemetery Draws Visitors," *The New York Times*, June 7, 1931, E6.

125 "Want Buffalo Marker," *The New York Times*, January 28, 1934, E5.

126 "'Cardiff Giant' Sale Barred by Fort Dodge," *The New York Times*, Associated Press, August 4, 1934, 14.

127 Other than the Fort Dodge chamber's attempt to hang onto the fake giant, the items in this paragraph are taking from the Wikipedia article on the Cardiff Giant.

128 Mark Kelly, *A Powerful Presence: The Birmingham Regional Chamber of Commerce and the History of Birmingham* (Birmingham, Ala.: Birmingham Regional Chamber of Commerce, 2008), 43.

129 Kimblerly Barlag, "Back Roads: Sturgis: 'The Best Rally for Riding'," *American Motorcyclist*, November 2000, 33-6. See the sidebar on page 35, "From Zero to 60 . . . Years, That Is. . ."

130 "Notes From Here and There," *NACOS News*, November 1938, 6.

131 Eugene Moehring and Michael Green, *Las Vegas: A Centennial History* (Reno: University of Nevada Press, 2005), 109-110. Many other authors also mention the Cashman-Griffith-Hull story. The Las Vegas Chamber connections of Cashman and Griffith are unusually strong. James Cashman Sr. was a local auto dealer and an active chamber member since his arrival in town in 1904. He was still involved with the chamber after 1950, and his son James Cashman Jr. became president of the chamber in 1970, while his grandson James Cashman III also was involved in the organization. Griffith had been president of the chamber in 1938, two years before he and Cashman Sr. invited Hull to town. Robert Griffith's father, E.W. Griffith, was president of the chamber in 1913, 1914, and 1916. (C.P. Squires's "Early History of the Las Vegas Nevada Chamber of Commerce" lists the Las Vegas Chamber presidents through 1940.)

132 Eliot Ness with Oscar Fraley, *The Untouchables* (Cutchogue, N.Y.: Buccaneer Books, 1957), 11-12.

133 Jonathan Eig, *Get Capone: The Secret Plot That Captured America's Most Wanted Gangster* (New York: Simon & Schuster, 2010), 238.

134 Dennis E. Hoffman, *Scarface Al and the Crime Crusaders: Chicago's Private War Against Capone* (Carbondale, Ill.: Southern Illinois University Press, 1993), 18-20. Hoffman describes the CCC's founding and early days in this passage. The quotation, on page 19, is taken by Hoffman from Chamberlin's talk to the annual meeting of the American Institute of Criminal Law and Criminology in Indianapolis on September 17, 1920. Hoffman's book is by far the most complete description of the role of business in taking down Al Capone, although many other sources also acknowledge business's role in fighting Capone.

135 Jonathan Eig, *Get Capone: The Secret Plot That Captured America's Most Wanted Gangster* (New York: Simon & Schuster, 2010), 11-12.

136 Jonathan Eig, *Get Capone: The Secret Plot That Captured America's Most Wanted Gangster* (New York: Simon & Schuster, 2010), 27.

137 Jonathan Eig, *Get Capone: The Secret Plot That Captured America's Most Wanted Gangster* (New York: Simon & Schuster, 2010), 41. The entire McSwiggin episode is described in this chapter, "A Man of Destiny," from pages 38 through 44.

138 Dennis E. Hoffman, *Scarface Al and the Crime Crusaders: Chicago's Private War Against Capone* (Carbondale, Ill.: Southern Illinois University Press, 1993), 24.

139 Dennis E. Hoffman, *Scarface Al and the Crime Crusaders: Chicago's Private War Against Capone* (Carbondale, Ill.: Southern Illinois University Press, 1993), 31.

140 Dennis E. Hoffman, *Scarface Al and the Crime Crusaders: Chicago's Private War Against Capone* (Carbondale, Ill.: Southern Illinois University Press, 1993), 32-33.

141 Jonathan Eig, *Get Capone: The Secret Plot That Captured America's Most Wanted Gangster* (New York: Simon & Schuster, 2010), 194.

142 Dennis E. Hoffman, *Scarface Al and the Crime Crusaders: Chicago's Private War Against Capone* (Carbondale, Ill.: Southern Illinois University Press, 1993), 51.

143 Dennis E. Hoffman, *Scarface Al and the Crime Crusaders: Chicago's Private War Against Capone* (Carbondale, Ill.: Southern Illinois University Press, 1993), 74.

144 Dennis E. Hoffman, *Scarface Al and the Crime Crusaders: Chicago's Private War Against Capone* (Carbondale, Ill.: Southern Illinois University Press, 1993), 84. Hoffman indicates that Samuel Insull gave $15,000 and Julius Rosenwald additional funds toward the high-tech crime lab that would be established at Northwestern University (at the university in order to be free from political interference). These two men were soon to be members of the famous "Secret Six" of the Chicago Association of Commerce. The crime lab, moreover, had been advocated by the Chicago Crime Commission, which, as we have seen, was a child of the CAC.

145 Dennis E. Hoffman, *Scarface Al and the Crime Crusaders: Chicago's Private War Against Capone* (Carbondale, Ill.: Southern Illinois University Press, 1993), 88.

146 Thomas Barnard, "The Secret Six," 2003-2009: http://thomasbarnard.com/Articles/secretsix.htm

Barnard is a writer and the grandson of Harrison Barnard, who owned the construction company employing Meagher. An alternate version of the shooting, with two strangers coming to the construction site in the black sedan and asking "Where's Meagher?", is offered in a newspaper analysis two years after the shooting: Neil M. Clark, "Inside Facts of How Chicago Vigilantes Are Routing Gangsters Revealed – Mysteries of the Secret Six," *The Washington Post*, August 21, 1932, SM1. Clark's version is picked up almost verbatim by Dennis Hoffman in *Scarface Al.* Barnard's version, however, appears more genuine, with realistic details, such as: "The job foreman, Slim Ebert, pulled him [Meagher] down behind a pile of bricks." Barnard's sources include his grandfather's scrapbooks and conversations with his father, who continued to employ Meagher for many years.

147 Thomas Barnard, "The Secret Six," 2003-2009: http://thomasbarnard.com/Articles/secretsix.htm

148 James D. Nowlan, *Glory, Darkness, Light: A History of the Union League Club of Chicago* (Evanston, Ill.: Northwestern University Press, 2004), 93.

149 This analogy is not original to the author of this book. A Web commentator, Chris McAvoy, who did research on Isham Randolph, saw his son Robert Isham Randolph as a good stand-in for Batman.

150 Thomas Barnard, "The Secret Six," 2003-2009: http://thomasbarnard.com/Articles/secretsix.htm

151 Robert Isham Randolph, "Head of Chicago's 'Secret Six' Tells of the War Upon Gangs," *The New York Times*, April 17, 1932, XX3.

152 "Business Men Fight Chicago Criminals," *The Washington Post*, Associated Press, February 9, 1930, M6.

153 Barnard indicates the Swanson meeting was on February 11 and the Mid-Day Club meeting was the following day. But Randolph's secret committee of six (or seven), which we know included Samuel Insull, had been announced on February 8. How could Swanson have first introduced the idea of a secret investigation on February 11 if a secret committee was already announced three days earlier? In any case, we know these events all occurred close together in time and just after Meagher's shooting by gangsters.

154 Robert Isham Randolph, "Head of Chicago's 'Secret Six' Tells of the War Upon Gangs," *The New York Times*, April 17, 1932, XX3. Randolph is recalling what Insull said. In this article Randolph does not mention Insull's name, but other sources indicate he was the man making the 10 percent offer.

155 Thomas Barnard, "The Secret Six," 2003-2009: http://thomasbarnard.com/Articles/secretsix.htm

156 Thomas Barnard, "The Secret Six," 2003-2009: http://thomasbarnard.com/Articles/secretsix.htm

157 Thomas Barnard, "The Secret Six," 2003-2009: http://thomasbarnard.com/Articles/secretsix.htm

158 Dennis E. Hoffman, *Scarface Al and the Crime Crusaders: Chicago's Private War Against Capone* (Carbondale, Ill.: Southern Illinois University Press, 1993), 111. The phrase "public enemies," however, was not as new as Hoffman suggests. The *Chicago Daily News* used the expression earlier in 1930 when it provided the names and addresses of Chicago criminals to goad the police to take action against them. This earlier and very public usage of "public enemies" is cited here: "Chicago Turns on the Gunman," *The Literary Digest*, March 8, 1930, column one.

159 Robert Isham Randolph, "Head of Chicago's 'Secret Six' Tells of the War Upon Gangs," *The New York Times*, April 17, 1932, XX3.

160 Robert Isham Randolph, "Head of Chicago's 'Secret Six' Tells of the War Upon Gangs," *The New York Times*, April 17, 1932, XX3.

161 "Names Make News," *Time*, October 5, 1931.

162 Thomas Barnard, "The Secret Six," 2003-2009: http://thomasbarnard.com/Articles/secretsix.htm

163 Thomas Barnard, "The Secret Six," 2003-2009: http://thomasbarnard.com/Articles/secretsix.htm

The dialogue appears to be straight from Randolph's scrapbook and the explanatory prose is evidently Barnard's.

164 Cited by Thomas Barnard, "The Secret Six," 2003-2009: http://thomasbarnard.com/Articles/secretsix.htm

The article is: "'I'm Through! Secret Six Licked Me,' Says Al in Interview," *Chicago Herald Examiner*, July 30, 1931.

165 James L. Merriam, *Grafters and Goo Goos: Corruption and Reform in Chicago* (Carbondale, Ill.: Southern Illinois University, 2008), 126.

166 Thomas Barnard, "The Secret Six," 2003-2009: http://thomasbarnard.com/Articles/secretsix.htm

167 Neil M. Clark, "Inside Facts of How Chicago Vigilantes Are Routing Gangsters Revealed – Mysteries of the Secret Six," *The Washington Post*, August 21, 1932, SM1.

168 Dennis E. Hoffman, *Scarface Al and the Crime Crusaders: Chicago's Private War Against Capone* (Carbondale, Ill.: Southern Illinois University Press, 1993), 171.

169 "Kansas City Forms Committee," *The New York Times*, Associated Press, June 14, 1930.

170 "House Group Hears Kidnapping Terrors," *The Washington Post*, Associated Press, February 26, 1932. See also "Kidnapping Torture Bared to Congress," *The Washington Post*, Associated Press, February 27, 1932.

171 It's an ill wind that blows nobody any good. Hauptmann's trial included prominent testimony by a retired school teacher, Dr. John Conlon, who had been the intermediary for ransom money from the Lindberghs. During the trial, the affable Conlon (called "Jafsie" because of the sound of his initials, J.F.C.), was asked where he lived. "In the most beautiful borough in the world – the Bronx," he replied. For this, the Bronx Chamber of Commerce made him an honorary life member. See: "Bronx Chamber Pays Tribute to 'Jafsie,'" *The Washington Post*, Associated Press, March 28, 1935, 11. There are a few different versions of the quote; the AP article seems to have embellished the original slightly. Incidentally, this is far from the only time that local chambers of commerce obtained publicity from evil deeds or evildoers. In March of 1930, after Capone was being released from federal prison, Dan Evans, secretary of the chamber in Rapid City, South Dakota, invited Capone to live in a community where "the stranger is not judged by reports of his past record." Evans offered Capone "the glad hand of welcome in a community practically free of crime." The governor of South Dakota took a dimmer view, and Capone responded that he didn't want to live there. See: "Black Hills Invite Capone as Resident," *The New York Times*, Associated Press, March 29, 1930, 6. Also: "Capone Refuses to Live in Black Hills," *The New York Times*, Associated Press, March 30, 1930, 20.

172 A young man in Cleveland, Jerry Siegel, would create a character named "Clark" whom he named, as he later admitted, after a well-known actor. That actor debuted in 1931 in *The Secret Six* and stole the show. The actor was Clark Gable, appearing in the movie as a newspaper reporter crusading against crime. Siegel lost his father to criminals in 1932 and imagined some tie-wearing do-gooder who could have prevented that crime. Siegel's full name for his hero was Clark Kent, aka Superman. This author does not know if Siegel saw *The Secret Six*, but given that this was Clark Gable's first movie and Superman was invented soon afterward, there is a chance. For more information on the original Secret Six movie see: "The Secret Six," www.moviediva.com, 2001-2. The movie, however, departed wildly from the real Secret Six story.

173 "Protests Island Prison: San Francisco Objects to Use of Alcatraz for Desperadoes," *The New York Times*, October 14, 1933, 32.

174 "City Would Like to Know Who Are 'Secret Seven,'" *The Washington Post*, Associated Press, March 3, 1935, B10.

175 For the crash, see: "Mayor Ruffu Killed with Three Others as Train Hits Auto," *The New York Times*, Associated Press, June 23, 1930, 1. For the chamber involvement and the charges of white slavery (prostitution), there are a number of references in early 1930, including: "Ruffu Refuses to Quit," *The New York Times*, January 30, 1930, 14; also "Larson Keeps Aloof in Atlantic City Vice," *The New York Times*, February 3, 1930, 17. For Ruffu's estate, see: "Ruffu Estate May Net $250,000," *The New York Times*, October 14, 1930, 9.

176 The victim, Mrs. Massie, identified her five assailants, all ethnically Japanese, but it wasn't clear if she was correct, and it appears her husband and mother in law had a hand in murdering one suspect. The Honolulu Chamber, not surprisingly in view of the importance of racial harmony in this mixed-race community, insisted that the overall incident wasn't a reflection on local racial relations. It offered a reward for evidence and its law and order committee worked to increase protection for the families of military personnel in the territory. See for example: Wallace B. Farrington, "Farrington Denies That Hawaii is Race Mad," *The New York Times*, January 15, 1932, 4; also Russell Owen, "Hawaii is Rent Over Massie Case," *The New York Times*, March 1, 1932, 7.

177 "Colored CCC Camp Protest is Ignored," *The Washington Post*, August 7, 1934, 9.

178 Read Lewis, "Registration of Aliens: Proposal of State Commerce Chamber Called Danger to Liberty," Letter to the Editor, *The New York Times*, January 8, 1931. This letter notes that the U.S. Chamber of Commerce had a much more liberal and fair attitude on this topic than had the New York Chamber. The letter also eviscerates the New York Chamber's wildly exaggerated claims on the number of illegal and deportable aliens.

179 "State Chamber Assailed by Jews," *The New York Times*, May 7, 1934, 7.

180 "State Chamber Assailed by Jews," *The New York Times*, May 7, 1934, 7.

181 "Sermon Scores Report: Wise Calls State Chamber a Group of 'Stuffed Shirts'," *The New York Times*, May 7, 1934, 7.

182 This organization changed its name from the Harlem Board of Commerce (sometimes called the Harlem Board of Trade or Harlem Chamber of Commerce) in 1933. See: "Harlem Group Changes Name," *The New York Times*, January 11, 1933, 13.

183 "Harlem Compact Gives Negroes Third of Jobs in Stores There," *The New York Times*, August 8, 1938, 1.

184 Mabel Dugan, "Woman – The New Force in Public Affairs," *NACOS 18th Annual Meeting: Readjustment, Reconstruction, Recovery* (Memphis: NACOS, October 23-26, 1932), 236-41.

185 Mabel Dugan, "Woman – The New Force in Public Affairs," *NACOS 18th Annual Meeting: Readjustment, Reconstruction, Recovery* (Memphis: NACOS, October 23-26, 1932), 236-41.

186 "Pastor Scores Chamber," *The New York Times*, Associated Press, March 23, 1931, 4.

187 "Rockaway Yields to the Shorts Fad," *The New York Times*, July 29, 1935, 17.

188 "Shirtless Men Bathers Face Aldermanic Ban," *The New York Times*, June 18, 1936, 24.

189 "Lost Lansing: Elton Shaw Promoted Temperance and Sunbathing," *Lansing Online News*, January 23, 2011. Votta calls the association the American Sunbathing Association, but it's referred to elsewhere as the International Nudists Association or the International Nudists Conference. Shaw's other work includes a book called *The Curse of Drink*.

190 "Church Denounces Easter 'Travesty'," *The New York Times*, April 6, 1935, 17.

191 "This Morning . . . With Shirley Povich," *The Washington Post*, April 1, 1936, 23.

192 The story, as taken from a Shirley Povich column, is as follows: At one time Ganzel had managed a team from Rochester that played an exhibition game with the St. Mary's Industrial School in Baltimore. A pitcher from St. Mary's held his team to five hits. Ganzel saw something in this "big, overgrown left-hander," and he recommended the young man to Jack Dunn, manager of the Baltimore Orioles. When Dunn later sold the young man, Babe Ruth, to the Boston Red Sox, Ganzel received some of the purchase money. This information comes from: "This Morning . . . With Shirley Povich," *The Washington Post*, March 1, 1939.

193 John Kieran, "Sports of the Times," *The New York Times*, December 30, 1931, 23.

194 "Ty Cobb, Sued for Divorce, Shocked by Wife's Action," *The Washington Post*, April 16, 1931, 1. His wife withdrew that suit but filed a few more, finally divorcing him in 1947.

195 "Geisha Girls Not Invited to Dance at Festival Here," *The Washington Post*, January 12, 1930, 13.

196 This source mentions that Shultz had the idea: "1939 Turkey Festival," Massanutten Musings, November 18, 2011, Blog of the Massanutten, Va., Regional Library. For the figure of 350,000 turkeys, see: "Turkey Festival Dates Arranged," *The Free-Lance Star* (Fredericksburg, Va.), July 12, 1939, 8. For the consultation with the Virginia State Chamber of Commerce and the protest of the Society for the Prevention of Cruelty to Animals, see: "Fete Heads Plan to Drop Turkeys With Parachutes," *The Washington Post*, Associated Press, July 7, 1939, 14. The *Post* article implies that this festival existed before 1939, but other sources differ. In the first year, turkeys were thrown from the First National Bank Building (see Massanutten Library source), despite the consultation about parachutes and SPCA fears, and so presumably the parachutes came in subsequent years. Several sources confirm that the birds were indeed dropped from the sky with parachutes in 1940 and/or 1941. This author will leave to future researchers to get the full story on the blimp-flung parachuting turkeys of Rockingham County.

197 "Rattlesnakes Taken as Tickets," *The Washington Post*, Associated Press, August 30, 1933, 5.

198 Anne Harding, "90 Years of Building a Better Dallas: The History of the Greater Dallas Chamber, 1909 to the Present," 5. This is a 15-page paper made available by the Greater Dallas Chamber in 1999.

199 "City's Fair Assured of Widespread Aid; Business is Elated," *The New York Times*, September 24, 1935, 1.

200 "Mayor to Mobilize All City for Fair," *The New York Times*, October 4, 1935, 23.

201 "Television Theatre Will Open Monday," *The New York Times*, April 5, 1930, 16. See also "Get Television Broadcast: Jersey City Radio Shops Hear and See Hague, Carroll and De Forest," *The New York Times*, April 8, 1930, 31. Additionally: C.E. Butterfield, "Theater Given Sound Talkies by Television," *St. Petersburg Times*, Associated Press, April 8, 1930, 1. For a more detailed description of what the vaunted "first" meant (not too much), see: Richard Koszarski, *Hollywood on the Hudson: Film and Television in New York From Griffith to Sarnoff* (Rutgers University Press, 2008), 419-21.

202 Kyle Crichton, "Will the Boosters Stay Mum?", *Scribners*, February 1932, 111-2.

203 Willard Hammer, "In Union There is Strength," *Nation's Business*, November 1935, 39-42.

204 Byron Darnton, "California Pulls in Her Adjectives," *The New York Times*, May 12, 1940, 115.

205 James M. Cain, "Paradise," *The American Mercury*, March 1933, 278.

206 James M. Cain, "Paradise," *The American Mercury*, March 1933, 278-9.

207 Elizabeth Tandy Shermer, *Sunbelt Capitalism: Phoenix and the Transformation of American Politics* (Philadelphia: University of Pennsylvania Press, 2013), 66. This page mentions Goldwater's involvement in the Thunderbirds; his activism in the chamber as a whole is mentioned in many parts of the book.

208 Elizabeth Tandy Shermer, *Sunbelt Capitalism: Phoenix and the Transformation of American Politics* (Philadelphia: University of Pennsylvania Press, 2013), 2.

209 Elizabeth Tandy Shermer, *Sunbelt Capitalism: Phoenix and the Transformation of American Politics* (Philadelphia: University of Pennsylvania Press, 2013), 274-6.

Notes

210 This section on Phoenix is deeply indebted to Shermer's book, *Sunbelt Capitalism*. While her political point of view is different from the author's, her conclusions as to the importance of an active chamber in promoting business expansion and community growth are almost identical to his. And her identification of the Phoenix Chamber leaders with government activism (despite their ideological bent in favor of small government) is right on the mark, and not far from chamber traditions dating back to 1768. Moreover, the politician-chamber booster alliance was at work in many places at this time. In Austin, the chamber forced the resignation of its anti-growth secretary and pushed for expansion-oriented policies, aided by another youngish politician, Congressman Lyndon Baines Johnson. See: Elizabeth Tandy Shermer, *Sunbelt Capitalism: Phoenix and the Transformation of American Politics* (Philadelphia: University of Pennsylvania Press, 2013), 61.

211 This recounting of the much-told BAWI story, apart from the discussion of what it eventually meant to chambers of commerce, comes primarily from a single, excellent source: James Cobb, *The Selling of the South: The Southern Crusade for Industrial Development, 1936-1980* (Baton Rouge: Louisiana State University Press, 1982). A shorter version of the story, drawing on Cobb but also on other sources, is a good place to start and was helpful to this author as well: Connie Lester, "Economic Development in the Thirties: Balance Agriculture with Industry," *Mississippi History Now*, an online publication of the Mississippi Historical Society:

http://mshistory.k12.ms.us/articles/224/economic-development-in-the-1930s-balance-agriculture-with-industry

212 While this Marion County story is well documented by modern commentators, it's important to realize that contemporary experts also found it interesting and that the chamber was not simply a creature of the mayor but had some energy of its own. See the contest award application to NACOS by the Marion County Chamber in 1931: W.C. Flanders, Secretary, Marion County Chamber of Commerce, Columbia, Mississippi, "Relief From One Crop System of Farming," *NACOS 17th Annual Meeting: Organization Responsibilities* (Toledo: NACOS, October 18-21, 1931), 295. A similar, longer article appeared in a Southern Commercial Secretaries Association annual report at about this time.

213 Samuel Engle Burr, "How Chambers Help Schools," *Nation's Business*, October 1930, 114-116. The quotation is on page 116.

214 "Dewey Hits Teachers' Pay Cuts," *The New York Times*, Associated Press, January 30, 1933, 4. A more extensive criticism of business interests by Dewey, also mentioning the U.S. Chamber, can be found here: "Charges Economy Menaces Schools," *The New York Times*, March 2, 1933, 18.

215 "History," Greater Tampa Chamber of Commerce Web site:

http://www.tampachamber.com/Ci_History.Asp

216 Mark Taylor Dalhouse, *An Island in the Lake of Fire: Bob Jones University, Fundamentalism and the Separatist Movement* (Athens, Georgia: University of Georgia Press, 1996), 47.

217 Frederick Forbes, "California in the Midst of University Row," *The New York Times,* March 9, 1931, E6. See also: Frederick Forbes, "California May Get Its Chain Colleges," *The New York Times*, April 10, 1932, E5.

218 Frederick Forbes, "California in the Midst of University Row," *The New York Times*, March 9, 1931, E6.

219 Westbrook Pegler, "Fair Enough: The First American Duce," *The Washington Post*, October 19, 1936.

220 L.H. Robbins, "The Triborough Bridge: A Vast Project," *The New York Times*, August 27, 1933, XX2.

221 L.H. Robbins, "The Triborough Bridge: A Vast Project," *The New York Times*, August 27, 1933, XX2.

222 "Smith Hails Moses as City Parks Head," *The New York Times*, January 19, 1934, 2.

223 "Mayor's Support for Moses Seen," *The New York Times*, January 18, 1935, 10.

224 "Moses is Attacked Over 'Unfit' Parks," *The New York Times*, April 6, 1935, 17.

225 "Californians Ask Bridge Loan Today," *The Washington Post*, Associated Press, September 27, 1932, 8.

226 "Backing is Sought for Bridge Plan," *The Washington Post*, February 20, 1930, 5.

227 "Trade Bodies Favor Memorial Parkway," *The Washington Post*, October 19, 1930, M16.

228 Among chambers' many activities connected with Skyline Drive was a successful push by the Charlottesville and Waynesboro chambers to get a reluctant landowner to let the road go through his property, creating a more elevated route that served the two communities better than the alternative. See: "Skyline Drive Offer by Scott Wins Approval," *The Washington Post*, December 4, 1934, 5.

229 "WPA Aids Boston Channel," *The New York Times*, Associated Press, December 30, 1935.

230 Charles Beard, "The Myth of Rugged American Individualism," *Harper's*, 1931. Issued as a separate pamphlet in 1932, published in 1932 by John Day Company, New York.

231 "Calls for Action in Housing Problem," *The New York Times*, March 22, 1931, RE2.

232 "A New Frontier," *The New York Times*, July 20, 1931, 15.

233 Joseph Platzker, "Broad Plan Urged for New Housing," *The New York Times*, July 9, 1933, RE10.

234 "10,000 Hear Mayor Say Unsafe Slums Will Be Wiped Out," *The New York Times*, April 9, 1934, 1.

235 "From the East Side," *The New York Times*, July 27, 1935, 12.

236 Report of the Committee on Highways and Bridges to the board of directors of the Pittsburgh Chamber of Commerce, approved by the board on December 14, 1933. This exhibit was connected with the minutes of the board meeting of the same date. The same report notes that Ickes's speech was in Baltimore on October 8, 1933.

237 It's important to note that the idea of a transcontinental highway was not unique to Ickes. Planners had thought of such roads at least since World War I, and young Dwight Eisenhower was impressed by the need for such a project when he took a convoy across the nation on the Lincoln Highway in 1919. Indeed, who didn't have such an idea? As one writer indicated in 1935, "The daydream of a wide, lonely, straight and stopless concrete *highway* is common to all Americans who have ever jammed on their brakes for a red light, or followed the tail light of a ten-ton truck on a narrow road, or been caught in Sunday traffic in the suburbs, or realized that their itinerary took them through the heart of Chicago." (Robert Littel, "Hypnotic Highway," *Today*, Volume V, 1935, 118.)

238 The group convened without Chamber President John Fisher, who had just got into hot water for anti-FDR remarks he made at a private dinner. See "NRA Head Out at Pittsburgh," *The Washington Post*, Associated Press, December 13, 1933, 5.

239 Minutes of the board of directors of the Pittsburgh Chamber of Commerce, December 14, 1933. The superhighway suggestion was Exhibit "B" and the slow lane suggestion was Exhibit "C." These minutes are kept at the Historical Society of Western Pennsylvania.

240 Edward Snodgrass, Jr., "Trans-Continental Super Highway Needed," *Greater Pittsburgh*, November 1934.

241 Minutes of the board of directors of the Pittsburgh Chamber of Commerce, March 14, 1935.

242 Reginald Cleveland, "A Super-Highway for America," *The New York Times*, November 10, 1935, XX1.

243 "Turnpike Gets Federal Funds," *The Pittsburgh Press*, United Press, July 30, 1938, 1.

244 "Turnpike Marks 60 Years of Service and Safe Travel," *Traveler*, December 2000, www.paturnpike.com.

245 "Tunnel Road Yields $168,037 in 3 Weeks," *Reading Eagle*, Associated Press, November 8, 1940, 13.

246 "The Log of Organized Business," *Nation's Business*, December 1922, 63.

247 Lincoln Steffens, *The Autobiography of Lincoln Steffens* (New York: Harcourt, Inc., 1931), 600-601.

248 "Sweet Briar to Hear Watson," *The New York Times*, January 8, 1938, 13. The article indicates that Watson has been involved with the ICC for 15 years.

249 Here at the Merchants' Association, Watson worked with the executive who was the grand old man of chamber management himself: S. Cristy Mead, the founding president of the National Association of Corporate Organization Secretaries and the top executive of the Merchants' Association since 1897.

250 Thomas Watson, Jr. with Peter Petre, *Father Son & Co.: My Life with IBM and Beyond* (New York: Bantam Books, 1990), 54.

251 "See Soviets' Doom in Stalin's Waste," *The New York Times*, August 18, 1931, 9.

252 "Home Town to Supply Funds for Miss Stephens," *The Washington Post*, Associated Press, July 9, 1936, X19.

253 "U.S. is Favored to Gain Major Honors in Berlin Olympics," *The New York Times*, July 26, 1936, S2.

254 "Owens is Honored in Columbus Fete," *The Washington Post*, August 29, 1936, X14.

255 "The Camera Overseas: Big U.S. Businessman Does His Duty in Berlin and Paris," *Life*, July 26, 1937, 68-9.

256 "Crisis Casts Cloud on World Chamber," *The New York Times*, June 30, 1937, 16. See also: Edwin Black, *IBM and the Holocaust: The Strategic Alliance Between Nazi Germany and America's Most Powerful Corporation* (New York: Three Rivers Press, a division of Random House, 2001), 132-3.

257 Thomas Watson, Jr. with Peter Petre, *Father Son & Co.: My Life with IBM and Beyond* (New York: Bantam Books, 1990), 54-5.

258 Edwin Black, *IBM and the Holocaust: The Strategic Alliance Between Nazi Germany and America's Most Powerful Corporation* (New York: Three Rivers Press, a division of Random House, 2001), 127.

259 Edwin Black, *IBM and the Holocaust: The Strategic Alliance Between Nazi Germany and America's Most Powerful Corporation* (New York: Three Rivers Press, a division of Random House, 2001), 176.

260 Edwin Black, *IBM and the Holocaust: The Strategic Alliance Between Nazi Germany and America's Most Powerful Corporation* (New York: Three Rivers Press, a division of Random House, 2001), 214.

261 "David Kirschbaum Ends Life with Chain," *The New York Times*, June 11, 1938, 32.

262 For the mummy story: "Fair Not Courting a 'Chief Speaker,'" *The New York Times*, May 7, 1940, 27. For the fair ladies of the fairs story: Meyer Berger, "At the Fair," *The New York Times*, May 23, 1940, 24.

263 "Czecho-Slovakia at the Fair," *The New York Times*, March 22, 1939, 19.

264 Erik Larson, *In the Garden of Beasts* (New York: Broadway Paperbacks, 2011), 147-151. The speech was on Columbus Day: October 12, 1933.

265 "U.S. Business Aide Arrested in Soviet," *The New York Times*, December 6, 1937, 6.

266 "American Chamber in Moscow Closes," *The New York Times*, February 9, 1940, 7.

267 S.T. Williamson, "Why Britain Slept While Hitler Prepared for War," *The New York Times*, August 11, 1940, 70.

268 "Says Entry in War Would Ruin Nation," *The New York Times*, May 19, 1940, 10.

269 "Prentis Condemns Draft of Wealth," *The New York Times*, December 13, 1940, 19.

270 "Hitler May Strike Soon, Says Lothian," *The New York Times*, April 20, 1940, 6.

271 "Chamber Favors Armed Aid by U.S.," *The New York Times*, June 7, 1940, 10.

272 "Shoe Imports May be Stopped," *The Southeast Missourian*, Associated Press, March 16, 1939, 1.

Notes

273 This quotation of a New York Chamber report comes from this source: "City as Style Hub Urged by Chamber," *The New York Times*, September 30, 1940, 16.

274 James M. Smallwood, *Urban Builder: The Life and Times of Stanley Draper* (Norman, OK: The University of Oklahoma Press, 1977), 99-102. All the information in this paragraph comes from this source.

275 Bill Waller, *History of the Tulsa Metro Chamber* (Tulsa: Tulsa Metro Chamber, 2003), 45-47.

276 Don Woodward and Joel Campbell, *Common Ground: 100 Years of the Salt Lake Chamber* (Montgomery, Alabama: Community Communications Inc., 2003), 97.

277 Charles Hurd, "St. Louis Industry Takes Cue From '18," *The New York Times*, February 27, 1941, 14.

278 Betty Burnett, "For 173 Years, a Force for Progress: RCGA History, Part II," *St. Louis Commerce*, May-June 2009, 104-5.

279 Charles Hurd, "St. Louis Industry Takes Cue From '18," *The New York Times*, February 27, 1941, 14.

280 Judith Kennedy, *Bicentennial History, 1801-2001* (Philadelphia: Greater Philadelphia Chamber of Commerce, 2000), 23.

281 This information came chiefly from a timeline of the Jacksonville Regional Chamber of Commerce web site in approximately 2008 but no longer is there. The exact wording from the web site (except for this author's "*sic*") was as follows: "1937 - formed the Military Base Committee, which lead [*sic*] to the creation of NAS Jacksonville in 1939."

282 Anne Harding, "90 Years of Building a Better Dallas: The History of the Greater Dallas Chamber, 1909 to the Present," 6. This is a 15-page paper made available by the Greater Dallas Chamber in 1999.

283 Paul Shafer, "Local Politics – Menace to Defense," *The American Mercury*, May 1940, 54-59.

284 Paul Shafer, "Local Politics – Menace to Defense," *The American Mercury*, May 1940, 54-59.

285 Ben Lawshe, Manager, Commercial Organization Division, Chamber of Commerce of the United States, "Gearing into the National Defense Program," *NACOS 26th Annual Meeting: Meeting the Needs of the Community* (Boston: NACOS, October 20-23, 1940), 48. Lawshe's paper begins on page 46. Donald Nelson, whom Lawshe quoted at some length, had this full title: Coordinator of Purchases, National Defense Advisory Commission.

286 "Knox Calls Fleet World's Greatest," *The New York Times*, Associated Press, September 15, 1940, 33.

Local Chambers in a Global War (1941-1945)

1 "Army 'Over Hump,' Marshall Asserts," *The New York Times*, April 23, 1941, 1.

2 A triangular division of infantry, for example, would include three separate regiments under one divisional command.

3 "'Business as Usual' Impossible Under Arms Program, U.S. Chamber Told," *The Washington Post*, April 30, 1941, 1. See also W.H. Lawrence, "Stark Hints at Aid for British Fleet," *The New York Times*, April 30, 1941, 1.

4 Charles Hurd, "Fort Bragg Made Giant Cantonment," *The New York Times*, February 13, 1941, 10.

5 Frank Fogarty, "The Role of the Chamber of Commerce in National Defense," *NACOS 27th Annual Meeting: "Meeting the Problems of the Emergency* (Los Angeles: NACOS, October 19-22, 1941), 210-216. The quote is on page 211.

6 "Alexandria Area Will See Army Maneuvers," *NACOS News*, March 1940, 3.

7 Leo M. Cherne, "Your Business and the Unlimited Emergency," *Nation's Business*, July 1941. This very lengthy article begins on page 17 but the mention of the more than 700 defense committees is on page 54. Their activities are evident from a wide variety of other sources. It's worth noting that Cherne first mentions trade associations and gives them greater weight than the local chambers of commerce.

8 "Chamber Finds His Dream Girl," *The Spokesman-Review*, October 16, 1941, 2.

9 Alfred Friendly, "Priorities Force a Lively Town to Take a Back Seat," *The Washington Post*, September 24, 1941.

10 Leverett Lyon, "Service to Industries in War Production," *NACOS War Conference: The War Work of Chambers of Commerce*" (Detroit: NACOS, October 18-21, 1942), 68-71. The quote is on page 71.

11 Frank Green, "The MAP of the Nation's Business," *Nation's Business*, August 1941, 30.

12 For the overcrowding of Los Angeles area airports: James Bassett, "Seek More Air Fields," *The New York Times*, February 2, 1941, XX5. For the 5,000 workers per month figure: Robert O. Foote, "A New Migration Toward the West," *The New York Times*, July 20, 1941, E8.

13 Edward T. Folliard, "Krivisky's Dramatic Career Comes to Shadowy End Here," *The Washington Post*, February 16, 1941, B6.

14 "Laborite Says Attack on Russia Probably Will Avert British Defeat," *The Washington Post*, June 26, 1941, 11.

15 "U.S. Building Site Up Today," *The Washington Post*, August 8, 1941, 4.

16 Herbert Houston, "Moves for Organized World," Letter to the Editor, *The New York Times*, October 20, 1943, 20.

17 Ruth Cranston, "Myths of the League Battle," *The New York Times*, August 20, 1944, SM14. See column 1 in the continuation of the article, on SM37.

18 Urges U.S. Assume World Leadership," *The New York Times*, May 21, 1943, 29. Quotation is on the continuation page, 34.

19 As mentioned in the acknowledgments, Walter Russell Mead is the author's elder brother.

20 "Calls on Business to Fight War Steps," *The New York Times*, January 9, 1941, 19.

21 Merle Thorpe, "National Defense – For War? For Peace?", *Nation's Business*, February 1941, 13.

22 Merle Thorpe, "If Only," *Nation's Business*, April 1941, 13.

23 Merle Thorpe, "A Liberty Loan Payable in Full," *Nation's Business*, June 1941, 13.

24 Merle Thorpe, "The Job is War, Not Reform," *Nation's Business*, March 1942, 13.

25 Myrtle Shaw Lord, *A Sacramento Saga: Fifty Years of Achievement – Chamber of Commerce Leadership* (Sacramento: Sacramento Chamber of Commerce, 1946), 331, 336.

26 Fred Setterberg, editor, *America: True Stories of Life on the Road* (Sebastopol, California: Travelers' Tales, 1999), 335. Yreka is an inland town in northern California and is not the same as the larger coastal community of Eureka.

27 "Retires as Secretary of Merchants' Group," *The New York Times*, January 7, 1941, 21.

28 "Merchants Association Becomes C.I.A. Today," *The New York Times*, August 27, 1941, 33.

29 NAMD, later called the National Association of Membership Development, would exist until 2003, when it became a part of the American Chamber of Commerce Executives (now the Association of Chamber of Commerce Executives).

30 Jeff Davis and Al Eufrasio, *Weird Washington: Your Travel Guide to Washington's Local Legends and Best Kept Secrets* (Toronto: Sterling Publishing Co., 2008), 152.

31 "Atlantic City Welcomes 43 Beauty Queens," *The Washington Post*, Associated Press, September 2, 1941, 15.

32 "Victim of Own Crusade," *The New York Times*, July 29, 1941, 17.

33 Jeff Burbank, *Las Vegas Babylon: True Tales of Glitter, Glamour and Greed* (London: Robson Books, 2006), 29.

34 Jeff Burbank, *Las Vegas Babylon: True Tales of Glitter, Glamour and Greed* (London: Robson Books, 2006), 48-9.

35 Hedda Hopper, "Hedda Hopper," *The Washington Post*, January 26, 1941.

36 Marsha Henry Goff, *The Lawrence Chamber of Commerce, 1878-2000* (Lawrence, Kan.: Lawrence Chamber of Commerce, 2000), 9.

37 Louella Parsons, "Louella O. Parsons' Close-Ups and Long-Shots of the Motion Picture Scene," *The Washington Post*, January 31, 1941. Fibber's real name was James Jordan. For that fact and the Wistful Vista connection, see: *NACOS News*, June 1942, 1.

38 Louis B. Mayer, "Wednesday Morning Remarks," *NACOS 27th Annual Meeting: "Meeting the Problems of the Emergency* (Los Angeles: NACOS, October 19-22, 1941), 242-44.

39 "Short Urges Hawaii to Organize Defense," *The New York Times*, United Press, April 8, 1941, 13.

40 "Knox Tells Japan We Won't Budge," *The New York Times*, November 12, 1941, 2.

41 William Robert Faith, *Bob Hope: A Life in Comedy* (Cambridge, Mass.: Perseus Books, 2003), 129.

42 John Hamilton, Secretary, Chamber of Commerce, Honolulu, Hawaii, "Chamber Responsible for Saving Many Lives During Pearl Harbor Attack," *NACOS News*, January 15, 1943, 1. Bold-print emphasis is that of the author or of *NACOS News*.

43 John Hamilton, Secretary, Chamber of Commerce, Honolulu, Hawaii, "Chamber Responsible for Saving Many Lives During Pearl Harbor Attack," *NACOS News*, January 15, 1943, 1, 10.

44 The holdout was Rep. Jeannette Rankin (D-Montana), a pacifist.

45 "Business Men's Organizations and the War Program," *Nation's Business*, January 1942, 33.

46 "All-Out Business Pledge," *The New York Times*, December 11, 1941, 34.

47 Morton Grodzins, *Americans Betrayed: Politics and the Japanese Evacuation* (Chicago: University of Chicago Press, 1949).

48 Jacobus tenBroek, Edward Barnhart, and Floyd Matson, *Prejudice, War, and the Constitution: Causes and Consequences of the Evacuation of the Japanese Americans in World War II* (Berkeley, Calif.: University of California Press, 1954).

49 Jacobus tenBroek, Edward Barnhart, and Floyd Matson, *Prejudice, War, and the Constitution: Causes and Consequences of the Evacuation of the Japanese Americans in World War II* (Berkeley, Calif.: University of California Press, 1954), 374. Many other sources also cite this quotation. The LA Chamber, ironically, had another "first" related to Japan. Apparently it had been the first organization to send a representative to meet the "Last Emperor," Pu Yi. This gentleman was the puppet who was in nominal charge of the area that the Japanese had invaded in 1931, Manchukuo. Pu Yi was installed by the Japanese in 1932. For the Pu Yi meeting, see the very brief mention in this article: Ben Bruce Blakeney, "Pu Yi," *Life*, July 16, 1945, 78-86. The mention is on page 85.

50 Telephone conversation, DeWitt with Gullion, December 26, 1941, WDC-CAD 311.3 Tel Convs (DeWitt, 42-43). This conversation (and this citation of that conversation) comes from the following source: Martin Blumenson et al., *Command Decisions* (Washington, D.C.: U.S. Government Printing Office, 1960), 128.

51 Telephone conversation, DeWitt with Gullion, January 24, 1942, WDC-CAD 311.3 Tel Convs (DeWitt, 42-43). This conversation (and this citation of that conversation) comes from the following source: Martin Blumenson et al., *Command Decisions* (Washington, D.C.: U.S. Government Printing Office, 1960), 132.

52 Greg Robinson, *By Order of the President: FDR and the Internment of Japanese Americans* (Cambridge, Mass.: Harvard University Press, 2003), 97.

53 Morton Grodzins, *Americans Betrayed: Politics and the Japanese Evacuation* (Chicago: University of Chicago Press, 1949), 68-69.

54 Morton Grodzins, "Interview with James [sic] Read, Managing Director, Los Angeles Chamber of Commerce, July 20, 1943." From the Japanese-American Evacuation and Resettlement Records [ca. 1941-1953], Collection No.: BANC MSS 67/14/c, Reel 8, BNEG: 1858.

55 Morton Grodzins, "Interview with James [sic] Read, Managing Director, Los Angeles Chamber of Commerce, July 20, 1943." From the Japanese-American Evacuation and Resettlement Records [ca. 1941-1953], Collection No.: BANC MSS 67/14/c, Reel 8, BNEG: 1858.

56 Morton Grodzins, "Interview with James [*sic*] Read, Managing Director, Los Angeles Chamber of Commerce, July 20, 1943." From the Japanese-American Evacuation and Resettlement Records [ca. 1941-1953], Collection No.: BANC MSS 67/14/c, Reel 8, BNEG: 1858.

57 Morton Grodzins, "Interview with James [*sic*] Read, Managing Director, Los Angeles Chamber of Commerce, July 20, 1943." From the Japanese-American Evacuation and Resettlement Records [ca. 1941-1953], Collection No.: BANC MSS 67/14/c, Reel 8, BNEG: 1858. See the final page of the Read interview. Alexander Meiklejohn, "an old teacher of McCloys," said John McCloy admitted the Congressional and public-opinion influence on his department's policy on the Japanese.

58 Morton Grodzins, "Interview with James Ingebretsen," October 14, 1942, Report #14, pp. 3-4. From the Japanese-American Evacuation and Resettlement Records [ca. 1941-1953], Collection No.: BANC MSS 67/14/c, Reel 4, BNEG: 1854.

59 Morton Grodzins, *Americans Betrayed: Politics and the Japanese Evacuation* (Chicago: University of Chicago Press, 1949), 69.

60 Jacobus tenBroek, Edward Barnhart, and Floyd Matson, *Prejudice, War, and the Constitution: Causes and Consequences of the Evacuation of the Japanese Americans in World War II* (Berkeley, Calif.: University of California Press, 1954), 4.

61 One of Grodzins's critics at JERS scrawled something interesting next to a remark in Grodzins's notes. The commenter wrote that Grodzins didn't include in Grodzins's book an important remark by Leonard Read, in which (as we have quoted above in the body of this book) Read said he thought the Japanese-Americans were good for the local economy and should be welcomed back at the appropriate time. So much for Grodzins's theory that greed was behind the clamor for internment. The JERS commenter makes the point in two separate places (in handwritten form, on top of Grodzins's typewritten interview notes) that Grodzins passed over this vital quote. The implication is that Grodzins discarded evidence that did not prove his case (that greed was behind the clamor for internment).

62 Greg Robinson, *By Order of the President: FDR and the Internment of Japanese Americans* (Cambridge, Mass.: Harvard University Press, 2003), 90.

63 Mary Sennholz, *Leonard E. Read: Philosopher of Freedom* (Irvington-on-Hudson, N.Y.: Foundation for Economic Education, 1993), 20.

64 Mary Sennholz, *Leonard E. Read: Philosopher of Freedom* (Irvington-on-Hudson, N.Y.: Foundation for Economic Education, 1993), 6-42.

65 Mary Sennholz, *Leonard E. Read: Philosopher of Freedom* (Irvington-on-Hudson, N.Y.: Foundation for Economic Education, 1993), 43-49.

66 Mary Sennholz, *Leonard E. Read: Philosopher of Freedom* (Irvington-on-Hudson, N.Y.: Foundation for Economic Education, 1993), 59.

67 Gerald D. Nash, *The American West Transformed: The Impact of the Second World War* (Bloomington, Ind.: Indiana University Press, 1985), 7-8.

68 Charles Sims, *Sow Your Fallow Ground* (Trafford Publishing, 2012), 19.

69 Leonard Read, Letter "To the Senators and Congressmen of Washington, Oregon and California," February 2, 1942. From the Japanese-American Evacuation and Resettlement Records [ca. 1941-1953], Collection No.: BANC MSS 67/14/c, Reel 4, BNEG: 1854.

70 Thomas Nixon Carver, "How Can There Be Full Employment After the War?" from the *Economic Sentinel*, April 1945. Cover indicates the paper was "Prepared for the Los Angeles Chamber of Commerce." Excerpts from this paper are reprinted in: David M. Levy, Sandra J. Peart, and Margaret Albert, "Economic Liberals as Quasi-Public Intellectuals: The Democratic Dimension," from *Documents on Government and the Economy*, edited by Marianne Johnson (Bingley, U.K.: Emerald Group Publishing Company, 2012). The quote is on page 27 of this book.

71 *Intelligence Activities and the Rights of Americans, Book II: Final Report of the Select Committee to Study Governmental Operations with Respect to Intelligence Activities*, April 26, 1976 (Washington: U.S. Government Printing Office, 1976). This is better known as the Church Committee report. Under C. Excessive Use of Intrusive Techniques, a subsection called D. Mail Opening, Subfinding (c), indicates:

The application of the "national security" rationale to cases lacking a substantial national security basis has been most apparent in the area of warrantless electronic surveillance. Indeed, the unjustified use of wiretaps and bugs under this and related labels has a long history. Among the wiretaps approved by Attorney General Francis Biddle under the standard of "persons suspected of subversive activities," for example, was one on the Los Angeles Chamber of Commerce in 1941. 108 This was approved in spite of his comment to J. Edgar Hoover that the target organization had "no record of espionage at this time." 109

Both footnotes, 108 and 109, refer to a memorandum from Attorney General Francis Biddle to J. Edgar Hoover, November 19, 1941.

72 At this time, such wiretaps were easier to obtain than they are today, and President Roosevelt seemed to find the relatively new process of wiretapping useful but also, at least in one case, amusing. After J. Edgar Hoover's FBI had been caught wiretapping labor leader Harry Bridges, and Hoover was publicly embarrassed for being responsible, Hoover presented the situation to President Roosevelt. Then FDR laughed, slapped the FBI chief on the back, and said, "By ___, Edgar, that's the first time you've been caught with your pants down!" See George Lardner, "FBI Wiretap Use Laid to Presidents," *The Washington Post*, May 10, 1976, 1, 4.

73 There is a good amount of material on Ingebretsen's spiritual awakening, including his own account, *Apprentice to the Dawn: A Spiritual Memoir*. A good capsule biography of him hits some of the main points: "Historical Note" from "Guide to the James C. Ingebretsen Papers," Northwest Digital Archives, nwda.orbiscascade.org.

74 A book with extraordinary insights and research into the roots of Goldwater Republicanism and the Reagan Revolution describes Read, Mullendore, and other anti-New Deal activists: Kim Phillips-Fein, *Invisible Hands: The Businessmen's Crusade Against the New Deal* (New York: W.W. Norton and Co., 2010).

75 Read could be sharply critical of the Roosevelt Administration, and he brought in ultraright friends such as W.C. Mullendore and Thomas Nixon Carver to address NACOS executives and his own members. But he also saw the captivating, inspiring side of freedom and expressed it well. For example, in the NACOS convention of 1943, he reminded his peers of Britain's economic agonies after the Napoleonic Wars and what brought the country out of its woes: "The businessmen of Manchester under the leadership of two economic thinkers, Cobden and Bright, and operating through the Manchester Chamber of Commerce, were the initiators of a freedom movement." Their persistent efforts led to economic liberalization such that: "Within a few years England entered into the most prosperous period of her long history." (See: Leonard Read, "Keynote Address," *NACOS Second War Conference: Home Front Battles of Chambers of Commerce* (Pittsburgh: NACOS, October 24-27, 1943), 43-50. The quote is on page 48.

76 This theme may have been a conscious echo of the "Get it Done" campaign of the Kansas City Chamber of Commerce in the early 1920s. The earlier effort began after people noted a number of unfinished projects around town, and the chorus erupted, "Let's get it done." The Kansas City campaign enabled the chamber and the community to finish many items on their list. See: "The Log of Organized Business," *Nation's Business*, March 1921, 59.

77 John Chamberlain, "Eric Johnston," *Life* magazine, June 19, 1944, 96-108. The discussion of the coup is on page 105.

78 Ralph Edgerton, "The Eric Johnston Story," *The Pacific Northwesterner*, Vol. 33, No. 4 (Fall 1989), 55-62. The version cited was edited by David Wilma and appears as Essay 7339 on HistoryLink.org: The Free Online Encyclopedia of Washington State History.

79 John Chamberlain, "Eric Johnston," *Life* magazine, June 19, 1944, 96-108. The Manchurian whack on the head is on page 102.

80 Ralph Edgerton, "The Eric Johnston Story," *The Pacific Northwesterner*, Vol. 33, No. 4 (Fall 1989), 55-62. The version cited was edited by David Wilma and appears as Essay 7339 on HistoryLink.org: The Free Online Encyclopedia of Washington State History.

81 "Eric Johnston Finishes Work at Chamber Helm," *Spokane Daily Chronicle*, March 1, 1933, 33.

82 John Chamberlain, "Eric Johnston," *Life* magazine, June 19, 1944, 96-108. The tally of editorials is on page 108.

83 William Shurtleff and Akiko Aoyagi, *Henry Ford and His Researchers: History of Their Work With Soybeans, Soyfoods and Chemurgy, 1928-2011* (Soyinfo Center, 2011), 256.

84 John Chamberlain, "Eric Johnston," *Life* magazine, June 19, 1944, 96-108. The quote is on page 98.

85 John Chamberlain, "Eric Johnston," *Life* magazine, June 19, 1944, 96-108. The item is on page 96.

86 Louis Stark, "Labor, Employers Meeting for Unity," *The New York Times*, July 24, 1942, 7.

87 Drew Pearson, "The Washington Merry-Go-Round," *The Washington Post*, August 21, 1942, 12.

88 John Chamberlain, "Eric Johnston," *Life* magazine, June 19, 1944, 96-108. The quote is on page 106.

89 Paul Hodges, "Let's Get It Done," *Nation's Business*, June 1942, 33-48. The quote is on page 46.

90 "Eric Johnston Dies; Aided Three Presidents," *The New York Times*, August 23, 1963, 1.

91 John Chamberlain, "Eric Johnston," *Life* magazine, June 19, 1944, 96-108. The quote is on page 108.

92 The suggestion for football to be added back into the Tournament of Roses festivities (they had been discontinued in 1902) had been made at a dinner at the Pasadena Chamber of Commerce in 1915. Speaker Ralph Glaze, the coach at the University of Southern California, made the proposal. See: Mark F. Bernstein: *Football: The Ivy League Origins of an American Obsession* (Philadelphia: University of Pennsylvania Press, 2001), 104-5.

93 For the Durham information, see: Hal Twitty, "Durham, With 60,000 Population, Prepares to Care for Almost That Number at Bowl Game," *Pittsburgh Press*, United Press, December 16, 1941, 29. For Southern Pines, see: "Oregon State Gridders Take a Lesson – in Golf," *The Washington Post*, Associated Press, December 29, 1941, 16.

94 "'Merciless' Bombings Predicted For Capital Within 6 Months," *The Washington Post*, February 21, 1942, 1.

95 Charles Mathis, "Wildwood, N.J.," *Billboard*, December 26, 1942, 40.

96 "Coney Plans a Dimout Curtain 18 Feet High and 14 Blocks Long," *The New York Times*, July 6, 1942, 1.

97 "Moses Rules Out Coney Light Shield," *The New York Times*, July 7, 1942, 21.

98 Dismayed at the pain that gas rationing would cause the local oil industry, the Tulsa Chamber of Commerce attempted to stir up oil-country opposition to gas rationing. But soon it bowed to the inevitable and to its patriotic duty to comply with the restrictions. See: Bill Waller, *History of the Tulsa Metro Chamber* (Tulsa: Tulsa Metro Chamber, 2003), 50-51.

99 Advertisement, "Ocean City, Md.," *The Washington Post*, July 2, 1944, S5.

100 "Bob Run Closed for Year," *The New York Times*, February 4, 1943, 30.

101 For New York and a report on its regional population and wealth by the Commerce and Industry Association of New York, see: "40,395,435 Persons Live Near This City," *The New York Times*, August 2, 1942, 40. For the Atlantic City Chamber of Commerce dinner where its rosy wartime tourism future was predicted, see: "Travel in Great Smokies Far Ahead of Last Year," *The Washington Post*, February 22, 1942, S9. For Ocean City, Md., see: "Trek Begins to Ocean City, Md.," *The Washington Post*, May 31, 1942, L9.

102 "Travel Bureaus Given Data on Sarasota," *The Washington Post*, October 25, 1942, L10.

103 "Atlantic City is Hopeful," *The New York Times*, June 20, 1943, 18.

104 "Hits at Army Hotel Plan," *The New York Times*, August 4, 1944, 8.

105 "Change in WAAC Plans Leaves Room for Daytona Guests," *The Washington Post*, December 27, 1942, L6.

106 "Community Hit in Child Discussion," *The Washington Post*, May 14, 1943, B1.

Notes

107 "Phoenix Ousts City Officials in War on Vice," *Sarasota Herald-Tribune*, Associated Press, December 17, 1942, 2.

108 Agnes Meyer, "Army Town Rots Under Layers of Vice and Greed," *The Washington Post*, April 18, 1943, B1.

109 Agnes Meyer, "Problem in Wilmington Is to Get Something to Eat," *The Washington Post*, April 30, 1943, 15.

110 "West Coast Farms Appeal for Labor," *The New York Times*, June 21, 1942, F5.

111 "Chamber Opens Drive to Ban Return of Japs for Duration," *Los Angeles Times*, April 23, 1943, A1.

112 Fred McCargar, Secretary, Salinas Chamber of Commerce, "Japanese Internees," Letter to the Editor, *The Washington Post*, July 3, 1943, 6.

113 Clarence L. Hodge and Peggy Ferris, *Building Honolulu: A Century of Community Service* (Honolulu: Chamber of Commerce of Honolulu, 1950), 55.

114 Clarence L. Hodge and Peggy Ferris, *Building Honolulu: A Century of Community Service* (Honolulu: Chamber of Commerce of Honolulu, 1950), 55. This source also mentions that the 100th was taken to basic training in Wisconsin by Lieutenant Colonel Farrant L. Turner. He would become the president of the Honolulu Chamber in 1951. The 442nd was featured in a 1951 movie starring Van Johnson and including several veterans of the unit, *Go for Broke*.

115 "New Britain, Conn., Salutes," *The New York Times*, Associated Press, December 18, 1943, 2.

116 "Famous Mustache to Be First Casualty as Charlie Chaplin Becomes 'Lady Killer'," *The New York Times*, October 16, 1942, 21.

117 Leonard Lyons, "Broadway Bulletins," *The Washington Post*, November 20, 1943, B6. Lyons also recounts here that on a different room of the Stork Club, another person who was present who had something to do with publicizing Oklahoma. It was John Steinbeck, the author of *The Grapes of Wrath*.

118 Caption to AP wirephoto, *The Washington Post*, October 3, 1942, 7.

119 Thomas Brady, "Studio Sales Plans Again in Flux," *The New York Times*, August 23, 1942, X3. There is also a much briefer mention in: Leonard Lyons, "Loose-Leaf Notebook," *The Washington Post*, July 2, 1942, 23. Hitchcock would return to the area to film *The Birds* in 1963.

120 Randy Roberts and James S. Olson, *John Wayne: American* (First Bison Books, 1997), 333-4.

121 Another cultural figure who made a connection to chambers in this period, but who seemed to be looking past them, was the poet Wallace Stevens. This man was politically conservative and had been a vice president of Hartford Accident and Indemnity Company. But he was no conformist: he married a woman his parents considered lower class and in 1940 he broke his hand while slugging Ernest Hemingway in Key West. Two years later, Stevens famously wrote that poets need to address their work "not to a chamber of commerce but to a gallery of one's own." See: Wallace Stevens, "The Noble Rider and the Sound of Words," reprinted in *Toward the Open Field: Poets on the Art of Poetry: 1800-1950*, edited by Melissa Kwasny (Middletown, Conn.: Wesleyan University Press, 2004), 328.

122 Thomas Swift, "St. Louis Rushes War Production," *The New York Times*, February 8, 1942, 1.

123 "Mayor of St. Louis, Others Die in Glider's Plunge," *The New York Times*, August 2, 1943, 1.

124 Mark Kelly, *A Powerful Presence: The Birmingham Regional Chamber of Commerce and the History of Birmingham* (Birmingham, Ala.: Birmingham Regional Chamber of Commerce, 2008), 55.

125 Mark Kelly, *A Powerful Presence: The Birmingham Regional Chamber of Commerce and the History of Birmingham* (Birmingham, Ala.: Birmingham Regional Chamber of Commerce, 2008), 55-56. For a description of the employment program, also called simply the "Birmingham Plan," see "Scratchpaddings," *The Rotarian*, April 1944, 49. The *Rotarian* article mentions the 35 interested chambers. See also: James F. King, "Current Benefits Set Outline for Future," *The Washington Post*, February 27, 1944, B3.

126 Don Woodward and Joel Campbell, *Common Ground: 100 Years of the Salt Lake Chamber* (Montgomery, Alabama: Community Communications Inc., 2003), 97.

127 James M. Smallwood, *Urban Builder: The Life and Times of Stanley Draper* (Norman, OK: The University of Oklahoma Press, 1977), 103-5.

128 "Business Urges Billion More Tax," *The New York Times*, Associated Press, August 16, 1941, 8.

129 "Sales Taxes Or - ", *The Washington Post*, April 21, 1942, 8.

130 Dennis J. Ventry Jr. and Joseph J. Thorndike, "The Plan That Slogans Built: The Tax Revenue Act of 1943," Tax History Project, Tax Analysts, www.taxhistory.org, September 1, 1997. This article is a good summary of the various threads of policy and ideas that resulted in the passage of the Tax Revenue Act of 1943.

131 "Ruml Plan Backed by State Chamber," *The New York Times*, September 11, 1942, 11.

132 "Study of Post-War Problems Under Way," *Activities of the Indianapolis Chamber of Commerce*, Volume 57, January 1942, No. 12, page 1.

133 Merryle S. Rukeyser, "The Outlook: Problem of Skilled Arms Workers From Enlisting Grows in Industrial Areas," *The Washington Post*, February 4, 1942, 23. The article is datelined February 2.

134 "100 Agencies Draft Post-War Plans," *The New York Times*, April 6, 1942, 23.

135 "Offer Post-War Program," *The New York Times*, June 20, 1942, 4.

136 "U.S. Chamber Sees Postwar Buying Rush," *The Washington Post*, August 9, 1942, C7.

137 Much was written about this high-profile committee during World War II. A relatively early and helpful article is the following: Claude A. Jagger, "Plan Mapped to Provide Postwar Jobs," *The Washington Post*, January 2, 1943, 1.

138 Hoffman helped rescue Studebaker during the 1930s but left the company from 1948 to 1953 (handling Marshall Plan aid to Europe and then heading the Ford Foundation). By the time he returned to the firm in 1953, it was seriously troubled and, despite a merger with Packard Company in 1954, was close to expiring in 1956. At that time the Eisenhower Administration placed it in Curtiss-Wright, a stronger company. But the cars couldn't compete with Detroit's Big Three and the last Studebaker rolled off a Canadian assembly line in 1966. (This footnote is drawn from Wikipedia articles on Paul Hoffman and on Studebaker.)

139 Lawrence Davies, "'Work-Pile' Scheme Pushed on Coast," *The New York Times*, July 4, 1943, S7. Note how the U.S. Department of Commerce adopted the plan, suggesting it for hundreds of communities: "Local Job Planning Seen Post-War Aid," *The New York Times*, September 13, 1943, 27. And for the San Francisco Chamber's proud perspective on the idea, see: Ernest Ingold, "San Francisco: No. 1 Work Pile City," *The Rotarian*, November 1943, 8-10.

140 Seldon Menefee, "America at War: Pacific Rim Movement," *The Washington Post*, September 14, 1944, 9.

141 Seldon Menefee, "America at War: Pacific Rim Movement," *The Washington Post*, September 14, 1944, 9.

142 Julia Beeson, "Planting Roots and Sowing Green," *San Diego Magazine*, March 2006, 85-89. See the timeline on page 87. The 1944 item also indicates that in the late 1940s, the community began dredging Mission Bay Park to create "the largest man-made aquatic park in the country."

143 Ann Reed Burns, "How Does Boom End? Portland Soon to See," *The Washington Post*, April 1, 1945, B6.

144 General Dwight Eisenhower apparently said this after the D-Day invasion, but also on other occasions. He attributed this quote to German Field Marshal Helmuth von Moltke, winner of the Franco-Prussian War.

145 "Our Poor Schools," *Kiplinger Magazine*, September 1948, 5-11. See p. 11.

146 "Postwar Training Asked by Chamber," *The New York Times*, July 29, 1943, 21.

147 Trinity University Web site: http://web.trinity.edu/x836.xml

148 Marguerite Johnston, *Houston: The Unknown City, 1836-1946* (Texas A&M University Press, 1991), 361.

149 Marguerite Johnston, *Houston: The Unknown City, 1836-1946* (Texas A&M University Press, 1991), 361.

150 Anne Harding, "90 Years of Building a Better Dallas: The History of the Greater Dallas Chamber, 1909 to the Present," 6. This is a 15-page paper made available by the Greater Dallas Chamber in 1999.

151 University of Texas Southwestern Medical Center Web site:

http://www.utsouthwestern.edu/utsw/cda/dept353744/files/609082.html

152 Mark Kelly, A Powerful Presence: *The Birmingham Regional Chamber of Commerce and the History of Birmingham* (Birmingham, Ala.: Birmingham Regional Chamber of Commerce, 2008), 56.

153 Mark Kelly, A Powerful Presence: *The Birmingham Regional Chamber of Commerce and the History of Birmingham* (Birmingham, Ala.: Birmingham Regional Chamber of Commerce, 2008), 56

154 Historian David Kennedy describes the story as "rambling and perplexing." See: David M. Kennedy, *Freedom From Fear: The American People in Depression and War, 1929-1945* (New York: Oxford University Press, 1999), 804. On the other hand, the Secretary of State at the time, Edward Stettinius, found the story to the point and helpful toward negotiations. (See the note below for his treatment of the story.) Stettinius had a motive to see an effective President here: the State Department chief wished to portray Yalta as an effective conference that did not give away the store to the Communists.

155 Edward Stettinius Jr., *Roosevelt and the Russians* (Kessinger Publishing, 2005), 275.

156 This author would have preferred to write here "the rear end of the rear admiral," but Halsey actually was a vice admiral, one rank up. His measurements were provided by his daughter. Fred Lohlein, a saddle maker with 50 years' experience, created the item, attaching 116 pieces of engraved silver to it. A good writeup of the process is: Guy Clifton, "Admiral Halsey's Saddle Heading Home to Nevada," www.RGJ.com, October 15, 2012.

157 Guy Clifton, "Admiral Halsey's Saddle Heading Home to Nevada," www.RGJ.com, October 15, 2012.

158 Judi Daly, "Equestrian Deception: The Mythical Capture of Emperor Hirohito's Horse," The Long Riders Guild Academic Foundation, www.lrgaf.org.

159 "Home to Roost," editorial, *The Washington Post*, August 14, 1945, 6.

160 "Back World Body to Maintain Peace," *The New York Times*, January 9, 1944, 44.

161 Selden Menefee, "America at War: Conference City," *The Washington Post*, April 30, 1945, 5.

162 "Out Of Its Name," *The Washington Post*, March 14, 1945, 8. Not only the chamber of commerce (mentioned in this response to a letter to the editor) but many people in San Francisco have attempted to eliminate the name "Frisco" over the years, never successfully.

163 "Editorial - A Dream: In Which the UNO Goes To Palestine and Really Starts Building Peace," *Life* magazine, December 10, 1945, 32.

164 "Roosevelt Home Offered as United Nations Center," *The New York Times*, September 21, 1945, 7.

165 "Editorial - A Dream: In Which the UNO Goes To Palestine and Really Starts Building Peace," *Life* magazine, December 10, 1945, 32.

166 "UNO Commission to Postpone U.S. Permanent Site Selection," *The Washington Post*, December 18, 1945, 8.

167 "Aided by John D. Rockefeller Sr. and Jr., Latter's Sons Join Chamber of Commerce," *The New York Times*, March 8, 1935, 31. This article describes how John D. Rockefeller III and Nelson Rockefeller became members of the New York Chamber on March 7, 1935, joining their grandfather, John D. Rockefeller Sr. (who joined the chamber in 1889) and their father, John D. Rockefeller Jr. (chamber class of 1900) in the 167-year-old institution. This was the first time that three generations of any family had been in this chamber. John D. Rockefeller Sr. was also a longtime member of the Cleveland Chamber of Commerce, having joined it in 1870 and, in 1923, sending that chamber greetings on its 75th birthday.

168 A total of 94 NACOS members served in the war – not a huge number in a group of around 1,200 members, but this low number is probably explainable because these members were mostly chamber managers (CEOs) and hence unlikely to be of prime military drafting age. If all the employees within these chambers were included, the number who went to war likely would have been much higher. For the citation of the figure of 94, see: D.W. Campbell, "Report of the Resolutions Committee," *NACOS Victory Conference Proceedings: Thirty-First Annual Meeting of the National Association of Commercial Organization Secretaries* (Columbus, Ohio: NACOS, November 18-21, 1945).

169 Gerald Movius, "Adventures in Thinking Ahead," *Nation's Business*, August 1945, 23-24, 78-82. The quote is on page 82.

170 "To Hold Baby Parade," *The New York Times*, Associated Press, December 19, 1945, 41.

Epilogue (1946-Today)

1 John F. Kennedy, "Remarks at the Breakfast of the Fort Worth Chamber of Commerce," November 22, 1963, John F. Kennedy Speech No. 476, The American Presidency Project, University of California at Santa Barbara:

http://www.presidency.ucsb.edu/ws/?pid=9538

2 Mark Kelly, *A Powerful Presence: The Birmingham Regional Chamber of Commerce and the History of Birmingham* (Birmingham, Ala.: Birmingham Regional Chamber of Commerce, 2008), 82.

3 Notes 12 and 13 of a 2009 presentation to the board of the Hollywood Chamber of Commerce by Leron Gubler, president and CEO. Provided to the author by Leron Gubler.

4 Ward Winslow and the Palo Alto Historical Association, *Palo Alto: A Centennial History* (Palo Alto, Calif.: Palo Alto Historical Association, 1993), 159.

5 Greater San Antonio Chamber of Commerce Web site, ca. 2008. This Web page has been removed by the chamber but the original is an impressive list of chamber accomplishments, many of which have been documented elsewhere in this book (HemisFair, Trinity University, Brooks and Kelly air force bases, the Riverwalk, etc.). The controversial McAllister Freeway was open to traffic in 1978 and the Northwest Freeway was completed in 2004.

6 Marvin Hurley, *Decisive Years for Houston* (Houston: Houston Chamber of Commerce, 1966), 120; 150-51; 185.

7 Jessica I. Elfenbein in association with Howard Gillette, Jr. and William H. Becker, *Civics, Commerce, and Community: The History of the Greater Washington Board of Trade, 1889-1989* (Dubuque, IA: Kendall/Hunt Publishing Company, 1989), 36-37. The Board of Trade's 1936 advocacy of the metro was also mentioned in the 200-year chamber anniversary article in *Nation's Business* (April 1968, 44).

8 Many a southern civic activist and fundraiser has brought up the Atlanta-Birmingham airport story, or the overall comparison of the two cities, as a goad for other cities to take the initiative in one arena or another. Mark Kelly describes the airport story well *A Powerful Presence: The Birmingham Regional Chamber of Commerce and the History of Birmingham* (Birmingham, Ala.: Birmingham Regional Chamber of Commerce, 2008), 77-79. It's hard to say that sluggishness on one decision (the airport) could determine the future of a great city, but it does appear to have acted as a drag on the Alabama city's growth.

9 The president of the Greater Providence Chamber at the time was Jim Hagan, who informed the author of this letter-writing campaign in 2004 or 2005. It is common for chambers of commerce to attempt to drum up support to convince carriers to make a stop in their airports. The Providence example was unusual in that it represented a drastic strategy change for what had been a regional carrier (Southwest Airlines) and had a striking impact on airfares in Providence, which suddenly plunged from among the highest to among the lowest in the nation.

10 The airport was endorsed by voters 11 years after the Denver Metro Chamber of Commerce assembled a group of interested people and organizations. The complex nature of the project, involving everything from annexation of land to the blessing of it by native American holy men, was a group effort if ever there was one. In the public mind, however, it's normally associated with one key figure, the mayor, who in that case was Federico Pena, later to become Secretary of Transportation. The story, and the chamber's critical role in it, is well described in – indeed dominates – a retrospective history of the Denver Chamber, *The Persistence of Vision*, by Fred Brown (Golden, Colorado: Fulcrum Group, 2011).

11 Notes 11, 14, and 15 of a 2009 presentation to the board of the Hollywood Chamber of Commerce by Leron Gubler, president and CEO. Provided to the author by Leron Gubler.

12 The Seattle World's Fair of 1962, also known as the Century 21 Exposition, originally was conceived as a 50-year celebration of the Alaska Yukon Pacific Exposition in Seattle in 1909. That highly successful fair, with 3.7 million visitors, had been championed by the local business community; the fair's president, Ed Chilberg, had been a two-term president of the Seattle Chamber of Commerce. The idea of a new world's fair for Seattle was broached by a city councilman, Al Rochester, who had attended the 1909 event and still remembered it fondly. He got a "mixed response" until: "One day, at an informal luncheon at the Washington Athletic Club, Don Follett, executive vice-president of the Chamber of Commerce, took an interest in Al's idea. Also at the luncheon were Denny Givens, the chamber's director of public affairs, and Ross Cunningham, an editor of *The Seattle Times*. They too expressed an interest." (Source: Alan J. Stein, "Century 21 – The 1962 Seattle World's Fair, Part I," Historylink.org essay 2290, 2000, updated 2003, www.historylink.org.) Longtime civic leader Edward Carlson, who had served among other things as a board member of the Seattle Chamber of Commerce, was picked to head the fair. The press of his responsibilities forced him to step down in 1960, when he was replaced by Joseph Gandy. Like Ed Chilberg of the Alaska Yukon Pacific Exposition, Gandy was a two-time past president of the Seattle Chamber of Commerce. In a key move, he visited Paris and got the Bureau of International Expositions to provide Seattle the official "World's Fair" designation.

The Seattle fair of 1962 had 10 million visitors.

13 In 1958, at a San Antonio Chamber of Commerce meeting, chamber officer Jerome Harris came up with the idea and the name of a "hemis-fair." This comes from the following source: Mike Gregory, *Expo Legacies: Names, Numbers, Facts and Figures* (Bloomington, Ind.: Authorhouse, 2009), 277. The chamber co-sponsored a world trade seminar in 1962 for which the HemisFair concept was again invoked, and to which the chamber's board pledged its cooperation (board minutes, July 10, 1962, 4). As the event approached, the San Antonio Chamber of Commerce was involved in many activities connected to it, including the extension of the Riverwalk. The chamber also spearheaded the public campaign for the election for citizens to approve $5.5 million in funding for the Tower of the Americas, which was to be the centerpiece of the HemisFair. This was not an easy task for the chamber, as time was short and volunteers had distractions: "the hunting season was on, and in San Antonio this is something to contend with" (board minutes, December 13, 1966, 2).

14 There are many sources describing the role of Elliot Tiber in getting the permit for the Woodstock Music & Art Fair, including the 2009 Ang Lee film *Taking Woodstock*. One source citing the chamber connection is Conor Dougherty's *Wall Street Journal* article about the effort to write this book (*The Magicians of Main Street*). That August 17, 2012 article, "Don't Yawn – Chambers of Commerce are Really Quite a Kick," includes a brief interview with Tiber: "They needed a permit, and I had a permit,' says Mr. Tiber, who recalls his chamber had four members including himself, and the right to have a festival."

15 Impresario George Wein had been asked by New Orleans groups, including the "mayor and the board of trade and the chamber of commerce," as early as 1962 to bring a jazz festival to New Orleans, much like the famous one he had started at Newport. But local segregation laws got in the way. Not only were many jazz musicians African-American, but he was married to an African-American woman. A couple of years after 1968, however, he learned that the New Orleans Chamber's opinions had changed – including a mayor's concerns about his wife's race - and he agreed to set the show up and run it. "It's OK with the Chamber of Commerce," he said wryly. See for example: Liz Scott Monaghan, "The Founding of Jazz Fest," taken from March/April 2005 issue of *Prime Magazine* but originally from *New Orleans Magazine*, April 1994. Web link to retyped article: http://www.nojazzfest.com/chat/showthread.php?t=52. See also: John Pope, "Obituaries: Joyce A. Wein, 76, N.O. Jazzfest adviser," *New Orleans Times-Picayune*, August 17, 2005. Web link (p. 5): http://www.sueauclair.com/pdfs/aug05/JoyceWeinPasses.pdf

16 There are several sources indicating that Payne's efforts got a boost from the chamber and from its chair, Bob Holder. One of them is: C. Richard Yarbrough, *And They Call Them Games: An Inside View of the 1996 Olympics* (Macon, GA: Mercer University Press, 2000), 23. Another source is Jerry Bartels, who was the president of the Atlanta Chamber of Commerce at the time. Bartels noted a variety of other chamber contributions to the bid and to the Games. The contribution of which he is the proudest, and which he considers the most lasting legacy of the Games, is the chamber's role in raising the seed money for Centennial Park. This park has been vital for Atlanta, he told the author, because before that, "Atlanta didn't have a good front door." A good deal of new downtown development took place as a result of the park's creation.

17 The chamber's account of the bid can be found in "Snaring the Olympics," a chapter in the chamber history: Don Woodward and Joel Campbell, *Common Ground: 100 Years of the Salt Lake Chamber* (Montgomery, Alabama: Community Communications Inc., 2003), 176-185.

18 "History of the River Walk," Timeline, Official Website of the San Antonio River Walk, http://www.thesanantonioriverwalk.com/history/history-of-the-river-walk

19 "Chamber History," Greater Oklahoma City Chamber of Commerce:

http://www.okcchamber.com/index.php?src=gendocs&ref=ChamberHistory&category=About

20 James Cobb, *The Selling of the South: The Southern Crusade for Industrial Development, 1936-1980* (Baton Rouge: Louisiana State University Press, 1982), 138.

21 Harold H. Martin, *Atlanta and Environs: A Chronicle of Its People and Events*, Volume III (Athens, Ga.: University of Georgia Press, 1987), 319-20. Martin's book quotes Ivan Allen Jr.'s memoirs as mayor. See also: Stephen B. Oates, *Let the Trumpet Sound: A Life of Martin Luther King Jr.* (New York: HarperCollins, 1892, 1994), 171.

22 Christopher Silver and John V. Moeser, *The Separate City: Black Communities in the Urban South, 1940-1968* (Lexington, Ky.: University of Kentucky Press, 1995), 119-20.

23 Mark Kelly, *A Powerful Presence: The Birmingham Regional Chamber of Commerce and the History of Birmingham* (Birmingham, Ala.: Birmingham Regional Chamber of Commerce, 2008), 87-185. The civil rights story is the heart of Kelly's history of the Birmingham Chamber. The Trailways terminal episode and Smyer's Tokyo experience is described on 106-9. Other books mention the Birmingham Chamber's involvement in the civil rights movement, including Diane McWhorter's Pulitzer Prize-winning *Carry Me Home: Birmingham, Alabama – The Climactic Battle of the Civil Rights Revolution* (New York: Simon & Schuster, 2001). A word search in McWhorter's book finds Smyer's name 91 times.

24 John Reed and Daniel Singal, editors, *Regionalism and the South: Selected Papers of Rupert Vance* (Chapel Hill, N.C.: University of North Carolina Press, 1982), 177.

25 Marvin Hurley, *Decisive Years for Houston* (Houston: Houston Chamber of Commerce, 1966), 178-9, 206-8.

26 The massive electoral vote prize of Texas (the same prize that brought President Kennedy to Fort Worth and Dallas in 1963) put Vice President Johnson in a strong position to advocate for the Houston Chamber's suggestion.

27 This author vividly recalls, soon after his arrival at Stanford University as an MBA student in the fall of 1978, placing a call to Frederick Terman. At this time the professor had retired from his regular duties. I asked Terman, "Can you tell me something about how you created this valley?" He responded somewhat gruffly (at least as I remember it now): "All that stuff about the creation of this valley is a waste of time. Young man, you need to hurry up and study and make something of yourself. Now get going and stop sitting around and thinking about what other people have done."

28 Moffett Field, an Army and Navy training facility until closure in 1994, and the home of the still existing NASA Ames Research Center, arose in 1931with considerable (and not surprising, given chambers' historic interest in attracting military bases) chamber support. The original idea for the base, in a place in Mountain View where fog rarely appears, may have come from a real agent named Laura Thane Whipple. Whipple initially presented the idea at a luncheon of the Mountain View Chamber of Commerce. Later, as the need for local fundraising and political support increased, other chambers raised their voices and helped raise funds. The San Jose Chamber of Commerce has indicated it was one of those chambers; here is an item from the chamber's Web site circa 2010, since removed: "Raising money for key projects: San Jose State Normal School, predecessor to today's 25,000-student San Jose State University, and Moffett Field, today a vital part of the Silicon Valley's R&D infrastructure as home to NASA Ames Research Center." For a good article about Whipple and the Mountain View Chamber, see: Daniel DeBolt, "One Woman's Indelible Mark on Silicon Valley," *Mountain View Voice*, August 5, 2013.

29 "I'm a pushover for pitchmen," he said in one article (Russell E. Pettit as told to Frank Taylor, "I've Got the Craziest Job," *Saturday Review*, September 11, 1954, 40 and continuing on 132 through 137). In the same article, he claimed to have been a "yell leader" in high school and, at the University of Chicago, to have "helped start the card system for bleacher stunts at football games." He engaged in multiple silly promotions at the Santa Clara County Fair, which he ran in connection with his chamber work. One was to paint splotches of vegetable dye on a horse so that it would be a "horse of a different color."

30 An excellent treatment of this topic is found in: Philip J. Trounstine and Terry Christensen, "Flashback: A Short Political History of San Jose," excerpted from their book, *Movers and Shakers* (New York: St. Martin's Press, 1982).

31 Norman Kuhne, "Towns Are Sold From the Ground Up," *Nation's Business*, August 1949. Article begins on page 42; cited portion is on page 75.

32 Much of the growth, admittedly, was from annexation, in which Hamann was expert. The city was 17 square miles in 1950 and 149 in 1970.

33 Leslie Berlin, *The Man Behind the Microchip: Robert Noyce and the Invention of Silicon Valley* (New York: Oxford University Press, 2005), 55-57.

34 David W. Breneman and Susan C. Nelson, *Financing Community Colleges: An Economic Perspective* (Washington, D.C.: The Brookings Institution, 1981), 1.

35 "About Community Colleges," Web site of the American Association of Community Colleges: http://www.aacc.nche.edu/AboutCC/Pages/default.aspx

36 From speech by George W. Bush, March 30, 2004, Appleton, Wisconsin, hosted by the Fox Cities Chamber of Commerce, from *Public Papers of the Presidents of the United States: Public Papers of George W. Bush, January 1 – June 30, 2004* (Washington, D.C.: U.S. Government Printing Office, 2004), 487.

37 Kevin James Dougherty, *The Contradictory College: The Conflicting Origins, Impacts, and Futures of the Community College* (Albany, N.Y.: State University of New York Press, 2001), 133-4.

38 Kathleen Krebbs Whitson, *Bill Jason Priest, Community College Pioneer* (Denton, Texas: University of North Texas Press, 2004), 31.

39 "History of DCCCD," Dallas County Community College District Web site: http://www.dcccd.edu/About%20DCCCD/History/Pages/default.aspx

40 Kathleen Krebbs Whitson, *Bill Jason Priest, Community College Pioneer* (Denton, Texas: University of North Texas Press, 2004), 32.

41 Kathleen Krebbs Whitson, *Bill Jason Priest, Community College Pioneer* (Denton, Texas: University of North Texas Press, 2004), 33.

42 Barbara Jones-Kavalier et al., *The Hiring Game: Reshaping Community College Practices* (Washington, DC: Community College Press, American Association of Community Colleges, 2008), 34.

43 Whitson, Kathleen Krebbs Whitson, *Bill Jason Priest, Community College Pioneer* (Denton, Texas: University of North Texas Press, 2004), 34.

44 Interview with Dave Cooley, June 2010.

45 This item from Horace Mann's diary surely should endear him to those attempting to promote education from the standpoint of improving standards of living:

Sept. 14. Today I have been to Lowell, and have had a very pleasant interview with Mr. Clark and Mr. Bartlett, superintendents of some of the largest [business] establishments in that city, on the subject of the superiority of educated as contrasted with uneducated people, in the amount and value of their products of labor. My object is to show that education has a market value; that it is so far an article of merchandise, that it may be turned to a pecuniary account: it may be minted, and will yield a larger amount of statutable coin than common bullion. It has a pecuniary value, a price current. Intellectual and moral education are powers not only insuring superior respectability and happiness, but yielding returns of silver and gold. This is my idea.

The diary item is cited in: Mary Mann, *Life of Horace Mann: By His Wife* (Boston: Walker, Fuller and Company, 1865), 151-52.

46 Chamber sources describe the rivalry and the annexation push, which had motives not only of limiting the number of governments in the area but also, even more importantly, of providing bragging rights and appearance on important lists of large cities (in population, which inevitably increased when land area was annexed). A good non-chamber source on the annexation struggle is: "A History of Tulsa Annexation," Tulsa City Council, 2004. The report quotes Tulsa Mayor James Maxwell as saying regarding the Oklahoma City rivalry, "If this is an annexation war, then it will be clear that Tulsa did not fire the first shot" (page 14).

47 Interview with Dave Cooley, June 2010. The chamber's involvement is corroborated from other sources, including this article: "200 Years of Business Leadership," *Nation's Business*, April 1968, 45.

48 The decline and fall of the Chamber of Commerce of the State of New York is surely a difficult topic for those interested in the future of other chambers of commerce. Perhaps it had become a "Heritage Club," as the film *Trading Places* termed it. Several sources describe its declining influence in the 20th century. See these essays in Kusserow's *Picturing Power - Portraiture and Its Uses in the New York Chamber of Commerce* (New York: Columbia University Press, 2013): Karl Kusserow, "Portraiture's Use, and Disuse, at the Chamber of Commerce and Beyond,"94; and Elizabeth Blackmar, "Exercising Power: The New York Chamber of Commerce and the Community of Interest," 216-224. (The entire essay is helpful but the cited pages are directly on point.)

49 Change certainly is happening quickly. One female chamber executive, interviewing at a southern chamber of commerce a couple of years ago, referred to the selection committee facing her as "pale, male, and stale." But she got the job and is still there.

50 Two essays mention the movie in Kusserow's *Picturing Power - Portraiture and Its Uses in the New York Chamber of Commerce* (New York: Columbia University Press, 2013): Karl Kusserow, "Portraiture's Use, and Disuse, at the Chamber of Commerce and Beyond,"96; and Elizabeth Blackmar, "Exercising Power: The New York Chamber of Commerce and the Community of Interest," 222.

51 L.E. Foster, General Manager, Chamber of Commerce, Birmingham, Ala., "Keeping Our Work in Step With the Times," *NACOS 21st Annual Meeting: "What's Next?"*, (Washington, D.C.: NACOS, October 20-23, 1935), 106-12. Foster said (page 107) that in the cauldron of the Depression, "I submit that there has not been a Chamber of Commerce of any consequence in this country that has closed its doors and folded up."

52 Russell Rhodes, "The President's Address," *NACOS War Conference: The War Work of Chambers of Commerce* (Detroit: NACOS, October 18-21, 1942), 28-32. The quotation is on page 29.

Appendix B: Chamber Founding Dates

1 This state-chamber information comes from various sources, but one stands out: an article from the proceeds of NACOS in 1928: George B. Chandler, Secretary, Ohio State Chamber, "The History and Present Status of State Chamber of Commerce Organization," *Fifteenth Annual Meeting of the National Association of Commercial Organization Secretaries* (Milwaukee, Wisc.: NACOS, Oct. 21-23, 1929), 78-82. Chandler's information isn't perfect as he didn't have access to records of incipient state chambers of earlier days, but nevertheless he did a very solid job of compiling his list.

Selected Bibliography

Histories and Studies Longer Than Article/Essay Length

United States

175: A History of Mobile's Progressive Business Advocate – Mobile Chamber of Commerce 1836-2011 (Mobile, Ala.: Mobile Area Chamber of Commerce, 2011).

Albany, Ga. Reflections: 100ᵗʰ Anniversary Celebration (Albany, Ga.: Albany Area Chamber of Commerce, 2010).

Batcheller, Robert, *The Commercial Club of Boston, Organized November 7, 1868: Constitution, Officers, Chronology, Retrospect* (Boston: Riverside Press, 1906).

Bishop, John Bucklin, *A Chronicle of 150 Years: The Chamber of Commerce of the State of New York 1768-1918* (New York: Charles Scribner's Sons, 1918).

Blasig, Carl, *Building Texas* (Brownsville, Texas: Springman-King Company, 1963). This book looks at Texas chambers' role in the growth and development of their state.

Brecher, Barbara, *Celebrating 100 Years: Alexandria Chamber of Commerce, 1906-2006* (Alexandria, Va.: Brecher Design, 2006).

Brown, Fred, *The Persistence of Vision: The Denver Metro Chamber of Commerce* (Golden, Colo.: The Fulcrum Group, 2011).

Bruce, William George, Editor, *Commercial Organizations: Their Functions, Operation and Service* (Milwaukee: The Bruce Publishing Company, 1920).

The Charleston Chamber of Commerce: List of Members, Arrears Lists, and Treasurer's Annual Statements, 1838-1863, South Carolina Historical Society library, Charleston, S.C.

Claiborne, Jack, *Crown of the Queen City: The Charlotte Chamber from 1870 to 1999* (Charlotte: Charlotte Chamber of Commerce, 1999).

Clark, Neil M., *These Tremendous Years, 1912-1937: Flashes from the History of a Quarter Century of Business Achievement* (Washington, D.C.: U.S. Chamber of Commerce, 1937).

Commercial and Industrial Organizations of the United States: Revised to November 1, 1919 (Washington: Government Printing Office, 1919), issued by the U.S. Department of Commerce's Bureau of Foreign and Domestic Commerce, Miscellaneous Series, No. 99.

Decisions of the New-Orleans Chamber of Commerce from its Formation, in 1834 to August 4ᵗʰ, 1856 (New Orleans: Printed at the Price Current Office, 1857).

Dodd, Monroe, *Business and the Making of Kansas City* (Kansas City: Rockhill Books, 2012).

Elbert, David, *Standing on the Shoulders of Giants* (Des Moines: Greater Des Moines Partnership, 2013).

Elfenbein, Jessica I., in association with Howard Gillette, Jr. and William H. Becker, *Civics, Commerce, and Community: The History of the Greater Washington Board of Trade, 1889-1989* (Dubuque, IA: Kendall/Hunt Publishing Company, 1989).

Fifty-Years [sic] of the Chamber of Commerce of Pittsburgh, 1874-1924 (Pittsburgh: Pittsburgh Chamber of Commerce, 1924).

Flynn, Shirley E., and William Robert Dubois, *We've Worked Hard to Get Here: The First 100 Years of the Cheyenne Chamber of Commerce* (Cheyenne, Wyo.: Greater Cheyenne Chamber of Commerce, 2007).

Frazier-Hedberg, *A History: The Delaware State Chamber of Commerce, 1837-1987* (Wilmington, Del.: Delaware State Chamber of Commerce, 1987).

Geib, George and Miriam,, *Indianapolis First: A Commemorative History of the Indianapolis Chamber of Commerce and Local Business Community* (Indianapolis: Indianapolis Chamber of Commerce, 1990).

Graham, Lloyd, and Frank Severance, *The First Hundred Years of the Buffalo Chamber of Commerce* (Buffalo, N.Y.: Foster & Stewart Publishing Corp., 1945).

Greater Scranton Chamber of Commerce, 1867 – 1967: 100 Years of Service (Scranton, Pennsylvania: Greater Scranton Chamber of Commerce, 1967).

Herring, Henry Stonewall, *History of The New Orleans Board of Trade Limited, 1880-1930, and Annual Report for Year 1929* (New Orleans: New Orleans Board of Trade, 1930).

Hodge, Clarence L., and Peggy Ferris, *Building Honolulu: A Century of Community Service* (Honolulu: Chamber of Commerce of Honolulu, 1950).

A Journal of the Charleston Chamber of Commerce, Commencing 6, of February 1784. South Carolina Historical Society, Charleston, S.C.

Kelly, Mark, *A Powerful Presence: The Birmingham Regional Chamber of Commerce and the History of Birmingham* (Birmingham, Ala.: Birmingham Regional Chamber of Commerce, 2008).

King, Charles, *History of the New York Chamber of Commerce: With Notices of Some of Its Most Distinguished Members. An Anniversary Discourse, Delivered Before the New York Historical Society, November 21, 1848* (Ithaca, N.Y.: Cornell University Library digital edition, 1993).

Kullenberg, Roger, and Dave Hager, *Kalamazoo: Kalamazoo Regional Chamber Celebrating 100 Years/ 1903-2003* (Kalamazoo: Kalamazoo Regional Chamber, 2003), 25.

Kusserow, Karl, *Picturing Power: Portraiture and Its Uses in the New York Chamber of Commerce* (New York: Columbia University Press, 2013).

Langsam, Walter Consuelo, *Centennial History of the Commercial Club of Cincinnati, 1880-1980* (Cincinnati: The Commercial Club of Cincinnati, 1981).

Law and Order in San Francisco: A Beginning (San Francisco: San Francisco Chamber of Commerce, 1916).

Levi, Steven C., *Committee of Vigilance: The San Francisco Chamber of Commerce Law and Order Committee, 1916-1919* (Jefferson, N.C.: McFarland & Company, 1983).

Lord, Myrtle Shaw, *A Sacramento Saga: Fifty Years of Achievement – Chamber of Commerce Leadership* (Sacramento: Sacramento Chamber of Commerce, 1946).

Minutes of the Board of Directors of the Pittsburgh Chamber of Commerce, 1874-1987, housed in the Historical Society of Western Pennsylvania, Heinz History Center, Pittsburgh, Pa.

Minutes, Chamber of Commerce of Kansas City. These are housed at the Greater Kansas City Chamber of Commerce. The first volume includes handwritten minutes from the first volume of the collected records of this chamber. The first entry is dated October 1, 1856.

Minutes, Charleston Chamber of Commerce: 1866-1878, handwritten manuscript, South Carolina Historical Society library, Charleston, S.C.

Moseley, Edward A., *List of National, State and Local Commercial Organizations; National, State and Local Agricultural Organizations; and Railway Associations* (Washington, D.C.: Interstate Commerce Commission, February 1898).

Origin, Growth and Usefulness of the Chicago Board of Trade: Its Leading Business Men, and Representative Business Men in Other Branches of Trade (New York: Historical Publishing Co., 1885-6).

Rich, Marshall N., *History of the Work of the Board of Trade of Portland, Maine* (Portland, Maine: Press of Ford & Rich, 1887).

Rosser, Howard W., editor, *The First Fifty Years: A History of the East Texas Chamber of Commerce* (Longview, Texas: *East Texas Magazine,* 1976).

Selected Bibliography

Shermer, Elizabeth Tandy, *Sunbelt Capitalism: Phoenix and the Transformation of American Politics* (Philadelphia: University of Pennsylvania Press, 2013). This book, although the title indicates a wider subject, is surprisingly centered on the activities of the leaders of the Phoenix Chamber of Commerce, including Barry Goldwater and a variety of other people better known for their later activities in the federal government and judiciary.

Smallwood, James M., *Urban Builder: The Life and Times of Stanley Draper* (Norman, OK: The University of Oklahoma Press, 1977). Although a biography, this book is an in-depth look at the Oklahoma City Chamber of Commerce through its colorful and charismatic leader, Stanley Draper.

Smith, Charles, *San Antonio Chamber of Commerce: A History of Its Organization for Community Development and Service, 1910-1960,* thesis for M.S. degree, Trinity University (San Antonio: Trinity University, May 1965).

Starke, William, Editor, *Century of Progress, 1899-1999: Fort Atkinson Area Chamber of Commerce* (Fort Atkinson, Wis.: Badger Press, Inc., 1999).

Stevens Jr., John Austin, *Colonial Records of the New York Chamber of Commerce, 1768-1784* (New York: John F. Trow & Co., 1867), 204.

Stowits, George H., *History of the One Hundredth Regiment of New York State Volunteers* (Buffalo, N.Y.: Printing House of Matthews & Warren, 1870; courtesy of BiblioLife Reproduction Series).

Sturges, Kenneth, *American Chambers of Commerce* (New York: Printed for Williams College by Moffat, Park and Co., 1915).

Summary of the Minutes of the Denver Board of Trade and the Denver Chamber of Commerce, 1867 to 1949, housed at the Denver Metro Chamber of Commerce.

Walker, Louise Drusilla, *The Chicago Association of Commerce: Its History and Policies* (Chicago: University of Chicago, June 1941), a Ph.D. dissertation submitted to the Faculty of the Division of Social Sciences, Department of History, University of Chicago.

Waller, Bill, *History of the Tulsa Metro Chamber* (Tulsa: Tulsa Metro Chamber, 2003).

Willard, Charles Dwight, *The Herald's History of Los Angeles City* (Los Angeles: Kingsley-Barnes & Neuner Co., 1901), The appendix covers the chamber during the decade after 1901.

Willard, Charles Dwight, *History of the Los Angeles Chamber of Commerce* (Los Angeles: Kingsley-Barnes & Neuner Company, 1899).

Woodward, Don, and Joel Campbell, *Common Ground: 100 Years of the Salt Lake Chamber* (Montgomery, Alabama: Community Communications Inc., 2003).

Woolf, Joni, *Sesquicentennial of the Macon Chamber of Commerce* (Macon, Georgia: Macon Chamber of Commerce, 2011).

International

Bennett, Robert J., *Local Business Voice: The History of Chambers of Commerce in Britain, Ireland, and Revolutionary America 1760-2011* (Oxford: Oxford University Press, 2011), 93-98. All the information in this paragraph comes from Bennett's excellent description of the intellectual origins of chambers in the English-speaking world.

Bennett, Robert J., *The Voice of Liverpool Business: The First Chamber of Commerce and the Atlantic Community* (Liverpool: Liverpool Chamber of Commerce, 2010).

Cuthbertson, Brian, *Voices of Business: A History of Commerce in Halifax 1750-2000* (Halifax, Nova Scotia: Metropolitan Halifax Chamber of Commerce, 2000).

Fedotov, Victor I., *Business Associations Study: Organizational and Legal Models of Chambers* (Washington, D.C.: Center for Private Enterprise, April 20, 2007), Table 24, 61.

Gilpin, John F., *Century of Enterprise: The History of the Edmonton Chamber of Commerce* (Edmonton: The Edmonton Chamber of Commerce, 1988).

Ilersic, A.R., *Parliament of Commerce: The Story of the Association of British Chambers of Commerce, 1860-1960* (London: The Association of British Chambers of Commerce, 1960).

Latimer, John, *The History of the Society of Merchant Venturers of the City of Bristol* (Bristol, U.K.: J.W. Arrowsmith, 1903).

Peach, Jack, *The First Hundred Years: The History of the Calgary Chamber of Commerce, 1891-1991* (Calgary: The Calgary Chamber of Commerce, 1990).

Ridgeway, George L., *Merchants of Peace: Twenty Years of Business Diplomacy Through the International Chamber of Commerce* (New York: Columbia University Press, 1938).

Stanford, G.H., *To Serve the Community: The Story of Toronto's Board of Trade* (Toronto: The Board of Trade of Metropolitan Toronto, 1974).

Taylor, Ron, *A History of Chambers of Commerce in the United Kingdom, 1768-2007* (London: British Chambers of Commerce, 2007), 10.

Other Chamber Books

The National Association of Commercial Organization Secretaries (NACOS) published annual proceedings of its meetings beginning in 1915. These books, ranging from about 200 to 400 pages, are a wealth of information about local-chamber activities from 1915 through 1945. The author went carefully through all of them from 1928 through 1945 and through most if not all of those available on the Web, up to about 1923. He similarly examined minute books of the Southern Commercial Secretaries Association of this period.

Shorter Histories, Articles, Essays, and Web Postings

Hundreds of chambers – but still a minority of the roughly 7,000 chambers in the United States - have a notice, usually very brief, on their Web sites with a "History of the Chamber" or similar item. Most are not cited here unless particularly useful or lengthy. Some of the histories cited below are not on Web sites but were distributed in other ways, such as at annual dinners or anniversary celebrations.

"100 Years of Achievement," history item on the Oakland Chamber of Commerce Web site: http://www.oaklandchamber.com/chamber_100years_first100.shtml

"100 Years of Business Growth," Greater Akron Chamber, *2006 Annual Report*, foldout section, p. 11 and following.

"125 Years of Big Ideas: 125th Annual Meeting & Luncheon of the Fort Worth Chamber of Commerce, Thursday, June 7, 2007."

"200th Anniversary Chronology," Savannah Area Chamber of Commerce.

"200 Years of Business Leadership," *Nation's Business*, April 1968, 40-57.

"1914-1923 – The Great War and the Roaring '20s: The Detroit Board of Commerce is the 'Spokesman of Optimism' and a Hub of Activity," *The Detroiter*, June 2003.

"1924-1933: From Boom to Gloom – the Detroit Board of Commerce is Active on the Air, at Sea and on the Ground," *The Detroiter*, June 2003. Other decades were also covered in this series.

"2002 Annual Meeting Centennial Celebration," Anderson Area Chamber of Commerce, Anderson, S.C., September 5, 2002.

Ambrosius, Spencer, "Traverse City Chamber of Commerce Historical Timeline," Powerpoint presentation, circa 2009.

Balser, John, "Pardners in Prosperity," *Cheyenne Business Monthly*, July 2009.

Brill, Edmond H. Jr., "History of the Richmond Chamber of Commerce," Richmond, Va., 1967.

Burks, Chester W., *Annals of the Chamber of Commerce of San Francisco* (San Francisco: Neal Publishing Company, 1909).

Burnett, Betty, "For 173 Years, a Force for Progress: RCGA History, Part I," *St. Louis Commerce*, March April, 2009.

Burnett, Betty, "For 173 Years, a Force for Progress: RCGA History, Part II," *St. Louis Commerce*, May-June 2009, 104-5.

Carbone, Ray, and Gemma French, *Celebrating 100 Years of Manchester's Most Memorable Moments, Decade by Decade* (Manchester, N.H.: Greater Manchester Chamber of Commerce, 2011).

"Chamber of Commerce's (Lexington) History," Commonwealth of Kentucky, Record No. 31019, created July 4, 2009.

"Chamber History," Wichita Metro Chamber of Commerce.

"Chamber Milestones," Santa Fe (NM) Chamber of Commerce, 1983.

"Chamber Shaped: Las Vegas Success Story," Greater Las Vegas Chamber of Commerce, 1972/1973. Provided by the Las Vegas Metro Chamber of Commerce.

"Chamber Timeline," Wilmington, N.C. Chamber of Commerce, circa 2009.

Cincinnati USA Regional Chamber History, Part 1: 1839-1911: http://www.cincinnatichamber.com/cham_a.aspx?menu_id=146&id=6786

Donahue, Louise Gilmore, *Pathways to Prosperity: A History of the Greater Omaha Chamber of Commerce* (Omaha: Greater Omaha Chamber of Commerce, 1993).

"Edmond Area Chamber of Commerce: One Hundred Years, 1907-2007," Edmond, Okla., Area Chamber of Commerce, 2007.

"Florida Chamber History," Florida Chamber of Commerce Web site: http://flcc.harvestmanager.net/mx/hm.asp?id=about_history

Goff, Marsha Henry, *The Lawrence Chamber of Commerce, 1878-2000* (Lawrence, Kan.: Lawrence Chamber of Commerce, 2000).

"Greater Austin Chamber of Commerce," from *Austin: Celebrating the Lone Star Millennium* (Austin, Texas: Greater Austin Chamber of Commerce, 1999), 330-1.

"Greater Chambersburg Chamber of Commerce, 1911-2011," Greater Chambersburg Chamber of Commerce, 2011.

"Greater Columbus Georgia Chamber of Commerce History Time Line," provided by the chamber in about 2009.

Greater Little Rock Chamber of Commerce, 1867-2004, Greater Little Rock Chamber of Commerce Web site:

http://www.littlerockchamber.com/CWT/EXTERNAL/WcPages/Membership/Lending_a_Helping_Hand.aspx

Greater Memphis Chamber Web site, history section: http://www.memphischamber.com/The-Chamber/History.aspx

Greater Spokane Incorporated's Agricultural Bureau: "The Past, Present and Future" – 1890 to 2010 and beyond. . . Powerpoint presentation provided by Greater Spokane Inc. circa 2010.

Grey, Peter, *The First Two Centuries: An Informal History of the New York Chamber of Commerce* (New York: New York Chamber of Commerce, 1968).

Hanes, Patrick, "History of the Lansing Regional Chamber of Commerce," 2012.

Harding, Anne, "90 Years of Building a Better Dallas: The History of the Greater Dallas Chamber, 1909 to the Present," This is a 15-page paper made available by the Greater Dallas Chamber in 1999.

"Historic Essay Written at the State Chamber's 50th Anniversary," New Jersey Chamber of Commerce, 1961. Available on this Web site in 2013: http://www.njchamber.com/index.php/about-us/our-history/44-historic-essay-written-at-the-state-chamber-s-50th-anniversary

"History of the Chamber," Web site of the Beverly Hills Chamber of Commerce: http://www.beverlyhillschamber.com/general.asp?id=590

"History of the Charleston Chamber of Commerce," created by the Charleston Chamber of Commerce in 1973. About seven pages long.

History of Clarksville Chamber, Clarksville Area Chamber of Commerce Web site: http://www.clarksvillechamber.com/about/history-clarksville-chamber/

"History," Greater Tampa Chamber of Commerce Web site: http://www.tampachamber.com/Ci_History.Asp

History of the Organization of the Nevada State Board of Trade: Its Aims and Purposes, Constitution and Bylaws (Nevada State Board of Trade, circa 1890).

"History of the Savannah Area Chamber of Commerce," six-page document published by the Savannah Area Chamber of Commerce on its 200th anniversary in 1906, 4.

History timeline from the Denver Metro Chamber of Commerce, provided about 2009.

Holladay, Bob, "Leading Change: The Nashville Area Chamber of Commerce: A Historical Perspective on 150 Years of Providing Support for Nashville's Business and Removing Obstacles for Nashville's Progress," white paper, 1997, 3.

Hope-Hempstead County Chamber of Commerce Web site: www.hopechamberofcommerce.com/festival

"The Houston Chamber of Commerce Celebrates its One Hundredth Anniversary: And Related Here is the Story of the Founding of This Organization," *Houston*, the magazine of the Houston Chamber of Commerce, April 1940.

"The Kalispell Area Chamber of Commerce Celebrates 100 Years of Regional Leadership in Northwest Montana," November 2004.

Kennedy, Judith, *Bicentennial History, 1801-2001* (Philadelphia: Greater Philadelphia Chamber of Commerce, 2000).

Krohe, James Jr., *Shoulder to the Wheel: A Centennial History of the Greater Springfield Chamber of Commerce* (Springfield, Ill.: Greater Springfield Chamber of Commerce, 1976).

Langdon, Bonnie, and Phillip Parker, *Dayton Area Chamber of Commerce* (New York: Newcomen Society of the United States, 1996).

Mark, Jay, "The Tempe Chamber of Commerce," *The Arizona Republic*, June 21, 2008. Other materials and notes from the Tempe Chamber of Commerce provided by Mary Ann Miller, 2009.

Marshall, Robert, (1978), updated by Harry McCawley (1999), "A Brief History of the Columbus Area Chamber of Commerce," provided by the Columbus, Ind., Area Chamber of Commerce.

McKibben, James A., *The Structure or Organization of a Chamber of Commerce* (Evanston, Ill.: National School for Commercial Secretaries, 1922). This 40-page booklet was the first in a series provided as text for the second gathering of this NACOS-U.S. Chamber project for the training of commercial secretaries, the school that today is the U.S. Chamber program known informally as "Institute."

Plunkett-Cole, Anna, "Early Years of the Jersey Chamber of Commerce," This is Jersey Website: http://www.thisisjersey.com/2008/11/27/early-years-of-the-jersey-chamber-of-commerce/

Quackenbush, Gary, "A Century with the Chamber," *North Bay Business Journal*, September 18, 2006, 24. History of the Santa Rosa, Calif., Chamber of Commerce.

Rittenberg, Sidney, publicity secretary, Charleston Chamber of Commerce, "The Charleston Chamber One Hundred Years Ago," from *The American City*, Volume 15, No. 2, August 1916, 168.

Rules and Regulations of the Savannah Chamber of Commerce (Savannah: Seymour and Woolhopter, 1807).

Savannah Area Chamber of Commerce Web site: http://www.savannahchamber.com/about-the-chamber/history

Shumway, Floyd M., and Richard Hegel, "The First Century of the Greater New Haven Chamber of Commerce, 1794 – 1894," *Journal of The New Haven Colony Historical Society*, Volume 40, No. 2, Spring 1994.

Smith, Edward, and Pat Filer, "The Chamber's Amazing Story: 150 Years of Vision, Faith and Courage," *Panorama* (publication of the Hamilton and District Chamber of Commerce, Hamilton, Ont.), September 24-26, 1995.

Squires, Charles P., "Early History of Las Vegas Nevada Chamber of Commerce," a 12-page typewritten manuscript from 1940 (UNLV Library, Call Number F 849 L35 5678 1940).

Stauffer, Thomas, "A History of the San Francisco Chamber of Commerce, 1850-2000," from *San Francisco: From the Gold Rush to Cyberspace* by Charles A. Fracchia and Thomas Stauffer (San Francisco: San Francisco Chamber of Commerce and Marcoa Publishing Inc., 2000), 90.

Steve Stone, *Dynamic Decades: The Salem Story as Seen Through a History of the Salem Area Chamber of Commerce* (Salem, Oregon: Salem Area Chamber of Commerce, 1965).

"Together for Our City: A Brief History of The Commercial Club of Chicago" (Chicago: Commercial Club of Chicago, 1996).

U.S. Chamber 100th Anniversary timeline: http://www.uschamber.com/about/100th-anniversary

U.S. Chamber of Commerce: The Early Years, U.S. Chamber of Commerce, 2012.

Washington Centennial '89, Spokane Area Chamber of Commerce
(Spokane: Spokane Area Chamber of Commerce, 1989).

"Yuba Sutter Chamber of Commerce History," Web site, Yuba Sutter Chamber of Commerce:
http://www.yubasutterchamber.com/index.php?option=com_content&view=article&id=163&Itemid=167

Chamber Annual Reports and Proceedings

The author examined many chamber annual reports for this book. Many individual volumes are cited in the Notes section. Among the chambers whose annual reports were studied were:

Board of Trade of the City of La Crosse, Wisconsin

Boston Chamber of Commerce

Boston Board of Trade

Chamber of Commerce of Richmond, Virginia

Chamber of Commerce of San Francisco

Chamber of Commerce of the State of New York (aka New York Chamber of Commerce)

Cincinnati Chamber of Commerce and Merchants' Exchange

Chicago Board of Trade

Cleveland Chamber of Commerce

Honolulu Chamber of Commerce

Los Angeles Chamber of Commerce

Memphis Chamber of Commerce

Milwaukee Chamber of Commerce

National Board of Trade

National Negro Business League

Philadelphia Board of Trade

Saint Paul Chamber of Commerce

Washington Board of Trade

Other Books of Special Interest

Thousands of books, mostly online, were briefly touched on as the author perused material connected with chambers of commerce. Some of these appear in the notes with specific citations. Those listed here are chosen, somewhat arbitrarily, for being more helpful than most. Some were useful simply for general historical background for the periods in question. Other books, such as collections of letters, speeches, or Congressional testimony, are skipped here because they are only relevant for the specific letter or testimony in question, and can be found in the Notes section for that specific information.

Allen, Ivan Sr., *Atlanta from the Ashes* (Atlanta: Ruralist Press, 1928).

Alperin, Lynn, *History of the Gulf Intracoastal Waterway* (National Waterways
Study, U.S. Army Engineer Water Resources Support Center, 1983).

America's Gibraltar: Muscle Shoals – A Brief for the Establishment of our National Nitrate Plant at Muscle Shoals on the Tennessee River (Nashville: Muscle Shoals Association, 1916).

The American Remembrancer; or, an Impartial Collection of Essays, Resolves, Speeches, &c. Relative, or Having Affinity, to the Treaty with Great Britain (Philadelphia: Mathew Carey, August 20, 1795).

The American Remembrancer; or, an Impartial Collection of Essays, Resolves, Speeches, &c. Relative, or Having Affinity, to the Treaty with Great Britain, Volume II (Philadelphia: Mathew Carey, October 10, 1795).

Bain, David Haward, *Empire Express: Building the First Transcontinental Railroad* (New York: Viking Press, 1999).

Bancroft, Hubert Howe, *History of the Life of William T. Coleman: A Character Study* (San Francisco: The History Company, 1891).

Beckert, Sven, *The Monied Metropolis: New York City and the Consolidation of the American Bourgeoisie, 1850-1896* (Cambridge, U.K.: Cambridge University Press, 1993).

Bergreen, Laurence, *Capone: The Man and His Era* (New York: Touchstone Books, 1994).

Bernstein, Peter L., *Against the Gods: The Remarkable Story of Risk* (New York: John Wiley & Sons, 1996).

Bernstein, William J., *A Splendid Exchange: How Trade Shaped the World* (New York: Grove Press, 2008).

Black, Edwin, *IBM and the Holocaust: The Strategic Alliance Between Nazi Germany and America's Most Powerful Corporation* (New York: Three Rivers Press, a division of Random House, 2001).

Bokovoy, Matthew F., *The San Diego World's Fair and Southwestern Memory, 1880-1940* (University of New Mexico Press, 2005).

Brown, William Adams, *Morris Ketchum Jesup: A Character Sketch* (New York: Charles Scribner's Sons, 1910).

Bunau-Varilla, Philippe, *Panama: The Creation, Destruction, and Resurrection* (New York: McBride, Nast & Company, 1914).

Burrows, Edwin G. and Mike Wallace, *Gotham: A History of New York City to 1898* (Oxford: Oxford University Press, 1999).

Campbell, Carlos C., *Birth of a National Park in the Great Smoky Mountains* (Knoxville: University of Tennessee Press, 1960; paperback edition, 1993).

Cardozo, Jacob Newton, *Reminiscences of Charleston* (Charleston, S.C.: Joseph Walker, 1866).

Chambers, Adam B., *Proceedings of the St. Louis Chamber of Commerce, In Relation to the Improvement of the Navigation of the Mississippi River, and Its Principal Tributaries and the St. Louis Harbor* (St. Louis, Mo.: Chambers & Knapp, 1842).

Chernow, Ron, *Alexander Hamilton* (New York: Penguin Press, 2004).

Chernow, Ron, *The House of Morgan: An American Dynasty and the Rise of Modern Finance* (New York: Grove Press, 2001).

Childs, Harwood Lawrence, *Labor and Capital in National Politics* (Columbus, Ohio: The Ohio State University Press, 1930).

Cobb, James, *The Selling of the South: The Southern Crusade for Industrial Development, 1936-1980* (Baton Rouge: Louisiana State University Press, 1982).

Conners, John A., *Shenandoah National Park: An Interpretive Guide* (McDonald and Woodward Publishing Company, 1988).

Cronon, William, *Nature's Metropolis: Chicago and the Great West* (New York: W.W. Norton, 1992).

Crosby, Molly Caldwell, *The American Plague: The Untold Story of Yellow Fever, the Epidemic That Shaped Our History* (New York: Berkley Books, 2006).

Currey, J. Seymour, *Chicago: Its History and Its Builders: A Century of Marvelous Growth* (Chicago: S.J. Clarke Publishing Company, 1912), Volume II.

Cutlip, Scott, *Fund Raising in the United States: Its Role in America's Philanthropy* (New Brunswick, N.J.: Transaction Publishing, 1990; an expanded book from the original, which was published by Rutgers University in 1965).

Selected Bibliography

Dible, Louise Nelson, *Paying the Toll: Local Power, Regional Politics, and the Golden Gate Bridge* (Philadelphia: University of Pennsylvania Press, 2009).

Doig, Jameson W., *Empire on the Hudson: Entrepreneurial Vision and Political Power at the Port of New York Authority* (New York: Columbia University Press, 2001).

Downs, L. Vaughan, *The Mightiest of Them All: Memories of Grand Coulee Dam* (American Society of Civil Engineers, 1993).

Doyle, Don Harrison, *New Men, New Cities, New South: Atlanta, Charleston, Nashville, Mobile, 1860-1910* (Chapel Hill, N.C.: University of North Carolina Press, 1990).

Dray, Philip, *There is Power in a Union: The Epic Story of Labor in America* (New York: Doubleday, 2010).

Egan, Timothy, *The Worst Hard Time: The Untold Story of Those Who Survived the Great American Dust Bowl* (New York: Houghton Mifflin, 2006).

Eig, Jonathan, *Get Capone: The Secret Plot That Captured America's Most Wanted Gangster* (New York: Simon & Schuster, 2010).

Ellsworth, Scott, *Death in a Promised Land: The Tulsa Race Riot of 1921* (Baton Rouge, La.: Louisiana State University Press, 1982).

Fischer, David Hackett, *Champlain's Dream* (New York: Simon and Schuster Paperbacks, 2008).

Gordon, John Steele, *An Empire of Wealth: The Epic History of American Economic Power* (New York: HarperCollins Publishers, 2004).

Gotham, Kevin Fox, *Authentic New Orleans: Tourism, Culture, and Race in the Big Easy* (New York: New York University Press, 2007).

Green, James, *Death in the Haymarket: A Story of Chicago, the First Labor Movement, and the Bombing that Divided Gilded Age America* (New York: Random House, 2006).

Grodzins, Morton, *Americans Betrayed: Politics and the Japanese Evacuation* (Chicago: University of Chicago Press, 1949).

Hamby, Alonzo L., *Man of the People: A Life of Harry S Truman* (New York: Oxford University Press, 1995).

Harris, Joel Chandler, *Joel Chandler Harris' Life of Henry W. Grady Including His Writings and Speeches* (New York: Cassell Publishing Company, 1890).

Harrison, Eliza Cope, editor, *Philadelphia Merchant: The Diary of Thomas P. Cope, 1800-1851* (South Bend, Ind.: Gateway Editions, 1978).

Hoffman, Dennis E., *Scarface Al and the Crime Crusaders: Chicago's Private War Against Capone* (Carbondale, Ill.: Southern Illinois University Press, 1993).

Hill, Hamilton, *A Review of the Proceedings of the Detroit Convention* (Boston: J.H. Eastburn's Press, 1866).

Houston History, 174 Years of Historic Houston, a Web site: http://www.houstonhistory.com/decades/history5a.htm

Hurley, Marvin, *Decisive Years for Houston* (Houston: *Houston Magazine*, Houston Chamber of Commerce, 1966).

Ingebretsen, James, with Madeline Coulombe, *Apprentice to the Dawn: A Spiritual Memoir* (Los Angeles: The Philosophical Research Society, 2003).

Jaher, Frederic Cople, *The Urban Establishment: Upper Strata in Boston, New York, Charleston, Chicago, and Los Angeles* (Urbana, Ill.: University of Illinois Press, 1982).

The Jews in Nazi Germany: The Factual Record of Their Persecution by the National Socialists (New York: The American Jewish Committee, 1933), 13. This disturbing book, published in June 1933, provides much early documentation of the outrages of the Nazis.

Karcher, Alan J., *New Jersey's Multiple Municipal Madness* (Piscataway, N.J.: Rutgers University Press, 1998).

Koeppel, Gerard, *Bond of Union: Building the Erie Canal and the American Empire* (Philadelphia, Pa.: Perseus Books, Da Capo Press, 2009).

Kolko, Gabriel, *The Triumph of Conservatism: a Reinterpretation of American History, 1900-1916* (New York: The Free Press, 1963).

Kotler, Philip, Donald H. Haider, and Irving Rein, *Marketing Places: Attracting Investment, Industry, and Tourism to Cities, States, and Nations* (New York: The Free Press, 1993).

Larson, Erik, *In the Garden of Beasts* (New York: Broadway Paperbacks, 2011).

Lathers, Richard, *Reminiscences of Richard Lathers: Sixty Years of a Busy Life in South Carolina, Massachusetts and New York* (New York: The Grafton Press, 1907), edited by Alvan F. Sanborn.

Lewis, David L., *W.E.B. Du Bois: A Biography* (New York: Holt Paperbacks, 2009).

Lewis, Sinclair, *Babbitt* (New York: Grosset & Dunlap, 1922).

Lewis, Sinclair, *Main Street* (Project Gutenberg ebook, no. 543, www.gutenberg.org).

Lindbergh, Charles A., *The Spirit of St. Louis* (New York: Scribner, 1953).

Lipsky, William, Images of America: *San Francisco's Panama-Pacific International Exposition,* (San Francisco: Arcadia Publishing, 2005).

McWhorter, Diane, *Carry Me Home: Birmingham, Alabama – The Climactic Battle of the Civil Rights Revolution* (New York: Simon & Schuster, 2001).

Moehring, Eugene, and Michael Green, *Las Vegas: A Centennial History* (Reno: University of Nevada Press, 2005).

Moeller, Beverley Bowen, *Phil Swing and Boulder Dam* (Berkeley: University of California Press, 1971).

Mulholland, Catherine, *William Mulholland and the Rise of Los Angeles* (Los Angeles: University of California Press, 2002).

Ness, Eliot, with Oscar Fraley, *The Untouchables* (Cutchogue, N.Y.: Buccaneer Books, 1957).

Phillips-Fein, Kim, *Invisible Hands: The Businessmen's Crusade Against the New Deal* (New York: W.W. Norton and Co., 2010).

Power, J.C., *History of Springfield, Illinois: Its Attractions as a Home and Advantages for Business, Manufacturing, Etc., Published Under the Auspices of the Springfield Board of Trade* (Springfield: Illinois State Journal Print, 1871).

Proceedings of the Commercial Convention, Held in Detroit, July 11th, 12th, 13th and 14th, 1865 (Detroit: Advertiser and Tribune Company Print, 1865).

Putnam, Robert, *Bowling Alone: The Collapse and Revival of American Community* (New York: Simon & Schuster, 2000).

Ranck, George Washington, *History of Lexington, Kentucky: Its Early Annals and Recent Progress* (Cincinnati, Ohio: Robert Clarke & Co., 1872).

Reilly, Thomas, *Jannus, an American Flier* (Board of Regents of the State of Florida, 1997).

Report of the Monetary Commission of the Indianapolis Convention of Boards of Trade, Chambers of Commerce, Commercial Clubs, and Similar Bodies of the United States (Chicago: the University of Chicago Press, 1898).

Russell, Francis, *A City in Terror: Calvin Coolidge and the 1919 Boston Police Strike* (Boston: Beacon Press, 1975).

Save the Adirondack Forests and the Waterways of the State of New-York: Opinions of the Press (New-York: Press of the Chamber of Commerce, 1883).

Scherer, James A.B., *"The Lion of the Vigilantes": William T. Coleman and the Life of Old San Francisco* (Indianapolis: The Bobbs-Merrill Company, 1939).

Schlesinger, Arthur M., *The Colonial Merchants and the American Revolution, 1763-1776* (New York: Columbia University Ph.D. Thesis, 1917).

Semmes, Admiral Raphael, *Memoirs of Service Afloat, During the War Between the States* (Baltimore: Kelly, Piet & Co., 1869).

Sennholz, Mary, *Leonard E. Read: Philosopher of Freedom* (Irvington-on-Hudson, N.Y.: Foundation for Economic Education, 1993).

Sherman, William Tecumseh, *Memoirs* (New York: Penguin Classics, 2000).

Shingleton, Royce, *High Seas Confederate: The Life and Times of John Newland Maffitt* (Columbia, S.C.: University of South Carolina Press, 1994).

Smith, Carl S., *The Plan of Chicago: Daniel Burnham and the Remaking of the American City* (Chicago: University of Chicago Press, 2006).

Smock, Raymond, *Booker T. Washington in Perspective: Essays of Louis R. Harlan* (University Press of Mississippi, 1988).

Soule, Frederick Judson, *An American Village Community: A Sociological Study of Village Association* (New York: Columbia University Department of Political Science, Ph.D. Thesis, 1909).

Stevens, John Austin Jr., *Colonial New York: Sketches Biographical and Historical 1768-1784* (New York: John F. Trow & Co., 1867).

Stevens, John Austin, *Proceedings of the Mass Meeting of Loyal Citizens on Union Square, New-York, 15th Day of July, 1862* (New York: George F. Nesbit & Co., Printers, 1862).

Strouse, Jean, *Morgan: American Financier* (New York: HarperCollins, 2000).

tenBroek, Jacobus, Edward Barnhart, and Floyd Matson, *Prejudice, War, and the Constitution: Causes and Consequences of the Evacuation of the Japanese Americans in World War II* (Berkeley, Calif.: University of California Press, 1954).

Tocqueville, Alexis de, *Democracy in America*, quoted in *The Perfect Gift: The Philosophical Imagination in Poetry and Prose*, by Amy Kass (Bloomington, Indiana: Indiana University Press, 2002).

Todd, Francis Morton, *The Story of the Exposition: Being the Official History of the International Celebration Held at San Francisco in 1915 to Commemorate the Discovery of the Pacific Ocean and the Construction of the Panama Canal* (New York: G.P. Putnam's Sons, The Knickerbocker Press, 1921), Volume Five.

Tyack, David, *The One Best System: A History of American Urban Education* (Cambridge, Mass.: Harvard University Press, 1974).

Ward, Stephen V., *Selling Places: The Marketing and Promotion of Towns and Cities, 1850-2000* (New York: Spon Press, 1998).

Watson, Thomas Jr., with Peter Petre, *Father Son & Co.: My Life with IBM and Beyond* (New York: Bantam Books, 1990).

Wehr, Kevin, *America's Fight Over Water: The Environmental and Political Effects of Large-Scale Water Systems* (New York: Routledge, an imprint of the Taylor & Francis Group, 2004).

Wiebe, Robert H., *The Search for Order: 1877-1920* (New York: Hill and Wang, 1967).

Whitney, Albert, *Report of the Special Committee of the Board of Trustees of the Chamber of Commerce of San Francisco on Insurance Settlements Incident to the San Francisco Fire, Approved at a Meeting of the Board of Trustees on November 13, 1906* (San Francisco: Chamber of Commerce of San Francisco, 1906).

Wilentz, Sean, *The Rise of American Democracy: Jefferson to Lincoln* (New York: W.W. Norton & Company, 2006).

Williams, Mary Floyd, *History of the San Francisco Vigilance Committee of 1851* (Berkeley, California: University of California Press, 1921).

Wilson, Lucius E., *Community Leadership: The New Profession* (New York: The American City Bureau, 1919).

Wolff, David A., *Seth Bullock: Black Hills Lawman* (Pierre, S.D.: South Dakota Historical Society, 2009).

Some Articles of Interest

Of course many articles were perused for this book. *The New York Times* and *The Washington Post* were particularly used, especially in the period from 1923 through 1945, when copyright rules made it difficult to access chamber annual reports (which are relatively plentifully online before 1923, as of this writing). From 1923 through 1945, there are 32,704 articles or advertisements in *The New York Times* database within ProQuest with the words "chamber of commerce." The author examined the titles of all of them, looked at most of the articles, and read many or most of those opened. There were 18,318 similar articles and advertisements in *The Washington Post* over the same years, and these were treated in the same way. The author also looked at selected articles in these newspapers before 1923, and at articles in other newspapers in the years before and after 1923. He also checked listings (not all of them, but selected) with the words "board of trade" or "association of commerce" or "commercial club" in various newspapers and periodicals. Particularly relevant articles from newspapers are cited in the Notes section; relatively few appear below, which are mostly devoted to magazine articles and other material, and even then, a limited selection.

The magazine that was most helpful was *Nation's Business,* the periodical issued by the U.S. Chamber of Commerce in 1912 and thereafter. Other periodicals with useful material included *Life, The American City, Town Development, The Rotarian, Niles' Weekly Register, Hunt's Magazine and Commercial Review,* and *DeBow's Review of the Southern and Western States.* Also, NACOS had a newsletter, *NACOS News,* which provided numerous items of interest. The author reviewed the issues in the possession of NACOS (now called the Association of Chamber of Commerce Executives) from 1924 through 1945.

Abbe, Cleveland, "Historical Notes on the Systems of Weather Telegraphy, and especially their Development in the United States," *The American Journal of Science and Arts,* edited by James B. Dana and B. Silliman, Third Series, Volume II, No. 7-12, July to December, 1871 (New Haven: Tuttle, Morehouse & Taylor, 1871).

"Achievements of Commercial Organizations," *Nation's Business,* January 14, 1914.

"An Address: Read Before the Annex, February 25 [or possibly 23 or 28], 1890 by Mrs. Carrie Williams," *The Great Southwest: A Monthly Journal of Horticulture,* March 1890, 14.

Barnard, Thomas, "The Secret Six," 2003-2009: http://thomasbarnard.com/Articles/secretsix.htm

Beard, Charles, "The Myth of Rugged American Individualism," *Harper's,* 1931. Issued as a separate pamphlet in 1932, published in 1932 by John Day Company, New York.

Berner, George, "Just Dogs," *The Washington Post,* September 27, 1936, R19.

"Biographical: Thomas P. Cope," *The American Merchant,* July 1858, 139.

Blakeney, Ben Bruce, "Pu Yi," *Life,* July 16, 1945, 78-86. The mention of the Los Angeles Chamber is on page 85.

"Boston vs. New York," *American Railroad Journal,* March 13, 1847, 170.

"Brutal 1917 East St. Louis (IL) White-on-Black Race-Riot Disaster: Worst in American History," Suburban Emergency Management Report, Biot #414, March 20, 2007: http://www.semp.us/publications/biot_reader.php?BiotID=414

"Business Men's Organizations and the War Program," *Nation's Business,* January 1942, 33.

Butterfield, Roger, "'Los Angeles is the Damnedest Place. . ',' The City That Started with Nothing but Sunshine Now Expects to Become the Biggest in the World," *Life* magazine, November 22, 1943, 104.

"Chamber Acts to Bar Movie: Alleged Slanderous Picture May Be Boycotted by State Group," *St. Petersburg Times,* July 30, 1926, Section One, page 11.

Chamberlain, John, "Eric Johnston," *Life* magazine, June 19, 1944, 96-108. The discussion of the coup is on page 105.

Chapman, Lee Roy, "The Nightmare of Dreamland," This Land Press, originally published September 1, 2011.

"City Enlarged by Merger of Several Towns; Daytona Beach Now Ranks as One of Largest Cities in State," *Sarasota Herald,* January 3, 1926, section one, page 4.

"The 'City Manager' Plan Adopted by Sumter, S.C.," *The American City,* July 1912, 38.

"Clarence D. Chamberlin Recalls Historic Flight, Explains Why Lindbergh Beat Levine Across the Atlantic," 1965, Yiddish Radio Project: http://yiddishradioproject.org/exhibits/levine/chamberlin.php3?pg=1.

Clark, Neil, "Inside Facts of How Chicago Vigilantes Are Routing Gangsters Revealed – Mysteries of the Secret Six," *The Washington Post,* August 21, 1932, SM1.

Cleveland, Reginald, "A Super-Highway for America," *The New York Times,* November 10, 1935, XX1.

Clifton, Guy, "Admiral Halsey's Saddle Heading Home to Nevada," www.RGJ.com, October 15, 2012.

"Commercial Organization: An Address by Mr. Ryerson Ritchie, of Boston," *City Club Bulletin,* City Club of Philadelphia, March 3, 1910.

Dawe, G. Grosvenor, "Commercial Organization in Good Roads Campaign," address to the American Road Congress, reprinted in *Nation's Business,* November 18, 1912, 6.

Selected Bibliography

Depew, Chauncey, "Address Before the Detroit Chamber of Commerce, May 2, 1895," from *Orations, Addresses and Speeches of Chauncey M. Depew*, Volume II, edited by John Denison Champlin (New York: Privately Printed, 1910), 51.

DeWitt, John, and Allen Gullion, telephone conversation, December 26, 1941, WDC-CAD 311.3 Tel Convs (DeWitt, 42-43). This conversation (and this citation of that conversation) comes from the following source: Martin Blumenson et al., *Command Decisions* (Washington, D.C.: U.S. Government Printing Office, 1960), 128.

DeWitt, John, and Allen Gullion, January 24, 1942, WDC-CAD 311.3 Tel Convs (DeWitt, 42-43). This conversation (and this citation of that conversation) comes from the following source: Martin Blumenson et al., *Command Decisions* (Washington, D.C.: U.S. Government Printing Office, 1960), 132.

"Drift-Wood: Public Spirit," from *The Galaxy*, edited by William Conant Church and Mark Twain, April 1874, from Volume 17, January to June 1874 (New York: Sheldon & Company, 1874), 553.

"Dog Sellers Weep at Virginia Mart," *The New York Times*, October 15, 1937, 25.

Edgerton, Ralph, "The Eric Johnston Story," *The Pacific Northwesterner*, Vol. 33, No. 4 (Fall 1989), 55-62. The version cited was edited by David Wilma and appears as Essay 7339 on HistoryLink.org: The Free Online Encyclopedia of Washington State History.

"An Editor Who Shoots: A Politician Wants Satisfaction or Fight, and Gets the Last," *The Providence Morning Star*, October 15, 1882.

"Effect of the Disturbances Upon Business. Appeal from the Merchants of Kansas. From the *St. Louis Globe Democrat*," *New York Daily Times*, February 28, 1856.

"F.D. Roosevelt Turns Columnist: In Beacon Standard, He Comments for 'Neighbors' of Dutchess County," *The New York Times*, August 3, 1928, page 38.

"Fall of a Crown: Hawaii's Kingdom is a Thing of the Past; Annexation is the Cry," *The Washington Reporter*, January 31, 1893, 6, column 1.

"Fined for Violating the Pure Food Law," *The Deseret News*, April 16, 1908.

"The First Confederate Flag," *The Confederate Veteran Magazine*, 1895 (Nashville, Tenn.: Blue and Gray Press, 1971), Volume 3, No. 10, October 1895, 315.

Franz, Mary, "The Real Men of Deadwood," *Wild West Magazine*, August 2006.

Garvey, Marcus, "The Conspiracy of the East St. Louis Riots," Speech on July 8, 1917, from *The American Experience* by PBS: http://www.pbs.org/wgbh/amex/garvey/filmmore/ps_riots.html

"The Goat Island Grant," a pamphlet on the proceedings of a mass meeting on March 16, 1872 (San Francisco: San Francisco Chamber of Commerce, 1872), 3-6.

Gould, Kathrine Clemmons, "Women in Trade Reconstruction," *The Forum*, October-November 1919 issue, 471-79.

"The Great Pacific Railroad. New York Chamber of Commerce.", *The American Whig Review*, September 1849, 311-2.

Grodzins, Morton, "Interview with James [*sic*] Read, Managing Director, Los Angeles Chamber of Commerce, July 20, 1943." From the Japanese-American Evacuation and Resettlement Records [ca. 1941-1953], Collection No.: BANC MSS 67/14/c, Reel 8, BNEG: 1858.

Grodzins, Morton, "Interview with James Ingebretsen," October 14, 1942, Report #14, pp. 3-4. From the Japanese-American Evacuation and Resettlement Records [ca. 1941-1953], Collection No.: BANC MSS 67/14/c, Reel 4, BNEG: 1854.

"Harlem Compact Gives Negroes Third of Jobs in Stores There," *The New York Times*, August 8, 1938, 1.

"Hawaiian News: Talk of All Sorts Concerning Annexation," *Morning Missoulian*, February 1, 1893, 1.

Heinly, Burt A., "Carrying Water Through a Desert: The Story of the Los Angeles Aqueduct," *National Geographic*, July 1910, 582.

"Henry Grady, 'The New South' Speech (December 22, 1886), Web Document: Primary Source," from History 367, the University of Puget Sound: http://www.anselm.edu/academic/history/hdubrulle/CivWar/text/documents/doc54.htm

Hill, Hamilton Andrews, "Memoir of Isaac Chapman Bates," *The New-England Historical and Genealogical Register*, April 1877, 142-145.

Holzer, Harold, "Pre Civil War Peace Conference," Weider History Group, www.historynet.com. This article was published online on November 8, 2010. It was originally published in *America's Civil War*, a magazine.

Hoover, Herbert, "The Chamber of Commerce," *Nation's Business*, December 1921, page 46.

Hoover, Herbert, "Conquering an American Nile," *Nation's Business*, August 1922, 9-11.

Hunt, Thomas, and Jno. Toof of the Memphis Chamber of Commerce, letter to CSA President Jefferson Davis, October 30, 1861, from *The War of the Rebellion: A Compilation of the Official Records of the Union and Confederate Armies* (Washington: Government Printing Office, 1898), Series I – Volume LII – in two parts; Part II – Confederate Correspondence, etc., 189.

"'I'm Through! Secret Six Licked Me,' Says Al in Interview," *Chicago Herald Examiner*, July 30, 1931.

"It's Time for Conventions – and for Festivals," *Kiplinger's Personal Finance*, May 1948, 44-46.

"James Gore King," *The National Cyclopaedia of American Biography*, Volume1 (New York: James T. White & Co., 1898), 498-99.

"Jane Addams Our Guest," *The Detroiter: Spokesman of Optimism*, October 1912, 33.

Johnson, Gerald W., "Greensboro, Or What You Will," from *South-Watching: Selected Essays by Gerald W. Johnson* (Chapel Hill, N.C.: The University of North Carolina Press, 1983), 45. This essay first appeared in the *Reviewer* in April 1924.

"Jurist Drops Dead Before Peace Board: Ex-Justice Burke Expires in Arms of Dr. Butler at Carnegie Endowment Meeting," *The New York Times*, December 5, 1925, 1.

Kaufman, L.G., "Report of the Chamber of Commerce of Juneau, Alaska," from *Bulletin of the Department of Labor, Volume III – 1898*, edited by Carroll D. Wright, Commissioner (Washington: Government Printing Office, 1898), 419-425.

"Ladies Annex," *The Great Southwest: A Monthly Journal of Horticulture*, September 1889, 10.

"Ladies' Annex: A Wonderful Growth and Much Good Work," *The Great Southwest: A Monthly Journal of Horticulture*, October 1889, 8. (This page of this issue of the magazine mistakenly shows "1886" but the other pages correctly show the date as 1889.)

"The Ladies' Annex: An Able Ally of the Chamber of Commerce," *The Great Southwest: A Monthly Journal of Horticulture*, January 1890, 3.

Leahy, W.H., "Atlanta, City of the Present," *Town Development*, January 1914, 15.

Lincoln, Abraham, "Argument in the Rock Island Bridge Case," Daily Press of Chicago, September 24, 1857, from *The Writings of Abraham Lincoln, Volume 2*: http://www.classicreader.com/book/3331/101/.

Martin, Wilbur "How Men of Commerce Made New York," *Nation's Business*, April 1968, 62.

Maxwell, Sidney, Cincinnati Chamber of Commerce Superintendent, letter to S.S. Guthrie of the Buffalo Board of Trade, December 12, 1888, reprinted in: *Annual Report of the Boston Chamber of Commerce, Compliments of Wm. Herbert Pearson, Secretary* (Boston: C.M. Barrows and Co., 1889), 4.

McKee, Logan, "Civic Work of the Pittsburgh Chamber of Commerce," *The American City*, July 1911, Vol. 5 No. 1, 12.

McMasters, William Henry, "On Chambers of Commerce," from *Originality and Other Essays* (Boston: The Four Seas Company, 1921), pages 67-71.

Mead, S. Cristy, "I Believe in My Work," *Nation's Business*, May 1929. The article is on pages 31, 33, 186, 188, and 190.

Mentor, "State of Opinions on the Treaty," from the *Lancaster Journal*, published in *The American Remembrancer; or, an Impartial Collection of Essays, Resolves, Speeches, &c. Relative, or Having Affinity, to the Treaty with Great Britain*, Volume II (Philadelphia: Mathew Carey, October 10, 1795), 201.

"Mercantile Miscellanies: The Boston Board of Trade," *Hunt's Merchant Magazine and Commercial Review*, Volume 34, January-June 1856 (New York: Freeman Hunt, 1856), 261.

"Million-Dollar Civic Fund Raised by Middletown Chamber," *The American City*, June 1920, 627.

Selected Bibliography

Moore, W.B., "Oklahoma City Unique in Nation: Wondrous Town Made in 23 Years," *Nation's Business*, October 21, 1912.

"National Association of State Chambers of Commerce Organized," *The American City*, Volume XXXI, July-December 1924, 599.

"A Nationwide Campaign for Free Ports Takes Definite Shape," *Greater New York*, June 30, 1919, 8.

"A Negro Business Men's League," *The American City*, June 1917, 633.

"The New South: As Shown by a Georgia Editor to New Englanders – High Tribute to Lincoln – The Way Mr. Grady Talked to the Yankees," *The Meriden Journal*, December 23, 1886.

Nye, Matthew, *"A Life Remembered: The Voice and Passions* of Feminist Writer and Community Activist Flora Kimball," California History, *September* 2010, page 3, www.Findarticles.com

Orr, A.E., "Commercial Organizations," *The Encyclopedia Americana*, edited by Franklin Converse Beach (New York: The Americana Company, 1904), volume 5.

Parsons, Albert, "The Autobiography of Albert Parsons," published in 1887, available on this link: http://law2.umkc.edu/faculty/projects/ftrials/haymarket/autobiography1.html

Pegler, Westbrook, "Fair Enough: The First American Duce," *The Washington Post*, October 19, 1936.

"Plan to Make Memphis the 'Best Negro City,'" *Lumber (Manufacturers' Edition)*, October 20, 1919, 30.

Powell, Willis, "Simply Staggering," *Nation's Business*, May 1925, 19-21. For the hunting dog quote and others like it, see: "The Log of Organized Business," *Nation's Business*, January 1921, 37.

"President Taft's Speech at Annual Banquet," *Nation's Business*, January 28, 1913.

Randolph, Charles, "The Year, Seen from the Board of Trade," *The Lakeside Monthly*, Volume VIII, July to December, 1872 (Chicago: The University Publishing Company, 1872), October 1872, 254.

Randolph, Robert Isham, "Head of Chicago's 'Secret Six' Tells of the War Upon Gangs," *The New York Times*, April 17, 1932, XX3.

Read, Leonard, Letter "To the Senators and Congressmen of Washington, Oregon and California," February 2, 1942. From the Japanese-American Evacuation and Resettlement Records [ca. 1941-1953], Collection No.: BANC MSS 67/14/c, Reel 4, BNEG: 1854.

Ritchie, Ryerson, "The Modern Chamber of Commerce," *National Municipal Review*, April 1912, 161-169. The full chart, including population figures, is on page 166.

Roosevelt, Theodore, "Speech at the Chamber of Commerce Banquet," November 11, 1902, from *The Triumphant Life of Theodore Roosevelt: Citizen; Statesman; President*, by Shelby Cullom, William Loeb, George Perkins, et. al., edited by J. Martin Miller (Washington, D.C.: J. Martin Miller, 1905), 358.

Roosevelt, Theodore, "Desirability of a Secretary of Commerce and Labor," from the President's message to the opening of the first session of the fifty-seventh Congress, December 3, 1901, reprinted in *The Roosevelt Policy: Speeches, Letters and State Papers, relating to Corporate Wealth and Closely Allied Topics, of Theodore Roosevelt* (New York: The Current Literature Publishing Company, 1908), Volume One, 170-1.

"Ryerson Ritchie Resigns," *San Francisco Chamber of Commerce Journal*, March 1912, 12.

"Ryerson Ritchie to Resign: His Organization Work in the Chamber of Commerce Practically Completed," *Boston Evening Transcript*, October 15, 1909.

Sandburg, Carl, "Fixing the Pay of Railroad Men – Third Article," from *International Socialist Review*, Volume 15, June 1915, 711-712.

Saunders, W.O., "My Town Has Too Many Organizations," *Nation's Business*, June 1928, 36-37.

Schiff, Jacob, letter to Lord Rothschild, April 4-5, 1904. From Cyrus Adler and Mortimer Schiff, *Jacob H. Schiff: His Life and Letters, Part 2* (Garden City, New York, 1929), 122.

Shafer, Paul, "Local Politics – Menace to Defense," *The American Mercury*, May 1940, 54-59.

"Sit Down Love Strike Ended; Girl Says Yes," *Sarasota Herald*, Associated Press, February 7, 1937, 2.

Slatta, Richard W., "Deadwood Dick," *The Mythical West: An Encyclopedia of Legend, Lore, and Popular Culture* (Santa Barbara, Calif.: ABC-Clio Inc., 2001), 119-20.

"Sophia E. Delavan, Who changed her whole source of workers to meet her 'labor problem,'" *The Magazine of Business*, edited by A.W. Shaw, Volume 38, July to December 1920, September issue, 421-22, 447-49.

Sprague, J.R., "A Civic Campaign," parts one and two. Part one: *Nation's Business*, January 1924, 52, 54. Part two: *Nation's Business*, February 1924, 44, 46.

"Storms," *The American Cyclopedia: A Popular Dictionary of General Knowledge*, Volume 15, edited by George Ripley and Charles A. Dana (New York: D. Appleton and Company, 1883), 405.

Strong, Howard, "Leading the Way in War's Confusion," *Nation's Business*, August 1917, 28.

Taft, William Howard, "Remarks at the Banquet Tendered Him by the Chamber of Commerce at Los Angeles, Cal. (October 11, 1909)," from *Presidential Addresses and State Papers of William Howard Taft: from March 4, 1909 to March 4, 1910* (New York: Doubleday, Page & Company, 1910), Volume One, 345.

Thorpe, Merle, "Why They Cheered – 'He Built Seattle,'" *Nation's Business*, August 1925, 30.

"Tiffin Goes to War," *Nation's Business*, March 1918, 44. This article provides a good overview of one chamber's involvement in the home front of the war.

Totten, W.W., and others from the Nashville Chamber of Commerce to President Andrew Johnson, May 22, 1865, from *The Papers of Andrew Johnson: May-August 1865*, Paul H. Bergeron, editor (University of Tennessee Press, 1989), 103.

Trenholm, William L., "The Centennial Address Before the Charleston Chamber of Commerce, 11th February 1884" (Charleston, S.C.: The News and Courier Book Presses, 1884), 23.

"Two Years' Progress: The Second Annual Meeting of the Chamber of Commerce of the United States of America Reveals the Wonderful Growth and Invaluable Work of the Most Potent Commercial Organization in the World," *Town Development*, March 1914, 67, column 2.

Wheeler, Harry A., "The National Citizens' League: A Movement for a Sound Banking System," from *The Federal Reserve System: Its Purpose and Work*, in *Annals of the American Academy of Political and Social Science*, January 1922, 27.

White, Jeremy, "The Los Angeles Way of Doing Things: The Olympic Village and the Practice of Boosterism in 1932," *Olympika: The International Journal of Olympic Studies*, Volume XI, 2002, 79-116; quotation on 82.

"Why Plane is Named 'Spirit of St. Louis,'" *The New York Times*, June 13, 1927, page 7.

Wiggins, Frank, "Advertising California," *Official Report of the Twenty-Eighth Fruit-Growers' Convention of the State of California, Held Under the Auspices of the State Horticultural Convention, at Los Angeles, Commencing Tuesday, May 5th, and Ending Friday, May 8th, 1903* (Sacramento: W.W. Shannon, Superintendent of State Printing, 1903), 117.

Photo Bibliography

Photo and Illustration Credits

22 Cruger, John. [Drawing]. (1765). *The First Two Centuries . . . An Informal History of the New York Chamber of Commerce.* By Peter P. Grey. New York, NY: Partnership for New York City, Inc.

23 The Great Seal of the New York Chamber of Commerce. [Plaque]. *The First Two Centuries . . . An Informal History of the New York Chamber of Commerce.* By Peter P. Grey. New York, NY: Partnership for New York City, Inc.

33 Hamilton, Alexander. [Painting]. *The First Two Centuries . . . An Informal History of the New York Chamber of Commerce.* By Peter P. Grey. New York, NY: Partnership for New York City, Inc.

45 SS Savannah. (1819). [Photograph of a painting of the SS Savannah]. Hunter Wood. Retrieved from http://en.wikipedia.org/wiki/File:SS-Savannah.jpg.

51 Jackson, Andrew. (1845). [Photograph]. Public Domain. Retrieved from http://commons.wikimedia.org/wiki/File:Andrew_Jackson_Daguerrotype-crop.jpg.

52 de Tocqueville, Alexis. (1850). *Alexis de Tocqueville.* Public Domain. Retrieved from http://commons.wikimedia.org/wiki/File:Alexis_de_tocqueville.jpg.

63 Coleman, William Tell. (1851). *"The Lion of the Vigilantes": William T. Coleman and the Life of Old San Francisco.* By James A. B. Scherer. Indianapolis: The Bobbs-Merrill Company.

68 Rock Island Bridge. [Sketch of bridge burning]. (1856). Rock Island County Historical Society: Moline, IL.

69 Lincoln, Abraham. (1857). *Abraham Lincoln* [Photograph]. Washington, DC: Library of Congress Prints and Photographs Division. Retrieved from http://www.loc.gov/pictures/item/98504484/.

72 Great Eastern Laying Atlantic Cable. (1866). *A Cable Laying Ship.* [Painting]. Henry Clifford (1821-1905). Image courtesy of Atlantic-Cable.com. Retrieved from http://atlantic-cable.com/Article/Clifford/Clifford-Great-Eastern-t.jpg.

77 Charleston Harbor (S.C.). (1862). *Sketch of Charleston Harbor* [Map]. Williams, W. A.: L. Prang & Co. Charleston Harbor, SC. Retrieved from Boston Public Library Flickr Stream.

81 Low, Abiel Abbott. [Oil on canvas portrait]. (Date Unknown). Public Domain. Retrieved from http://en.wikipedia.org/wiki/File:Aalowpic.jpg#filehistory.

81 CSS Alabama. (1862-1864). [Photo of sepia wash drawing by Clary Ray]. Washington, DC: Navy Art Collection. Retrieved from http://www.history.navy.mil/photos/sh-us-cs/csa-sh/csash-ag/ala-a.htm.

84 Trenholm, George A. [Portrait of George A. Trenholm]. (1862). Public Domain. Retrieved from http://commons.wikimedia.org/wiki/File:George_Alfred_Trenholm.jpg.

85 New York Riots. [Sketch of the Draft Riots]. (1863). Public domain. Retrieved from http://en.wikipedia.org/wiki/File:New_York_Draft_Riots_-_fighting.jpg.

102 Boss Tweed, by Thomas Nast. (October 21, 1871). Wood engraving, *The "Brains" Boss Tweed* depicted in *Harper's Weekly.* Public Domain. Retrieved from http://commons.wikimedia.org/wiki/File:Boss_Tweed,_Thomas_Nast.jpg.

114 Field, Marshall. [Photograph]. Public Domain. Washington, DC: Library of Congress Prints and Photographs Division. Retrieved from http://www.loc.gov/pictures/item/ggb2006006097/.

118 Bullock, Seth. [Photograph]. Public Domain. Retrieved from http://commons.wikimedia.org/wiki/File:Seth_Bullock.gif.

120 Chinese Immigrants, [Cartoon]. (Date Unknown). Public Domain. Retrieved from http://sunsite.berkeley.edu/cgi-bin/flipomatic/cic/images@ViewImage?img=brk00001713_16a.

122 Yellow Fever [Poster]. (c1873-78). *In Memoriam of the Lamented Dead.* Public Domain. Southern Publishing Co.: New Orleans, LA. Retrieved from http://www.memphishistory.com/portals/0/Lamented%20Dead.jpg.

127 Grady, Henry. [Portrait of Henry Grady]. (1890). Public Domain. Retrieved from http://en.wikipedia.org/wiki/File:Henry-grady-1890.jpg.

137 Jefferson Davis Monument. (2005). [Photograph]. Public Domain. Retrieved from http://en.wikipedia.org/wiki/Image:Monument_avenue_richmond_virginia.jpg.

137 William T. Sherman Statue. (2008)). [Photograph]. Public Domain. Retrieved from http://commons.wikimedia.org/wiki/File:Sherman_gilded_jeh.JPG.

138 Schiff, Jacob. (1903). Portrait of Jacob Schiff. [Scan of Photograph]. Public Domain. *The World's Work, 1903.* By Aime Dupont. Doubleday, Page & Company, New York, NY: Retrieved from http://archive.org/stream/worldswork06gard#page/3602/mode/2up.

145 New York City Subway Chamber Plaque. [Scan of Photograph]. *Rapid Transit in New York City and in the Other Great Cities (1906).* New York, NY.: Chamber of Commerce of the State of New York. Public Domain. Retrieved from http://www.nycsubway.org/wiki/Station:_City_Hall_%28IRT_East_Side_Line%29.

146 Hurricane , Galveston, Texas. (1900) [Stereograph]. Public Domain. Washington, DC: Library of Congress Prints and Photographs Division. Retrieved from http://www.loc.gov/pictures/item/98503822/.

147 The Parthenon, Nashville, Tenn. [Photograph]. (c1900). Public Domain. Washington, DC: Library of Congress Prints and Photographs Division. Retrieved from http://www.loc.gov/pictures/collection/det/item/det1994014657/PP/.

Tennessee Centennial Exposition. (1897). [Photograph]. Public Domain. Retrieved from http://commons.wikimedia.org/wiki/File:PyramidParthenon.jpg.

152 Du Bois, William Edward Burghardt "W. E. B.". (1907). [Photograph]. Public Domain. Retrieved from http://commons.wikimedia.org/wiki/File:Du_Bois,_W._E._B..jpg.

153 Washington, Booker T. (Taken between 1905 and 1915). Public Domain. Washington, DC: Library of Congress Prints and Photographs Division. Retrieved from http://www.loc.gov/pictures/item/hec2009002812/.

167 Wilson, George. (1889). [Portrait]. Public Domain. *Picturing Power: Portraiture and Its Uses in the New York Chamber of Commerce.* By Karl Kusserow. New York, NY: Columbia University Press. 35.

168 Wiggins, Frank. (c1897/1924). [Photograph]. Los Angeles, CA: University of Southern California, on behalf of the USC Special Collections. Retrieved from http://digitallibrary.usc.edu/cdm/singleitem/collection/p15799coll65/id/2701/rec/29.

170 Wiggins, Frank. (c1897-1924). [Photograph]. Los Angeles, CA: University of Southern California, on behalf of the USC Special Collections. Retrieved from http://digitallibrary.usc.edu/cdm/singleitem/collection/p15799coll65/id/21319/rec/15.

172 Chamber of Commerce, Cleveland. (1900). [Photograph]. Public Domain. Washington, DC: Library of Congress Prints and Photographs Division. Retrieved from http://www.loc.gov/pictures/item/det1994014215/PP/.

175 Mead, S. Cristy. (1914). [Photograph]. Association of Chamber of Commerce Executives (ACCE), formerly National Association of Commercial Organization Secretaries (NACOS). Alexandria, VA.: Archives.

179 Los Angeles Aqueduct. (1912). [Photograph]. Public Domain. Retrieved from http://commons.wikimedia.org/wiki/File:LA_Aqueduct_Pipe.jpg.

180 Aviation Meet. (1910). [Poster]. Public Domain. Retrieved from http://commons.wikimedia.org/wiki/File:1910_Airmeet_Poster.jpg.

181 *Plan of Chicago.* (1909). [Illustration]. Public Domain. Retrieved from http://commons.wikimedia.org/wiki/File:Plan_of_Chicago_Plate_CXII.jpg.

187 Oklahoma City. (1910). [Photograph]. Public Domain. Washington, DC: Library of Congress Prints and Photographs Division/ Panoramic photographs. Retrieved from http://lccn.loc.gov/2007662689.

Photo Bibliography

197 Colonel Sanders, Harland. (ca 1930). [Photograph]. Public Domain. Retrieved from http://commons.wikimedia.org/wiki/File:Sanders_cafe_2.png.

208 Goethals Bridge. (1991). [Photograph]. Public Domain. Washington, DC: Library of Congress Prints and Photographs Division. Retrieved from http://www.loc.gov/pictures/item/ny1806.photos.351427p/.

212 Rockefeller, John D. (1885). [Photograph]. Public Domain. Retrieved from http://commons.wikimedia.org/wiki/File:John_D._Rockefeller_1885.jpg.

213 Law & Order Committee of the SF Chamber of Commerce. (1916). [Photograph]. San Francisco History Room, San Francisco Public Library, San Francisco, CA.

231 Gorman, Margaret. (1921). [Photograph]. Public Domain. Washington, DC: Library of Congress Prints and Photographs Division. Retrieved from http://www.loc.gov/pictures/item/npc2007004969/.

232 Santa Claus Lane. (1928). [Photograph]. Purchased, Bruce Torrence Hollywood Photograph Collection. http://hollywoodphotographs.com.

233 Dempsey, Jack. (c1921). [Photograph]. Public Domain. Washington, DC: Library of Congress Prints and Photographs Division. Retrieved from http://www.loc.gov/pictures/resource/cph.3b35134/.

234 Brooklyn New York Chamber of Commerce led by Raymond H. Fiero, posed standing with President Coolidge. (1929). Public Domain. Washington, DC: Library of Congress Prints and Photographs Division. Retrieved from http://www.loc.gov/pictures/item/94509094/.

244 Lindbergh, Charles. (c1927). [Photograph]. Public Domain. Washington, DC: Library of Congress Prints and Photographs Division. Retrieved from http://www.loc.gov/pictures/item/2002721494/.

247 The Golden Gate Bridge. (1934). [Photograph]. Public Domain. Washington, DC: Library of Congress Prints and Photographs Division. Retrieved from http://www.loc.gov/pictures/item/99403559/.

249 Hoover Dam. (1932). [Photograph]. Washington, DC: U.S. National Archives and Records Administration. Retrieved from http://upload.wikimedia.org/wikipedia/commons/8/8a/Looking_upstream_into_Black_Canyon_toward_Hoover_Dam_site_showing_outlet_portals_of_four_diversion_tunnels_and..._-_NARA_-_293789.tiff .

251 Grand Coulee Dam. (1935). [Photograph]. Washington, DC: U.S. National Archives and Records Administration. Retrieved from http://commons.wikimedia.org/wiki/File:The_southeast_corner_of_the_immense_3,000_foot_Grand_Coulee_cofferdam_-_NARA_-_293984.tif

254 Moffat Tunnel. (1928). [Postcard]. Retrieved from http://commons.wikimedia.org/wiki/File:Moffat_Tunnel_Western_view_circa_1928.jpg.

255 Great Smoky Mountains. (1931). [Photograph]. Public Domain. Retrieved from http://commons.wikimedia.org/wiki/File:NPS_Preliminary_Survey_Personnel_GSNP.jpg.

261 Ponzi, Charles. (1920). [Photograph]. Public Domain. Retrieved from http://commons.wikimedia.org/wiki/File:Charles_Ponzi.jpg.

270 NACOS School. (1927). [Photograph]. Association of Chamber of Commerce Executives (ACCE), formerly National Association of Commercial Organization Secretaries (NACOS). Alexandria, VA.: Archives.

273 NACOS 15th Annual Meeting. (1929). [Photograph]. Association of Chamber of Commerce Executives (ACCE), formerly National Association of Commercial Organization Secretaries (NACOS). Alexandria, VA.: Archives.

277 Tenino Wooden Money. (2012). Photograph by Joe Mabel. Attribution: Joe Mabel. Retrieved from http://commons.wikimedia.org/wiki/File:Tenino_wooden_money_02A.jpg.

287 Cheyenne Frontier Days. (c1910). [Photograph]. Public Domain. Washington, DC: Library of Congress Prints and Photographs Division. Retrieved from http://www.loc.gov/pictures/item/2004674923/.

294 The Vulcan statue, Birmingham, Alabama. (2006). Photograph by Andre Natta. Attribution: Andre Natta. Retrieved from http://commons.wikimedia.org/wiki/File:Vulcan_statue.jpg.

295 Colossal iron statue of Vulcan. (1904). [Stereograph]. Public Domain. Washington, DC: Library of Congress Prints and Photographs Division. Retrieved from http://www.loc.gov/pictures/item/95508072/.

295   El Rancho Hotel. (c1941-1960). [Photograph]. Pitchford,
      G. I. Las Vegas, NV: Special Collections, University Libraries, University of Nevada,
      Las Vegas. Retrieved from http://digital.library.unlv.edu/objects/pho/330.

299   Harrison Barnard. (c1930). [Photograph]. Permission, William Barnard & Thomas
      Barnard. Retrieved from http://thomasbarnard.com/Articles/secretsix.htm.

300   Randolph, Charles Isham. (c1930). [Photograph]. Permission Chicago
      History Museum. Chicago, IL: Chicago History Museum.

304   Capone, Alphonse Gabriel "Al". (1931). [Photograph]. Permission,
      Chicago Tribune. Chicago, IL: *Chicago Tribune*.

      Capone, Alphonse Gabriel "Al". (1931). [Photograph]. Public Domain. United States Department of
      Justice. Retrieved from http://commons.wikimedia.org/wiki/File:AlCaponemugshotCPD.jpg.

309   Shaw, Elton Raymond. (1893). [Book]. Public Domain. *The Body Taboo: Its Origin, Effect, and
      Modern Denial.* By Elton Raymond Shaw, M.A. Washington, DC: Shaw Publishing Co.

311   Cherry Blossom Queen. (1939). [Photograph]. Public Domain. Washington, DC: Library of Congress
      Prints and Photographs Division. Retrieved from http://www.loc.gov/pictures/item/hec2009013098/.

327   Larger photo: Thomas J. Watson (1937). AP Photo/File. New York, NY: Associated Press.

      Three smaller photos: Thomas J. Watson and ICC proceedings in Berlin. *Life* magazine, July 26, 1937, 68.

343   DeWitt, John Lesesne. (c1941). [Photograph]. Public Domain. Washington, DC: United States Army Center
      of Military History. Retrieved from http://commons.wikimedia.org/wiki/File:John_Lesene_Dewitt_copy.png.

349   Read, Leonard E. (c1946). [Photograph]. Permission, Foundation for Economic Education.
      Irvington, NY: Foundation for Economic Education. Retrieved from http://www.fee.org/
      about/page/2013-leonard-e-read-distinguished-alumni-award#axzz2pUJhcVVA.

353   Advisory Board of the Office of War Mobilization and Reconversion. (1946). [Photograph]. Permission,
      Harry S Truman Library and Museum. Independence, MO.: Harry S Truman Library and Museum.
      Retrieved from http://commons.wikimedia.org/wiki/File:Photograph_of_President_Truman_posing_with_
      members_of_the_Advisory_Board_of_the_Office_of_War_Mobilization_and..._-_NARA_-_199371.jpg.

356   442nd Regiment. (1946). [Photograph]. Public Domain. Washington, DC:US
      Army Signal Corps. Retrieved from http://commons.wikimedia.org/wiki/
      File:442nd_Infantry_regimental_colors_on_display_in_Hawaii_1946.jpg.

363   Admiral Halsey's Saddle. [Photograph]. Permission, Peter Barton,
      administrator. Nevada State Division of Museums and History.

368   John F. Kennedy at the Fort Worth Rally. (1963). . [Photograph]. Public Domain.
      Boston, MA.: John F. Kennedy Presidential Library and Museum. Retrieved from http://
      commons.wikimedia.org/wiki/File:Fort_Worth_rally,_22_November_1963.jpg.

377   Hurley, Marvin. (c1946). [Photograph]. Permission, Central Fort Bend Chamber. Rosenberg, TX:
      Central Fort Bend Chamber. Retrieved from http://www.cfbca.org/Chamber/History.aspx.

377   Port of Houston, Texas. (1939). [Photograph]. Public Domain. Washington, DC:
      United States Office of War Information Overseas Picture Division. Retrieved from
      http://lcweb2.loc.gov/service/pnp/fsa/8b23000/8b23100/8b23130v.jpg.

Index

Index

Index

Index

Index

Index

About the Author

Chris Mead is senior vice president of the Association of Chamber of Commerce Executives, an organization representing 1,200 local, state, and regional chambers of commerce. He also is executive director of the foundation affiliated with ACCE, Community Growth Educational Foundation (CGEF). His previous experience includes economic development and other consulting, publishing newsletters on international trade, and serving as vice president of the Council for Urban Economic Development (now the International Economic Development Council).

Chris holds an MBA degree from Stanford University and a BA degree in English from Oberlin College. Chris is married to Laura Lewis Mead and has two daughters and a son. They live in Oakton, Va.